COMMUNICATION
RESEARCH

JOHN E. HOCKING

University of Georgia

DON W. STACKS

University of Miami

STEVEN T. MCDERMOTT

*California Polytechnic State University,
San Luis Obispo*

Boston ■ New York ■ San Francisco
Mexico City ■ Montreal ■ Toronto ■ London ■ Madrid ■ Munich ■ Paris
Hong Kong ■ Singapore ■ Tokyo ■ Cape Town ■ Sydney

Executive Editor: *Karon Bowers*
Series Editorial Assistant: *Jennifer Trebby*
Marketing Manager: *Mandee Eckersley*
Composition and Prepress Buyer: *Linda Cox*
Manufacturing Manager: *JoAnne Sweeney*
Editorial-Production Coordinator: *Mary Beth Finch*
Editorial-Production Service: *Modern Graphics, Inc.*
Electronic Composition: *Modern Graphics, Inc.*

For related titles and support materials, visit our online catalog at www.ablongman.com.

Copyright © 2003 Pearson Education, Inc.
Previous edition copyright © 1999 by Addison-Wesley Educational Publishers Inc.

Between the time Website information is gathered and then published, it is not unusual for some sites to have closed. Also, the transcription of URLs can result in unintended typographical errors. The publisher would appreciate notification where these errors occur so that they may be corrected in subsequent editions.

Hocking, John E.
    Communication research / John E. Hocking, Don W. Stacks, Steven T. McDermott.—3rd ed.
        p. cm
    Updated ed. of: communication research / Don W. Stacks. 2nd ed. 1999.
    Includes bibliographical references and index.
    ISBN 0-321-08807-7
        1. Communication—Research. I. McDermott, Steven T.   II. Stacks, Don W.
    Communication research c1999. III. Title

P91.3 .S7 2002
302.2'072—dc21

                                                                        2002071683

Printed in the United States of America
10 9 8 7 6 5 4 3 2 1   07 06 05

CONTENTS

CHAPTER THREE
Considerations: Knowledge, Ethics, and Science   46

PART II   METHODS OF COMMUNICATION RESEARCH   77

CHAPTER FOUR
Getting Started: Retrieving and Evaluating Information   81

CHAPTER FIVE

**Evaluating Information:
Historical/Rhetorical-Critical Methodology   104**

CHAPTER EIGHT
Describing Information: Content Analysis   **170**

CHAPTER NINE
Qualitative Methodology   **193**

CHAPTER TEN
Quantitative Sampling   216

CHAPTER ELEVEN
Quantitative (Survey) Research   237

CHAPTER TWELVE
The "True" Communication Experiment   273

CHAPTER THIRTEEN
Experimental Strategies and Designs   298

PART III   MODES AND USES OF ANALYSIS   323

CHAPTER FOURTEEN
Descriptive Statistics   325

CHAPTER SEVENTEEN
**Disseminating Information: Writing and
Presenting Research   419**

PREFACE

As with the first edition, the objectives of *Communication Research* are to provide: (a) an introduction to social scientific thinking as it applies to human communication; (b) awareness of ethical issues associated with conducting research with human participants; (c) exposure to the major empirical research methods, particularly surveys, field studies, and experiments; (d) the opportunity to experience designing and collecting data for an empirical study; (e) an opportunity to learn and apply some of the statistical techniques which are important to interpret fully and accurately the results of communication research; (f) exposure to writing a final research report; and, most importantly, (g) an emphasis on information processing and independent critical thinking as the ultimate goal of the book, the course, and a liberal education.

When the book and course have been mastered, the student will be better able to efficiently find and evaluate information presented in other courses, on the job, on the Internet, or as concerned, constructive citizens. Further, he or she may be able to conduct or participate in his or her own empirical research studies. In short, one of the major purposes of this book is to make neophyte communication scientists out of the reader—to develop an attitude such that he or she anticipates future research projects (and the consumption of the research of others) with excitement and enthusiasm instead of boredom or intimidation.

We find ourselves at the foot of the third millennium looking forward towards unimaginable challenges and opportunities. All of us have experienced the last part of the most breathtaking and important century in human history, a century that began with *animals* being the primary means of transportation and with letters, newspapers, and the telegraph, using dots and dashes, being the most sophisticated and fastest modes of communication. The twentieth century really was, as Charles Dickens characterized a part of the eighteenth, the best of times and the worst of times. Wars, weapons, social injustices, environmental destruction, and squalor of unthinkable horror; but also peace, human rights triumphs, *and discovery of the means to turn our planet into a paradise for every living thing, forever*—all in the last hundred years. Wow, what a ride!

Is the world a better place now than it was in 1900? Will it be better or worse in 2100? Although no one knows the answer to these questions, there is no doubt that the extent to which human communication is understood and used will play a vital role in determining the future.

Two things we are quite sure about are these: (1) Communication will continue to be the lifeblood of interpersonal relationships. It will be the means with which we control, and are controlled by, our social environments. Communication will make us happy or sad, fulfilled or lonely. It will remain essential to what it means to be a human being. And, (2) *Information*, knowledge, and how it is created, transmitted, diffused, found, selected, that is, *communicated*, and ultimately, used, has and will be *the* critical factor in determining the answers to these questions. The study of information and how it is processed and used transcends time and space and topic in its importance. And most fundamentally, that's what this book, and the college course in which it is used, and for that matter, a liberal education itself, are about. It is about creating, finding, transmitting, evaluating, and using information in an efficient and skillful manner. It is about distinguishing between chaff and wheat, the sublime from the ridiculous, the stuff from the nonsense. It is about *information processing*, a phrase, in our view, so closely linked to *communication* that they are almost synonyms.

Since the first edition of this book appeared in 1992, it is estimated that the *total* amount of information in existence has increased expotentially. In 1992 the Internet, the World Wide Web (WWW), and e-mail barely existed. Phrases like "search engines," "Web Pages," and "spam" had not been invented. "Information age?" Ah, in 1992, compared to today, it was more of a cliché than reality. But guess what? Boom. The information explosion has happened. It's here; this time, it's real.

It has become almost a cliché to say that we live in an "information age," a time when information is more valuable than physical things. Bill Gates's name has become so well known, it has essentially entered the English language as a noun. Similarly, Enron will probably enter as a noun meaning "corporate scandal." Bill Gates, at this writing, has more money than anyone has had in history. He doesn't build cars or own buildings or real estate. He owns stock in a company that dominates the ways in which information is processed.

Most students of communication understand the important role that communication plays in our work and personal lives. Communication is fundamental to survival. But what do research and research methods have to do with a communication major? Many students ask in frustration, "Why do I have to learn about surveys and experiments and all the rest? I want to study communication!—to learn about it and to become more effective at it—and let's get on with it. A research methods course seems like a waste of time." Every instructor of a communication research methods course has heard comments similar to these. We think they are fair questions and deserve our best answers.

The sheer quantity and ease of accessibility of information is a double-edged sword. Sure, there's more of it—a lot more. And it's much easier to access. But the fundamental problem that existed in 1992 is a dramatically bigger problem today. Much of this easily available information is wrong, or misleading, or worse—designed to manipulate us to our detriment. The information comes in many forms, it comes from diverse sources, and is based on all sorts of evidence, of varying degrees of validity. How do we know what to believe and what to doubt?

Consider the following examples. A new AIDS drug is reported by the company that discovered it to be extraordinarily effective at slowing, or perhaps even eradicating, this horrific disease. They report the results of an experiment in which none of twenty HIV-positive research participants who were given large doses of the new drug over a period of two years had developed any symptoms of AIDS. Patients in a second group were given modest doses of the drug; and several began to develop symptoms of full blown AIDS. A final group, who received none of the drug, had nearly all of the participants develop AIDS and several died from the disease before the two-year period was over. Hearing of this research, one's reaction is, "Geez, let's get this drug on the market. Why is the FDA so slow to approve important and obviously effective new drugs?"

A serious crime is allegedly committed and the police arrest a suspect. He voluntarily takes a polygraph examination and fails. He is judged by the examiner to be lying. Let's have the trial and lock this guy up as quickly as possible.

A phone survey released by a local congressman shows that his constituents are overwhelmingly against a substantial tax increase on cigarettes because the money, while purporting to be used to combat smoking in young people, is really going to create bigger government and bureaucracy. Thus, his vote to kill the tax was true representation of the voters in his district and thus fully justified.

One of the goals of this book is to help create a healthy degree of skepticism—to contribute to the critical thinking skills—among the reader/students. It can be risky to automatically and uncritically accept information as true, even when it is labeled "scientific," and even when it appears in "reputable" sources such as a prominent newspaper or magazine or in other forms of the news media. Important information such as that in the above examples should be viewed with a certain degree of suspicion until additional information is provided, certain questions answered.

All three of our examples could result in harmful conclusions. In the first, the pharmaceutical company assigned the least sick HIV-positive participants to the experimental group who received large doses of their new drug, the next healthiest patients received a moderate amount of the drug, while the sickest patients, some of whom already were showing symptoms of AIDS, were put in the group that received none of the new drug. The participants should have been randomly assigned to the various treatment conditions. The method used essentially invalidates the results of the study. Any subsequent actions taken regarding that drug would have been based on a study so flawed as to border on being fraudulent. The FDA was quite correct to go slow and we, as readers of the initial news report, should have been armed with hats of skepticism to protect us from being smothered by the chaff as we search for a bit of wheat.

In the second example, careful scientific study of polygraph exams have shown them to be no more accurate than random chance. That the accused individual flunked the exam means next to nothing. Nearly half of people who are telling the truth fail polygraph exams. In our opinion, the entire polygraph industry and those "professionals" who claim near virtual accuracy are also committing borderline fraud. We will have more to say about this in Chapter 16.

In the third example concerning the congressman and the phone survey, we would like to know, at least: (1) who paid for the survey; was it the same cigarette companies who donated millions of dollars to the campaigns of those who voted to defeat the cigarette tax increase and who spent tens of millions of dollars taking out ads calling the tax increase a "big government tax-and-spend scheme designed to hurt the little guy"; (2) how was the sample selected—was it a true probability sample in which each voter in his district had an equal opportunity of being selected; (3) how were the key questions worded—did they use code phrases like "tax-and-spend" and fail to mention what the additional revenue was to be used for? Very subtle changes in the wording of survey questions has been shown to affect response patterns profoundly.

A thorough understanding of the elements of communication research is essential to being a good communications student. The content of this book and this course will help the reader perform better in upper level communication courses precisely because those courses report the results of communication research, research that varies in validity. Skeptical hats should be worn when reading the daily paper or watching CNN; they should also be worn to class every day. Do not forget to put them on when reading the course texts as well, including this one. Be an informed critical thinker. Hopefully this text will help you do that.

In addition, a good student of communication research methods should be in a strong position to move into a job in which research skills are helpful to job advancement, if not necessary for job success. Increasingly, communication students move into positions in marketing or sales—positions that require that research, at a minimum, be understood, and perhaps even positions in which the communication student is required to conduct a valid empirical study, one on which important job decisions are based.

FEATURES OF COMMUNICATION RESEARCH, THIRD EDITION

A New Chapter on Applications of Communication Research

We love to teach Research Methods ourselves and were excited to be asked to update and improve this edition. The question we often hear is: "How can I use this stuff?" "How will it help me at work or as a person?" In the first two editions we tried to address these questions often, but perhaps danced around them. We tried to address them more directly in this third edition. We have taken the bull by the horns and devoted an entire chapter to applications of communication research. Ultimately, the goal of this chapter is to give the reader a glimpse of the ways in which communication research can improve our lives in the many roles we play; as workers, consumers, voters, parents, friends—as concerned, constructive, and happy people. The chapter is a collage of the interrelationships between science, the methods and techniques presented, and critical thinking in life's many arenas.

An Expanded Treatment of Ethical Issues

The first edition (1992) was, we believe, the first communication research methods book to devote an entire chapter to ethics. We continued this emphasis in the second (1999) edition and have expanded this treatment still further here to include not only the issue of the ethical treatment of human participants in research, but also issues such as plagiarism and ghost writing. We revisit ethics again and again throughout the book. For example, in our new applications, Chapter 16, we raise the issues of scientific chicanery and the influence of money on science, even touch on scientific fraud, a seemingly near-taboo topic. In this context, we discuss how much of a society can be duped in the name of science.

Minimal Jargon

We continue to try to cover fundamental issues with minimal jargon and yet explain ideas in a way that acknowledges and explains the complexity of issues in a clear and readable way, providing an abundance of communication examples. We do our best to be conversational and readable without oversimplification. We are well aware that we are writing for smart people on a subject that at first glance might appear dull. It may seem occasionally dull, but we are taking you to interesting places if you will share with us our enthusiasm for discovering new things.

Hands-On Projects

At the request of some of the many adopters of the first edition, we integrated a series of student projects into almost every chapter of the second edition. In this new edition, we have taken this further: we suggest more projects, most of which we have used ourselves or heard about from other teachers. Increasingly, we have come to believe that learning is accomplished in direct proportion to the level of hands-on involvement in conducting research. These projects are feasible and often exciting. We do not believe there is one project in the text that cannot be successfully tackled by an individual or group. At a minimum, we recommend that the reader think through or discuss in class the steps that would be involved in many of these projects.

Flexible Design and Broad Coverage

The book maintains its broad coverage, including many different methods and wide ranging examples of communication substance in various contexts. Examples are drawn from interpersonal communication, mass communication, public relations, intercultural communication, and organizational communication. Regardless of the name and emphasis of the communication department in which the book is used, we have attempted to be inclusive of communication in all its forms and contexts.

We also discuss the entire research process from the research question to method selection, design, operationalization, data collection and analyses, and writing the final report.

This book is designed to be an introduction to research methods in any communication field: speech communication, mass communication, public relations, marketing, organizational communication, as well as other social sciences. Knowledge and methodology do not exist in the discrete categories reflected in academic departments, which exist primarily for political reasons.

Even though the book is geared toward undergraduates, it also may provide a nice review for the graduate student who wants to get up to speed for advanced courses or for those who need a background refresher.

A Balance Between Science and Rhetoric

There is an undeniable dialectical tension in the communication discipline between science and rhetoric. We do not side step this tension but discuss it head on. Our book includes some philosophy of science, and we take stances on issues that result from this tension. For example, we explicitly acknowledge the importance of rhetoric in informing and complementing empiricism. We discuss the questions that can be answered by each "method" and identify the importance of each one. We do our best to show the value of historical, humanistic, and historical research. Ultimately, we emphasize these research traditions as complementary to social science methods and try to demonstrate the utility of each methodology. However, let us make clear that we have written a text that emphasizes social science research.

The Ultimate Goal: Critical Thinking and
Independent Student Thought

We believe that critical thinking and independent thought are the ultimate goals of this book and of a liberal education; there's no absolute truth here, only ideas for the reader to consider and embrace, or not. We make a clear distinction between information processing and information storage, and argue that processing, that is, finding, evaluating, synthesizing, creating and using information to guide our behaviors, is what science and education are about. Education is no longer just memorizing facts. It is being able to find, create, evaluate, and use these facts that counts. Most books or classes in which the student writes down ten pages of notes every day and then spits back this information on an exam probably belong in the 1950s or 1960s or 1970s. Critically analyzing information and creatively using information turn the key to success in this new era.

ACKNOWLEDGMENTS

We were excited to be asked to write a third edition of *Communication Research*. We have worked to write a significantly better book than the second edition that appeared in 1999. For starters, we added Steve McDermott as an author. Steve has contributed since the inception of this project in the mid 1980s, with individual chapters. This edition sparkles with Steve's lively writing, fresh examples, and conversational prose. John Hocking assumed overall responsibility for the new book, and Don Stacks graciously asked Dr. Hocking to become senior author. We will probably switch back for the fourth edition. The core of the book that has proven so popular and been changed minimally may be safely attributed to Dr. Stacks. We are delighted to have the rare opportunity to have a third try at "getting it right." There are no perfect research studies or textbooks. But it is a privilege to have this third chance. We want to especially thank Karon Bowers of Allyn & Bacon and Martha Tenney of Modern Graphics for their superb guidance, patience, and most of all, for giving us this opportunity. They want the best from their authors, and we hope we have not disappointed.

Book are not written in a vacuum. They are in a very real sense collaborative efforts in which the influence and support of many people blend in a transactional, dynamic process to produce pages of good advice and occasionally even wisdom.

As we note early on in the text, research is a rigorous process. The process of writing and updating this book has been no exception. We wish to acknowledge a number of people who reviewed earlier editions, as well as those who reviewed the manuscript of this edition, and made us work harder to hone our own understanding of the research process. We gratefully appreciate the insight and stimulating questions provided by the following reviewers: Ferald J. Bryan, Northern Illinois University; Julie A. Burke, Bowling Green State University; Kenneth D. Frandsen, University of New Mexico; Kay F. Israel, Rhode Island College; David Myers, Loyola University; Kartik Pashupati, University of West Florida; Judi Sanders, California State Polytechnic University; Ronald M. Sandwina, Indiana University/Purdue University; Xuejian Yu, Stonehill College; and Christopher J. Zahn, Miami University.

I (John Hocking) would like to acknowledge and thank, albeit inadequately: the loves of my life—my wife, Ruth Ann, and daughter, Anna Lauren; my mentors, role models, and friends—Cal Hylton, Gerald Miller, Ed Fink, Dale Leathers, Don Stacks, and Carol Roberts; and my parents—Julia and Ernie Hocking. A special thanks to Alicia Beckworth who meticulously put hundreds of changes into the final manuscript before it was sent to Allyn & Bacon. I owe a special debt to two of the best colleagues and friends that I could have—Jerry Hale and Don Rubin. These gentlemen helped me more than they can ever know.

I (Don Stacks) would like to acknowledge and thank my wife, Robin, and daughters Stacy, Katie, and Meg for putting up with long days and nights in front of the computer and grousing about editors and publishers' requirements. Also, I gratefully acknowledge my mentors, role models, and friends who insisted and continue to insist that I always go back to the "original sources" in my research: Judee Burgoon and Michael Burgoon, Mark Hickson and Jack Orwant (who started me on a career in academia and research), Don Richardson, Marvin Shaw, John Hocking, Mitch Shapiro, and John D. Stone; and my parents—Margaret and Fred Stacks.

I (Steve McDermott) would like to embrace and thank my wife, Marilynn, for all her years of love, patience, and support; and my daughters, Nicole and Michelle, for their love and all the wonderful times we've shared. I also want to thank my supportive colleagues, especially Mike Fahs, Raymond Zeuschner, Jim Conway, Terry Winebrenner, and Chris Shea. I want to give special recognition to all my excellent teachers and role models, most notably Cal Hylton, Brad Greenberg, Chuck Atkin, and G. R. Miller; and my friend and theoretical buddy, Mike Sunnafrank. Finally, I want to thank John Hocking and Don Stacks for graciously inviting me into this project over the years.

We also want to thank other research methods instructors with whom we have discussed both the project and our feelings about teaching this important course in research methods.

John E. Hocking
Athens, GA

Don W. Stacks
Coral Gables, FL

Steven T. McDermott
Los Osos, CA

PART I

THEORY AND RESEARCH METHODS

This section introduces the study of **communication** theory and method. It establishes our view of communication study. Research is only as good as the questions asked and, therefore, in establishing a base for research in communication we begin by considering the kinds of questions addressed. Asking a trivial question results in a bad research study regardless of the methodological sophistication of the attempt to answer it. Chapter 1 lays the foundation for asking *good* research questions, questions that concern communication across a variety of areas.

Chapter 2 builds on this foundation by examining the study of *communication* from a number of theoretical and applied perspectives. The chapter begins with some general comments about research in communication and moves toward an examination of **science** as one model of research and **humanistic research** as a second model. These two models are presented as different, yet complementary to one another. In examining the two orientations, emphasis is placed on what each does best. Both serve as foundations for later discussion of more specific methods.

Chapter 3 enters the humanistic arena of ethics. All good research meets certain **ethical standards**, requirements that are fundamental. The discussion begins with the fundamental rules of **scholarship**. Discussion then centers on the more specific questions of what an ethical topic for research is and how we can ethically prepare, collect, and analyze data. In the past there have been problems associated with the use of human beings in research (communication researchers use *humans* as the **subjects** (i.e., participants) of their studies either implicitly or explicitly), and we devote most of the chapter to a discussion of the ethical treatment of human participants. Our purpose is to create a "social etiquette" for conducting research, regardless of the method chosen. But we go one step further—we must also explore the ethical use of research after it has been reported and present the National Communication Association standards regarding our ethical responsibilities when we communicate.

Part I establishes the reasons and the ground rules for conducting research. It should guide your later consideration of both methods and modes of analysis. Research, as we will note throughout our treatment, is asking the appropriate question based on a theoretical understanding of communication and then collecting and analyzing **data** in such a way as to advance our knowledge of how humans communicate. Ultimately, the goal of communication research is the betterment of the human condition.

CHAPTER ONE

EXPLORING INFORMATION: ASKING AND ANSWERING QUESTIONS

INFORMATION AND COMMUNICATION
Information age
Information sources
Information consumption

COMMUNICATION QUESTIONS
Definition
Fact
Value
Policy

EPISTEMOLOGY
Tenacity
Authority
Intuition
Science

APPLYING KNOWLEDGE IN COMMUNICATION

OBJECTIVES

By the end of this chapter you should be able to:

1. Distinguish between information and communication.
2. State those things communication researchers hold in common across disciplinary lines.
3. Distinguish the four major questions that communication researchers ask.
4. Describe how we as communication researchers "know what we know."
5. State a research question in either a face-to-face or mass communication context.

We are well into the new millennium. Even though a recently popular television show, *Who Wants to be a Millionaire*, and the longest-running one, *Jeopardy*, emphasize the memorization of *facts*, the fact is that we are not in a historical, but an information age. We are bombarded with information. When you were born, the Internet did not exist. The desktop computer was not an everyday part of people's lives, cable TV was just beginning to spread, and TV stations, not individual viewers, used satellite dishes. There were no CDs, MP3s, Palm Pilots, pagers, cell phones, videos-on-demand, or international news programs such as CNN or MSNBC.

The information and communication age has arrived with a bang! This new age requires that you select and *process information* in ways that have never before been required. Memorizing and regurgitating facts is no longer relevant because people have instant access to an unparalleled amount of them. In this age, every citizen needs to know how to select, evaluate, and act on the information to which they have easy access in order to function within society. The valuable people in society are not those gameshow contestants with trivia, but those who can evaluate information and solve problems. As Bill Gates (1995) declares: "More than ever, an education that emphasizes general problem-solving skills will be important. In a changing world, education is the best preparation for being able to adapt" (p. 254).

Just a few years ago, students followed a standard model of a college education. They did what they were told, asked very few questions, and were usually pleased with just a passing grade. "Speech" students learned about public speaking, great speakers in history, interpersonal and small group communication, and persuasion. "Journalism" students learned how to write press releases and some very basic information about advertising and public relations. "Broadcast" students learned how to write television and radio copy and the basics of camera angles and movement.

Education in general was largely still viewed as the learning of *facts*. The general public—not unlike the general public of today—thought an educated person was someone who knew lots of things and had lots of information stored ready for retrieval at the appropriate time. However, arcane and obscure information (e.g., What is the capital of Madagascar?) is now readily available at the click of a mouse. For example, if you look up "interpersonal communication" using any good search engine on the Internet, you will retrieve millions of sites! Which sites should you choose? Which sites are credible? Which sites give you accurate information? Which sites give you enough information so that you can make a reasonable assessment of the information? So, we argue that an educated person today needs to sift and evaluate information—maybe even to produce it—in order to function in the information age. Education in this new millenium is not about students becoming encyclopedias of information, but rather people capable of processing the abundant information that is available.

Fundamentally, that is what this book is about. Instead of memorizing facts, you will be expected to know how to find out what is already known (*information retrieval*), how to understand and evaluate new information (*information processing*), and even how to discover things that were previously unknown (*new information*) so that you and others may know it. It is also about how to communicate that information to others in society. Thus, the purpose of this book is to provide you with a comprehensive foundation to the essentials of communication research methods.

RESEARCH AND SOURCES OF INFORMATION

Social psychologist Elliot Aronson (1972) once wrote in tribute to his friend and mentor Leon Festinger: "I *could* say that he taught me all I know about social psychology, but that would be a lie. He taught me something much more valuable than that: he taught me to find out the things that neither I nor anybody else knew" (p. viii).

Indeed! Much of the important information learned by students in the past is now obsolete. And most of the information we learn today about communication simply did not exist then. More importantly, much of the information that will be known in ten years is not known today. How is this possible? Ours is an information age. Knowledge about communication and the world is exploding. For many communication professionals, keeping up with this new information will be a critical determinant of career success. To find, evaluate, and use relevant information may be the single most valuable skill taught by colleges today. We will be so bold as to assert categorically that **information processing**—selectively choosing or discarding, combining or synthesizing, finding or creating, and most importantly, evaluating information to reach conclusions—will be the name of the game during the rest of your time in college, and in your careers in the twenty-first century.

Information comes, indeed, bombards us, from all directions. It comes from our personal experiences. It comes from family, friends, and work associates. It comes from the ancient sages Aristotle and Plato and from the more modern ones, McLuhan and Gerbner, Lazarsfeld and Rogers, Burke and Bitzer, McCroskey and Miller, Atkin and Greenberg, J. Cambell and Knapp. It comes from the print and broadcast media. It is stored in archives and arrives with the evening news. But most importantly for our purposes, it takes the form of **communication research**—the patient, systematic study to learn new things about communication: things, to paraphrase Aronson, that neither you nor I, nor anybody else, ever knew before. The modern student of communication, regardless of his or her concentration, needs a grounding in understanding, planning, conducting, consuming, and evaluating communication research.

RESEARCH AND THE CONSUMPTION
OF INFORMATION

More than ever before, today's college student (and graduate) is a hungry consumer of knowledge generated by diverse sources. To succeed in upper-level communication courses and in most postgraduate careers, skillful consumption of knowledge is paramount. In order to be a good consumer of knowledge, one must know how that knowledge was generated and must learn to be critical of **research methodology**. It is equally important to note that with increasing frequency, this same consumer of knowledge is frequently a supplier of knowledge for his- or herself, and for others. Thus, today's communication student and professional need to understand how and why research is conducted.

Communication scholars conduct research on many different subtopics using many different methods (see Figure 1.1). These methods have some elements in common as well as some differences. Throughout this book we will be pointing out these similarities and

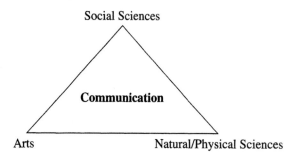

FIGURE 1.1 Communication is essential.

differences. Here, we will emphasize some very basic things that those of us who study communication all have in common.

1. *All methods of inquiry about communication have as their ultimate goal the generation of knowledge that may then be used to improve the human condition.*

This will sound grandiose to some, pompous to others, and perhaps patently obvious to all. However, we feel that this point is so important that it deserves special emphasis, lest we lose sight of the big picture and get lost in the details of research procedures. Ideally, the humanities (arts) and the sciences exist to enrich lives, to make the world a better, more prosperous, fairer place. A particular scientist or artist might look at his or her creations as ends in themselves, but humanities and science, like other collective human endeavors such as government, exist and are worthy of our support because they can and often do make it a better world.

2. *All methods of inquiry about communication involve studying how humans encode, transmit, and receive symbols to influence one another.*

The use of symbols, both verbal and nonverbal, is unique to our species. Our discipline focuses on symbol usage in all contexts, whether it be a comic telling a joke to millions or a mother whispering to her child. To be sure, there is an overlap between what communication researchers study and what is studied by social psychologists, sociologists, political scientists, historians, and others. Knowledge does not always organize itself into the apparently discrete, but largely artificial, categories between various academic disciplines reflected in academic departments. But whereas the social psychologist, for example, sometimes studies symbol usage, the communication researcher *always* has this as his or her focus.

3. *All methods of inquiry about communication follow certain prescribed rules.*

Some of these rules are universally accepted as ethical, for example, providing credit and proper citations for the source of one's information and ideas. However, some of the rules are less explicit and vary with the type of research undertaken. For example, the methods of the communication researcher who takes a scientific approach generally dictate more explicit and stricter rules regarding research procedures than do the methods of the researcher who is engaging in rhetorical criticism or postmodern interpretation. Nonetheless, each method has a structure, a system of prescriptions about the right and wrong way to engage in research.

   4. *All methods of inquiry about communication involve the collection and analysis of data.*
   The form the data take, the way they are analyzed, and the type of conclusions drawn often vary by method of inquiry. The historian may gather newspaper accounts of an event, the rhetorical critic might gather the texts of a speech, and the social scientist might gather the responses to a questionnaire, but every communication researcher systematically and carefully collects and analyzes communication data in some form.

   5. *All methods of inquiry about communication begin with a question, an interrogative, asking about something that is unknown.*
   At the core of any research project is a good research question, a question addressing an important aspect of communication. Sometimes it is easy to get lost in a sea of detail about research procedures and to lose sight of this extremely important part of the process. If an important question is not being addressed, no matter how carefully the researcher proceeds to gather data, no matter how powerful and sophisticated the statistical or other analytic tools he or she applies, no matter how well written the paper that reports the research, the project is of little value, and the energies of all involved have been wasted. All good research begins with a *good* **research question**, a question the researcher hopes to address through research that will advance knowledge of the world. One of the hardest things in research is asking the *right* question, a question whose answer is important for a culture, society, or humanity as a whole.
   Let us start at the very beginning. Let us start our presentation of research methods about communication with a discussion of the kinds of questions your field—communication—addresses.

ASKING QUESTIONS ABOUT COMMUNICATION

Inquiry of any kind, regardless of the perspective from which it is conducted, has, at its core, the process of asking questions that the investigator uses to guide him- or herself through the research process. There are many kinds of questions that can be asked. Our primary aim in this section is to make the most fundamental distinction between the kinds of questions that can be asked about communication, specifically, the distinction between questions of *fact* and questions of *value*. Later in this section, we will discuss questions of *policy*. As we shall see, questions of policy require a blending of factual and value considerations before they can be adequately answered. Questions of *definition* are important to begin any study of communication. For this reason, we turn first to questions of definition.

Questions of Definition

Critically important to asking and answering questions about communication is the definition of the terms used in the questions. Whether one is asking questions of fact, value, or policy, it is vital that the questioner, and others interested in the inquiry process, clearly understand what is being asked. If terms are not defined in an unambiguous way, the questioner cannot know exactly what question he or she is asking or even be confident that it has been adequately answered. Thus, we turn to an area that permeates all research about communication, questions of definition.

Abstraction.   Everything written in this book, including the questions to be posed, has been written in a language (English, obviously). Language is a system of symbols and accompanying rules about how the symbols should be ordered that is shared by those who understand the language. Communication is only possible if two users of the language share the same or similar meaning for the same symbol. Presumably, if you are reading this book, you are fluent in English, and therefore the ink on the page does not appear to you as random markings. A book written in a language in which you are not fluent, particularly one that did not use the twenty-six alphabetic characters of the English language, would literally be meaningless. There is no meaning in the ink on these pages. The meaning lies in those of us who are writing these sentences and those who are reading them. A famous scholar, David Berlo, once stated that communication is in people, not words.

Where do we learn meanings? We learn them from our parents, our playmates, our teachers and classmates, from authors, from friends and lovers, from movies and television, from music and art. We never stop learning meanings nor do the meanings we already have ever stop evolving and changing, albeit, usually in subtle ways. In short, we learn meanings from our past experiences.

No two people, however, have exactly the same past experiences, therefore no two people will have exactly the same meaning for the same symbol. When someone says *dog*, you may think of your collie back home while he was thinking of their neighbor's friendly little mixed breed, Suzie. But at least all were thinking about four-legged animals that bark. You were not thinking about a tree while he was thinking of Tuesday. Fortunately, we share considerable overlap in our meaning for most words, especially words with low levels of abstraction. The more abstract the word, the more potential **referents**—specific meanings the word can refer to—the word has. The word *dog* is a symbol with a low level of abstraction. It can refer to many types and sizes of dog, but at least it does not refer to birds as well. The word *pet* is more abstract because it might refer to dogs (in all variations) or to birds, or to cats, or turtles, or whatever. The word *animal* is even more abstract.

As a general rule, the more abstract the word, the more important are clear definitions to reduce potential for misunderstandings. Most of the questions communication researchers pose about communication include abstract, equivocal, vague, or technical terms that require clear definition. There is a tendency among all of us, including experienced communication researchers, to assume that when we use a term in a particular way, others are using it in the same way. But just as we think of two different dogs when we see the symbol, *dog*, we may have different meanings for the terms in our important questions about values, facts, and policy. What we mean by such abstract terms as social justice, ethically appropriate, morally acceptable, TV ministry, lying, celebrity endorsement, greatest performer, terrible-looking roommate, better painter, corporate divestment, date other people, and so on, may or may not be what you mean by these terms. The bottom line is that question-asking begins with definition. No question can be adequately answered unless everyone involved understands what is meant by the words in the question.

Categorizing Definitions.   There are many ways to categorize kinds of definitions, and these will be discussed in more detail in later chapters. Here, it will suffice to make a distinction between a reportive definition and a stipulative definition. Basically, a **reportive definition** reports how a particular term has been customarily used; what the conventional meaning for a term is. Dictionary definitions can be thought of as reportive because they report to the reader how people in general use a term.

In contrast, a **stipulative definition** involves specifying how a term will be used—to what it will be used to refer. In other words, the researcher stipulates what he or she is referring to by using a particular word. For example, he or she might say, "by 'inappropriate self-disclosure,' I mean revealing highly personal information to someone who is known to the discloser for less than one hour." We used a stipulative definition earlier, when we defined communication as centering on humans use of symbols. It is quite silly to argue about whether a stipulated definition is true or false, right or wrong, correct or incorrect. Stipulative definitions are thus not true or false, rather they are statements or declarations about how a person intends to use a term. Stipulative definitions should thus be judged on their *usefulness*. Do they effectively convey a clear idea about the term being defined? Does a particular definition facilitate answering some important research question? Generally, researchers try to find consensus on stipulated definitions. Later, in Chapter 2, we will discuss in some detail a particular kind of stipulative definition, the **operational definition**, that defines variables with such specificity and concreteness that they make scientific research possible.

Questions of Fact

Whereas questions of definition deal with making *judgments* about the way we describe the world, questions of fact are concerned with *describing the world as it is according to what we know at that time*. A question of fact poses an inquiry about the nature of the world that is external to our minds. And whereas the answers to questions of definition are largely found within us, the answers to questions of fact are found "out there" in the observable environment. Questions of fact are often called **empirical questions**, capable of being verified or refuted by observation. The following questions are empirical:

Is the average cost of a Monet painting at auction higher than that of a painting by Manet or Renoir?

Did hip-hop music sell more CDs in the 1990s than rock music?

Did Bruce Springsteen play ten consecutive sold-out concerts in Madison Square Garden in 2000?

Is capital punishment a deterrent to murder and other serious crimes?

Are commercials that advertise candy, toys, and cereal effective at changing the attitudes and behaviors of children under the age of seven?

If your roommate looks terrible for a date and you tell him so, what effect will this have on his self-concept, on his success during the date, and on your relationship with him?

How much money do people send in to the television evangelists as a result of hearing that good things will come if they send money?

Do combat veterans believe that *Saving Private Ryan* is a more realistic depiction of what it was like to be in combat than *Black Hawk Down*?

Did more people listen to Franklin Roosevelt's fireside chats than listen to our current president's Saturday morning addresses?

The answer to each question can be found, at least potentially, through observation. If two people observe in the same way, that is, go through the same steps in the process of finding answers, follow the same observational rules, and if the rules are specific enough, they should arrive at the same answer. The answers are not within the researcher, but rather are out there in the world. We can look for them and we can agree, at least theoretically, on what the answers are.

If these questions of fact were stated in the declarative form instead of their current interrogative form, these statements could, after appropriate research, be found to be true or false. Consider the statement, Bruce Springsteen sold out ten consecutive concerts at Madison Square Garden in 2000. This statement is true or false, and it can, in fact, be determined to be so. He either sold out the concerts or he did not. It is one or the other. And what the researcher may think about Springsteen's music, or whether or not the researcher believes that human life is sacred, capital punishment is morally wrong, and so on, is not going to have any effect on how many concerts Springsteen sold out in 2000. Contrast this with the value statement, Bruce Springsteen is the greatest performer in the history of rock music. This statement *cannot* be determined to be either true or false, but is a value judgment for humanistic researchers to argue.

Questions of fact are amenable to empirical answers. This does not mean that they are easy to answer, nor does it mean that there will not be disagreements about the answers. Some questions of fact are complex, and despite being studied for years, different empirical studies may point to different answers.

Questions of fact may yield answers that seem contradictory. However, many questions of fact are answered by *different* people, using different methods, and different definitions.

For example, does the depiction of violent acts by the mass media contribute to violent behavior by those exposed to the media? This question has been studied empirically and the answers debated for over forty years. The causes of violence in our society are many, and sorting them out in a definitive way is an incredibly complex task. Think of all the other factors that may contribute to a violent act besides exposure to a "slasher" movie or a "Road Runner" cartoon. But ultimately, violence in the media either does or does not play some contributory role. The difficulty in answering a question does not determine whether the answer is out there in the external environment. It is possible to make observations relevant to the answer.

Questions of fact can be about the past, the present, or the future. Questions about the present and future lend themselves to *direct observation*. It is often possible to observe the answer first-hand. The Super Bowl is played every year. Who wins, what the score is, and how many people were at the game are all factual questions. We can observe the answers directly for games to be played in the future. Questions of fact about past events can only be observed indirectly.

When Franklin Roosevelt made his famous fireside chats in the 1930s, what was their impact? Did he restore national confidence at a time when it was at an all-time low? Did he energize people to apply themselves with new vigor to solving some of the great problems of the time? Even though these are questions of fact, we cannot *directly* observe the answers. Certainly, there are historians who will assert that his chats did, in fact, have these effects. However, their assertions about these "facts" are based on *indirect observations*. They may have read newspaper accounts of the chats and the listeners' reactions to them. They may have interviewed people who were old enough to remember hearing the broadcasts. They may even have listened to tapes of the radio programs. Nonetheless, there will be historians who disagree and who have their own indirect observations to support opposite conclusions. Thus, while historians frequently deal with questions of fact, they use indirect observation methods to address such questions. This is why historians, intellectuals, and especially those with a political agenda attack historical "fact" that they do not like by calling it "revisionist history," implying that the "true facts" have been revised in the process of a new interpretation. For example, since few people are alive today who directly witnessed or experienced the Holocaust, some right-wing extremists claim it did not happen, something that would have been impossible to claim fifty or even twenty years ago.

Questions of fact can be answered in many ways, and we will discuss these later in the chapter. Communication researchers who address questions of fact about present and future events generally do so using the methods of *science*. Scientific research requires carefully controlled and defined observations that can be repeated again and again. The methods of science are designed to detect and correct mistakes in answering questions of fact. An assumption is that human beings are fallible, even prone to having biases and to making mistakes. Thus, the rules of science are designed to minimize these influences on descriptions of the world.

As noted earlier, deciding if an important question—or a good question—is being asked can be one of the most difficult and subjective parts of the research process. Students of communication, whether they be neophytes taking their first course in the field or seasoned veterans of many research projects, spend great amounts of time deciding which questions are important and which are not. Although there are no surefire principles for determining if an important question is being asked, there are some guidelines that may help. When trying to decide whether a question of fact is worthy of our research energies, the checklist in Box 1.1 may prove useful.

Questions of Value

Questions of value pose inquiries about whether an object, situation, or behavior is perceived as good or bad, right or wrong, beautiful or ugly. They concern the world as it *ought* to be, not necessarily as it is (Miller & Nicholson, 1976).[1] Let us examine some questions of value:

Is Monet a better painter than Michelangelo or Renoir?

Is Bruce Springsteen the greatest rock 'n' roll performer ever?

Is it morally justifiable for the president to order the assassination of the leader of an enemy nation?

Is capital punishment wrong?

■ ■ ■ ■ ■

BOX 1.1
CRITERIA FOR EVALUATING QUESTIONS OF FACT

1. Is it a factual question?
2. Is it about communication; that is, human symbolic transactions?
3. Is it clearly and unambiguously stated?
4. Is it about the relationship among two or more variables?
5. Is the question of potential theoretical interest? Is there reason to believe that the variables are related? Are there other variables possibly related to both? (Is there potential for the study to be of interest to the scientific community and therefore the results may be published and part of "public knowledge"?)
6. Is there previous research examining this or related questions?
7. Are we personally interested in devoting our energies to answering this question?
8. Would we be able to answer this question in an ethical way? Would our procedures pass the human subjects committee on campus?
9. Is it feasible for us to answer this question? That is, are we capable, given our resources, of doing the research? How would we operationalize the variables? What procedures would be necessary to address the question?
10. Is there the potential, however distant, that the world would change for the better if we knew the answer?

Is it ethical to aim commercials advertising candy, toys, and cereal at children under seven years of age and who are predictably watching Saturday morning television?

Is it ethically acceptable for various TV evangelists to tell people that good things will happen if they send money to the ministry?

Is *Saving Private Ryan* a better film about war than *Schindler's List*?

Was Franklin Roosevelt's use of the radio, specifically his fireside chats, a more moral use of the mass media than the current president's press conferences?

All of these questions could be interesting to research. Even though all of them can be answered, will everyone agree about the answer? Probably not, because the answer to each of these questions of value lies to a great degree within the person who is asking and answering the question; that is, the answer lies in our internal mental judgments. Philosopher Dewit H. Parker (1931) writes that "values belong wholly to the inner world, to the world of the mind. . . . A value is always an experience, never a thing or an object. . . . We project into the external world" (pp. 20–21). This is why there is great disagreement regarding the answers to many questions of value.

McGuire (1984) wrote a very interesting essay about Bruce Springsteen's music in which he describes the music and identifies several central themes to which Springsteen appears to return again and again. McGuire, who likes Springsteen, gives his opinion of the quality of the music. His essay is an excellent example of contemporary rhetorical criticism. If someone else wrote an analysis of Springsteen's music, would they write the same essay, identify the same themes, and have the same opinions about the quality of the music? Perhaps, but probably not.

Why? Because in McGuire's essay the reader learns about two very different things, in arguably equal amounts. First, of course, the reader learns something about Springsteen and his music. Second, and vitally important to note, he or she learns a great deal about the essay's author. When he praises Springsteen's music, the statements he makes are as much about himself as they are about Springsteen. When he says Springsteen is a great songwriter and performer, he is really saying, *I believe* Springsteen is a great songwriter. *I like* Springsteen. The subject of these sentences is *I*—McGuire—not Springsteen. And to a greater or lesser degree, the same is true about all questions of value. Their answers lie largely within the person answering them.

We think McGuire's essay is excellent. However, a colleague of ours disagrees. In fact, she thinks that popular music is not an appropriate subject for rhetorical criticism. What do you think? As you think about it, you are looking within yourself to answer still another value question—one about the world of communication research as it *ought* to be.

Questions of value can be about big issues that affect society. They can also be about the small day-to-day judgments we make about what is right or wrong in our interpersonal interactions. Although debatable, we take the position that there are no absolute right or wrong answers to most questions of value. People will disagree about them, argue about them, sometimes resolve them temporarily, but any issue remains, ultimately, open to debate. This is because the answer is within each of us. No two of us are exactly alike. We come into the world with a *tabula rasa*, a blank slate. We become what we are, think what we think, and have those values that we have as a result of our past experiences, but no two people have identical past experiences, therefore no two people's internal mental states will ever be exactly the same. Because we share a common culture and common language system, we share many of the same values. For example, it would be a safe bet that most people believe that human life is sacred, individual initiative is good, and education is important.

But our differences are profound. Some people believe in God, others do not. Some people believe that capital punishment is wrong, most people do not. The fact that American culture is pluralistic contributes to the diversity of our value systems. Ours is probably the most heterogeneous society in the world. Many of us have different attitudes, opinions, beliefs, and values. Values are within us, and it is ultimately within ourselves that we must turn for answers to questions of value.

Before leaving this discussion of questions of value, one final point deserves emphasis. Because the answers to questions of value lie largely within us, does this mean that all value judgments are equally good?[2] Does this mean that the answers to questions of value are equally valid? Some people argue for an extreme form of **ethical relativism**—the belief that all ethical judgments are equally valid because they depend on the situation in which the judgment is being made and the personal ethical beliefs of the individual making the judgment. This position would be in sharp contrast to **ethical absolutism**—the belief that ethical judgments are absolutely right or wrong, true or false, regardless of the situation or the beliefs of the individual (Titus, 1964).

We prefer a middle ground between extreme forms of ethical relativism and absolutism. Not all value judgments are equally correct. Value judgments based on established principles that are widely accepted within a culture and that are advanced with thoughtful argument are much more likely to be agreed-upon judgments than those resulting from spontaneous emotional reactions. And, although value questions are internal mental judgments, the information on which these judgments are based certainly can be influenced by external sources. The Christian Bible, other religious doctrines, and other sources of moral authority provide guidance that aid many people in making these judgments. Similarly, many professions have codes of ethics that their members are required to follow. Simply knowing that almost everyone makes a similar value judgment may help us to make the same judgment. However, let us not ever forget that everyone once thought that the world was flat. Moral or even factual truth is not decided by popular vote.

What happens when a question of value requires the reconciliation of two deeply held values that come into conflict? For example, the belief that human life is sacred is held almost universally, certainly within the western world. It follows from this that purposefully ending a human life is wrong. Here it appears that we are coming pretty close to a posture accepting ethical absolutism. Killing is wrong. Absolutely and always. But what if the person who was killed had been suffering from some disease, and, after years and years of suffering, had begged to be killed? To illustrate the power that a simple word change can influence answers on a survey, consider the difference between "killed" and "allowed to die with dignity." In this situation two powerful human values have come into conflict. Killing is wrong and should never be allowed. Terrible human suffering is wrong and should not be allowed. Perhaps in this situation causing the death of another person might be ethically appropriate. And many people, if apprised of the details, would agree. But not everyone. Even with careful study, thought, and use of ethical principles, people will often come up with different value judgments.

Questions of value deal with ethical, moral, aesthetic, and artistic concerns. There are many important and interesting questions of value that have to do with communication. Communication researchers who take a humanistic (rhetorical, critical, historical) approach to inquiry focus their research energies and resources addressing questions of value. But questions of value influence all research projects.

Before ending our discussion of questions of fact and value, a final point—a qualification—must be made. For clarity's sake, we have purposefully presented the distinction between questions of fact and questions of value in its simplest form, that is, as a dichotomy. However, this dichotomy is not quite as straightforward and tidy as our presentation has implied. While we can frequently distinguish between a question of fact and a question of value, we cannot separate them completely. There is an interaction between facts and values. The researcher addressing a question of fact is not a totally objective seeker of the truth in the external world. He or she is a fallible and probably biased individual whose personal value judgments permeate most aspects of a research project. The specific factual questions they address and the procedures they use to answer the question are both influenced by the values they hold.

Nor is an individual whose concern is a question of value isolated from external observable events. The observable characteristics of things enter into our evaluations of them. All knowledge is to some extent the result of a transaction between the internal mental states of the researcher and the outside observable world. Thus it is probably most useful to think of questions of fact and questions of value as falling along a continuum, as shown in Figure 1.2.

As shown, the extremes, which are anchored by "Answer Lies Purely Within the Questioner" and "Answer Lies Purely Within the External World," are never the realm in which the answer to either type of question lies. Rather, the answers to both questions of fact and value are found to varying degrees in the internal and external worlds, with the answers to questions of value tending to lie toward the left of the center.[3]

Questions of Policy

Questions of policy are concerned with deciding wise and prudent courses of action in the management of affairs. Policies prescribe what to do under certain circumstances. Policies take the form of formal or informal rules regarding courses of action or behavior. Usually, when we think of policies we think of formal organizations such as governments, businesses, and educational institutions. Consider the following policy questions:

> Should the United States send troops to join United Nations peacekeeping missions to prevent genocide?
>
> Should state governments lower the drinking age to eighteen?
>
> Should the Federal Trade Commission (FTC) ban the use of celebrity endorsements in alcohol advertising?
>
> Should tobacco be regulated as a drug?
>
> Should colleges and universities maintain separate dormitory facilities for athletes?
>
> Should Congress and the states pass a constitutional amendment banning the burning of the flag of the United States?

Questions of policy are frequently very complicated, requiring much varied information to answer. Questions of policy require not only an agreement on definition, but both factual information and value information. The following example illustrates this.

Should the FTC ban the use of celebrity endorsements in alcohol advertising? What are some of the kinds of information we would need, to know what national policy should

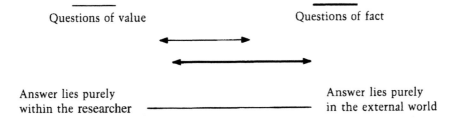

Questions of value   Questions of fact

Answer lies purely   Answer lies purely
within the researcher —————————————— in the external world

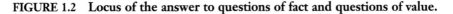

FIGURE 1.2   Locus of the answer to questions of fact and questions of value.

be on this matter? Or, put another way, what questions of fact and value would we have to answer before we could answer this question of policy? First, however, we need to agree on what we are studying, that is, on questions of definition: What is advertising? What constitutes a celebrity endorsement? And so forth.

At a minimum, we would need to know the answers to value questions associated with several related concerns. (1) Regarding alcohol consumption—some people believe that no one should consume or be allowed to consume alcohol under any circumstances. (2) Regarding government regulation—some people believe that federal government regulation of any kind is wrong and that federal government has no role in public affairs, other than perhaps national defense. (3) Regarding censorship—some people believe that the government has no role to play in regulating communication of any kind, whether broadcast via the mass media or spoken on a street corner.

Furthermore, we would probably want to know the answers to questions of fact, such as (1) How widespread is the use of celebrities to endorse alcohol products? (2) What are the intended and actual audiences at which these advertisements are aimed—do young people see these ads? (3) What is the effect of these messages—for example, do people who see former athletes like Willie Mays or Bill Russell in Coors beer ads drink more Coors? Do they drink more beer in general? If we had clear-cut definitions and answers to all these questions—answers that were widely agreed upon—setting a policy would be relatively simple. As with most policy questions, however, we usually do not have definitive answers to either the value questions or the factual questions. So policy questions are open to debate, and ultimately answered through discussion, argument, and reason.

If you have taken or will take an argumentation class as part of your communication studies or plan to be on the debate team or advertising team, much of your energies will be spent researching the answers to questions of fact and value as they relate, ultimately, to questions of policy. **Argument** is the use of reason and evidence to persuade someone that a policy is correct. And the evidence for correctness of a policy is usually information about answers to questions of fact and value based on accepted definitions.

So far, we have been concerned with examples of a policy question about the course of action to be taken by a large structured organization. But policies, and questions about them, also exist in informal organizations such as families and dyadic relationships, for example:

Should we buy what we want (e.g., an HDTV, a computer, a new dress) on credit or should we operate strictly on a cash basis?

Should Bob and Molly date other people over the summer vacation?

Should you take turns with your roommates doing the dishes or let the person who dirtied them wash them?

Should you persuade your best friend to loan you money?

Relevant factual and value information would also be important to have in deciding policy questions about these more mundane and informal situations. Although structured debates in government, industry, and academia are frequently the mechanisms by which questions of policy are answered, more informal discussions are usually the way policies in interpersonal and small group communication systems are decided. The important point is that regardless of the level of the policy question, whether it concerns the entire world or your relationship with your roommate, questions of policy require that answers to questions of fact and value be addressed first. These answers are then (or should be) applied with the use of cogent reasoning to the policy question.

Now that we have an introduction to the categories of questions people ask about communication, we will turn to the question of where we might look to answer them. Specifically, we are going to turn to the general issue of how people come to believe the things they believe.

EPISTEMOLOGY

We began this chapter by noting some of the changes that have taken place in education. These changes are especially apparent in fields such as computer science, but we feel they are equally important in communication. Thirty years ago speech students studied public speaking and group discussion, while their journalism brothers and sisters studied news and editorial writing. Today, we still study these topics, but also much more. Communication as a discipline covers an enormous range of subject matter. Students take courses that present information about communication in relationships, both fleeting and long term; in social and work groups; in political campaigns and social movements; in courtrooms and churches. They study nonverbal communication and persuasion and cross-cultural communication. They study advertising and public relations and mass communication effects, and on and on.

From where does this information—the knowledge that constitutes the content of these courses and specializations—come? How do we know what message exchanges characterize the beginning and ending stages of a relationship? How do we know that one presidential candidate uses more ethically appropriate message appeals than another? How do we know what role communication plays in a group's decision making? How do we know the effects of a political debate on voters' perceptions of the credibility of the candidates? How do we know what arguments will be most effective in convincing jurors that a defendant is guilty? How do we know if Martin Luther King's "I Have a Dream" speech was a better speech than John F. Kennedy's inaugural address or Abraham Lincoln's "Gettysburg Address"? How do we know the impact of an automobile commercial or a violent music video on adolescent viewers? The following discussion, in a general way, presents how our discipline, communication, comes to "know" the things that we teach.

Epistemology is the study of how we come to know things. It deals with how individuals and groups come to believe what they believe. Educational psychologists Kerlinger and Lee (2000) have presented a widely cited category system for organizing the various ways we come to arrive at beliefs. Their treatment is useful for both understanding how *individuals* come to hold the beliefs they hold and how communication *researchers* reach conclusions about the answers to research questions. This treatment centers on four approaches: tenacity, authority, intuition, and science.

Tenacity

The first method discussed by Kerlinger and Lee is *tenacity*. Some things we believe simply because we have always believed them. We know these things to be true because, well, we know it. We have never even thought to consider the possibility that they might not be true. We take them for granted to the point that we will cling to these beliefs *tenaciously*, regardless of conflicting information. Centuries ago humans believed that the world was flat, and that heavenly bodies—the sun, moon, and the stars—revolved around the Earth, which was the center of the universe. To believe differently was heresy, and some individuals were put to death for failing to conform to the conventional wisdom, as was the case during the Spanish Inquisition of the 1500s.

These kinds of beliefs come from traditions we inherit from our culture or subcultures. One of us observed a Ku Klux Klan (KKK) rally as part of a study of group communication rituals and noted that the individuals in attendance expressed beliefs about black people and a whole host of other "out" groups that we know to be false. But frequent repetitions of "truths" seems to reinforce their veracity. These people grew up hearing these "facts" from the time they were small children. (In fact, there were small children at the rally.) One can imagine the number of times members of the KKK and their ilk repeat and reinforce their shared beliefs—beliefs that they have learned from their culture, or in this case, from their small, isolated subculture. Unfortunately, for the time being it appears that these people are clinging to their beliefs with great tenacity. We can only hope it will not take the centuries to change these beliefs that it took to convince people that the world is round.

This is not to say that to believe something our culture has ingrained in us is necessarily bad or even that the belief is necessarily incorrect. Many such beliefs are probably quite proper, and especially in the area of fundamental human values, we probably should accept them. Take the belief that brushing your teeth is good for you. We accept this blindly. We know it is true. We will cling to it tenaciously. We are also as sure as anyone can be sure of anything that human life is sacred. So the problem with tenacity as a method of knowing is not that the beliefs are wrong. Sometimes they are and sometimes they are not. The problem is that if they *are* wrong, they may be difficult to change (the question of whether tenaciously held beliefs are especially difficult to change is itself an empirical question that has not been answered definitively). If a belief is factually or morally wrong, desirable changes may be slow in coming.

Clearly, all of us, as human beings, believe some of what we believe because of tenacity. Does tenacity as a source of knowledge operate with communication researchers as well? Most assuredly. Many researchers train within research traditions that *emphasize* certain kinds of questions, and certain approaches to answering them, to the point of excluding other questions and other methods. In our field, considerable journal space and researcher energies have been devoted to stating in some form or another, "my way is best." Or worse, "my way is the only way." Communication researchers sometimes believe things because they have been told them over and over again by their "culture"—that is, their colleagues who subscribe to the same beliefs. Academicians sometimes cling to their beliefs as tenaciously as anyone. We discuss this in more detail in Chapter 2.

Thomas Kuhn (1962), in his influential book, *The Structure of Scientific Revolutions*, writes of research paradigms. To Kuhn, a *paradigm* is a dominant way of conceptualizing a phenomenon, of approaching it methodologically, and of looking for solutions to research problems. A paradigm may dominate for decades, even centuries, with its adherents defending it bitterly in the face of conflicting information, until, ultimately, a revolution occurs and a new paradigm takes over. The new paradigm offers radically new conceptualizations, research strategies and methods, and suggestions for solutions (Kuhn, 1962). Again, the problem is not that the particular set of beliefs that constitute a paradigm are necessarily wrong, but that beliefs held because of tenacity may be extremely difficult to change.

Authority

A second method of knowing discussed by Kerlinger and Lee is *authority*, a source of some kind that has established knowledge and shares it with us: "The Bible says it, therefore it must be true." "Tom Brokaw said so on television; it must be so." "My research methods instructor disagrees with your view, so you clearly are mistaken." This method has also been called the *granny method*. One can imagine the oldest member of a family, the grandmother, sitting in a rocking chair on the front porch. When an important question needed to be answered, a family member would go up to the porch for an audience with Granny, sit at her feet, and let this wise old woman tell the truth.

Much of what we know, both as individuals and as students of communication, we know because some authority has told us. For many things that we know this is entirely sensible, especially if the authority is speaking within the realm of his or her expertise. If our dentist tells us that we need a cavity filled, we almost certainly do. She is knowledgeable about teeth in general and about our teeth in particular. Further, she is trustworthy. She is not going to lie to us. Nevertheless, authorities can be wrong and second opinions should be obtained. Even the best people at times make mistakes; there is nothing wrong in getting a second opinion, in dentistry or communication. A good rule of thumb: The more important it is that the authority be correct, the more important it is to obtain the opinions of additional authorities. We probably will not seek a second opinion about a bad tooth. However, open heart surgery would be a different matter. Note that the second opinion should be completely independent, the second doctor should not know the first doctor's opinion.

The key to using an authority as a source of information is an accurate appraisal of the extent that he or she (or it, in the case of an inanimate object such as the Bible or the U.S. Constitution) really is an authority. A special problem exists when the authority steps outside his or her area of expertise. We see this commonly in advertisements. Golfer Tiger Woods is the spokesperson in ads for everything from cars to breakfast cereals. Obviously, the company believes that he will be viewed as an authority by many people. But what does he know about nutrition? (And it stretches credulity to believe that Tiger drives a $28,000 Buick.) Evaluating the credibility of an authority is an important part of the research process, particularly when conducting historical, critical, and rhetorical research. People in academia, including communication researchers, sometimes espouse truths in areas outside their area of expertise. And some of them are right or wrong with equal confidence. How to evaluate sources of information, including authorities, is a major theme of Chapter 4.

Intuition

A third method of knowing discussed by Kerlinger and Lee is the **a priori method**; also called the method of *intuition*. Basically, this is the idea that the truth tends to be self-evident, and that if reasonable people engage in open-minded discussion, the correct answers to problems will tend to surface. This is similar to one of the premises on which democratic governments are based—that other things being equal, open discussion inclines us toward the truth. Kerlinger and Lee are critical of this method as a way of knowing, stating, "The difficulty with this position lies in the expression 'agree with reason.' Whose reason?" (p. 7). However, they are concerned primarily with answering questions of fact that are amenable to scientific inquiry. For questions of value and questions of policy, in particular, the *a priori* method of allowing reason to prevail is a good way to proceed.

There is nothing to preclude the open discussions in which reason prevails from including arguments that contain a variety of kinds of evidence, including statements from authorities and even relevant scientific findings. If, for example, a national policy is to be decided, this method has generally served our country well.

Science

For questions of fact that do lend themselves to empirical study, we agree with Kerlinger and Lee. The fourth method of knowing, *science*, is best. Communication researchers who take a scientific approach, like other scientists, model their methods after those used in the physical sciences and as articulated by philosophers such as John Locke, Karl Popper, Carl Hempel, and John Dewey. In brief, the scientist starts with a problem or obstacle, proposes a solution—a **theory**—which predicts that if the proposed solution is correct, certain events ought to occur under certain circumstances, creates those circumstances in a manner that allows for careful observations to determine if the prediction was correct, and uses the results of the observation to confirm, modify, refine, or reject the theory.

Science has one advantage over other ways of knowing—and it is a big one. If an error has been made with the scientific method there are built-in checks explicitly designed to maximize the likelihood that the errors will be detected and corrected. The *ideal model of science* includes the following features. First, science is authority-free. Research is evaluated not by who did it, but by how it was done, whether proper procedures were followed, objective methods used, and so on. Thus, research papers submitted to journals for publication or for presentation at scientific gatherings are usually evaluated by reviewers who do not know who wrote the paper. It is not who you are that counts; rather, it is the quality of your research. As with most methods, however, practice sometimes does not meet the ideal; the fact is we do have authorities, not all journals use blind reviews, and some published research is invited, based on the reputation of the researcher.

Second, scientific knowledge is always *public* knowledge. The researcher describes not only his or her results, but also the methods used to obtain those results. Furthermore, the methods are described with enough detail to allow other researchers to evaluate and reproduce them. Flaws in the method used are described openly. Honesty and openness characterize science.

Third, because of the openness and detailed descriptions of procedures, other researchers are free to attempt to reproduce the results using the same or slightly modified procedures. If researcher A believes that researcher B has biased the results in some way, A is free to repeat B's observations with the alleged biasing elements eliminated. A is then free to present his or her observations and results for public scrutiny. Over time, since science is addressing questions of fact, which are empirical questions, we can become more and more confident of their utility, as we describe the way the world is.

Like all research methods, science has its limitations and disadvantages. It does not address, directly at least, questions of value. (Although the results of scientific research might help an individual reach a decision about a value question.) The methods of the scientist have become an essential set of tools for contemporary communication researchers.

APPLYING KNOWLEDGE IN COMMUNICATION

All research begins with the asking of a question. That question may be something simple or it may be complex. The process by which we conduct research is the same regardless of the communication area we are interested in studying. Some areas of communication research, however, are more appropriately studied from different types of perspectives using a variety of methods, only one of which is science. For example, much broadcast research tries to answer policy and value questions. This is not to say that broadcasters do not answer questions of definition or fact; indeed, they do. Advertising research addresses questions of fact: What commercial message is most effective in selling a product?

In Part II we will explore a variety of research methods that answer one or more of the questions posed by the communication researcher. Figure 1.3 expands upon Figure 1.1, the relationship between the sciences, humanities, and research methodologies. When approached from a research orientation, the differences between science and humanities may best be viewed in terms of rigor. Rigor, in this usage, concerns the specificity of the rules followed by the researcher to answer his or her question. We might conceptualize rigor in the following manner:

Humanities   Social Sciences   Natural/Physical Sciences

Less Rigorous   ◄─────────────────────────► Most Rigorous

Chapter 2 (and much of the rest of the book) will discuss rigor in greater detail. However, we should note that the humanities "less rigorous" label may be misleading. What the humanities are primarily concerned with are questions of definition and value—what it is and how well it was done. Humanities-oriented research explores in-depth a particular event, message, individual, or historical outcome as an end in itself. As we shall see, science, on the other hand, seeks to generalize findings as widely as possible. The more rigorous the control, the better the generalizability and the credibility of those generalizations. The rigor difference between the social and natural sciences comes from the subject of study: humans and their interrelationships are the study of the social sciences, and humans are difficult to "control," especially when dealing with communication variables such as attitudes, beliefs, and values. As noted earlier in this chapter, each approach to the study of communication focuses on a particular aspect of the research question.

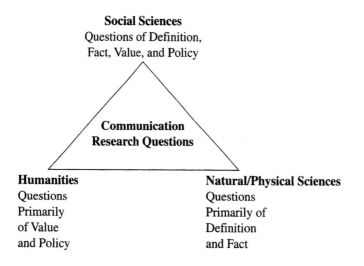

FIGURE 1.3   **Relationship of an approach to research questions.**

The natural and physical sciences include chemistry, biology, and physics; social science research includes communication, psychology, anthropology, and sociology. All approaches, however, contribute to our understanding of human communication.

In Chapter 2 we will explore theory as it relates to understanding communication behavior. We will examine in some detail the different ways that researchers answer their questions based on whether they approach those questions from a scientific or humanistic approach.

SUMMARY

This chapter focused on the beginning stages of the research process. It was noted that all communication research: (1) is designed to generate knowledge that may be used to improve the human condition; (2) involves studying how humans encode, transmit, and receive symbols to influence one another; (3) follows certain prescribed rules; (4) involves the collection and analysis of data; and (5) begins with a question that asks about something that is unknown. Questions about human communication can be divided into questions of definition, fact, value, and policy. Four methods or ways of answering questions were presented: tenacity, authority, intuition (or reason), and science. We argued that for addressing questions of fact, science has an advantage over these other "ways of knowing." The scientific method includes procedures that increase the likelihood that if an error has made, it will be detected and corrected. While the focus of this book is on scientific research, other approaches to research, if well conducted, can contribute to our understanding of human communication.

PROBES

1. Why *do* people conduct research? From your point of view, what is important about the research process? Based on what you have learned thus far in your communication courses, what has research provided that allows us to understand better how humans communicate?

2. All research begins with a question. What does this statement mean? How do we go about finding a good question to study?

3. There are three major questions posed by researchers (value, fact, and policy). Take an interest area and pose one question for each of the three types. Looking at these questions, do they suggest any particular *process* or *systematic* relationships between the concepts in the question? Take a concept from an earlier communication course and provide any reportive and stipulative definitions you can find. Are some better than others? Why?

4. Write several questions of fact and several of value about important communication issues. Which seem more easily answered? Which seem more important to answer?

5. The study of how we come to know things is called "epistemology." Looking through the literature in your area of interest, list examples you believe reflect knowledge through tenacity, authority, intuition, and science. How do you define "best"?

6. We argue that the ultimate goal of communication is improving the human condition. Explain how correct answers to questions of fact can do this.

7. How can answers to questions of fact help us make value judgments?

8. What are the advantages and the dangers, if any, in putting total faith in one authority to guide us in making value judgments?

RESEARCH PROJECTS

Throughout this book we will suggest sample research projects. Some, found within the chapters as "mini-projects," can be used to extend your understanding of the material. Others, located at the end of the chapter, offer more ideas for communication research and may be used for class project assignments.

1. We have used the phrase "consumer of information" in this chapter. What are "consumers of information"? How do they differ, if they do, from "nonconsumers" of information? Is the distinction something that communication researchers will find valuable? Why? How do you know? Provide an analysis of the concept "consumer of information."

2. What is the history of research contributions in the areas of journalism, interpersonal communication, organizational communication, public relations, rhetoric, broadcast, or advertising? What types of questions were addressed at what particular stages ("paradigms") of the area's development? Provide an analysis of the development of any of these communication areas with an emphasis on *how*, that is, the methods used to learn new information.

3. Identify some cultural ideals that are "known" through intuition and tenacity. What scientific evidence refutes those beliefs?

NOTES

1. Our treatment of this distinction between types of questions is heavily influenced by Miller and Nicholson (1976).

2. Some complex philosophical issues that are beyond the scope of this book are raised by this seemingly simple distinction. *Subjectivism* is a philosophical view that ob-

jects do not exist independent of our awareness of them, whereas *objectivism* is the view that there is a reality that exists independent of human perception. When dealing with questions of fact or value, an intermediate view between these two extremes is probably the most useful. See Titus (1964) pages 44–52, for a discussion.

3. However, we should note that while this is our po-sition on the nature of value judgments, there is a con-trasting view that values are objective and out there in the world to be discovered. Critical thinking involves not only deciding what is right and wrong, that is, making value judgments, but also in deciding on *how* best to make our value judgments.

REFERENCES

Aronson, E. (1972). *The social animal*. San Francisco: W. H. Freeman.

Gates, W. (1995). *The road ahead*. New York: Viking Press.

Kerlinger, F. N., & Lee, H. B. (2000). *Foundations of behavioral research*, 4th ed. New York: Harcourt College Publishers.

Kuhn, T. (1962). *The structure of scientific revolutions*. Chicago: University of Chicago Press.

McGuire, M. D. (1984). Darkness on the edge of town: Bruce Springsteen's rhetoric of optimism and de-spair in M. J. Medhurst & T. Benson (Eds.), *Rhetorical dimensions in media: A critical casebook*. Dubuque, IA: Kendall-Hunt.

Miller, G. R., & Nicholson, H. (1976). *Communication inquiry: A perspective on a process*. Reading, MA: Addison-Wesley.

Parker, D. H. (1931). *Human values*. New York: Harper.

Titus, H. H. (1964). *Living issues in philosophy*. New York: American Book.

CHAPTER TWO

THE ROLE OF THEORY IN COMMUNICATION RESEARCH

APPROACHES TO COMMUNICATION

THEORETICAL ORIENTATIONS

SCIENTIFIC RESEARCH AND THEORY
    Description
    Explanation
    Prediction
    Control
    Utility

    Deductive vs. inductive theory
    Self-correctiveness

HUMANISTIC RESEARCH AND THEORY
    Practice
    Questions of Value

APPLYING KNOWLEDGE IN COMMUNICATION

OBJECTIVES

By the end of this chapter you should be able to:

1. Explain the role that theory plays in communication research.
2. Distinguish between the major theoretical orientations to communication study.
3. Explain the concepts of description, explanation, prediction, control, and self-correctiveness as they relate to communication research.
4. Differentiate between inductive and deductive theoretical approaches to communication research.
5. Decide whether the research question posed is best suited to be addressed by a scientific or humanistic approach.

There are many ways to categorize the communication discipline—to make sense of the "buzzing, blooming confusion" that sometimes seems to characterize our field. A number of often ambiguous terms are used to describe the variety of research approaches used in communication studies. Rhetorical, historical, critical, humanistic, scientific, quantitative, and qualitative are the most commonly used labels (c.f., Salwen & Stacks, 1997), but there is by no means universal agreement about what each means or about the nature of research conducted by someone who calls him- or herself by one of these labels. In this chapter we are going to build on the foundation laid in Chapter 1, specifically on the distinction between questions of fact and questions of value, and use this distinction to clarify some key terms. In the process we will provide an introduction to the role of theory in addressing both kinds of questions.

APPROACHES TO STUDYING COMMUNICATION

Gerald R. Miller (1975) argues that there are three primary purposes for studying communication. First, "in some situations, students of . . . communication observe communication phenomena primarily for the purpose of making factual generalizations about similar phenomena not encompassed by the observations" (p. 232). In other words, sometimes we are interested in observing events not because of the event itself, but because of what the event will tell us about communication in general. This is what the communication scientist is interested in—always. (As will be explained later, this is what the rhetorician is interested in much, if not most, of the time.) The scientist wants to make statements about the relationships between concepts, constructs, or variables that, although observed in one setting, exist in others as well. The researcher is interested in a relatively few factors that provide explanations for a broad range of human behavior. The communication researcher in these instances is interested in questions of fact about the relationship between variables or concepts in the present and the future.

For example, imagine that a researcher is interested in the kinds of messages people exchange in initial encounters, specifically the depth of self-disclosure achieved during a one-hour encounter. She brings forty strangers together in her laboratory, places them in dyads (pairs) and videotapes their initial interaction. Later, she observes these videotapes, and based on carefully stipulated definitions, categorizes the information exchanged in terms of "depth of self-disclosure" during the first 20 minutes, the middle 20 minutes, and the final 20 minutes of a one-hour meeting. The researcher is not interested in the specific information an individual pair exchange, per se, or even what all 20 pairs collectively say to one another. The researcher is interested in the *relationship* between the two abstract variables—time (the first, second, or third 20 minutes of an hour) and depth of disclosure (level of intimacy)—in general. She wants to make statements about the way these variables relate in this situation not as an end in itself, but as evidence about the way these variables relate in other situations.

Second, according to Miller (1975), "[in other situations, students of communication] study and observe phenomena so they can draw factual conclusions about the observed phenomena themselves" (p. 232). In other words, sometimes we are interested in observing the event as an end in itself. We are not interested in learning about other events; rather, this event is of such interest that learning about it is ample justification for its study. This approach is sometimes called an **ideographic model of explanation** (Babbie, 1986). The researcher is interested in identifying as many factors that contribute to a particular event as possible, even if these factors are unique to this event. If the event is in the present or future, the researcher can conduct a **case study**, which might involve direct observations of the event, interviews with participants before, during, or after it, and a host of other data-gathering techniques that will be discussed in detail in later chapters.

For example, a researcher might be interested in the depth of self-disclosure President Clinton achieves when talking about his involvement with a student intern. The researcher might videotape Clinton's various interviews and news conferences on the topic and carefully categorize and describe when and how he reveals various information. The researcher is not interested in self-disclosure generally or even self-disclosure by United States presidents; he is interested in this specific president's disclosure on this specific issue—his relationship with Ms. Lewinsky. The issue might be viewed, at least by this researcher, of such great importance that it is worthy of study as an end in itself.

Since, by definition, the events being studied are communication events, the researcher is focusing on the processes by which human beings exchange symbols and influence one another. The researcher is likely to use the methods of rhetoric to understand the event and to call him- or herself a *rhetorician*. The rhetorician in this case is addressing questions of *fact* about specific communication events. The study of the specific event, however, may suggest to the rhetorician general principles about how communication works in other situations. And, in fact, in many cases, this is a major purpose of a rhetorical study.

A rhetorical *case study* may suggest relationships between variables that apply in other situations. This is often called a *grounded theory* approach. Some of these generalizations may lend themselves to carefully repeated, objective observation. To the extent that the rhetorician does this, he or she is behaving very much like a social scientist engaged in qualitative field research. It is also here that the rhetorician and scientist may be able to complement and supplement one another's research efforts. A rhetorical study of a specific communication event may suggest questions that a scientist could test. There are examples of principles or theories that were suggested in a case study later being tested in the controlled conditions of a laboratory.[1]

If the event was in the past, the researcher would use the methods of the historian to "observe" it indirectly. The methods of the historian include examining diaries, newspapers, and other documents, film clips, interviews, and a host of other techniques (see Chapter 5). If asked what he or she did for a living, the response might be, "I am an historian," or perhaps, "a rhetorical historian." In these situations the researcher is interested in questions of *fact* about *specific* communication events that have occurred in the past. Specific facts, in turn, may illuminate larger issues. The issue of whether historical/rhetorical research has as its purpose theory building, the explication of historical facts, or an examination of discourse as an end in itself, has been debated long and hard by rhetorical critics (c.f., Baskerville, 1977). Suffice it to say that there is disagreement among rhetoricians on this issue.

Finally, Miller (1975) states that we "study communicative phenomena for the purpose of arriving at ethical or aesthetic judgments about the phenomena themselves, or about the event, or events, with which the phenomena are associated" (p. 235). Here, Miller is talking about questions of *value*. Individuals who address questions of value do so using the methods of the critic. The critic often attempts to apply some established ethical or aesthetic principles to a situation in an effort to answer a question of value.

The use of these labels becomes more complicated because the nature of the inquiry is often not clearly of one kind or another. Rather, there may be some overlap between these seemingly discrete categories of research questions. For example, a researcher might be interested in both describing an event and offering a critical evaluation of it. In fact, Bill Clinton claimed several times that he did not "have sex with" Ms. Lewinsky, his intern. A historian could examine the facts of this incident, come to conclusions about whether, in fact, Mr. Clinton's claim was truthful or not, *and then* go on to offer criticism of the event, including judgments about Clinton's integrity and, perhaps morality. This researcher would be addressing questions of fact and questions of value within the same overall research project. We would say that this person was conducting a historical (it happened in the past, or near past), rhetorical (the focus is on a persuasive speech or speeches), critical (value judgments are made, either explicitly or implicitly, concerning the events surrounding the speech[es] and the speech[es] themselves) study.

Who employs rhetorical, historical, or critical approaches to research? We all do. However, there are those who rely more on some of these approaches than do others. The television critic, the reporter who investigates a particular candidate, person, or event in great detail utilizes one of these approaches. Scientists who study persuasion, attitude change, or propaganda often begin with hypotheses that are derived from aspects of a rhetorical approach. Advertising and public relations is often taught from a case studies approach. The general idea is that the better we understand a particular promotional campaign, the better we can prepare for a future one. Much of business and organizational communication is taught this way as well.

THEORETICAL ORIENTATIONS

Few words in the English language are used in more different ways than **humanism**. In the most general sense it is used to refer to an attitude or philosophy in which human beings are of paramount importance, that human interests and values are worthy of study as ends in themselves. When research questions focus on single events, as ends in themselves, or with a more **qualitative**—as contrasted with **quantitative**—approach to communication, the label humanistic is often used. Thus rhetorical-historical-critical research, which often examines questions of value and uses qualitative research methods, is frequently referred to

■ ■ ■ ■ ■

MINI-PROJECT:

Pick up another class textbook and open it to any page. Pick out several paragraphs and read them. Write out the paragraph's thesis. How is that thesis supported? Which theoretical approach do you think was used primarily? Was the thesis derived from a particular approach? If so, which? What does this knowledge provide you in terms of the section's thesis?

as *humanistic;* we will use this definition to identify any method that focuses on specific events that have occurred in the past and ask questions of value.

One final point should be made. Humanistic research is often contrasted with, or seen as the opposite of, social scientific research. This is unfortunate. Our view is that both kinds of research have the same general goal: *The improvement of the human condition.* The questions each is able to address are different, and the methods used to answer them are different, but, as noted earlier, both make an important contribution.

We are going to collapse Miller's (1975) distinction between the communication researcher who is interested in an event as an end in itself and the researcher who is concerned with questions of value. Although it may be an oversimplification, we believe this is a sensible approach because, in practice, the rhetorician, whether studying a present or past event as an end in itself, is also usually offering **critical analysis** of the event. In short, all rhetorical studies require description, but many rhetorical studies use rhetorical theory to evaluate and interpret the meaning of the event. We will distinguish between the two dominant methods used by communication researchers by using the term **humanistic** to refer to rhetorical-historical-critical research and the term **scientific** to refer to social scientific, or **empirical** research. The word empirical simply means "capable of being verified through observation."

Humanism and science have some fundamental things in common as well as some significant differences. In this chapter we will describe these similarities and differences, particularly as they relate to the use of theory in the field. Again, we hope to show that the two approaches complement one another. First, we will take a look at science, its method, and specifically the role of theory.

SCIENTIFIC RESEARCH AND THEORY

As stated in Chapter 1, we believe that any collective human endeavor, including research of all kinds, must have as its ultimate goal the betterment of the human condition. Science contributes to this lofty goal through building theory. Fundamentally, the purpose of any science is to build theory about the phenomena that fall within the range of that scientific discipline. Communication theories provide explanations for, and predictions about, observed communication phenomena and their effects. In this section we are going to define theory formally, show how theory is built using the scientific method, and illustrate how theories are *useful* to researchers and practitioners alike.[2] Finally, we are going to take an example that demonstrates how science is self-correcting; that is, when mistakes are made, when theory is in error, the design of the methods of science maximizes the likelihood that a hypothesis or error will be detected and corrected.

The term **theory** is used in many different ways. In everyday language we use the word as a synonym for a conjecture or a guess. For example, someone might say, "I have a theory that he is lying," or, "my theory is the Democrats will pick a female candidate for president in the next election." People talk about something working in theory, but not in practice. They say that an idea is *merely* a theory.

In science, the word theory has a special use. Although scientists sometimes use the word in different ways, fundamentally, to a scientist, theories are *statements about the relationships among abstract concepts or variables.* A simple theory might specify how only two or three variables are related. For example, a researcher who is interested in the effects of self-disclosure on relationship development might reason thusly:

> Self-disclosure by person A to person B results in B coming to the decision that A trusts B. It is rewarding to be trusted. People like to be trusted. It feels good. Therefore, people who indicate that they trust people are likely to be liked by other people. Thus, self-disclosure leads to increased liking. Person B will like person A as a result of A's self-disclosure to B.

This is a small theory, to be sure. It has only three variables: self-disclosure, perceived trust, and liking. We are going to use Kerlinger's (1986) definition of scientific theory:

> A theory is a set of interrelated constructs (concepts), definitions, and propositions that present a systematic view of phenomena by specifying relations among variables, with the purpose of explaining and predicting the phenomena. (p. 9)

A theory, simply put, answers the question why are those concepts and variables related?

It is often said that science has four purposes: **description, explanation, prediction,** and **control**. The following sections examine the key features of Kerlinger's definition and observe how theory contributes to each of these purposes. Obviously, the kinds of research questions we ask are influenced by our purpose.

Description

A theory includes definitions of *variables*. But what is a variable? It is literally any attribute we can think of that is changeable, that varies. Variables require definition. A good theory stipulates to what a variable, concept, or construct refers. Note that Kerlinger speaks of concepts and constructs. The term **construct** is carefully selected. Quite literally, the scientist builds or *constructs* the variables. They literally are "made up" to describe or explain phenomena. They did not exist before the scientist, working in the abstract world of symbols, created them. And, since they are abstract creations, we need to know to what they

■ ■ ■ ■ ■

MINI-PROJECT:

Construct your own mini-theory using the variables self-disclosure, trust, and liking as they might relate to your communication major. Are these variables generalizable to situations or contexts beyond interpersonal communication? Do they operate, for instance, in broadcasting, advertising, or public relations?

refer. Constructs include such things as credibility, intelligence, violence, attitudes, message intensity, communication goals—the list is endless.

Explanation

A theory involves specifying the *relationships* among variables. A theory provides an explanation by stating *why* the relationship exists. For our self-disclosure example, self-disclosure leads to trust, and trust is related to liking. So the reason, or the *why*, according to this particular theory, is that self-disclosure is related to liking because of trust which is the explanation. If we know the conditions under which events will occur, we can say that you have explained the event. The specification of the relationships between independent and dependent variables constitutes scientific explanation. An **independent variable** is the variable that is the cause of, or the antecedent to, or the predictor of, the dependent variable. The **dependent variable** gets its name because it depends on the independent variable for its value.

The concept of cause is controversial among philosophers and social scientists. Some treatments of explanation emphasize the specification of causal relationships as the ultimate goal to which science aspires (c.f., Blalock, 1970). Other writers, including Kerlinger, feel that the notion of causality is not necessary for scientific understanding. Our position is that causal thinking is such an integral part of human thinking that it is difficult to conceive an orderly universe without it. Theories tell us why independent variables cause which dependent variables to take on particular values.

Prediction

If we know the way that variables are related, it follows quite closely that knowledge of the value of an independent variable will allow us a good chance of predicting the value of the dependent variable to which it is antecedent. If X occurs and we know that Y follows, then we can predict: If X, then Y. If we know that high source credibility results in more audience member attitude change than low source credibility, we can predict that when there is high source credibility there will be more attitude change than when there is low source credibility among audience members. The test of a theory is whether the explanations it provides, that is, whether the relationships among the variables that are contained in its statements (frequently called *propositions*), allow for accurate explanations of observable events. Theories that allow accurate predictions are useful. We can think of them as supported or correct. Theories that do not allow accurate predictions are not useful. We can think of them as rejected, not supported; that is, as incorrect.

Hypotheses.   How do we know if a theory predicts accurately? We test it empirically. While the variables in a theory may be abstract, when the time comes to test that theory, to make observations about whether the variables are related in the presumed ways, concrete definitions are necessary. These definitions *allow us to make hypotheses*. A *hypothesis*, like a theoretical proposition, is a statement of the relationship between variables. However, whereas theoretical propositions are abstract, hypotheses are more concrete statements. Hypotheses are to be tested. A *research hypothesis* predicts that changes in the dependent variable(s) will occur in specified ways due to changes in the independent variable(s). Hypotheses, then, include variables that are less abstract and suggest implications for testing the prediction empirically. Hypotheses are phrased as declarative sentences. Here are some examples of hypotheses:

> The more often teenagers attend movies, the more likely they are to use tobacco products.
>
> Self-disclosure is related to liking among romantic dyads.
>
> Advertisements that use repetitive images will attract more attention than those that do not.
>
> Organizations with supportive climates have lower absenteeism than those that do not.
>
> A job interviewee who uses proper grammar during the interview will be evaluated more favorably by the interviewer than his or her counterpart who uses poor grammar.

Operational Definitions.   To test theories, the variables must be defined operationally. *Operational definitions* specify the procedures—literally the operations—the researcher engages in to observe the variable. Conceptually, we all know what a German chocolate cake is. But we need a recipe to follow to actually produce one. That recipe describes all the procedures we have to follow to produce a German chocolate cake. The recipe is the operational definition, and the social scientist must follow and publish their operationalizations so that other researchers can understand and reproduce the procedures or recipe. Both the independent and dependent variables require operational definition. There are two general categories of operational definitions: *manipulated* and *measured*. We will discuss manipulated operational definitions first.

If a researcher wanted to test the relationship between self-disclosure and liking, she might conduct an experiment in which a **confederate**—a person who appears to naive research participants to be another participant, but who in reality has been trained by the researcher—engaged in either a high or low degree of self-disclosure to the participant. The specific context that was created, the verbal and nonverbal messages emitted by the confederate in the two experimental conditions—high and low self-disclosure—would constitute the operationalization of the independent variable. The operational definition would be so specific as to include the actual message. For example:

> In the *high* self-disclosure conditions the confederate stated to the participants that (1) she had just taken an exam and failed it; (2) that she had caught her boyfriend on a date with another woman; and (3) that she was deathly afraid of catching herpes. In the *low* self-disclosure condition the confederate states that (1) she has just taken an exam and does not know how she has done; (2) she has a boyfriend; and (3) she was afraid of spiders.

Note that with this much detail other researchers have the potential to evaluate the research procedures and repeat the study.

The second kind of operational definition involves stating the procedures used to measure the concept. In the self-disclosure experiment, the researcher would need some way to assess the impact of high or low self-disclosure on the participants' degree of liking for the confederate. Most variables have many potential operational definitions and "liking" could be assessed in a variety of ways. The researcher might give a paper and pencil measure to the participants and ask them, "How much did you like the person you were paired with in this interaction?" The participant could be given scaled response options, such as: "I Like Them: A Great Deal, Somewhat, A Little, or Not at All." Or, the participant might be given an opportunity to sit next to the confederate on a sofa and the number of inches they sat apart could become the operationalization of "liking."

Independent variables can be manipulated *or* measured. Dependent variables are *always* measured. We shall have a good deal more to say about manipulated operational definitions and measured operational definitions in later chapters.

Control

If we know that under certain conditions certain things will happen, we can sometimes control these conditions and achieve outcomes that are more favorable than they would have been otherwise. It is for purposes of **control** that the notion of causality becomes especially useful. If an independent variable is known to cause a dependent variable to take on a particular value, we have the potential to change the independent variable so that the dependent variable will take on the value *we want*. It is through the increased ability to control our social environments that communication theory offers the potential to contribute to a better world.

This basic idea is applicable at several levels. On the personal level, if we know that, under certain conditions, self-disclosure generally results in increased liking, we can self-disclose to someone under these conditions and increase the probability of their liking us. On a more global level, if we know that segregation leads to racism, we can make integration a national policy and reduce racism. Or, if we know that a particular message strategy used in public service advertisements will reduce the incidence of smoking among adolescent girls, we can use this strategy to achieve such an outcome. In short, theory creates the potential for controlling communication and its effects. And the better the theory, the more potential for control—for changing the world from the way it is to something better.

No doubt some are concerned that scientifically derived knowledge about human communication, that is, communication theory, has the potential to be put to evil ends—perhaps to control people for evil outcomes. (Hitler's use of propaganda is a commonly cited example.) There are several responses to this legitimate concern. First, remember that real scientific knowledge is *public* knowledge; it is available to all scientists, and, in fact, quickly diffuses to the population as a whole. It shows up quickly in college and (later) high school textbooks, and it appears in such popular magazines as *The Atlantic, Harpers, The New Yorker, Maxim,* and even *Cosmopolitan.* Just as knowledge of how to control people can be used to control them, the knowledge also can be used to prevent people from being controlled in undesirable ways. Second, everything turns out some way. Allowing "what will be to be" obviously results in a good many poor outcomes—loneliness, suicide, relational dissatisfaction, job unhappiness, poor group decisions, political fiascoes—and each such outcome shows that the world deviates from perfection. Knowledge gives us the potential to change these poor outcomes to more positive ones. Our view is that the potential benefits far outweigh the risks.[3]

The Utility of Scientific Theory

Karl Sagan, the famous astrophysicist, (1996) wrote, "Science is more than a body of knowledge; it is a way of thinking" (p. 25). And what scientists think about much of the time is theory. To the scientist, theories are both an end in themselves and the means to an end. Theory begets better theory, and on and on. A theory tells a researcher what variables to look at and, by implication, what variables to ignore. If the theory is supported, that is, if observations reveal the variables to be related in the way stated by the propositions of the theory, then the scientist has increased confidence in it. If it is not fully supported, the theorist may refine it by adding new variables or expand its scope by making further observations to test it in other situations. If the theory is not supported by observation, the researcher must either modify the method of observation or modify the theory. Much like definitions of terms, theories are not true or false in any absolute sense. Rather, they are useful or not useful. To the extent that a theory provides explanations that allow accurate predictions, they are useful. To the extent they do not provide explanations that provide accurate predictions, they are not useful.

Theory tells the communication researcher what variables to study, what to observe. If you are interested in understanding the role that communication plays in relational satisfaction, you might start with a simple hypothesis: Employees who talk a lot will be more satisfied than those who do not talk very much. Although the hypothesis only has two variables—"amount of talk" and "relational satisfaction"—it nonetheless serves the important function of directing the researcher to look at certain variables and to ignore others. In this case, observations would be made about the amount of talk and about relational satisfaction. If the hypothesis were more developed into a theory it might make statements about the relationship between the kinds of information exchanged during the talk periods and relational satisfaction. You would then be able to look for the effect of the exchange of these types of information on satisfaction (either in general or examined as levels, such as high, moderate, and low satisfaction). As the theory was expanded, tested, modified, retested, refined, tested again, you would move closer and closer to a fuller understanding of communication and relationship satisfaction. The better the theory, the better able you will be to specify new variables to study.

Let us look at a concrete example of how theory is useful to the scientist. In January, 1986, a national tragedy occurred when the space shuttle *Challenger* exploded, killing all seven people on board, including schoolteacher Christa McAulliffe. Until this event, all twenty-four shuttle launches had been successful. "Shuttle launch success" was not a variable. This concept was a constant. Sadly, "launch success" turned into a variable with launch number twenty-five. We can think of the shuttle "launch success" as a dependent variable. It is a variable because it can *vary*, that is, take on different values. The shuttle can be launched successfully or it can explode. The problem the various scientists and engineers faced immediately after the accident was to find out which of an almost limitless number of potential independent variables caused this launch to fail. For several days after the accident there did not seem to be a clue as to what went wrong. The U.S. Navy and Coast Guard began collecting every bit of physical evidence they could find. Radio messages received from the shuttle were examined, as were vocal transmissions and photographs. For several days, it looked pretty hopeless. There was even speculation that we might never find out why *Challenger* exploded.

Then NASA found a still photograph that appeared to show a plume of smoke emitted from one of the solid fuel booster rockets. Almost immediately, those investigating the accident focused on the booster rocket seals as a *possible* cause, that is, an independent variable. They now had a hunch, the beginnings of a theory. It told them what to look at and what to possibly ignore. Very quickly it was discovered that there had been trouble with and concern about the "O rings" that sealed the booster rockets' sections. They now were able to piece together the evidence and create their explanation as to why *Challenger* exploded. It was learned from past research that cold affected "O ring integrity;" further photos showed a puff of white smoke from one of the seals at the moment of ignition of the rockets. (Note that the scientists and engineers did not know to look closely at that specific photo out of thousands available until they had a theory to guide them.) Although government officials were cautious about making a hasty conclusion, and it was a full year before the O ring problem was officially proclaimed to have been the cause, it became very clear that this, in fact, was the key independent variable. As a result of this investigation, the booster rocket seals were redesigned.

This example also shows how theory is useful in controlling the environment. By identifying the independent variable, "O ring integrity," that caused the particular effect on the dependent variable, "shuttle launch success," the engineers and scientists were able to change the independent variables as a means of exerting control over the dependent variable. In this case, a change in the way in which the O rings were used, or even eliminated from future booster rocket designs, affected the future shuttle launchings (environment). The ability to explain and predict provides the potential for control. And, as we now know, shuttle launches since the *Challenger* disaster have been controlled in a manner that has resulted in successful outcomes.

It may not be quite so obvious how theory is useful to the nonscientist. Imagine that you have just graduated from college and have taken a job as an organizational communication consultant. Your firm has been commissioned by a company to make recommendations about how to correct problems they are having at one of their manufacturing plants. Employee morale at the plant is at an all-time low. Absenteeism, turnover, tardiness, and poor work quality are all indications of the seriousness of the problem. Company management has no idea what is wrong, but, in desperation, they think it may have something to do with "communication." Thus your firm has been hired to make specific recommendations to correct the problem. They send you out to the plant to appraise the situation. Imagine, furthermore, two variations on the basic scenario: You arrive with no theory; or, you arrive with a whole briefcase full of theories.

Scenario 1: No Theory. What do you do? What do you look for? What could be the cause of these problems? What independent variables could be causing this dependent variable, employee morale, to take on such a low value? You have no idea. You are theoryless. Soon, you will also be jobless.

Scenario 2: Theory. What do you do? What do you look for? What could be the cause of these problems? What independent variables could be causing the problems? Your theories (those that you learned in your classes while in school as well as those you learn, refine, and test as a communication professional) will tell you exactly where to look, what to observe, whom to interview, what to study, and how to proceed.

You know, for example, that a well-supported theory indicates that employees who are allowed or encouraged to have input into decisions that affect their jobs are more likely to be committed to, and involved with, their jobs than are employees who have no such input. This theory is sometimes given as one of the reasons that Japanese managers, who typically use a more participatory form of management than their more autocratic American counterparts, have been so successful in producing high-quality goods. Armed with this knowledge, you examine the communication flow within the plant, specifically with an eye toward determining if employees are given the opportunity to have input into decisions that affect their jobs. If further investigation reveals that they have no such input opportunity, you have a good candidate for an independent variable that may provide a solution. If, on the other hand, your study reveals that the plant already has a well-run and thoroughly diffused quality circle program, a program specifically designed to provide such input, you will have to look in your briefcase again. Fortunately, it is full of theory, and will direct you what to look at next.

It has been said that nothing is as practical as a good theory (Lewin, 1951). What differentiates a scientist, in general, and a communication researcher/scientist in particular, from the average person just trying to understand the world around him or her is the degree of rigor used to identify problems and those things that may be causing them. Philosopher Robert Dubin (1976), writing on how science and theory can be applied to the work place, notes:

> The scientist's and practitioner's views of what constitutes a 'problem' clearly differ. The practitioner operates with a finite world and continually grounds his decisions and predictions about how that finite world will be ordered. Problems occur when the predictions go wrong and decisions deriving from the predictions become inaccurate. . . . Absenteeism is a problem to a business executive because he would like to make decisions based on a prediction that would mean low absenteeism for his organization. For the scientist, the nature of an individual's attachment to an organization may be his analytical problem and he views absenteeism as a form of temporary disengagement, the reasons for which is one of his analytical tasks to discover. (p. 21)

Knowledge of theory allows both the practitioner and the scientist to solve their respective problems better.

Deductive Theory or Inductive Theory

As noted, the research process begins with a question about something that is unknown. There is a problem or obstacle that is not understood. The traditional approach to science would be to propose a solution, a theory. Then observations would be made about whether the proposed theory is correct. The model is basically **deductive**; the researcher *presumes* a relationship between particular variables ahead of time and then deduces a testable hypothesis. The theory precedes the research. It has to because the theory tells the researcher what variables to study.

Some philosophers of science, for example, Sir Francis Bacon, have advocated an **inductive** approach to scientific theory building. Basically, an inductive approach would involve selecting a particular communication phenomenon and observing every identifiable variable that might conceivably be related to the phenomenon. The researcher would then sort through the data and look for patterns that may allow him or her to make a generalization. In short, the research precedes the theory. (This closely resembles the grounded theory method of the rhetorician that we mentioned earlier.)

This is also essentially the approach that was used to study the space shuttle disaster. The engineers and scientists were looking at *everything*. However, they were in a unique situation of having virtually limitless resources and many extant measures of variables already available. Paul Reynolds (1971) is particularly critical of an inductive approach to theory building, and we agree. In the natural and social sciences, there are just too many *possible* variables to observe and too many ways that they might be related to expect patterns simply to "emerge." Communication research is equally complex. An inductive approach is, in general, terribly inefficient. Recall how slowly the space shuttle investigation proceeded *until* a theory was developed. We prefer the traditional deductive model of science: theory, then research, then better theory, then more research, and so on.

Self-Correctiveness

We asserted in Chapter 1 that science has a major advantage over other ways of answering questions; specifically, it is *self-correcting*. The rules of openness, of describing procedures in great detail, of tying claims about the nature of the world to systematic and reproducible observations, increase the chance that if mistakes are made, if claims about the relationship between variables are wrong, these procedural rules will help us identify and correct them. This is the ideal, the goal, but does it actually work? An examination of the risky-shift phenomenon shows one instance where it did.

The Risky-Shift Phenomenon: A Mistake Corrected.   Group discussion and decision making has been written about and studied by communication researchers since the 1930s. How do groups reach decisions and how do these decisions compare to decisions made by individuals? In 1962, Wallach, Kogan, and Bem reported an interesting finding in which groups of people were found to make decisions that were riskier than these same decisions made by individuals.[4] The finding was replicated among different populations and in a very short time became known as the *risky-shift phenomenon*. The finding quickly diffused into textbooks in group and interpersonal communication and in social psychology. The risky-shift phenomenon was now a "fact."

The methodology of the studies on this topic involved asking people how risky or conservative they would be in a variety of hypothetical "life dilemma" situations. Twelve such situations were described and the respondent was asked how great the chances of success would have to be before he or she would recommend that the riskier of two alternatives be selected. After they responded to all twelve situations individually, they were put into groups and asked to make group recommendations on the same twelve situations. As noted, the groups of people generally recommended increased risk taking, compared to their earlier individual responses. Virtually all of the earlier research on the risky-shift was conducted using the "life-dilemma" technique.

A number of years later, different researchers (Clement & Sullivan, 1970), using different measures of risk taking, failed to reproduce a group shift towards risk taking. Other researchers (Clark & Willems, 1969) subsequently went back to the early research and carefully examined the procedures that were used. (Of course they were only able to do this because the procedures, including the operational definition of risk taking, were published in sufficient detail.) After careful consideration, the researchers felt the instructions might be conveying to respondents the idea that the original researchers wanted to find increased risk taking. Thus, they changed what they suspected were biased instructions and repeated Wallach, Kogan, and Bem's research. *Their results showed no risky-shift.* In fact, they found that if the instructions were changed so that participants were leaning toward a conservative direction prior to group discussion, the group decision would shift toward a more conservative position than had been the individual's prediscussion opinion.

To make a long story short, and many studies into a succinct point, we now know that under some circumstances groups will make systematically more *extreme* decisions than would be made by the individuals who constitute the group. This is referred to as a *group polarization phenomenon*. On any decision-making continuum, if the majority of the members of a group lean slightly in one direction or the other, they have a tendency to shift to a more extreme—a more polar—position as a result of group discussion (Myers & Kaplan, 1976).

The important point is that a mistake was made about a question of fact. Carefully controlled, systematic observation of the world "out there" resulted in the mistake being identified and corrected. The methods of science, then, are designed to minimize human biases and fallibility as theory is tested and reevaluated.

HUMANISTIC RESEARCH AND THEORY

Inquiry into human communication is at least 2,500 years old, probably older. The dialogues of Plato and Aristotle's work, *Ars Rhetorica*, demonstrate that understanding the process by which we communicate is a fundamental area of human inquiry. These ancient Greeks, as well as the Romans such as Cicero and Longinus who followed them, were

MINI-PROJECT:

Take a research result from one of your readings in this or other communication classes that you *personally* do not think (for whatever reason) should have occurred as it was reported. Find the original study and carefully go through it and see if something in the method—the operational definitions, the control, the use of inductive or deductive theory—may have contributed to the findings. How would you go about reconceptualizing this study? What results do you think you would find from this new perspective? Why?

interested primarily in the "one-to-many" communication event, that is, public speaking. They focused on factors that made a public speech effective at influencing others such as the type of argument used and the ethos (credibility) of the speaker. These earliest of communication "theorists" wrote prescriptively; that is, they prescribed the ways to be persuasive when making a public speech. This knowledge about how to be an effective speaker was called *rhetoric*—the use of all available means of persuasion—and those who studied and described it were called *rhetoricians*.

Although this text emphasizes science, we are including a brief introduction to humanistic approaches to studying communication. Our view of humanistic research is that it usually has as its end the understanding of a particular event, person, or thing, and frequently, to critically evaluate the object of study as good or bad, ethical or unethical, or beautiful or ugly, that is, to evaluate communication. This body of research in communication is typically labeled historical, rhetorical, or critical method. The common thread running through each of these methods is their concern with the *uniqueness* and the *individualness* of the particular event, person, or thing; this uniqueness is sometimes studied as an end in itself, while at other times it is studied to shed light on a larger issue. As noted, the humanistic researcher's goals are similar to those of the scientist; that is, the humanistic researcher is striving to make the world a better place. The major differences, however, are the type of questions asked and the degree of subjectivity allowed in the methods used to obtain an answer. First, while the scientist is concerned with questions of fact, the humanistic researcher's questions usually deal with both questions of fact and questions of value, the world as it *ought* to be. How *was* something done and how *well* was that something done? Second, while the goal of science is objectivity and bias-free results, humanistic research tends to be more subjective and the answers to research questions more affected by the personal views of the researcher (Wander & Jenkins, 1972).

Another difference between the humanistic method and the scientific method is found in *control* and *prediction*. Both methods strive to describe the phenomena they are studying. Both methods try to understand the communication process. Science is concerned with predicting the *relationships* between abstract variables. For the most part, humanistic research emphasizes specific communication events, frequently focusing on events in the past—historical events.

Before we continue, we should also note that many treatments of humanistic theory are available for both historical and rhetorical theories. It is important to understand the variety of other modes of analysis and perspectives on theory that exist. Although this book is mostly about empirical research and the social sciences, we feel that ignoring the contributions of humanism in communication theory—rhetorical theory, history, or rhetorical criticism—would produce a rather lopsided and shortsighted view of research and the process of research.

As you will find in the later chapters that emphasize scientific method, the type of theory that is formally stated is *empirically* oriented and involves the relationship between abstract variables. The theory of the humanistic researcher tends to be more *qualitatively* or value-oriented. As Miller (1975) noted:

> *Often students of . . . communication study communicative phenomena for the purpose of arriving at ethical or aesthetic judgments about the phenomena themselves, or about the event, or events, with*

which the phenomena are associated. In short, they strive to articulate reasoned value judgments about a communicative act or acts. (pp. 234–236)

Thus, Miller argues that there are particular questions that can be better answered by methods other than science. These questions, he suggests, are those associated with specific events or people and questions dealing with whether the communication is good or bad, ethical or unethical, beautiful or ugly.

The traditional humanistic model presupposes emphasizing the particular over the general. This model suggests, rightly or wrongly, that an understanding of the practices will yield some general knowledge about human behavior.[5] This is not atheoretical, but presupposes that the communication act, behavior, or event will yield the theory. It is an inductive approach. As Michael C. Leff (1980) notes, "Theory [from the perspective of traditional humanistic critic] is the outcome of critical practice, not its starting point" (p. 343). That is, beginning from the *act* is as valuable as observing that same act after establishing your theoretical perspective. Action, then, may, at a later time, yield theory.

Practice Versus Theory

As noted earlier, scientific method generally presupposes a deductive model; that theory comes before testing. In humanistic methods this, however, is not usually the case. Rather, the humanistic method is more concerned with the unique contributions of a particular person, event, or movement; that is, the norm is an in-depth understanding of a particular speech or related event; the focus is on the individual "act" or "event," not the wider ramifications and generalizability of such communication. This approach is not universally accepted, however. Leff (1980), for example, notes that:

> [One] approach, which has dominated contemporary criticism, follows the model of conventional scientific and logical theories. It seeks to discover high order abstractions that inform or govern rhetorical practice, and these abstractions enjoy a privileged status whether the system works from general precepts to particular cases or from particular cases to general precepts. Thus, [traditional] theories eventuate in predicative generalizations or in extremely abstract models of the rhetorical transaction. Such theories provide an orderly direction for inquiry, and their proliferation has proved useful in breaking down the staid monism of earlier criticism. (p. 348)

In contrast, the traditional approach seems to suggest that theory is not paramount, except insofar as it illuminates and helps explain the unique contributions of the individual person, event, or thing.

What type of research would you conduct if you adopted the traditional approach? What if you were interested in the impact of former Alabama governor George Wallace's communication during the school desegregation years. What kinds of questions might you ask? Some interesting questions might include: Were Wallace's words his own or simply reflective of the sentiments of the specific time and constituents Wallace represented? Were Wallace's communications morally justified if they prevented violence and ultimately contributed to peaceful, albeit slower, desegregation? To answer these questions you would need to understand in great detail events during the early 1960s in Alabama. You would have to know a lot about George Wallace, his background, and the situation as it existed at that time. Your answers would not generally be valid if compared to another politician, but would instead reflect your ability to get under his skin, or into his psyche so to speak. You would study his speeches, his stances, and look for central themes, you would look to see how he presented his messages, and you might center on one or two major themes as representative of his work.

On the other hand, you might address questions derived from a general rhetorical theory. In this use of theory, however, a real danger can be that the humanistic researcher will only see what he or she wants to see (e.g., Black, 1980). If we were interested in Wallace's political communication and our theory suggested that he only communicated from a "populist" perspective, then we would be looking for support for that theory. While you are working with an abstract theory, that theory may direct your "world view," and subsequently what you find.

Which of the two views is correct and which incorrect? Probably neither. Both approach an understanding of a communication event, communicator, or communication object with the intent of asking questions that require value or value-like responses. How well? Why? Answers to these questions do not always yield truth-like generalizations that can be applied to all communicators. Instead they tell us something about the aesthetic, ethical, and descriptive aspects of the communication. Their value lies in the uniqueness of the event, person, or object.

While the scientist strives to be an impartial observer, the humanistic researcher is sometimes a subjective participant in the communication event, whether that communication took place today, a hundred, or a thousand years ago. The humanistic researcher becomes a critic looking at or for specific phenomena. Once these phenomena are found, he or she examines how well certain principles were applied and with what effect. It is a distinct advantage that he or she already knows the outcome and can work out specifically what was "good" or "bad" about the communication.

The question of a methodological or theoretical "superiority" is not of concern here. The questions we ask will dictate the method we choose. If, as we have suggested, the type of question you seek to ask and the outcome you seek are amenable to one particular method, *adopt it!*

APPLYING KNOWLEDGE IN COMMUNICATION

We need to comprehend how all approaches and areas contribute to our understanding of communication and its effects on us across a variety of contexts (see Figure 2.1). At the most basic, intrapersonal level our research is based on a combination of physiological and psychological theory and research from a scientific approach. Yet, much of what we know about intrapersonal processes we know from humanistic study of individual people and their highly individualized perceptions of themselves and their communication. As we move upward to the mass communication level, one context area of interest continues to borrow from the others.

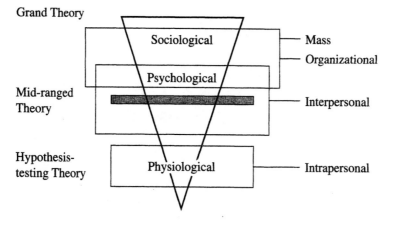

FIGURE 2.1   Levels of communication and theory.

Source: Adapted from: L Thayer [1967]. Communication and organizational theory. In F. E. X. Dance [Ed.], *Human communication theory: Original essays.* New York: Holt, Rinehart & Winston [page 87].

Quite simply, to understand the communication process requires that you become versed in all approaches and methods. Our emphasis in this book is science, yet to understand it we must also have an understanding of research past and a feeling for the actual theorists and researchers. Since our particular orientation is social scientific, that orientation tends to blind us toward certain types of research and ways of thinking. Therefore, we hope you are critical consumers of the information in this book and consider these caveats.

SUMMARY

This chapter suggests some theoretical foundations for conducting research in communication. It has extended the material in Chapter 1 by presenting two basic approaches to research: the scientific method and the humanistic method. In instances when you are interested in factual observations, empirical research and the method of science will be adopted. With this adoption you choose a method that begins with description, moves to explanation, and yields prediction. In order to use this method you must be prepared to take abstract concepts and create "concrete" variables. Ultimately, environmental control through theory building is the goal of scientific research.

The choice of science also provides the researcher with a self-correcting method. What we mean by this is that the method of achieving results is done in such a way (is reported through the literature) that others can seek to replicate or extend the research. In this regard other findings will either support or call into question the usefulness of the theory which is used to answer new research questions.

Finally, we examined humanistic research. We noted that, unlike science, the humanistic approach examines the unique contributions of the communicator or communication. This approach usually seeks answers to both questions of fact *and* value.

In the end, the method you adopt should parallel your research question. The quality of research is directly dependent upon the quality of the research question. A good question almost always suggests the methodological approach you should be taking.

PROBES

1. What relationships, if any, exist between research aimed at making generalizations and research aimed at making value statements?

2. How does the scientist differ from the humanist? Or, is this a moot question since both are interested in understanding the human condition as it relates to communication?

3. What does *theory* provide the scientist? The nonscientist? Can both look at the same phenomenon? If they do, will they ask the same questions? Take a concept from your particular area of interest and examine it from first the scientist's point of view and then from the humanist's point of view.

4. If we were to assume that *all* communication researchers could be divided into either scientific or humanistic camps, into which would you fall? Why? What types of questions would you ask? What types of answers would you expect from your research approach?

5. Gerald R. Miller argues that communication researchers must *understand* both the scientific and humanistic approaches to research. Why? Can you provide examples where this is true?

6. As scientific research is designed to answer questions of fact, does this mean that the research is value free; that the researcher's values as a human being have no influence on the research process? If an individual scientist allows her values to bias her research, how do the methods of science eliminate such biases?

7. The late Carl Sagan wrote, "Science is more than a body of knowledge; it is a way of thinking" (1996, p. 25). What do you think he meant by this? As a fallible human being, did Sagan's values influence his "way of thinking"?

RESEARCH PROJECTS

1. Find an area of communication you find interesting (see Salwen and Stacks, 1997, for a number of different theoretical models) and trace its theoretical development from inception to date. This is sometimes called an "area paper" in which the researcher is preparing a "literature review" of a particular theory or approach.

2. Most theory, whether it be humanistic or scientific, operates on what is called a "central assumption." Take a theory discussed in this or other classes and find and evaluate its central assumption. Has the research supported the theory's central assumption? If not, why? (For instance, central to the attitude change theories of balance, congruity, symmetry, and dissonance is the assumption that people actively avoid situations that are inconsistent with our perceptions. Research shows that this is not always the case.)

3. "Theory begets more theory." Test this assumption by tracing the development of a particular communication "theory." How did research (and the approach taken) affect that theory?

4. Many communication areas (e.g., persuasion, public relations, organizational communication, intrapersonal communication) have been developed from a humanistic approach. What has this approach provided communication theorists in their movement to building communication theory? Are there particular areas

within the humanistic approach that have been more beneficial to theory development than others? Why or why not, and what implications does this finding have for future communication theory and research?

SUGGESTED READING

Dubin, R. (1969). *Theory building*. New York: The Free Press.

Littlejohn, S. W. (2002). *Theories of human communication*, 7th ed. Belmont, CA: Wadsworth.

Miller, G. R. (1975). Humanistic and scientific approaches to speech communication inquiry: Rivalry, redundancy, or rapprochement. *Western Journal of Speech Communication, 49*, 230–239.

Reynolds, P. D. (1971). *A primer in theory construction*. New York: Bobbs-Merrill.

Salwen, M. B., & Stacks, D. W. (Eds.) (1997). *An integrated approach to communication theory and research*. Mahwah, NJ: Lawrence Erlbaum Associates.

Skinner, B. F. (1971). *Beyond freedom and dignity*. New York: Alfred A. Knopf.

NOTES

1. Many of the self-concept studies—and most that take their origins from symbolic interactionism, clinical psychology, and from instances where something has occurred with a particular speaker that is then generalized to other speakers—come from this tradition. In the area of organizational communication, because of its obvious closeness to management, many case studies produce findings that are then tested in the controlled conditions of the laboratory or in field experiments.

2. A thorough discussion of communication theory is beyond the scope of this book. For detailed treatments, see Stacks, Hickson, & Hill, 1991; Trenholm, 1986; Littlejohn, 2002; and Anderson (1996).

3. See Skinner (1948; 1971) for a discussion of the issue of controlling human behavior through the knowledge gained through the methods of science.

4. The finding was originally reported in P. Stoner, "A Comparison and Group Decisions Involving Risk," unpublished master's thesis, Massachusetts Institute of Technology.

5. For an excellent example of this model, see Black (1980).

REFERENCES

Anderson, J. (1996). *Communication theory*. New York: Guilford Press.

Babble, E. (1986). *The practice of social research*, 4th ed. Belmont, CA: Wadsworth.

Baskerville, B. (1977). Must we all be rhetorical critics? *Quarterly Journal of Speech, 63*, 107–116.

Black, E. (1980). A note on theory and practice in rhetorical criticism. *Western Journal of Speech Communication, 44*, 331–336.

Blalock, H. M., Jr. (1970). *Theory construction: From verbal to mathematical formulations*. Englewood Cliffs, NJ: Prentice-Hall.

Clark, R. D., & Willems, S. E. P. (1969). Where is the risky shift: Dependence on instructions. *Journal of Personality and Social Psychology, 13*, 215–221.

Clement, D. E., & Sullivan, D. W. (1970). No risky shift with real groups and real risks. *Psychonomic Science, 18*, 243–244.

Dubin, R. (1969). *Theory building*. New York: The Free Press.

Hill, F. (1969). Conventional wisdom—traditional form—the president's message of November 3, 1969. *Quarterly Journal of Speech, 58*, 373–386.

Kerlinger, F. N. (1986). *Foundations of behavioral research*, 3rd ed. New York: Holt, Rinehart & Winston.

Leff, M. C. (1980). Interpretation and the art of the rhetorical critic. *Western Journal of Speech Communication, 44*, 343.

Lewin, K. (1951). *Field theory in social sciences*. New York: Harper.

Littlejohn, S. W. (2002). *Theories of human communication*, 7th ed. Belmont, CA: Wadsworth.

Miller, G. R. (1975). Humanistic and scientific approaches to speech communication inquiry: Rivalry, redundancy, or rapprochement. *Western Journal of Speech Communication, 49,* 232.

Myers, D. G., & Kaplan, M. F. (1976). Group induced polarization in simulated juries. *Personality and Social Psychology Bulletin, 2,* 63–66.

Reynolds, P. D. (1971). *A primer in theory construction.* New York: Bobbs-Merrill.

Sagan, C. (1996). *The demon-haunted world: Science as a candle in the dark.* New York: Ballantine Books.

Salwen, M. B., & Stacks, D. W. (Eds.) (1997). *An integrated approach to communication theory and research.* Mahwah, NJ: Lawrence Erlbaum Associates.

Skinner, B. F. (1948). *Walden two.* New York: Macmillan.

Skinner, B. F. (1971). *Beyond freedom and dignity.* New York: Alfred A. Knopf.

Stacks, D. W., Hickson, M., III, & Hill, S. R., Jr. (1991). *An introduction to communication theory.* Fort Worth, TX: Holt, Rinehart & Winston.

Trenholm, S. (1986). *Human communication theory.* Englewood Cliffs, NJ: Prentice-Hall.

Wallach, M. A., Kogan, N., & Bem, D. J. (1962). Group influence on individual risk-taking. *Journal of Abnormal and Social Psychology, 65,* 75–86.

Wander, P., & Jenkins, S. (1972). Rhetoric, society, and the critical response. *Quarterly Journal of Speech, 58,* 441–450.

CHAPTER THREE

CONSIDERATIONS: KNOWLEDGE, ETHICS, AND SCIENCE

RULES OF SCHOLARSHIP
Ethical considerations
Crediting others
Reporting
Honesty and integrity

TREATMENT OF HUMAN SUBJECTS (PEOPLE)
Ethical codes
Deception
Confidentiality and anonymity

DEBRIEFING
Eliminating harmful effects
Professional ethics
The research experience

ETHICAL APPROPRIATENESS
What to study
Use of data

APPLYING KNOWLEDGE IN COMMUNICATION

OBJECTIVES

By the end of this chapter you should be able to:

1. Distinguish between ethical and unethical research.
2. Explain why ethics is important to communication research.
3. Explain how research participants should be treated.
4. Discuss the importance of informed consent, deception, and debriefing in conducting research.
5. Explain the proper use of data.
6. Discuss the professional research codes.

Ethics deals with questions of value about whether something is right or wrong. Consciously or unconsciously, we make ethical judgments every day. These daily judgments shape many of our daily behaviors. Ethical judgments are made in research situations just as they are made in social and business situations. Ethical questions include: Is it okay to cite an original source in a paper we are writing for a class even though we only read about what the original source said in another source; in other words, is it ethical to cite a secondary source? Does a political candidate's campaign commercial unfairly distort his opponent's record? Should we tell a friend that his female friend has been dating another male? Should we as professors give a highly physically attractive member of the opposite sex "the benefit of a doubt at grade time" because he or she came by our office and was friendly several times during the term? Must we leave a note on the windshield of a car that we barely scratched in the parking lot? Should we allow our friend to cut in line to get good concert tickets even though the people behind us have waited all night for the same coveted tickets? Like most questions of value, the answers to these questions are not always simple or obvious.

Early social science research texts gave scant attention to ethics. For example, the first edition of Kerlinger's (1964) definitive *Foundations of Behavioral Research* not only has no chapter devoted to research ethics, the word "ethics" does not even appear in the index. Kerlinger's fourth edition includes a fine, albeit brief, presentation of ethical considerations in conducting behavioral research (Kerlinger & Lee, 2000, pp. 437–448). More current texts (Stacks, 2002) discuss ethics at length. There are probably several reasons for this neglect. First, ethics, by definition, concerns questions of value: What is right and wrong, what is good and bad. And, as we noted in Chapter 1, science cannot do much to answer such questions. Sometimes the results of empirical research can help us decide if something is right or wrong, but, ultimately, it is the individual who makes this decision. The locus of the answer to value questions lies within us.

Second, some ethical issues are so fundamental, so universally accepted, that they may be taken for granted. Here we are speaking of basic **rules of scholarship**, such as giving appropriate credit for ideas, reporting the results of research in an impartial and complete way, and describing openly and honestly any flaws or weaknesses in research procedures. Unfortunately, many of us have assumed that these kinds of basic rules of scholarship are so obvious that everyone, including graduate as well as undergraduate students, are explicitly aware of them. It is almost as if some things are known at birth—they never need mentioning.

An especially important area of ethics concerns how humans who participate in our research projects are treated. Yet even this area was scarcely mentioned until about the mid 1970s. Most researchers, we believe, just assumed that they themselves treated their human participants (sometimes called "subjects," a label we will explore later in this chapter) ethically, and so did their colleagues. To even raise the question of ethical treatment seemed to imply that they, or their colleagues, might be doing some things that were "wrong," which, of course, they would not do. And, anyway, the researcher seemed to be saying: We are after *knowledge* here. If some people are damaged in the process, that is just a necessary price to pay for the advancement of the common good. And finally, experimental researchers could be secure in the knowledge that if their research procedures did harm the subjects, the *debriefing* would erase any negative effects. There is a general human tendency to place a high value on one's activities, including one's research projects. Some researchers seem to believe that the intrinsic value of their research off-sets any harm that might accrue to participants. This is referred to as the cost versus benefits ratio.

We will address four ethical issues relevant to all research. (1) Are the basic rules of scholarship being followed? (2) Have the participants in the project been adequately in-formed of the procedures involved, including any potential risks that may be involved (physical and psychological), and with this knowledge, freely consented to participate? If deception was involved, was it absolutely necessary? (3) Have research participants been ad-equately "debriefed" following participation in research? Are they in some way better peo-ple than when they arrived to participate? (4) Is the topic being studied ethically appropriate? Are the data gathered maintained and reported in such a manner as to ensure confidentiality and anonymity? We begin our analysis of these issues with the one we feel is most basic to *all* research methods: rules of scholarship.

RULES OF SCHOLARSHIP

In our careers as educators, we have had several experiences that brought into sharp focus the importance of including an explicit discussion of some of the basic rules of scholar-ship. In the first case a student turned in a paper that reviewed the literature of a nar-row subarea of communication. The student, a well-intentioned, bright, and hard-working individual, was attempting to summarize the results of several research articles and then offer some ideas of her own that would reconcile inconsistencies between several stud-ies. Being somewhat of a neophyte at writing papers of this sort, the paper was awk-wardly worded. Embedded within the paper were bits and pieces—a sentence here, a paragraph there—of professional level social scientific writing, however, no quotations were indicated. How could the student be so uneven in her style? An examination of the articles reviewed in the paper revealed the answer. A sentence here, a paragraph there—had been copied directly from the papers being reviewed. There is nothing wrong with doing this, *except*—and this is extremely important—there was no indication of the fact that this material was not original. The reader of the paper could not discern, except by writing ability in this case, which parts of the paper came from the student and which came from the articles being reviewed. Was the student behaving unethically? Yes. Ig-norance of the law, of the rules of scholarship in this case, is not an excuse. She did not know that what she had done was inappropriate. When the problems with her paper were discussed, she was embarrassed, upset, and apologetic. She was simply ignorant of how to **reference** sources appropriately.

The second experience was more serious. In one instance an upperclassman was re-quired to write a review of a particular theoretical perspective in a persuasion course. The paper he turned in was excellent; it was well written, used jargon appropriately and in con-text, and even began with an abstract. A close reading, however, found an opening quotation mark at the start of the title and a closing quotation mark at the end of the reference section. The student had copied, word for word, an article that reviewed this particular area. The stu-dent claimed to believe that since he enclosed it in quotation marks that he had fulfilled his ethical obligations. This case was adjudicated fully at a major university. The student was found "not guilty" on the grounds that he did not know he had engaged in plagiarism. The "not guilty" verdict was greeted with such outrage by university faculty that the case resulted in a complete revamping of the academic honesty policy at the university. This included the implementation of carefully designed and elaborate procedures that would protect the fundamental integrity of a college education and the rights of the student. Had this same incident occurred at this same university today, the student would almost certainly have been expelled from the university for a year and had a permanent notation put on his transcript, or worse. Plagiarism is cheating, pure and simple, and a crime on college campuses.

The third case was more clear-cut. It dealt with the buying of a paper for a class. In this instance students were required to write short five-to-ten-page papers for the course. A number of students in this class needed a passing grade in this course in order to graduate. When reading the papers it quickly became apparent that several students had chosen the same topic and even the same sources to quote. After reading several papers it was clear that the papers *were* the same, only a few sentences here and there were modified to make the papers "different." When this was brought to the students' attention they, like others, were embarrassed, upset, and apologetic. However, they freely admitted to *buying* the papers. In their minds, while the purchase would be wrong and unethical if they had turned in the papers without revision, that revision made it ethical. The penalty for such an obviously unethical practice was severe.

Scholarship Considerations

Unfortunately, these are not isolated cases. It happens every day on campuses all over the country. A survey conducted by Jerold Hale (1987) suggests that *most* college students have plagiarized written work for college classes at least once. We believe the problem is not that students intentionally do unethical things, although, of course, some do. The problem is that there is no formal and systematic way to assure that everyone knows the rules of scholarship. That is why we review these rules here, in an effort to clear up the sometimes blurred distinction between ethical and unethical scholarship.

1. *Give appropriate credit for one's ideas.* The most fundamental rule of all scholarship is to credit other people's ideas and statements, whether a direct quotation from a source or the paraphrasing of ideas. Furthermore, you must completely give credit, in terms of textual statements (through quotation marks or setting off the material if it is a long quote) and referencing. There is a surprising amount of misunderstanding surrounding the issue of cheating and plagiarism. What is it? When does it occur? Why is it so seriously wrong? The University of Georgia booklet, *A Culture of Honesty* (2002), puts it this way:

> "Academic Honesty" means performing all academic work without plagiarism, cheating, lying, tampering, stealing, or receiving unauthorized or illegitimate assistance from any other person, or using any other source of information that is not common knowledge. "Academic Dishonesty" means knowingly performing, attempting to perform, or assisting any other person in performing academic work that does not meet this standard of Academic Honesty. (p. 5)

Much, if not most, academic honesty problems seem to involve confusion about what constitutes plagiarism. Simply put, plagiarism is presenting information as one's own, either orally or in writing, when in fact those words, writing, concepts, definitions, ideas, research findings, and so on, are not common knowledge. Here are some guidelines from the University of Georgia.

1. Quoting another person's written or spoken word without quotation marks and appropriate credit;
2. Summarizing or paraphrasing another person's words, again, written or spoken, without notes or statements in the body of the work itself indicating the source of the words;
3. Describing an idea, concept, or theoretical proposition originated by another person as the original work of the person submitting the work;
4. Reproducing or repeating anecdotes, statistics or tables, *which are not common knowledge*, and which originated from another person;
5. Receiving or purchasing in any manner (e.g., over the Internet, from a term paper company or from a roommate) a term paper or any assignment, and submitting it as the student's own work.

Third-millennium students should know that the full weight of the advanced technology of the Internet that allows a cheat to type in complex set of key words into a search engine to find a unique term paper is also being used to identify plagiarized work. University computer scientists, working hand in hand with other professors, have already developed clever ways to catch a thief. In the years subsequent to the publication of this book, we believe that some student educational careers will be damaged or ended. *Beware.* As plagiarism grows, so will the mechanisms to catch it.

It has become almost a mantra that the cheat is only cheating him- or herself, but is this really true? Most people are hard working and honest and would rarely, if ever, cheat.

The cheaters are cheating you. Here is why. All achievements in life are the result of comparisons. If *everyone* graduated Harvard with a 4.0 G.P.A., that achievement would be worthless, because, compared to others it meant nothing. The very integrity of what it means to have a college degree is diminished *every time* someone cheats. The cheater most certainly does turn in higher quality work than he or she could otherwise do. Would the cheater quote or paraphrase someone else's stupid idea or copy poor writing? Cheating steals from *everyone* against whom the cheaters work is compared.

If a person found a formal speech manuscript in a fraternity file, practiced delivering it over and over, and then went to class and delivered the term's best speech in front of an impressed audience of classmates and a teacher who assigned an "A," the bar for comparison for what constitutes an "A" speech has been raised for every honest student in that class. The honest students in the class are not being compared to the cheater, they are being compared to a perhaps brilliant student who left his or her award-winning speech in that file.

A very challenging ethical dilemma confronts us when we observe others cheating. It is a serious matter to turn in another human being when they do wrong; science cannot help you decide what to do. As presented in Chapter 1, science deals with the world as it is.

Questions of value, and this is a tough question of value, deal with the world as it ought to be. This question can only be answered from within each of us.

2. *Report conflicting evidence and all that you find.* Not all that you read or learn will support your own personal view of the world. In research you will almost always find results that differ from each other. It is your responsibility to report *all* that you find, refuting what you can, accepting as valid other views if they cannot be refuted. Remember, in many instances you will be more knowledgeable in the area than your reader and you have a certain responsibility to make sure that he or she understands both sides of the issue or question being addressed.

There is a natural tendency to put our best foot forward. We all like to find what we set out to find, to support some hypothesis or refute some question. Unfortunately, many times we either fail to get results that support our thesis or only partially support it at best. In such cases it is easy to gloss over that which was *not* found in favor of the more favorable results. Part of doing research is to accept the responsibility for failure. In so doing, you may actually help yourself or others later by a frank assessment of why you did not find what you expected. The reasons may be many, but perhaps you found new documents, a new way to analyze the facts you explored, or (in the scientific method) were unable to duplicate exactly the conditions of the study as you proposed. These problems must be emphasized, not deemphasized.

3. *Describe the flaws in your research.* This follows from the previous requirement. What problems came up that may have invalidated your results? What were the flaws? If your study dealt with physical attraction, for instance, were your manipulations of attraction too subtle? Not subtle enough? In a humanistic study, did you choose the most appropriate documentation? Did you have access to the *original* materials? By including your flaws you allow others to understand why your interpretations are as they are and provide information for new and perhaps better research.

4. *Use primary sources whenever possible.* A primary source is the research as presented by the author in whatever form it was originally distributed to the public. Careful citation requires more than the correct use of quotation marks and footnote systems. Be clear when you are paraphrasing: Do not just provide the explanation, include phrases such as "the authors go on to explain." After doing an enormous amount of research you would probably like to be cited in someone else's work. It is a courtesy to reference others' work, but it is also a necessity and allows the reader to understand the theoretical background from which

---

MINI-PROJECT:

Conduct a small, unscientific survey of your friends regarding referencing. How many of them know the rules of scholarship? How many of them have unwittingly violated at least one of the rules? How many of them have knowingly violated at least one of the rules?

you are coming. In general, when not sure whether to reference or not, it is much better to include the reference.

Part of the method of research deals with understanding that all people perceive things differently. Whenever possible, get to the original source. It is very tempting to rely on others, but your interpretation of the event fits your theory much more closely than even that of your best friend. As will be pointed out in Chapter 4 and Chapter 5, **secondary** (another source referencing the primary source) and even **tertiary sources** (a reporting of secondary source's report of the primary source) have their place in research, but only under certain conditions. If you do use secondary or tertiary sources, write "cited in . . . ." As a general rule, however, primary sources are usually the ones on which we depend.

5. *Honesty and integrity go hand in hand.* We assume that research and the reporting of that research is done in an honest manner. The integrity of the author (and, to a degree, the integrity of all those with whom you have studied or worked) is on the line. Most academic institutions have academic integrity codes. It is in your best interest to investigate your institution's integrity statement.

6. *When working in groups do your best to give credit for work in fair proportions.* When the end product is in final form (paper, article, book, film, tape, or in-house monograph) *all* associated with the project are assumed to share responsibility and credit, but authorship order may be affected by varying contributions. If one person contributed more than others, they should be senior author (this is usually done when there are multiple authors and responsibility is shared by all). In classroom projects, for example, failure to include a co-author's name could result in that person failing the assignment. Similarly, it is frequently a good idea to include footnotes thanking others who helped significantly during the design and analysis stages. As noted earlier, this rule also applies in the "real" or business world.

7. *All research is conducted under a general ethical code.* Major professional associations have specific codes of ethics. These codes provide the basic rules for scholarship in a given field. You should be familiar with how each field views scholarship. Ignorance is no excuse for unethical scholarship.

All these rules are enforced most rigorously in an academic environment. But they are rules that should be used in other environments as well. Consider the following example: An associate of ours worked as a city planner. It was routine when putting together zoning reports in the planning office to pull entire paragraphs from other zoning reports, even from textbooks on how to write zoning reports. There is nothing wrong with this, per se, *if* appropriate credit is given. Certainly those individuals whose lives are being affected by the zoning decisions have the right to know from where the specific wording and justification for the decisions that are made are coming.

In business and politics, do the same principles apply? Recently there has been a general questioning of the ethics of people in general and certain groups—lawyers, stockbrokers, accountants, and CEOs—in particular. Louis A. Day (1997) notes that:

All of the major professional media organizations, representing a broad constituency, have developed formal codes. For example, the Society of Professional Journalists (SPJ) has adopted standards for such things as truth, accuracy, objectivity, conflicts of interests, and fairness. . . . Likewise, the Public Relations Society of America (PRSA) has adopted a Code of Professional Standards [see Box 3.1] to guide its members through the moral thicket of corporate responsibility. . . . While the PRSA can expel a member for violation of its code, it has no legal authority to prohibit an expelled member from continuing to practice public relations. (pp. 43–44)

BOX 3.1

CODE OF PROFESSIONAL STANDARDS FOR THE PRACTICE OF PUBLIC RELATIONS

DECLARATION OF PRINCIPLES

Members of the Public Relations Society of America base their professional principles on the fundamental value and dignity of the individual, holding that the free exercise of human rights, especially freedom of speech, freedom of assembly, and freedom of the press, is essential to the practice of public relations.

In serving the interests of clients and employers, we dedicate ourselves to the goals of better communication, understanding, and cooperation among the diverse individuals, groups, and institutions of society, and of equal opportunity of employment to the public relations profession.

WE PLEDGE:

To conduct ourselves professionally, with truth, accuracy, fairness, and responsibility to the public;

To improve our individual competence and advance the knowledge and proficiency of the profession through continuing research and education;

And to adhere to the articles of the Code of Professional Standards for the Practice of Public Relations as adopted by the governing Assembly of the Society.

CODE OF PROFESSIONAL STANDARDS FOR THE PRACTICE OF PUBLIC RELATIONS

These articles have been adopted by the Public Relations Society of America to promote and maintain high standards of public service and ethical conduct among its members.

1. A member shall conduct his or her professional life in accord with the *public interest*.
2. A member shall exemplify high standards of *honesty* and *integrity* while carrying out dual obligations to a client or employer *and to the democratic process*.
3. *A member shall deal fairly* with the public, with past or present clients or employers, and with fellow practitioners, giving due respect to the ideal of free inquiry and to the opinions of others.
4. A member shall adhere to the highest standards of *accuracy and truth*, avoiding extravagant claims or unfair comparisons and giving credit for ideas and words borrowed from others.
5. A member shall not knowingly disseminate *false or misleading information* and shall act promptly to correct erroneous communications for which he or she is responsible.

(continued)

BOX 3.1   CONTINUED

6. A member shall not engage in any practice which has the purpose of *corrupting* the integrity of channels of communications or the processes of government.
7. A member shall be prepared to *identify publicly* the name of the client or employer on whose behalf any public communication is made.
8. A member shall not use any individual or organization professing to serve or represent an announced cause, or professing to be independent or unbiased, but actually serving another or *undisclosed interest.*
9. A member shall not *guarantee the achievement* of specified results beyond the member's direct control.
10. A member shall *not represent conflicting* or competing interests without the express consent of those concerned, given after a full disclosure of the facts.
11. A member shall not place himself or herself in a position where the member's *personal interest is or may be in conflict* with an obligation to an employer or client, or others, without full disclosure of such interests to all involved.
12. A member shall *not accept fees, commissions, gifts or any other consideration* from anyone except clients or employers for whom services are performed without their express consent, given after full disclosure of the facts.
13. A member shall scrupulously safeguard *the confidences and privacy rights* of present, former, and prospective clients or employers.
14. A member shall not intentionally *damage the professional reputation* or practice of another practitioner.
15. If a member has evidence that another member has been guilty of unethical, illegal, or unfair practices, including those in violation of this Code, the member is obligated to present the information promptly to the proper authorities of the Society for action in accordance with the procedures set forth in Article XII of the Bylaws.
16. A member called as a witness in a proceeding for enforcement of this Code is obligated to appear, unless excused for sufficient reason by the judicial panel.
17. A member shall, as soon as possible, sever relations with any organization or individual if such relationship requires conduct contrary to the articles of this Code.

Reprinted with permission of the Public Relations Society of America.

A related issue concerns the use of ghostwriters to produce political speeches. Political leaders are frequently judged by the quality of their speeches. However, many of these speeches are written by someone other than the speaker. For example, former President Ronald Reagan's speeches were so good that he was sometimes described as "the great communicator." George Bush's acceptance speech at the 1988 Republican National Convention was generally judged to be outstanding, and to have contributed significantly to his successful fall campaign. As it turns out, many of Mr. Reagan's speeches, such as his *Challenger* disaster eulogy, and Mr. Bush's acceptance speech were written by one of their employees, Peggy Noonan. All contemporary presidents have speech writers. This same ethical issue exists in business: Corporate executives often have their speeches ghost-written. If we may offer a value judgment, the basic rules of scholarship should apply here as well. (See Box 3.2.) Part of a liberal education should be to reinforce such fundamental values as truth and honesty, the basis of the rules of scholarship.

TREATMENT OF HUMAN SUBJECTS (PEOPLE)

Imagine that you have been given an assignment in an introductory communication class to participate in a research project being conducted in the department that is offering your class. Furthermore, imagine this is your first term and you have been having a rough time of it so far. You have not made too many friends. Your self-concept, never as high as you would like, is at an all-time low. You have even considered quitting school and returning to mom's home cooking. But if you do, your parents, who have taken second jobs to help send you here, will be disappointed.

Well, at least you are in an *interpersonal* communication course, with no required speeches. A poll you once read showed that public speaking is Americans' biggest fear, ranking even ahead of death. No wonder—you do not have to make any speeches when you are dead.

So you show up at the designated time and place to participate in a research project to complete the course assignment. A distinguished, authoritative, and important-looking man comes into the waiting room, introduces himself as Dr. Smith, the project director, and goes on to explain that the research involves studying how effective people can be when they make speeches on various topics, and that you are going to be required to make a speech to a group of visiting high school students. Dr. Smith escorts you to another room and explains your topic: You are going to have to try and convince the students that marijuana should be legalized. This is something that you definitely do not agree with and you wonder how on earth you are going to make the speech. Dr. Smith gives you a sheet of paper with the outline of a few arguments that he tells you to use in your speech. You will have 15 minutes to prepare. You start to shake. You are panic-stricken. There is no way you can make any speech, let alone one advocating the legalization of marijuana.

Gamely, you do your best to prepare, you jot down some notes and in 15 minutes Dr. Smith returns and escorts you to a room full of videotape equipment. He explains that a nearby room is full of high school students who are anxious to hear you speak. They will be watching you on television. Your heart is pounding, your palms are sweating, your knees are literally knocking, you start to talk into the camera, but you are so nervous you can barely speak. All you can think of is how embarrassing this is, how everyone watching can tell how nervous and inarticulate you are. Near the end of the speech, which lasts for 5 minutes but seems like 30, you nearly break down and start to cry.

A few minutes later, Dr. Smith enters the room and walks with you down a very long corridor to still another room. As you walk along he is looking through some sheets of paper and casually mentions that these are evaluations of your speech that were just filled out by the students who watched you on television. He gives them to you, explaining that he is sure you will be interested to see how you did. As you read the evaluation forms your worst feelings are confirmed. You did make a fool of yourself. The student comments indicate that you are stupid, nervous, tongue-tied, crazy for wanting to legalize marijuana, and worse. You have never felt lower. After arriving at the last waiting room, you are given a questionnaire to fill out. It asks, among other things, how you feel about the legalization of marijuana.

Finally, you are taken into still another room where another researcher asks you what your understanding is of the purpose of this research project. You explain, as best you can, that it was a study of how effective people can be in making speeches. The researcher then proceeds to debrief you. He explains that the research was an *experiment*, the purpose of which was to see if people who advocated a position that was different from what they believed would change their beliefs to be more consistent with what they stated in the speech.

BOX 3.2

TURNING SOME LIGHT ON "1,000 POINTS"

Mike Royko

Let's have a brief literary quiz. Please, don't run away, it won't be heavy stuff.

I will give you a phrase, and you name the author. If you miss it the first time, don't worry. You get three guesses.

The phrase is: "A thousand points of light."

See? I told you it wouldn't be hard. You said George Bush. You may even know when and where he used it.

The first time was at the Republican convention, when he accepted his party's nomination in a finely crafted speech.

He said: "This is America . . . a brilliant diversity spread like stars, like a thousand points of light in a broad and peaceful sky."

And he used it again in his inaugural address when he said: "I have spoken of 'a thousand points of light' of all the community organizations that are spread like stars throughout the nation, doing good."

So if you identified the author of that phrase as George Bush, uh, sorry, but you're wrong.

But you have two more guesses, so try again.

If you are a student of politics, a Washington insider, or a political journalist, I know what you're saying. You probably had it as your first guess.

Peggy Noonan, right? Ms. Noonan is an outstanding political speech writer, and it's generally acknowledged that she wrote Bush's acceptance speech.

The White House press office won't come right out and say that she wrote the "thousand points of light" phrase. But a White House source says, yes, she did.

So if you guessed that Ms. Noonan authored the "thousand points of light" phrase, sorry, you're wrong, too.

But don't feel bad. I would have flunked my own quiz. My first guess would have been Ms. Noonan, since I knew she wrote the speech.

I knew it couldn't have originated with President Bush, because he would have been more likely to say: "I want to tell you about this points of lights thing. We have about one thousand of them. They represent this goodness thing."

(continued)

BOX 3.2   CONTINUED

So you have one more guess. Take your time. You have three seconds.

Give up?

The answer was provided for me by an irate and sharp-eyed man named Ray Riley, who lives in Seekonk, Mass.

Mr. Riley says: "I would like to suggest that George Bush's main campaign theme was borrowed unlawfully, in other words plagiarized.

"The definition of plagiarism is to steal and pass off the ideas or words of others as one's own; use without crediting the source; to commit literary theft; present as new and original an idea or product derived from an existing work."

And what is this existing work? Actually, there are two. Both are books written by novelist Thomas Wolfe, who died in 1938.

In "You Can't Go Home Again," Wolfe describes America this way: (the italics are mine.)

"It's your pasture now, and it's not so big—only three thousand miles from east to west, only two thousand miles from north to south—but all between, where ten thousand points of light prick out the cities, towns and villages, there, seeker, you will find us burning in the night."

OK, I concede that Wolfe saw 10,000 points of light, while Bush-Noonan saw only 1,000 points of light.

But wait. We then have Wolfe writing in "The Web and The Rock" about a character's longing to be back in his home.

Wolfe wrote: "And instantly he would see the town below now, coiling in a thousand fumes of homely smoke, now winking into a thousand points of friendly light . . ." Because of this, the irate Mr. Riley said:

"The political right has heaped praise on Bush for his points of light theme, calling it brilliant and visionary. There is nothing brilliant, nothing visionary, nothing even remotely admirable about stealing."

Oh, I don't know.

Assuming that Bush-Noonan did pilfer the thousand points of light from Thomas Wolfe, they should at least be credited with having good taste. Wolfe isn't easy to read, but he's generally accepted as something of a literary genius.

So in that regard, Bush has already moved beyond Ronald Reagan, who plucked many of his lines and anecdotes from old B-movies.

Reprinted by permission: Tribune Media Services.

Furthermore, the researchers wanted to see how the speaker's beliefs about the success of their speech affected any change in their opinion about the topic of the speech. There were, in fact, no high school students watching your speech. The forms you saw were filled out ahead of time and half the "subjects" in this experiment were shown forms that indicated that their speeches were well received.

In other words, you have been lied to, repeatedly and convincingly. You not only bought the lie, but you just went through one of the most miserable experiences of your life. How do you feel?

This example is real, and the experience of designing and participating in this study served at least one very important function: It made one of us (Hocking) realize the importance of ethical treatment of human participants. This sensitivity is important because there have been many abuses of human subjects in the past. For many years, there was no formal code of ethics regarding the treatment of human subjects. However, as examples of abuses came to light in the early 1970s, the American Psychological Association, an organization representing over 35,000 psychologists as well as a good many communication researchers, appointed a committee to develop standards for ethical conduct. Because of the importance and almost universal acceptance of these standards, we believe that you should be both familiar with and understand what they say and mean. Box 3.3 lists the ten "principles" of ethical behavior the researcher should follow.

From your reading of these principles you should identify six major themes. First, the researcher must accept **ethical responsibility** for the research project. This responsibility goes beyond simply saying "I am responsible for the research." It includes a clearly thought out research plan tied closely to the research question or hypotheses under test. The researcher must also ensure that those who are working with him or her understand the implications of the research and must take responsibility for the actions of these assistants, as well as ensure that all involved are treated fairly and equitably.

Suppose for a moment that you are interested in conducting a research project that will examine the effect of distraction on persuasion. In carrying out this study you must carefully weigh the possible benefits with potential risks. Will your research cause harm? Will psychological damage occur? Will the strength of the message, without their knowledge, cause message recipients to change their attitudes in a way to which they object?

The question is then, is a topic such as the legalization of heroin ethically appropriate? Several studies have used a message on this topic in persuasive research (Burgoon, Cohen, Miller, & Montgomery, 1978; Miller & Burgoon, 1979; Stacks & Burgoon, 1981; Stacks & Sellers, 1986). While preparing the stimulus messages much thought was given to this, especially the ethical ramifications of whether or not the message created problems for the *research itself*. These questions are concerned with value; hence, the researcher shoulders the ethical responsibility.

The second theme you should observe in the principles concerns **informed consent**. First, you must tell your participants *basically* what they will be doing. This is not to say that you must tell them exactly what your purpose is, as that could cause problems with the study, but you must inform them of the procedures and any possible risk. Second, you must allow your participants to decline participation. You must allow those who do not wish to participate, for whatever the reason, to withdraw *at any point in the study*. This should be made clear in the Participant's Informed Consent Form or the introduction to the survey (see Box 3.4). Use of such a form protects both the participant and the researcher. On this form you will tell the prospective "subject" approximately what you are doing and how it will be done (more on this follows). The general procedures the participant will follow should be outlined and any potential risk identified. Both researcher and volunteer sign the form.

Consider the speech research project described earlier. If you had been informed in advance that you had the right to withdraw from the project, would you have? We are going to let you in on a secret: If you are a member of a "subject pool" and arrive at a designated time and place with the intent of participating in research, if after reading the consent form you

BOX 3.3
APA CODE OF RESEARCH ETHICS

PLANNING RESEARCH
Psychologists design, conduct, and report research in accordance with recognized standards of scientific competence and ethical research. Psychologists plan their research so as to minimize the possibility that results will be misleading. In planning research, psychologists consider its ethical acceptability under the Ethics Code. If an ethical issue is unclear, psychologists seek to resolve the issue through consultation with institutional review boards, animal care and use committees, peer consultations, or other proper mechanisms. Psychologists take reasonable steps to implement appropriate protections for the rights and welfare of human participants, other persons affected by the research, and the welfare of animal subjects.

RESPONSIBILITY
Psychologists conduct research competently and with due concern for the dignity and welfare of the participants. Psychologists are responsible for the ethical conduct of research conducted by them or by others under their supervision or control. Researchers and assistants are permitted to perform only those tasks for which they are appropriately trained and prepared. As part of the process of development and implementation of research projects, psychologists consult those with expertise concerning any special population under investigation or most likely to be affected.

COMPLIANCE WITH LAW AND STANDARDS
Psychologists plan and conduct research in a manner consistent with federal and state law and regulations, as well as professional standards governing the conduct of research, and particularly those standards governing research with human participants and animal subjects.

INSTITUTIONAL APPROVAL
Psychologists obtain from host institutions or organizations appropriate approval prior to conducting research, and they provide accurate information about their research proposals. They conduct the research in accordance with the approved research protocol.

RESEARCH RESPONSIBILITIES
Prior to conducting research (except research involving only anonymous surveys, naturalistic observations, or similar research), psychologists enter into an agreement with participants that clarifies the nature of the research and the responsibilities of each party.

INFORMED CONSENT TO RESEARCH
Psychologists use language that is reasonably understandable to research participants in obtaining their appropriate informed consent (except in the case of "Dispensing with Informed Consent"). Such informed consent is appropriately documented. Using language that is reasonably understandable to participants, psychologists inform participants of the nature of the research; they inform participants that they are free to

(continued)

BOX 3.3 CONTINUED

participate or to decline to participate or to withdraw from the research; they explain the foreseeable consequences of declining or withdrawing; they inform participants of significant factors that may be expected to influence their willingness to participate (such as risks, discomfort, adverse effects, or limitations on confidentiality, except as in "Deception in Research"); and they explain other aspects about which the prospective participants inquire. When psychologists conduct research with individuals such as students or subordinates, psychologists take special care to protect the prospective participants from adverse consequences of declining or withdrawing from participation. When research participation is a course requirement or opportunity for extra credit, the prospective participant is given the choice of equitable alternative activities. For persons who are legally incapable of giving informed consent, psychologists nevertheless provide an appropriate explanation, obtain the participant's assent, and obtain appropriate permission from a legally authorized person, if such substitute consent is permitted by law.

DISPENSING WITH INFORMED CONSENT

Before determining that planned research (such as research involving only anonymous questionnaires, naturalistic observations, or certain kinds of archival research) does not require the informed consent of research participants, psychologists consider applicable regulations and institutional review board requirements, and they consult with colleagues as appropriate.

INFORMED CONSENT IN RESEARCH FILMING OR RECORDING

Psychologists obtain informed consent from research participants prior to filming or recording them in any form, unless the research involves simply naturalistic observations in public places and it is not anticipated that the recording will be used in a manner that could cause personal identification or harm.

OFFERING INDUCEMENTS FOR RESEARCH PARTICIPANTS

In offering professional services as an inducement to obtain research participants, psychologists make clear the nature of the services, as well as the risks, obligations, and limitations. Psychologists do not offer excessive or inappropriate financial or other inducements to obtain research participants, particularly when it might tend to coerce participation.

DECEPTION IN RESEARCH

Psychologists do not conduct a study involving deception unless they have determined that the use of deceptive techniques is justified by the study's prospective scientific, educational, or applied value and that equally effective alternative procedures that do not use deception are not feasible. Psychologists never deceive research participants about significant aspects that would affect their willingness to participate, such as physical risks, discomfort, or unpleasant emotional experiences. Any other deception that is an integral feature of the design and conduct of an experiment must be explained to participants as early as is feasible, preferably at the conclusion of their participation, but no later than at the conclusion of the research.

SHARING AND UTILIZING DATA

Psychologists inform research participants of their anticipated sharing or further use of personally identifiable research data and of the possibility of unanticipated future uses.

MINIMIZING INVASIVENESS

In conducting research, psychologists interfere with the participants or milieu from

BOX 3.3   CONTINUED

which data are collected only in a manner that is warranted by an appropriate research design and that is consistent with psychologists' roles as scientific investigators.

PROVIDING PARTICIPANTS WITH INFORMATION ABOUT THE STUDY

Psychologists provide a prompt opportunity for participants to obtain appropriate information about the nature, results, and conclusions of the research, and psychologists attempt to correct any misconceptions that participants may have. If scientific or humane values justify delaying or withholding this information, psychologists take reasonable measures to reduce the risk of harm.

HONORING COMMITMENTS

Psychologists take reasonable measures to honor all commitments they have made to research participants.

PLAGIARISM

Psychologists do not present substantial portions or elements of another's work or data as their own, even if the other work or data source is cited only occasionally.

PUBLICATION CREDIT

Psychologists take responsibility and credit, including authorship credit, only for work they have actually performed or to which they have contributed. Principal authorship and other publication credits accurately reflect the relative scientific or professional contributions of the individuals involved, regardless of their relative status. Mere possession of an institutional position, such as Department Chair, does not justify authorship credit. Minor contributions to the research or to the writing for publications are appropriately acknowledged, such as in footnotes or in an introductory statement. A student is usually listed as principal author on any multiple-authored article that is substantially based on the student's dissertation or thesis.

DUPLICATE PUBLICATION OF DATA

Psychologists do not publish, as original data, data that have been previously published. This does not preclude republishing data when they are accompanied by proper acknowledgment.

SHARING DATA

After research results are published, psychologists do not withhold the data on which their conclusions are based from other competent professionals who seek to verify the substantive claims through reanalysis and who intend to use such data only for that purpose, provided that the confidentiality of the participants can be protected and unless legal rights concerning proprietary data preclude their release.

PROFESSIONAL REVIEWERS

Psychologists who review material submitted for publication, grant, or other research proposal review respect the confidentiality of and the proprietary rights in such information of those who submitted it.

Source: From "Ethical Principles of Psychologists and Code of Conduct," *American Psychologist, 47,* 1597–1611. Copyright © 1992 by the American Psychological Association. Adapted with permission.

■ ■ ■ ■ ■

BOX 3.4
PARTICIPANT'S INFORMED CONSENT FORMS

Written:
Project Director:

Project Title: Analysis of Behavior in Problem-Solving Groups

The purpose of this research project is to examine how people operate in problem-solving groups. Students are being asked to view a segment of a group interaction that was conducted for an advanced course in group processes. After viewing the group in operation each student will be asked to complete a series of scales and respond to a number of questions about their perceptions of the group.

By signing this form you agree to view the videotaped group segment and evaluate the group via the scales and questions provided. No attempt will be made to identify you through your responses to the questions and scales; please do not make any identifying marks on your response packet.

Signing this form also acknowledges that you have been given the opportunity to withdraw from participation in this project without penalty.

_____   _____
Student's Signature   Date

_____
Project Director

_____

Oral:

SURVEY INTRODUCTION
Hello, my name is _____. I'm calling for _____. We are conducting a survey of randomly selected residents concerning the upcoming presidential election. Your telephone number was selected at random for inclusion in this study and your responses to our questions will remain confidential and your identity anonymous. I'd appreciate it very much if you would answer a few questions, it should only take _____ minutes. **(IF YES, CONTINUE; IF NO, THANK THE RESPONDENT AND MOVE ON TO THE NEXT CALL.)**

decide that participation in the research would put you at risk, or make you uncomfortable, or that you would rather not volunteer to participate for any reason, you may get up and leave and you will receive full credit towards participation. We are aware of research protocols that do not make this clear to participants; that imply that the person must participate in the study to receive credit. This simply is not true and social researchers should make clear that when they say, "no penalty will be assigned for declining to participate."

Let's think for a moment why this is the case. Voluntary participation is a core ethical principle in conducting research. If a person has taken the time and effort, in good faith, to participate in a study, or if they were required to participate after reading the consent form to receive the promised credit, the researcher would be exercising a degree of coercion to induce participation.

Special care must be taken when research participants are especially vulnerable to coercion such as might be with prisoners. A study was recently proposed to the Institutional Review Board at the University of Georgia in which the researcher was interested in childhood sexual abuse and subsequent delinquent behavior. She wanted to conduct in-depth interviews with teenage juveniles who were being held in a correctional institution. For every willing participant, she wanted to write a letter and have it placed in the file of that person indicating that he had been willing to assist in the research. It was implied to the institutionized juveniles that letters of this sort could be indications of good behavior, of willingness to cooperate, and could reflect positively on their subsequent treatment, including release date.

This letter consituted coercion to participate because *any individual who declined to participate would have no letter* and the accompanying positive implications. In such a situation, vulnerable populations may feel desperate and might "volunteer" for any research project, regardless of the risks involved. No letter was allowed. All participants had to be treated the same with regard to their institutional situations, regardless of participation.

There are also ethical considerations when dealing with children. In all cases, guardians must be informed and give consent for their children's participation in research.

The third theme follows from this discussion. At times the researcher must engage in **deception** to get genuine reactions or behaviors. Such practice must be justified, and immediately after participation the "subject" must be told of such deception and the reason for it explained. Much social science research engages in some form of deception. Imagine what the results of your study might be if you told your participants exactly what you were trying to find. Would they behave normally, or would they try to "help" you get the results for which you are looking? Obviously, many would try to help.[1]

The practice of deception also may be necessary with your helpers, people we call confederates. A confederate is someone helping with the research by engaging in some form of deception. We must be careful that the confederate does not try to "help" get results. In most instances it is best if the **confederate** knows only as much as is needed to do his or her job. After the research has been completed, you have an ethical responsibility to debrief all confederates and other helpers as to the "real" procedures of the research.

The fourth theme concerns the **risk** you put participants to in the study. In some studies psychological damage can occur. Imagine if you were engaged in a study of negotiation and, although you were told that nothing would actually happen to your "hostage" or "workers," your negotiation caused those people "harm." Such a study might entail you creating messages to another party and getting back bogus messages that attack your negotiating skills. What *potential* damage might this cause to your psyche at a later time and place, perhaps when you actually began negotiating for a pay raise? The researcher must keep this in mind. Part of accounting for risk concerns the debriefing the participant will receive after completing the project.

Most communication research has minimal risk attached to it. But, for example, some of the research into message processing is beginning to use physiological measures. In accessing physiological data the researcher must "hook" the participant to electrical equipment. The risk involved here is minimal, but the participant must be informed that he or she will be hooked to a machine with electrodes. In studies of deception the researcher may use an electrocardiograph to assess heart rate as the participant is asked questions. Although there is very little risk here, the participant must know the procedures involved and feel confident that the researcher can use the equipment competently.

When using procedures that may constitute high risk, the researcher must accept any future responsibility to correct for any long-term consequences. No waiver of responsibility actually reduces the ethical responsibility of the researcher here. Although very few communication research projects will deal with physical harm, the question of psychological damage is always a possibility and should be considered when designing the study.

Fifth, the researcher must ensure anonymity or confidentiality of the data collected. **Anonymity** means that no one, including the researcher, knows who gave which responses. **Confidentiality** means that only the researcher knows who gave the responses. This means that once the participant has completed the study, his or her responses are maintained in such a way that only the researcher actually knows who responded in what way. In cases where participants must be identified later to assess whether time factors in the study, confidentiality may become a problem, but can be dealt with by assigning numbers to participants or using special codes. Ethically, however, the researcher must protect the confidentiality of the participant. Obviously, if he or she must know who is who, then the data must be guarded carefully.

Sixth, the researcher is responsible for **debriefing** the participant. Because the debriefing process is so very important, and because it is controversial, we will treat this aspect of research in detail. The quality of the debriefing may determine whether or not the entire project is ethical.

DEBRIEFING

Debriefing refers to the postexperimental explanation that is provided to research participants at the conclusion of participation. There are at least four important purposes to be served by debriefing. First, a debriefing should erase any negative effects that may have resulted from participation. Second, debriefing should establish or maintain a favorable relationship between participants and researchers. Third, debriefing should make participation in the research educational for participants by explaining thoroughly what has been done, how, and why. Finally, competent debriefing procedures provide researchers with feedback relevant to the efficacy of the research procedures. Unfortunately, the topic has seldom been mentioned in research methods textbooks. The intent of the following discussion is to emphasize the importance of the debriefing.

Eliminating Harmful Effects

Many kinds of communication research have potentially harmful consequences for participants. In the "counterattitudinal advocacy" study that was described earlier in this chapter, first-year college students were presented with a situation in which they were required to

MINI-PROJECT:

Interview a faculty member other than your research methods professor about his or her research. Concentrate on understanding first what it is that he or she does, then on the ethics of it. Ask questions regarding treatment of participants and data. Is the research conducted in an ethical manner? Is deception employed? If so, how is the deception clarified? How does he or she debrief the participants?

give a short speech in front of a television camera. They were told falsely that an audience in another room was watching their presentation. The situation was carefully controlled to ensure that even though participants were nominally told they could decline to make the speech, few of them would exercise this option. Some of them were extremely anxious in this situation and, as described in the example, some were visibly shaken by the experience. At least one experienced such a high degree of anxiety that she could not finish the speech. It is highly probable that participating in this research was harmful to the self-concepts of at least some participants.

If research procedures do result in harm of any kind, the debriefing must eliminate this harm. The effectiveness of debriefing thus becomes a crucial determinant of whether or not the research project is ethical. Unfortunately, little is known about the effectiveness of debriefing in such situations. The one empirical study that has addressed this question explicitly provides results that are so important and illuminating that we will describe it in some detail.

Elaine Walster and her colleagues (1967) conducted an experiment designed to see if a careful debriefing eliminated any lingering negative effects resulting from participation in an experiment even after participants were thoroughly and carefully debriefed. Participants were told that the study dealt with how socially skilled individuals were. They were required to respond to a questionnaire that was purported to measure their social skills. Half of the participants, selected at random, were falsely told that they had scored at the eighteenth percentile, meaning that fully 82 percent of the people who took the test were more skilled socially than they were. Furthermore, they were given a written profile stating that "they were reluctant to become involved with others, they could not express their real feelings to others, and that they lacked self-insight to the point of being largely unaware of these shortcomings." The participants then were given time to read and think about this highly critical feedback. The other half were given positive feedback about their social skills. They were told that they scored at the ninetieth percentile, meaning that only 10 percent of those taking the test were more skilled. They also received highly favorable written evaluations.

All participants were given a thorough, individual debriefing that took a minimum of 20 minutes. They were told that the questionnaire they had filled out had no validity whatsoever, that the feedback they received was completely false, and that they had been assigned to the positive and negative feedback conditions randomly. They were shown the version of the feedback material that the participants in the other conditions received. The debriefing was terminated only after it was clear that the participants understood that the feedback reports had nothing to do with their actual degree of social skills. Finally, they were asked to provide self-report measures of their perception of their own level of social skills.

The critical finding was this: Participants who were given unfavorable feedback about their social skills now rated themselves as less socially skilled than did those who received the favorable feedback. In other words, the debriefing was not entirely successful in eliminating a very obvious negative effect that resulted from participation in a research project. Whether a different debriefing strategy would have been more effective is unknown. Perhaps participants, given time during the experiment to think about their critical feedback evaluations, recalled and reinterpreted events in their lives in a manner that was consistent with this new evaluation. Whatever the explanation, it was obvious that their self-concepts were altered more profoundly than even a careful debriefing could erase. The important point is that we cannot immediately assume that a debriefing erases negative effects, and, in fact, the only available evidence suggests that the debriefing may *not* undo negative effects. We believe that if there is likely to be harm to participants resulting from research participation, serious ethical questions about the research itself are raised, regardless of the care given to debriefing participants. We will now turn to the other important reasons for conducting debriefing.

The Research Experience

For both ethical and practical reasons, participation in a communication research project should be a positive experience. Ethically we believe that it is simply wrong to take from people without providing something in return. It would be impossible to conduct social research without research participants. The participant provides time and energy to the researcher and makes it possible for the researcher to further his or her own career as well as make a contribution to knowledge about communication. It is reasonable for the participant to gain from the research experience, and he or she should gain more than whatever minimal grade or monetary incentive may have been used to induce participation. What the researcher can offer in return is a positive educational experience and the debriefing provides the opportunity to provide it. (See Boxes 3.5 and 3.6 for sample debriefings.)

The second reason to make participation in experiments a positive experience is practical. College students do not frequently come into contact with social scientists. A large component of the impression that participants and others have of social science is probably a result of whatever personal contact they may have had with social scientists. Any time a communication researcher comes into contact with a participant, he or she is, in a sense, representing both the communication discipline and social research in general. This is also true of the "student" researcher. This is an important responsibility, one that should be taken seriously.

The primary mechanism for assuring that research participation is a positive, educational experience is the debriefing session. This is the researcher's chance to communicate with the participant in a manner from which everyone involved—the researcher,

---

BOX 3.5
DEBRIEFING STATEMENT

The study you have just participated in examined perceptions of small group behavior and communication. Because participation in research of this kind should be part of all students' education, both as consumers of research in life and as critical readers of research, this sheet provides you the initial data you need to better understand why the study was undertaken. Please read the following paragraph and then sign this sheet to indicate (1) that you have been debriefed and been able to ask questions concerning the research by either the investigator or his representative and (2) (because the project will run over several days) that you will refrain from discussing the research project until the date specified has passed.

This study sought to examine the impact of touch and topic involvement on perceptions of the group. Specifically, students viewed a videotape in which the issue was "involving" or "not involving" and in which the confederates engaged in the discussion were either touching each other frequently or not. Additionally, some students simply read transcripts of the interaction. The two conditions (touch and topic) were the manipulations and we were interested in how they interacted to produce different perceptions of the observed group's credibility, attraction, cohesiveness, involvement and satisfaction, and how you felt about joining the group you observed in a future interaction. Your responses will be treated confidentially, in no way will your responses be made public. The results of the research should be available by next Fall Semester, please feel free to drop by the Department of Communication Arts and read them.

By signing this form you indicate that you have read the debriefing statement and have been given a chance to have any questions answered. Your signature also indicates that you agree not to disclose what you have seen or the scales you completed until after _____.

I have read and agree to abide by the wishes of the research director.

_____   _____
Volunteer's Signature   Date

---

the communication discipline, social researchers in general, and especially, of course, the participant—will benefit. If participants leave a research project with bad feelings about their participation, bad feelings about the researcher, or bad feelings about social science, then ethical questions about the researcher's behavior should be raised. Thus a major, and often overlooked, purpose of the debriefing is to make participation in the research a positive educational experience for the participant and, in the process, create or maintain a favorable relationship between the researcher (and all that he or she represents) and the participant.

Earlier we mentioned that the label *subject* has a negative connotation.[2] Because of this we have consciously avoided the term wherever possible because it tends to dehumanize the process of research. In some fields the subject may not be human; indeed, it may not even

BOX 3.6
DEBRIEFING LETTER

Dear _____:

Your participation in this research project is very important for a variety of reasons. First, when the data you provided are analyzed fully and written up for publication, our knowledge of the behavioral basis for accurate judgments of lying will have been advanced. This individual study, by itself, makes only a small contribution to our understanding of human behavior and its effects. However, other researchers interested in this same area will be able to examine our procedures and results and be able to extend and refine the knowledge gained. In this way, as more studies are completed, the accumulation of knowledge grows steadily and systematically.

Second, there are practical applications of this study. It was paid for by a National Science Foundation grant which is looking at the effects of using videotape during court proceedings. If, in the future, trials are recorded on videotape and shown to juries on television monitors, it will be important to know under what conditions jurors would have the best chance to detect lying by witnesses.

Third, the researchers have benefited from your participation in this research. It is necessary to conduct major research projects to complete graduate studies in all social science disciplines, including Communication. Your participation has been important to us personally for this reason.

Finally, you personally may have benefited from this experience. By participating in this experiment, by listening to the description of the research which was provided during the class period in which you participated, and by reading this letter, you may have learned a little bit about how Social Science research is conducted. Hopefully this project has been an educational experience for you. Also, much of the content of courses comes from research projects like this one. Thus, future communication students may benefit from your participation just as you have likely benefited from the contributions of past participants.

In short, your participation in this experiment was extremely valuable. We sincerely appreciate your help and would like to thank you very much.

---

be an animal. We prefer to think of our participants as people who think, feel, and react to stimuli. One thing that communication researchers should always remember is that they deal with people and any process that dehumanizes those helping in research is likely to contribute to negative feelings toward future participation. Some academic journals, for example, now require that the term *subjects* be changed to refer to *respondents* or *participants*, hence humanizing the research.

The attitude of many subjects toward social research is captured in this hypothetical letter from a subject to a researcher written by psychologist Sidney M. Jourard (1968):

My name is S. You don't know me. I have another name my friends call me by, but I drop it and become number 27 as soon as I take part in your research. I serve in your surveys and experiments. I answer your questions, fill out questionnaires. . . . I have started to wonder why I do these things for you. What's in it for me. . . ? I feel myself being pressured, bull-dozed, tricked, manipulated everywhere I turn. You really seem to be studying me in order to learn how to influence my actions without my realizing it. I resent this. . . . I feel used, and I don't like it. But I protect myself by not showing you my whole self, or lying. Did you ever stop to think that your articles, and the textbooks you write, the theories you spin—all based on your data (my disclosures to you)—may actually be a tissue of lies and half-truths (my lies and half-truths) or a joke I've played on you because I don't like or trust you? That should give you some concern. (pp. 9–12)

Indeed it should. Examining questionnaires that have been filled out at random or ob-serving these attitudes being manifested in other ways happens all too frequently.

Suspicions and mistrust regarding the ethics of social researchers are not limited to research subjects. Even today, decades after David Berlo (1960) wrote *The Process of Communication*, a book that contributed greatly to the diffusion of empirical approaches to studying human communication, there are some communication professionals who vocally denounce scientific research, or at least suggest that such inquiry leads to mistreatment of subjects. Your authors know of an attempt in a large Communication Studies Department at a major university to systematize procedures for obtaining student research participants, which was met by opposition from faculty whose orientation was "humanistic." According to a document circulated by an opponent, "the overriding reason has to do with treating people as instruments for professional ends."[3] We believe that such sentiments exist because many researchers have, in fact, shown a callous disregard for assuring that the research par-ticipants do, in fact, gain something from participation. As Herbert Kelman (1967) notes, "[the participant] should in some positive way be enriched by the [research] experience, that is he [or she] should come away from it with the feeling that he has learned something, un-derstood something, or grown in some way" (p. 1).

Does the impression that people form of a specific study as a result of their participa-tion in it affect their attitudes toward social science in general? One experiment involved purposely putting participants through experiences designed to suggest to them that re-search was either interesting and important or dull and a waste of time. Those people in the positive experience condition subsequently felt more favorably toward research in general, and performed more conscientiously during a later study than did those in the negative pre-vious experience condition (Holmes & Applebaum, 1970).

The quality of the debriefing influences participants' judgments of the value of a spe-cific project and of social science research in general (Hocking, Bauchner, Kaminski, & Miller, 1979). One study examined the detection of deceptive communications. The partic-ipants observed videotapes of sixteen people who were either lying or telling the truth, and were asked to attempt to determine which was which. A third of the participants received no debriefing, a third received a minimal debriefing (Box 3.6), and a third received a de-tailed and thorough debriefing that described the purpose of the study, how the results would fit into a larger framework, the practical and theoretical value of the research, and the potential benefits that could result for all involved, including the researchers, future communication students, mankind, and the participants themselves. In short, the detailed debriefing attempted to make sure that participation was a positive educational experience for participants and that there was a positive relationship between the researcher and participants. Several weeks later all subjects filled out a purportedly unrelated questionnaire that asked how valuable communication research was, how concerned researchers in general were for the "welfare of their participants," and how reasonable was a use of class time for research participation. The people who received the detailed debriefing indicated more favorable views of research and researchers than did those who received no debriefing; those who received minimal debriefing fell in the middle.[4]

Debriefing Children. It is important to debrief children. Obviously, the nature of the debriefing, like all communication messages, needs to be adapted to the audience and the situation, but children have great potential to benefit from a debriefing. In a study examining adolescent drinking patterns (Atkin, Hocking, & Block, 1984), the youngest group in the sample was made up of seventh-graders, all about twelve years old. Their participation involved observing some alcohol advertisements and filling out a lengthy questionnaire. The debriefing, which lasted over an hour, resulted in a stimulating class discussion about not only the specific research project and social science research in general, but also the effects of alcohol advertising and advertising in general, the propriety of alcohol use in a variety of situations, and the pros and cons of alcohol use in general. The teacher later reported that the students had learned a great deal about an important topic as a result of their participation in the research, especially from the debriefing.

Can the debriefing affect children's attitudes about social research? An experiment by Carol Weissbrod and Thomas Mangran (1978) suggests that the answer is "yes." Fifth-grade boys and girls were deceived as part of an altruism experiment. Debriefed children subsequently indicated that they believed the research to be more "worthwhile" than children who were not debriefed. The authors conclude "that the debriefing may give children information that adds to their positive perception of the value and potential of experimental studies" (p. 72).

Debriefing Procedures. How does one go about debriefing in such a way that participants will "in some positive way be enriched by the experience, that is he [or she] should come away from it with the feeling that he has learned something, understood something, or grown in some way" (Weissbrod & Mangran, 1978, p. 72). First, let participants know that you appreciate their participation. Thank them for helping you. Second, be as open and honest as you can be at that particular time. (See, for example, the sample debriefing statement presented in Box 3.5.) Debriefing statements also frequently ask, in the name of the research, that the participant not divulge to other potential participants the purposes and procedures of the research.

Third, describe for the participants what you were attempting to do, the hypotheses or questions you asked, and your procedures. This not only educates them, but also provides feedback at times when your procedures are not working the way you thought they would. In this way the debriefing serves a corrective function. Fourth, if you are not conducting the debriefing yourself (as is the case with field experiments conducted by several confederates or helpers in the field), provide the participants with an address and telephone number through which they can contact you. Finally, attempt to contact them after the fact. If you used a class, go to a meeting of that class and present your results. If the participants came from a number of classes, either provide the instructors with a summary of what you found or send participants a letter thanking them for helping and giving them your major findings. This extra step almost always ensures the participant an educational experience and usually leaves him or her with a positive feeling about the research.

ETHICAL APPROPRIATENESS

Are there certain topics for research that may not be appropriate to study? The question of ethically appropriate topics is especially troublesome for researchers of communication.

The decision regarding what to study and how to study it is an individual choice and the individual must live with that choice. It is a value judgment tempered by an understanding of possible risk. In general, we believe that researchers should be given maximum freedom to study whatever they want and to go wherever their theory and findings lead them. Nonetheless, there are some points of concern. For example: Is it ethical to try to determine if a particular racial group has different characteristics, such as communicative competencies? Such questions may be debated as to whether they are ethically appropriate for study under current ethical standards.

There is a related ethical concern that has been referred to but not discussed. This concern deals with data. Data, as we will discuss in later chapters, are the "things" we observe in a study. Data may be numbers, names, concepts, and so forth. Data, too, must be treated appropriately. Singletary (1994) goes so far as to suggest that you must consider data ethics from the moment you conceptualize how you will collect the data (questionnaire, observation, physiological device) and begin to operationalize your constructs. Part of data ethics includes the training of confederates or interviewers, the drawing of your sample, recording and storing data, and the final analysis of that data. In general terms, you should treat your data as you do your participants—as an integral part of the research process.

A PARTING NOTE

We will finish our discussion of research ethics by concluding Sidney Jourard's (1968) letter. Read carefully what he is saying and see if you agree.

> If you'll trust me, I'll trust you, if you're trustworthy. I'd like you to take the time and trouble to get acquainted with me as a person, before we go through your experimental procedures. And I'd like to get to know you and what you are up to, to see if I would like to expose myself to you. Sometimes, you remind me of physicians. They look at me as the unimportant envelope that conceals the disease they are really interested in. You have looked at me as the unimportant package that contains "responses," and this is all I am for you. Let me tell you that when I feel this, I get back at you. I give you responses, all right; but you will never know what I meant by them. You know, I can speak, not just in words, but with my action. And when you have thought I was responding to a "stimulus" in your lab, my response was really directed at *you*; and what I meant by it was, "Take this, you unpleasant so-and-so." Does that surprise you? It shouldn't.
>
> . . . I'll make a bargain with you. You show me that you are doing your researches *for me*—to help me become freer, more self-understanding, better able to control *myself*—and

I'll make myself available to you in any way you ask. And I won't play jokes and tricks on you. I don't want to *be controlled*, not by you or anyone else. And I don't want to control other people. I don't want you to help other people to understand how I can be "controlled," that they can then control me. Show me that you are for me, and I will show *myself* to you. (pp. 11–12)

Jourard wrote this letter after serving as an unknowing subject in another researcher's project. Obviously, had he known he was going to be a participant, had the chance to withdraw from the project, and been fully debriefed afterward, he may have felt differently. Ethically, you need to treat your participants as feeling, thinking, and emoting people. In other words, treat them as you yourself would like to be treated.

APPLYING KNOWLEDGE IN COMMUNICATION

Ethical responsibility comes with conducting research. Questions of academic research ethics arose out of examples of mistreatment of human participants in both medical and social science research (e.g., Zimbardo, Ebbesen, & Maslach, 1977). Much of what we have studied in this chapter is focused on one particular research methodology: the experiment. Why? In part this is because the researcher, to observe impartial and honest responses to some manipulation, must deceive participants from trying to respond in a way they *think* is what she *wants*. Also, in an experiment, participants are actually subjected to a stimulus (a speech, carefully constructed press release, a newspaper page with changes that only certain groups of participants will see) and respond without sometimes knowing that they have actually been manipulated.

However, all forms of research have ethical problems. Survey research often leads the respondent into thinking that the survey will take a very short time (after all, what is "a few minutes"?), or that the sponsor is one organization while another is actually sponsoring the research, or that the people surveyed actually represent the population from which they were selected. Focus groups, especially those conducted by organizational communication researchers, often pose ethical problems for participants. Should I, a subordinate, be openly critical of my superior in a focus group, even if guaranteed confidentiality and anonymity—and what if my supervisor is part of the focus group? As we will note later, a nominal group technique often eliminates some of the ethical questions raised.

Knowing about ethics and ethical quandaries makes for better research. As communication research deals with messages and the way messages are presented, we should be very concerned that our research in no way endangers our research participants. And, because academic research seeks to produce knowledge that others will use and trust *because* it was produced by academic researchers, we must be very careful to follow some ethical code.

But what of those conducting research outside of academia? Obviously, research is conducted in the "real" world. Advertising agencies, marketing firms, public relations people, organizational consultants, media specialists, and journalists all conduct research. As was noted earlier, there are codes for ethical conduct; however, enforcement is questionable. Taking what you have learned about scholarship, treatment of research participants, and ethical appropriateness and applying it in the "real" world will make you not only a better researcher, but a better person as well—you will have helped to improve the human condition.

Although the focus of this chapter has been on ethics as they apply to (1) rules of scholarship and (2) the treatment of human participants, the National Communication Association (1999) has developed a "Credo" to cover all communication. We feel that an appropriate way to end this chapter is to present this "Credo," shown in Box 3.7.

BOX 3.7

NCA CREDO FOR ETHICAL COMMUNICATION (APPROVED BY THE NCA LEGISLATIVE COUNCIL IN 1999)

Questions of right and wrong arise whenever people communicate. Ethical communication is fundamental to responsible thinking, decision making, and the development of relationships and communities within and across contexts, cultures, channels, and media. Moreover, ethical communication enhances human worth and dignity by fostering truthfulness, fairness, responsibility, personal integrity, and respect for self and others. We believe that unethical communication threatens the quality of all communication and consequently the well-being of individuals and the society in which we live. Therefore we, the members of the National Communication Association, endorse and are committed to practicing the following principles of ethical communication:

We advocate truthfulness, accuracy, honesty, and reason as essential to the integrity of communication.

We endorse freedom of expression, diversity of perspective, and tolerance of dissent to achieve the informed and responsible decision making fundamental to a civil society.

We strive to understand and respect other communicators before evaluating and responding to their messages.

We promote access to communication resources and opportunities as necessary to fulfill human potential and contribute to the well-being of families, communities, and society.

We promote communication climates of caring and mutual understanding that respect the unique needs and characteristics of individual communicators.

We condemn communication that degrades individuals and humanity through distortion, intimidation, coercion, and violence, and through the expression of intolerance and hatred.

We are committed to the courageous expression of personal convictions in pursuit of fairness and justice.

We advocate sharing information, opinions, and feelings when facing significant choices while also respecting privacy and confidentiality.

We accept responsibility for the short- and long-term consequences of our own communication and expect the same of others.

SUMMARY

This chapter has examined a topic that is central to conducting quality research. We began with a general discussion of ethics, with an emphasis on the rules of scholarship in particular. All methods of research must adhere to the rules of scholarship. We then examined the ethics of choosing a topic; again, an ethical decision that transcends method and encompasses *all* types of research. We then moved to examine problems associated with the scientific method, specifically, the treatment of human beings as participants in research. We noted that the term "subject" connotes something subhuman and urged you to avoid thinking of your participants as subjects, but rather as participants or respondents.

We believe that this chapter serves as a sort of social etiquette for conducting research. According to that etiquette, you treat those you work with as you would treat your family or significant other.

PROBES

1. What is ethics? When attempting to define this concept, what do you think is ethical research? To meet your definition, what are the minimal considerations the researcher must consider before saying that his or her research is ethical?

2. We have made a point in labeling the people involved in a research project as participants rather than subjects—or worse yet, victims. What does each label mean to you? Which would you rather be, assuming that you were involved as a student in another student's research? Why?

3. When we talk about the "rules of scholarship" we are talking about giving consideration to others. How much of a research report is actually the researcher's? Where do you draw the line between others' work and your interpretation of others' work as original? When do you cite their work? In research is it possible to really have a truly unique idea?

4. Suppose you are placed in the following situation. You have worked hard to prepare a research proposal for class, one that can be turned in either under single authorship or in conjunction with a classmate. The day before

it is due your best friend comes to you and asks you to "return a favor" for something she helped you with earlier. That return favor is to be named as coauthor of the proposal. How would you handle the situation? Do you think a similar situation might occur to others? Why?

5. You become aware that a classmate or a friend of yours has purchased a term paper that he intends to turn in as his own work. What action, if any, do you take? What if you found out *after* the paper had been turned in?

6. Discuss the balance between deception and debriefing. How would you handle conducting an advertising study in which the message advocated the public listing of AIDS carriers? What ethical considerations would you have to weigh in conducting this research project? Which are most important? Which are least important? Why?

7. Read the NCA's Credo for Ethical Communication. Are these guidelines realistic? Too narrow? Too broad? Can you find examples in contemporary American discourse that violate these guidelines?

RESEARCH PROJECTS

1. Compare and contrast the ethical codes of professional associations (Advertising Federation, Public Relations Society of America, Radio-Television News Directors Association, Society of Professional Journalists) to those of academic associations (such as the American Psychological Association, National Communication Association, Association for Education in Journalism and Mass Communication, Broadcast Education Association).

2. The study of ethics is much more detailed than presented in this chapter. Conduct a study that looks at the philosophical reasons underlying "ethics." Are there any "schools" or "approaches" to ethics that help us to better understand what ethics are? How are they related to communication research?

3. Prepare a questionnaire that focuses on (1) defining ethics in the research environment and (2) how researchers perceive ethics in research. Interview both "academic" and "professional" ("real" world) researchers about their perceptions of ethics and write up your results.

4. Address the question, "Can ethics be learned?" and design a research study to answer the question. Point out in the design how you have been ethical in the conduct of this research.

5. Identify examples of communication in American public discourse (politics, media news, ads) that violate the NCA Credo.

SUGGESTED READING

Holmes, D. S., and Applebaum, A. S. (1970). Nature of prior experimental experience as a determinant of performance in subsequent experiments. *Journal of Personality and Social Psychology, 14*, 195–202.

Jourard, S. M. (1968). *Man disclosing to himself.* New York: D. Van Nostrand Company.

Johannesen, R. L. (1990). *Ethics in human communication,* 3rd ed. Belmont, CA: Wadsworth.

Kelman, H. (1967). Human use of human subjects: The problem of deception in social psychological experiments. *Psychological Bulletin, 67,* 1–11.

Merrill, J. C., & Barney, R. D. (Eds.) (1975). *Ethics and the press: Readings in mass media morality.* New York: Hastings House.

Seib, P., & Fitzpatrick, K. (1995). *Public relations ethics.*

Fort Worth, TX: Harcourt Brace College Publishers.

Stacks, D. W. (2002). *Primer of Public Relations Research.* New York: Guilford.

Walster, E., et al. (1967). Effectiveness of debriefing following deception experiments. *Journal of Personality and Social Psychology, 14,* 371–380.

Weissbrod, C. S., & Mangran, T. (1978). Children's attitudes about experimental participation: The effect of deception and debriefing. *Journal of Social Psychology, 106,* 59–72.

Wright, D. K. (1993). Enforcement dilemma: Voluntary nature of public relations codes. *Public Relations Review,* Spring, 13.

NOTES

1. See, for example, the Hawthorne studies, in which people changed their behavior because they thought they were being observed.

2. Equally negative is to say "bring in the next one," which many beginning student social researchers use, either consciously or unconsciously, to refer to the people on whom they test their ideas.

3. Ethics requires that we not disclose either the

institution or individual. By so doing we have assured that individual that those comments are both anonymous to readers and confidential to us.

4. The participants in the minimal and no debriefing conditions then were given the thorough debriefing.

REFERENCES

Atkin, C., Hocking, J., & Block, M. (1984). Teenage drinking: Does advertising make a difference? *Journal of Communication, 34*, 157–167.

Berlo, D. K. (1960). *The process of communication.* New York: Holt, Rinehart & Winston.

Burgoon, M., Cohen, M., Miller, M. D., & Montgomery, C. L. (1978). An empirical test of a model of resistance to persuasion. *Human Communication Research, 5*, 27–39.

Day, L. A. (1997). *Ethics in media communications: Cases and controversies,* 2nd ed. Belmont, CA: Wadsworth.

Hale, J. L. (1987). Plagiarism in classroom settings. *Communication Research Reports, 4*, 66–70.

Hocking, J. E., Bauchner, J., Kaminski, E. P., & Miller, G. R. (1979). Detecting deceptive communication from verbal, visual, and paralinguistic cues. *Human Communication Research, 6*, 33–46.

Holmes, D. S., & Applebaum, A. S. (1970). Nature of prior experimental experience as a determinant of performance in subsequent experiments. *Journal of Personality and Social Psychology, 14*, 195–202.

Jourard, S. M. (1968). *Disclosing man to himself.* New York: D. Van Nostrand.

Kelman, H. (1967). Human use of human subjects: The problem of deception in social psychological experiments. *Psychological Bulletin, 67*, 1.

Kerlinger, F. N. (1964). *Foundations of behavioral research.* New York: Holt, Rinehart & Winston.

Kerlinger, F. N., & Lee, H. B. (2000). *Foundations of behavioral research,* 4th ed. New York: Harcourt College Publishers.

Miller, M. D., & Burgoon, M. (1979). The relationship between violations of expectations and the induction of resistance to persuasion. *Human Communication Research, 6*, 300–313.

Singletary, M. (1994). *Mass communication research: Contemporary methods and applications.* New York: Longman.

Stacks, D. W., & Burgoon, J. K. (1981). The role of nonverbal behaviors as distractors in resistance to persuasion in interpersonal contexts. *Central States Speech Journal, 32*, 61–73.

Stacks, D. W., & Sellers, D. E. (1986). Toward a holistic approach to communication: The effect of 'pure' hemispheric reception on message acceptance. *Communication Quarterly, 34*, 266–285.

University of Georgia Vice President for Instruction. (2000). *A Culture of Honesty: Policy on Academic Honesty.* Athens, GA: The University Council.

Walster, E., et al. (1967). Effectiveness of debriefing following deception experiments. *Journal of Personality and Social Psychology, 14*, 371–380.

Weissbrod, C. S., & Mangran, T. (1978). Children's attitudes about experimental participation: The effect of deception and debriefing. *Journal of Social Psychology, 106*, 72.

Zimbardo, P. G., Ebbesen, E. B., & Maslach, C. (1977). *Influencing attitudes and changing behavior.* Reading, MA: Addison-Wesley.

PART II

METHODS OF COMMUNICATION RESEARCH

Now that the bases of theory and research and the relationship between them have been covered, we can move into the realm of research *methodologies*. Understanding the various available research methodologies is a necessary step in consuming and conducting research.

The foundation laid in Part I emphasized the types of questions different methodologies are best at answering. In this section we discuss those questions specifically asked by researchers attempting to build a knowledge base. Based on the foundation of theory and science/humanism, method provides the blueprints from which we will build our research projects.[1]

Before you can begin to create a blueprint, however, you must first understand the materials with which you build. These are typically found in the *literature* appropriate to the area(s) you are studying. The literature you review creates the foundation from which questions and/or hypotheses are drawn. Regardless of the research method chosen, all researchers begin by reviewing previous studies and existing theory. In the case of the historical method, the library becomes the major research source and analysis is rooted in those sources found in depositories of knowledge: academic libraries, personal libraries, archives, and so on. Previous editions of this book (1992, 1999) pointed to the library as the starting point. In the first century of the third millennium we will instead say: Once you have a question to answer, the first place to start is probably the virtual library you have on your computer screen, which gives you access to hundreds of academic databases and millions of Web sites.

Chapter 4 addresses the problems and resources involved in conducting documentary research. We begin by establishing what a document is and how to select appropriate

---

[1] The analogy of building blocks is similar to that suggested by Don W. Stacks, Sidney R. Hill, and Mark L. Hickson in *An Introduction to Communication Theory* (New York: Holt, Rinehart & Winston, 1991). In their metaphor theory is perceived as the foundation for understanding. In our metaphor theory is viewed as the foundation upon which method is built, the type of question helps to establish particular method. The frame, therefore, is method and method rests upon a theoretical foundation.

documentation for particular research needs. We then move toward the literature review, or the formal analysis of the documents obtained in the search. The aim of this chapter is to provide the knowledge necessary to (1) decide what documents are necessary, (2) locate where they may be found in the library or on the internet, (3) determine what resources may be available that make the search process easier, and (4) establish systematic procedures for putting research together.

Chapter 5 examines the historical/rhetorical-critical method from two perspectives: social science and humanism. The questions best addressed by historical methods are presented as an introduction to the methods themselves. Finally, rhetorical-critical method is addressed. Rhetorical-critical method is defined as research involving value judgments about communication, with emphasis given to oral communication, such as that found in rhetorical analysis and speech criticism.

Chapters 6 and 7 set the stage for three methods that constitute the social scientific method by discussing how we *measure* the various cognitive and behavioral variables of interest to communication researchers. These chapters discuss reliability and validity and introduce the reader to commonly used scales and other measurement techniques.

Chapters 8 through 13 present the four major social scientific methods—content analysis—as both an extension of measurement, but primarily as a method; participant observation, focus nominal group techniques, and in-depth interviewing; survey; and experiments. Remember, the purpose of science is to build theory—systematic statements of relationships between variables. Thus, each of these methods has as its goal the identification or confirmation of relationships between variables. Each method differs with regard to the degree of confidence the researcher can place in findings about whether variables are related and the degree of artificiality used to study the relationships between variables. On the one hand, the participant observer studies behavior from a qualitative/descriptive model that takes advantage of communication in naturally occurring contexts, but statements about whether the variables under observation are related to each other must be carefully qualified. The importance here is placed on *naturally occurring behavior*. Rigor is sacrificed in favor of realism. The survey represents a quantitative model that allows increased confidence in the results, but at some expense of control. The experiment can provide great rigor and allows high degrees of confidence to be placed in statements concerning the relationships between variables, but often at the expense of control. Thus, as we shall see, each method has its advantages and limitations.

Chapter 8, Describing Information: Content Analysis, looks specifically at messages; it provides a systematic base for the analysis of messages through carefully constructed category systems and an analytical technique that provides indices of reliability. Since messages are what communication researchers focus on in their research, being able to construct systematic and reliable measures of the content of messages is an essential research tool.

Chapter 9 examines the several social scientific research methods that, while rigorous in themselves, tend toward more humanistic interpretation: participant-observation, focus and nominal groups, and in-depth interviewing. These methods are the most subjective of the social science approaches and provide ways of observing how people communicate in their environments under real-world conditions. Usually no effort is made to predict or to generalize the findings of the research to a larger population; instead participant-observation, focus group, and in-depth interviewing are addressed from a purely exploratory and descriptive viewpoint.

Chapters 10 and 11 present a more rigorous method of research: Survey research, a method that seeks to generalize findings to a larger population based on a subpopulation of people "selected" for study (Chapter 10). This method examines the concepts of *surveying* a population by selecting a representative sample and asking that sample questions relevant to the variables under study. Survey design is discussed in Chapter 11, as well as data collection techniques.

Chapters 12 and 13 examine the experiment. These chapters present experimental and quasi-experimental designs, focusing on features of designs that may invalidate the research, and how the researcher "creates" his variables through operational definitions.

Part II, then, builds upon the theoretical foundation laid in Part I. An understanding of the various methods provides the knowledge necessary to make intelligent decisions about which method best answers which research questions. It also provides a strategy for collecting and accessing the type of data needed before addressing the research question or hypothesis.

CHAPTER FOUR

GETTING STARTED: RETRIEVING AND EVALUATING INFORMATION

OBJECTIVES

By the end of this chapter you should be able to:

1. Explain how to obtain and evaluate research sources.
2. Discuss the different roles of documentary research and their function in research.
3. Explain how to conduct a computer-based documentary search.
4. Construct a literature search.
5. Discuss the criteria employed in appraising a document's credibility.
6. Create a "literature review."

Perhaps the hardest part of conducting research is getting started. After you get an idea— or perhaps have a topic assigned to you—you must begin *systematically* to search available sources of information, make decisions, prepare arguments, and develop answerable questions or testable hypotheses. After you have thought about the topic, you need to investigate what others have said and researched about it. You need to assess the available repositories of information. The repository you usually check first is the library, increasingly accessed and searched by a desktop computer either physically or at the library, from a computer lab, dorm room, or literally anywhere there is a computer and a modem. Of course, there are other sources for the information, such as authorities—people who have expertise in a given area. This chapter will prepare you for your first step in research: collecting the relevant information from which to make choices.

If we were to think of one thing that has revolutionized the research process over the last several decades, it would be the advent of the personal computer. Initially created to process mundane mathematical tasks, the computer has become a necessary requirement for modern research. Not only does the PC compute like a calculator, but it can serve as a conduit to large databases—sources of information of all kinds ranging from newspaper articles to historical documents to Web sites that have graphs of everything from the population of your home town to statistics on condom use.

First, remember that all research begins with a theoretical statement derived from some literature review. This literature review is necessary for identifying all the important, previous knowledge in the area of your topic of investigation. Today, the computer can make literature reviews easier and also help in preparing the written product. We can begin by attaching our computer to a document database, such as a library or other online document depository. By asking for certain key words or authors we can establish a listing of available sources, which then can be copied and printed for later use. The Internet has opened a wide variety of resources, from specialized research "home pages" to networks in specialized areas. There are specific content networks such as CRTNET, PSYCHNET, CELEX, COMSERVE, ISAAC, and LEXIS/NEXIS. Access to LEXIS/NEXIS allows you to conduct world-wide searches of most business, communication, information, and government databases. Using computers, it is even possible to ask other researchers, all over the world, for help. For example, you might ask if anyone on the CRTNET network knows of sources or information concerning your interest area.

Simply put, the personal computer has become one of the most important tools that you will use in both school and on the job. It has become a major fixture in our lives, for work *and* play. As a research tool, however, it opens new vistas in terms of obtaining information from which to derive hypotheses or ask research questions. This availability, however, is like

MINI-PROJECT:

You have grown up with computers and take as commonplace what they can do. Talk to faculty about what research was like before the mainframe computer and the PC. How has the computer advanced our knowledge of communication?

a two-edged sword: it possesses both an advantage—we have access to more information than ever before—and a disadvantage—we have access to too much information and that information's credibility is sometimes suspect. In any event, we are acquiring "documents" that must be evaluated whether they are in print or electronic.

OBTAINING DOCUMENTS

Before we get to the nuts and bolts of conducting a documentary search, two comments are in order. Any time you begin to conduct a research project, even in conducting a literature review, you must have a *plan of action*. Such a plan allows you to make the best use of a commodity of which there is far too little: time. By carefully considering just what is needed, how you will attack the task of finding what you need, and what criteria you will use in deciding what to save and what to discard, you have taken your first step toward establishing your research methodology. This step is important in that it establishes the *parameters*—the limits or boundaries—of what you consider relevant to your topic. Establishing parameters, however, does not mean that you have irrevocably limited yourself. As more and more information is garnered the process of research often produces changes.

Indeed, one of the major differences in documentary research today and just thirty years ago is found in the complexity of the search. Figures 4.1 and 4.2 are two models of documentary research and illustrate the changes in complexity between 1970 and the present. What caused this increase in complexity? The answer is simply access to documents and others who might help in obtaining basic information increased dramatically with the advent of computer-based documentary searches.

A second philosophical consideration deals with the type of analysis involved in a documentary search. Documentary research establishes the first *critical* analysis of sources and resources (Hickson & Stacks, 1992). This means that while you are establishing how you will conduct the documentary search, you are also making decisions as to what is important and unimportant. This analysis is discussed in more detail later in the chapter. Given the explosion of information availability, it is important that you quickly establish a document's credibility: Is it true? Does it come from a reputable source? Has it been reviewed before publication? These are the first few questions you must ask before accepting the documents as worthy of inclusion.

Finally, there are different types of documentary research. Just as different types of research produce different answers, different types of library research produce different outcomes. There are at least three types of library research (Tucker, Weaver, & Berryman-Fink, 1981). The first is that which seeks to **organize existing knowledge**. The purpose is to take some of the randomness out of your search. Here you decide the what's and when's of the searches; you establish cutoff dates for sources, establish descriptors (**key words** or **terms**) that will serve to guide your search, and generally establish the limits of the search.

Second, a search may **establish relationships** between the topics or concepts of interest. In so doing, you should be able to specify the strengths of the research base, the weaknesses, and areas in which further research is needed. This type of research is based on a knowledge of existing sources and is the first step toward establishing a theoretical perspective. At this time you are ready to prepare a formal review of the literature.

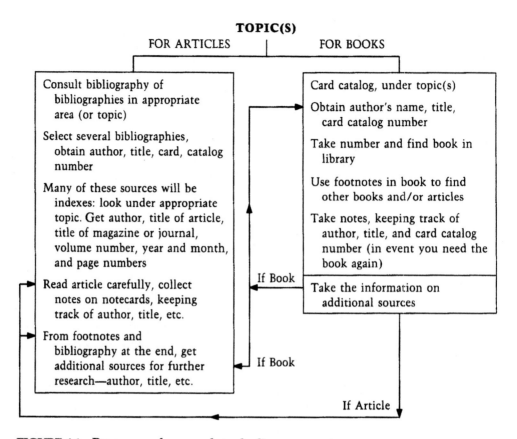

FIGURE 4.1 Programmed approach to the literature review.

Source: Don W. Stacks and Mark Hickson, III, "Research: A programmed approach." *Florida Speech Communication Journal,* 2 [1974], 22.

    The **literature review** represents the third type of library research. In the literature review you present the *relevant* literature pertaining to your topic. As Paul Leedy (1985) notes, the literature review's function is "to 'look again' (*re* + *view*) at the 'literature' (the reports of what others have done) in a *related* area: an area not necessarily identical with, but collateral to, your own area of study" (p. 69). This third type of research, then, establishes *your* perspective of the relevant literature. It should be thorough and should include all the important aspects that are related to your area of investigation.

    It is important to note that *all* research, regardless of the approach taken, requires a literature review and selected parts of the review will be written in a final article, paper, or report. Most published research *begins with a literature review,* a review that sets the author's rationale, his or her theoretical perspective, and presents the context, the previous research he or she feels lead up to the research questions or hypotheses addressed. The literature review will normally culminate in a written argument for conducting your research. In social science research, it constitutes the evidence and argument for the advancement of testable

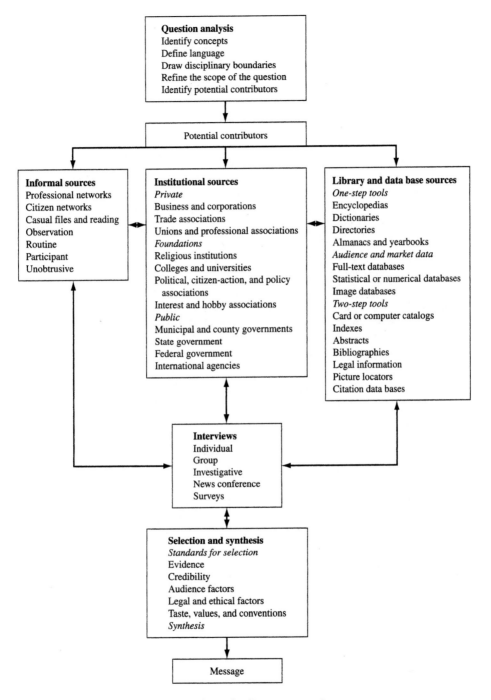

FIGURE 4.2   Alternative approach to the literature review.

Source: J. Ward and K. A. Hansen, *Search strategies in mass communication*, 2nd ed., 1993, New York: Longman.

hypotheses and/or research questions. We will address this as a way of rounding out the chapter at its end.

ESTABLISHING THE PARAMETERS OF STUDY

Documentary research begins with a decision of just *what* you will examine. In part this decision is cast in terms of the research question(s) being asked. Hence, if we were interested in a study of nonverbal communication that examined the impact of personal space on the persuasiveness of a source, our questions might include: How is personal spacing perceived in persuasive settings? What is the impact of differing personal spacings between a source and her receiver? In asking these questions we begin to establish the parameters of study—we have *delineated* the study via research questions into areas of study amenable to research.

But from where will your sources come? For the established researcher, one who has been working on his research questions for some time, a base of knowledge has already been amassed. For the researcher seeking to break new ground, however, the keys to establishing the parameters of study come from two forms of knowledge: tradition and authority (Babbie, 1994). **Tradition**, in some ways similar to what Kerlinger and Lee (2000) calls tenacity (see Chapter 1), is that which our culture presents to us. Tradition is what we are brought up to believe and generally accept without testing. Babbie suggests that tradition provides a cumulative body of knowledge that allows us to begin our research with a database of sorts. Tradition, however, provides a biased and often unscientific base of knowledge. As a point of departure, however, tradition provides us with the necessary information to begin the documentary search.

Sometimes tradition also provides us with counter ideas and new thoughts. These thoughts reject the knowledge based on time and culture and suggest new vistas of knowledge. In rejecting tradition, however, you must be prepared to advance solid arguments and provide evidence that supports or will support your position. In such an instance, you will be relying on **authority**. Authority is steeped in the credibility of the source (Babbie, 1994). Within all fields of study, there are people we consider *experts*. An expert is one who has thoroughly researched the literature in his or her area and who usually has made important additions. Often what an expert says is accepted simply on the authority of the statement or the source.

Tradition *and* authority, then, provide the basis from which we can begin our research. Knowing who the authorities are also will provide an edge in your documentary search; by using authorities as the first line of sources you can effectively reduce the amount of time necessary to get your initial grasp of an area. Also, by identifying authorities you can use their bibliographies as a basis for future searches. To do this, you search databases for the most current articles and work backwards, looking up references to previous articles.

TYPES OF DOCUMENTS

For the most part, the nature of library research is found in *documentation*. Documents can be of a variety of forms. The most familiar form of documentation is the book, followed closely by the periodical, including professional journals, and the newspaper. Other sources are available, however, and are extremely important. These sources include electronic materials that have been made available through computerized networks.

Print

Perhaps the most significant feature of any document is that it is out-of-date before it is released to the public; this is especially true of books. This is because the document is written long before it appears in print. A **book** can present an in-depth analysis of its topic and provide a rich historical perspective and a clearly developed theoretical perspective. A book, however, takes longer to read and analyze. Books usually fall into one of two general classes. First we have books for the general public or beginning student—for example, textbooks. They are written to explain things rather simply, thus the nuances of the research are not noted. Because of this they are not very useful to the careful researcher. The advantage, however, is that books provide you with a simplified version of the topic. The second class are those that are written for the advanced reader. These are "academic" books and take a more detailed and in-depth look at the topic under study. They are especially useful for generating *new* sources of information and providing overviews of significant areas of study. Of particular importance in this category are the handbooks, yearbooks, and books published in an annual series, which present reviews of major topics or concerns. (For example, the *Communication Yearbook* series, the *Handbook of Interpersonal Communication*, and so forth.)

The second type of documentation comes in the form of **periodicals**. Again, there are a number of different types of periodicals. Most of us are familiar with the **magazines** we purchase at the local newsstand: *Life, Newsweek, Time, People, Rolling Stone*, and so forth. These magazines are designed for the general public and provide topical information in an interesting format and at a level that most people can comprehend. Magazines do not usually provide thoroughly tested and reviewed sources of information, but provide timely opinion and data; they generally reflect the world in the way our culture perceives it.

A second type of periodical is the **journal**. A journal is usually produced by a professional organization and reflects the ideas and interests of that organization. The journal typically presents more technical and theoretical information and may be more abstract and complex than publications intended for a general audience. Journals typically have expert review boards that serve to select the material (articles) to be published. The journal provides a *scholarly* source of information about the concept or topic under study. Table 4.1 presents a representative list of communication and communication-related journals. Articles related to communication may also be found through the use of published indexes that provide abstracts of relevant articles. These indexes may be found in university reference rooms. *Communication Abstracts, Psychological Abstract*, and *Sociological Abstract* are all good sources of abstracts.

A third type of periodical is the **newsletter**. Newsletters, produced by special interest groups to present ideas and events, often provide information that the more formal sources cannot. Here you might follow a controversy or find new sources of information. Most divisions of such national or international associations as the National Communication Association, Association for Education in Journalism and Mass

TABLE 4.1   Key Journals with Articles Relating to Communication

Academy of Management Journal	*Journal of Business Research*
American Anthropologist	*Journal of Clinical Psychology*
American Behavioral Scientist	*Journal of Communication*
American Journal of Psychology	*Journal of Communication Therapy*
American Journal of Sociology	*Journal of Conflict Resolution*
American Political Science Review	*Journal of Consumer Research*
American Psychologist	*Journal of Cross-Cultural Psychology*
American Sociological Review	*Journal of Educational Psychology*
Archives of Psychology	*Journal of Experimental Psychology (General)*
Audio-Visual Communication Review	*Journal of Experimental Psychology (Human*
Basic and Applied Social Psychology	*Perception & Performance)*
Behavioral Science	*Journal of Experimental Social Psychology*
Behaviour	*Journal of General Psychology*
British Journal of Psychology	*Journal of Intergroup Relations*
British Journal of Social and Clinical Psychology	*Journal of Marketing Research*
British Journal of Sociology	*Journal of Marriage and the Family*
Canadian Journal of Behavioral Science	*Journal of Nonverbal Behavior*
Central States Speech Journal	*Journal of Personality and Social Psychology*
Columbia Journalism Review	*Journal of Popular Culture*
Communication Education	*Journal of Popular Film and Television*
Communication Monographs	*Journal of Psychology*
Communication Quarterly	*Journal of Social Issues*
Communication Research	*Journal of Social Psychology*
Communication Research Reports	*Journal of Speech and Hearing Research*
Critical Studies in Mass Communication	*Journal of the American Forensic Association*
Editor and Publisher	*Journal of Verbal Learning and Verbal Behavior*
ETC: A Review of General Semantics	*Journal of Written Communication*
European Journal of Social Psychology	*Journalism Educator*
Family Process	*Journal of Public Relations Research*
Human Communication Research	*Journalism Monographs*
Human Organization	*Journalism & Mass Communications Quarterly*
Human Relations	*Language and Speech*
Intermedia	*Language in Society*
International Journal of Psychology	*Learning and Motivation*
International Organization	*Management Science*
International Political Science Review	*Mass Communication Review*
International Social Science Journal	*Media, Culture, and Society*
Journal of Abnormal and Social Psychology	*Memory and Cognition*
Journal of Advertising Research	*Newspaper Research Journal*
Journal of Advertising	*Organizational Behavior and Human*
Journal of Anthropological Research	*Performance*
Journal of Applied Behavior Analysis	*Personality and Social Psychology Bulletin*
Journal of Applied Communication Research	*Personnel Psychology*
Journal of Applied Psychology	*Philosophy and Rhetoric*
Journal of Black Studies	*Political Behavior*
Journal of Broadcasting and Electronic Media	*Political Communication Review*
Journal of Business	*Political Science Quarterly*

TABLE 4.1   Continued

Politics and Society	*Social Forces*
Progress in Communication Science	*Social Science Research*
Psychological Bulletin	*Sociological Inquiry*
Psychological Record	*Sociological Methods and Research*
Psychological Reports	*Sociological Quarterly*
Psychological Review	*Sociology: Journal of the British Sociological*
Psychology of Women Quarterly	*Association*
Public Administration Review	*Sociometry: Social Psychology Quarterly*
Public Opinion Quarterly	*Southern Communication Journal*
Public Relations Journal	*Television Quarterly*
Public Relations Quarterly	*Vital Speeches of the Day*
Public Relations Review	*Washington Journalism Review*
Quarterly Journal of Speech	*Western Journal of Speech Communication*
Semiotica	*Women's Studies*
Sex Roles: A Journal of Research	*Women's Studies in Communication*
Signs: Journal of Women in Culture and Society	*Women's Studies International Quarterly*
Small Group Behavior	*World Communication*

Communication, Broadcast Education Association, and the International Communication Association publish newsletters.

The fourth type of document is the **newspaper**. Like the general-audience magazine, the newspaper presents information from less technical and theoretical perspectives but provides an extremely *timely* source of information. If you are interested in following something over a period of time, then you would go through the relevant newspapers of the day. Newspapers are extremely important in conducting historical research, providing the text of major speeches of the day.

Electronic Documents

The final type of documentation includes published and unpublished resources stored in computer systems. More and more documents are found in computer-based retrieval systems. More about these will follow in later sections, but it is important to note that some nonpublished documents can be obtained through such services as ERIC (Educational Resources Information Center). Included in ERIC are previously unpublished convention papers, literature reviews, and other materials that might be of interest. Many university and public libraries now offer access to documents online or through CD-ROM access. ERIC and *First Search*, which replaced the old *Reader's Guide to Periodical Literature*, provide you with not only the citation, but actual copies of the document which can be downloaded or printed.

Documentation also takes the form of audiovisual materials. Some libraries have special collections of film, videotape, and audiotape. For instance, Vanderbilt University serves as the repository for the "CBS Evening News" tapes. Purdue University has tapes of all programs appearing on C-SPAN. The University of Georgia has all the political ads that Jimmy Carter used in his run for president. Interviews with visiting scholars or dignitaries sometimes find their way into such special collections or are found in individual collections (e.g., The Martin Luther King Center, or presidential libraries). Documents, then, may be more than simply the written word. A good researcher will use all the documents available.

TYPES OF SOURCES

As noted, there are at least two types of source material available. Researchers would like to use as much **primary** material as possible. Primary material comes from original sources: It is the actual study, text, or data; it may be an experiment, a film, or a journal article. The main point here is that *it is what was reported or conducted*; with it you have the author's own reporting. **Secondary sources**, on the other hand, are compilations of others' work. In using secondary sources you must rely on the authors' interpretation of what was presented (and cite the author accordingly). While it is permissible to use secondary sources, you should always try to obtain the primary source (see Chapter 5). Textbooks are secondary sources.

FINDING SOURCES

Ten years ago you would begin and end your documentary search in the library. As noted, the personal computer, however, has changed this dramatically. Although you will probably still have to physically visit the library to obtain certain documents, most of your document searches can be done from a computer terminal located almost anywhere.

Getting Started

Any documentary search plan should be *systematic*. You should have an idea of where you want to begin and then how you will use the information you find to move on to the next phase. Figures 4.1 and 4.2, presented earlier, offer two different programmed approaches to getting started. Both, however, are similar in that they *presume* you know where you want to begin your search.

MINI-PROJECT:

Explore how your textbooks are documented. How many books, periodicals, and electronic sources are used? How are they reported? Can you make any personal judgments regarding how documentation helps you understand what is presented? Try reading the notes at the end of various chapters—do they help you understand what is being presented?

Periodical Indexes.   Sometimes it is best to begin with a periodical index. There are a number of general periodical indexes, but the best-known one is *First Search*. This index will provide information concerning popular periodicals broken down by general subjects. Additionally, there are other, more specialized indexes available online or through CD-ROM.

Bibliographic Indexes.   A number of bibliographic indexes exist to help you find information. The most general index is the *Bibliographic Index: A Cumulative Bibliography of Bibliographies*, which provides information about more specific indexes (see Table 4.2). Use it to gain mastery of the various indexes available. Some of the more specific indexes include *CommSearch*. This work indexes journals pertaining to *communication* from their first issue to date (see Figure 4.3). *CommSearch* is available on CD-ROM and, for several journals, includes the articles from 1991 to date. *Current Index to Journals in Education* (CIJE) and *Resources in Education* (RIE) index ERIC materials and provide an outlet for unpublished materials. Finally, newspaper indexes, such as the traditionally found *The [London] Times Index* and *The New York Times Index* provide comprehensive indexes to a number of newspapers. Most major newspapers now have their own electronic indexes available for libraries and personal use; they may require a subscription fee.

TABLE 4.2   Selected Indexes

Alternative Press Index	*National Union Catalog of Manuscript*
Agricultural Index	*Collections*
Applied Science and Technology Index	*Newsbank*
Bibliograhic Index: A Cumulative Bibliography	*Newspaper Index*
of Bibliographies	*New York Times Index*
Biography Index	*New York Times Films Reviews*
Book Review Index	*Obituary Index to the New York Times*
British Humanities Index	*Pool's Index to Periodical Literature, 1902–1989*
Business Periodicals Index	*Public Affairs Information Service Bulletin*
Canadian Periodical Index	*Reader's Guide to Periodical Literature*
CBS News Index	*Serial Bibliographies in the Humanities and*
Comprehensive Dissertation Index	*Social Sciences*
Current Index to Journals in Education	*Social Sciences Citation Index*
Education Index	*Social Sciences Index*
First Search	*Special Issues and Indexes of Periodicals*
Humanities Index	*Speech Index: An Index to Collections of World*
Index to Journals in Communication Studies	*Famous Orations and Speeches for Various*
Through 1985	*Occasions*
Index to Legal Periodicals	*Summary of World Broadcasts by the British*
Index of Publications of Bureaus of Business and	*Broadcasting Corporation*
Economic Research	*Television News Index and Abstracts*
Index to Selected Periodicals	*Topicator*
International Index to Periodical Literature in	*United Nations Documents Index*
the Social Sciences and Humanities	*Wall Street Journal Index*

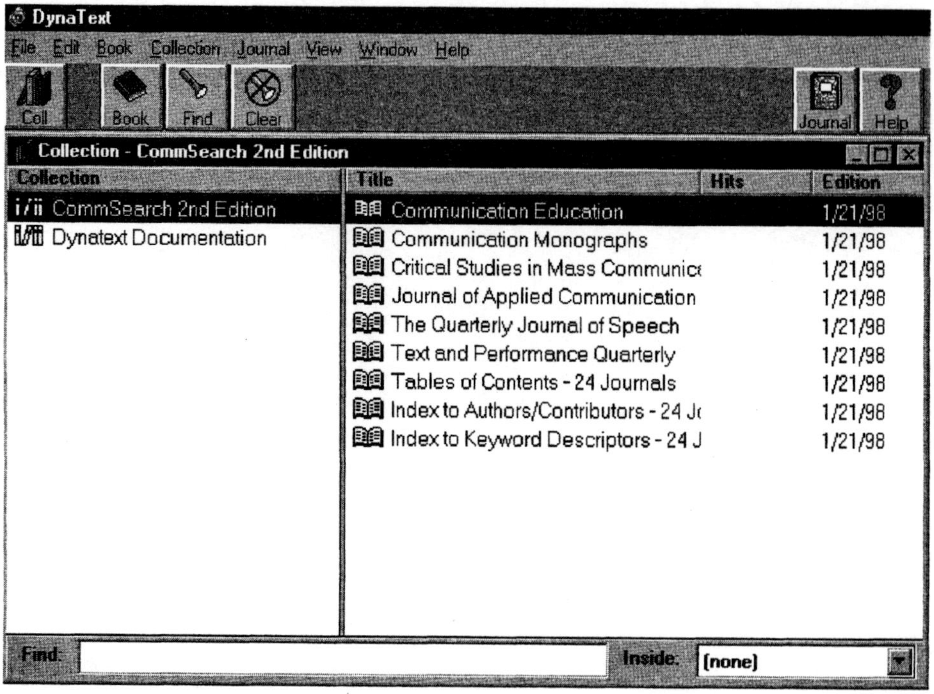

FIGURE 4.3 *CommSearch*—CD-ROM-based index.

Source: Used with permission of the National Communication Association.

Social Sciences Citation Index. The *Social Sciences Citation Index* provides citations for specified key word entries and may be cross-referenced for specific searches. A subscription fee is required for its services. Of course, this and other databases that once had to be searched by hand and trial and error can now be investigated using a personal computer, which has access to a larger computer at a library.

Government Documents. One final index to note is the U.S. government documents catalogue. To use the government documents system you must first access through its Web site the *Monthly Catalog*, the primary index to U.S. government documents. The *Monthly Catalog* document contains both indexes and entries broken into twelve monthly issues (or yearly volumes). The *Monthly Catalog* has several indexes that include author, title, title key word, subject, and series statement or report number. You can use one or all to cross-index your research.

Abstracts. A number of sources available to you are found as abstracts. At least three abstract publications should be of value to you. *Communication Abstracts* provides coverage of about 200 journals in advertising, broadcasting, public relations, and speech communication indexed by author and subject. *Psychological Abstracts* and *Sociological Abstracts* provide summaries of research in journals and papers published all over the world indexed according

TABLE 4.3   Selected Abstract Services

Child Development Abstracts	*Public Administration Abstracts*
Communication Abstracts	*Race Relations Abstracts*
Criminal Justice Abstracts	*Sage Public Relations Abstracts*
Dissertation Abstracts	*Sage Urban Studies Abstracts*
Historical Abstracts, 1775–1945	*Sociological Abstracts*
International Political Science Abstracts	*Urban Affairs Abstracts*
Language and Language Behavior Abstracts	*Women Studies Abstracts*
Psychological Abstracts	

to major area by subject and author. Other abstracts that may be of interest are listed in Table 4.3.

Online Searches.   As noted, most significant databases may be efficiently searched using the computer through e-mail, the World Wide Web, and Lexis/Nexis, which allow written materials of all types to be searched quickly and accurately. Access to these data banks is through a personal computer, telephone line, and modem, or through direct hard wiring (sometimes called a broadband connection) to a mainframe computer. Most data banks charge a fee for their services; however, there are increasingly more data banks being provided free of charge through Web pages. Table 4.4 lists some of the databases of interest to

TABLE 4.4   Selected Databases

AB/INFORM (Business database)
ADTRACK (Advertising database)
AP NEWS (Newspaper database)
BRS (Bibliographic Retrieval Services)
CENDATA (Demographic database)
CIS (Database of U.S. Congress reports)
COMPUSERVE (General database)
DONNELLEY DEMOGRAPHICS (Demographic database)
DIALOG (General service access to over 200 databases)
DOW JONES NEWS/RETRIEVAL (Business database)
ENCYCLOPEDIA OF ASSOCIATIONS (Association database)
ERIC (Educational Resources Informational Center)
GPO MONTHLY CATALOG (Government Printing Office)
INFOSERVE (General database)
LEXIS-NEXIS (Newspaper database)
LLBA (Language and Language Behavior Abstracts)
MAGAZINE INDEX
MARQUIS WHO'S WHO (Biographical database)
MEDLINE (Biomedical database)

communication researchers. Many of the abstract services mentioned earlier (e.g., *Psychological Abstracts*) are now available online or via CD-ROM.

Of course, searches through your library allow you to receive help from the librarians. However, searching the World Wide Web has become a mainstay of document research. Netscape and Microsoft Explorer are the dominant software packages that allow "Web surfing" (searching). Both have **search engines** developed to conduct very fast searches using key words.

Although a detailed discussion of the use of computers in research is beyond our scope, a brief mention of the **World Wide Web** (WWW), which has opened up documentary research to anyone with a computer and Internet access is required. The Web is a graphically based information system that links various sites (URLs—Uniform Resource Locators—the "Web Page") together. As you know, the Web has resulted in a virtual explosion of the availability of new information. Anyone can create a Web site and post whatever information he or she wishes. This, of course is a double-edged sword. The information can be on or off target and true or false. The very ease of its use is a shortcoming for the researcher: Documents found on Web sites may or may not be credible.

It also should be noted that normal electronic mail (e-mail) can be used for both formal and informal documentary searches. Many scholarly associations and research groups have created **Listservs**—automated distribution lists—that send information between members. The National Communication Association is an example of an interactive Listserv, whereas other NCA and AEJMC Listservs offer information to members and ways of getting in touch with other members.

Before conducting a computer-assisted search, first identify any **key words** you think will help to specify the needed information. (Key words are terms that describe some topic addressed by the article and are used to identify it in a computerized database—concepts, author's name, methodology, and so forth.) Key words can be used strategically. Simply using "public relations" will yield more information than you can use. However, using a *Boolean* operator, such as AND, can limit the search. For instance, searching by "public relations" AND "corporate" will only yield those documents that have public relations AND corporate as key words. Using OR would include all those documents with *either* key word. Bibliographic databases such as *CommSearch* search for the key word throughout the title, abstract, and actual document if it is stored.

A note of caution must be interjected here. Just because a source is listed in a database does not necessarily mean it is good or even relevant. All too often articles or papers may be omitted, may slip through the acquisition process, or the source needed may not be tied into the particular database. Much of what you receive may be inapplicable; a good researcher will use the abstract as a filter for selecting documents for further analysis. A good rule of thumb is to check for links that connect to reputable sites such as universities. Be careful when evaluating the credibility of the Web site based on the name of the site alone. Sometimes what sounds like a legitimate source is not. Two of your authors wanted to study the influence of smokeless tobacco on adolescents (McDermott et al., 1989). We tried to seek funding but did not know where to look. We investigated sources that sounded good and identified one called "The Smokeless Tobacco Institute," thinking that an "institute" must be an unbiased sort of "think tank." What we found was a lobbying group for the tobacco industry. So, check your sources very carefully. For a good example of Internet credibility, try the following site: http://www.improb.com/archives/classical/cat/cat.html.

ESTABLISHING A NOTATION SYSTEM

How do we go about reducing the volumes of material found? There are several options. First, we can copy or store all documents, or portions of documents, found. Obviously, this is expensive and creates a storage problem. There are times, however, when duplication of the materials is both appropriate and necessary. When you feel a document will be cited or used many times, it may be economically feasible to reproduce or store it. If the document is important, copy or store it. Second, we can create a bibliographic note system. This system should consist of note cards (4 × 6 inch note cards seem best). The "card" should contain all important information: *complete* citation, including page numbers, issue number or month issued, and a short one- or two-line annotation of what the document contained. Additionally, you should include a list of key words you can later cross-reference (see Figure 4.4). Obviously, this system will not provide complete recall of the material, but it will provide the first listing of information. Using a word processor, you can create your own database of citations, complete with key words.

The third strategy is to *abstract* the document. The abstract "card" provides the same information as the bibliographic note card—a complete bibliographic citation—but expands upon the annotation to include a complete abstract of the document (again, this can be done with a word processor and stored for retrieval). For a physical abstract card, 5 × 8 inch note cards work best (set your paper size for 5 × 8 inches if doing this on the computer). Under the complete citation (and any key words you may want to include) you should *briefly* abstract the major concepts, the hypotheses, questions, or theoretical statements made, the design of the study (the method used to collect whatever data was obtained: historical/critical, descriptive, experimental), the results, the conclusions, and your evaluation of the study (excellent, good, average, poor, terrible) and why (see Figure 4.5). In using an abstract system you must learn to be concise yet accurate. Any quotations should

> Stacks, Don W., and Sellers. Daniel E. "Toward a holistic approach to communication: The effect of 'pure' hemispheric perception on message acceptance. COMMUNICATION QUARTERLY 34 (Summer, 1986), 266–285.
>
> Key Concepts: message processing, hemispheric style, language intensity, persuasion information processing, neurocommunication, auditory processing
>
> Notes: behavioral measures ONLY.

FIGURE 4.4   Sample note card.

John E. Hocking, "Sports and Spectators: Intra-Audience Effects," *Journal of Communication* 32, 1 (1982), 100–108.

"Intra-audience effects" refers to the impact of audience members overt responses to any stimulus on other members of an audience. This descriptive study, supplemented with reviews of relevant literature, examined how crowd behavior and spectator's reactions can contribute to the entertainment value and involvement that result from watching sports in a live context. Specifically, Hocking argues that crowd response contributes to the degree of arousal, excitement, and enjoyment experienced by crowd members.

Four theoretical perspectives, each of which postulates different social influence processes, were proposed as being useful for understanding intra-audience effects at sports events: contagion theory, convergence theory, emergent norm theory, and information theory. Each perspective is described.

Future research directions and methods for conveying the "stadium event" through the broadcast media are suggested.

FIGURE 4.5   Sample abstract card.

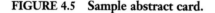

be placed on the back of the note card—in quotation marks—along with the page location of the quotation (or as part of the file the abstract is stored on if being done electronically). If handwriting the card, be sure that you are legible, accurate, and complete.

ESTABLISHING A DOCUMENT'S CREDIBILITY

Although the computer and the accompanying communications and search capabilities make finding documents easier than was the case just a few years ago, the quality of the documents or information must still be evaluated. For example, your plan of attack should include the basic criteria by which you will select a document for possible inclusion at a later stage. Although there probably are as many criteria as there are research questions and researchers, several rules of thumb may be applied to any document you encounter in your search. Use these as your initial screening criteria.

Content

The first criterion applied to any document deals with its content. To what degree does the document deal with your research questions? Is it central to your topic, on the periphery, or irrelevant? Does it report the findings of a particular research project or is it a summary of existing research? A literature review? A critical analysis of your area of interest? Does the article add anything *new*? These questions can be answered in part by reading the abstract that accompanies most scholarly articles.

■ ■ ■ ■ ■

MINI-PROJECT:

You have been asked to conduct a background review of a communication concept for a class. How would you go about doing that? State the concept, list the key words you would use to search, establish your search parameters. Limit your parameters until you have fewer than twenty-five sources.

Authority

The second rule of thumb deals with authority: Is the document from a reputable source? This appraisal would be based on knowledge concerning the type of document (book, journal, and so forth), the authors of the document, and their backgrounds. In appraising the document you might consider whether it was subjected to a peer review or was invited by the editor. The publisher also should be considered. Is the publisher (in the case of a book) large and well respected in the particular area you are researching? Is the publisher a major association (in the case of a journal) and what type of circulation (international, national, regional, local) does it have? What about computer searches? Is the site the authorized site of an association? Can you document the site's credibility? Is there any screening, or is everything and everyone allowed to list on the site?

This is not to suggest that smaller circulation works or presses—or their electronic equivalent—should be evaluated as less important. In many cases a small journal in a particular area may be the *only* outlet for research and theory. In many instances the "academic" presses (e.g., The University of Chicago Press) fall into this category, as do some journals (e.g., *Journal of Communication Therapy*). Do not overlook these documents in your search.

Critical Standards

A third selection criteria is more subjective and deals with your ability to evaluate critically the content of the documents. This appraisal takes the form of a critical analysis of document content. According to Mona McCormick (1985), critical standards are something that can be learned as a skill. As you go through the literature in your area you should become relatively skilled at answering the following questions:

1. Are the main issues or points clearly identified? Does the author(s) clearly explain and define the issues and assumptions being made? Is the theoretical perspective of the author(s) addressed?

2. Are the underlying assumptions of the arguments advanced by the author(s) generally acceptable? Are the questions asked or hypotheses advanced testable or have the potential to be tested? In applying this criteria you must obviously have some background in the area of study.

3. Is the evidence presented adequate, evaluated clearly, and does it support the conclusions drawn?

4. Is there any bias and is that bias addressed by the author(s)? Does the author(s) admit to a particular bias and address that bias?

5. How well is the document written? Are concepts clearly defined? Are they operationalized (made testable) in ways that allow for testing? Is the language concise, clear, and concrete? Often the best writing is concise, to the point, and streamlined. This is most often found in the academic journals and professional books.

Obviously, not all documents will meet these criteria all the time, but those that come closest will probably be more important to you than those that do not. As noted, the process of appraisal should begin as soon as the document is *first* obtained and some type of systematic analysis tells you the importance of the document to your topic or area of interest.

PUTTING IT ALL TOGETHER: THE LITERATURE REVIEW

The literature review represents a way to interpret formally the documents you have reviewed. In preparing the literature review, you put those documents together in a way (1) that provides a clear rationale and history of the area of study, (2) prepares the reader for your theoretical perspective, and (3) serves to establish your hypotheses or research questions. For the novice, the literature review has as its basis a plan of study that should reduce the time and effort spent in document searches. It is important to note that the literature review is necessary for *all* methods of research.

Statement of the Problem

A good literature review begins with the statement of *the problem*. Basically, to say that there is "a problem" means that there is something that is not known, but that should be known, and the fact that it is *not* known is "the problem." The problem should be stated in such a way that it is restricted in scope. In stating the problem, then, the topic should be limited to something "doable." For instance, a study that tried to examine how male and female communication differs would be too broad and not doable. The problem may be a reaction to something you have read or it may be something you have been thinking about for a long time. The problem statement should accurately reflect the essence of what you will be examining. It may evolve as a result of the search, or you may start with the problem and search the literature to find what is already known about the topic and determine what needs to be known. The researcher might find that his or her initial question has been answered, but a related one has not.

Historical Review.   The historical review section is where the documents are reported. Although there are any number of organizing patterns to the review, most reviews are constructed around one of the following patterns:

1. *Chronological* patterns report the topic in a time sequence. You might begin at a particular time and trace your topic through its development. For instance, you might examine propaganda from 1900 to date.
2. *Cause-effect* patterns begin with a problem and review the various solutions. You might examine the reduction of communication apprehension as the product of speech rehearsal.

3. *Inductive-deductive* patterns begin with a general concept or problem and deduce to more specific concepts and problems (deduction) or begin with a specific idea or problem and build to a larger problem or idea (induction). You might consider how brainstorming affects group behavior in general (inductive) or how personal space violations influence attitudes depending on the type of violator (deductive).

4. *Topical* patterns break the topic into subtopics and examine each individually. This pattern sometimes includes the other three within it. For example, you might be interested in source credibility and break it into topical areas such as expertise, attraction, or dynamism. You would then present the research addressing each topic separately.

Critical Analysis

The next stage is a critical analysis of what has preceded it. This analysis is sometimes done in the historical review, but should be undertaken here even if it is not done earlier. It is at this stage that you critically review the research with an eye toward establishing patterns, relationships, strengths, weaknesses, and future research needs. The critical analysis establishes *your* theoretical perspective as it relates to those of others who have researched similar areas. The critical analysis, then, serves as your contribution to study in the area.

A second form of critical analysis is more specific and called *meta-analysis* (e.g., Hunter, Schmidt, & Jackson, 1982; Rosenthal, 1984). In its simplest form a meta-analysis is an analysis of previous literature in an area that has been studied *quantitatively*. A meta-analysis provides information on the comparative effectiveness of a number of variables that may influence a given area. For example, a meta-analytic study by Allen, Hunter, and Donahue (1989) examined the impact of public speaking anxiety as self-reported data on communication apprehension reduction programs. The meta-analysis they conducted provided information on which treatment techniques, if any, were preferred, and the relative effectiveness of each or combinations of each by looking at all the major research articles in the area.

Generation of Questions and/or Hypotheses

After the critical analysis consider asking questions or stating hypotheses. This stage of the literature review allows you to question past research (Will it [the problem or solution] still hold true today? Given this new information does the same relationship still hold?) in such a way that you propose new research projects. You may ask value questions (How well did President John F. Kennedy manipulate the media? What were the rhetorical principles of Nazi Germany?). For certain types of research, you may see new relationships emerging from your review and formally state them as hypotheses (Given direct eye contact to an audience, perceptions of source credibility will increase.). Not all literature reviews generate research questions or hypotheses, instead they may point out areas where more research is needed before such statements can be made or questions asked.

Summary

What does the literature review do? Leedy (1985) suggests seven benefits of a literature review:

1. It can reveal investigations similar to your own, and it can show you how the collateral researcher handled these situations.
2. It can suggest a method or a technique of dealing with a problematic situation which may also suggest avenues of approach to the solution of similar difficulties you may be facing.
3. It can reveal to you sources of data that you may not have known existed.
4. It can introduce you to significant research personalities [authorities] of whose research efforts and collateral writings you may have had no knowledge.
5. It can help you to see your own study in historical and associational perspective and in relation to earlier and more primitive attacks on the same problem.
6. It can provide you with new ideas and approaches that may not have occurred to you.
7. It can assist you in evaluating your own research efforts by comparing them with related efforts done by others.

In preparing to enter the library, the literature review, in its outline form, provides a plan of attack. In short, the literature review, whether it is actually written or not, provides the basic strategies necessary to conduct a research project effectively.

CREATING THE END PRODUCT

Once a documentary search has been completed, what do you do with the material? This depends, of course, on the nature of the research you plan on doing. If, for instance, you did a search for a specific paper, you would then gather your information together and use it to write the paper, the literature review section of the study, often called the *rationale*. If you are writing a comprehensive overview on your topic (sometimes called an *area paper*) then you need to go over the Literature Review material presented earlier. However, there are other things that can be produced from a documentary search.

It is important to remember that the method you choose may dictate how your end product is written. If you are preparing to conduct social science research your paper may examine, for example, the effects that a series of variables have on other variables—you may conduct your own meta-analysis of the relevant research. If you are dealing with a project focusing on the more value-oriented or humanistic dimensions of research, such as those found in historical analysis or in the critical analysis of a particular speech event or movement, your search will center on the more qualitative dimensions of interpretation of past events. As was noted in Chapter 2, there are significant differences in each method's approach to research and these are usually borne out in the end product, as discussed in Chapter 5.

Finally, one important step is left: the creation of a **bibliography**. The bibliography provides a list of all the sources you found in your library search. The bibliography simply lists—usually in alphabetical order—the citations you have on your cards or in your database. The bibliography, however, could be broken into sections relating to the key words you used in your search. Again, the listings would usually be in alphabetical order, but possibly in some other order as well (chronological or topical, for instance).

Another type of bibliography is the **annotated bibliography**, which is similar to the straight bibliography or topical breakdown bibliography, but also includes brief synopses—

descriptions—of each source. This bibliography can be important if you plan on using the sources in a programmed series of projects.

There are several advantages to the bibliography. One is that you can locate all your sources in one document. A second is that you can carry the bibliography around without worrying about spilling all your cards or losing your data disk. Finally, the bibliography allows you to put your materials together in such a way as to create some form of perspective on your topic or area. Even after creating the bibliography (in whatever form) you should keep your cards—they are invaluable.

APPLYING KNOWLEDGE IN COMMUNICATION

By now it should be obvious that both computers and documents have a special place in the research process. The document is that which we use to gain an understanding of the concepts and ideas we set out to research. Regardless of the communication research area, mastery of that area comes through a thorough search of those documents—books, periodicals, online resources—that already exist in our knowledge repositories: libraries and databases. No research can begin without first undertaking a documentary search.

While documents have been with us for hundreds of years, computers are an amazingly recent development that has opened for you sources on a scale never thought possible just a decade ago. It is now possible for you to conduct a basic search from your own personal computer, store the information, sort it, enter it into a word processor and publish it. That same computer will take and analyze data, allowing you to insert tables and graphics into your final product, and even to create media shows of your results.

SUMMARY

This chapter established how you obtain the information—documents—that establish the base for your research projects. We examined search strategies and methods of gathering information. Sources and methods have been described that should enhance your ability to gather information for whatever type of research you conduct. Taken together, these strategies become skills that you can use to utilize your time better and produce better products.

PROBES

1. What has the computer done for research? Has it changed the *process* of research? If so, how?

2. How would you use a "bulletin board" or a computer service specializing in research? Take an area of interest and generate the key words necessary to do a computer search in that particular area.

3. How computerized is your school's library? How is it used? Take the concept and key words you generated for the mini-project on page 97 and use the library's computers to do a literature search. What additional elements would enhance that search? (Can you get a printout of the listings? Can you order a book or journal through the computer?)

4. Why is documentary research important? Why should a researcher be concerned with spending hours in the library? What does the library research process establish for you?

5. How does documentary research establish parameters of study? Assume that you have been asked to research in the area of message

credibility, how would you attempt to begin your research? From what perspective?

6. "All research begins with a literature review." What does that statement mean to you? What does the literature review do? Can you think of any reasons for making the literature review the major thrust of your research? Why or why not?

RESEARCH PROJECTS

1. Conduct a documentary search on the use of computers in communication research. What problems did you have? What can you do to make this research more efficient?

2. Produce a literature review on a communication concept that interests you. In this literature review, focus on the type of research you found—the methods used and the use of findings.

3. Conduct a computerized document search on a general communication area (e.g., "persuasion," "messages," "interpersonal communication," "organizational communication," "journalism," "advertising," "public relations," "broadcasting"). Pare down the search with Boolean operators until you have found a number of recent documents that you can read in a week. What decisions did you make to select the links? Discuss the process and problems you faced in getting the documents.

SUGGESTED READING

Anderson, P. J. (1974). *Research guide in journalism.* Morristown, NJ: General Learning Press.

Asimov, I. (1984). *How did we find out about computers?* New York: Walker.

Dertouzos, M., & Moses, J. (Eds.). (1979). *The computer age: A twenty-year view.* Cambridge, MA: MIT Press.

Doyle, T., Rivard, J. D., & Branscomb, H. E. (1997). *Quick guide to the Internet for speech communication.* Boston: Allyn & Bacon.

Etizoni, A. (1975). Effects of small computers on science. *Science, 189,* 19–75.

Kardas, E. P., & Milford, T. M. (1996). *Using the Internet for social science research and practice.* Belmont, CA: Wadsworth.

Kerlinger, F. N. (1986). *Foundations of behavioral research,* 3rd ed. New York: Holt, Rinehart and Winston.

Lawlor, S. C. (1990). *Computer information systems.* New York: Harcourt Brace Jovanovich.

Rubin, R. B., Rubin, A. M., & Piele, L. J. (2000). *Communication research: Strategies and sources,* 5th ed. Belmont, CA: Wadsworth.

Ward, J., & Hansen, K. A. (1993). *Search strategies in mass communication,* 2nd ed. New York: Longman.

REFERENCES

Allen, M., Hunter, J. E., & Donahue, W. A. (1989). Meta-analysis of self-report data on the effectiveness of public speaking anxiety treatment techniques. *Communication Education, 38,* 54–76.

Babbie, E. (1994). *The understanding of social research,* 7th ed. Belmont, CA: Wadsworth.

Hickson, M., & Stacks, D. W. (1992). *NVC: Nonverbal communication, studies and applications,* 3rd ed. Dubuque, IA: William C. Brown.

Hunter, J., Schmidt F., & Jackson, G. (1982). *Meta-analysis.* Beverly Hills, CA: Sage.

Kardas, E. P., & Milford, T. M. (1996). *Using the Internet for social science research and practice.* Belmont, CA: Wadsworth.

Kerlinger, F. & Lee, H.B. (2000). *Foundations of behavioral research*, 3rd ed. New York: Holt, Rinehart and Winston.

Leedy, P. D. (1985). *Practical research planning and design*, 3rd ed. New York: Macmillan.

McCormick, M. (1985). *The New York Times guide to reference materials*, rev. ed. New York: Times Books.

McDermott, S. T., Hocking, J. E., Johnson, L., & Atkin, C. K. (1989). Adolescents' responses to sports figure product endorsement. *The Southern Communication Journal, 54*, 4, 350–363.

Rosenthal, R. (1984). *Meta-analytic procedures for social research*. Beverly Hills, CA: Sage.

Tucker, R. K., Weaver, R. L., & Berryman-Fink, C. (1981). *Research in speech communication*. Englewood Cliffs, NJ: Prentice-Hall.

CHAPTER FIVE

EVALUATING INFORMATION: HISTORICAL/RHETORICAL-CRITICAL METHODOLOGY

RESEARCH CLASSIFICATIONS
Humanistic
Social Scientific
Philosophical Orientations

HISTORY'S MEANINGS
Research Approaches
Advantages and Limitations

HISTORICAL METHODOLOGY
Establishing Facts
Identifying Documents
Methodological Issues

RHETORICAL-CRITICAL METHODOLOGY
Artistic Standards
Rhetorical Criticism
Critical Examinations of *Message Text*
Symptom Criticism
Didactic Criticism
Thematic Criticism

LIMITATIONS AND HAZARDS

**APPLYING KNOWLEDGE IN
COMMUNICATION**

OBJECTIVES

By the end of this chapter you should be able to:

1. Compare and contrast the historical method with the rhetorical-critical method.
2. Demonstrate an ability to conduct a historical study.
3. Demonstrate an ability to conduct a rhetorical-critical study.

There are three traditional classifications of research methods: historical, descriptive, and experimental. These three classifications can be further divided into two groups: humanistic (historical and rhetorical-critical) and scientific (associational and experimental). Although this book reflects more of the scientific approach, we would be remiss if we did not provide a brief introduction to the humanistic method. The purpose of this chapter is to examine the humanistic methodology associated with history, rhetoric, and criticism.

Some research questions are more appropriately addressed by humanistic methodology, which is considered to be *qualitative*, not quantitative. The logical progression of research methodology is from the building of the bibliography and literature review to the scrutiny of the obtained materials discussed in Chapter 4. While this process is found in *all* types of research, those mastering the humanistic method do so in much finer detail, and move from a simple *description* to a critical analysis and interpretation of the event or person of interest.

All of these methods are ways of illuminating key aspects of communication or discourse. These methods function by examining communication in a way so as to point out aspects of the communication that the reader should be aware of, acting in a way as a flashlight to show the important parts of communication that need to be recognized. These methods are not about generalization. As Bowers (1999) points out: "Social scientists (those that do descriptive and experimental research) want method, unassailable evidence and logic, even if their generalizations almost always must apply to large aggregates, seldom to individuals. Rhetoricians want to take the search where it leads them, to delightful and controversial surprises" (p. 2). Black (2000) says about criticism (one of the methods of humanistic researchers): ". . . you do not read criticism solely in order to have your own opinions confirmed, but that you read criticism in order to be brought to see something that you hadn't noticed on your own" (p. 2). So, as Black articulates, criticism has no set formula. It is a creative activity that relies on the interpretive and observational powers of the critic.

The rhetorical-critical historian often studies a single communicator and his or her messages, a single message, or messages at a certain time (or over a period of time). For example, Benoit and McHale (2000) examined how special prosecuter Kenneth Starr, who was in charge of the Clinton investigations, tried to repair his image in an interview by Diane Sawyer on *20/20*. One of the things Benoit and McHale examined was an aspect of the rhetoric of apologies labeled *denial*. They pointed out that Starr denied introducing graphic sexual information to embarrass President Clinton, and went on to state: ". . . when Sawyer pressed Starr to explain the relevance of apparently gratuitous comments made by him (e.g., concerning the size of a woman's breasts), his only answer was: 'I don't think that it serves any purpose to continue' with these examples" (p. 274). Thus Benoit and McHale have made an argument by showing the reader examples of what they found to illustrate their point. They have flashed a light on those parts of the message to illuminate factors that illustrate their argument.

We look first at the logic associated with historical method, including some philosophical assumptions associated with qualitative and quantitative historical methods. We then turn to the historical method as a general way of studying communication. Then, because many people (for instance, journalists as "rhetorical critics") are turning to a *critical analysis* of some event, speech, play or movie, person, or institution we will differentiate between historical and critical methods. Finally, we will examine some of the advantages and problems associated with the historical/rhetorical-critical methodology.

Before moving into the realm of humanistic methodology, remember that *all* methodology, whether humanistic or scientific, can make an important contribution to the study of communication. In choosing this type of research question and thus one method over others, the researcher indicates a philosophical stance toward the phenomenon studied. This choice most likely originates from those with whom you study. If, for instance, your background is rhetoric, public address, or in the history of institutions or social movements, you will probably opt for the historical/rhetorical-critical, humanistic approach. If, on the other hand, you are more interested in questions of fact about the relationship between variables, descriptive analyses of larger groups of people, or more natural science-like research then you will gravitate toward the scientific.

When one chooses a methodology he or she also chooses a degree of generality from which you can then explain your results and apply them to a larger population. In choosing the historical/critical methodology you generally choose to study the concept, event, or person in great detail. This detail places limitations on the extent to which you can generalize your findings to other people or events. When you use the survey or experimental methodology, your ability to generalize may be expanded and your ability to establish or test scientific *theory* is expanded.

How do you decide which methodology is appropriate? Regardless of your preference, the *research question* provides the answer in that the question dictates the methodology to be used. Having said that, it is important to note that at some stage, *all* researchers use historical methods.

AN OVERVIEW OF HISTORICAL RESEARCH

Historical research requires following systematic rules and procedures rigorously. According to William Lucey (1958), historical methodology employs a rigorous set of standards aimed at ordering knowledge in such a way as to pass several tests of critical analysis. These tests are what the historian utilizes in his or her quest for knowledge, that is both "correct" and "appropriate." In examining the past, the historian attempts to build upon known "facts" and "evidence" in such a way as to understand better the quality of what happened and how certain events may have contributed to that event.

Raymond K. Tucker, Richard L. Weaver, and Cynthia Berryman-Fink (1981) have suggested that the historical methodology can be used to study several general areas of investigation. Historical research can be used to "ascertain the meaning and reliability of past facts" (p. 68). It can evaluate past "facts." It can examine how and why events happened as they did and make comparisons and contrasts of major figures or movements. Historical study can also examine how an individual contributed to change within a particular strand of society or social structure. Historical research can help us to understand better how we arrived where we are today and even provide insight into the future.

Understanding the Meaning of History

Paul Leedy (1985) suggests that history "is the means by which the researcher deals with the latent *meaning* of history" (p. 119). The researcher must get as close to the original sources of information about the **original event** as possible. We can do this by looking at history either as a **chronology of events** or as a reflection of an event occurring in **time and space**. In studying history as chronology the researcher merely traces the events as they occurred in some **time pattern**. Although this provides insight into cause-effect relationships, it does not help us to understand *what* happened; instead it serves as a road map that simply chronicles events as they happened over time. To understand what happened better the researcher needs to go beyond the chronology (use it as a stepping off point) and examine what happened during this period (for instance, during the Middle Ages, did rhetoric develop or stagnate? What was the impact of Darwin on the study of communication? How did the Hellenistic rhetoric differ from later Greek rhetoric?). This is the *first* step in analysis.

Once the concept of time has been established, the researcher needs to examine the spatial dimension of history. The events had to occur *somewhere*. How did the geographical location affect the events or people? For example, is there a difference between Asian rhetoric and Western rhetoric (e.g., Smith, 1994)? Does the geographic location influence our communication patterns (e.g., Chaudhary & Starosta, 1992)? How does location reflect itself in terms of the institutions of communication? By taking location into account the historical researcher is better able to key in on the unique contributions of the person, event, or institutions and make his or her analysis.

Areas of Potential Historical Research

An appraisal of research conducted by the communication historian suggests that historical study falls into seven areas (Phifer, 1961):

1. *Biographical or biographical/critical studies.* Research concentrates on the life of a particular person, such as Abraham Lincoln, Ronald Reagan, Adolf Hitler, Susan B. Anthony, or even Dan Rather. These studies explore not only what the individual under study has said or done, but also his or her biographers. Thus, if we were to look at Ronald Reagan's use of communication and his rise to the presidency, we would want to explore not only his speeches, interviews with him, what others said about his communication, but also those who seriously studied him. In evaluating his communication, we might want to incorporate a rhetorical perspective, such as the Pentad or thematic analysis (see the next section).

2. *Movement or idea studies.* These studies center on the development of social movements (political, social, economic) such as the Green Movement, anti-war protest, the Black Panthers, Black rhetoric, freedom of press and speech movements. The focus here is more sociological, with the study of discourse—oral or written—on large portions of society. Hickson and Jandt (1976), for instance looked at Marxian perspectives on communication, applying Marxist principles to communication.[1] They identified several principles directly applicable to communication practice.

3. *Regional studies.* Regional studies examine the impact of geographical location, such as a city, state, or nation. Research areas might include American journalism, British oratory, or German film criticism. Crossing region with time also produces areas of research, for instance, American journalism since Watergate, First Amendment attacks by the Reagan presidency, Nazi rhetoric, and hip-hop music in the 1990s.

4. *Institutional studies.* Institutional studies center on the history of particular institutions, such as IBM, the *New York Times*, CBS, or particular schools of thought (i.e., the Chicago School of Symbolic Interactionism). As with regional studies, they may be located in time and space, yielding specific histories of specific institutions at specific times. Institutional studies are very important in understanding the specific events or personalities that influenced particular institutions, concepts, and understandings that shed more light on contemporary communication concerns. For instance, an interesting study might look at how an "upstart" like Ted Turner changed the way we perceive television news reporting today or his impact on film media via his company's "colorization" of classic movies.

5. *Case study.* Case studies center on specific events, institutions, or persons at a specific point in time. Case studies could be conducted on institutions or people. One could research the impact of Watergate on Nixon's rhetoric, or a particular event, such as when the National Guard fired on and killed students at Kent State in 1970.

6. *Selective studies.* Selective studies examine one particular aspect of a complex process, for example, the rhetoric of Abbie Hoffman during the Vietnam War period or the impact of "happy talk" in television news, 1970–1979. Selective studies may examine particular aspects of one person's or institution's communication; they may also take on the trappings of a case study. Dionisopoulos and Goldzwig (1992), for instance, examined then-Secretary of State George P. Shultz's 1985 speech, "The Meaning of Vietnam." They concluded that "Shultz's address provides an excellent case study for examining the rhetorical demands facing a politician offering a revisionist perspective on cultural history, potentially useful strategies for meeting those demands, and an opportunity to see how a troublesome past can be reframed to make it more 'useful' in the present" (p. 61).

7. *Editorial studies.* This area of research focuses on translation of texts or discovery of new texts. Much of this research focuses on the *meaning* of particular statements and their translation to English. Swartz's (1995) study of Foucault is one example, as is much of the analysis of Aristotle and Plato's works written in the third century B.C.

J. Jeffery Auer (1959) suggests two other potential areas of study. Auer suggests that **bibliographic study** is an alternative historical research area. Bibliographic study focuses

■ ■ ■ ■ ■

MINI-PROJECT:

Conduct an informal historical study of your communication department from at least two of the seven areas discussed. What research questions does each answer? (For example, how did it begin? Who were its founders? Did it ever cover more or fewer communication areas? Who graduated from the department and what contributions have they made to the study of communication? What does your informal study tell you about the department? Based on this analysis, can you predict where it will go in the future?

on documentary research and the creation of an information base, such as those discussed earlier in this chapter. A second area is the **study of sources**, that is, a study of those with whom the person studied (teacher, mentor) or someone acknowledged as influential in the subject's life. Hence, you might note who influenced the communication style of Bill Clinton (i.e., John F. Kennedy), the type of reporting of a specific journalist (Dan Rather or Carl Woodstein) or the speeches of a particular speaker.

Completing a good historical research project requires a lot of access to information, perseverance, and a little luck. The historical researcher must be willing to spend time gathering and reading primary sources of information: documents (which may include books, photographs, audiotapes, videotapes, and so forth). Once the documents have been read (or heard or viewed), categorized, and scrutinized, the researcher can begin to make the interconnections between the "facts" as seen by the particular source and those that he or she can verify.

Advantages and Disadvantages

Historical research has both advantages and disadvantages. Advantages include the ability to know how the event turned out (e.g., the reported impact of a particular speech on foreign policy, or the popularity of a particular singer). So, while obtaining sources the researcher can ascertain whether or not the source agrees or disagrees with history *as it happened*. As the researcher works through the documents certain patterns that may help to explain why others saw or reported the event or person differently may become evident. Finally, as the historian adds to the corpus of knowledge about the topic, he or she gains an insight into how a speaker, for instance, may have acted or thought.

There are also significant disadvantages facing the historical researcher. First and foremost is the problem of *accuracy*. Although we will cover this in detail later, it should suffice here to note that the historian is faced with a major hurdle in determining accuracy. Records may be incomplete or lost. Some records are simply inaccurate, reflecting some bias. Mistakes are made by other historians both in terms of data collection (such as premature closure in the document search, note mix-ups, accidental destruction of documents) and in writing the results of the study for publication. Once the research has been written, publishers may make subtle changes that alter the editorial tone. Often space considerations make it necessary to leave out portions of the text originally scheduled for publication. Historical accuracy may then be a relative term.

A second disadvantage is the result of the *new sources of data acquisition and retrieval* available. Today a researcher can use a computer and modem to access databases and documents in a way never imagined in the past (see Chapter 4). This availability produces two major problems. First, rather than reading all the documents identified, we may rely instead on the services of others, hence our access may actually take us further from the sources we need (these become, as we will discuss, secondary sources). Second, since information is constantly and quickly being added to the Internet, we may wait forever to conclude our search. If we keep both problems in mind, treating the data we have as a continual process of gaining knowledge, we can draw conclusions as accurate as the information we have and feel fairly confident in what we report.

HISTORICAL METHODOLOGY[2]

Historical research reflects the careful and systematic assembling of all the authentic "facts" that may have a bearing on the target of study. The historian's methodology is tied to how he or she gathers information. In some cases the interview may yield the information necessary to make conclusions. However, more commonly this information takes the form of extant documents and records (visual, written, or auditory).

Historical Facts

In examining these sources the researcher is seeking the "facts" as they might have been known at that time. These "facts" may be different from those we believe or know today. For instance, at one time or another it was believed to be a "fact" that the earth was flat and that the sun revolved around the earth. A fact, in terms of history, is not simple. Facts are created through human perception, perceptions that may change as times or locations change. Therefore, the historical fact is something the researcher sees and uses to make a particular event clear. Facts are usually derived either directly or indirectly from historical documents and verified by others. Hence, the historical fact is dependent upon verification, even if that "fact" is different from what we know today.

Historical Documents

The historical fact arises from documentation. **Historical documents** may be defined as any evidence the researcher uses to establish or help explain the event or person under study. In most instances a document is any original written, auditory, or visual record, official or unofficial. It may take the form of a report, newspaper article, editorial, transcript of a speech, tape (audio or video) of a speech, diary, letter, correspondence, or even garbage. A document, then, is something the researcher seeks that may add to his or her knowledge of the period, person, event, or institution.

■ ■ ■ ■ ■

MINI-PROJECT:

Trace the development of the "mass media" and the facts that have been associated with it over time. For example, begin with the first printing press (is it Gutenberg's?) and explore how the printed word influenced such social perceptions as religion, politics, and social movements. A second project requires that you take the opening statement of the Declaration of Independence or the preamble to Patrick Henry's "Give me liberty or give me death" speech and read it to several friends. Ask them (1) who wrote it, (2) when it was written, and (3) what it means to them.

Historical Research

The historical method blends the data (or facts) obtained from various sources into a lucid and flowing narrative. The major goal is to explicate some event from the past in a manner that illuminates the communication and its effects. To do so the researcher collects **surviving objects**—the printed, written, and oral materials that may be relevant and can be authenticated. After this he or she extracts the material that he or she believes is (and tests out as) credible. Finally, he or she organizes that material into a reliable narrative or exposition.

One of the major functions of historical research, then, is to (1) set out to find all available information, (2) scrutinize that information in terms of accuracy, and (3) get the "story" (or narrative) out. (Gathering information is discussed in Chapter 4.) We now need to examine more closely the sources of information we gather and how we can test for authenticity.

Sources, Information, and the Test of Evidence.   Broadly speaking, there are two sources of information. We actively seek **primary evidence**, that is, evidence from the source itself. Primary evidence consists of testimony, documents, and evidence that comes from those actually engaged in the activities of the period. At times, however, we are forced to deal with **secondary evidence**, that is, evidence from those of the time period who may have observed but did not actually engage in the activities in question. Secondary evidence also represents sources whose credibility or testimony cannot be verified through primary sources. Sometimes we are forced to begin our research with **tertiary evidence**, or evidence based on the accounts of the primary source (Phifer, 1961). Obviously, tertiary evidence must be approached with even greater caution, but it may yield important clues to securing secondary or primary evidence.

In general, it is best to use evidence from primary sources. When we cannot get to the primary source, secondary evidence should be carefully cross-checked for accuracy. In establishing criteria for secondary and tertiary evidence, the researcher must establish both the context of the source and the accuracy of the researcher. If the context can be established and the source is reputable, secondary evidence may be accepted. Tertiary evidence, however, is accepted less frequently and must be viewed skeptically.

Testing for **external evidence** concerns the following questions: Is the information the real thing? Is it genuine? Is it authentic? There are certain physical tests that can establish authenticity. Authenticity could be established through scientific tests on the documents found. Such tests include examination of handwriting, paper and ink used, and whether the language reflects the period under study. Additionally, you have to ask yourself whether or not, based on the reporter's abilities, the materials you are working with are accurate. At least eight questions should be asked in establishing textual authenticity (Ewbank & Auer, 1951):

1. Was the person in a position to perceive the event clearly? With little distraction?
2. Was the source *physically* able to observe the communication? (Unable to be close enough to the speaker?) Was he or she blind? Deaf?
3. Was the person *intellectually* able to perceive the event?
   a. Was the testimony or material presented in a clear, concise, and intelligible fashion?
   b. Did the reporter present the material in a clear, concise, and intelligible fashion?

4. Was the person able to *morally* report what occurred? (Did the event run against current religious or social norms? What pressures may have been on the witness or reporter?)
5. Was the person aware of the significance of his or her reporting? (Was the person accurately reporting the event or how it should be for posterity?)
6. Was the person reluctant to report all relevant parts of the event? (The reluctant reporter is generally perceived to be more credible. Did the person have an "ax" to grind?)
7. Did the person have a personal interest in the event or the way in which the evidence was presented? (Knowledge of potential bias? Was any such bias made clear in the document?)
8. Is the person supported by other sources and evidence? (pp. 108–109)

In addition, you might consider the source's training as an observer and establish the source's relationship to the event, person, or institution. You might consider how long it was between the event and the writing about the event. Obviously, the longer the time period between event and document, the less reliable it is likely to be. Make certain, especially in the case of speeches, that the text you work with is the one actually presented. In the case of speeches before Congress, make certain that the indicated speaker actually delivered the speech. In fact, the text of the speech in the record does not necessarily reflect what was actually said on the floor. Also, ascertain whether you are working with the speaker's own words. Finding two or more forms of the same material is not uncommon. Check variant forms against each other for verification.

Testing for **internal evidence** follows external testing. Now that the authenticity of the material has been established to some degree of satisfaction, the researcher begins to evaluate the statements made within the material. The criteria we examine at this stage of research concern the source's *meaning*. Here we are asking: What is the person trying to say? What is behind the statements made, and the way they are made? The focus is on the meaning of the words or symbols used in communication.

Internal testing focuses on the credibility of the document. When testing the internal criteria the focus is on the **literal meaning of the document**. What does any given statement really say? Are there technical, foreign, archaic, or unfamiliar terms? If so, the researcher must delve into the symbols and slang of the period to gain an understanding of what the source was trying to say. Finding the meaning the source intended is difficult. Rarely, for instance, do two people agree on what someone else has said. The researcher must take into account ambiguity and the use of figurative language in the original source's words. Also, because most of the documents will be in written form, sarcasm and humor may be difficult to spot, let alone analyze. The researcher must also watch for statements taken out of context. A statement taken in context provides a wealth of information; a statement taken out of context is next to worthless, unless, of course, the researcher is interested in how original communications are used out of context by others.

Ultimately, the researcher must decide whether or not the statements reviewed and analyzed are believable. Much like external evidence, a statement's believability is based upon confirmation. Confirmation in this case, however, may deal with the internal consistency of the document or statement, the ability to verify that this was indeed communicated in the way it was and in the correct context. Finally, the researcher must decide whether the statement made reflects the person or institution he or she has been studying all along.

Skepticism.   The acceptance or rejection of a document or the testimony of a source must be approached with skepticism. In attempting to arrive at truth, the historical researcher must wade through streams of manuscripts, notes, and other relics that may help or hinder the quest. In the end, the historical researcher must be prepared for conflicting testimony and information. In some instances what was true may have been repressed or rewritten by the powers that be. Only a careful analysis of all sources of information allows the researcher to arrive at a decision regarding the *degree* of truth to be found in any one document or statement.

Analytical Strategies.   Historical research is both inductive and deductive. In some cases the historian relies on the deductive approach, reasoning from an idea or thesis, looking for evidence to support the thesis, then leading to new ideas or thesis statements. In other cases the historian relies on a keen sense of induction. Sometimes a particular piece of evidence will derive theses or ideas concerning relationships or events.

Some argue, however, that historical research is **adductive**, that the process of inquiry is neither deductive nor inductive. Rather, inquiry takes the form of "adducing answers to specific questions, so that a satisfactory explanatory 'fit' is obtained" (Fisher, 1970, p. 1). That is, it follows a *general systems* approach to the event being studied (Stacks, Hickson, & Hill, 1991).[3] This approach suggests that communication (or other phenomena) are best *described* when *all* possible causes are examined for their impact on some event. As such, the historical researcher would examine the *interactive* impact of all possible causes, rather than singling out one or two for specific attention.

According to Smith (1989), then, "Adduction permits the historian to respond to a research question with multiple measures" (p. 326). Hence, the historian takes a "holistic" approach to research, taking all the information and extrapolating meaning based on a viewing of the whole corpus of data without the dictum of some form of reasoning (deductive or inductive). This is what Edward DeBono (1968) calls **lateral think**—rather than digging a deeper hole based on the analytical techniques of induction or deduction, the historian may widen the hole as he or she digs deeper into the research. In this way a "new" depth and breadth of understanding may be reached.

There are times when, as noted, the historian must borrow from social scientific colleagues. At times there may be too much data to comprehend or there may be large gaps in the data. In such cases statistical methods can be brought to bear on the problem, sampling frames designed, and reliability and validity ascertained. The historian may also wish to conduct a content analysis, described in detail in Chapter 8, in which a category system that allows for an objective and systematic classification of communication content is created.

Thus, when the research question suggests it is appropriate to do so, the historian can turn from a humanistic, qualitative approach to a more quantitative, social scientific, behavioral approach. This requires that the historian understand quantitative methodology. Later chapters in this text will help provide that understanding. There are times, however, when objective methods do not answer the research question. It may be that the researcher must make artistic (aesthetic or ethical) decisions based on a *communicative performance* that has occurred at some time (either historically or in the immediate past). In times like these the researcher must become a *critic*. The next section examines rhetorical-critical research.

Before we turn to a discussion of critical research, we offer an example of historical research. Voss and Rowland (2000) examined the rhetoric of Frances Wright. In this case the authors identified a major orator from the early 1800s who was representative of the time before the inception of a the women's suffrage movement. They make the argument that Wright was a significant part of the period that immediately preceded the women's suffrage movement, a time when certain speeches had an impact on the trajectory of the emerging movement and its rhetoric. They chose to analyze a single speech given by Wright on the Fourth of July in 1828.

Voss and Rowland identified three major themes in Wright's speech: change, patriotism, and how humans can use reasoning to improve the world. They illustrated each of these themes with passages taken from the speech. They noted that at the time the speech was a failure, which the authors attribute to the unconventional and controversial stand she took that was contrary to the conservative views of the time. However, they argue that the speech provided a sort of "consciousness raising" function that led to the future rhetoric of the suffrage movement. Thus, they placed the speech in a historical time frame and noted how the speech contributed to the history of the suffrage movement.

RHETORICAL/CRITICAL METHODOLOGY

The application of critical analysis to a communication event or communication performer is increasingly finding its way into applied communication research and reporting. Hardly a day passes without news reporters delivering critical commentaries about some speech or communication. You can probably recall all the praise given by TV commentators to President Bush for his speech following the September 11, 2001 attacks on the World Trade Center. While the reporter may be trained in traditional journalism, seldom does he or she understand critical methodology. Critical method is part of the humanistic approach to historical research. We also view it as an extension of the tests of internal evidence or criticism the researcher uses when examining the question of how well the act was accomplished. This section examines how to use critical methodology.

■ ■ ■ ■ ■

MINI-PROJECT:

When new evidence accumulates that relates to a problem or research question but cannot be reasoned deductively or inductively, the reasoning used is adductive, or via "lateral thinking." Consider how the computer has changed the way we do both humanistic and social scientific research, what conclusions can be reached by tracing the computer's development and use in communication research, adductively, deductively, *and* inductively? Using the same types of reasoning, where do you think the computer will take us as far as communication research is concerned?

Critical research requires that the criteria or standards appropriate to the communication be chosen and analyzed (Carter & Fife, 1961; Thonssen, Baird, & Braden, 1970). In conducting a critical study the researcher should examine at least four aspects of the communication: the results, the artistic standards, the basis of the ideas, and the motives and ethics behind the communication. In examining the results of the communication, the researcher attempts to answer the questions: What was the purpose of the communication? What was the *true* purpose of the communication? And, what connection can be found between the communication and the results?

Artistic standards refer to the use of appropriate rhetorical methods and principles to examine how effectively or perhaps how *gracefully* the intended affect of the communication was accomplished. There are many sets of artistic standards. For example, there are the five traditional canons of rhetoric—invention, arrangement, style, delivery, and memory—although such classical models of proof themselves have been criticized, by which the critic examines how the communication was put together, the language used, the units of "proof" employed, and how it was delivered (Black, 1965).

Critical research has evolved beyond looking at how well a speaker delivers the message to other forms of communication such as the mass media. For instance, Collins and Clark (1992) examined the *Nightline* program, "This Week in the Holy Land," as it related to the *intifadeh* uprising in Israel's West Bank. They concluded that "*Nightline*'s structural choices privileged a particular reading of the conflict and belied their overt effort to let the participants tell their own story. [Anchor Ted] Koppel took local narratives which gave shape to cross-cultural conflict and forced a rereading of the events through his authoritative voice, interview interventions, and editing" (p. 25). Critical studies have explored such diverse topics as feminism (e.g., Pearce & Rossi, 1984), the television industry (e.g., Bodroghkozy, 1991), and singers and their lyrics (e.g., Rein & Springer, 1986; Weisman, 1985).

Rhetorical Criticism

A second critical method often employed is that of critical discourse, or **rhetorical criticism** or theory. Farrell (1980) has identified three "models" of performance of discourse, each slightly different in its approach to the communication event or person.[4] The first model, **symptom criticism**, approaches the communication event or person as a symptom of some larger social concern. This approach tends to be more sociological in nature, examining the social features or themes underlying the culture of the communication. For instance, suppose you were interested in addressing the question of culture and alienation in a modern media presentation, such as the film *Taxi Driver* (e.g., Hickson, 1977). You might examine how the artifacts of alienation (which you define) are exhibited by the particular culture and are identified by themes within the film and its impact on that culture. You might do the same by looking at the ways in which film portrays the "Vietnam experience," through both the rhetoric of *Rambo* and, later, *Platoon* and *Full Metal Jacket*.

Farrell's (1980) second model is more traditional. The critic using this model follows the notion that the study of the event or person is the model. Farrell calls this **didactic criticism**. Here the critic is interested in the particular communicator and how he or she uses communication as a tool. For instance, we might be interested in the use of metaphor as a rhetorical tool in the lyrics of a particular composer. We might want to know the particular **themes** that are found in the communications of a particular person, the personal meanings associated with the communication. Hickson and Stacks (1981) explored the theme of "class consciousness" from a Lucacs' perspective as a "new Marxian" approach to communication. They noted, "Knowing that we are individuals first and students second, and knowing how we have been treated in the past, opens the way to consciousness. Once consciousness has been achieved, communication can be used to improve our lives as students. *Much of the student movement of the middle to late 1960s can be analyzed in such a light* (emphasis added)" (Stacks, Hickson, & Hill, 1991, p. 238).

Finally, Farrell (1980) suggests a third model, one he labels **thematic criticism**. Here the critic is interested in how the communication is constructed. A particular model is constructed and the messages of the communicators are examined in light of that particular model. Gronbeck's (1980) assessment of thematic critical method is found in Figure 5.1. This model suggests that we can analyze communication based on the communicators' (actors as performers and actors as audience) meanings and actions (verbal and nonverbal communication) as they interact with and within particular social and cultural contexts. Hence, the theme becomes a way of analyzing the mental constructs that created the communication.

Bormann's (1972, 1973, 1982) fantasy theme analysis is a form of rhetorical analysis that looks for underlying themes that influence people's interpretation of reality. Fantasy themes are stories present in messages that convey certain character representation, such as

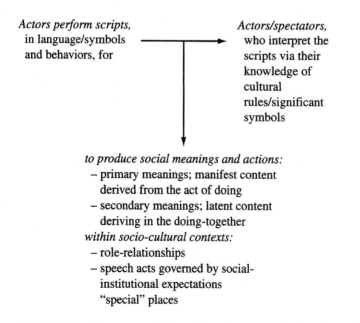

FIGURE 5.1   Dramaturgical models of communication in society.

Source: B. E. Gronbeck (1980). Dramaturgical theory and criticism: The state of the art (or science)? *Western Journal of Speech Communication, 44,* 317.

on the integrity of ideas presented in the communication. The motives and ethics concern the unstated reasons for the communication. By specifying the motives and ethics the critic gets a better understanding of the psychological being of the speaker. Finally, the critic examines how each of the four categories relate to one another.

Conducting a Critical Examination of Communication

In conducting a rhetorical-critical study the researcher begins by describing what has happened. This sets the stage, so to speak. In this analysis the researcher focuses on two sets of factors: those that are extrinsic to the communication and those that are intrinsic to the communication.

Extrinsic Factors.   In describing the event the researcher seeks to: (1) describe and analyze the period in which the communication occurred. The time in which the communication occurred is extremely important; it sets the stage against which other communication could be compared or contrasted. (2) The researcher describes the audience, both in terms of the intended and the real audience. What audience was the speech written for, and which audience actually received it? (3) The occasion for the speech is then described and analyzed. In the case of Martin Luther King's "I Have a Dream" speech, for instance, what was the occasion? Was the occasion used for a particular effect? (4) The researcher describes and analyzes the speaker (or organization), giving attention to the speaker's background and training. And (5) the communication itself is described and analyzed.

Intrinsic Factors.   This leads to the analysis of the communication itself and the evidence with which it was constructed. Here attention is placed on the interpretation and evaluation of the ideas and supporting logic presented. Analysis is focused on how the logic fits with the period in which the communication was presented. Next, the analysis and description turns on the speaker and his or her ability. What sort of speaker was he or she? What were his or her strengths and weaknesses? How well were verbal and nonverbal skills incorporated? Hence, the intrinsic features stress the individual's skills at creating and presenting the communication.

LIMITATIONS OF HISTORICAL RESEARCH

Just as with all methods, the historical method has certain limitations and hazards. In historical research the researcher must be prepared for fragmentary and incomplete records. In many cases you will not be able to find all the available data. A second limitation concerns the facts with which you work. Facts change as language and meaning change. As these facts change, any attempt at fixing cause and effect becomes problematic. Finally, there are certain limitations on the researcher him- or herself. These limitations include personal bias, selective perception of what is "right" and what is not, and faulty interpretation.

APPLYING KNOWLEDGE IN COMMUNICATION

The humanistic approach to research focuses on the human aspects of communication. As such, the method *tends* toward subjective interpretation of the event, person, or institution. As we stated at the beginning of this chapter, the methods illuminate key aspects of discourse. What we gain from both historical and rhetorical-critical research is an emphasis on the message and message source. Although humanistic studies are frequently not generalizable, they offer a richness and depth of understanding not found in many social scientific studies.

Historical and rhetorical-critical methods provide the framework from which to make sense of what you observe. The *rigor* of the method is tied to the extrinsic and intrinsic factors identified and analyzed. Two different researchers, employing the same methodology, would probably find different results; this holds both the promise and problems of the humanistic method.

SUMMARY

This chapter has examined a methodology that almost all researchers must learn to some degree: historical research. By conducting historical research we learn something of our past. From this past we can then better understand contemporary actions and feelings. For some, the historical methodology serves as the appropriate methodology for the particular research question. It may be that the type of research you are interested in stresses the unique and particular; and through historical research you may gain greater understanding of the complexities of the past.

We examined several difficulties in conducting historical research. Then the concept of the historical document and fact were discussed. Finally, historical methodology was pursued as a base for conducting research and critical methodology was examined as a special tool for examining *communication* events on a qualitative level. It was noted, however, that the historical researcher may borrow quantitative and statistical tools from the social sciences. In many ways, the good historical researcher must know a little about several methods and choose the most appropriate method or tools within the method.

PROBES

1. What differentiates the historical/critical method from other methods? Practically, what can the historical/critical method do that the scientific method cannot?

2. Assume for the moment that you have an assignment that requires that you get to know a particular speaker or editor. How would the historical/critical method help you gain a better understanding of this person? What research questions might you ask when approaching the research?

3. What is the "latent meaning of history"? How does this approach to historical research differ from a chronological or time and space analysis of some event or person?

4. How does the historical researcher go about testing his or her data? What limitations are you faced with when you take the historical method and apply it to communication? Using the Vietnam War as your event, what type of research could you conduct from this perspective?

5. How does critical method differ from historical method? What does critical method provide that historical does not? Taking the Vietnam War as your concern, what research questions might you ask about that era? How would you analyze the communication(s)?

RESEARCH PROJECTS

1. There are many approaches to the study of conflict resolution. Most are approached from a social scientific method. Outline how you would conduct a humanistic study on conflict resolution. Extend this to marital communication.

2. Conduct an institutional study on one of the major advertising or public relations firms in the country. What do we know about that firm after the study that we did not know before? What limitations must you place on your reporting of the study's results?

3. Analyze the communication strategies of the "Right to Life" faction in the abortion dispute.

4. Using Bormann's fantasy theme analysis, conduct a study of organizational communication in down-sized organizations.

5. Examine the speeches of an important local figure. Cross-apply at least two historical approaches with either a critical or rhetorical criticism method.

SUGGESTED READING

Auer, J. J. (1959). *An introduction to research in speech*. New York: Harper & Row.

Black, E. (1965). *Rhetorical criticism: A study in method*. New York: Macmillan.

Bormann, E. G. (1982). A fantasy theme analysis of the televised coverage of the hostage release and the Reagan inaugural. *Quarterly Journal of Speech, 68*, 133–145.

Campbell, K. K. (2000). Man cannot speak for her. In Brummet, B. (Ed.). *Reading Rhetorical Theory* (pp. 895–926). New York: Harcourt College Publishers.

Carter, E. S., & Fife, I. (1961). The critical approach. In C. W. Dow (Ed.), *An introduction to graduate study in speech and theater* (pp. 81–103). East Lansing: Michigan State University Press.

Fisher, D. H. (1970). *Historians' fallacies*. New York: Harper & Row.

Mishler, E. G. (1986). *Research interviewing: Context and narrative*. Cambridge, MA: Harvard University Press.

Nord, D. P. (1989). The nature of historical research. In G. H. Stempel, III, & B. H. Westley (Eds.), *Research methods in mass communication*, 2nd ed. (pp. 290–315). Englewood Cliffs, NJ: Prentice-Hall.

Phifer, G. (1961). The historical approach. In C. W. Dow (Ed.), *An introduction to graduate study in speech and theater* (pp. 52–80). East Lansing: Michigan State University Press.

Smith, M. Y. (1989). The method of history. In G. H. Stempel, III, & B. H. Westley (Eds.), *Research methods in mass communication*, 2nd ed. (pp. 316–330). Englewood Cliffs, NJ: Prentice-Hall.

Thonssen, L., Baird, A. C., & Braden, W. W. (1970). *Speech criticism*, 2nd ed. New York: Ronald Press.

NOTES

1. For more on different movement or "cultural" approaches to communication, see Stacks, Hickson, & Hill (1991), Chapters 9–12.

2. The material in this section has been gathered from two basic sources: Auer (1959) and Phifer (1961). Additional sources include Smith (1989), and Leedy (1985).

3. Stacks, Hill, and Hickson (1991) examine systems theory as a way to approach inquiry that differs from deductive and inductive methods; some define this as "adductive."

4. For an excellent overview of the rhetorical critical methods in general see Gronbeck (1980).

REFERENCES

Auer, J. J. (1959). *An introduction to research in speech*. New York: Harper & Brothers.

Benoit, W. L., & McHale, J. P. (2000). Kenneth Starr's image repair discourse viewed on *20/20*. *Communication Quarterly, 47*, 3, 265–280.

Black, E. (1965). *Rhetorical criticism: A study in method*. New York: Macmillan.

Black, E. (2000). On objectivity and politics in criticism. *American Communication Journal, 4*, 1 (http://acjournal.org).

Bodroghkozy, A. (1991). "We're the young generation and we've got something to say:" A granscian analysis of entertainment television and youth rebellion of the 1960s. *Critical Studies in Mass Communication, 8*, 217–230.

Bormann, E. G. (1972). Fantasy and rhetorical vision: The rhetorical criticism of reality. *Quarterly Journal of Speech, 58*, 396–407.

Bormann, E. G. (1973). The Eagleton affair: A fantasy theme analysis. *Quarterly Journal of Speech, 59*, 143–159.

Bormann, E. G. (1982). A fantasy theme analysis of the televised coverage of the hostage release and the Reagan inaugural. *Quarterly Journal of Speech, 68*, 133–145.

Bowers, J. W. (1999). Scientizing rhetoric. *Communication Studies, 50*, 1, 45–53.

Burke, K. (1965a). *A grammar of motives*. New York: Meridian.

Burke, K. (1965b). *A rhetoric of motives*. New York: Meridian.

Carter, E. S., & Fife, I. (1961). The critical approach. In C. Dow (Ed.), *An introduction to graduate study in speech and theatre* (pp. 81–103). East Lansing: Michigan State University Press.

Chaudhary, A. G., & Starosta, W. J. (1992). Gandhi's salt march: A case of *Satyagraha* with rhetorical implications. *World Communication, 21*, 1–12.

Collins, C. A., & Clark, J. E. (1992). A structural narrative analysis of *Nightline*'s "This Week in the Holy Land." *Critical Studies in Mass Communication, 9*, 25–43.

DeBono, E. (1968). *New think*. New York: Avon.

Dionisopoulos, G. N., & Goldzwig, S. R. (1992). "The meaning of Vietnam." Political rhetoric as revisionist cultural history. *Quarterly Journal of Speech, 78*, 61–79.

Ewbank, H. L., & Auer, J. J. (1951). *Discussion and debate*, 2nd ed. New York: Appleton-Century-Crofts.

Farrell, T. B. (1980). Critical models in the analysis of discourse. *Western Journal of Speech Communication, 44*, 300–314.

Fisher, D. H. (1970). *Historians' fallacies*. New York: Harper & Row.

Gronbeck, B. E. (1980). Dramaturgical theory and criticism: The state of the art (or science?). *Western Journal of Speech Communication, 44*, 315–330.

Hickson, M., III. (1977). The anti-art: Marxist thought. *The Center Design, 1*, 24–25.

Hickson, M. III, & Jandt, F. E. (Eds.) (1976). *Marxian perspectives on human communication*. Rochester, NY: PSI.

Hickson, M. III, & Stacks, D. W. (1981). The communication theory of Georg Lukacs. *The Researcher, 9*, 41–60.

Leedy, P. D. (1985). *Practical research: Planning and design*, 3rd ed. New York: Macmillan.

Lucey, W. J. (1958). *History: Methods and interpretation*. Chicago: Loyola University Press.

Pearce, W. B., & Rossi, S. M. (1984). The problematic practices of "feminism:" An interpretive and critical analysis. *Communication Quarterly, 32*, 277–286.

Peterson, V. (2000). Mars and Venus: The rhetoric of sexual planetary realignment. *Women and Language, 23*, 2, 1–8.

Phifer, G. (1961). The historical approach. In C. Dow (Ed.), *An introduction to graduate study in speech and theatre* (pp. 52–80). East Lansing: Michigan State University Press.

Rein, I. J., & Springer, C. M. (1986). Where's the music? The problems of lyric analysis. *Critical Studies in Mass Communication, 3*, 252–256.

Smith, C. R. (1994). Deducing a rhetorical theory from Confucius using the Aristotelian model. *World Communication, 23*, 35–41.

Smith, M. Y. (1989). The method of history. In G. H. Stempel, III, & B. H. Westley (Eds.), *Research methods in mass communication*, 2nd ed. (pp. 316–330). Englewood Cliffs, NJ: Prentice-Hall.

Stacks, D. W., Hickson, M. L., III, & Hill, S. J. (1991). *An introduction to communication theory*. Fort Worth: Harcourt Brace Jovanovich College Publishers.

Swartz, O. (1995). On power: A discussion of Richard Rorty and Michel Foucault. *World Communication, 25*, 13–20.

Thonssen, L., Baird, A. C., & Braden, W. W. (1970). *Speech criticism*, 2nd ed. New York: Ronald Press.

Tucker, R. K., Weaver, R. L., III, & Berryman-Fink, C. (1981). *Research in Speech Communication*. Engle-

wood Cliffs, NJ: Prentice-Hall.

Voss, C. R. W., & Rowland, R. C. (2000). Pre-inception rhetoric in the creation of a social movement: The case of Frances Wright. *Communication Studies, 51*, 1, 1–14.

Weisman, E. R. (1985). The good man singing well: Stevie Wonder as noble lover. *Critical Studies in Mass Communication, 2*, 136–151.

CHAPTER SIX

FOUNDATIONS OF MEASUREMENT

OBJECTIVES

By the end of this chapter you should be able to:

1. Discuss how measurement is used in communication research.

2. Describe and explain the use of nominal, ordinal, interval, and ratio measurement in communication research.

3. Explain why it is important to report reliability estimates and validity concerns in reporting research findings.

4. Differentiate between different types of reliability and explain how they are obtained.

5. Explain the different types of validity and how each influences communication research.

6. Explain the relationship between reliability and validity.

In Chapter 2 we introduced the notion of the operational definition, the social scientist's bridge between the abstract world of theories about the relationships between variables and the observable world in which the variables either are or are not related as stated in the theory. Operational definitions specify the procedures for observing: They state how we will know a particular variable when we see it and the values the particular variable takes on. Operational definitions, then, constitute the rules that spell out, in a very specific and concrete way, how to assess the existence of a variable. Earlier we described two kinds of operational definitions, manipulated and measured, and noted that an independent variable may be manipulated, as in an experiment, *or* measured, as a dependent variable in an experiment, or as either the independent or dependent variable in a survey. Dependent variables are always measured. Measurement is a crucial part of any research project that addresses a question of fact. Issues of measurement are an integral part of doing scientific or social scientific research.

WHAT IS MEASUREMENT?

Any observation or sensation can be thought of as a measurement. When we look out the window and see trees we are involved in measurement. We have a sense of what a tree is, we know when we see one, and we know when we do not. Thus, when we look out the window and see trees we are observing the amount of "treeness" in what we see, we note its color, we can smell it, and we can even touch it. Like all measurements, our observation of trees involves a *comparison*. We compare what we see with what we have seen at other times and in other settings. We can see trees because we know that at other times we have seen no trees. To be sure, these sorts of measurements are casual and imprecise, and we are generally unconscious of the process, but they are measurements nonetheless. If you arrived home one evening and the trees were not there, you would know it, *through measurement*, broadly defined.

In fact, whenever we process incoming data through any of our five senses, we are involved in measurement. When you touch your pet, smell the coffee brewing, hear a mail truck, taste a doughnut, see a computer, you are making observations—measurements, comparisons—regarding your immediate environment. The difference between the measurements that all of us spend most of our waking hours making and the measurements made by scientists revolves around the care and precision with which they are made. We measure casually, without much thought. However, when we take on a social scientist role, we measure variables with great care and give them a great deal of thought.

Suppose that someone tells you that it is raining right now. You would know this because you have seen rain previously and you also know what "not raining" is and can compare the two. The variable "amount of rain," however, can take on many different values, as many as our language can describe. It is presently "sprinkling lightly." Later, it might rain harder. It might "pour," or "rain cats and dogs." It could even develop into a "torrential downpour," or possibly into a real "gully washer," or even a "toad choker." Each of these labels is an attempt to *quantify* the variable, "amount of rainfall."

Unfortunately, our language can be terribly imprecise. A meteorologist attempting to develop theories that would allow her to explain and predict the amount of rainfall would be severely handicapped if she had to assess her dependent variable, "amount of rainfall," with terms such as "toad choker." Instead, she uses mathematics. And, to a greater or lesser extent, all scientists do the same thing. Using precisely described rules, we assign numbers to our observations. In fact, measurement is commonly defined as the process of assigning numbers to observations according to specified rules (e.g., Stevens, 1951; Torgerson, 1958). The problems associated with something as simple as describing (measuring) the "amount of rain" are simple when compared to the abstract nature of most communication research where researchers are attempting to measure such things as attitudes, values, beliefs, and intentions.

In measuring rainfall, the notion that 1 inch of rain is half as much as 2 inches is taken for granted. It is obvious. Likewise, the difference between 3 inches of rain and 2 inches is the same as the difference between 32 inches and 33 inches. It might seem tempting to conclude that all measures that associate numbers with observations of variables allow similar conclusions. However, the "level" at which a variable is measured determines what kind of conclusions can be drawn and how the data may be analyzed (usually with statistics).

Levels of Measurement

What is the "appropriate" level of measurement? The answer is found in the particular research question you ask and the degree of precision you require. There are four levels of measurement: nominal, ordinal, interval, and ratio.

Nominal Measurement. "The nominal scale represents the most unrestricted assignment of numerals" (Stevens, 1951, p. 25). Nominal measurement involves assigning numbers to categories that have *qualitative* rather than quantitative differences. For example, the numbers on uniforms worn by athletes serve this function. The numbers they wear differentiate football players. Yet a player who wears number 34 does not have more of something than a player who wears number 17, let alone twice as much of it. The numbers only serve as substitutes for the names of the players. They allow the spectators to tell which player is which and sometimes what position each plays.

Variables of interest to the communication researcher, which are generally measured at the nominal level, include sex, ethnicity, political party affiliation, and communication media (face-to-face, telephone, mediated). Nominal data is typically used when researchers are requesting **demographic data**, or data that differentiates between groups of people or things (see Table 6.1). The researcher arbitrarily assigns a number to each category. For instance, the research may code a male as a 1 and a female as a 2. The numbers have no mathematical value *per se*, but allow a statistical program to recognize the categories. The advantage of labeling a variable 1, 2, or 3 instead of Democrat, Republican, or Independent, is that variables with numeric category labels can be summarized and related to one another using special statistical techniques designed for nominal variables.

Ordinal Measurement. Most variables of interest to communication researchers are measured at least at the next level of measurement precision, the ordinal level. Ordinal measures involve being able to say that something or someone has more or less of whatever is being measured than someone else. A person could be asked to list the message strategy that

TABLE 6.1   Demographic Data Sheet with Nominal- and Ordinal-level Data

DEMOGRAPHIC DATA

Please complete the following information. DO NOT write your name on this sheet. This information is strictly CONFIDENTIAL and your identity will remain anonymous at all times.

1. Your student number: _____
2. Your age (in years): _____
3. Your sex (circle one):   Male   Female
4. Your race (circle one):   Caucasian   African American   Native American
                              Asian   Hispanic   Other
5. Marital status (circle one):   Married   Divorced   Never Married
6. Major: _____
7. Grade Point Average: _____, if you are a first quarter freshman, what was your high school academic average? _____
8. Within the past 5 years, have you held a job which required you to write?
   _____ Yes   _____ No
   If yes, how frequently did you write:
   memorandums: ___every day   ___1 or 2 times a week   ___seldom   ___never
   letters: ___every day   ___1 or 2 times a week   ___seldom   ___never
   reports: ___every day   ___1 or 2 times a week   ___seldom   ___never
9. Within the past 5 years, have you enrolled in a high school or college course that required you to write? _____ Yes   _____ No
   If yes, how frequently did you write:
   in-class essays: ___every day   ___1 or 2 times a week   ___seldom   ___never
   journals: ___every day   ___1 or 2 times a week   ___seldom   ___never
   discussion questions
      on exams: ___every day   ___1 or 2 times a week   ___seldom   ___never
   term papers: ___every day   ___1 or 2 times a week   ___seldom   ___never
10. What is your academic classification?   ____freshman   ____sophomore
                                             ____junior   ____senior
                                             ____graduate   ____unclassified

he or she would be most likely to use to end a relationship, then to indicate the next most likely strategy, then the third most likely strategy, and so on. The researcher would assign a 1 to the individual's most favored strategy, a 2 to the next strategy, a 3 to the third listed strategy, and so on. The variables in Table 6.1 that ask for writing frequency and academic classification are ordinal.

Note that nothing about the *size* of the differences between the various strategies is known. The difference between the most favored strategy and the second favored strategy might be small or large, and it might or might not be the same as the difference between the second and third preferred strategies. Further, nothing is known about the absolute *magnitude* of the individual's favorableness toward any of the strategies. The person might be highly favorable toward all three strategies, or may not like any of them at all and merely have viewed the "ranking ordering" as choosing the lesser of several evils.

Any time values for variables are **rank ordered**, the ordinal level of measurement is being used. Mass media researchers have asked people to list their most important sources of news information. For about the past twenty years, television has ranked first, with newspapers second. Unless follow-up questions are asked, all we know is that people believe television to be a more important source of information than newspapers. We do not know if the difference between television and newspapers is large or small. We merely know the order of importance people place on the two information sources.

Interval Measurement.   Interval measures meet the criteria of ordinal measures, but importantly, the *distance* between adjacent scores are assumed to be of equal intervals at all points along the measure. Thus, the difference between a score of 4 and 5 is assumed to be the same as the difference between 5 and 6. Further, the difference between a score of 22 and 31—8 units—is assumed to be the same as the *difference* between any two scores that are 8 units apart. Although the issue is somewhat controversial, most measurement scales, including all of those described in Chapter 7, are treated as if they provide interval data.

An advantage to using interval data is that they can be analyzed using a special, more sophisticated and powerful category of statistics called *parametric*, the importance of which we will explain a bit later in this chapter. Table 6.2 provides two ways to interpret one kind of interval data, **Likert-type**, which is presented in Chapter 7. Note that we can approach the response to the questions by counting the number who "Strongly Agree," "Agree," "Uncertain," "Disagree," or "Strongly Disagree." This analysis would treat the data as ordinal. To treat the data as numbers, each equally apart from the other, would be to treat the data as interval and, given the assumption that the distance between each response category is equal, analyze the data as a response from 1 ("Strongly Agree") to 5 ("Strongly Disagree"). As we will note later when discussing statistical analyses, ordinal data is reported as counts,

TABLE 6.2   Equal Appearing Interval Data

A. AS UNITS AN EQUAL APPEARING DISTANCE APART
Instructions: Please indicate your evaluation of each statement as it applies to you by circling whether you (SA) strongly agree, (A) agree, (U) are undecided, (D) disagree, or (SD) strongly disagree with each statement.

Communication measurement is easy.	SA	A	U	D	SD
Research methods is a fun class.	SA	A	U	D	SD

B. AS NUMBERS APPEARING TO BE EQUALLY DISTANT
Instructions: Please indicate your evaluation of each statement as it applies to you by circling whether you (1) strongly agree, (2) agree, (3) are undecided, (4) disagree, or (5) strongly disagree with each statement.

Communication measurement is easy.	1	2	3	4	5
Research methods is a fun class.	1	2	3	4	5

frequencies, and percentages, whereas interval data may have arithmetic averages, such as the mean, calculated. The data derived from Table 6.2 are generally treated as interval.

Ratio Measurement.   The fourth level of measurement is ratio measurement. Ratio measures meet all the criteria of interval measures, but also have *a meaningful absolute zero point*. This zero point allows statements about the ratios of numbers to be made so the full range of mathematical tools are available for analysis. Thus, one person can have a score that is twice or three times as high as someone else's. Time and age are commonly used ratio variables. For example, someone can be in a relationship for any length of time, from zero to many years. A couple who have been involved in a relationship for two months have been involved for twice as long as a couple who have been involved for one month (ratio—2:1) and two-thirds (also a ratio) as long as a couple who have been involved for three months. Ratio measurement in communication is found primarily in physiological studies that use as their measures such things as heart rate (EKG), brain waves (EEG), and the like. As we will find in Chapter 7, ratio measurement used in paper and pencil testing (self-administered testing or interviews) is found primarily in multidimensional scaling or a scaling technique called "thermometer scaling" (Wimmer & Domminick, 1994) and with variable measurement dealing with counts—program length, age, number of words in a story, and so forth (c.f., Bowers & Cartwright, 1984).

Of the demographic data listed in Table 6.1, age in years and grade point averages would meet the criteria of ratio-level data. Obviously, as with interval measures, we can decide to design measures that measure something that may be assessed as a ratio with the less powerful interval, ordinal, and/or nominal ways. For instance, we can ask for the exact age at the time we are collecting data (ratio). We can ask for age in groupings of years: 10 and under, 11 to 20, 21 to 30, 31 to 40, 41 to 50, and 51 and older (ordinal). Or, we could ask for age by some descriptive criteria, such as "old enough to drive" and "not old enough to drive" or vote or drink and so forth. As the answers to these questions would be zeroes and ones, it appears to be measuring at the nominal level (sex is nominal; e.g., 1 is male, 2 is female). However, not old enough to drive (0), old enough to drive (1) is measuring at the ordinal level, not nominal, because the respondent has more of what is being measured—the ability to drive.

The important point is that nominal measures serve merely as a naming function. Ordinal measures literally provide order—a 2 is more than 1. Interval measures allow us to assume that the distance or magnitude between a 1 and a 2 is the same as the distance between a 2 and a 3, or 57 and 58. Ratio measures mean that a 2 is twice as much of something. For example, someone who has watched four hours of the coverage of the September 11 atrocities has watched twice as much as someone who has watched two hours.

Precision and Power.   As noted in the preceding examples, interval and ratio measures are more precise than nominal and ordinal measures. It follows logically that if two variables that are predicted by some theory to be related, are, in fact, related, the more precise the measures of these variables, the greater the probability of the researcher detecting this relationship empirically. For instance, assume that self-disclosure and interpersonal attraction are, in reality, positively related. If a researcher has a theory that predicts that these variables are related, he or she wants to have every opportunity to observe this relationship.

MINI-PROJECT:

Create your own demographic data sheet (see Table 6.1) that employs all four measurement levels. Ask several friends to complete it. Were there any variables that they had trouble responding to? Did you miss any important information? Did you get too much? What conclusions can you draw from each variable? Reduce or collapse the ordinal-level measures to nominal, the interval measures to ordinal and nominal, and the ratio measures to interval, ordinal, and nominal.

Accurate and precise measures of self-disclosure and interpersonal attraction are much more likely to provide confirmation of the theory than less accurate, less precise measures.

Contributing further to the advantage of interval and ratio measures at detecting existing relationships between variables are the statistical techniques for analyzing data derived from these measures. Variables that are measured at the nominal and ordinal levels must be analyzed with **nonparametric statistics.** In contrast, interval and ratio data can be legitimately analyzed using **parametric statistics.** Parametric statistics are more "powerful," in that they provide a greater likelihood of detecting whether two or more variables are related. We will later see that parametric statistics allow us to use powerful mathematical formulas to determine relationships among variables. Thus, the more precise the measures and the more powerful the statistical techniques, the better the chance the researcher has of showing that two related variables are, in fact, related. (This point will become clearer in Part III, when we discuss nonparametric and parametric statistical techniques and tests.)

RELIABILITY

Regardless of the level of measurement, variables must meet certain criteria regarding their usefulness. These criteria fall into two areas: reliability and validity.

Reliability refers to the extent to which measurement yields numbers—data—that are consistent, stable, and dependable. Social scientists use the term reliability in association with measurement much the same way that it is used in everyday parlance. A reliable student, for example, is one who is dependable and predictable. He will perform in class pretty much the same way today, tomorrow, next week, and next term. An unreliable student is not so stable, dependable, or predictable. He may do well today, but may not do so well tomorrow or next week. Next term he may not even be in school.

A completely unreliable measure would not be measuring anything at all. Imagine a researcher who is trying to assess an individual's level of communication apprehension. Suppose we have a measure that revealed a particular individual's level to be 27 on a possible 100-point scale. Then suppose we tested that same measure again and the same individual scored 74, then 11, then 59, then 48, then 65, then 22, then 82. In other words, it looks like the measure yielded *random* results. This measure would not be useful. Data from such a measure could be worse than no data at all; time spent gathering and analyzing it would be completely wasted. A completely unreliable measure of a variable could never be demonstrated to be related to another variable. Randomness is, by definition, related to nothing.

On the other hand, to the extent that a measure yielded very similar answers each time it was applied to the same person or group of people, to the extent that all the scores were consistent, stable, predictable, and dependable, it would be a reliable measure. If the measure of communication apprehension was administered to the same person again, and this time the individual scored 28, then 25, then 24, then 29, then 26, then 27, it would be a reliable measure. It would be measuring *something*, even if it were not communication apprehension.

To aid in understanding measurement reliability it may be useful to think of any measure as being composed of two separate components. One component is **systematic measurement**—here repeated applications yield identical responses. The other component is **randomness**, and is not a measure of anything. Perhaps a question was worded ambiguously or the person was distracted as she placed a pencil mark on a scale or missed the intended mark. Whatever the reason, all measures are to some extent affected by randomness. This nonsystematic random fluctuation is **measurement unreliability**. The more a measure reflects systematic factors, the more reliable it is—the more it reflects randomness the more *un*reliable the measure. This randomness is a source of error. By that we mean that if we are going to predict something, this randomness will make prediction impossible for us to predict accurately.

Factors Influencing Reliability

Looked at another way, reliability deals with the amount of error in measurement. There are several types of error that are attributed to measurement (Singletary, 1994). There is **instrumental error**, error that occurs because the measuring instrument was poorly written. Instrumental error can occur when measure instructions are incomplete or ambiguous or when a question may have more than one possible response (it is **double-barreled**). For instance, the question, "Do you like to watch and play basketball?" requires two questions because a person may like to watch but not play basketball. Second, there is **application error**, error attributable to lack of control over how the measure was distributed or completed. In mail surveys, for instance, we never know who actually completed the measurement, it could be anyone at that address. And, third, there is **random error**, error that arises out of the interaction of all other forms of error—it is unpredictable, hence random. A slip of the pencil, filling in the wrong bubble on a test form, a mistake by the person who counts the vote all can contribute to error. As Singletary notes, "It is the duty of the researcher to *control* random errors to the greatest extent possible" (p. 77).

As we will note later in this chapter, most sources of error can be controlled. It takes an understanding of the variables you seek to measure, patience and pretesting your measures, and establishing as much control over how the data is acquired to establish control. Even given all this, some random error will occur. However, forewarned is forearmed and, as we will discuss in the chapters on specific methodology, certain research methods produce results that are more reliable than others.

All measures suffer from some degree of unreliability. And, while several factors have been identified as contributing to this, perhaps the most important reason lies in asking people to make extremely fine or difficult judgments. The more difficult the judgmental task or the more ambiguous the rules for assigning numbers to persons, objects, or events, the more a measure will tend to be unreliable. For instance, suppose your teacher asks you to estimate the size of your classroom in inches. Your class would offer a wide range of numbers. On the other hand, what if your teacher instead asked you to estimate its size as small, medium, or large? In this case, the estimations would be in three groups and reliability would be greater.

Coder Reliability

Researchers often attempt to train two observers (called "coders") of communication behavior to observe such things as videotapes or live action and rate the degree of inconsistency between verbal and nonverbal messages. It is often difficult to find coders who will agree on what they observed. Two coders, even after considerable training, consistently will come up with different judgments of the degree of inconsistency between, for example, eye contact and gestures. On the other hand, you might have no trouble training the *same* coders to reliably count the number of verbal nonfluencies, the amount of eye contact, and a whole host of other variables. The more subtle the communication cues the researchers attempt to measure, the more difficult it is to train the coders to agree in their judgments.

We can assess intercoder reliability by comparing how many times coders "agree" on their observations. If we find the coders agree on their observations over 90 percent of the time, we might accept that as "reliable." There are several statistical ways to assess intercoder reliability, such as Cohen's *kappa* (Cohen, 1960) or Scott's *pi* (Scott, 1969) coefficients. Each can be computed and compared with previous research. There are no absolute set guidelines for establishing reliability because it depends on the difficulty of the measurement.

Measurement Item Reliability

Similarly, if you were asked how much you liked the president of the United States, on a 100-point scale, with 0 representing Strongly Dislike and 100 representing Strongly Like, you will be likely to give slightly different responses every time the question is asked. You may say 85 one day, 82 the next day, 79 the next, 88 the next, and so forth. A 10-point random variation would not be uncommon on this scale. To decide exactly where one stands on a 100-point scale is a fairly tough judgment to make. On the other hand, if you were asked the same question on a 10-point scale, with 10 representing Strongly Like, you would be much more likely to respond consistently day after day. This is because it is much easier to pinpoint a rating on a 10-point scale than it is on a 100-point scale. A "Like," "Don't Like" scale would be very reliable, but would lack precision.

Measurement item reliability also can be computed. Much like intercoder reliability, item reliability looks at how respondents answer the questions or statements provided them. Their answers are their observations. For interval and ratio measures we can compute the **Coefficient Alpha** statistic (Cronbach, 1951) that tells us how consistent the respondents

MINI-PROJECT:

With a friend watch two evening newscasts, one local and one national. Count the number of times the anchor in each broadcast makes a mistake. Before conducting the project, however, operationally define what a "mistake" is. Tell your friend what you are looking for and then without discussing it place a mark on a piece of paper (coding sheet) each time you observe the communicative behavior(s) defined as "mistakes." Do not work together, instead simply each of you does your own coding. After a half-hour, how consistent is your coding?

are in their responses. For nominal and ordinal measures, consistency of response is computed by the **Kuder-Richardson formula 20** (or KR–20) statistic. Consistency falls between 0 (totally random responses) to 1.0 (total consistency in responses). In each case we would like our computed consistency to be at least 90 percent (.90); however, there are times when reliabilities between .70 and .90 may be acceptable, especially when new measures are being created.

It is important that researchers report their obtained reliabilities. Although some journals require such reporting, not all do so. *Research should always report the appropriate reliability of the measures used.*

Establishing Reliability

Reliability is always established by showing that two or more measures of the same variable are in agreement. Reliability applies to all types of measurement. With these fundamental ideas in mind, we will examine ways of increasing and establishing reliability in four common research measurement settings.

Self-Administered Questionnaires

A very common data-gathering technique used by communication researchers is the self-administered questionnaire. Whether the researcher is conducting an experiment or a survey, part of the research procedures may involve the distribution of a paper and pencil test or response sheet on which participants indicate their responses to the researcher's questions (**application error**). Several factors may reduce the reliability of this kind of self-report measure. First, unclear or ambiguous instructions, which may be interpreted in alternative, random ways, detract from reliability (**instrumental error**). Thus, researchers attempt to write instructions and questions as clearly and unambiguously as possible. It is common to "pilot test" a questionnaire on a small group of people similar to those who will participate in the actual study as a means of identifying, rewriting, or eliminating poorly worded items and/or instructions.

Reliability can be improved by increasing the number of specific measures of the same variable. At least two such measures, items, or subscales are required to establish any degree of reliability at all. Also, as the number of items measuring the variable increase, the randomness component of a person's answers to individual questions becomes less influential in determining the overall score assigned to the variable. As the number of items measuring the variable increases, the random fluctuations on particular items tend to cancel one another out. Additionally, as the number of measures of the same variable increases, reliability increases in generally systematic and predictable degrees.

Another factor that increases reliability concerns the circumstances under which the questionnaires are administered (**application error**). Many researchers have experienced the frustration of examining questionnaires that seemingly have been filled out in odd or unpredictable, even random, ways. Respondents who have been motivated to participate in a research project in a serious, conscientious manner are not likely to provide such useless data. For this and for some of the ethical reasons discussed in Chapter 3, participants should feel free to choose to participate in the research or not. They should be genuine volunteers who volunteer only after being properly informed about the nature of the research, including any risks involved.

Questionnaires should be administered under standardized and well-controlled circumstances. Reliability decreases as the number of ways in which a questionnaire is administered increases. So, for example, the instructions—including the written ones accompanying the questionnaire and the verbal statements made by the researcher or confederates during the administration of the questionnaire—about how to fill out a questionnaire from administration to administration should vary as little as possible.

For many communication variables studied repeatedly, there exist standard measures for which reliability has been established. For example, there are generally accepted self-report measures of such variables as communication apprehension, perceptions of source credibility, and attitudes toward a variety of objects and topics (e.g., Tardy, 1988). If extant measures adequately operationalize the variables under study, their selection may facilitate measurement reliability, as well as allow for more direct comparisons between the results of the current study and those of other studies using the same measures. When no such measures are available, the researcher must design his or her own questions or response scales. In either case, an effort is usually made to assess the reliability of the measures used. There are three general ways of establishing reliability.

Test-Retest Reliability. The first is the test-retest method, designed to assess reliability *over time*. Test-retest reliability is assessed by administering the same measures, for example a self-report questionnaire, to the same respondents under as nearly the same conditions as possible at different points in time. To the extent that each respondent's second score agreed with his or her first score, the measure is reliable. The degree of reliability is formally assessed by computing the correlation between the two sets of scores. The correlation coefficient, sometimes the **Pearson *r*** if the measures are at the interval or ratio level, is commonly treated as a good statistical assessment of the degree of reliability. This coefficient can range from +1.0, perfect reliability (responses to the first item are identical to the second), to 0, no reliability (responses on the first have no relationship to the second).

Split-Half Reliability. The second way to establish reliability is to assess how one part of the measure relates to the second. This is called split-half reliability. Just as the label implies, with split-half reliability you assess the degree of correspondence or correlation of half the measure's items with the other half. It is generally used with instruments that mea-

■ ■ ■ ■ ■

MINI-PROJECT:

You should be able to find a number of self-administered questionnaires (an examination could be considered one). Go through two or three and see if you can identify things that may affect the questionnaires' reliability. Are there some things that you find similar across the questionnaires? If so, what were they and how might they affect reliability?

sure a variable that has but one dimension, although variables with subdimensions (e.g., credibility, attitude) should produce items that correlate highly within subdimensions. Remember that the more measures you have that seem to measure the same thing, the more confidence you have in the results. Again a correlation coefficient such as the Pearson r is typically used as the test statistic and we would expect a positive high correlation between halves (.90 or greater).

Internal Consistency.   A third way to establish reliability is to assess the internal consistency of a measure. This is done by examining the extent to which several measures that appear on the same questionnaire, *and* are designed to measure the same variable, are in agreement. For example, if the researcher were measuring public speaking apprehension, a respondent might be asked at one point on the questionnaire to state his or her degree of agreement or disagreement with the statement, "I look forward with pleasure to opportunities to speak to large groups of people." Later, the respondent might be asked to respond to a similar statement, such as: "I enjoy making presentations in front of large audiences." To the extent that a specific respondent provided similar or identical responses to each of these statements, the overall measure would have internal consistency; it would be reliable. Consistency would be assessed by either the coefficient alpha or KR–20 test. The formal statistical assessment of the reliability of the measure is generally included in the research report to give the reader additional information to aid in evaluating the research and interpreting the results.

Acceptable Reliability Coefficients.   Regardless of the specific statistical indication of reliability used, they are all examining the same fundamental thing: the extent to which multiple measures of the same variable agree. To the extent that they do agree, the measure is reliable, to the extent that they do not, the measure is unreliable.

It has become somewhat of a *convention* within communication journals for scaled responses to achieve reliability coefficients of .70 or better to be considered "acceptable." As with other conventions in the social sciences, however, this figure is somewhat arbitrary. The underlying concern that makes highly reliable measures desirable is this: The more reliable the measure, the more probable it is that systematic relationships that exist between variables, and are predicted by theory, will be found empirically. Unreliable measures decrease the chances of obtaining research results that support or refute the theory.

Ronald Reagan's portrayal of the former Soviet Union as the "evil empire." Fantasy themes that are found throughout a society take on the form of fantasy types, which become important and strong rhetorical symbols. As fantasy types become shared, they turn into rhetorical visions, used by rhetorical communities and identify themselves through their use. Bormann's (1982) rhetorical analysis of the 1981 Iranian hostage release and Reagan inaugural, for instance, found that

> The critical analysis reveals similarities between rhetorical fantasies and televised news [coverage of the hostage release and inaugural address on January 20, 1981] by comparing the subliminal impact of the enactment of the transfer of power and end of the [hostage] crisis by the coverage of the inaugural and hostage release to the way Reagan's speechwriters used the fantasy type of restoration to meet the needs of a conservative political movement in the 1980s. (p. 133)

One particular thematic method that has enjoyed particular attention by communication researchers is that of Kenneth Burke (1965a, 1965b). Burke's approach is to examine the language as if it were used "on stage." In Burke's method the language employed is examined in terms of action rather than information. Burke's analysis has been labeled the *Pentad* and examines the interrelationships between symbol use and the *act* (communicative message), *scene* (the situation or background against which the act is performed), *agent* (the source of the communicative message), *agency* (the means or instruments used to communicate, or how the agent went about carrying out the act), and the *purpose* (the aim or goal of the message act). An example of this method might be Burke's analysis of *Mein Kampf* as a critical event: Adolph Hitler (agent) delivering a propagandistic message (act) at mass rallies (agency) with the setting of post–World War I economic and political turmoil (scene) with the goal (purpose) of uniting Germany and securing political power. Each element of the Pentad may be analyzed for results and artistic standards or they all may be analyzed.

Many researchers use **feminist** ideas as a basis of criticism. An example of this is a study done by Peterson (2000). She did a feminist critique of the hugely popular sex manual written by a man that was based on the book *Men Are from Mars, Women Are from Venus*. The book was entitled *Mars and Venus in the Bedroom*. Although her criticism covers a large portion of the book, she focuses on how the author polarizes the sexes, assigning power to the male and submissiveness and even objectification to the female. For part of the analysis she made the decision to analyze the lists in the book. That decision was made because the lists are easily distinguishable from the obtusely organized text.

Peterson notes that one of the lists provided by the author identifies "Twenty Sexual Turn-on Phrases" that purport to be statements that men can use to "turn on" women. She cites several examples that the author uses, such as "Your breasts turn me on," "Your lips are perfect," and "I love touching your soft skin," as evidence that the author reinforces traditional gender differences, writing that ". . . men are physical, women are mental; men are agents, women are scenes" (p. 5). Peterson continues by stating that these demonstrate that the author's rhetoric implies that "While men are gratified by vigorous physical contact and orgasm, women are gratified by compliments on their looks" (p. 5).

The basis of ideas concerns what was actually communicated. Here the critic is interested in establishing whether or not what was said was worthy of being said. Analysis centers

Note, however, the arbitrary nature of a .70 "required" reliability figure. If a variable was particularly difficult to measure, perhaps being measured reliably at .50 or less, and was still found to be related to another variable, this would be an indication that the relationship between the two variables is probably quite powerful since this systematic relationship was detected *in spite of* considerable randomness in the measurement process. It also might be your purpose to *create* a measure if no other exists. For instance, assume you are interested in investigating the messages of the Taliban immediately following the attack by Osama bin Laden on September 11, 2001. There are no existing measures for you to use, so you have to create them. Since this type of research could be considered exploratory, you might set your acceptable reliability standards lower, hoping that refinements in the measure will later yield higher reliability coefficients. Either way, the decision to accept a particular reliability coefficient is, indeed, arbitrary and up to the researcher and ultimately the consumers of the research to evaluate. As noted earlier, whenever possible reliability coefficients should be reported in the research report.

Not all researchers would agree. There are those who would dismiss the value of a study on the grounds that one or more measures failed to achieve reliability figures at a certain level. These people may have lost sight of why we do research: to construct and test theory. Instead of looking at what was measured and to what other variables the measure was found to relate, many people rely on accepted levels of reliability as a fiat, instead of evaluating the research by reason. There are times when any of a number of factors can reduce reliability. It is important to understand that measurement is a relative phenomenon and that reliability lower than .70, or some other arbitrary target figure, will sometimes be unavoidable.

Interviews

Interviews are conducted either face-to-face or, more frequently, over the telephone. Most of the same guidelines that apply to the self-administered questionnaire also are useful for increasing the reliability of interview responses. There are two key differences, however. (1) Questions used in the interview must be written even more simply and clearly since they will be heard and not read. There is a difference between how a question "sounds" and how it "reads," the researcher should be aware of such differences. (See Figure 6.1, a sample telephone questionnaire.) (2) The interviewers must be trained with meticulous care. Poorly trained interviewers reduce measurement reliability in a number of ways. Interviewing training procedures are discussed in later chapters, but here it will suffice to note that all interviewers should behave as nearly identically as possible in each interview, which is why training is so important. Questions must be asked—and answers recorded—*in the same way each time, over and over*. To the extent that there are variations, either within the same interview or from one interview to the next, or between interviewers, reliability is reduced.

Reliability of measures used in interview situations can be assessed in the same ways as measures on self-report questionnaires. Either the same questions can be asked of the same respondents at a later time (test-retest reliability), or multiple questions, each designed to measure the same variable, can be asked during the same interview (internal consistency). Additionally, as a check on *interviewer* performance, which directly affects measurement reliability, different interviewers may be required to interview the same

FIGURE 6.1 Sample telephone interview questionnaire.

Interviewer: _____
Telephone #: _____
Date/Time: _____

UM Vision Survey

Hello, my name is _____. Our communication research methods class is conducting a student survey of campus viewing habits. May we ask you a few questions concerning your television viewing? (IF NO, THANK THEM FOR THEIR TIME.)

1. To begin, do you or your roommate own a television?
   _____ Yes
   _____ No
   IF YES, GO TO 2.
   IF no, Do you have access to television on campus?
   IF NO, CONCLUDE AND THANK THE RESPONDENT.
   If yes, where: _____
   If yes, how often do you watch television there?
   _____ less than 5 hours per week
   _____ between 5 and 10 hours per week
   _____ between 10 and 15 hours per week
   _____ between 15 and 20 hours per week
   _____ more than 20 hours per week
   IF YES, GO TO 2.
2. Do you ever watch student programming on the University of Miami's Cable Channel 24?
   _____ Yes   _____ No
   2a. If yes, have you ever watched any of the following UM Vision programs:
       (READ ENTIRE LIST)
       _____ a. News Vision   _____ e. Gablus Profile
       _____ b. Local Color   _____ f. Calendar
       _____ c. To the Point   _____ g. Contact
       _____ d. Fit for Life   _____ h. Night Out
   2b. If no, you don't watch student programming on UM Vision because   (READ LIST)
       _____ a. Never heard of it
       _____ b. Programming does not interest you
       _____ c. Inconvenient timing
       _____ d. Do not know when it is on the air
3. How would you rate student programming? Is it
   _____ poor
   _____ unsatisfactory
   _____ neither unsatisfactory nor satisfactory
   _____ satisfactory
   _____ excellent
4. Do you ever watch CNBC, which airs nightly from 7 p.m. to 8 a.m. on UM Vision?
   _____ Yes   _____No

FIGURE 6.1 Continued

4a. If yes, you watch CNBC because it is
_____ interesting and informative
_____ the only programming available
_____ Other (_____)

4b. If no, you do not watch CNBC on UM Vision because:
_____ have never heard of it
_____ were not aware it was on UM Vision
_____ CNBC does not interest you
_____ Hours are not convenient
_____ Other (_____)

5. How would you rate CNBC? Is it
_____ poor
_____ unsatisfactory
_____ neither unsatisfactory nor satisfactory
_____ satisfactory
_____ excellent

6. What types of programming do you watch most often? (DO NOT READ LIST, MARK ALL CHOSEN)
_____ Cartoons
_____ Movies
_____ News
_____ Educational programs
_____ Sitcoms
_____ Soap Operas
_____ Sports
_____ Other (_____)

7. If you could add cable networks to UM Vision, which networks would you add? (PROBE FOR UP TO THREE)
a. _____
b. _____
c. _____

8. Finally, I'd like to ask you a few questions for statistical purposes.

9. What time do you usually watch television most?
_____ 7 a.m. to noon
_____ noon to 5 p.m.
_____ 5 p.m. to 9 p.m.
_____ 9 p.m. to midnight
_____ midnight to 7 a.m.

10. What is your major? _____

11. What is your student classification? Are you a
_____ Freshman _____ Sophomore _____ Junior _____ Senior or a
_____ Graduate Student?

12. Record respondent's sex here (ASK IF NECESSARY):
_____ Male _____ Female

Thank you, that concludes our survey. You have been very helpful.

respondent independently. This person could be a confederate of the researcher, a person trained to give identical responses over and over to each interviewer. An examination of the recorded responses for each interviewer provides an opportunity to assess the extent to which each interviewer is providing reliable and accurate data. In this manner, interviewers who are not behaving in a professional or conscientious manner, or who have been inadequately trained, can be identified.

Trained Observers

Here we are referring broadly to individuals who have been trained to observe and assign numbers to any variable of interest to a researcher. Observers are sometimes called *coders* because they replace observations with numeric codes. The material being observed might be written text, such as a transcript of an interaction, or newspaper editorials that are being analyzed for their content. Or, the focus of observation might be individuals, either live or on videotape, who were making speeches or engaged in group discussions. The material being observed might be radio or television broadcasts. In all cases the observers have been trained to assign numbers to their observations according to carefully specified rules. To the extent that they are able to do this in a consistent, dependable, and stable manner, reliable measures of the variables being observed will result.

Again, the key to having reliable measures is careful training of the observers. They should be given clear, concise definitions of what they are looking for, shown examples of material that falls within the various categories, given the opportunity to practice their observation tasks, given feedback about how they have done, have errors pointed out to them, and given an opportunity to practice again. Only when an observer has demonstrated his or her ability to assign the same numbers to the same observations consistently should he or she be allowed to proceed.

Reliability can be established in one of two ways. Two or more observers are trained to observe and code the same material independently. The extent to which they agree on the assignment of numbers to their observations is a measure of their reliability, usually reported as a correlation, or percentage of agreement of *interrater* or *intercoder* agreement. As with other measurement procedures, the more difficult the judgmental task, the more difficult it is to develop reliable measures. For example, it will be more difficult to train observers who are analyzing the latent meaning of poetry than it would be to train them to count the number of times a specific word appears in that same poetry. As with other measures, the key to establishing reliability is showing that there is *agreement*. Thus, two or more observers must be shown to code the same material using the same category system with the same outcome.

As noted earlier, several procedures are available for estimating interobserver reliability. As with other statistical techniques, the specific method selected depends on the level at which the observers are measuring the variables. Cohen's *Kappa* or Scott's *pi* provide an assessment of the reliability of observers who are assigning observations to *nominal* categories. They provide a statistical assessment of the degree of agreement between the observers, allowing for the level of agreement that would be expected by chance. Other procedures are available for higher levels of measurement (e.g., Krippendorf, 1980).

Alternatively, the same observer might observe the same material at different times and, purposely avoiding knowledge of how he or she coded it the first time, code it again a second time. An example of this would be a teacher grading essays and assigning a number of points to each essay. To assure reliable grading, a good habit is to grade a few of the essays independently a second time, of course taking care to remain ignorant of the grade given the first time. If the same grade is given both times, reliability has been established (test-retest reliability).

Participant-Observation

Chapter 9 examines participant-observation and deals with the special problems associated with establishing the reliability of this type of research. It is extremely difficult to have observational rules that are detailed enough to specify clearly how all the many nuances of behavior are to be coded in the natural setting. While it may not be possible to achieve the high level of reliability achievable on a self-report questionnaire, there are ways of increasing reliability in qualitative research. Again, the key is to establish agreement or consistency. Thus, two participant observers might make at least some of the same observations and compare results. Unfortunately, participant-observation research frequently allows only one observer, making reliability extremely difficult, if not impossible, to establish. However, if the researcher is careful, the consistency by which he or she observes the same behaviors over time will produce a form of reliability. However, as discussed in Chapter 9, reliability is a major problem with the method. We must point out, however, that participant-observation is less concerned with reliability than with an introspective and subjective perception of the communication event *as it happens in its natural setting*. Nonetheless, as will be noted when we discuss the relationship between reliability and validity, some minimal level of reliability is needed before a measure, and the study itself, has any validity whatsoever.

VALIDITY

"Does the measure you measure what it is supposed to measure" is the central notion of establishing validity. To the extent that scales or questions do measure what they are thought to measure, they are valid. To the extent that the scales or questions measure something else, or nothing at all, they are not valid. While this is the most common conception of measurement validity, there are several more specialized uses of the term, for example criterion-related validity, content validity, and construct validity. It should be emphasized that a measure is valid only in the context in which it is being used. A measure of a variable that is valid for one purpose may not be valid for another.

Content Validity/Face Validity

The first kind of measurement validity is content validity, and, its very close cousin, face validity. Content validity refers to whether a measure captures the content or the meaning of the variable being measured. You might, for instance, be interested in measuring someone's level of communication apprehension in general and writing apprehension in particular. It would be possible to write scores of relevant statements (called *items*) about this concept and ask respondents to state their agreement or disagreement with each statement. You cannot ask respondents to answer several hundred questions. Instead, you select a sample of items, a smaller subset of items from your pool of questions, ones that seem to be both indicators of apprehension and fit your particular conception of what apprehension is.

Whether a measure has content validity is somewhat of a subjective judgment. The relevance and representativeness of specific items would need to be judged by the researcher and perhaps other "experts." An item that stated "Writing is fun" probably would be relevant to the content of the writing apprehension variable. The statement, "I use the dictionary a lot" probably would not be relevant to the same concept (see Box 6.1).

Content validity and face validity are virtually indistinguishable; we might think of them as close cousins. Face validity is achieved if a measure appears, on the face of it, to be valid. Content validity has been achieved if a measure is judged to capture the content of whatever is being measured. Both types of validity require the use of common sense and logic to form a judgment about whether the variable is being validly measured. Put another way, a decision is made about whether the operational definition is consistent with the conceptual definition of the variable. Is this operationalization "capturing" the meaning of the conceptual definition? The key point is that both types of validity require a *judgment* to be made by someone—usually the researcher, but often by experts on the specific topic about which the measures were asking. Usually the researchers in the communication field agree on a construct's validity; this can be identified through a literature search.

Criterion-Related of Predictive Validity

Criterion-related validity focuses on the notion that a measure is valid to the extent that it enables the researcher to **predict** a score on some other measure or to predict a particular behavior of interest. The concern is not with what is being measured, but whether the measure predicts relevant behaviors and responses on a second measure. For example, if the goal of a study is the practical concern of predicting voter turnout, a measure yielding responses that allows you to do this accurately is valid, regardless of what it is measuring. The interest is more in the **criterion** itself—the variable the research wants to predict (voter turnout)—than in the *relationship* between what is being measured and the criterion. Thus, a measure labeled "Voter Turnout Instrument" might ask questions about past voting behavior, campaign interest, attention to campaign advertising, and educational level. Although this measure would seem to be measuring a variety of different things, it would have criterion-related validity if the responses could be combined or weighted in such a way that voting could be accurately predicted. This type of validity is often more useful in applied research than in theoretical research.

An example of criterion-related validity is a measurement instrument with which most college students are quite familiar: the Scholastic Aptitude Test (SAT). Most users of the SAT are solely interested in its criterion-related validity. To the extent that it predicts student performance in college, the SAT is viewed as valid. Controversy about *what* is being measured surfaces periodically. SAT critics claim, among other things, that it is *really* measuring socioeconomic status (SES) and the concomitant degree of understanding of white,

BOX 6.1

THE MASS COMMUNICATION WRITING APPREHENSION MEASURE (MCWAM)

Riffe and Stacks (1988, 1992) were interested in creating a measure of writing apprehension for mass communication students. They began in 1988 with over 100 items or statements about feelings and attitudes concerning writing. Some of these items reflected behavioral implications of writing ("I enjoy playing with words," "I'm a good speller," "I usually make deadlines"), while others reflected attitudinal implications ("It is very difficult for me to write when I know my writing will be evaluated," "I'm nervous about writing," "I write only when I have to"). From the item pool about 75 items were selected as representing the various subdimensions of writing apprehension the researchers felt the literature supported (*face validity*). These questions were then submitted to a panel of professional educators, journalists, and public relations practitioners (*content validity*). Each read the list and commented on the items. Based on their comments the researchers revised several items, dropped others, and added even more.

The revised MCWAM instrument was then given to over 400 students, along with a series of questions concerning their writing habits and other questions of theoretical interest (see Table 6.1). Student responses were then submitted to statistical testing to see if the subdimensions predicted would hold up to actual testing. Employing a statistical procedure called factor analysis, which establishes commonalities among items or unites items into dimensions—factors, thus "factor analysis." Measurement items that are correlated tend to "hang together" in the different factors, although some items may tend toward two or more factors ("double-barreled" or bad items) and will not be considered in the final subdimension. In this case, Riffe and Stacks (1988) found six factors comprising 37 items, but the mass communication factor failed to materialize (construct validity). They had hypothesized a number of relationships between demographic variables (sex, major, professional writing major versus non-writing major) which the MCWAM scores supported (criterion-related validity).

Riffe and Stacks (1992) then reworked the MCWAM. They added items thought to reflect a true mass communication orientation (items dealing with deadlines, audiences, being edited). They were then added to the items from the 1988 test and once again given to a panel of experts. After review and some alteration, the revised MCWAM was given to over 700 students, and submitted for analysis. This time they found eight subdimensions, but no true mass communication factor emerged. Two new factors, "audience salience" and "facts versus ideas," however, did emerge from items thought to be mass communication-related.

The measure's criterion-related validity was then tested. Significant differences between majors, student classifications, age, race, and gender were obtained, all as expected. Further, differences for respondent grade point average, anticipated grade point average, or their scores on a basic (writing) skills test were found on all but one MCWAM dimension ("facts versus ideas").

Source: Riffe, D., & Stacks, D. W. (1988). Dimensions of writing apprehension across mass communication students. *Journalism Quarterly, 65,* 384–391; Riffe, D., & Stacks, D. W. (1992). Student characteristics and writing apprehension. *Journalism Educator, 47,* 39–49.

upper-middle class American culture (Cleary et al., 1975; Goldman & Widawski, 1976; Jencks & Crouse, 1982). This controversy seems to miss the point. The purpose of the SAT is to *predict* college performance; this it does, albeit imperfectly. The test survives not because it *really* measures aptitude or, for that matter, because it *really* measures anything at all. It survives because students who score 1400 tend to do better in college than those who score 1100, who, in turn tend to do better than those who score 800, and so on. It has criterion-related validity.

Construct Validity

While criterion-related and content/face validity are fairly straightforward, construct validity is more difficult to grasp. **Construct validity**, Kerlinger (1973) writes, "bores into the essence of science ... it is concerned with the nature of reality and the nature of properties being measured" (p. 473). In brief, construct validity is concerned with *what* is being measured.

The "known-group" method is a commonly described way to establish construct validity (Shaw & Wright, 1967). Let us suppose that as the researcher, you are interested in a valid measure of extroversion-introversion. You develop a paper and pencil measure designed to assess this variable, which includes statements such as: "I am very talkative around other people." "In some group situations I speak up more than the average person." And, "I enjoy interacting with strangers." To the extent that people agree with these and related statements, they will be considered extroverted. To the extent they disagree, they will be categorized as introverts. But is the instrument valid? The known-group technique involves identifying groups of people known to exhibit whatever variable or concept you are interested in analyzing. Perhaps you have access to a group of students who live in a particular dorm. You could ask each to identify the five most introverted and the five most extroverted residents of the dorm. Residents who showed up on at least five of the students' lists might be labeled, accordingly, "highly extroverted" or "highly introverted." Then you could administer your instrument to the two groups. To the extent that the two groups differed on the measure as anticipated, the measure could be said to have construct validity.

Another way to establish construct validity involves showing that the variables being measured behave in theoretically expected ways in relation to other variables. For example,

■ ■ ■ ■ ■

MINI-PROJECT:

Remember the famous controversy over the Bush/Gore 2000 presidential election? First there were issues about the count in Florida, then there were issues about the "chads." There were "pregnant chads," "dimpled chads," etc. You may recall the picture of a man holding a ballot up to the light to check the chad. Then there were issues about absentee ballots. What other factors of the "measurement" process went wrong? How would you improve the reliability and the validity of this process?

you might hypothesize that trust of another person leads to increased levels of negative self-disclosure (bad things stated about oneself). Trust is an elusive concept and one that is difficult to measure. One way to provide evidence for the construct validity of your measure of trust would be to show that, as predicted by the theory, trust was related to negative self-disclosure. There also might be theoretical reasons for expecting trust not to be related to other variables. By demonstrating that these variables were not related to trust would provide evidence for the construct validity of the trust measure. In short, a pattern of findings that shows that relationships that are predicted by a theory are found, while other not-predicted relationships are not found, would be evidence for the construct validity of the measure. Box 6.1 demonstrates how a measure is created and its reliability and validity is determined.

THE RELATIONSHIP BETWEEN RELIABILITY AND VALIDITY

A good measure is both reliable and valid. However, reliability must be present or validity is impossible. Recall that a completely unreliable measure would not be measuring anything at all, so it obviously could not be measuring validly. Reliability is a necessary, although not sufficient condition for validity.

If you were interested in assessing people's attitudes toward a topic about which they had just received a persuasive appeal—armed air marshalls on airliners, for example—and you asked your respondents how many siblings they had, the result would likely be reliable, but invalid data. Someone who said he had two siblings would very likely give the same dependable, stable, consistent answer again and again, as would someone else who had none and someone else who had six siblings. But these numbers would not be indications of the respondents' views on armed air marshalls. To summarize, without measurement reliability, the researcher has measured nothing. But reliability by itself is equally useless unless, within the context of the purpose of a study, the measure is also valid.

Figure 6.2 suggests an analogy between the accuracy of a marksman firing a rifle at a target and the relationship between measurement reliability and validity.[1] A measure is valid to the extent that it consistently hits the target. In the case of target (a), the marksman shoots a random pattern of shots and therefore necessarily misses the target with most shots. He is not firing reliably, so his shooting is inaccurate, that is, not valid. In (b), his firing is reliable, the shots are grouped closely together, but he is missing the target, thus validity is absent. Finally, in (c), he is both firing consistently and hitting the target. This is analogous to a measure that is both reliable and valid.

APPLYING KNOWLEDGE IN COMMUNICATION

Why is it important for communication researchers to know the basics of measurement? Knowing what kind of measurement level you are working with helps us to better understand the kinds of conclusions being drawn by the researcher. Nominal and ordinal data provide classification, it puts people and things into groups that can be counted. In-

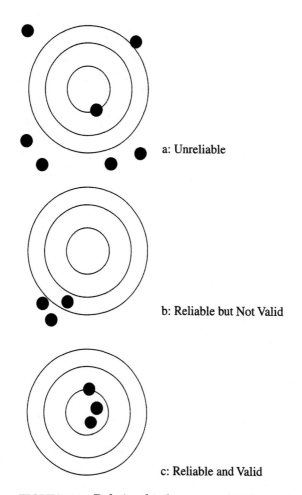

a: Unreliable

b: Reliable but Not Valid

c: Reliable and Valid

FIGURE 6.2   Relationship between reliability and validity.

terval and ratio data provides a more powerful and precise way of interpreting our findings. Later we will find that using interval and ratio data gives us powerful tools for data analysis. Interval data allows us precision not afforded by groupings, and ratio data is even more precise.

Understanding the related concepts of reliability and validity and how they are assessed allows us to measure a study's credibility. If we read of a study that found that the majority of people preferred a certain brand, and then found out that the measurement instrument used had a reliability of .65, we might question the findings and conclusions. The same is true with validity. The over-used examples of a clock set 10 minutes early to keep someone on time and the scale that weighs people in five pounds over the actual weight are both clearly reliable, they just are not valid measures of the *actual* time or weight. Considering that much of what you will read and do concerns things you cannot see (attitudes, beliefs, values) or things that we must operationally define to observe (what constitutes a multisyllable word or a "wry" smile?), validity becomes extremely important. Whether a measure has only face/content validity or it has withstood the tests of criterion-related and construct validity tells us much about not only the state of research but how theoretically developed the research is.

SUMMARY

By now you should realize that measurement is a complex, but doable, process when careful attention is paid to selecting measurement levels, and ensuring reliability and validity. We establish an instrument by which to measure objects through the specification of rules. We create our instrument to generate different types of data; it can be ordinal or nominal or it can be interval or ratio.

Measures can be assessed for their reliability and their validity. We have several methods available to assess reliability. We can look at internal consistency of items, we can break the test into subcomponents, or we can administer it to a group of people twice. In each case we will look for some indication of consistency, as indicated by statistical tests such as Cohen's *Kappa*, Scott's *pi*, *KR–20*, or coefficient alpha. What we get, however, is consistency; we still do not know if we are measuring what we think we are measuring.

Establishing validity is more problematic but no less important than establishing reliability. Of the types of validity examined, two (face or content) rely on judgments of whether a measure's content reflects what we say we are measuring. Criterion-related validity is established when the researcher demonstrates that the measure actually relates to something similar, such as a behavior or scores on a related measure. Finally, construct validity refers to the actual reflection of the measure being composed of items that reflect the measure; construct validity can be assessed through the "known group" method or by statistical tests such as factor analysis. We must weigh reliability and validity to assess our potential for contributions to error in our conclusions.

We turn next to creating the measuring instruments used in research. These instruments, in turn, are composed of scales, whose construction we will deal with in Chapter 7.

PROBES

1. Is measurement important to research? Why or why not? In answering this probe, take a variable of interest to you and create a measurement scheme that represents each of the four levels of measurement.

2. What is the tension between reliability and validity?

3. Can you think of a measure that is valid but not reliable? One that is reliable but not valid?

Look at ways a variable from your area of interest is measured and examine available evidence concerning its criterion-related validity, its content/face validity, and its construct validity. Are there any problems with this measure?

4. How would you approach a measurement for a study that was being conducted via the telephone? What levels of measurement would be most appropriate? Why?

5. What would you think of a study that reported as its reliability a coefficient of .73? Of .93? What does each tell you about sources of error?

RESEARCH PROJECTS

1. Obtain and read an article in a recent issue of a top journal such as *Communication Monographs* or *Human Communication Research*. Determine the measurement instruments used in the study (you may have to contact the authors—they should quickly provide them) and evaluate the reliability and validity of these measures. From a purely measurement theory perspective, review and criticize the use of measurement in communication research.

2. Conduct a study of research reliabilities reported in your particular area of communication. This will require that you read the "methods" sections of the articles, noting the measures used and their reported reliabilities. How many failed to report their reliabilities? How many relied on previous research reporting? What are the ramifications for neophyte researchers reading these studies?

3. Assume that you are interested in creating a new measure for a communication concept of interest. Operationally define it and determine what "kind" of data would produce the best measure.

4. Invent a measure of a communication variable and determine its face validity.

SUGGESTED READING

Emmert, P., & Barker, L. L. (Eds.). (1989). *Measurement of communication behavior*. New York: Longman.

Guilford, J. P. (1954). *Psychometric methods*. New York: McGraw-Hill.

Kerlinger, F. N. (1986). *Foundations of behavioral research*, 3rd ed. New York: Holt, Rinehart, and Winston.

Kirk, J., & Miller, M. L. (1986). *Reliability and validity in qualitative research*. Newbury Park, CA: Sage Publications.

Nunnally, J. (1978). *Psychometric theory*. New York: McGraw-Hill.

Shaw, M. E., & Wright, J. M. (1967). *Scales for the measurement of attitudes*. New York: McGraw-Hill.

Tardy, C. H. (Ed.). (1988). *A handbook for the study of human communication: Methods and instruments for observing, measuring and assessing communication processes*. Norwood, NJ: Ablex.

Torgerson, W. (1958). *Theory and methods of scaling*. New York: Wiley.

NOTE

1. This analogy was suggested by Kerlinger (1973).

REFERENCES

Bowers, J. W., & Cartwright, J. A. (1984). *Communication research methods*. Glenview, IL: Scott, Foresman.

Cleary, T. A., Humphreys, L. G., Kendrick, S. A., & Wesman, A. (1975). Educational uses of tests with disadvantaged students. *American Psychologist, 30*, 15–41.

Cohen, J. (1960). A coefficient for nominal scales. *Educational and Psychological Measurement, 20*, 37–46.

Cronbach, L. J. (1951). Coefficient alpha and the internal structure of tests. *Psychometrika, 16,* 297–334.

Goldman, R. D., & Widawski, M. D. (1976). An analysis of types of errors in the selection of minority college students. *Journal of Education Measurement, 13,* 185–200.

Jencks, C., & Crouse, J. (1982). Should we relabel the SAT or replace it? In W. Schrader (Ed.), *New directions for testing and measurement: Measurement, guidance, and program improvement.* San Francisco: Jossey-Bass.

Kerlinger, F. N. (1973). *Foundations of behavioral research,* 2nd ed. New York: Holt, Rinehart & Winston.

Krippendorf, K. (1980). *Content analysis: An introduction to its methodology.* Beverly Hills, CA: Sage.

Kuder, G. F., & Richardson, M. W. (1937). The theory of estimation test reliability. *Psychometrika, 2,* 151–160.

Riffe, D., & Stacks, D. W. (1988). Dimensions of writing apprehension across mass communication students. *Journalism Quarterly, 65,* 384–391.

Riffe, D., & Stacks, D. W. (1992). Student characteristics and writing apprehension. *Journalism Educator, 47,* 39–49.

Scott, W. A. (1969). A reliability of content analysis: The case of nominal scale coding. *Public Opinion Quarterly, 19,* 321–325.

Shaw, M. E., & Wright, J. M. (1967). *Scales for the measurement of attitudes.* New York: McGraw-Hill.

Singletary, M. (1994). *Mass communication research.* New York: Longman.

Stevens, S. S. (1951). Mathematics, measurement, and psychophysics. In S. Stevens (Ed.), *Handbook of experimental psychology.* New York: Wiley.

Tardy, C. H. (Ed.). (1988). *A handbook for the study of human communication: Methods and instruments for observing, measuring and assessing communication processes.* Norwood, NJ: Ablex.

Torgerson, W. (1958). *Theory and methods of scaling.* New York: Wiley.

Wimmer, R. D., & Dominick, J. R. (1994). *Mass media research: An introduction,* 4th ed. Belmont, CA: Wadsworth.

■ ■ ■ ■ ■

CHAPTER SEVEN

MEASURING INSTRUMENTS

MEASUREMENT

INTERVENING VARIABLES

TYPES OF MEASUREMENT SCALES
  Thurstone
  Likert-type
  Guttman
  Semantic Differential

Thermometer
Multidimensional Scaling

OTHER MEASUREMENT TECHNIQUES
  Open-Ended Questions
  Unobtrusive Measures

APPLYING KNOWLEDGE IN COMMUNICATION

OBJECTIVES

By the end of this chapter you should be able to:

1. Discuss how measurement scales are used in communication research.
2. Identify and explain the differences between different kinds of measurement scales.
3. Construct a Thurstone, Guttman, Likert-type, semantic differential, thermometer, and multi-dimensional scale.
4. Discuss the controversy found in using "equal appearing interval scales" as true interval-level measures.
5. Discuss other measurement techniques used in communication research, such as unobtrusive measures and open-ended questions.

In Chapter 6 we learned about measurement in general and some of the different ways that we can systematically collect observations. In this chapter we explore how to create measurement **instruments**. A scale is a form of measurement composed of items that reflect some underlying concept and may range from a single item to hundreds of items. Social scientists in general, and communication researchers in particular, are interested in explaining and predicting human *behavior*. That is why they are sometimes called *behavioral scientists*. Behavior is overt. It can be observed directly. However, although this is true in principle, in practice many behaviors are extremely difficult to observe and require a different kind of "observation."

Consider the following research questions:

Does exposure to pornography increase spousal abuse?

Are speeches that use fear appeal messages more likely to affect teenage sexual practices than ones that do not?

Do presidential debates contribute to voting decisions?

Is a particular compliance-gaining strategy more effective than another?

Is one relationship-disengagement strategy more effective at minimizing depression and suicide of the partner than another?

Does violence observed in the media contribute to violence in society?

All of these are important research questions about the effects of communication. The independent variable in each of the examples is *communication*. The dependent variable (the thing the researcher believes to be affected by the independent variable) is, in each case, the receivers' *behavior*. Unfortunately, the affected behaviors may be very difficult to observe. Spousal abuse, voting, sexual practices, compliance with requests, suicides, and many other important variables occur in private, or, if they do occur in public, you are not likely to be there to observe them. This difficulty in assessing the effect of various messages on behaviors is alleviated by constructing **intervening variables** to account for internal psychological processes that, in turn, account for overt (observable) behaviors.

EXAMPLES OF INTERVENING VARIABLES

An *attitude* is a common example of an intervening variable. An attitude is a "relatively enduring predisposition to respond favorably or unfavorably to an attitude object" (Simons, 1976, p. 80). As predispositions, attitudes exist in people's minds and cannot be observed directly. Their existence must be inferred, usually from responses to **attitude scales**. Thus, researchers construct the variable—attitude—to intervene between a stimulus—exposure to a message of some type or form—and a response—sexual behavior, spouse abuse, voting, suicide, compliance, and so on. As the researcher, you presume that the message does not have a direct effect on these behaviors, but rather it influences receiver attitudes (or some other internal state) which, in turn, influences behavior.

The most common way intervening variables such as attitudes are measured in communication research is through the use of *measurement scales*. Scales are generally used on questionnaires, which respondents complete either as part of a survey or after receiving some type of experimental stimulus. Scales also can be used in face-to-face interviews and, with more difficulty, in telephone interviews. Measuring a variable via a scale technique often involves the placing of a mark somewhere along a linear continuum. Numbers are then assigned systematically (according to rules) to points along the line that composes the scale. Responses to such scales are assumed to be indications of the internal psychological states of the participant. Such scales are assumed to provide interval data; they assume that distances between assigned numbers are an equal distance apart. The difference between a one and a three is assumed to be the same as between three and five, and so on.

The scales described here are frequently constructed according to detailed procedures and pilot-tested, that is, tried out, prior to use in the actual research. A **pilot test** is a preliminary data-gathering effort whose purpose is to examine the research procedures, including the measures used, in order to correct any problems before the full study is conducted. If confusing scale items are present, the pilot test allows them to be identified and changed before investing time in flawed data-gathering procedures. When conducting pilot tests, whether testing the efficacy of an experimental manipulation or the clarity of the measurement procedures, participants and circumstances under which the test is conducted should be as similar as possible to those that will exist during the actual research. If, for example, the people who participate in the actual research will do so in a classroom setting, the individuals who participate in the pilot test should also be in a similar classroom setting. A pilot test helps the researcher to eliminate potential sources of application and instrumentation error (see Chapter 6).

All the scales described here, if constructed carefully and used properly, can be reliable and valid measures of variables in communication research. We turn now to four popular types of measurement scales.

TYPES OF MEASUREMENT SCALES

Thurstone Scales

It would be hard to overemphasize the contributions of Louis Leon Thurstone to the development of measurement theory in general, and attitude measurement in particular. The main technique associated with Thurstone is also called the **equal appearing interval** scale (Thurstone & Chave, 1929). The Thurstone scale has predefined values associated with each statement. As might be expected, these scales can be a little more difficult to construct than others created via other techniques.

Constructing a Thurstone scale involves at least five steps:

1. Create a large number (100 or more) of positive *and* negative statements about the object to be evaluated.
2. Have the statements, the scale *items*, sorted by a number of judges (usually twenty to thirty people) into eleven piles, which represent categories of similar items that appear to your judges to be equally distinct from one another. The categories are assigned numbers from 1, Very Unfavorable, to 11, Very Favorable. For each statement an average is calculated based on the categories to which the judges have assigned it. So, for example, a statement that was assigned to category 8 by all the judges would have a value of 8. One that was assigned exclusively to category 11 would have a score of 11. One that was assigned by half of the judges to category 1 and by the other half to category 2 would be assigned a 1.5, and so on.

3. Calculate the degree to which the judges are in agreement with their category assignment. Items about which the judges agree are desirable. It would make little sense to choose an item that some judges placed in category 1 or 2, while other judges thought it was moderately favorable and placed it in category 6 or 7.
4. Choose a small number of items, usually twenty to thirty, that appear to best represent the measure.
5. The items that have high judge agreement (judgments correlated highly with one another) and that represent *all* points—unfavorable to favorable—along the 11-point continuum are selected and reproduced.

Examples of Thurstone items appear in Box 7.1. You would ask each respondent to indicate with which statements he or she agreed. The scale in Box 7.1 was designed to measure attitudes toward any school subject (Silance & Remmers, 1934, as cited in Shaw & Write, 1987). We have taken writer's license and substituted a communication research methods course as the subject being evaluated. (Note, the scale values for each item, which are shown in parentheses, would not appear on the actual scale.) Your participants would be instructed to select the items with which he or she agrees. Each person's score is the average of the scale values with which he or she agrees. As can be seen, each participant should agree with a large number of scales, all of which have similar values. When respondants agree with a large number of items, they validate the scale.

Thurstone scales are time-consuming to construct and for this reason they are used much less frequently than semantic differential or Likert-type scales. However, there are many extant Thurstone-type scales that have already been constructed and validated.[1]

BOX 7.1
THURSTONE SCALES

1. The very existence of humanity depends upon this communication research methods course. (10.3)
2. Communication research methods is one subject that all Americans should know. (9.4)
3. All of our great men (and women) studied communication research methods. (8.4).
4. Communication research methods is not receiving its due in public schools. (7.6)
5. Communication research methods might be worthwhile if it were taught right. (6.0)
6. Communication research methods is all right, but I would not take any more of it. (4.7)
7. Communication research methods reminds me of Shakespeare's play, *Much Ado About Nothing*. (2.6)
8. Communication research methods is more like a plague than a study. (1.3)
9. Words cannot express my antagonism for communication research methods. (1.0)

MINI-PROJECT:

List ten communication concepts that you believe cannot be observed. For each list an intervening variable (construct). Indicate how you might measure each intervening variable.

Likert-type Scales

Likert-type scales are another commonly used measurement technique. Named for their developer, Rensis Likert (1932), they are also called **summated rating** scales. Likert-type items are statements that yield responses that range from favorable to unfavorable toward an object (the object could be anything—a person, a rock 'n' roll band, an abstract concept, a public policy, etc.). The respondent is presented with a series of these statements and indicates his or her degree of agreement or disagreement with each. It is important to note that a *neutral point* must be provided, usually termed "Uncertain," "Undecided," or "Neither Agree nor Disagree." The most appropriate neutral point, however, is the last; "Neither Agree nor Disagree" is more descriptive of the midpoint than "Uncertain" or "Undecided," which may connote a different meaning. All, however, are found in the research literature.

Creating a Likert-type scale involves three stages:

1. Generate a large number of favorable and unfavorable statements about the object of interest.
2. Pilot test these items on people who are asked to indicate their degree of agreement or disagreement with each statement along a 5- (or sometimes 7-) point continuum. For favorable statements about the object in question, a Strongly Disagree might be scored 1; Disagree, 2; Neither Agree nor Disagree, 3; Agree, 4; and Strongly Agree, 5. The scoring is reversed for unfavorable statements (i.e., 5 = 1, 4 = 2, 3 = 3, 2 = 4, 1 = 5). Each of the respondent's answers are *summed* to produce a composite score.
3. Select a smaller number of items as being representative of the measure for administration; these are the responses that tend to agree with an individual respondent's overall score.

Thus, if your overall score indicates that you are unfavorable toward the object, items would be selected that also indicated this unfavorable attitude. Figure 7.1(a) provides examples of Likert-type items designed to measure attitudes toward dating (Bardis, 1962). Figure 7.1(b) presents an alternative way to present the same scales. Both are assumed to be equally reliable and valid. Box 7.2 presents an alternative way of presenting Likert-type statements to participants.

Likert-type scales are composed of a number of subdimensions. In writing the actual scale items you try to create items that reflect the most unfavorable to the most favorable statements you can think of regarding the **attitude object**. A problem with Likert-type scales comes when a statement contains information that could be responded to in more

(a)

Is it all right to kiss on the first date

Strongly Disagree	Disagree	Neither Agree nor Disagree	Agree	Strongly Agree

Girls should be allowed to ask boys for dates

Strongly Disagree	Disagree	Neither Agree nor Disagree	Agree	Strongly Agree

It is all right for dating partners to talk about sex

Strongly Disagree	Disagree	Neither Agree nor Disagree	Agree	Strongly Agree

Dating couples between 18 and 20 should be allowed to stay out as long as they wish

Strongly Disagree	Disagree	Neither Agree nor Disagree	Agree	Strongly Agree

It is *not* all right for a girl to invite a boy to her home when no one is there

Strongly Disagree	Disagree	Neither Agree nor Disagree	Agree	Strongly Agree

Young people should make love as much as they wish on a date

Strongly Disagree	Disagree	Neither Agree nor Disagree	Agree	Strongly Agree

(b)

SD = Strongly Disagree
D = Disagree
N = Neither Agree nor Disagree
A = Agree
SA = Strongly Agree

Place a check opposite each of the following statements to indicate your degree of agreement or disagreement.

	SA	A	N	D	SD
It is all right to kiss on the first date.	[ ]	[ ]	[ ]	[ ]	[ ]
Girls should be allowed to ask boys for dates.	[ ]	[ ]	[ ]	[ ]	[ ]
It is all right for dating partners to talk about sex.	[ ]	[ ]	[ ]	[ ]	[ ]
Dating couples between 18 and 20 should be allowed to stay out as long as they wish.	[ ]	[ ]	[ ]	[ ]	[ ]
It is *not* all right for a girl to invite a boy to her home when no one is there.	[ ]	[ ]	[ ]	[ ]	[ ]
Young people should make love as much as they wish on a date.	[ ]	[ ]	[ ]	[ ]	[ ]

FIGURE 7.1 Likert-type scale. Two Likert-type scales on (a) attitudes toward dating and (b) an alternate presentation of the same scale.

153

than one way or asks for two or more judgments in one statement (is "double-barreled"). Likert-type statements are simple statements, like "I love to write," "I'm afraid to speak in front of groups," and "The speaker was very persuasive." Statements such as "I'm afraid of the HIV virus and syphilis" ask the respondent to react to two objects—both negative—but we do not know which the response was for.

■ ■ ■ ■ ■

BOX 7.2
LIKERT-TYPE SCALE

Instructions: This instrument is composed of 24 statements concerning your feelings about communication with other people. Please indicate in the space provided the degree to which each statement applies to you by marking whether you (1) Strongly Agree, (2) Agree, (3) Are undecided, (4) Disagree, or (5) Strongly Disagree with each statement. There are no right or wrong answers. Many of these statements are similar to other statements. Do not be concerned about this. Work quickly, just record your first impression.

___ 1. I dislike participating in group discussions.
___ 2. Generally, I am comfortable while participating in a group discussion.
___ 3. I am tense and nervous while participating in group discussions.
___ 4. I like to get involved in group discussions.
___ 5. Engaging in a group discussion with new people makes me tense and nervous.
___ 6. I am calm and relaxed while participating in group discussions.
___ 7. Generally, I am nervous when I have to participate in a meeting.
___ 8. Usually, I am calm and relaxed while participating in meetings.
___ 9. I am very calm and relaxed when I am called upon to express an opinion at a meeting.
___ 10. I am afraid to express myself at meetings.
___ 11. Communicating at meetings usually makes me uncomfortable.
___ 12. I am very relaxed when answering questions at a meeting.
___ 13. While participating in a conversation with a new acquaintance, I feel very nervous.
___ 14. I have no fear of speaking up in conversations.
___ 15. Ordinarily I am very tense and nervous in conversations.
___ 16. Ordinarily I am very calm and relaxed in conversations.
___ 17. While conversing with a new acquaintance, I feel very relaxed.
___ 18. I'm afraid to speak up in conversations.
___ 19. I have no fear of giving a speech.
___ 20. Certain parts of my body feel very tense and rigid while giving a speech.
___ 21. I feel relaxed while giving a speech.
___ 22. My thoughts become confused and jumbled when I am giving a speech.
___ 23. I face the prospect of giving a speech with confidence.
___ 24. While giving a speech I get so nervous, I forget facts I really know.

Once you have your Likert-type scale you have to assess its construct validity. This is frequently done by submitting the pilot-tested measure to **factor analysis**, a technique briefly noted in Chapter 6 and explained later in this chapter. Factor analysis is a tool available on most advanced statistical packages (SPSS, SAS) used by communication researchers and has been available for the personal computer for a number of years. Simply put, factor analysis looks for items in common with each other (items that correlate highly).[2] If, for example, more than one "factor" (dimension) is found, then the scale measures more than one thing. Riffe and Stacks (1988, 1992), for instance, found multiple factors, while Daly and Miller (1975) found only one factor for writing apprehension.[3] For each dimension found in factor analysis, a number of "item loadings" are obtained. The item loadings are the actual scale items. Interpretation is subjective, but most researchers follow three simple rules:

1. To be considered for further analysis, a group of items must contribute significant amounts of variance explained (usually determined by a cutoff on a statistic called "Eigenvalue" of 1.0 or higher).
2. For a factor to be retained, at least two scale items must "load" on a factor.
3. For an item to "load" on a factor, its minimal item coefficient is set (usually ±.60, but the sign makes no difference) and it must not appear on any other factor with a loading greater than ±.40 (it must load "cleanly").

Box 7.3 presents a typical factor analysis solution for a Likert-type scale of nineteen items designed to measure audience perceptions of a convention panel conducted by one of the authors. The highlighted scores represent interpretable items that "loaded" on each of the dimensions. A more conceptual discussion of factor analysis can be found on page 158, where semantic differential scales are discussed.

■ ■ ■ ■ ■

BOX 7.3
SAMPLE FACTOR ANALYSIS—SPSS BASE
FINAL STATISTICS

VARIABLE*	COMMONALITY	FACTOR	EIGENVALUE	PCT OF VAR	CUM PCT
V1	.7343	1	6.4571	34.0	34.0
V2	.6797	2	1.5307	8.1	42.0
V3	.5497	3	1.3958	7.3	49.4
V4	.5762	4	1.2253	6.4	55.8
V5	.6350	5	1.1100	5.8	61.7
V6	.7523				

(continued)

BOX 7.3   CONTINUED

VARIABLE*	COMMONALITY	FACTOR	EIGENVALUE	PCT OF VAR	CUM PCT
V7	.6357				
V8	.5641				
V9	.6193				
V10	.5641				
V11	.6733				
V12	.5543				
V13	.4751				
V14	.6019				
V15	.6844				
V16	.4114				
V17	.6685				
V18	.4400				
V19	.7586				

VARIABLE	F1	F2	F3	F4	F5
V1	.830	.170	.124	−.003	.023
V2	.365	−.042	.730	.062	−.081
V3	.399	.384	.455	.031	.175
V4	.664	.216	.112	.248	.114
V5	.056	.214	.670	.307	.203
V6	.138	.218	.820	.088	.064
V7	.717	.110	.178	.263	−.089
V8	.344	.312	.386	.445	−.002
V9	.140	.589	.231	.442	.057
V10	.134	.149	.204	.740	.207
V11	.079	.088	.163	.740	−.201
V12	.599	.218	−.226	.791	−.210
V13	.028	.598	.120	−.227	.304
V14	.469	.533	.210	.097	.123
V15	.625	.468	.237	.193	.118
V16	.264	.243	−.029	.050	.519
V17	.123	.805	.067	.107	−.017
V18	−.309	.030	.085	−.003	−.218
V19	−.032	.061	.146	−.537	.855

* Scale item

Two additional points must be made at this time. First, Likert-type scales are *summated ratings*, that is, there must be more than one item to sum. They were not meant to be used in isolation. Second, there is a controversy as to whether Likert-type scales are truly interval scales or are actually ordinal scales. The argument for ordinal measurement suggests that participants do not respond to a continuum from favorable to unfavorable, but to the actual categories. The argument for interval measurement argues that the scale items are responded to on an equal appearing interval scale of favorable to unfavorable. Kerlinger (1973) argues that this controversy is a tempest in a teapot, but goes on to note that, "Still, we are faced with a dilemma: if we use the ordinal measures as if they are interval or ratio measures, we *can* err in interpreting the data and the relations inferred from the data, though the danger is probably not as grave as it has been made out to be" (p. 440).

Guttman Scales

While Likert-type scales may be multidimensional, that is, measuring several subcomponents of a larger construct, the Guttman (1944) or *cumulative* scale or **scalogram** is unidimensional; that is, it measures one and only one variable. The Guttman scale is a series of statements that reflect the strength of attitudes toward some object. Respondents check or circle the statements they agree with and each is ranked to determine the most likely responses.

Consider a person's attitude toward nuclear power. You want to assess the degree to which they are committed to doing something about it. You would have them circle items they would consider doing from the following list:

1. sign a petition
2. write a congressperson
3. march in a protest parade
4. hand out flyers in class
5. go to a site and protest

Although used often in the social sciences, Guttman scales are not used very much in communication research. There may be times when a Guttman scale meets your needs for assessing strength of attitudinal commitment or behaviors.

■ ■ ■ ■ ■

MINI-PROJECT:

You have been asked by the CEO of a local organization to create a measure of job satisfaction. Create a Likert-type scale that will measure "job satisfaction." (Remember: you must operationally define "job satisfaction.")

Semantic Differential

The *semantic differential scale* is a general scaling technique for measuring the meaning that a person, place, or thing has for an individual. Developed by Osgood, Suci, and Tannenbaum (1957), the semantic differential has been widely used in communication research. Osgood's technique is based on the notion of **semantic space**, the idea that people evaluate objects along spatial continua. Using the technique involves placing the name of the object at the top of a series of 7-point scales anchored by bipolar adjectives or adverbs. The respondent then places a check at the point along each scale that reflects his or her judgment about the object. For example, the following scales might be used to measure your view of your instructor.

My Instructor

Informed	___	:	:	:	:	:	Uninformed
Unfair	___	:	:	:	:	:	Fair
Prepared	___	:	:	:	:	:	Unprepared

Using factor analysis to determine if responses to a relatively large number of different scales (usually ten or more) will result in a smaller number of underlying dimensions or factors. Osgood concluded that people evaluate objects along three general dimensions of meaning—activity, potency, and evaluation (see Figure 7.2).

The evaluation dimension has proved especially useful to communication researchers as it generally measures attitudes—predispositions to *behave* favorably or unfavorably toward attitude objects. Thus, we often use these scales as measures of attitudes because they are assumed to be predictors of behaviors that we can measure. Thus, assessing the effects of measures of attitudes is an important technique. The evaluation scales are anchored by items such as Valuable-Worthless, Honest-Dishonest, and Good-Bad. Typically, several

FIGURE 7.2 Semantic differential scales.

Evaluation:
Good	___	:	:	:	:	:	Bad
Beautiful	___	:	:	:	:	:	Ugly
Clean	___	:	:	:	:	:	Dirty

Potency:
Large	___	:	:	:	:	:	Small
Heavy	___	:	:	:	:	:	Light
Strong	___	:	:	:	:	:	Weak

Activity:
Active	___	:	:	:	:	:	Passive
Sharp	___	:	:	:	:	:	Dull
Fast	___	:	:	:	:	:	Slow

Semantic differential scales.

items are used to measure the meaning that an object holds for an individual. If the scales are all measuring the same underlying dimension, as already noted, multiple measures increase the reliability with which it is measured. The scale items are usually scored by assigning a 1 if the respondent marks the line next to the negative side of the scale, a 2 if the next line over is marked, and so on, up to 7, if the space next to the positive side of the scale is marked, as in the example:

My Instructor

Good	X :	:	:	:	:	Bad
Worthless	:	:	:	:	: X :	Valuable
Honest	:	: X :	:	:	:	Dishonest

These items would be scored 7, 6, 5 (good, valuable, honest), or total score 18, or 6.0 (18 ÷ 3 items) out of 7. Note that the items have been reversed so that a **response set**, a pattern the respondent might get into based on simply marking down one side or the middle, is less likely to be induced. The reversal of items also provides an indication when people simply "fill out" the scales rather than thinking about how each item relates to the object.

One of the most widely cited uses of the semantic differential is that of David Berlo and associates (e.g., Berlo, Lemert, & Mertz, 1967; McCroskey, 1966). These researchers administered hundreds of semantic differential scales to people and asked them to evaluate the credibility of message sources (see Box 7.4). Berlo et al. found three independent subcomponents of source credibility: trustworthiness (sometimes called character), expertise (also called authority), and dynamism (Cronkhite & Liska, 1976). Trustworthiness is measured by scale items anchored by such adjectives as Honest-Dishonest and Trustworthy-Untrustworthy. Expertise is measured with scale items anchored by adjectives such as Wise-Foolish and Knowledgeable-Not Knowledgeable, whereas dynamism is measured by scale items such as Interesting-Dull and Active-Passive. Each of these dimensions of source credibility is *independent*. That is, a source evaluated as being high on one dimension could be low on another or high on one and high on another.

For example, suppose that you were interested in the concept of presidential credibility. You might use Berlo's semantic differential scales and, depending on your research question, measure presidential credibility in general or the credibility of certain specific presidents. Imagine, for example, that you are interested in the credibility of the current president. You administer your measure to a group of people, compute the various "scores," and find that the president was viewed as highly trustworthy—he was viewed as an honest person who would not knowingly lie—but low on expertise—he is not knowledgeable about as many areas as he should be. The current president, on the other hand, was perceived by your participants as high in expertise—he is a smart man who knows a lot—but low in trustworthiness—he might very well lie to you. Hence, the independence of the scales allows for multiple interpretations.

When measures are added to form a composite score, as we just did, it is extremely important that they be measures of the same thing. Thus, only measures of the expertise dimension of source credibility should be added together. If the scales measuring trustworthiness, for example, were added to the expertise scales, to the extent that individual

BOX 7.4

SAMPLE SEMANTIC DIFFERENTIAL SCALES

SCALES USED TO MEASURE IDEAL AND ACTUAL SELF CONCEPT AS A WRITER

INSTRUCTIONS: Please rate **YOURSELF** as a *WRITER* on the following 12 scales. The closer your mark is to one of the two terms, the more you feel that term applies to you. Please make sure that you have marked *each* scale.

Wise	_____ : _____ : _____ : _____ : _____ : _____ _____	Foolish
Unimportant	_____ : _____ : _____ : _____ : _____ : _____ _____	Important
Interesting	_____ : _____ : _____ : _____ : _____ : _____ _____	Uninteresting
Forceful	_____ : _____ : _____ : _____ : _____ : _____ _____	Forceless
Bad	_____ : _____ : _____ : _____ : _____ : _____ _____	Good
Successful	_____ : _____ : _____ : _____ : _____ : _____ _____	Unsuccessful
Pleasant	_____ : _____ : _____ : _____ : _____ : _____ _____	Unpleasant
Safe	_____ : _____ : _____ : _____ : _____ : _____ _____	Dangerous
Crude	_____ : _____ : _____ : _____ : _____ : _____ _____	Gracious
Authoritative	_____ : _____ : _____ : _____ : _____ : _____ _____	Unauthoritative
Strong	_____ : _____ : _____ : _____ : _____ : _____ _____	Weak
Timid	_____ : _____ : _____ : _____ : _____ : _____ _____	Bold

INSTRUCTIONS: Please rate how you **WOULD LIKE TO BE** as a *WRITER* in the following 12 scales. The closer your mark is to one of the two terms, the more you feel that term applies to you. Please make sure that you have marked *each* scale.

Wise	_____ : _____ : _____ : _____ : _____ : _____ _____	Foolish
Unimportant	_____ : _____ : _____ : _____ : _____ : _____ _____	Important
Interesting	_____ : _____ : _____ : _____ : _____ : _____ _____	Uninteresting
Forceful	_____ : _____ : _____ : _____ : _____ : _____ _____	Forceless
Bad	_____ : _____ : _____ : _____ : _____ : _____ _____	Good
Successful	_____ : _____ : _____ : _____ : _____ : _____ _____	Unsuccessful
Pleasant	_____ : _____ : _____ : _____ : _____ : _____ _____	Unpleasant
Safe	_____ : _____ : _____ : _____ : _____ : _____ _____	Dangerous
Crude	_____ : _____ : _____ : _____ : _____ : _____ _____	Gracious
Authoritative	_____ : _____ : _____ : _____ : _____ : _____ _____	Unauthoritative
Strong	_____ : _____ : _____ : _____ : _____ : _____ _____	Weak
Timid	_____ : _____ : _____ : _____ : _____ : _____ _____	Bold

respondents had different evaluations of the expertise and trustworthiness of the president as a source, reliability and validity would be reduced. For this reason, like the Likert-type scales, factor analysis is frequently performed on the responses to scales before any substantive analysis is performed. (These scales form factors or dimensions that can be safely *added* to form a composite score.) Thus, those scales that are measuring the same underlying dimensions can be added together to increase measurement reliability.

Thermometer Scaling

Sometimes it is easier to present a scale graphically. The University of Michigan Survey Research Center developed a special scale for "feelings." The scale, in the design of a thermometer asks responsondents to indicate their degree of like or dislike, favorableness or unfavorableness, agreement or disagreement on a 0 to 100 degree scale (Wimmer & Dominick, 1994). Thus, the scale provides ratio-level measurement. This type of scale is used most often in advertising and public relations.

The use of graphically oriented measures is not limited to thermometers. Measurement with children or with impaired people often uses happy faces, sad faces, and neutral faces in an attempt to measure attitudes with those populations. Pressner (1978), for example, used happy to sad faces in a study examining how patients related to their therapists.

Multidimensional Scaling

Multidimensional scaling (MDS) is a complex but valuable communication research technique. Its usefulness has been demonstrated in the communication discipline primarily by Joseph Woelfel and Edward L. Fink (1980; Fink, Robinson, & Dowden, 1985; Saltiel & Woefel, 1975). The basic assumption of this technique is that we can draw an analogy between a *physical* space and distances and a similar space and distances in our *minds*. In this way the technique is similar to Osgood's notion of semantic space. However, unlike semantic space, which is limited to seven units of length, objects in the "multidimensional space" of our minds can be *any* distance apart—from zero to any number. Just as we know that it is about 2500 miles from Chicago to Los Angeles, we also might know that it is about 188 mental units from new wave rock music to country and western music. MDS assumes that all evaluations are interrelated. For example, it assumes that our view of "World Peace" is a complex idea that involves our attitudes on, say, democracy, the Pentagon, poverty, oil, ethnicity, the U.S. flag, young soldiers, and so on and so forth, all of which are interrelated.

MDS uses information about how similar or how different certain objects are perceived to be; it then places the objects in a spatial relationship to one another. Respondents are given a list of objects and asked to make judgments about how different or similar they are. In making this request, the researcher provides respondents with an arbitrary psychological yardstick to apply in making their judgments about the distance between the objects. The yardstick is of the form: If Object A and Object B are X units apart, how far apart are Object C and Object X? So, for example, a researcher who was studying an election might assess perceptions of the distance between the following five objects: (1) personal voting intentions; (2) a political candidate; (3) arms control; (4) the federal deficit; and (5) inflation.

To do so, the researcher might provide the following yardstick for respondents:

If the President and the leader of the opposition party are 100 political inches apart, how far apart are:

Then, as shown in Figure 7.3, each respondent would be asked to compare each of the objects with each of the others. For instance:

Inflation and the president   *36*
The federal deficit and the president   *166*
Arms control and the federal deficit   *54*
Arms control and the president   *44*
Inflation and the federal deficit   *101*
Arms control and inflation   *86*
The president and my vote   *39*
Arms control and my vote   *5*
Inflation and my vote   *200*
The federal deficit and my vote   *452*

To compare each of the objects with all other objects, the respondent is required to make $[n(n - 1)]/2$ different judgments, where n is the number of objects being judged. In

FIGURE 7.3   Hypothetical multidimensional scale.

If the president and your governor are 100 "political inches" apart, how far apart are:

Inflation and the governor   _____
The federal deficit and the governor   _____
Arms control and the federal deficit   _____
Arms control and the president   _____
Inflation and the federal deficit   _____
Arms control and inflation   _____
The president and my vote   _____
Arms control and my vote   _____
Inflation and my vote   _____

MINI-PROJECT:

Create a measurement instrument that will access elementary school students' perceptions of a planned bicycle safety program.

our example there are five objects, thus ten $[5(5 - 1)] \div 2 = 10$ judgments are required. Ten objects would require forty-five judgments.

Using special statistical techniques developed for this type of scaling technique, respondents' perceptions of the objects' distances from one another can be "plotted" in hypothetical space. The procedure is designed so that the distance between any two objects approximates the average distance between the two objects indicated by the entire group of respondents. Thus, the plot results in an approximation of the *relationship* of each of the objects to every other object in hypothetical multidimensional space for the group as a whole.

The value of the technique lies in its potential for assessing cognitive *changes* that result from receiving messages. This tells the researcher what concepts are close together in cognitive space and which are not. By administering the MDS questions before *and* after messages are received, for instance, changes in spatial relationships between the objects can be plotted.

In the example, "my vote" is presumed to represent voting intention and the closer a candidate is to "my vote," the more likely the candidate will be to receive the respondent's vote. Similarly, the closer the candidate is to issues that are also close to the concept, "my vote," the more favorable the voter is presumed to be toward the candidate. Conversely, if the candidate is perceived to be close to issues that the respondents collectively view as a great distance from their vote, the candidate would be well advised to generate messages that would move him or her away from that issue and toward "my vote."

Table 7.1 shows data resulting from a hypothetical administration of the MDS questionnaire shown in Figure 7.3. Respondents might collectively indicate that "arms control" was an average of 7 "political inches" from their vote, whereas the federal deficit was 426 inches from their vote. These responses would be interpreted as meaning that this particular group was much more favorable to the concept "arms control" than they were to the "federal deficit." The president would be well advised to generate messages that would move him toward identification with arms control and away from the federal deficit. In fact, MDS has been used to advise political candidates about the nature of campaign messages to generate to move the candidate closer to "my vote" (Barnett, Serota, & Taylor, 1976). Changes following the receipt of messages could be assessed by administering the MDS questionnaire a second time and comparing the results.

TABLE 7.1   Multidimensional Scaling Distance Matrices

	1	2	3	4	5
1. Arms control	—				
2. Inflation	55	—			
3. The president	37	16	—		
4. My vote	07	189	46	—	
5. Federal deficit	29	64	132	426	—

MDS has several disadvantages associated with its use. Large groups of people, usually of at least 100 people, and frequently many more, may be required to ensure that the results will be reliable. Additionally, as the number of objects being compared increases, the number of comparisons required of respondents increases dramatically. Thus, MDS questionnaires are typically tedious and time-consuming to fill out; hence, respondent motivation is often difficult to maintain. Nonetheless, MDS has been shown to be a viable measurement technique that in some research applications can be superior to more traditional scaling techniques. Its use will likely increase in the future.

OTHER MEASUREMENT TECHNIQUES

There are other measurement techniques that may be used in collecting data. These techniques, however, are often more ambiguous than those discussed earlier and the researcher must be concerned with the reliability and validity of each.

Open-Ended Questions

Scales provide respondents with a set of categories from which to select a response. Open-ended questions differ in that no such predetermined response options are provided. Rather, the respondent is free to provide whatever responses he or she chooses. Open-ended questions may be used in either face-to-face or telephone interviews (discussed in detail in Chapters 9 and 11), or on self-administered questionnaires. Examples of open-ended questions include, "How do you feel about the job the president is doing these days?" and "In what way have the revelations about the use of assault weapons by drug dealers affected your perceptions of gun control laws?"

Open-ended questions can be extremely useful. They allow the researcher the potential to identify respondent views that may not have been anticipated when the questionnaire was designed. They also offer the opportunity for more in-depth responses. Thus, open-ended questions are especially useful in providing qualitative data that may supplement that provided by participant observation, telephone or mail surveys, or face-to-face interviews. Open-ended questions are the staple of "focus groups" (see Chapter 9). A focus group is a group "interview" in which the researcher uses open-ended questions and follow-up questions (*probes*) to stimulate a controlled discussion among a small group of respondents. Focus groups are frequently used as a preliminary research step from which qualitative information is gathered to help design a subsequent quantitative study.

During interviews or on self-administered questionnaires, a few open-ended questions also can help increase rapport with the respondent, who may feel frustrated by having to answer a long series of closed-ended scaled responses that do not always fit what he or she wants to say.

Open-ended questions often provide information about important things that you, as the researcher, cannot or did not think of in creating your measure. They can also provide important information about perceptions. For instance, one of your authors conducted a survey for a local television station during a county election. As part of the questionnaire, he employed two sets of open-ended questions used often in political research.

He asked respondents to think about and then list four things they liked about each candidate and then to think about and list four things they disliked about each candidate (there were four candidates). Interviewers were instructed to probe for responses if necessary. The information was then content analyzed (see Chapter 8). Based on that analysis he was able to extend the findings of the closed-ended questions employed and, through more sophisticated analyses, use the data to successfully predict the order of finish one month prior to the election.

Open-ended questions, however, have several disadvantages and should be used sparingly in most research projects. First, they are time-consuming to gather and to interpret. Long irrelevant answers are not uncommon. Second, it is often difficult to reliably code (assign numbers to) the answers. In effect, open-ended responses frequently need to be content analyzed, a measurement discussed in detail in Chapter 8. Further, as with other self-report measurement techniques, there is always the danger of a respondent telling you what he or she thinks you want to hear, or give you a desirable answer. One way to avoid some of these pitfalls is to use unobtrusive measures.

Unobtrusive Measures

Research participants are almost always aware that they are being studied. Sometimes this awareness becomes manifest in an effort to help the researcher—to behave in ways you believe the researcher wants you to behave, to answer questions in ways you believe the researcher wants them to be answered. The phrase **demand cues**, has been coined to describe the sometimes subtle, unconscious cues that the researcher may emit to let the participant know what the researcher wants to find. These cues "demand" of the participant certain behaviors, certain responses (Rosenthal & Rosnow, 1969). These can be as subtle as wearing a tie. Merely knowing that research is taking place has been shown to affect respondent behavior. The term *Hawthorne effect* (Mayo, 1933) refers to this well-known phenomenon.[4] In a series of research studies at Western Electric in the 1920s, researchers were looking for ways to increase productivity. They increased plant lighting and production went up. They piped in music and production went up. In fact, for everything they did, production increased. So they reduced lighting to its previous level; production went up again! The workers were responding to the fact that they were part of a research project. Apparently they were stimulated by this knowledge and worked harder and harder, but the variable that explained this was not lighting or music—it was researcher presence. Thus, the novelty of being studied has the potential to change behavior in and of itself.

MINI-PROJECT:

You have been asked to measure student readability and attitudes toward your campus newspaper. Create a measurement instrument that will do both. (Make sure that it covers all the relevant features and columns as well as what the students like the most and why they like or dislike them.)

In their highly influential book on unobtrusive measures, Eugene Webb, Donald Campbell, Richard Schwartz, and Lee Sechrest (1966) argue for the use of measurement techniques that do not require respondent awareness of the fact they are being measured. They suggest that unobtrusive measures should not replace the interview or questionnaire but should "supplement and cross-validate it [the interview or questionnaire] with measures that do not themselves contaminate the response" (p. 2). They describe three general types of such measures: physical traces, archives, and observations.

Physical Traces.   Physical traces include "erosion measures, where the degree of selective wear on some material yields the measure" and "accretion measures, where the research evidence is some deposit of materials" (Webb et al., 1966, p. 36). An example of an erosion measure with a nonverbal application might be an assessment of traffic patterns and, hence, the popularity of exhibits in a museum. Such a study examined the frequency with which floor tiles around various exhibits had to be replaced (Webb et al., 1966). An accretion measure might include assessing the readership levels of advertisements by counting the number of fingerprints on the pages of selected magazines in public places. A researcher could count the number of flyers that were handed out at a rally that were discarded.

Archives.   Archives include *running records*, the ongoing, continuing public records of a society, such as the *Congressional Record*, or actuarial records, such as birth and marriage records. For example, library records have been used to study the effects of introducing television into a community. Withdrawals of fiction titles were found to have dropped, while withdrawals of nonfiction titles did not. A second type of archival records are defined as *episodic* and *private* records, such as sales records, institutional records, and personal documents. (Archival records stored in libraries are discussed in detail in Chapters 4 and 5.) However, many archival records are not available in libraries. Here we will simply note several unusual examples provided by Webb et al. (1966). Several researchers attempted to measure airline passenger anxiety after major air crashes by assessing sales of airline tickets, trip life insurance policies, and airport bar liquor sales.

Observation.   The final type of unobtrusive measure presented by Webb et al. is *observation*. For example, racial attitudes in two colleges were compared by observing the groupings of whites and blacks in classrooms. The degree of fear created by ghost stories has been measured by observing the shrinking diameter of a circle of children (Webb et al., 1966). Measurement through the observation of behavior is the subject of Chapter 9 on participant-observation, wherein several types of observation are discussed.

APPLYING KNOWLEDGE IN COMMUNICATION

Measurement and measurement scales are central to social science research and communication research that seeks to understand how people communicate, as well as how well their communications are received. Through measurement we evaluate our theories of human communicative behavior. We always measure dependent variables, whether we are doing a survey or an experiment, and frequently we also measure the independent variables, as would be the case in a survey.

Since communication researchers often look for the effect of messages—verbal and nonverbal, written and graphic, across various channels (face-to-face, Internet, television, phone, etc.)—on peoples' beliefs, attitudes, values, and predispositions to behave, measurement scales must be carefully designed and tested. The subject of study often dictates this (especially in the area of broadcasting and journalism where fast-breaking events like September 11 are the norm). An understanding, then, of proper scale creation and a knowledge of what constitutes reliability and validity is of paramount importance to the communication student and researcher.

Reporting of measurement scales should include both reliability data and indications of how those scales were validated. At the minimum, reliability and validity tests (coefficients, factor analyses, and the like) should be run for each group of participants. This gives the study credibility.

Measurement is important. Measurement can be difficult. However, the concepts underlying the how and why of measurement conduct is straightforward. Your research (and the research you read) is only as good as the measurement employed. What and how you report it goes a long way in determining how beneficial your research efforts are to others.

SUMMARY

In this chapter we have explored how to measure things that are hard to observe. Based on the concept of the intervening variable, we noted that there are many times when researchers must create instruments that tap people's perceptions of how they might behave and what their attitudes and beliefs are, and use them in testing theory. Communication researchers, especially those who take a social science bent, depend heavily on measurement scales; they allow them to test theories of human behavior and predict communication strategies.

The chapter explored six types of measurement scales used in communication research: Thurstone, Guttman, Likert-type, semantic differential, and multidimensional scales. By now you should be able to construct and evaluate each. We also noted the benefits and limitations of each scale.

We ended with a discussion of other ways to measure communication—unobtrusive measures and interviews. With unobtrusive measures, however, there are concerns with reliability (not with validity—what you saw was what you saw). The chapter also examined the types of measurement employed in telephone and in-person interviewing.

We leave measurement with a reminder: Regardless of the type of measurement scale employed, reporting should include operational definitions, reliability coefficients, and why the scale is a valid measure of the concept under study. Quite simply, the better you report your measures, the more others will respect your research and the more likely your research will be used to advance knowledge in communication.

PROBES

1. What is a measurement scale? Assume that we are interested in assessing interest in an event on campus, what things would you have to consider in creating a scale to measure this event? Which of these considerations is most important? Least important? Why?

2. We are interested in tapping attitudes about AIDS on your campus. How would you go about measuring this topic using semantic differential scales? Using Likert-type scales? Using Thurstone scales? Using multidimensional scaling? Try to create several items for each of the scales.

3. Why might a researcher have to employ techniques other than scaling to answer a research question? What research question would be best answered using open-ended questions as your measurement technique? Using unobtrusive measures? Compared to scaling techniques, what do you gain and what do you lose by adopting each?

RESEARCH PROJECTS

1. Take one of the measurement scaling techniques covered in this chapter and present a literature review of its history and use in contemporary communication research.

2. Take a communication area and explore the different types of measurement employed in testing theory in that area. Have the measurement scales changed over time or are the same scales or techniques being used over time? What advantages or limitations does this have on our knowledge of communication?

3. Go to a campus event and report communication behavior by using unobtrusive measures.

SUGGESTED READING

Daly, J. A., Vangelista, A. L., & Daughton, S. M. (1987). The nature and correlates of conversational sensitivity. *Human Communication Research, 14,* 167–202.

Guilford, J. P. (1954). *Psychometric methods.* New York: McGraw-Hill.

Kerlinger, F. N. (1986). *Foundations of behavioral research,* 3rd ed. New York: Holt, Rinehart, and Winston.

Likert, R. (1932). A technique for the measurement of attitudes. *Archives of Psychology, 40,* 1–55.

Mayo, E. (1933). *The human problems of an industrial civilization.* New York: Macmillan.

Nunnally, J. (1978). *Psychometric theory.* New York: McGraw-Hill.

Osgood, C., Suci, G. J., & Tannenbaum, P. (1957). *The measurement of meaning.* Urbana, IL: University of Illinois Press.

Shaw, M. E., & Wright, J. M. (1967). *Scales for the measurement of attitudes.* New York: McGraw-Hill.

Stacks, D. W., & Murphy, M. A. (1993). Conversational sensitivity: Further validation and extension. *Communication Reports, 6,* 18–24.

Thurstone, L. L., & Chave, E. J. (1929). *The measurement of attitude.* Chicago: University of Chicago Press.

Torgerson, W. (1958). *Theory and methods of scaling.* New York: Wiley.

Webb, E., Campbell, D. T., Schwartz, R. D., & Sechrest, L. (1966). *Unobtrusive measures: Nonreactive research in the social sciences.* Chicago: Rand-McNally.

Woelfel, J., & Fink, E. L. (1980). *The measurement of communication processes: Galileo theory and method.* New York: Academic Press.

NOTES

1. Shaw and Wright (1967) contains 175 attitude scales that can be used by communication researchers, many of which are in a Thurstone format.

2. A detailed treatment of factor analysis is beyond the scope of this book. For an excellent explanation of factor analysis, see Kerlinger (1986). For an excellent *and* simplified explanation, see Williams (1992).

3. Daly and Miller (1975) actually found two factors,

but one was the mirror of the other, thus they concluded that writing apprehension, as they measured it, was unidimensional.

4. For a discussion of the *Hawthorne effect*, see Goldhaber (1986), page 86.

REFERENCES

Bardis, P. D. (1962). A dating scale: A technique for the quantitative measurement of liberalism concerning selected aspects of dating. *Social Science, 37*, 44–47, cited in Shaw & Wright (1967).

Barnett, G. A., Serota, K. B., & Taylor, J. A. (1976). Campaign communication and attitude change: A multidimensional analysis. *Human Communication Research, 2*, 227–244.

Berlo, D., Lemert, J. B., & Mertz, R. J. (1967). Dimensions for evaluating the acceptability of message sources. *Public Opinion Quarterly, 33*, 563–577.

Cronkhite, G., & Liska, J. (1976). A critique of factor analytic approaches to the study of credibility. *Communication Monographs, 43*, 91–107.

Daly, J. A., & Miller, M. D. (1975). The empirical development of an instrument to measure writing apprehension. *Research in the Teaching of English, 99*, 242–249.

Fink, E. L., Robinson, J. P., & Dowden, S. (1985). The structure of music preference and attendance. *Communication Research, 12*, 301–318.

Goldhaber, G. (1986). *Organizational communication*, 4th ed. Dubuque, IA: William C. Brown.

Guttman, L. L. (1944). A basis for scaling qualitative data. *American Sociological Review, 9*, 139–150.

Kerlinger, F. W. (1973). *Foundations of behavioral research*, 2nd ed. New York: Holt, Rinehart & Winston.

Kerlinger, F. W. (1986). *Foundations of behavioral research*, 3rd ed. New York: Holt, Rinehart & Winston.

Likert, R. (1932). A technique for the measurement of attitudes. *Archives of Psychology, 140*, 1–55.

McCroskey, J. C. (1966). Scales for the measurement of ethos. *Speech Monographs, 33*, 65–72.

Osgood, C., Suci, G. J., & Tannenbaum, P. (1957). *The measurement of meaning*. Urbana, IL: University of Illinois Press.

Pressner, B. (1978). The therapeutic implications of touching during articulation therapy. Unpublished M. A. thesis, University of Florida.

Riffe, D., & Stacks, D. W. (1988). Dimensions of writing apprehension across mass communication students. *Journalism Quarterly, 65*, 384–391.

Riffe, D., & Stacks, D. W. (1992). Student characteristics and writing apprehension. *Journalism Educator, 47*, 39–49.

Rosenthal, R., & Rosnow, R. L. (1969). *Artifact in behavioral research*. New York: Academic Press.

Saltiel, J., & Woelfel, J. (1975). Inertia in cognitive process: The role of accumulated information in attitude change. *Human Communication Research, 1*, 333–344.

Shaw, M. E., & Wright, J. M. (1967). *Scales for the measurement of attitudes*. New York: McGraw-Hill.

Silance, E. B., & Remmers, H. H. (1934). An experimental generalized master scale: A scale to measure attitudes toward any school subject. *Purdue University Studies in Higher Education, 35*, 84–88, cited in Shaw & Wright (1967).

Simons, H. W. (1976). *Persuasion: Understanding, practice, and analysis*. Reading, MA: Addison-Wesley.

Thurstone, L. L., & Chave, E. J. (1929). *The measurement of attitude*. Chicago: University of Chicago Press.

Webb, E., Campbell, D. T., Schwartz, R. D., & Sechrest, L. (1966). *Unobtrusive measures: Nonreactive research in the social sciences*. Chicago: Rand-McNally.

Williams, F. N. & Monge, P.R. (2001). (1992). *Reasoning with statistics*, 5th ed. New York: Holt, Rinehart & Winston.

Wimmer, R. D. & Dominick, J. R. (2003). *Mass media research: An introduction*, 7th ed. Belmont, CA: Wadsworth.

Woelfel, J. & Fink, E. L. (1980). *The measurement of communication processes: Galileo theory and method*. New York: Academic Press.

CHAPTER EIGHT

DESCRIBING INFORMATION: CONTENT ANALYSIS

OBJECTIVES

By the end of this chapter you should be able to:

1. Define content analysis and discuss its relative advantages and limitations as a communication research tool.
2. Differentiate between "manifest" and "latent" content analysis.
3. Explain what a unit of analysis is and differentiate between the five major unit types.
4. Create an exclusive and exhaustive category system for coding.
5. Explain how you would select content for analysis.
6. Discuss the process of training coders and establishing coding reliability and validity.
7. Explain the role of computers in content analysis.

There is an ongoing debate in society about whether society shapes television programming or TV programs shape society. In order to address this question, communication researchers describe what actually is shown on TV. They must assess the types of messages that are shown, that is, the content of the programs. To do so they conduct **content analysis**. An example of this can be seen in a study by Brown (2001). She did a comparison between FBI crime statistics and a content analysis of "realistic" crime shows (such as *Law and Order*). For her analysis she selected a sample of a show and categorized the depictions of the crimes shown into such categories as murder, rape, assaults, etc. She also noted who committed them (by gender, age, socio-economic status). Then she saw if those depictions were similar to the actual crime statistics (they were). This is just one example of the value of describing information in communication research. This chapter outlines the foundations for doing content analysis, which is often an important first step in studying communication.

One of the most important distinguishing characteristics of research in communication is its focus on human symbolic exchanges; that is, on both verbal and nonverbal communication *messages*. As communication researchers we are interested in the antecedents of messages, the effects of messages, and, frequently, in the messages themselves and the inferences we can make about their creators or the circumstances under which the messages were created. One special method of communication research, which focuses specifically on such messages in a systematic, rule-governed and rigorous way, is **content analysis**, a research method or measurement technique that involves the systematic study and quantification of the content or meaning of communication messages. As we will see, a content analysis involves the creation of categories that are designed to allow a particular research question to be answered by counting the instances of content within a message that fall within a certain predetermined category.

Before we examine content analysis in detail, a short overview of the method will provide a perspective on why content analysis is conducted and how it fits with the scientific study of communication. We begin with its uses and an example.

USES OF CONTENT ANALYSIS

Any message of which there is an obtainable record can be content analyzed. Speeches, dialogue (as in a play, film, or television show), conversations, letters, mail appeals to sell a product or support a cause, marketing messages, and newspaper or magazine articles or editorials are potential sources for content analysis. Other messages might include fiction or nonfiction books, music lyrics, poetry, courtroom testimony, advertisements (in newspapers, magazines, or on television, radio, or billboards), editorial or humorous cartoons, graffiti in restrooms or on mass transit cars, and so forth; all can be content analyzed. Of course, it is important to keep in mind that while any kind of communication message can be content analyzed, there must be a good reason to do so; that is, the analysis must help us answer an important research question. Content analysis can be used in research projects that seek to describe or explain communication. We will examine each of these in turn.

Description

Researchers often start by describing communication messages before they go on to look at relationships. Thus, many research projects have as their goal the description of some communication phenomenon. In Chapter 7 we introduced some unobtrusive measurement techniques and, in Chapter 9, we will examine other field research techniques, such as participant-observation, focus groups, and in-depth interviewing. The researcher's goal with these techniques is to observe behaviors and then write down what he or she observes. Similarly, a researcher might be interested in observing communication content and describing what was observed. Content analysis can be used to add accuracy and precision to such observations.

In Chapter 2 and Chapter 5 we pointed out that researchers who take a qualitative (historical/rhetorical-critical) approach are frequently interested in describing a particular event. Content analysis provides a method for quantifying the messages that were produced during the event. For example, Franklin Roosevelt's fireside chats were an historically important use of the mass media. "What did he say in them?" Skillful use of content analysis could answer such questions as: "What topics did he speak about?" "What was the frequency of selected topics?" "What types of persuasive appeals did he use?" And, by drawing inferences, we could also consider such questions as "Whom did he address?" and "What were his motives?"

An important use of content analysis as a descriptive method is as a starting point for establishing the effects of particular messages. A researcher who wanted to study the effects of Roosevelt's speeches might first want to know their precise content. Similarly, if a researcher was interested in examining whether rock music contributed to drug use among teenagers, he or she would first want to know the content of the lyrics under scrutiny. Or, a researcher who was studying whether violence on Saturday morning television shows aimed at children contributed to viewer violence would probably first want to know exactly the quantity of violence on the selected shows under study. Or, if a researcher was interested in how downsizing affected organizational communications, she might conduct a content analysis of company memoranda about the planned changes.

Explanation

Content analysis can be used in research that has as its purpose the explanation of observed communication phenomena. In this way, it can be used as a *measurement technique* to provide measures of independent and dependent variables in research designed to test hypotheses derived from theory. Good explanatory research questions compare something to something else; that is, as we have discussed, they involve examining the relationship between variables.

A careful content analysis study, for instance, might reveal that 23 percent (a fictitious number for example purposes) of the "Doonesbury" comic strips sampled over the past year contained attacks on the current president's administration. As a descriptive method this finding may be interesting, but it begs the question. Why do we want to know this? On the other hand, if we suspected that "Doonesbury" was harsher on the current administration than it was on the previous administration, we could then compare the 23 percent finding

MINI-PROJECT:

Obtain several politically oriented cartoon strips from the newspaper (e.g., "Doonesbury" cartoon strips) (you might want to go to the library or get them online) and see if you can determine how they treat politicians. What do you look for? How do you "count" them? Answering these questions requires you to select your "unit of analysis" and create your "coding categories."

with a figure derived from analyzing "Doonesbury" comic strips when one president was in office as compared against the incumbent. If 23 percent attacked the incumbent and only 10 percent involved attacks on a former president, this might be interpreted as evidence that the strip was biased. In other words, bias would help *explain* something—the percentage of "Doonesbury" cartoons that attacked the administration in power.

In this example, content analysis is used to measure the *dependent* variable. To compare violence on television now versus ten years ago, a researcher might content analyze a random sample of current programming and compare the incidence of violence on these shows with shows that were on ten years ago. The amount of violence would be the dependent variable, while time, "now" or "ten years ago," would be the independent variable. Or, to assess the effect of the manipulation of an independent variable in an experiment, a researcher might have participants in experimental and control groups write essays, which then could be content analyzed and compared.

Content analysis also can be used to measure the independent variable. Several researchers (Jesse G. Delia, Ruth Ann Clark, James L. Applegate) have operationalized the variable *cognitive complexity* by content analyzing essays written by their participants. Cognitive complexity is then used as a predictor of a wide number of dependent variables, including communicator effectiveness.[1]

Steps in Content Analysis

The methods of content analysis follow directly from and are largely guided by the research question. The steps in conducting a content analysis are outlined briefly here and explained in detail in the rest of the chapter. The first step in any content analysis is a review of the literature, a review that helps focus and clarify the research questions or hypotheses that guide the study.

The second step is to define exactly *what* messages are to be studied. Here your **population** or **universe** of messages is defined. In the "Doonesbury" example this would probably be all the strips created by Garry Trudeau from the beginning of the strip to date. This step simply involves limiting the study by creating workable boundaries and parameters.

Although it would be possible to answer some research questions by analyzing all available relevant messages, more commonly the messages are so numerous as to be difficult to study in their entirety. Thus, a third step, in which a sample is selected, is required.

The sample consists of messages that are representative of the entire body of messages available for analysis. The sample must be large enough to be representative, yet small enough to be studied feasibly with available resources. An alternative would be to **sample** from selected administrations (sampling will be covered briefly later and in detail in Chapter 10). For example, you might take "Doonesbury" cartoons from only the Bush and Clinton administrations. Or, you could take cartoons from the *election years only* that were aimed at the Reagan, Bush, Clinton, and Bush administrations.

After you have defined and selected the messages, the fourth step involves defining the **units of analysis**, the thing that is actually counted and assigned to categories. Units of analysis might include a word, a sentence, a paragraph, a theme, a yell (at a football game, for instance), television news story, and so forth. In the "Doonesbury" example, the **theme** of the comic strip would be the unit of analysis, but since there usually is one theme per strip, the strip also could be thought as the unit of analysis.

Fifth, **categories** into which each unit of analysis is assigned are created. The creation of categories that are valid, that allow you to measure what you want to measure, is critical to a successful content analysis. Creation of categories is reflected by the research questions posed or hypotheses advanced. Frequently, however, the researcher begins with some preliminary categories and then refines or modifies them during a pilot-test phase of the project. In the "Doonesbury" example, the categories could be as simple as Attacks the Administration in Power/Does Not Attack the Administration in Power, or as complex as a semantic differential scale reflecting the degree of pro- or anti-administration sentiment. This leads to the sixth step, the creation of reliable coding procedures. As noted earlier, clear operational definitions must be provided and training procedures created that will ensure that coding reliability is high.

Finally, the actual **coding** is done. Coding is conducted carefully, systematically, and objectively. After the messages have been coded the results are tabulated, analyzed, and interpreted. With this in mind, we now turn to a more detailed examination of content analysis.

DEFINING THE METHOD

Just what *is* content analysis? As Bernard Berelson (1952) defined it, content analysis is "a research technique for the objective, systematic, and quantitative description of the *manifest* content of communication" (p. 18, emphasis added). And, although that is the predominant use of content analysis, there are two directions that content analysis researchers can take. Researchers may focus on the manifest and/or latent aspects of communication.

What is the **manifest content** of communication? Why is it important? Consider the following question: How many times is the reader referred to as "you" in this text? To answer this question you would count the number of times the word *you* was used. *You*, in this regard is *manifest* in that it is on the surface and obvious; the content exactly as it appears. The researcher can assign numbers and determine the frequency of the use of *you* by the communicators (the authors). Further suppose that you know that one or two chapters were written by others. Could the frequency of use of the word *you* provide an indication of which chapters were written by whom?

Other researchers argue that content analysis can be approached on a *qualitative* level. Based on such analyses you might seek to move one step further: to understand the **latent content**, or the deeper meanings that are intended or perceived. Holsti (1969) contends that content analysis *at the coding level* must be limited to manifest content; that is, by being objective and systematic we are limited to coding that which we observe. The latent question comes in when content analysis is used with research questions that go beyond the *pragmatic aspects of the messages themselves*. This approach, which opposes that offered by Berelson, has been advanced by Charles E. Osgood (1959) as a way of approaching questions dealing with the intended uses of the message or their intended effects. Holsti (1969) argues, however, that such definitional problems are overcome when you remember that content analysis is *objective*, it must deal with the manifest nature of the material observed. He also suggests that the latent meaning of a message may be inferred, but must be corroborated by independent evidence. An example of latent content analysis would be to determine if someone is sexist by examining the types of adjective they use to describe women. (e.g., chic, babe).

This chapter concentrates on the analysis of the manifest content of messages. When necessary, the researcher may make inferences based upon the objective and systematic study of the messages in question. You have, however, just seen one of the outcomes of content analysis; many times it functions as a preliminary mode of investigation to research from a different method.

An Illustration

Suppose, for instance, that you were interested in finding which research methods were being used in articles published in communication journals. There are a number of methods available to address this question. You might survey communication professionals for their opinions. But what you would get would be attitudes or beliefs regarding the methods they *thought* were being published, not the actual content of the journals. What you want to know is which research methods are actually being used in articles published in communication journals. The best way to answer this type of research question would be through a content analysis whereby you could carefully select communication journals and systematically check each for the research methods published in each article.

The key element here lies in the *content* of the journals. In answering this question you may be assuming that certain research methods may be more prevalent than others. You might also keep track of who is using what methods or when the method was employed (assuming that the date of publication represents a valid estimation of when the research was

MINI-PROJECT:

The illustrated example suggests an interesting and challenging project. Do certain journals and certain authors publish more of a particular methodology than others? How would you go about preparing to conduct such a content analysis study?

conducted). By identifying the major research methods thought to be prevalent in the journals, you might construct categories such as rhetorical/critical, historical, experimental, survey, content analysis, and so on. You might also have other subcategories, which could include, for example, the discipline of the author(s) (English, Psychology, Public Relations, and so forth). The content analysis will provide a listing within each category that will help you to answer your research question, and tell you which methods are used in empirical articles published in communication journals. It may also tell you who (from the identification of researchers employing each method) is using which method and which researchers employ more than one method. You may also want to report trends over time.

Content analysis, then, is a method of observing the communication of others and categorizing it according to some rigorous set of rules. Such rules determine what the content is that we are analyzing, and determine what categories we create to sort the content and to adequately sample the content under study.

CONDUCTING THE CONTENT ANALYSIS

In preparing to analyze any communication event or variable you must first decide *what* you will be studying; you must select your *unit of analysis*. Based on the unit of analysis you must then decide how to sort the data; you must create your category system. Both decisions, however, are guided by the research question and are dependent on the amount of data with which you can work. After selection of the units of analysis and creation of the category system, a sampling procedure must be established. Finally, you must acquire the data.

Research Questions

We conduct a content analysis if the method best answers the particular research question. As with other approaches to the study of communication, the research question helps the researcher define just what he or she will study. Conducting a content analysis just because the material exists does not help us to understand communication better; content analysis should be employed in research because it is best suited to answer the questions posed by the researcher.

The creation of the research question begins with a thorough literature review, which leads to either specific research questions or hypotheses that point out the category system ultimately employed. The research question *delimits* the content to be analyzed in such a way as to make the research doable and valuable to the researcher. Questions that can be answered primarily with content analysis include:

1. Does sexism exist in public school textbook portrayals of "appropriate" male and female roles?
2. Has the amount of sex and violence in rock music videos changed in the past ten years?
3. Do individuals who are lying engage in more self-references than their counterparts who are telling the truth?

Delimiting the Population

After deciding that a content analysis is the most appropriate method to answer a specific research question, the first step is to establish certain boundary conditions that will limit your search. Assuming that you still want to know which research methods are used in articles published in communication journals, you must first determine two things: what constitutes the "outlets" for publication and how far back in time you will go to establish a starting point. In determining the population under study, then, you must decide which journals are appropriate for publication of communication research. Look back over the journals listed in Chapter 4. Could you possibly cover *all* those journals? Or, are there certain journals that are more likely to publish communication research (as opposed to predominantly psychology or sociology research) or are more important to your specialty or field? Further, are you interested in communication as a general discipline or is your concern with one of the subdisciplines? In so doing you have established a boundary for your population: Perhaps you will look at only the ten most representative journals for communication. Obviously, this selection will limit the generalizability of your findings.

The second boundary you might consider is how many years will be covered in your study. This decision may be based on practicality and dictated by the resources available, such as coding assistance, time, and the journals themselves. The decision may be based on previous research. It may be that previous study covers only the period up to 1980; therefore, you might choose the time period 1980 to date as a second boundary on your population. (You should have a specific ending point—in this case one sufficiently close to the present but still allowing for at least, say, four issues *each* of your journals to be published and in circulation, 2002 might be a good ending date.)

In this example, then, let us say your population is composed of the twenty journals you feel best represent where communication research has been published and will cover fifteen years. You are now ready to move to the second step, selecting the things you will count, your units of analysis.

Units of Analysis

The *unit of analysis* is what you actually *count* and assign to categories. How your unit of analysis is defined depends on how you *operationally define* the variable(s) under study. As noted in Chapter 6, the concept of an operational definition is crucial when creating the variables for study. In content analysis the variables under study (the ones being counted) should be distinct and identifiable by coders after training. Potential units of analysis might include: words, sentences, paragraphs, and themes in written material; phrases, sentences, and turns in oral material; scenes, acts, and plays in dramatic material; or names, institutions, and dates in other material.

A major consideration at this stage of content analysis is how the definition of the unit of analysis will relate to how it is ultimately coded. How can you select your unit of analysis? As a start, we might consider the five *major* units suggested by Berelson (1952) (see Table 8.1). Keep in mind, however, that these units are suggestions and, at a minimum, will need further specificity. Berelson's smallest unit of analysis is the **word** or **symbol**. This can include units consisting of names, utterances, parts of speech, and so forth. The second unit

TABLE 8.1   Units of Analysis

UNIT	EXAMPLE
Word	Nouns, Proper names, Utterances (for example, "uh-huh")
Theme	Self-esteem, Positive news promotion, Democracy
Character	Sex (male/female), Occupation, Ethnicity (Asian American, Euro American, etc.)
Time/Space	Column inches, Type size, Air time provided a program
Item(s)	Speech, Interview, Television program(s)

of analysis is the **theme**, which may move away from the manifest content of the message towards the latent or underlying meaning. A theme consists of an idea, concept, or thesis. While the word is fairly simple to operationalize, the theme presents more of a problem. Kerlinger (1986), however, suggests that careful use of the theme provides "an important and useful unit because it is ordinarily realistic and close to the original content" (p. 480). For instance, if the unit of analysis is defined as an individual's self-concept, the theme would revolve around statements of self-esteem, self-worth, and so on. Within the major theme, then, we would have subthemes. Obviously, thematic variables are more difficult to use and should be carefully operationalized. Berelson notes that thematic units of analysis are more difficult to code reliably, a problem that can be minimized through clear defini-tion, careful training, and the use of more than one coder.

Themes provide the researcher with an idea of the *latent* meaning of the content at a quantifiable level of analysis. For example, if we assume that sexually related innuendo un-derlies more situation comedy today than in the 1960s, we could compare scripts of both periods. Our analysis would look for the absence or presence of innuendo, coded as "sex-ual" or "nonsexual." A count of use would provide support as to which was prevalent. For example, sexual innuendo might include such nonverbal *quasi-courtship* behaviors as long, lingering glances, eyebrow raises, or pelvis rotation (both sexes), breast thrusts or touching (females), pelvis thrusts or unbuttoned shirts (males).

The third unit of analysis discussed by Berelson (1952) is the **character**. The charac-ter is defined as an individual. In most research the character unit is composed of specific people, such as whites/blacks, males/females, or married/unmarried. However, you could define the character as being composed of specific communicative behaviors identified with a specific type of person. Suppose that you are analyzing the transcripts of a group discus-sion. You may choose as your unit of analysis the particular *roles* as the characters employed by members during the discussion. Hence, you might find that certain roles emerge at dif-ferent points in the discussion. In literary and some historical research characters as units of analysis take special importance.

The fourth unit of analysis is an increment of **time and space**. Just as it suggests, this reflects some physical or temporal measure. Spatial/temporal measures of content are often employed in media research. Wurtzel (1985), for instance, used the amount of air time given a particular event. Other time/space variables might be defined as the size of differ-ent pictures used in media, number of column inches a given story is allocated, or even the page where a particular story is placed in the paper.

The final unit of analysis in Berelson's (1952) system is the **item**. An item consists of an entire communication message. In Wurtzel's study of airtime given an event, the story (Republican-oriented or Democrat-oriented) was an item unit of analysis, while the time aired per story was a time unit of analysis. One advantage of item units is that they can be presented to trained judges (coders) with rating scales and compared on a dimension or range of dimensions.

Sometimes the researcher must use two or more different units of analysis. Again, it is important to keep in mind that the choice of the most appropriate units should reflect the research questions or hypotheses being tested. Use of multiple units can provide extra information and may help validate the measures.

Creating Categories for Analysis

Once you have decided on your units of analysis, the next step is to establish the categories in which to place them. The concern here is establishing how to separate the units of analysis into *meaningful* categories. As with selecting unit(s) of analysis, the decision of *which* and how many categories to use must reflect the objectives of the research project. Quite simply, choosing the proper category system is critical in conducting a content analysis.

Guidelines.   When creating a category system, five general guidelines should be followed (Holsti, 1969). Content analysis categories should (1) reflect the purpose of the research, (2) be exhaustive, (3) be mutually exclusive, (4) allow for independence (assigning an item to one category should not influence the assignment of other items to other categories), and (5) all categories within the system should reflect one, *single* classification principle. These guidelines underlie the systematic and objective nature of content analysis, which makes it a scientific method.

At the core of categorization, then, is the definitional process. Suppose again that your research project deals with identifying different *types* of research methods published in communication journals. The unit of analysis is the article published. The categories might reflect those established in this book: historical/critical, survey/descriptive, participant-observation/descriptive, focus group/descriptive, interview/descriptive, experimental/quasi-experimental, and, of course, content analysis. Given this category system, will all units identified fit into only one of the categories? If they do, you have created a category system that is **mutually exclusive**, a particular entry will fall into one of these seven areas and only one of these seven areas. What will you do with an item that fits none of your categories?

■ ■ ■ ■ ■

MINI-PROJECT:

You have the following research question: "Do talk shows reflect the concerns and problems of the average viewer?" Determine the population you would study and the units of analysis you would count (words/symbols, characters, themes, time and space, items).

In this case you might have an eighth category: *Other*. However, you should not expect that the number of items to be coded as *other* to be larger than any of the other categories.

In creating the subcategories you have created a category system that is not only *exhaustive* but also *exclusive*. Creating categories, then, involves making choices as to whether or not you will have the right number of categories. Sometimes it is necessary to pretest or pilot test a study to get a feel for the content and the *appropriate* number of categories necessary to answer the research question adequately.

Counting. Suppose you want to know how many articles communication researchers publish. To illustrate, consider the following ongoing research project one of your authors has been associated with, which is examining which individuals have published in major communication journals (Hickson, Stacks, & Amsbary, 1993).[2] The major research questions concerned learning who the "top" publishers in communication journals are. The universe for this study, then, consisted of people publishing in communication journals; specifically, by those publishing in journals recognized by the *Index to Journals in Communication Through 1990* (Matlon & Ortiz, 1992). This index includes only "major" communication journals.[3] Our unit of analysis is the equivalent to the "word" in Berelson's system, the author's name. Each author's listing, regardless of whether or not he or she was the sole author, was entered as well as the number of articles in each of the selected journals. By using the *Index* we were able to reduce the time it takes to draw our sample based on the earlier work put into the *Index*.

The most obvious and simple quantification system is to count the units being analyzed in each category. Typically, the researcher will create a tally sheet. In this example, the tally sheet would include those authors included in the journals. Hence, our category system is more complex and takes in a bigger picture than simply identifying authors.

Counting also may take the form of examining how many times a particular word or phrase is used in a message. In counting, no discrimination is made regarding subdivision within a category. If you were interested in how a writer perceived himself in his writing, and thought that as the writer gained self-respect and reduced apprehension more personal pronouns would appear in his writing, a simple count of the number of personal pronouns would constitute the results. Note that no further discrimination between *types* of personal pronouns is made. In the author's and his associates' studies, a simple count of citations was used for each journal regardless of *what* the article might have been about or what method was used.

MINI-PROJECT:

Extending the last Mini-Project ("Do talk shows reflect the concern and problems of the average viewers?"), create a category system for the talk show study and determine how you will count your units of analysis. How will you ensure that the category system is exclusive and exhaustive? What counts?

SAMPLING

Although we will cover sampling in more detail in Chapter 10, a quick introduction to sampling is important because you cannot always study an entire population of messages. Content analysis often requires that the elements chosen be representative of the larger universe or population. Although there are times when it is possible to include *all* messages in your content analysis, many times there is too much material with which to work efficiently.

Sampling Concerns

If the population you will be studying either is not large or is composed of a limited number of messages, sampling may not be of concern. In such cases you would in effect simply take a **census** of the material available—including all messages—as part of the content analysis. This may be possible with some content analyses, but usually there are more messages than can be efficiently and reliably studied. Of concern here is whether the messages are such that *any* message or item is representative of all possible messages. The following sections review different ways to draw sample messages from some population.

Random and Systematic Sampling.   A simple **random sampling** of works written or spoken by a communicator could be conducted. The research question here would concentrate on understanding the messages of this particular person. If you are concerned with messages from a variety of sources, and you have no reason to believe that your sources are dissimilar with regard to whatever attributes are of importance, then simple random sampling may be appropriate. If your research question concerns the content produced by one individual—a long complex speech, a book, or text of some message—then sampling may not be a major concern.

Simple random sampling, however is limited in its application. You might want to consider a **systematic sampling** of the content. Since you already have copies of the messages (in written, audiotape, or videotape form), systematic sampling may be a better approach. Systematic sampling involves compiling a list of messages and the selection of a random starting point and a constant skip interval. Based on the starting point, the next message for inclusion in the sample will be determined by the skip interval. Perhaps there are several hundred presidential speeches over the term of a single president. If you are not concerned with *change* in messages over time, a systematic random sample would be an efficient and accurate way to select the messages for content analysis. Thus, we might select every tenth speech (the **skip interval** chosen randomly) from the first speech of the second year (again, both—as starting points—chosen randomly).

Availability of Data.   Another consideration in sample selection is the availability of data. Suppose, for instance, that you are examining the mudslinging campaign of one candidate for a statewide political office. In this state there are five major cities, each with a population over 100,000. In four of the five cities the major media consists of one newspaper; in the other, there are two newspapers. Assume also that four of the five newspapers are clumped in a geographic area about 150 miles from the largest city and the fifth is some 250 miles from the closest city. Can you ignore the fifth city? Not if your questions deal with statewide impact, even though getting the paper may pose a problem. If, on the other hand, you are interested only in the coverage of newspapers from the large, perhaps more political parts of the state, then you might consider excluding the fifth paper. In any event, you must present a good argument for your sample selection.

Decisions regarding availability of sources should be considered at the research question/hypothesis stage. The availability of sources also should be considered before the sample is selected. In some instances you have available an existing database from which to draw your sample. Suppose that you are interested in what type of article is written in the popular press (magazines) following an important news event. One source to consider might be *INFOTRACK* (see Chapter 4), which is indexed by topic and title, for the content of the particular areas you need. In the author's project mentioned earlier, the *NCA Index* might be considered as the database, assuming that it is a reliable compilation of the data; however, care should be taken to double-check the accuracy of all the entries. As noted in Chapter 4, there are many abstract sources that provide potential sources of data; care must be taken, however, to ensure that they are representative of the population required for your research questions.

Quantification

How do we "enter" the data collected in a content analysis? That depends on the category system employed. The decision of how to quantify or "code" the categories should be approached early in the planning process. Remember, one of the major goals of the method is that all data should be potentially quantifiable (Kerlinger, 1986). Given today's use of computers, simple and straightforward coding has become even more important (we will cover this in more detail and depth in a later section of this chapter). This section will discuss ways to approach this stage of the content analysis.

Nominal Quantification. Coding requires that some distinction be made in the content. Here, the researcher is merely naming (nominal) the characteristics of the variables. Ethnicity, gender, job category, and region of the country are all nominal classifications. This distinction could be defined as simply as male/female or more complexly as in the case of personal pronouns, which might be first person, second person, or third person. As discussed in Chapter 6, a nominal variable does not assume that one category is more or less, better or worse, higher or lower than any other category. Assume for a moment that you are evaluating a number of messages written by respondents after exposure to

MINI-PROJECT:

Extending the previous Mini-Project ("Do talk shows reflect the concerns and problems of the average viewer?"), how will you sample from the population of talk shows? Draw a sample from your population using each of the sampling techniques discussed.

a persuasive message with which they did not agree. You might code each respondent's message's arguments according to the strategy he or she employed in reacting to the persuasive message. In coding each message you would assign an appropriate letter, number, or phrase to the particular message. The same could be done if your unit of analysis was the paragraph. For example, messages may be of three types: one-sided, two-sided, or emotional appeal. Coding of these messages could employ any of several strategies: 1 (one-sided), 2 (two-sided), 3 (emotional appeal); Type I, Type II, Type III; and so on. Another example of nominal quantification is found in Table 8.2.

Ordinal Quantification.   A second method of coding requires some decision regarding ranking the data. Ranking requires that the content be placed in categories that are mutually independent and ordered in some way. If you were working with a number of student news releases you might rank them as Excellent, Good, Bad, or Terrible. Each release could be coded as E, G, B, T or 4, 3, 2, 1. Or, you could assign a grade (A to F) for each. Other sample codings are found in Table 8.3. However, note that these codes are not mathematical in the sense that the fourth ranking is not two times more than the 2.

Interval Quantification.   A third method of coding is that of rating each item in the analysis according to some scale. These scales could be of any of the types discussed in Chapter 6. Often you will want to code your content according to some degree of something, perhaps positive to negative. In that case we are no longer simply creating a dichotomy but actually placing the item on some continuum:

Positive _____:_____:_____:_____:_____ Negative

Or, we could use multiple rating scales:

Positive _____:_____:_____:_____:_____ Negative
Hot _____:_____:_____:_____:_____ Cold
Active _____:_____:_____:_____:_____ Passive

Obviously, you obtain finer distinctions or categories from such scales. However, the price you pay is in the increased difficulty of establishing reliability. Content analysis, unlike

TABLE 8.2   Nominal Coding

CONTENT: NEWSPAPER EDITORIALS	
UNITS	**NOMINAL CODING**
Domestic affairs	1
International affairs	2
Environment	3
Local issues	4

TABLE 8.3   Ordinal Coding

AMOUNT OF VIOLENCE DEPICTED IN A TELEVISION SHOW

CATEGORY	CODING
A lot	1
A little	2
None	3

SEXUAL APPEAL IN A MAGAZINE CIGARETTE ADVERTISEMENT

CATEGORY	CODING
Blatant	1
Moderate	2
Slight	3
Subtle	4
None	5

earlier uses of these scales, requires that coders agree with one another regarding, for example, how positive or negative the message was.

Coding Reliability

Since content analysis is a type of measurement, as pointed out in Chapter 6, reliability is a vital element of the value of the research. When content analysis calls for simply counting manifest content, for example, the number of times a particular word appears, reliability is fairly easy to establish (Berelson, 1952). However, when more difficult judgments are required, increased attention is necessary to assure that coders place items in the correct categories with a degree of consistency.

When quantification requires that judgments be made, the researcher must be prepared to establish that the coders are consistently placing data into the correct categories. (Even with counting, it is necessary that someone other than the researcher double-check the counting.) The principles described in Chapter 6 clearly apply. For example, coding reliability is enhanced when the units of analysis are clearly defined and they are assigned to mutually exclusive and exhaustive categories. Even when these two conditions are met, there may be times when coders will be unable to agree upon the category in which the item should be placed. In such cases it is helpful to have all agree in which category the items should go, achieving a common frame of reference toward the content (Stempel, 1980). Therefore, practice sessions are very important. When coders have problems deciding where the particular item(s) go, they should talk over their differences and agree on a category for the item(s), if the category system has been adequately pretested before the act of analysis begins.

Intercoder reliability can be enhanced in several ways. Perhaps the most important of these is to make certain that all coders understand and can use the coding categories. It is important that they understand the definitions of the categories and how and why the units of analysis were chosen. Coders must understand the project well enough to make decisions about content but not so well as to know what the researcher is seeking. However, although the coders should be versed in how to categorize items, they should not be aware of the theory or hypotheses behind the coding scheme so that they do not introduce any bias in the coding, even if it is unintentional. For example, if the material being analyzed was derived from people who had participated in an experiment, the coders should be blind to (unaware of) the experiment's particular conditions (treatments). It is also important that they understand that certain items may not easily fit into the categories, that they might need to "talk it over" and agree where the item should be placed when such an item appears (but only during the practice, not during actual coding). For this purpose a pilot-test phase of research should be undertaken during which the categories and operational definitions are tested and coders trained.

After the coders have a good understanding of the project's definitions and categories, practice sessions should be run. In these sessions material randomly selected from the population under consideration should be presented and coded. Any disagreements over coding should then be discussed and agreements reached concerning the appropriate categories (if the researcher has reviewed the area well enough, category ambiguity should be minimal, but it should be expected that some content may still cause problems). The practice session should be used to work out procedures for solving disagreements and to ascertain whether or not the categories meet Holsti's (1969) criteria of reflecting the research question, being properly subdivided into useful groups, being exclusive and independent, and reflecting a single classification principle.

Coders should always use a standardized coding form to ensure reliability and accuracy from coder to coder. Such a form provides the necessary categories and allows for standardization.

Reliability Coefficients.   Once the data have been gathered some estimate of coding reliability must be determined. Hand-calculated reliability coefficients are not difficult to compute. One example is Holsti's (1969) reliability formula which is straightforward, requiring only information about the number of coding decisions the coders must make and the total number of decisions made by each coder:

$$\text{reliability} = \frac{2M}{N_i + N_j}$$

where M = total items agreed upon
$\quad N_i$ = total items coder i selected
$\quad N_j$ = total items coder j selected

As an example, we could have the following:

$$\text{reliability} = \frac{2(200)}{220 + 230} = \frac{400}{550} = 72.7$$

This means that our reliability is 72.7. Most researchers want to achieve a coefficient of about 90, although that is not set in stone. *If* it is not that high, a researcher can continue to train coders or modify the coding scheme.

This assumes that independent coders have been employed. In some cases you may use only one coder. *Intra*coder reliability may be computed the same as *inter*coder reliability; the coder codes the *same* material *twice*, without being aware of how it was coded the first time, and coefficients of reliability are then computed on both sets of data. Of course, this assumes a fairly large number of messages have been coded so that the coder would not remember how he or she coded it the first time.

Some coding requires more than simple categorization. This is especially true when the data is being coded for specialized computer analysis. For instance, H. Wayland Cummings' Syntactic Language Computer Analysis (SLCA) program analyzes messages for syntactical content (Cummings & Renshaw, 1979; Stacks, Boozer, & Lally, 1983). Box 8.1 presents an actual message and its SLCA-coded counterpart. SLCA allows researchers to conduct content analysis of grammatical and syntactical elements of verbal and written messages. Previous research typically relied on techniques such as "type/token ratios" (Cummings & Renshaw, 1979), rather simple message calculations. SLCA provides indicators of verb use, tense, pronoun and noun counts, and other language indicators. It is quite complex and provides considerable insight into message construction. Stacks, Boozer, and Lally (1983) used SLCA-generated dependent variables for an analysis of writing apprehension. Based on the SLCA-generated data they were able to produce predictive models of specific grammar and syntax use that predicted several types of writing apprehension.

A drawback of this method, however, is coding the message, which can be quite complex and requires both extensive training sessions and checking of the coding by the researcher.

Coding Validity

As noted in Chapter 6, reliability is a necessary but not sufficient condition for establishing measurement validity. Validity is most commonly defined as whether a coding system measures what you want it to measure. As with other methods, validity can be a real concern with content analysis. This concern can be traced to three possible sources of invalidity: definition, category, and sample.

Definitional Sources of Invalidity.   By now it should be apparent that the definitional process involved in determining what the units of analysis will be is critical to validity in content analysis. When units of analysis are defined, a set of boundary conditions are created which serve to limit what you will accept in the analysis. In setting these boundaries you may or may not reflect the same definitions others would have chosen. Many times definitional

BOX 8.1
COMPUTER-ASSISTED CODING FOR CONTENT ANALYSIS: SYNTACTIC LANGUAGE COMPUTER ANALYSIS (SLCA)

A. MESSAGE AS WRITTEN

Local officials met Tuesday with a chemical company about the development of a new chemical plant in the Tuscaloosa Area.

Dayton Chemical Inc. was named a "serious polluter" in 1984 by the Environmental Protection Agency. It produces many products, among them are compounds used in manufacturing medicines. Dayton is a pioneer in research on synthetic interferon, a compound some predict will be a significant breakthrough in the treatment of cancer.

In 1985, Dayton settled a damage suit over toxic waste dumping near the headquarters in Ohio. The total settlement was for $1.4 million.

Dayton could create as many as 200 new jobs for Tuscaloosa residents.

-30-

B. MESSAGE AS CODED FOR COMPUTER ANALYSIS

LOCAL + OFFICIALS – MET ++ TUESDAY WITH A CHEMICAL + COMPANY ABOUT THE ++ DEVELOPMENT OF A NEW CHEMICAL + PLANT IN THE ++ TUSCALOOSA + AREA. ++ DAYTON ++ CHEMICAL ++ INCORPORATED WAS – NAMED A SERIOUS + POLLUTER IN + 1984 BY THE ++ ENVIRONMENTAL ++ PROTECTION ++ AGENCY. + IT – PRODUCES MANY + PRODUCTS, AMONG + THEM – ARE + COMPOUNDS – USED IN + MANUFACTURING + MEDICINES. ++ DAYTON – IS A + PIONEER IN + RESEARCH ON SYNTHETIC + INTERFERON, A + COMPOUND + SOME – PREDICT WILL – BE A SIGNIFICANT + BREAKTHROUGH IN THE + TREATMENT OF + CANCER. IN + 1985, ++ DAYTON – SETTLED A DAMAGE + SUIT OVER TOXIC WASTE + DUMPING NEAR THE + HEADQUARTERS IN ++ OHIO. THE TOTAL + SETTLEMENT – WAS FOR 1 MILLION + DOLLARS. ++ DAYTON COULD CREATE AS MANY AS 200 NEW + JOBS FOR ++ TUSCALOOSA + RESIDENTS./

problems come up in training sessions; once pilot testing commences it is discovered that the definition decided on will not work with the material or the coders. If this occurs, your definition needs revision.

If your research project was interested in how communication apprehension was manifested verbally and nonverbally in an initial public speech, it would be important to define apprehension in such a way that it could be codeable in a manner consistent with your definition. Such coding might yield different results if we defined apprehension as a *fear of com-*

munication rather than as an *unwillingness to communicate* or *shyness*. Conceptually, there are major differences between being fearful of communication and being unwilling to communicate; being shy may be an altogether different reason for being apprehensive about communicating. Clearly, the way we define our units of analysis will alter how they are perceived by the coders, thus becoming a potential source of invalidity. In addition, we need to examine *what* content is being analyzed. If we were to take the actual text of the speeches, to include hesitations, stutter-starts, and so forth as the content, our definition would need to incorporate such instances of apprehension. Assume that our content is the self-statements made during the speaking situation. Although the definitions may appear similar, they really point to three different perspectives of apprehension. The same is potentially true of many concepts, such as violence, conservatism, liberalism, or even self-concept.

Your theoretical perspective will serve as the guiding force in definition. If your approach to apprehension is from a perspective suggesting unwillingness, then that definition will be valid for you. The validity of the analysis, then, lies primarily within the areas of face or content validity.

Category Sources of Invalidity. As should be evident by now, definition is closely tied to category selection. Creating a category system that is valid presents a second problem. Category systems should be exhaustive and mutually exclusive. To the degree that you are able to place units in categories without overlap, validity is increased. Here, validity is closely related to reliability. If your reliability is high, your validity should be increased. As noted earlier, *the categories must reflect the purpose of the research.*

For example, if you were interested in the portrayal of sex on MTV, VH1, and CMT, and you have a category that is defined as instances in which a female is treated violently, the category does not accurately reflect the variable *per se*. It is not valid. Or, if the number of times certain words—devil, Satan—were used as a measure of the extent of devil worship content it might not be valid. Christian rock might use the words "beat the devil" or "defeat Satan" and the category would validly reflect the variable. Thus, simple word counts would be inadequate to assess the content. Themes would probably be more appropriate.

Sampling Sources of Invalidity. The third problem facing the researcher deals with the sample. If your sample represents the universe or population from which it was drawn and the analysis of the sample is valid, inferences about the population should be valid. However, care must be taken to make sure that your sampling procedure reflects the aims of the research. This is especially true in content analyses that look at parts of a speech, newspapers, or a sample of one week of TV shows to find out about violence in prime time—whose validity was destroyed because one network ran a miniseries that week. Choosing the first 100 words of a number of randomly selected messages for analysis could invalidate the sampling procedure if your research question does not deal with just the introduction. If the research question deals with the *total* message, random sampling from sections of the message is probably more valid than fixing on a certain number of words at the beginning of the message. In general, if you are examining a number of messages, your sample should consist of the *population* of messages; if you are examining certain messages, the sample should be the *message itself*; and, if you are examining a specific message, you should examine the *entire* message.

USE OF COMPUTERS IN CONTENT ANALYSIS

The computer has allowed content analysis to accomplish things never thought possible thirty years ago, although it is, no doubt, still in its infancy compared to what will be possible thirty years from now. Computer programs such as The General Inquirer provided the first computerized analysis of messages and subsequently a number of other content analysis programs have become available (Stone, Dunphy, Smith, & Ogilivie, 1966).

Computerized content analysis often demands complex coding procedures. Such seemingly trivial things as spelling errors can cause problems. The human computer, the brain, may be the best content analysis tool yet devised.

Computerized content analysis, when set-up properly, can provide speed and precision not possible by human beings. It does *not* replace anything that the researcher could do, but it does make it easier to accomplish the often tedious chores associated with coding the data. Any of the research questions suggested earlier *could* be addressed through computerized content analysis. Obviously, the computer is an excellent tool for counting; but it has problems with establishing the *meaning* of the content. Most questions addressing the latent content of messages may best be approached by a noncomputerized method.

ADVANTAGES AND LIMITATIONS OF CONTENT ANALYSIS

Like any method, there are certain advantages and limitations to content analysis. By now you should be aware that content analysis can be both time-consuming and complex. The key point to remember is that content analysis *describes* the content of a message, but the message can be part of (or derived from) a larger study that has explanation as its goal. Content analysis provides the researcher with the *manifest* message content, which *may* lead to future research on the *latent* meaning of that content. In many ways content analysis should be considered a heuristic tool—serving to establish future research.

Finally, it should be emphasized that content analysis does not, and cannot, assess the *effects* of communication messages. Occasionally we hear, for example, that certain song lyrics advocate Satan worship or worse. This may or may not be true. But, if it is true, nothing has been learned about the effects of these lyrics on those who listen to them. In this regard, content analysis could be the impetus for other research questions that require different methodologies to arrive at the appropriate answer.

APPLYING KNOWLEDGE IN COMMUNICATION

Content analysis provides communication researchers with a descriptive and explanatory methodology and at the same time a potentially reliable form of measurement that focuses on the message. Because messages are the central focus of communication research—whether that research is verbal, written, graphic, or film/video—content analysis is a powerful tool for communication researchers. Content analysis can help us describe film genre, approaches to music and lyrics, roles that may be found in the organization, types of press releases, and types of advertisements to name but a few uses. Content analysis also allows the researcher to better understand the psychological aspects of message creation, such as a method of conducting research on an internal mental state (e.g., research on self-concept or cognitive complexity).

SUMMARY

Content analysis is an important measurement tool that can be used alone or in conjunction with other methods. It can be used historically and critically to examine messages people have produced. It can be used in both qualitative and quantitative descriptive research and to measure either the independent variable or dependent variable in research. As a measurement tool it can assess concepts included in research using other methods, such as experiments. As a method itself, content analysis can tell us a lot about the type of messages we see.

Content analysis can be a complex and time-consuming method of research. Its advantages lie in an ability to focus squarely on communication messages, the core of the communication discipline, and also to make inferences about the creator of the message, and to providing a unique heuristic. It is a powerful tool for describing information, but as with any method it should be carefully considered, to be used when the research questions or theoretical perspective call for it.

PROBES

1. As noted in opening sections of this chapter, content analysis focuses on messages. Are there *any* messages that may be inappropriate or impossible for content analysis? If there are, which ones and why?

2. What is the difference between *manifest* and *latent* content? Is the distinction really important, or is it a secondary consideration? Give an example of something that may be coded as manifest content.

3. From your area of communication interest, state a research question that is amenable to content analysis. Based on this question, what *type* of content will you be analyzing? (How would you operationalize the categories?) What unit(s) of analysis would you use? How would you sample the content, or would a census be best?

4. Assume that you are interested in conducting a content analysis of network news promotions. Specifically, you are interested in the types of promotions and the frequency with which they are used during prime time to hype the evening news. What would be an interesting question that content analysis would best answer? Based on this question, what category system(s) might you employ? What would your units of analysis be? Would you want to consider some time frame? Would you have to *sample* the content? If so, how? How would you analyze the data?

5. What reliability and validity concerns does content analysis present? Are these concerns unique to content analysis, or are they present in other research methods as well? Do you think that computer-assisted content analysis has any impact on reliability? Validity? Why or why not?

RESEARCH PROJECTS

1. Conduct the Mini-Project study that sought to answer the question, "Do talk shows reflect the concerns and problems of the average viewer?"

2. Editorial cartoons often take a hard look at political communication. Design a study that answers the research question, "Do modern political cartoonists portray politics any differently than did their counterparts in the 1800s?"

3. Conduct a research project that answers the following research question, "How violent are Saturday morning cartoons?"

SUGGESTED READING

Berelson, B. (1952). *Content analysis in communication research*. Glencoe, IL: Free Press.

Budd, R. R., Thorp, R., & Donohew, L. (1967). *Content analysis of communications*. New York: Macmillan.

de Sola Pool, I. (Ed.). (1959). *Trends in content analysis*. Urbana, IL: University of Illinois Press.

Gerbner, G., et al. (1969). *The analysis of communication content*. New York: John Wiley.

Holsti, O. R. (1969). *Content analysis for the social sciences and humanities*. Reading, MA: Addison-Wesley.

Kaid, L. L., & Wadsworth, A. J. (1989). Content analysis. In P. H. Emmert & L. L. Barker (Eds.), *Measurement of communication behavior* (pp. 197–217). New York: Longman.

Krippendorf, K. (1980). *Content analysis: An introduction to its methodology*. Beverly Hills, CA: Sage.

Laswell, H. D., & Associates (1942). The politically significant content of the press: Coding procedures. *Journalism Quarterly, 19*, 12–23.

Stone, P., Dunphy, D. C., Smith, M. S., & Ogilivie, D. M. (1966). *The general inquirer: A computer approach to content analysis*. Cambridge, MA: MIT Press.

NOTES

1. For several excellent examples, see *Communication Monographs 46* (1979), 231–281. Four articles using content analysis are presented.

2. This is an example of a program of research that has utilized a particular methodology—content analysis—to answer a research question.

3. A problem with indices such as Matlon and Ortiz's, however, is that they often contain errors that will affect both the validity and the reliability of the study.

REFERENCES

Berelson, B. (1952). *Content analysis in communication research*. New York: Free Press.

Bowers, J. W. (1970). Content analysis. In P. Emmert & W. D. Brooks (Eds.), *Methods of communication research*. Boston: Houghton Mifflin.

Brown, N. J. (2001). A comparison of fictional television crimes and crime index statistics. *Communication Research Reports, 18*, 2, 192–199.

Cummings, H. W., & Renshaw, S. L. (1979). SLCA III: A meta-theoretic approach to the study of language. *Human Communication Research, 5*, 291–300.

Hickson, M., III, Stacks, D. W., & Amsbary, J. H. (1993). Active prolific scholars in communication studies: Analysis of research productivity, II. *Communication Education, 42*, 223–233.

Holsti, O. R. (1969). *Content analysis for the social sciences and humanities*. Reading, MA: Addison-Wesley.

Kerlinger, F. N. (1986). *Foundations of behavioral research*, 3rd ed. New York: Holt, Rinehart & Winston.

Matlon, R. J., & Ortiz, S. (1992). *Index to journals in communication studies through 1990*. Annandale, VA: Speech Communication Association.

Osgood, C. E. (1959). The representational model and relevant research methods. In I. de S. Pool (Ed.), *Trends in content analysis* (pp. 33–88). Urbana, IL: University of Illinois Press.

Stacks, D. W., Boozer, R., & Lally, T. D. P. (1983, March). *Syntactic language correlates of written communication apprehension*. Paper presented at the Southwest American Business Communication Association Convention, Houston, TX.

Stempel, G. H., III (1980). Content analysis. In G. H. Stempel, III, & B. H. Westley (Eds.), *Research methods in mass communication*. Englewood Cliffs, NJ: Prentice-Hall.

Stone, P., Dunphy, D. C., Smith, M. S., & Ogilivie, D. M. (1966). *The General Inquirer: A computer approach to content analysis*. Cambridge, MA: MIT Press.

Wurtzel, A. (1985). Review of the procedures used in content analysis, in J. R. Dominick and J. E. Fletcher (Eds.), *Broadcasting research methods*. Boston: Allyn and Bacon, 1985.

CHAPTER NINE

QUALITATIVE METHODOLOGY

MARK HICKSON, III
University of Alabama at Birmingham

OBJECTIVES

By the end of this chapter you should be able to:

1. Distinguish between three qualitative/descriptive methodologies.
2. Explain how the concept of "control" differentiates participant-observation, focus group, and in-depth interviewing methods.
3. Discuss how to conduct a participant-observation study.
4. Explain what a focus group is, how it is conducted, and how it differs from a nominal group.
5. Discuss how to conduct an in-depth interview study.

Qualitative/descriptive research employs primarily nonquantitative observation techniques. The qualitative researcher often attempts to "discover" a variable and to define it. A number of research techniques may be used by the qualitative researcher, including, but not limited to, open-ended interviews, focus groups, and participant-observation. In addition, the qualitative method often employs two or more qualitative techniques along with one or more quantitative techniques for the purpose of verifying data; this is sometimes referred to as **triangulation** (Webb, Campbell, Schwartz & Sechrest, 1970). In this chapter we focus on three methods that have been adapted for use in the field of communication: participant-observation, focus groups, and in-depth interviewing.

Why would communication researchers be interested in qualitative/descriptive methods? In some ways the methods already discussed point us to them: One major flaw with historical and critical study is the inability to understand how the participants viewed the communication, the scene, the act. The historical/rhetorical-critical researcher most often examines the event after it has occurred and, even with much empathy, cannot understand the events as they occurred to the participants. Qualitative/descriptive methods, on the other hand, allow the researcher to record the actual messages presented in the situation in which they were presented and allow the researcher to *understand and feel* how the participants felt as they were involved in an ongoing event. These methods deal with *real behavior as it occurs in a naturally occurring setting*. With quantitative methods the ability to study communication in the actual setting is offset by being able to establish control over the research, as in other types of research that will be discussed in the next few chapters. We examine the selected qualitative/descriptive methods based on the ability of the researcher to exert some control over the research. We begin with the method with least control, participant-observation.

PARTICIPANT-OBSERVATION

If real-world behavior is the major concern of the researcher, then participant-observation is an appropriate methodology. This method, however, assumes some liabilities. The major liability is that participant-observation is more subjective than objective; the researcher lives the event, participates as do others, and then steps back and attempts to re-create what happened and how it fit expectations; that is, reliability may be reduced in favor of validity. In reality, this is a trade-off, one that the researcher is willing to make in order to understand better how the particular variables he or she is interested in operate unconstrained by the control that typifies other research methods. Participant-observation allows for this, but it does so within the constraints of systematic observation and relies on an understanding of **communication roles**, **rules**, and **routines** as they relate to the verbal and nonverbal messages present.

What Is Participant-Observation?

There are various modes for studying people. Each one has its positive and negative aspects. If we look at each of these from the standpoint of *subjectivity* versus *objectivity*, however, we find some differences that may at first appear inaccurate. The most direct way to describe the behavior of a person is to view the act from the viewpoint of the actor, to be a part of the occurring behavior as it exists in the natural world. A less satisfactory approach is to view the act from the intuitive judgment of an outside, omniscient forecaster (an author). (See Table 9.1.) What are the other possibilities? More on the objective side are video recordings of the act, followed by audio recordings, and written recordings of the act. This is followed by participant-observation, during which elaborate and extensive procedures are used to ensure that the information being recorded is exactly what happened. To this point, we have discussed acts, recordings, and fiction.

Participant-observation is, then, *a combination of a first-person and a second-person account, which takes place in a naturalistic setting, of the actions and behaviors of a specific group of people.* Participant-observation in communication research allows us to examine many types of communication *messages* as they occur naturally. For instance, we can examine how people *speak*, the language they use in the workplace or at home, without interjecting an outside presence which may change the way the speaking naturally occurs. Or, we can examine the *behaviors* (verbal and nonverbal) people exhibit in particular situations (at rallies, sports events, on the job, during family arguments). Finally, we can observe how people adopt and

TABLE 9.1 Levels of Social Research

	PERSON	NATURE	METHOD
More "objective"	1st	Act Recording	Act VTR Audio recording Paper recording Participant-observation ■ as participant ■ as participant-observer ■ as observer-participant ■ as observer
	2nd	Synthesis	Self-report (and interpretation by subject[s])
	3rd		Historical report and interpretation—from primary source Historical report and interpretation—from secondary source ■ Self-report ■ Historical report interpretation ■ Interpretation ■ Self-report with stimulus (lab) ■ Historical report with stimulus
More "subjective"	Omniscient narrator	Fiction contrived	

Source: Hickson, M., III, Roebuck, J. B., & Murty, K. S. (1990). Creative triangulation: Toward a methodology for studying social types. In N. K. Denzin (Ed.), *Studies in symbolic interaction*, vol. 2. Greenwich, CT: JAI Press (p. 121).

employ different *roles* in the real world and how these roles change verbal and nonverbal messages. The focus of participant-observation, then, *is on a variety of messages in naturally occurring situations.*

When and Where Participant-Observation Should Be Used

There are three basic types of questions that can be asked using the participant-observation method. First, does the social grouping *exist*—one that is communicatively different from others? Second, what is the *normative* behavior of such formal and informal groups—how do the people who compose these groups use verbal and nonverbal communication? Third, how does communication *function* in these groups? We will first discuss how one determines the existence of a social group.

Participant-observation, as a research method, should be used primarily to develop useful, beneficial research questions. For example, in 1982 Roebuck and Hickson entered the community of the southern redneck primarily to discover whether such a social group as a construct—*redneck*—actually existed, as well as to study the norms and characteristics of such a social group if, indeed, it did exist. The researchers found through a literature search that, in the past 100 years, such a group seemed to be associated with "poor whites" in the southern part of the United States. Following a detailed historical account of the group, the researchers entered their community.

The purpose of the second phase was to provide an account of the **social norms** of such a group as well as determine how the group described itself. This entailed visiting the redneck's social world: honky-tonks, the homes of rednecks, the places where they worked, and the places where they transacted business. This indicated that the redneck considered himself somewhat of a social rebel, choosing to place himself against other groups rather than holding a specific identity for himself.

Such an investigation would have been extremely difficult, if not impossible, to undertake using traditional methods. For example, rednecks would not be open to entering a laboratory situation because they do not like academia nor academicians, and therefore would not be willing participants. For similar reasons, it would be difficult to entice rednecks to answer questions honestly using a traditional survey approach; because they consider themselves social rebels, rednecks do not participate in anything that might be considered part of mainstream society. They do not like to talk to strangers.

Thus, it may be "dangerous" to use traditional methods of study. Liebow (1967), for example, found that while streetcorner blacks in Washington, DC, held their own set of norms, those norms were not typical of society as a whole. Assume, for example, that you are interested in studying prison behavior. Traditional methods will not give you the insight you need to explain the channels of communication, for instance, between prisoners and guards. Prisons have their own codes of behavior, which may or may not be consistent with mainstream society. Assuming a white, middle-class mentality may be both physically dangerous and theoretically unjustified. Participant-observation is an effective method to use to study whether a group exists in the sense of having its own system of normative behavior.

Another example of participant-observation occurs when the participants themselves are unaware of their own behavior. Hickson's (1977) study of people who rode commuter buses found that normative behavior changed over time. Had the participants been surveyed about their normative behavior, they probably would not have recognized that such changes had taken place. Thus, at certain times, in such an investigation, it is necessary to "test" the normative behavior of the group by violating what the researcher believes are the norms (e.g., Douglas, 1970; Garfinkel, 1967). As a member of the "group," the participant-observer is only one step removed from the behavior; the method provides the ability to examine differences over time because they have been noted *as they occurred*. The group members (the *actors*), because they are involved with everyday activity, caught up in their daily lives, are more likely to ignore such changes—unless, of course, the violations are so dramatic as to stimulate discussion.

Such violations involving **ethnomethodology** (how people make sense out of the situations in which they find themselves) not only provide answers as to what constitutes the norms but also what kinds of sanctions the group assesses for violations. Again, as a researcher, you must take care to watch for your own physical well being as well as assuring the accuracy of your data.

What if the people are acting in such a way *because* a researcher is present? Hickson (1974) dealt with this problem in a study of the communication patterns in a community action agency in Illinois. He made three recommendations regarding studying an organization: (1) the researcher must be able to communicate with personnel on all levels, (2) it is probably better if the researcher is assigned a volunteer job in a low-status position, and (3) the researcher should attempt to balance the roles of participant and observer.

When studying the communication of organizations, it is important to remember that the low status workers' communication patterns are as important, if not more so, than the communication of the higher status staff. In a hierarchical organization, the bottom part of the pyramid holds many more people than does the top. It has, therefore, a greater opportunity to affect the relationships with individuals outside the organization. In addition, the lower status workers tend to establish the norms for external communication behavior. Thus, you need to be accepted as an insider among the low status workers, use their language, and dress the part. To engage in the research you should be a volunteer; entering the organization as a paid worker may be perceived as threatening to other low status workers. As a researcher, it is important that you make it clear that you are not interested in having a long-term, paid position in the organization and that you do not associate with the value system of upper-level management. You must stay in the organization for a long period of time (probably at least six months), but also have a deadline for a final exit.

Conducting a Participant-Observation Study

There are seven basic steps to undertaking a participant-observation study: (1) establish the general research questions; (2) review the literature on the subject group; (3) develop a **theoretical model** (based on the literature) that provides an understanding of what *should* be observed given this particular group of people, organization, or event; (4) collect the data; (5) analyze the data; (6) develop an **empirical model**; and (7) compare and contrast the theoretical model with the empirical model to determine the conclusions and implications of your research.

MINI-PROJECT:

What group on campus would make a good participant-observation study? An athletic team? The debate team? A fraternity or sorority? Choose a group and list what you know about it and its members. How would you "fit in" as a participant?

Research Questions.   Participation-observation requires a flexible, adaptive researcher and research technique. The following questions are appropriate for participant-observation:

1. Is there such a phenomenon as the southern "redneck"?
2. Do African American streetcorner people have a set of communicative norms? If so, what are the nonverbal ways they communicate (the nonverbal norms)? What are the verbal norms? (Do they employ slang, street English, obscenities?)
3. To what extent do these communication norms change as a result of changes in the environment?
4. What communicative behaviors are associated with a newsroom? Are there special nonverbal behaviors employed? Is there a special layout that provides clues as to status or power? Are there special vocabularies?
5. What types of verbal and nonverbal communication occur in families undergoing marital stress?

Review of the Literature.   While the traditional literature review may be undertaken using a library search of books and articles, various subject groups for qualitative studies require the use of nontraditional methods of understanding the subject "pool" as well. For example, it may be necessary to read newspaper articles about organizations as diverse as the National Socialist Party, the Black Panthers, or even the Kiwanis. Such a review of articles could provide you with information on what is going on in the organization as well as the media's views of the importance of that organization's activities. A thorough review of the subject pool should enable you to discriminate the differences between the First Presbyterian Church in Terre Haute, Indiana, and the First Presbyterian Church in Savannah, Georgia.

The literature review should provide certain demographic data (age, sex, race), the level of formality of the group (amount of policies and procedures in written form), and the identity of group leaders (names, demographics, biographical data). In addition, it should provide an historical account of the group. The review should provide data about how you could go about being assimilated into the group; the group's systems of rewards and sanctions should be available.

Developing a Theoretical Model.   From an extensive literature review the researcher should have a number of clues about: (1) why the group is unique, (2) why the event is unusual, (3) how similar organizations function from an idealistic perspective, and/or (4) why most people would consider the behavior and communication processes deviant in comparison with a norm. Thus, the theoretical model is an outline of what the researcher presumes will be the case, taken from the context of the review of literature and his or her knowledge of the communication event itself.

An example can be taken from a study of the communication that occurs at a communication convention. The research question you would consider might be, "What type of communicative behaviors occur at conventions of people engaged in the study of communication?" The specific questions would center on what particular convention(s) you were interested in examining. Suppose, for reasons of access, expense, and interest, you are interested in how people at regional communication conventions communicate.

The following are typical examples of occurrences a researcher interested in convention communication might expect to find; that is, the research question is concerned with how the role of conventioneer alters both communication role and the resultant communication norms—both verbal and nonverbal messages. First, there is a registration for both the convention hotel and the convention itself. Second, there is a placement service available for employers and potential employees to meet, greet, and talk with one another. Third, there are a large number of presentations and seminars. Fourth, there are a number of events that call for the participation of all persons gathered at the convention (receptions, association business meetings, association social events, addresses to the association, and so forth). Given these factors, you might begin by asking questions about which members would attend which of these events.

In establishing this *typicality mode*, you must first visualize the physical areas of interaction. There are individual rooms for the members, a registration area, large convocation rooms for receptions and major addresses, smaller rooms for the presentation of papers and seminars, restrooms off the lobby area, and the lobby area itself. Since we know that there is a need for eating meals at such conventions, you should be aware that there may be one or more restaurants and bars in a hotel, and bars and restaurants near the hotel at which individuals can meet and interact with one another.

Second, you must anticipate *expected* behavior. A researcher might expect, for instance, that the convention attendees would register early to get a name tag so that others would recognize them by name. When people see one another once a year or less, it is easy to remember the face but not the name.

You might expect that employers and potential employees would look for the placement service space very early upon arrival. In other words, a researcher should expect that each person involved in the event under study has a *role*. In this instance the roles might include potential employer and potential employee, paper presenter, seminar leader, or simply observer; that is, each person has a pragmatic reason for attending the convention and this reason—or role—will influence the messages he or she produces. In addition, you would expect that people attending for a particular reason would also have *rules*. Rules are unwritten behaviors dictated by the norms present as established by the group. For example, it might be that the potential employer feels at ease going to a bar in the hotel and having a few drinks. Such behavior may be against the rules for the potential employees, lest they run into one of the potential employers in the "wrong" place. It also may be a rule violation for the potential employer to be seen "interviewing"—even if that person is just talking to a potential job seeker—at an inappropriate time and place.

Finally, you might expect that a person would get into a *routine*; that is, employers and employees might go back and forth to check the job and interview possibilities at the placement service periodically. Individuals who are not seeking a job might never go to the placement service. Thus, through this review of literature and commonsensical evaluation, we have developed a theoretical model. The communication—at communication conventions, as our example indicates—should encompass roles, rules, and routines (Hickson & Hill, 1979). Hence, our theoretical model must define the general roles, rules, and routines we expect to be typical of the event and the group. Based on these definitions, we create expectations of what communicative messages (both verbal and nonverbal) we would expect to observe, given the circumstances. Obviously, each may change as either the group or the event changes, something over which the researcher has *no control*.

For the theoretical model to be helpful, however, the researcher should be more specific; that is, what verbal and nonverbal communication roles seem to go with what verbal and nonverbal rules and the resultant routines (the *application* of the roles and rules)? Table 9.2 provides a listing of convention roles. Understanding that these roles are not mutually exclusive, the researcher can then go about determining which communicative roles are attached to which communication rules and the resultant routines. Following through on this process, you, as the researcher, will have developed a *theoretical model*.

TABLE 9.2   Possible Communication Roles

1. *The job seeker:* What communication strategies does the person seeking a job adopt? Are there any particular rules that he or she employs communicating with others, both potential employers and competitors?

2. *The politician* (the person holding or seeking office at the convention for the particular group [the office-seeker may be seeking an organization-wide office or may be seeking an office in a smaller division of the organization, and this should be taken into account as the expectations might change according to the participant's role]): What communication strategies does this person use? Here we might note the particular types of language employed; where (the nonverbal aspects) this person communicates with others; and whether or not a particular routine is followed by each politico.

3. *The information-seeker* (the person there to learn, to be trained, to compare different ideas): How does this person communicate? Where does he or she sit in meetings? In what type of verbal questioning does he or she engage? With whom does he or she normally spend her time? Is there a common purpose in the group?

4. *The presenter* (the person there to deliver a paper or lead a seminar): How does he or she communicate? What verbal or nonverbal skills are employed? By what set of "rules" is he or she constrained? How does the presenter approach his or her task?

5. *The conventioneer* (the person present to "see the city"): As a group, how do these people act? Do they spend their time at the convention? Individually, does he or she establish a minimal time to be spent in meetings? Does he or she dress differently?

6. *The socialite* (the person there to "see old friends"): What distinguishes this person from the politician? What verbal behaviors are observable that would establish a "rule" that there should be only social talk? Does this person use different nonverbal codes or systems to indicate the communication norm is social and not business?

Data Collection. The theoretical model is simply a preliminary stage for establishing a sense of what is being studied. Participant-observation requires that *careful notes* be taken of all observations. Two different types of notes are taken when conducting participant-observation research: immediate records and delayed, reflective log observations. You might call the former field notes and the latter refined notes. One drawback of participant observation is found in taking notes. In places where you are surreptitiously recording behavior, the taking of notes may be too overt, it may create behaviors in the population under study not normally found in either the group or the situation. Therefore, you should try to limit the number of notes taken if you feel that in the process of note taking you are observing behaviors created because of your presence. This, of course, leaves much to memory and requires you to find an isolated spot to record your observations. If you are in a position to observe without it being obvious to the group, then you might consider taking more complete notes.

Obviously, it would be easier if we could audio- or videotape the interactions. Tape recordings should only be used in cases where a person could be *publicly* overheard talking with another person. There is a fine line between participant-observation and violating another person's right of privacy.[1]

Immediate records should be as factual as possible. In general, you should record your observations as carefully and completely as possible. Use the margins around your notes to review and elaborate behaviors that might have gone unnoticed at first but, when reviewed, come to mind. When doing such a review, you should be careful to avoid interpreting what you observed; the immediate notes should reflect the actual *behaviors as they occurred and without interpretation or analysis*.

The delayed, reflective log of observations, however, will certainly incorporate your feelings as a researcher and, to the extent possible, the researcher should take great pains to differentiate his or her own interpretations from the more objective behavior which was observed. As a participant-observer, it is important that you get into the habit of writing the reflective log at the end of each day. In writing this log, use the immediate observations as a guide to reconstructing what was observed, trying both to describe and interpret the behaviors and situations. What was typical and atypical might be noted as well as how the participants in your study reacted on that day. Among other items, the reflective log should tell the reader how you were influenced by the observations and to what extent you may have influenced the behaviors of other participants.

The methods for collecting data may change in the process of actual observation. You may decide that open-ended interviews are needed to gain additional information from some of the participants. The observations may call for you to mail a questionnaire to the participants *after the event*. The important thing to remember is that you should be open to such changes throughout the investigation. Participant-observation, as a method, must adapt to changes in both the group and the setting. A major strength of such change is the interpretation you would make on why changes were necessary in your later analysis and reporting.

Once the data collection has begun, your objectivity is paramount; that is, a person should not attempt to observe an organization or people to whom he or she is very familiar, nor should he or she try to observe organizations or people with whom he or she shares a close ideological agreement or has a major disagreement. The participant-observer is above all a researcher, a person trying to make objective, rational explanations for people's behavior. Attempting to infiltrate an organization or group that you either agree or disagree with will probably yield biased observations from the beginning, is unethical and should be avoided at all times.

One final comment. *Validity* of observation is a major concern with participant-observation research. Because you are actually observing behavior in the context of normally occurring communication, what you observe is as valid as the perceptions that you as the researcher have of the behavior; that is, to the degree to which you can observe what has happened, the language used, the norms established, you have at least face and content validity. *Reliability*, however, is limited in at least two ways. First, there are potential biases associated with observing others. The degree to which you can identify your biases, your reliability in observing and reporting is increased. Second, participant-observation is a personal experience and your interpretation is your interpretation. The decisions you make are based on your understanding of what should and did happen.

How can the problems of reliability be overcome? One way would be to employ more than one trained observer. To the degree that the two or more observers agreed on what they observed, reliability could be enhanced. This is no different than intercoder reliability, which was discussed in earlier chapters.

Data Analysis.   Once the observations have been collected and compressed into a form of data, you take a new role, that of telling a story to the reader. Here you are trying to provide an account of the everyday happenings under investigation; you try to present your findings in an account that is so real that the reader feels he or she is actually present in the situation. In conducting this phase of participant-observation you should take care neither to underestimate nor to exaggerate the findings. In selecting the information out of the notes, include information about similarities and dissimilarities among the participants, the actions taken by the participants, and your own feelings—your personal reactions to the observations collected. In particular instances you might excise certain interpretations and place them in explanatory footnotes attached to the report. Whether the analysis is in the text or in footnote form, it will be reporting what you as the *researcher* observed, hence it is based on your observations of what you observed as it occurred, including your personal biases. This lends a particular uniqueness to both the method and the style of reporting.

Development of an Empirical Model.   After the data have been collected and analyzed, you develop an empirical model. The empirical model is simply a summary of the

■ ■ ■ ■ ■

MINI-PROJECT:

Assume that you will be conducting a participant-observation study of classroom communication at your institution. What communication roles, rules, and routines would you expect to find? How would you test the theoretical model? How would you collect the data?

observations and the findings of the analyzed data. In its most simplistic form the empirical model presents what was observed in the naturalistic setting. The empirical model reflects data that are similar to that of other methods. The empirical model represents the world as it was when the observations were collected.

Model Comparison and Contrast.   The final phase is the reporting of similarities and differences between what was expected (theoretical model) and what was observed (empirical model). Guiding this stage of analysis is a number of general questions that are adapted to the specific questions asked in the study: How did the original review of the literature and subsequent theoretical model compare with the empirical model developed out of the data collection and analysis? That is, how similar or dissimilar are the two models? Where were the differences observed? Why? Where were similarities observed? Did the similarities hold up across time? Other questions guiding this analysis are found in Table 9.3. The ultimate purpose of this final comparison-contrast is to act as the theoretical model for the next investigator.

Advantages and Limitations

As with any method, there are certain advantages and limitations to research conducted by participant-observation. Participant-observation best answers certain kinds of questions. If the research question requires a qualitative but social scientific method, then participant-observation may be best suited to find the appropriate answers.

There are three limitations. First, good participant-observation research usually takes a long time. It may take a year or longer to complete; most researchers who use this method take a number of years to collect their data. Second, participant-observation studies are usually not too generalizable. They cannot be generalized to time nor to other similar groups. The results, while valid for the particular group observed, may not be reliable when compared to other, similar studies. The participant-observation method yields a **case study**. A third limiting factor is found in the realization that not all researchers can undertake studies using this method. Some people cannot set aside their biases; because there is no external source for accounting for biases (such as statistics or sampling procedures), many beginning participant-observers simply give up on this method.

TABLE 9.3   Model Comparison and Contrast Questions

1. What communication roles were observed?
2. What communication rules were observed?
3. What communication routines were observed?
4. What were the norms for communication, given this particular group, institution, or event?
5. How did roles, rules, and routines interact to create norms?
6. Under what circumstances were the rules and routines that made up the norms violated? Why were norms violated?
7. In what ways were the norms violated? Which norms were upheld? Why?

FOCUS GROUPS

While participant-observation allows researchers to study groups in their own setting and with no control over the events, a second qualitative/descriptive methodology allows you to study groups and to exercise considerable control: the **focus group**.

What Is a Focus Group?

A focus group is a group of people collected through some method that discusses some topic of concern to the researcher. The focus group usually does not meet in a naturalistic setting; instead, it meets where you can control the environment. Instead of uncontrolled interaction, you have a guide or questionnaire that a **moderator** or **facilitator** uses to stimulate discussion. You often will have materials with which to stimulate discussion, especially if your research project deals with the marketing of a product or service. What you have in effect is a "controlled group discussion" (Wimmer & Dominick, 1997, p. 97).

When and Where Should It Be Used?

Focus group method has been used primarily in mass communication and marketing communication research (Lederman, 1990). A review of the literature indicates that, although not used as a major academic research tool, the method is gaining acceptance in preparing for preliminary survey and experimental research and in applied research in the "real world." Using focus groups is a qualitative research method that attempts to probe a small group of people about their attitudes, values, and behaviors to identify deep feelings and motivations. It is basically a directed small group discussion on an issue that is guided or facilitated by a skilled leader. The moderator has a rough set of questions that are modified as the group discussion proceeds. Focus groups typically last an hour or more.

Pragmatically, we use focus groups all the time. Whenever we need ideas for a project we get a group of people together and "brainstorm." This form of brainstorming can be used to answer communication questions. For example, suppose you are interested in the following research question: "How can we increase attendance at women's athletic events on campus?" You could go to the events and observe those present, but that will not give you information about those who do not attend. You could conduct a telephone survey or interview students, but that takes time. A focus group composed of students who both attend and do not attend women's athletic events would give you the information you need to mount a communication campaign. An advantage of focus groups is that they are efficient, quick, and an inexpensive way to collect data. The disadvantage is that they have no hard or fast rules or procedures to follow; instead, you operate along general guidelines.

Focus groups are used in marketing communication, advertising, public relations, and organizational communication research. The method can be used to gather preliminary information to prepare for a larger survey or experiment. It also helps us to understand the reasons behind a communication phenomenon. From the perspective of this book, however, it helps us answer questions of definition, value, and policy. Focus groups are not good at answering questions of fact.

Preparing for a Focus Group

Preparing for a focus group requires that you first have a research question that is best answered by the method. For example, suppose you are conducting a promotional campaign for the tourist industry in the Florida Keys. One of the things you want to do is increase local use of attractions. A survey would be difficult, most of your population stays only on weekends and then they typically are out on the water. Participant-observation might work, but you want to generalize your findings to the larger population. A focus group is your best solution.

Now that you plan on conducting the focus group, how do you get your participants? You select people who have a range of feelings about the topic. In the Florida study, it would be important to get people who have visited the local attractions and those who have not. In thinking about the number of participants, you need to consider how many groups you will need. As a general rule of thumb, you need at least two groups. A second group allows comparison of responses between groups. Generally, you would want between two and ten groups. Because you are interested in their discussion of why they do or do not attend local attractions, you need to keep the group size down. You want somewhere between five and fifteen participants per group, depending on the questions being asked. Thus, your "sample" for five groups would run from twenty-five to seventy-five participants.

Sometimes you have to offer incentives to get participation. For instance, you might offer a free admission to an attraction or a free meal. If you are working with a product, the product might be part of the incentive package. In a study conducted for a university hospital, the incentive was time off work and the promise of a meal for participating in a "one to two hour" group looking at communication at the hospital. How many participants? Wimmer and Dominick (1997) suggest 150 percent of what you think you need. Experience, however, indicates that a good rule to follow is the "rule of 10." If you want 50 people for your groups, solicit 500. This is especially true when you are trying to recruit participants from a large, general population.

After deciding how many groups and participants you need, you need to find a location for the groups and establish the times they will meet. For obvious reasons, most focus groups are run at night, with one group following a second by 10 to 15 minutes. Because of the interaction required, most groups run between one and two hours, with at least one refreshment and bathroom break included. Some research companies have two-way mirrored and electronically monitored rooms that you can rent. You need a room that is conducive to communication and not too formal. Preferably, you want your participants to face each other, perhaps in a circle around a table. You may need more than one room. Minimally, you will want to tape record each session; ethically, you need your participants' agreement (see Chapter 3).

Once you have set up the room and decided on how you will record the interaction, you need to create a facilitator guide (see Box 9.1). The guide includes the opening statements and the general questions you want discussed. Because this is a discussion and not an interview, the questionnaire includes general questions and possible tag questions. If we

BOX 9.1

SAMPLE FACILITATOR GUIDE AND QUESTIONNAIRE FOR A STUDY ON INTERNAL COMMUNICATION

WELCOME AND INTRODUCTION

Good (morning/evening). I'm _____, a graduate student in the UM School of Communication, and I've been asked to lead you in a discussion about communications here at the medical school. This is _____, an employee in the Department of _____ and a member of the school's internal communications group, who will be assisting me today.

I'm sure you must have a lot of questions about why you're here today, how you were selected, and what's expected of you. To answer your questions, the members of the medical school's internal communications workgroup, who invited you here today, have written a brief letter which I've been asked to give you. _____ will pass those out to you now, along with a brief questionnaire on the nature and history of your employment at UM that will help assess the information we discuss here today. We are also giving each of you a name tag. Please write your first name, or a nickname, or a fictitious name if you prefer, on the tag and put it on so that I and everyone here may address you by name.

I'd like to let you know that the information you supply on the questionnaire and everything you say here today will remain entirely confidential. The discussion will be audiotaped and the transcription of the tape will be summarized in such a manner that no individual can be identified.

Please take a few minutes to read the letter and fill out the questionnaire. When your questionnaire is completed, please raise your hand and _____ will collect it.

Has everyone read the letter and turned in the questionnaire?

OK. (TURN ON TAPE)[a]

I'd like to open the discussion with introductions. Let's go around the room clockwise, beginning with _____. Please state your name, your position, how long you've worked at the School of Medicine, and anything else you care to mention.

DISPLAY MISSION STATEMENT OF SCHOOL

QUESTION: This is the mission statement of the School of Medicine. How many of you are familiar with it?

QUESTION: How many of you can relate your role or position here at the school with the mission statement? _____ Do you see how your job fits in?

QUESTION: Has anyone ever explained to you how your job relates to the mission? _____. Who?

QUESTION: Was the mission of the school explained to you before you were hired or shortly thereafter?

QUESTION: What picture of the UM School of Medicine did you have before you started working here? PROBE FOR MULTIPLE RESPONSES.

QUESTION: Has this picture changed since you started working here?

QUESTION: What was it that changed your picture of the school? Something you heard or read about? How did you learn about it?

[ISSUE—Are employees receiving the information they would like to receive and that they feel they need to do their jobs well?]

DISPLAY "INFORMATION CATEGORIES" CHART
[Faculty & Staff news, Clinical Practice news, Biomedical research programs, institutional goals/policy issues/strategic planning, institutional news (awards, initiatives, school-wide programs/events), administrative announcement, educational/training opportunities, employee benefits, campus events.]

INSTRUCTION: Take a minute to look over this list of different categories of information related to the School of Medicine.

QUESTION: Which three categories of information are you most interested in knowing? Why?

QUESTION: Which three categories of information do you feel you need the most to do your jobs effectively? Why?

ªBold-faced type and statements in brackets are for the facilitator's use and information only.

were asking questions about local Florida Keys attractions, we might ask how many attractions have the participants visited within the last year. As the question is answered, the facilitator may tag on the response, "Why?" or "Do any of you agree with that?" The tag question seeks to extend the answer, yet not provoke a simple yes or no response.

Some focus groups prescreen participants for attitudes and beliefs with some measurement instrument. They then provide some stimulus—such as a movie or advertisement—and then discuss it. At the end of the focus group, they may posttest participants to see if the stimulus and discussion altered attitudes or beliefs. This is a common focus group technique employed in the advertising industry. The motion picture industry often has focus groups view a production and then change parts of the film or video after analysis of participant comments.

The key to a successful focus group session is the facilitator or moderator. The facilitator must be able to handle diverse personalities, ethnicities, ages, and people of different socio-economic status (Davies, 1999). He or she must be a good listener, a skilled interviewer, and be nonjudgmental. He or she should be able to mask feelings and not give off nonverbal cues that may influence group responses. The facilitator must be thoroughly familiar with the nuances of the topic and be able to construct insightful probes. Most focus groups are run by highly trained professionals who are skilled facilitators.

As the researcher, you should refrain from serving as a facilitator, unless you are conducting the study as a preliminary step toward a larger project. Marketing research services often provide facilitators as part of their costs. A good facilitator, whether professional or not, is someone who knows when to allow the discussion to continue and when to break in. A good facilitator knows how to draw out reluctant participants and to shut off participants who dominate the group.

Conducting the Focus Group

Once the facilities have been set, the facilitator selected and trained, the discussion guide prepared, and the participants selected and in place, you are ready to conduct the focus group. Before each group is run, an equipment check should be run. The facilitator should provide a general overview of the session and what participants can expect; at this time confidentiality and anonymity should be stressed and participants allowed to back out of the project. Focus groups typically begin with participants introducing themselves or sharing some experience relevant to the project (the facilitator may ask each participant to indicate what local attractions they have or have not visited lately). This accomplishes two things. First, it "breaks the ice." Second, it gets names and voices on tape for later transcribing and analysis.

Analyzing the Results.   Once the focus groups have been run you need to analyze the results. This is done in two ways. First, immediately after the group is finished, you get the facilitator's reaction to the group and to individual participants. A good facilitator can tell you a lot about the discussion based on his or her first impressions. Second, transcripts may be made of the session. The transcripts are then analyzed via content analysis—units of analyses are selected, content categories are created, the data coded and analyses conducted. Usually, however, the facilitator acts as a reporter and writes up a qualitative analysis.

Known Group Technique

A special type of focus group is often used in situations where the participant population is extremely small. Problems are often encountered in organizational communication research, for instance, when subordinates and superiors are placed in the same group or when participants are selected for the same group (Hickson, Stacks, & Greeley-Padgett, 1998). A known group's participants are selected because of their position in the organization (Gwin, 1984). Often we want to include all levels of an organization in a group, to get as many different perspectives on a problem or product as possible. However, due to status differences,

---

MINI-PROJECT:

Design a study using focus group methodology that seeks to answer the following research question: "What can the [your institution] do to increase the local town population's participation in [your institution's] events?"

subordinates are often reluctant to talk or disagree with their superiors. To counter this, all initial communication is done in writing, often prior to the group's initial meeting. The responses are then evaluated by the facilitator, summarized in writing, and used as stimulus material for discussion. In this way no one knows whether the CEO or janitor came up with the statement and status differences quickly break down (Gwin, 1984).

Advantages and Limitations

Focus group methodology provides a quick and relatively inexpensive way to get qualitative information (Mitofsky, 1996). The data it provides is rich in that it often provides explanations for responses to questions that cannot be obtained by other methods because of time constraints. A major advantage of the focus group is that participants can "tag" off each others' answers, often arriving at conclusions that would differ greatly from a simple interviewer "Why?" probe. The focus group provides data that tend to be holistic and its outcome often is greater than the sum of its participants.

Focus groups are limited in two very important ways. First, they depend upon the facilitator to move the group along. The facilitator's abilities may make or break the project. Second, the participants themselves often limit the findings. They are usually volunteers—who self-select themselves in most cases. And, regardless of the facilitator's skill, one or more may not participate and others may succeed in monopolizing or even intimidating others from participation. Questions of validity and reliability should be considered carefully with this technique (Kirk & Miller, 1986).

IN-DEPTH INTERVIEWS

As noted earlier, sometimes the researcher needs to develop what Brenner (1985, p. 148) calls an "intimate familiarity" with the people involved in a research project. This familiarity allows you to understand the other individual's point of view and is achieved through an unstructured, or at best, very limited interview questionnaire. When we think of an in-depth interview, we usually think of the personality interview, such as those conducted by Barbara Walters or the interviews conducted by television magazine shows. When used in research, in-depth interviews can create an aura of empathy not found in participant-observation or focus group methods; they are a one-on-one, interpersonal interaction.

What Is the In-depth Interview?

As noted, the in-depth interview is a one-on-one, you and the interviewee, process. The in-depth interview requires respondents who are willing to give the time necessary to conduct the interview correctly. In some cases this requires payment, anywhere from a few dollars to thousands of dollars may be involved. The method also requires that you, as the researcher, know your subject matter very well. How well? Since the in-depth interview can go almost anywhere, you must be prepared to follow any of a number of paths. Because you are participating in an open-ended discussion, talking with the respondent, recording the interview becomes a problem. The intense nature of the interview almost certainly requires that the interaction be audio or video recorded and transcribed later for analysis. The in-depth interviewer is acting like a good news reporter who is objective and thorough in questioning and reporting.

When and Where Should It Be Used?

The research questions best answered by in-depth interviewing are value and policy-oriented. What you are asking for are personal interpretations of social events—their significance and how they influenced the individual being interviewed. Although you may exercise great control over the interview, the location, and interview format, your ability to generalize to others is extremely limited. Because of the intensity of interaction, interviews are held with only a few individuals. In general, you would conduct an in-depth interview when and if you can identify what many qualitative researchers call *key informants*, or people who are both willing and able to shed light on your research concern (Murphy, 1980). Alexis McKenna (1990), for instance, was interested in the socialization process that older, female, graduate students go through when they return to school after years in the work force. (McKenna was an older student who, after owning several businesses, decided to return to school and pursue her doctorate in communication. The interactions she had with other, younger male and female graduate students and faculty led her to her research.) To conduct the study, McKenna identified seven older female graduate students and interviewed them over a period of time. Her findings shed light on how these particular women socialized into their graduate programs and dealt with their younger male and female counterparts, to include some roles (i.e., mothering) that had been reported in other literature.

Conducting the In-depth Interview

Conducting an in-depth interview involves five steps. First, as noted earlier, the research question being posed should be best answered by the method. Second, the interviewees must be selected. Identifying key informants is the first step in selecting interviewees. Often a **snowball technique** is used to obtain interviews—each interviewee is asked to identify other interviewees. McKenna (1990) and many feminist researchers (e.g., Rush & Grubb-Swetnam, 1966) have used this technique to identify research participants. Peterson et al. (1994) conducted in-depth interviews with 46 Texas farmers on their farms to identify themes and issues that impacted a persuasive safety campaign. At this stage you also need to

■　■　■　■　■

MINI-PROJECT:

Plan an in-depth interview of a faculty member about his or her research and how it is conducted. Who will you select? When and where will you conduct the interview? Will the interviewee allow you to record it? What questions will you use as a guide to the interview? How will you analyze the data gathered?

consider whether you want to interview participants individually or in groups. Marital communication researchers, for example, often begin an interview with the couple and then separate them for the remainder of the interview (e.g., Surra, Chandler, & Asmussen, 1987).

After you have identified your participants, the third step is to schedule the interview. Consideration of locale is important (Frey, Botan, Friedman, & Kreps, 1991). Whether you interview participants in their territory, your territory, or some neutral place may alter how they view the interview situation. The rule of thumb is to interview people when and wherever it is most convenient to them. Hayden (1993) conducted in-depth interviews with 16 chronically ill patients:

> In order to find subjects willing to participate in interviews, I asked both private practitioners working with people who are chronically ill and various illness foundations to solicit volunteers for this project. After receiving a list of volunteers, I contacted each person by telephone and set up an interview at her or his convenience. I asked for permission to audiotape the session, and read each person a consent form. Subjects were promised complete anonymity, thus all names used in this work have been changed. Once all of the interviews were completed, they were transcribed in full, yielding 140 pages of transcript.[2]

Interviewing someone at his or her place of work as in an organizational leadership study, however, may yield many interruptions and distractions; on the other hand, interviewing at the place of work provides you with a better understanding of how that person communicates in that environment.

The fourth step involves the interview itself, or its format. Generally, in-depth interviews are conducted with minimal prepared questions. Prepared questions tend to be used in a funnel format, going from general, overview questions to specific questions. The fifth, and final, step involves analyzing the data gathered. Analysis begins much like the other methods (the facilitator's immediate reactions are assessed and participant-observer's immediate notes are analyzed): the subjective feelings of the interviewer must be drawn out and analyzed. How did you feel during the interview? Were the answers to your questions openly and honestly answered, or did the interviewee hedge and deceive? Careful attention and noting of not only the interviewee's verbal, but also nonverbal behaviors is required. It is a good idea to write in a journal your feelings immediately after the interview. The interviews are then transcribed and the data analyzed via historical/rhetorical-critical or content analysis. Final reporting often reads more like a novel than a formal research report.

Advantages and Limitations

The in-depth interview allows you to get intensely involved with the research. It provides a depth of understanding that is not found in the focus group or participant-observation study. The in-depth interview affords you as the researcher to go off in different directions, taking the time to see that all approaches, theories, or ideas have been explored. It also allows interviewees to tell their stories as they see them; the text is their story.

The major limitations to the method lie in the inability to establish reliability and the concomitant lack of generalizability and the enormous investment of time. With regard to reliability, the key issue is how much has the study revealed about the object of study and how much about the researcher and his or her own unique perspective. This is why rigor of detailed contemporaneous notes is so very critical.

Concerning the vital resource of time, since you are only interviewing a few individuals, you cannot generalize to others in similar instances; like the participant-observation study, the in-depth interview is much like a case study. What we know about the event, occasion, or person is rich in detail and understanding, but helps us little in projecting how others would communicate in similar situations. Second, in-depth interviewing is both expensive and time-consuming. Interviewing requires some form of recording; tapes and transcription can be expensive. In-depth interviewing also takes many hours and often even longer to get to location. Finally, even the validity of the data may be endangered; interviewers may inadvertently communicate their personal feelings and attitudes through verbal slips and nonverbal communication.

APPLYING KNOWLEDGE IN COMMUNICATION

Qualitative/descriptive methodologies offer communication researchers in-depth understanding of communication phenomena. The trade-off, of course, is that the results are very difficult to extend to other situations, even similar ones. However, participant-observation, focus group, and in-depth interviewing have been used to understand how people perceive and use communication in their daily lives. We get a feeling for the quality of life from qualitative methods. As we will find in later chapters, this is something that is missing from objective quantitative methods such as survey and experimental research.

Participant-observation provides you with an understanding of how communication operates that cannot be found in more controlled methods. The fact that you participated in the event adds a reality to the study that is not found in survey or experimental research. It provides a different perspective. Focus group method affords some control over the questions asked and the direction you want to go in answering your research question. Unlike the survey, which often requires participants to respond to forced-choice, Likert-like statements, the focus group method allows full responses and encourages others to tag on to a particular thought or statement. The in-depth interview allows you to *really understand the people you study*. It affords you the chance to dig for information and "get under the skin" of the people who lived the event or occasion.

Research in health communication, journalism, organizational communication, advertising, public relations, and feminist communication have employed qualitative/descriptive methods. Other areas are beginning to explore the potential it holds for them as they seek to triangulate different methodologies toward better answers to their research questions.

SUMMARY

In this chapter we have attempted to introduce the ideas behind qualitative descriptive research. We have outlined three methods: participant-observation, where the researcher "becomes one" with his or her research; focus groups, where the researcher is a part of the communication with a selected group of participants, but now in control of both the questions being asked and the environment; and the in-depth interview, where the researcher is one-on-one with participants, working without an extensive questionnaire or protocol that allows both structure and freedom to probe for more information. Much can be learned about how others communicate simply by listening and observing them communicate verbally and nonverbally.

PROBES

1. Why participant-observation? What does this method offer you that other methods do not? Can you think of a research question based thus far on your academic training in communication that would be best handled by participant-observation? Why?

2. In conducting a participant-observation study you must develop a theoretical model. How is this done? What is typicality in the model? Why is the establishment of typicality important? How does typicality relate to the concept of role in this method?

3. How would you conduct a focus group study that wanted to answer the research question, "What do you think about this television commercial for product X?"

4. When would you use the known group technique as a way to get a focus group to communicate? What advantages does the known group have over the focus group?

5. What advantages does in-depth interviewing offer the communication researcher that the participant-observation or focus group methods do not?

RESEARCH PROJECTS

1. This research project seeks to discover the roles, rules, and routines found in a newsroom, broadcast studio, advertising agency, public relations agency or department. This project might be combined with an internship or a part-time job.

2. What communication problems do freshmen on your campus encounter when they first come to campus? Conduct a focus group study to answer the question.

3. Identify several community leaders—journalists, police or fire chiefs, politicians, broadcasters, business leaders—and conduct in-depth interviews that focus on their jobs and what role communication plays in their day-to-day activities.

SUGGESTED READING

Bogdan, R., & Taylor, S. J. (1975). *Introduction to qualitative research methods: A phenomenological approach to the social sciences.* New York: John Wiley.

Brown, M. H. (1990). "Reading" an organization's culture: An examination of stories in nursing homes. *Journal of Applied Communication Research, 18,* 64–75.

Davies, R. (1999). *Focus groups in Asia: A guide.* http://www.researchinfo.com/library/focus_in_asia/index.shtml.

Greenbaum, T. L. (1988). *The practical handbook and guide to focus group research.* Lexington, MA: D. C. Heath.

Hayden, S. (1993). Chronically ill and "feeling fine": A study of communication and chronic illness. *Journal of Applied Communication Research, 21,* 263–278.

Hickson, M., III. (1974). Participant-observation technique in organizational research. *Journal of Business Communication, 11,* 37–42, 54.

Lederman, L. C. (1990). Assessing educational effectiveness: The focus group interview as a technique for data collection. *Communication Education, 39,* 117–127.

Morgan, D. L., & Krueger, R. A. (1998). *The focus group kit.* Thousand Oaks, CA: Sage.

Phillipsen, G. (1975). Speaking "like a man" in Teamsterville: Culture patterns of role enactment in an urban neighborhood. *Quarterly Journal of Speech, 61,* 13–22.

Roebuck, J. B., & Hickson, M., III. (1982). *The southern redneck: A phenomenological class study.* New York: Praeger.

Spradley, J. P. (1980). *Participant observation.* New York: Holt, Rinehart and Winston.

Van Maanen, J., Manning, P. K., & Miller, M. L. (Eds.). (1986). *Sage qualitative research methods series.* Beverly Hills, CA: Sage Publications.

NOTES

1. This differs legally by state, but typically you may not tape record another person without that person's expressed consent; this is particularly true for telephone conversations.

2. This citation has no page number. The article was cited in *CommSearch95*; the database and articles do not contain individual page numbers, making it difficult to follow a *normal* citation system (see Chapter 4). The actual page number for this cite is page 266, found by going to the library and looking up the article.

REFERENCES

Brenner, M. (1985). Intensive interviewing. In M. Brenner (Ed.), *The research interview* (pp. 147–162). London: Academic Press.

Douglas, J. D. (Ed.). (1970). *Understanding everyday life.* Chicago: Aldine Press.

Frey, L. R., Botan, C. H., Friedman, P. G., & Kreps, G. L. (1991). *Investigating communication: An introduction to research methods.* Englewood Cliffs, NJ: Prentice-Hall.

Garfinkel, H. (1967). *Studies in ethnomethodology.* Englewood Cliffs, NJ: Prentice-Hall.

Hayden, S. (1993). Chronically ill and "feeling fine": A study of communication and chronic illness. *Journal of Applied Communication Research, 21,* 263–278.

Hickson, M., III. (1974). Participant-observation technique in organizational research. *Journal of Business Communication, 11,* 37–42; 54.

Hickson, M., III. (1977). Communication in natural settings: Research tool for undergraduates. *Communication Quarterly, 25,* 23–28.

Hickson, M., III, & Hill, S. R., Jr. (1979, April). *Communicating at conventions: Roles, rules, and routines.* Paper presented at the convention of the Southern Speech Communication Association, Biloxi, MS.

Hickson, M., III, Stacks, D. W., & Greeley-Padgett, M. (1998). *Organizational communication in the personal context.* Needham Heights, MA: Allyn & Bacon.

Kirk, J., & Miller, M. L. (1986). *Reliability and validity in qualitative research.* Newbery Park, CA: Sage.

Lederman, L. C. (1990). Assessing educational effective-

ness: The focus group interview as a technique for data collection. *Communication Education, 39,* 117–127.

Liebow, E. (1967). *Tally's corner: A study of negro streetcorner men.* Boston: Little, Brown.

McKenna, A. (1990). *'The 'talk' of returning women graduate students: An ethnographic study of reality construction."* Unpublished dissertation, Florida State University.

Mitofsky, W. (1996). Focus groups: Uses, abuses, misuses. *The Harvard International Journal of Press/Politics, 1,* 2, 111–115.

Murphy, J. T. (1980). *Getting the facts: The fieldwork guide for evaluators and policy analysts.* Santa Monica, CA: Goodyear.

Peterson, T. R., Witte, K., Enkerlin-Hoeflich, E., Espericueta, L., Flora, J. T., Florey, N., Loughran, T., & Stuart, R. (1994). Using informant directed interviews to discover risk orientation: How formative evaluations based in interpretive analysis can improve persuasive safety campaigns. *Journal of Applied Communication Research, 22,* 199–215.

Roebuck, J. B., & Hickson, M., III. (1982). *The southern redneck: A phenomenological case study.* New York: Praeger.

Rush, R. R., & Grubb-Swetnam, A. (1996). Feminist approaches to communication. In M. B. Salwen & D. W. Stacks (Eds.), *An integrated approach to communication theory and research* (pp. 497–518). Mahway, NJ: Lawrence Erlbaum Associates.

Surra, C., Chandler, M., & Asmussen, L. (1987). Effects

of premarital pregnancy on the development of in-
terdependence in relationships. *Journal of Social and
Clinical Psychology, 5*, 123–139.

Webb, E. J., Campbell, D. T., Schwartz, R. D., & Sechrest,
L. (1970). *Unobtrusive measures: Nonreactive research
in the social sciences*. Chicago: Rand McNally.

Wimmer, R. D., & Dominick, J. R. (1997). *Mass media research: An introduction*, 5th ed. Belmont, CA:
Wadsworth.

QUANTITATIVE SAMPLING

OBJECTIVES

By the end of this chapter you should be able to:

1. Distinguish between quantitative and qualitative descriptive research.
2. Explain the difference between a population and a sample.
3. Describe and draw a sample.
4. Distinguish between probability and nonprobability samples.
5. Determine the appropriate sample size required for a study based on "acceptable" sampling error and confidence in the results.

Earlier chapters used the term **sample** as a way of obtaining a group of people or objects to study that were representative of a larger population or universe of interest. How and why researchers sample has been alluded to but not covered in any detail. This chapter introduces you to sampling and its importance in social scientific communication research. Although most people identify a "sample" with survey research, we have already noted that samples are employed in conducting almost all types of research, including all types of empirical social scientific research, content analysis, and rhetorical-critical historical-research studies. Thus an understanding of sampling is fundamental for all communication scholars, regardless of the questions asked and methods used. Sampling is particularly key in quantitative research, especially when the researcher intends to infer the results to the larger population from which the sample was drawn and, particularly, when employing survey and experimental methods.

This chapter introduces a *systematic* set of methods designed to help you have confidence that your theoretical thinking is **isomorphic**—has a one-to-one correspondence—with actual attitudes or behaviors. If you apply the principles of sampling theory well, your study will provide an *accurate* and *reliable* picture of how your respondents think or act and show a picture of how the larger population under study thinks and behaves.

SAMPLING THEORY

To make accurate descriptions that apply to all members of a **population** (people in general who possess some *characteristic* you wish to study; the characteristic under study is called a **parameter**) you can do two basic things: You may question every member of a population, or you can question only part of the population and infer from that part of the population to the entire population. If you question every member of the population, you have conducted a **census**. When conducting a study of objects (words, television shows, characters, themes), the population is called a **universe**. For example, in a legal communication research project that examined the type of rhetoric used in "winning" closing arguments, if we were to randomly sample the closing arguments of "winning" attorneys, we would sample from the universe of all closing arguments.

In many cases a census is practical, but more often than not it is quite impractical. If, for instance, you wanted to learn the opinions of the tenants of your apartment complex about a recent raise in rent, it may be practical to question all the residents, that is, to conduct a census. However, if you wanted to find out how the people of your state feel about putting warning labels on compact disks (CDs), you would have a difficult time trying to question all of the people. In this example the impracticality of questioning all of the people is obvious and **sampling** some of the people in the hope of making an accurate bet about how all the people would feel about warning labels is necessary.

Sampling, then, is the practical selection of people from some population in such a way as to ensure that they will meet whatever criteria you specify. The sample is simply a representative group of people similar to the population and, although these group members may differ from that population, they should not differ much.

In constructing your sample you will follow a set of fairly rigorous procedures. These procedures help ensure that the people you sample are representative of the target

---

MINI-PROJECT:

You have been given the assignment to choose the participants for a class study. Your research question is "What communication skills should students use when visiting a faculty member's office?" Briefly define your population or universe and what your sample will comprise.

---

population. Generally, there are two categories of sampling: **probability sampling** and **nonprobability sampling**. In probability sampling we select our respondents as randomly as possible; that is, every person in the population should have an equal chance of being chosen. In nonprobability (**purposive**) sampling we take certain subpopulations that we think match the parameters or population characteristics. Because not all possible respondents are represented in the sample, the amount of confidence we can place in their representativeness is less than that of people selected at random. Which method of sampling you use will depend on the degree of rigor that you require.

NONPROBABILITY SAMPLING

When we use a nonprobability sample we do so for a specific purpose. Generally, there are two reasons for using the nonprobability sample: **convenience sampling** and ensuring that a particular number of people meet certain criteria, or **quota sampling**. In addition, **volunteer** and **snowball sampling** techniques may be used when you are not sure of your population (snowball) or how to approach participants (volunteers). Use of nonprobability sampling should be approached with caution; researchers using this form of sampling usually tend to be very careful when interpreting their findings because the sampling procedure does not reflect the *entire* population, but only selected segments.

Convenience Sampling

Convenience sampling means that the researcher questions the people that are convenient to him or her. Convenience sampling may be necessary because of a limited amount of time or a limited access to people with whom to work.

A descriptive study conducted by McDermott and Greenberg (1984) on the effect of exposure to television family dramas that had black characters in them and children's attitudes toward black and white people in real life points out why nonprobability sampling is employed. This research project required that children be used as the population. One of the problems associated with using children in research is the difficulty in obtaining access to them. In this study it would have been impossible to question all children about their television viewing habits, and it would have been difficult to get anything more than a convenience sample. To get their sample, the researchers approached twelve different schools and asked permission to enter classrooms and hand out questionnaires. Out of these schools, only one allowed access to their students, thus a convenience sample was the only option. The *only* children who could participate in the study were those to whom access was given, and, because parental permission was not obtained from all parents, the representativeness of the sample was further reduced.

What can we conclude about children in general from a sample of convenient children? Obviously, the children who participated in this study do *not* generalize to the total population of children who watch family dramas on television. For example, what if this particular school was located near a large state university? Would this make the children different from those located in either rural or urban areas? Are there differences in the way the children are raised? What about access to television or to particular stations?

To use convenience sampling we must carefully and cautiously interpret the findings. We might try to find some other variables with which we can later see how well the children generalize to some other population. Questions concerning parental income, occupation, length of time they have been in the community, whether or not the parents owned or rented the place in which they lived, number of brothers and sisters, and so forth, help to identify the sample as compared to other samples from other descriptive research projects. To the degree that other samples might match on these demographic variables, some degree of generalization might be possible. However, *convenience sampling should only be used after all other attempts have been made to get a probability sample.*

Quota Sampling

Quota, or purposive, sampling is another nonprobability technique. It is similar to convenience sampling in that it also involves questioning people to whom the researcher has access, but it differs in that the characteristics of the population are identified and used to guide the selection of respondents. For example, suppose you are a consultant to an organization that is concerned about the quality and volume of message flow through its various departments. You have two options: you could conduct several focus groups, or you could conduct a survey. Money, however, is tight.

After careful consideration you decide that the best thing to do is to conduct several focus groups, but because you need to know about communication flow at all levels of the organization, you decide a known group method would work best. If you just started asking organizational members who walked by the rooms you reserved for the study on a particular day, you would end up with a convenience sample, but with a disproportionate number of workers who worked in the area. You need to decide how many workers you need from various departments, their gender make-up, their seniority, and so forth. This can be done by obtaining the data from the human resources department and from the organizational flow chart. You would then select your sample of respondents by using the proportion of each group in the population.

For instance, suppose that the general population in your organization is 56 percent female and 44 percent male. The percent of people aged 18 to 30 was 35 percent, of people aged 31 to 40 was 25 percent, and of people aged 50 or more was 40 percent. Finally, you found that 33 percent of your population were management, 33 percent were secretarial, and 33 percent were employed in blue-collar jobs. Assume that for reasons of limited time and money, you decided you only needed 100 total respondents. Your quota for your sample would then break down as being 56 females and 44 males. Your age quotas would run approximately 35 people under 30, 25 people between 30 and 50, and 40 people over 50. Finally, your quota would require that 33 people be management, 33 be secretaries, and 33 be engaged in blue-collar occupations. Obviously, the closer you try to match, the more complicated the quota sample technique becomes.

Quota sampling allows you to make certain that you have not excluded certain people from your sample. Although quota sampling helps with representativeness, it is still basically a convenience sample within groups; that is, you are still sampling whomever you can get, but now making sure that certain groups of people are represented via some quota system. Like the convenience sample, this technique should be used only after other probability sampling methods are deemed impractical.

Snowball Sampling

Snowball sampling occurs when you do not know much about the population you are attempting to study and use identified participants to identify new participants. For instance, Weitzel (1991) was interested in communication programs in other countries. He found that there was no central listing of either programs or people from which he could draw a sample to conduct a mail survey. Thus, he employed a snowball technique by asking participants found through his literature search to identify other potential respondents. Beginning with a small sample, Weitzel soon had a large sample of communication educators from around the world. The snowball sample, like the convenience and quota, is limited in its generalizability to the larger population, is potentially biased, and should be used only when other techniques are not feasible.

Volunteer Sampling

A final nonprobability sampling technique uses participants who volunteer for the study, often for pay. In advertising and public relations research, for instance, many focus groups are composed of volunteer participants who are either paid or provided some type of service or product. Medical communication research often employs volunteer sampling. Volunteers are recruited through a variety of means, usually through paid advertisements in newspapers or through the mail. Rosenthal (1965) has found that volunteers differ in a number of attributes (motivation, for instance) from a "normal" population, and results should be approached in the same manner as any nonprobability sample—with great caution. The result

MINI-PROJECT:

You have been asked to conduct a study of fraternity and sorority members' perceptions of community service at your institution. Describe how you would draw a nonprobability sample using each of the methods discussed.

of using volunteer sampling, and all nonprobability sampling techniques for that matter, is that we have no way of knowing if those sampled are indeed representative of the larger population, which is, after all, the purpose of sampling. Thus we turn to the meat and potatoes of sampling: probability sampling.

PROBABILITY SAMPLING

A **probability sample** ensures that *the chance for selecting a member of a population is known.* This means that no one person will be excluded due to researcher biases, accessibility of the respondent, or by questionnaire administration. Probability sampling generates the most *representative* sample that can be acquired, although it does not guarantee perfect population representativeness. In addition, this technique allows the researcher to estimate the probability that the sample represents the population through the use of **probability theory**.

Random Selection

The central requirement of probability sampling is the **random selection** of members of a population for inclusion in the sample. Random selection means that, since each person has an equal chance of being chosen, factors other than chance that might bias the sample will not influence the selection. For example, suppose that there are 10,000 marbles in a jar. Of these marbles, 8,000 are red and 2,000 are blue. As part of its marketing campaign, a local store is giving away a new car to the person who correctly guesses how many marbles are of each color. The catch is that you cannot count all the marbles, but, in the spirit of fairness, you are allowed to select 10 marbles before making your guess.

What is the likelihood that the first marble you pick out will be red (assume that you have been blindfolded and that someone has thoroughly mixed the marbles)? Eight out of 10, or 8,000 out of 10,000! But by chance you *may* pick out a blue marble. What is the chance of this happening again? Is it still 8 out of 10? No, since you have one marble already in your hand, there are only 9,999 marbles left from which to choose. So, the probability is now less than 8 out of 10. *The point is that unless you replaced the marble each time you made a new selection, your estimate of the population (of marbles) would be distorted.* By the tenth pick you would be down to having only 9,991 marbles from which to pick and the method you are using is no longer truly probabilistic! (You have removed a marble which, under true probability—random—sampling *could* theoretically be chosen again.)

MINI-PROJECT:

Test the concept of sampling by flipping a coin 100 times. How many times did it come up heads? How many times did you expect it to come up heads (i.e., what is the probability of heads occurring out of 100 tosses)? Try it a second and a third time. Did you get the same results? Why?

Although the number of marbles left is still quite large, you change the characteristics of the population with each choice. Therefore, to estimate the population characteristics (*parameters*) accurately, you would need to select a marble, note its color, replace it in the jar, mix the marbles up, and select again. If you follow this procedure you should be confident that your sample, within a certain degree of confidence (you may make an error somewhere), is likely to be representative to the extent that chance prevented you from selecting a sample that accurately reflected the color parameters of the population of marbles in the jar. Still, however, chance will influence your selections. By chance alone, you *could* pick blue marbles on all 10 tries. Probability theory, however, helps in determining how much *confidence* you can have that your sample is selected due to representativeness rather than chance.

Accuracy and Confidence in Sampling.   There is a limitation to our example. How representative a sample will 10 marbles be of 10,000? If you had selected 5,000 marbles, would your sample be more representative? In answering this question we begin to examine the related questions of accuracy and confidence. *Accuracy* depends upon three factors: (1) the parameters (population characteristics) you set out to represent, (2) the size of your sample, and (3) the amount of error you are willing to tolerate in making your selection (the *standard error* of the measurement).

Because sampling is based on probability theory, a subarea of mathematics, there are ways of estimating the accuracy with which a sample represents the population parameters. One way is to calculate the standard error we will have before selection. There are many ways to calculate this error, depending on the type of sample you select. Below is an example formula for a simple random sample. (Please do not be intimidated by a formula; it is only high school algebra, so please hang in there with us.) This simple formula takes into account the population parameters and the sample size in estimating the error in measurement (selection):

$$s = \sqrt{P(1 - P)/n}$$

where s = standard error
   n = number of cases
   P = population parameters

To calculate the standard error you need to know the population parameters of interest (P) and the sample size you plan on using or are using (n). The calculated standard error is s. Going back to the marble example, P is .80, representing that 80 percent of the marbles are red; $1 - P$ is .20, representing that 20 percent of the marbles are blue. If our sample size is 10 ($n = 10$), then the standard error is the square root of $(.8 \times .2) \div 10$, which is .126 or 12.6 percent. If the sample size were 100, the standard error would be .04 or 4 percent.

The Normal Curve

The standard error tells us the extent to which our sample will be like the population. Generally, 68 percent of the samples we might choose will fall within one standard deviation away from the true parameter value; that is, we know that as we choose our sample, the amount of error in our selection will approximate a *normal curve* (see Figure 10.1). As indi-

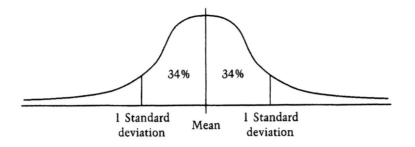

FIGURE 10.1   The normal distribution.

cated in Figure 10.2, a normal curve skews from the mean (the center of the curve) in a predictable way. As the size of the sample increases, the more normally distributed is the curve.
Hence, standard error is a function of both sample size and knowledge of population parameters.

The standard error, then, tells us the extent to which our samples will be like the
population from which they are drawn. Sixty-eight percent of samples we might choose
will fall within one standard error of the true parameter value. Thus, with a sample size
of 10, we know that 68 percent of the samples we could choose could be off by up to
12.6 percent on the population parameters. On the other hand, we could know that we
would be off only 4 percent each way with 68 percent of the total population if we increased the sample size to 100.

We also know from probability theory that 95 percent of our samples will fall within
one or two standard errors (deviations) from the true population value. So, we know that in
95 percent of our sample (with a sample size of 100), our selections should fall 8 percent
each way around our parameter value—between 72 percent and 88 percent of red marbles.

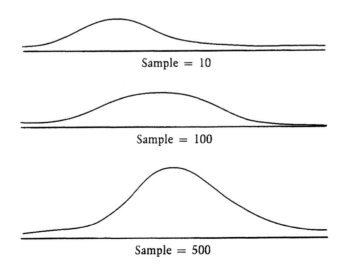

FIGURE 10.2   Possible distributions with increased sample size.

What does all this tell us? Basically, we know with a certain assurance that the people we select will reflect the population parameters we establish. From probability theory we also know that, by increasing sample size, we can reduce the error in sample selection. But we can also figure one more thing: confidence in the way in which people respond to the questions we ask.

A second way of looking at sampling error deals with the degree of confidence we can place in the responses people give us. Just as we can measure the amount of error in drawing the sample, we can also estimate the error in responses. Assume, for example, that you have been asked to survey people about their intent to vote in the next election. You choose your sample carefully, ensuring that respondents are of voting age and are registered to vote. The question you are concerned with most, however, is a simple yes/no response to the question: "Are you planning to vote in the upcoming election?" How many respondents do you need to be certain that their responses are accurate? What degree of accuracy (or, put another way, how much error) will we tolerate in their responses?

Convention assumes that we want to be within a 95 percent confidence level, or two standard errors in measurement for any response (Babbie, 1995). You could, if you so desired, move to a 99 percent confidence level. Here you know that your sample is within three standard errors of the true value, hence, you increase your accuracy. But, what is the cost of increasing our confidence level? Table 10.1 presents the number of people you would need to achieve both a 95 percent and a 99 percent confidence limit with varying degrees of tolerated error. Note that for the 95 percent confidence level and a 5 percent error tolerance you would have to include 384 people in your sample. Why so many? Table 10.1 provides a shortcut to selecting sample size and standard error. The population *size* the samples are drawn from, however, is assumed to be above 500,000.

TABLE 10.1   Simple Random Sample Size at 95 and 99 Percent Confidence with Tolerated Error[a]

ERROR	CONFIDENCE	
	95%	99%
1%	9,604	16,587
2%	2,401	4,147
3%	1,067	1,843
4%	600	1,037
5%	384	663
6%	267	461
7%	196	339

[a]Assumes that the population proportion is .50.

Source: Charles H. Backstrom and Gerald Hursh-Cesar, *Survey research*, 2nd ed. (New York: Macmillan, 1981). Reprinted by permission of Macmillan Publishing Company. Copyright © 1981 by Macmillan Publishing Company.

This means, for example, that a random survey of people in the state of New York would need only 384 respondents to ensure with a 95 percent confidence level that their responses would be off no more than plus or minus 5 percent.

Suppose, for example, that you did a statewide survey of voting intent in New York. The 384 people selected would have to come from all parts of the state (represent the entire population). You would analyze the results based on the total sample (not breaking down by sex, or age, or whatever—that would increase your tolerated error), and all people who meet your population parameters would have an equal chance of being selected. Should you desire ahead of time to see how males and females responded, to break your sample by sex, you would need 384 males and 384 females (doubling your sample size) to be 95 percent confident that your error would be no more than 5 percent on any response. So, by sampling 384 people in general, you might find that 63 percent said they were planning to vote and 37 percent were not. Your actual deviation from these responses would be between 68 percent and 58 percent voting and 42 and 32 percent not voting.

Your error of measurement, then, tells us how certain we can be that a response is accurate. In most *national* surveys (such as those reported on ABC, CBS, NBC, and CNN networks) the tolerated error is reduced to 3 percent, but at a confidence level of 95 percent. The sample size, drawn from throughout the country is *1,067* people. We can be 95 percent certain that these 1,000+ people represent our views and feelings! The condition that we be 99 percent certain that we have the true value of our population would almost double the number of people we must contact: at a 5 percent error rate we would need 663 people rather than 384; at a 1 percent error rate we would need 1,843 people rather than 1,067. If it takes 30 minutes to interview each person, you can see how increased accuracy will cost you in both time and money.

Sample Size.   What size should your sample be? That depends on how confident you need to be about sample representativeness and the degree of error you will tolerate. The larger the sample, the more representative of the population the sample will be and the smaller your error will be. The decision, then, is a personal one based on the confidence you have in your ability to ask good questions.

Up to now we have been dealing with extremely large populations. What about smaller populations? Philip Meyer (1973, p. 123) has worked out the different sample sizes you would need at the 95 percent confidence level for the following populations:

POPULATION SIZE	SAMPLE SIZE
Infinity	384
500,000	384
100,000	383
50,000	381
10,000	370
5,000	357
3,000	341
2,000	322
1,000	278

Notice the difference between 50,000 and infinity. These are the populations most of us sample. Generally, we will need about 384 people to be confident that we have sampled a representative group of people. If you have fewer than 1,000 people in your population, you should consider working out the error formula provided earlier or conducting a census of that population.

Before we provide several examples of sample selection, you might want to consider the information presented in Table 10.2. This table provides you with the error in response (again, at the 95 percent confidence level—a 20:1 safety factor) at differing sample sizes *and* responses. The far right column, the one labeled 50 percent, is the most conservative response we could hope for with a simple yes/no response: 50 percent of the respondents said "yes" and 50 percent said "no." Notice that the 5 percent error tolerance is found for a sample of 400 (the numbers have been rounded off for ease of use). To be within 5 percent of the response at the most conservative, you need 400 respondents. But, if your response is 25 percent "yes" and 75 percent "no," your error rate drops to 4.3 percent; at 90 percent "yes," the error is now 3 percent. Hence, you can determine your error not only from the sample size, but also the response rates you receive.

This information is useful if, for instance, you believe that your respondents are fairly decided in their attitudes and opinions. You could conceivably reduce the number of respondents and maintain a tolerated error rate. You can also establish how much error you have if some reason—time, money, or help restrictions—dictates a smaller sample. Suppose, for example, that you are doing an image study for a small town, population of 50,000 or more in the town and surrounding area. You have enough money and help to contact only 200 respondents. Your error rate at worst will be 7.1 percent. If you can live with that error rate then you only need 200 respondents.

Calculating Sample Size.   Sometimes tables are not good enough and you may want to calculate the sample size (N) required for your study. The calculation is not difficult, requiring that you simply know several parameters: your expected confidence (C) in the sample, how much error (E) you are willing to accept, and the expected outcome of your study (O). These are the same parameters you need to know to read one of the sample size tables.

Expected confidence is expressed in standard deviations under the hypothetical normal curve. We typically want to be either 95 percent or 99 percent confident that the sample represents the population or universe. This confidence is expressed as standard deviations and does not change. Thus, we know that when we want to be 95 percent confident, our value for C is 1.96; when we want to be 99 percent confident, our value for C is 2.58—always.[1] Our error level (E) is the amount of error we are willing to accept in responses, typically set at 5 percent (above *and* below the response. If the sample responded to a yes–no question 40 percent "yes" and 60 percent "no," the error in response would be between 35 and 45 percent "yes" and 55 and 65 percent "no"). Finally, our expected outcome (O) is usually set at the most conservative–50/50 or one half of respondents for and one half against. (In our earlier marble example, our outcome was 80 percent.) Table 10.2 provides different sample sizes based on different expected outcomes, while Meyer's calculations are based on the most conservative 50/50 split.

TABLE 10.2   Probable Deviation (Plus or Minus) of Results Due to Size of Sample Only

SAFETY FACTOR OF 20:1

SURVEY RESULT Sample of:	1% OR 99%	5% OR 95%	10% OR 90%	15% OR 85%	20% OR 80%	25% OR 75%	30% OR 70%	35% OR 65%	40% OR 60%	45% OR 55%	50%
25	4.0	8.7	12.0	14.3	16.0	17.3	18.3	19.1	19.6	19.8	20.0
50	2.8	6.2	8.5	10.1	11.4	12.3	13.0	13.5	13.9	14.1	14.2
75	2.3	5.0	6.9	8.2	9.2	10.0	10.5	11.0	11.3	11.4	11.5
100	2.0	4.4	6.0	7.1	8.0	8.7	9.2	9.5	9.8	9.9	10.0
150	1.6	3.6	4.9	5.9	6.6	7.1	7.5	7.8	8.0	8.1	8.2
200	1.4	3.1	4.3	5.1	5.7	6.1	6.5	6.8	7.0	7.0	7.1
250	1.2	2.7	3.8	4.5	5.0	5.5	5.8	6.0	6.2	6.2	6.3
300	1.1	2.5	3.5	4.1	4.6	5.0	5.3	5.5	5.7	5.8	5.8
400	.99	2.2	3.0	3.6	4.0	4.3	4.6	4.8	4.9	5.0	5.0
500	.89	2.0	2.7	3.2	3.6	3.9	4.1	4.3	4.4	4.5	4.5
600	.81	1.8	2.5	2.9	3.3	3.6	3.8	3.9	4.0	4.1	4.1
800	.69	1.5	2.1	2.5	2.8	3.0	3.2	3.3	3.4	3.5	3.5
1,000	.63	1.4	1.9	2.3	2.6	2.8	2.9	3.1	3.1	3.2	3.2
2,000	.44	.96	1.3	1.6	1.8	1.9	2.0	2.1	2.2	2.2	2.2
5,000	.28	.62	.85	1.0	1.1	1.2	1.3	1.4	1.4	1.4	1.4

Example: When size of sample is 500 and survey result comes out 25%, you may be reasonably sure (odds 20 to 1) that this result is no more than 3.9 off, plus or minus. Doubling this margin to 1,000 reduces this margin to 2.8.

Source: A Broadcast Research Primer. Washington, DC: National Association of Broadcasters, 1976, p. 19. Reprinted by permission.

Thus, we know that C will be 1.96 or 2.58; our error usually 5 percent, and our expected outcome whatever we know from previous research, or 50/50 if we are being extremely conservative. The calculation can be done by hand or with a simple calculator:

$$N = C^2 \div E^2 \times (O \times 1 - O)$$

where N = sample size required for
C = confidence in sample selection
E = amount of respondent error acceptable
O = expected outcome

To calculate a conservative expected outcome with 95 percent confidence in your sampling and a 5 percent acceptable error in response you would first square C (95% = 1.96^2 or 3.84), then square E (5^2 = 25), then divide C by E (3.84 ÷ 25 = 0.15). Next you would multiply O (50%) times $1 - O$ (50%) (50 × 50 = 2500). Finally, you would multiply 0.1537 × 2500 and get 384.25, or 384. To calculate an expected outcome (O) of 75 percent with 95 percent confidence and 5 percent error you would obtain a value of 0.1537 (C and E did not change), then multiply it by 5 × [1 − 75] to achieve 1875. N would equal 288.19 or a sample of 288 (0.1537 × 1875).

Suppose you wanted 95 percent confidence in sampling, but set your error at 1 percent, and still expected a 50/50 outcome? In this case C becomes 2.58, E^2 remains the same (25), as does O (50 × 50 = 2500). C^2 now is 6.6564, which is divided by 25 to equal 0.2663, which is multiplied by 2500 to equal 665.64, or the required sample size would be 666 respondents.[2]

Suppose we are interested in a population that is not infinite? A simple correction that requires an extra step provides the sample size for populations where size is known.

$$N = \frac{(O) \; \maltese (O) \; + \; \text{Std. Error}^2}{\text{Std. Error}^2 \; + \; \dfrac{(O) \times (O)}{N_1}}$$

where: Std. Error = acceptable error ÷ level of confidence

Thus, for a sample of 10,000 students with a 50/50 confidence and a 5 percent response error, you would need:

■ ■ ■ ■ ■

MINI-PROJECT:

Determine the sample sizes for the following studies: (1) A national study of television viewing habits with 95% confidence and 5% error; (2) a local study of school district attitudes toward a voting referendum with 95% confidence and 5% error; (3) a study of communication majors (N = your department, school, or college) with 95% confidence and 1% error.

$$N = \frac{(.50 \times .50) + (.05/1.96)^2}{(.05/1.96)^2 + \dfrac{(.50 \times .50)}{10000}}$$

$$= \frac{(.25) + .0006507}{.0006507 + \dfrac{(.25)}{10000}}$$

$$= 370.95$$

or 371 respondents.

After we have selected our sample size a question remains: How do we know that the sample selected represents our population or universe? In our earlier organizational example we alluded to a nonprobability sample where we would sample certain percentages of the population. In probability sampling, if done correctly, our final sample should reflect (within an acceptable sampling error) the population or universe parameters. Through a knowledge of the population or universe under study you should know the expected breakdown of the population or universe by parameter. Suppose, for example, that we know that our population consists of 42 percent male, 78 percent white, and that 22 percent are under age 25, 48 percent between 26 and 50, and 30 percent are 51 years or older. If we have a true probability sample, our sample percentages should come close (there will be some error depending on how many people were selected for the sample) to the population percentages.

However, in spite of the principles of probability sampling, we often are unable to stick to the procedures in the same way we have tried to do with the marble example at the beginning of this section (generating a true random sample where every object has an equal chance of being chosen, as compared to a systematic random sample, where a member is removed once selected).

SAMPLE SELECTION

An example from a study conducted by Greenberg and McDermott (1977) points out some of the problems faced when the research moves from the sample size question to the question of who to sample and how to construct the sample. This research project required a sample that drew from the population of the city of Detroit, Michigan. Detroit is a rather large city and presented several selection strategies. The researchers approached the task of selecting the sample in the following way. They needed a list of all the residents of the city to ensure that every member of the population had an equal chance of being chosen. But where could one find such a list? Here the actuality of conducting research interacts with the more abstract theory of research. Such a list is next to impossible to get. Therefore, the researchers had to decide on a method that would locate as many people as possible that met the parameters of the study. Several solutions were possible. The first possibility was to go door-to-door and interview respondents, but that still does not guarantee that all people could be contacted. Second, a telephone interview could be conducted using names and telephone numbers found in the city telephone directories. That still would not guarantee that the person would be home. And what if not everyone had a telephone? In the end the telephone interview was decided upon, as is the case with much of today's descriptive research. But how do you pick a sample that gives each listing in the phone book an equal chance of being selected? And, is this a representative sampling of *all* people with telephones?

Computer-Generated Sampling

Researchers do at least three things to select a sample randomly. The first, yet most difficult and costly, is to have a computer select from actual telephone numbers in the phone book. A computer-generated sample would provide not only the exchanges (and area codes for a national or international study), but also the individual unit digits. These are available through most major survey research firms or the telephone company for a fee. You could, however, generate a series of four digit random numbers and randomly select pages of them from selected exchanges in the population being sampled.

Sampling via a Random Numbers Table

A second method is to consult a table of random numbers that will instruct which numbers, say the 38th, 79th, 1,004th, 1,012th . . . to select from the telephone book. This is relatively inexpensive, but very time-consuming; you have to count down from the beginning to all the numbers in the telephone book—a task that would be difficult with a sample of about 400. If selected, the first step is to use a table of random numbers to tell you which telephone numbers to choose from each page of the directory. Then, take the total sample size, divided by the number of pages in the telephone book, and pick as many random numbers needed (between 0001 and the total possible on a given page) so you could sample from each page.

Weighted Sampling

A third way to select the sample would be through the use of the telephone exchanges (the three-digit numbers that begin all telephone numbers in the United States). By listing each exchange and the approximate population for the exchanges, the sample could be drawn by simple random selection. Stacks and Gordon (1974) did just this. They took the number of exchanges, found out how many people were in each exchange area and *weighted* the number of people from each exchange to the sample. For example, one exchange represented 45 percent of the population. Of the 384 respondents, 45 percent—173 people—were drawn from that exchange. Similar proportions were drawn for other exchanges. A table of random numbers provided the four-digit extensions. The use of microcomputers and random number generation programs simplifies this technique even more. Suppose that you need 100 numbers selected at random from all possible numbers for a given exchange. Your population for that subsample will be somewhere between 0 (0000) and 9,999. (The telephone company does not assign telephone numbers to exchanges sequentially, but does so randomly; you must include all 10,000 numbers as possible numbers.) You then ask for 100 numbers to be selected at random from between 0 and 9,999. The numbers you get will be random, just as with a random number table, but it is much easier to get than the time-consuming methods used previously.

Stratified Random Sampling

Sometimes simple random selection is insufficient to guarantee that certain groups within the population will be sampled. For instance, suppose you hypothesize that attitudes toward nuclear power plants vary with age. Specifically, you predict that people over the age of 50 and people under 30 are in favor of nuclear power plants, but people between 30 and 50 are generally opposed to them. If you left your sampling to random chance, you may not get representative samples of each age group. Thus, to ensure that each age group is adequately sampled, you need to conduct a **stratified random sample**. You determine the number of people you need in each age group, then randomly select from within each of the three age groups. This particular type of sampling is used by political opinion pollsters who need to stratify by demographic characteristics (e.g., sex, age, race) so their candidates know what issues affect each set of voters.

   Stratified sampling allows the pollster to anticipate accurately (± about 3 percent) the results of elections in which as many as 100 million people vote from a sample of about 1,200 voters. A stratum is a subgroup of the population whose members are *known* by the researcher to be more homogeneous, that is, more similar to one another, in terms of what is being measured than is the population as a whole. The more homogeneous a group, the fewer group members it takes in a sample to determine how the entire group feels. To take the most extreme example of this point, assume that you knew that all members of a group—say, Republicans from Indiana—agree completely on an issue, say capital punishment. How many of these Indiana Republicans would you have to survey to determine how the group felt about this issue? Only one! Since everyone in the group agrees, whomever is sampled at random can provide all the information you need to know about how the entire group feels. If this one person states that he is in favor of capital punishment, you know that the entire group feels this way.

   In reality, groups are seldom completely homogeneous in ways relevant to the questions being asked. And even if they were, the researcher would not be likely to know this. But many groups are *more* homogeneous on a relevant variable being measured than the larger population of which the group is a part. To the extent the researcher is aware of this homogeneity, the overall sample can be designed to sample systematically within various strata as a means of reducing sampling error or as a means of reducing the sample size necessary to achieve "acceptable" error goals. (It is important to note that *within* the stratum the sample must be selected using probability procedures, i.e., at random.) If groups that are homogeneous with regard to the variables being measured cannot be identified, stratified sampling is impossible and the researcher must rely on simple random sampling.

   Pollsters such as George Gallup and Louis Harris have been studying voting patterns among various groups (strata) for years. They use their knowledge of how individuals within particular strata vote to design a sampling plan that results in generally accurate estimates of voting outcomes.

Systematic Random Sampling

A second way to conduct random sampling is again with a telephone book or some other directory or listing of people. When you do this, however, you are conducting a *systematic random sample*. This technique requires three things: (1) that you start at some randomly chosen point in the directory, (2) that everyone has an equal chance of being chosen, and (3) that you choose a **skip interval**. The random start can be done with a random number table or computer-generated random number. Suppose that you are going to contact 200 recruiters for top Fortune 500 companies. To get your sample you could go to a directory of directors for these companies, and choose a random page number to begin (say, page 32 out of 100 pages). If the names are listed in one column per page you then choose a second random number (say, 17) and count down 17 people. This is your first person. To get your skip interval you would divide the total number of names and addresses in the directory by your sample size (assuming that there are 23 names per page, 100 pages, you would have 23 times 100 divided by 200 as your skip interval, or 11.5—which we would round to 12). You would then choose every twelfth person from the one with whom you started.

One advantage of this method is that you approximate stratification of your sample at the same time. Because most names are listed in alphabetical order your systematic sampling procedure will select from various nationalities, assuming, of course, that certain names are representative of certain ethnic backgrounds. Obviously, this method is not as precise as if you actually weighed your sample, but it does help with representedness as to ethnic origin.

Sampling in Experimental Research

Although examples in this section on sampling have centered on sampling populations for survey and descriptive research, the principles apply equally well in experimental research. When you are constructing the groups to constitute your experiment, you want to ensure that the participants in the groups are as close to identical as possible. Thus, any result that you find cannot be due to participant differences, but are due to the experimental treatment. For instance, suppose you decide to find out if males who use humor in classroom presentations are perceived differently than females who use humor. You find some classes and set up your experimental manipulation by having a female give a humorous speech and then have a male give the same humorous speech. The male gives his speech in a morning class

---

MINI-PROJECT:

How would you conduct a stratified random sample of students at your university or college? Establish the procedures and materials necessary to draw such a sample and then draw it. Remember that you need a characteristic in which known subgroups (strata) will be more similar with regard to the issues about which you are asking. (HINT: You will need to know the size of the population, the sample size for your accepted confidence and error rate, and have a directory of some form or another).

and the female gives her speech in an afternoon class. You do not have nearly equivalent samples. Perhaps the morning students are more alert and more susceptible to humor; the afternoon class is groggy from lunch. Perhaps the students who select morning classes are more serious; the afternoon more playful. Here, then, any differences you find could be due to the type of person in a class or the time of day, and not humor. To improve on this design, you need to use probability sampling, preferably a random sample, where you ask one set of randomly selected students to attend one presentation and another set of randomly selected students to attend the other *at the same time*. Randomization would offset any unknown biases that the students or time of presentation might have; the key is, however, that all participants have an equal chance of being in either presentation.

CONTACTING RESPONDENTS

Once you have drawn the sample, how do you contact them? Generally, there are three ways: telephone them, mail a questionnaire to them, or contact them on a one-on-one basis. Each is covered in more detail in Chapter 11, but because the method for contact may influence your sampling method, we briefly introduce them here. Although these methods are associated with survey research, they may be used with other methods, such as the random selection of participants in an experiment or for focus groups or for in-depth interviews.

Telephone Contact

The use of telephone interviews to contact respondents poses two problems. First, if you use a telephone book, are you assured that the numbers are current and that someone might answer the phone? Are you also assured that you are reaching a residence and not a store or hospital? There are also a large number of *unlisted* telephone numbers that you have excluded. To be representative you should include unlisted numbers. How do you get them? One possible way is to reverse the last two digits of the telephone numbers drawn. A second, often used method is called *random digit dialing*. Here the computerized random number generation program comes into play. You simply use the four-digit numbers drawn from the computer and assign them to one of your telephone exchanges. There is no guarantee, however, that you will hit upon any unlisted numbers. The only way you will know you are reaching unlisted numbers is if your respondents begin to ask how you got their unlisted number.

The second problem is ensuring that the person you are speaking with meets the parameters of the study. It is useless to interview a 14-year-old on voting behaviors, but finding out how old that person is something usually done last. In the same way, there may be times when you will have to ask for the "man of the house"; in most households the telephone is answered by the wife, hence you may have to ask for one or the other sex to balance out your sample.

Mail Contact

Sometimes you will contact participants or respondents by mail. Mail contact has the distinct disadvantage of not knowing who actually received the contact notice. Further, mail contact that requires potential participants to contact you produces a nonprobability sample more times than not. Your participants probably fall into the category of "volunteer" and do not reflect the actual population under study. Mail contact is costly, often requiring first class mail going out and coming back. It also takes a lot of time and may require that a follow-up notice be mailed to remind potential participants that they have been selected for the study. Error in sampling is increased through address changes, lost mail, and so forth.

Door-to-Door Contact

One form of sample selection in survey research has been door-to-door contact. This is an expensive and time-consuming contact approach and fraught with the hazards of being in the field. Consider, for example, a person chosen to participate in your study who lives in the worst part of town—what problems might you or your helpers run into contacting such people? Babbie (1995) and Backstrom and Hursch (1981) discuss the problems and procedures for door-to-door contact.

APPLYING KNOWLEDGE IN COMMUNICATION

For the communication researcher who seeks to study parts of a population or universe, sampling can be a critically important issue, particularly if you want to predict an election outcome or "know," within 3 percent error, how a large group feels about a woman's right to an abortion. (Can you identify the bias in the wording in the last sentence? If so, you are going to be a good survey writer.) This is true whether the research is qualitative or quantitative. Communication research often seeks to understand how messages are created, transmitted, and received. To study all the messages people communicate would be impossible. Studying a representative sampling of those messages makes communication study much easier. Sampling is very important in content analysis, focus group, in-depth interview, and survey methodologies. Random sampling is an important feature in experimental research, especially experimental research that employs "quasi-experimental" design (see Chapter 13).

Knowing how to sample, with what confidence you have in your sampling, and with the amount of respondent error you are willing to accept makes your job as a researcher easier. Understanding how samples were drawn, whether they were probability or nonprobability samples, the amount of confidence you can place in their generalizability to the larger population or universe, and the amount of response error found in any given study provides you with important and powerful tools in establishing the validity and reliability of the research you read as you prepare to conduct your own studies.

SUMMARY

This chapter has attempted to provide: (1) an understanding of what a sample is and how it reflects a population; (2) an understanding of how to sample that population in a way that accurately reflects the population's parameters within a prescribed confidence level and with an acceptable degree of error in the responses; and (3) information about how to collect data, whether it be by questionnaire or interview.

Sampling can be used by the historian and rhetorician as well as the social scientist. Understand also that probability sampling is a critically valuable and rigorous technique in most survey research. It provides a way of describing how people think and feel, or are *likely* to behave, with regard to a subject or issue, and allows generalizations to the larger population or universe from which the sample was selected.

PROBES

1. Sampling seeks to canvas a number of people to gain insight into their perceptions regarding selected variables or concerns. If you were asked to critique this method as a way of gaining understanding about human behavior, what would you say? What does sampling tell us that other methods do not? What limitations are placed on the researcher? Are these limitations important?

2. Assume for a moment that you want to know who will be the next president of the student body, how would you select your study participants?

3. What is the difference between probability and nonprobability sampling? Is probability sampling *truly* random? Why or why not?

4. Why would you want to use nonprobability sampling? Assuming you have to employ a nonprobability sampling technique, would you still have to calculate sample size? Why or why not?

5. How would you use sampling—both probability and nonprobability—in a qualitative or qualitative/descriptive research project?

RESEARCH PROJECTS

1. Probability theory, as a branch of applied mathematics, is very important to communication researchers who take a quantitative approach to research. Read up on statistical methods and apply probability theory to a communication research project.

2. Do different communication areas (e.g., organizational, journalism, advertising, public relations, broadcast, interpersonal) employ sampling procedures? Are there any sampling techniques that might be more appropriate to one area than another? Critique how sampling methods and techniques are used in communication research.

3. A major concern of politicians is the announcement of election results based on random sample surveys and exit interviews. Review the literature in this area and determine whether politicians and communication researchers should be concerned about this reporting. (Does it alter how people vote? How they communicate about voting? Whether or not they actually vote?)

SUGGESTED READING

Babbie, E. R. (1995). *Survey research*, 7th ed. Belmont, CA: Wadsworth.

Grusin, E. K., & Stone, G. C. (1992). Using focus groups to improve survey research. *Newspaper Research Journal, 13*, 72–83.

Kalton, G. (1983). *An introduction to survey sampling*. Beverly Hills, CA: Sage.

Mishler, E. G. (1986). *Research interviewing: Context and narrative*. Cambridge, MA: Harvard University Press.

Roll, C. W., Jr., & Cantril, A. H. (1972). *Polls: Their use and misuse in politics*. New York: Basic Books.

Rosenthal, R., & Rosnow, R. L. (1969). *Artifact in behavioral research*. New York: Academic Press.

Slonim, M. J. (1960). *Sampling*. New York: Simon and Schuster.

Weisberg, H. F., & Bowen, B. D. (1977). *An introduction to survey research and data analysis*. San Francisco: W. H. Freeman.

NOTES

1. This is the Z-score, or area under the normal curve, which will be discussed in Chapter 14, "Descriptive Statistics."

2. This differs from Table 10.1, which indicated a sample of 663. The difference is found in rounding.

REFERENCES

Babbie, E. R. (1995). *Survey Research*, 7th ed. Belmont, CA: Wadsworth.

Backstrom, C. H., & Hursh, G. D. (1981). *Survey research*, 2nd ed. New York: Macmillan.

Greenberg, B. S., & McDermott, S. T. (1977, August). *The debut of a black television station: Adoption of an innovation*. Paper presented to the Association for Education in Journalism and Mass Communication, Madison, Wisconsin. (ERIC ED 153-227.)

McDermott, S. T., & Greenberg, B. S. (1984). Black children's esteem: Parents, peers, and television. In R. Bostrom (Ed.), *Communication Yearbook 8* (pp. 164–177). Beverly Hills, CA: Sage.

Meyer, P. (1973). *Precision journalism*. Bloomington, IN: University Press.

Rosenthal, R. (1965). The volunteer subject. *Human Relations, 18*, 403–404.

Stacks, D. W., & Gordon, R. T. (1974). Does public speaking exist outside of academia? A look at one southeastern community. *Georgia Speech Communication Journal, 2*, 77–85.

Weitzel, A. (1991). Higher education communication curricula outside of the U.S.A. *circa* 1990: An inventory. *World Communication, 20*, 49–66.

QUANTITATIVE (SURVEY) RESEARCH

OBJECTIVES

By the end of this chapter you should be able to:

1. Describe when survey methodology is appropriate for communication research.
2. Distinguish between "surveys" and "polls."
3. Describe and differentiate between the two major survey designs.
4. Conduct a survey—structure your questionnaire, with your interviewers, and collect your data.
5. Explain ways to maximize response rates.
6. Discuss "new" survey techniques and problems associated with each.

As a communication professional, whether in public relations, an organization, marketing, sales, teaching, personnel, or whatever, you will design and create messages and programs that are intended to have worthwhile effects. To be successful at your job, you will be called upon to engage in a form of "audience analysis." A high-quality evaluation will require that you assess your intended receivers—be they clients, customers, students, subordinates, or the public—both *before* you design the intended communication and *after* your audience has been exposed to the communication. The names for these activities may differ for your specific communication profession. Some may call it *assessment*, others *evaluation, analysis,* and/or *reviews* (as in performance), but they all can be classified as types of **survey research**.

The answers you may have given in the 2000 census were a result of this kind of research. The teacher evaluations you fill out at the end of the term are as well. You may have filled out a small card at a motel or restaurant asking you about the service, or you might be asked to fill out a questionnaire about the parking problem or class priority registration at your school. After a presentation or workshop you may be asked about the facilitators and speakers. You may have participated in a CNN/Sports Illustrated Internet sports survey asking you to name the most outstanding athlete of the twenty-first century. And finally, you may be called on the telephone and asked questions about allowing oil drilling in national forests. All of these are types of survey research. In each instance a researcher has gathered information in such a way that he or she can paint a picture of what people think or do. He or she is using a questionnaire or some form of systematic observation to present a realistic representation of a topic by describing people's attitudes, beliefs, behaviors, or intentions at one level and the content of those same people's communication—whether it be via interpersonal communication or through the mass media.

The results of these efforts will be used to form the basis for determining whether what he or she *thinks* about reality (his or her theory or theoretical conceptualization) is *isomorphic* (relates to the behaviors under study) with what *is* reality. If the outcomes of the observations are the same as what he or she expects reality to "look like," then the description is isomorphic. For instance, suppose a researcher thinks that MTV portrays women as sex-starved. The researcher may hypothesize that young boys who watch excessive MTV programming believe older girls to be like those they see on MTV—sex-starved. For the researcher to conclude such a relationship, he or she must determine if what he or she thinks is on MTV is isomorphic with what is on MTV and what he or she thinks young boys believe about older girls is what young boys *really* believe about older girls.

To draw any conclusions about MTV and perceptions of sex, the researcher must conduct a survey research project. This project must do three things. First, it must determine the actual content (programming) of MTV. That is, it must discover if MTV portrays women as sex-starved. Second, it must accurately measure attitudes of young boys by questioning them. Third, it must reflect a sample large enough to say reliably that some relationship between viewing and attitude exists. This, obviously, is a project that asks questions of fact and definition and is amenable to scientific method. The survey is also used in qualitative research; however, such use generally precludes the researcher from generalizing to the larger population from what selected respondents report. Qualitative research may follow a similar questionnaire structure, but the *results* must be interpreted differently.

This chapter introduces a *systematic* set of methods designed to help you have confidence that your theoretical thinking is isomorphic with actual attitudes or behaviors. If you apply the principles of survey research well, your study will provide an accurate and reliable picture of how your respondents think or act.

TYPES OF QUANTITATIVE RESEARCH

Although there are many types of quantitative research, this chapter will concentrate on one method: *the survey*. This coverage is designed to familiarize you with how to conduct quantitative research with an emphasis on gathering the data. Hence, the *methodology* of quantitative research is emphasized. Appropriate analytical procedures (how you would analyze the data collected) are covered in Part III.

The method involves describing a subset of a population of people in such a way as to present accurate depictions of how the total population would respond. Some observational methods were presented in Chapter 9. Extending the observational method from the qualitative research to a more objective, quantitative approach is accomplished, in part, by specifying more thoroughly the *specific rules of observation*. Simply put, much of what is presented in this chapter applies to all research. The survey method, however, requires that, to the extent possible, the researcher remove his or her biases from the research. Thus survey methodology requires that specific procedures be followed with a set of measures for obtaining data.

SURVEY METHODOLOGY

When we speak about surveying people, we are talking about questioning individuals about their attitudes, emotions, beliefs, intentions, and behaviors. We are interested in how they *perceive* or *evaluate* some issue, event, or message.

Surveys and Polls

Although often used as synonyms, surveys and polls are different. A poll simply describes how or what participants think and is usually fairly short. It seeks simple answers to simple questions. A survey, on the other hand, is a more in-depth project, seeking to understand why people differ in their descriptions of perceptions of an event. And when the researcher uses the responses to examine the relationship between answers to different questions (variables or concepts), he or she is engaged in explanatory as well as descriptive research. For instance, we might conduct a poll of voting by asking whether people intended to vote and who they would vote for. What we know from the research is (a) the number of people who intend to vote, (b) who they intend to vote for, and (c) some demographic data (sex, race, age, etc.). This is important information, but it does not tell us much about why they intend to vote and who they might vote for, even more important data. A survey would go into more detail in questioning respondents, asking them to compare and contrast candidates, positions, promises made and kept, and so forth, along with typically asking for more demographic information. A poll might take one or two minutes, a survey typically takes 15 to 20 minutes.

A survey or poll asks people to respond to questions usually asked either orally—a **personal interview survey**—or through written questions—a **questionnaire survey**. Some of the questions (Q) and hypotheses (H) that can be answered by surveys include:

Q: How do people perceive decision-making style and satisfaction within an organization?

H: Extensive exposure to television shows with a great deal of violence/crime brings about fears of being an actual victim of crime.

H: Exposure to presidential debates leads to the perception that the U.S. system of elections is rational.

Q: What is the relationship between cognitive style and self-reported use of certain compliance-gaining strategies?

Q: How is a child's understanding of commercial disclaimers related to his or her requests for products?

Q: What is the relationship between exposure to alcohol advertising and drinking while driving among teenagers?

H: People who read editorial opinions will be more in favor of the person or event if the editorial is positive and full of intense language.

A second type of survey examines behavior and message content. The *observational* research methods examined also fall under the descriptive method. Here, the researcher is interested in the messages people use:

Q: What is the incidence of sexist language in national newspaper reports?

Q: How many references to war and peace do presidential candidates make during debates?

H: There are more references to sex in country songs than in rock 'n' roll songs (in the top 100 songs played in the United States).

H: Television reporting of the U.S. national elections was liberally biased during the last election.

These questions and hypotheses also require that elements of either a population of people or events be sampled. Often we cannot pick *all* people or events to study; we must choose in some orderly and rigorous fashion subelements that will within a certain degree of confidence possess those traits (see Chapter 10). This is a major advantage of survey research: We are able to construct a sample of people that will represent all those within the population we seek to describe.

Where do we begin? As with any type of research, questions or hypotheses are proposed and appropriate measures are chosen. Descriptive research using survey methods provides the researcher with a systematic way of measuring, including who, when, where, and how to measure the variables under study. The *who* involves sampling. The *when* is part of sampling, too, but refers to the measurement time frame. The place you collect the data

MINI-PROJECT:

> You have been hired to conduct a survey of attitudes toward faculty and class satisfaction of students at your school. Describe the steps you will take in selecting your sample and how you will actually draw that sample.

is the *where*. *How* you structure the observation (treated in this chapter as the interview, either face-to-face or via telephone or the mail) constitutes the last consideration.

Remember that there are two types of samples: nonprobability (which is used when you cannot guarantee that all possible respondents or elements have an equal chance of being included in the sample) and probability (when all possible respondents or elements have an equal chance of being included in the sample). Probability sampling provides us with a way of generalizing to the larger population, which would be no problem if you sample ALL members of that population (a census). Seldom, however, will you have the resources or time to conduct a census, therefore you must sample from a population or universe in order to obtain a sample of people or objects representative of that population or universe. Sampling theory provides us with information regarding the confidence we can place in how well we sampled (the amount of error we can tolerate in drawing the sample) and the amount of error we might find in the responses we get from asking questions and generalizing them to the larger population.

Sampling theory tells us how many people are necessary to meet the levels of acceptable error in both sample selection and the error we will allow in responses. In general, for an infinite population with acceptable sampling error of 5 percent and a 5 percent error in response, we need to *randomly select* 384 people to participate in our study. The key is that participants have been selected at random—each member of the population has an equal chance of being included in the study. This is generally accomplished through probabilistic sampling techniques: simple random sampling, stratified random sampling, or systematic random sampling.

Designs

Once you have determined the number of participants and the most efficient way of getting a sample, you need to consider how you will measure them. The type of hypothesis or questions you ask will determine the type of design you select. There are many variations of design, but survey designs typically follow two forms: **cross-sectional** and **longitudinal** design.

Cross-Sectional Design.   The cross-sectional design takes a cross section of a population to study *at a given time*. For example, suppose that you are interested in how the students at your institution perceive themselves. Are they liberal or conservative in their political attitudes? Are they supportive of causes or movements? To answer these questions you would develop a questionnaire that taps these questions, ask demographic questions to see how your sample might differ according to, say, student classification (Do first-year students differ from seniors?), and select a stratified random sample of college students. In this case, you would be conducting a cross-sectional study. You would draw your conclusions about the group of people you selected at that time and only about that group.

Notice, however, that you have not really measured or observed *changes* in people. You infer change on the basis of differences between demographic variables (if you found differences between demographic variables, such as student classification, sex, age, race, major, etc.). In fact, there could be other reasons for the differences. What you can infer from your sample only reflects that sample at that given time. You cannot really compare your findings to those of other times.

Similarly, a cross-sectional design might be used to examine the relationship between the number of hours a third-grader watches television programs and his or her reading ability. Your questionnaire would include measures of each variable. Assuming that you found a relationship between the two variables, that the children who watched a lot of television were poorer readers than those who did not watch a lot of television, could you conclude that watching television brought about the decrease in reading ability? *No*, because you have no way of knowing which occurs first, watching television or poor reading. Your survey of viewing and reading habits has only measured one variable at a time. Maybe poor reading ability brings about more watching of television. You have established a relationship between variables but only at one point in time; to say that one variable causes another, the effect must follow the cause. If time order is not necessary for your research question or hypothesis, then the cross-sectional design was adequate. Many times, however, a different design is needed.

Longitudinal Designs.   A design that allows for observations over time is labeled *longitudinal*. Longitudinal designs permit you to make statements about which variables occur first, although they *do not allow you to make statements about which variable causes another variable*. Only experiments, discussed in following chapters, allow you to draw causal conclusions about the relationship between two variables.

Trend and panel are two basic types of longitudinal sample designs. **Trend** designs allow you to collect *different* samples at *different* points in time (see Table 11.1). For example, you want to find out what people think about airline safety, and you have coincidentally collected data before a major airline disaster. If you wanted to see if perceptions about airline safety changed after the disaster, you would collect a second sample of people from the *same* population.

In the same way, you might be interested in how people's attitudes about using computers change over time. Because some members of your first sample will probably move away, some will die, while others will change their names through marriage or divorce, you will have to sample again from the *same* general population. If you wanted to trace what happened to people who went to college during the late 1960s and early 1970s (the baby boom generation), you would locate some data that measured students' attitudes and feelings at that time, and collect another sample from people who were now in their forties and went to

TABLE 11.1   The Difference Between Trend and Panel Designs

JANUARY	JUNE
PEOPLE SAMPLED—TREND DESIGN	
Linda ⟶	Debbie
Susan ⟶	Patricia
David ⟶	David
Mike ⟶	Ed
Joe ⟶	Jill
PEOPLE SAMPLED—PANEL DESIGN	
Linda ⟶	Linda
Susan ⟶	Susan
David ⟶	David
Mike ⟶	Mike
Joe ⟶	Joe

college. You would then compare the results. (If you want to know how "Generation X" people fare, you should measure them now.)

This study uses a **cohort trend** design. It is a cohort design because you are examining people who come from the same subgroup of the population over time. In this instance the cohort would be age. Trend designs are often necessary because of changes in your sample over time and are relatively easy to carry out (you simply ensure that your sample reflects the population). However, they do not permit actual examination of change over time. What you can measure is how two *different* groups sampled from the same population perceive your topic of interest.

Panel designs are those that measure the *same individuals over time* (see Table 11.1). This powerful design permits you to make statements of change. Panel designs are typically used in two ways. First, you might identify some condition (an intervening variable, or a variable that may cause people to change in some way) that is about to occur, sample and measure how people feel about the condition prior to the event, then measure the same people after the event has occurred. Second, you might follow a sample through a given time period to see what change, if any, has occurred regardless of specific events. The former design examines the impact of a specific event (condition or intervening variable) on a population while the latter examines simple change over time. The result, however, is the same: You can examine *how* people changed because you have studied the same sample over time.

An example of an intervening variable panel design is found in an unpublished study of the impact of the made-for-television movie, *The Day After*, on attitudes toward nuclear war. The movie dramatized the effect of a nuclear attack on a city in Kansas. John Hocking and Steven McDermott hypothesized that the movie might have a large impact on people in the United States and decided to test that hypothesis by a panel design of people contacted by telephone. The survey was run twice. The researchers contacted people two days before the broadcast, and then called the respondents back the day after the broadcast—a time-1, time-2 panel design. With this design the researchers would be able to note any change (or lack of change) due to seeing the movie.

Could it be said with assurance, however, that the broadcast *caused* the changes? Maybe the respondents simply changed from day one to day three. Maybe they were changed by the first set of questions. Maybe they were changed by interpersonal communication with others about the movie and not the movie itself. What if the design had included a separate sample of people who did *not* watch the broadcast? Could we then compare the two samples? No, because the respondents who watched may have been different from those who did not watch the broadcast; maybe those who watched the broadcast were more prone to change. Even though the time-1, time-2 design is valuable for investigating naturally occurring events, it does not permit us to infer causality.

Use of the second panel design might answer the question addressed earlier about reading and television habits. You might select a sample of children and follow them through preschool and elementary school and observe both their television habits and their reading ability. You could measure their television viewing and reading ability at regular intervals and note any changes over time. This type of sampling design is extremely powerful. If done properly you can make inferences of change and suggest causality; however, other factors—factors you cannot control—might influence your findings. (More about *control* will be discussed in Chapter 12.)

Although panel designs are more powerful, they are also much more expensive to conduct. You must locate and follow people across time. You must begin with an initial sample large enough so that when you lose sample members, you will still have a sample that is representative at a later time. Political studies that examine the electorate over a long period of time (say before the primaries, through the primaries, and after the general elections) are extremely time-consuming to conduct but tell the researcher much more than those that select separate samples at each surveying point.

Panel designs are very useful tools for people in public relations, advertising, and other communication professions that introduce products or ideas to the public. Health intervention programs, such as AIDS prevention, moderation in alcohol use, safe sex campaigns, and

MINI-PROJECT:

You are part of a team about to promote a new communication class that will be offered to all students. You have been charged with assessing how students felt about the class after its completion. What type of survey design will you use? In preparing a report back to the committee, what advantages or limitations will you discuss? What will you choose for acceptable sample and response error? Why? How many students will you sample? How will you draw the sample?

so forth, may all benefit by surveying before and after the communication messages are delivered to the public.

COLLECTING THE DATA

There are three basic ways of getting information from people in a survey: in person, by mail, or by telephone. In addition, there are "new" techniques for data gathering that have arisen from advances in computer use. Each of these methods has its advantages and disadvantages. In-person and telephone interviews, however, require another person, usually someone other than the researcher, to help gather the data. The degree to which your interviewers are trained will affect how the data are collected. Before examining each of the collection methods, we need to look at interviewer training.

Training Interviewers

You cannot simply give interviewers a questionnaire and send them on their way. The way in which the questionnaire is presented to the respondent will often introduce subtle biases and can alter the way the respondent chooses to answer each question. Also, as discussed in Chapters 6 and 7, variations in the way questions are asked can detract from measurement reliability. In general, all interviewers must go through a training phase, which includes an understanding of the questionnaire, how to deal with contingencies that may occur, and several practice rounds. First, the interviewer must understand what you are asking your respondents. He or she must be aware that the questionnaire must be followed *as it is written*; if not, the responses may be due to things other than the questions you have created. Second, the interviewer needs to know how to handle people. You are asking for their cooperation, so the interviewer must understand that the respondent may have other things to do at that time. In such cases you might instruct your interviewer to ask for a better time to call back. A respondent may, halfway through the interview, decide not to complete the interview; how should the interviewer tackle this? A respondent may wish to speak to "someone in authority" or ask "is there someone else who has the time?" Training should prepare the interviewer for such contingencies.

Finally, the interviewer must practice the questionnaire and the situation until he or she is at ease with both. In this mode of the training the interviewer should practice with other interviewers, both as interviewer and interviewee. After each session there should be a discussion of what was done right and what could be improved. At this stage you, as the researcher, could create different problems and have the interviewers work their way through them. Only after the interviewers feel comfortable with the questionnaire, understand how to conduct the interview, and have practiced the interview, should you allow them to contact a respondent.

There are five things interviewers need to be reminded of when contacting respondents (see Box 11.1). It is vital that the interviewer remember that the questionnaire is his or her "bible." Although the questions may be asked in a matter-of-fact, business-like fashion, the interviewer must ask the questions *exactly* as they appear on the survey instrument, even if they differ from the interviewer's own personal feelings or beliefs. In the same vein,

BOX 11.1
ASKING THE QUESTIONS

The questions are generally direct and straightforward. Emphasize the underlined words as you read them, and give the answers that are included in the wording of the question. Circle the capitalized response that is closest to the answer given. If you cannot clearly classify a response with one of the available choices, write it out in the margin. YOU, OF COURSE, HAVE FEELINGS ABOUT THESE ISSUES. THEY *MUST NOT* INFLUENCE YOUR RECORDING OF RESPONSES OR YOUR BEHAVIOR DURING THE INTERVIEW.

USE THE QUESTIONNAIRE, BUT USE IT INFORMALLY

The interview should be conducted in a relaxed manner; the interviewer should avoid creating the impression that the interview is a quiz or cross-examination. PLEASE BE CAREFUL NOT TO IMPLY CRITICISM, SURPRISE, APPROVAL, OR DISAPPROVAL OF THE QUESTIONS ASKED OR THE RESPONDENT'S ANSWERS.

But don't be sloppy in asking the questions. Know the questions so you can read each one smoothly and move on to the next without hesitancy. This means you should study the questionnaire carefully and practice asking the questions *aloud*, perhaps by doing a practice interview with someone.

ASK THE QUESTIONS EXACTLY AS WORDED IN THE QUESTIONNAIRE

Since exactly the same questions must be asked of each respondent, the interviewer should MAKE NO CHANGES IN THE PHRASING OF THE QUESTIONS. Also, guard against trying to be conversational by inadvertently adding a few words at the end of a question or leaving a few words out. The respondents should be aware of all of the alternatives for a particular question (except for yes/no questions).

Ask the questions in the order presented in the questionnaire. Question sequence is carefully planned for continuity and promoting a conversational atmosphere. The sequence is also arranged so that early questions will not have a harmful effect on the respondent's answers to later questions. Furthermore, the question order needs to be standardized from respondent to respondent if the interviews are to be comparable.

ASK EVERY QUESTION SPECIFIED IN THE QUESTIONNAIRE

In answering one question, a respondent will sometimes also answer another question appearing later in the interview. Or, from time to time, the interviewer needs to ask a series of apparently similar questions. In either case, DON'T SKIP QUESTIONS THAT ARE APPARENTLY ANSWERED BY AN EARLIER RESPONSE.

REPEAT QUESTIONS WHICH ARE MISUNDERSTOOD OR MISINTERPRETED

Questions may be repeated just as they are written in the questionnaire. If you suspect that the respondent merely needs time to think it over, simply wait and don't press for an immediate answer. If you think the respondent just needs reassuring, you may want to add to the question a neutral remark, such as: "We're just trying to get people's ideas on this," or "There are no right or wrong answers, just your ideas on it."

the interviewer must refrain from commenting or reacting nonverbally in a face-to-face or phone interview. (An exception would be if a "probe" was required as a follow-up to an open-ended question.) Again, we repeat: *The questions must be asked as they are written,* even if the interviewer thinks he or she could phrase them better (sometimes practice sessions conducted by the researcher produce clarity or other improvements in question wording). And, finally, when confusion is apparent (or the respondent asks for clarification), the question should be repeated exactly as written—the interviewer cannot be allowed to interpret the question for the respondent. Such deviations introduce measurement unreliability and ultimately threaten the validity of the research. Responses that require a reply, such as Strongly Agree, Agree, Disagree, Strongly Disagree, or Uncertain, should be repeated as often as necessary, just as if the respondent were responding to a *written* questionnaire.

Following these simple guidelines will produce an interview and data about which you can feel confident. As with most things, practice makes perfect. One final comment. If possible, as the researcher, you should be present when data collection is occurring. This provides you with an insight into any problems that may crop up *and* you will be available when questions arise. Your presence also ensures that the interviews are actually conducted and protects the integrity of the research itself. (Researchers frequently make random follow-up calls or monitor the calls to ensure that the call was made and that the interviewer conducted him- or herself exactly as he or she was trained.)

Interviewing Methods

In-person interviews, done door-to-door, on a street corner, or in a mall, allow for the greatest flexibility in terms of the type of information requested, but they are often the most time-consuming, difficult, and expensive to conduct (see Table 11.2). This method of collection also is most prone to **interviewer effects**, those outcomes that are produced in the responses as a result of behaviors of the interviewer, which may bias the answers a respondent provides. Showing approval or disapproval of responses, even with a smile, nod, or verbal hesitancy may influence the type and even the length of the response. Even the type of clothing worn may have a significant influence on answers (Hickson & Stacks, 1992; McPeek & Edwards, 1975).

In-Person Interviews. There are several advantages to the in-person interview. One advantage is that in-person interviews usually generate a good **response rate** (usually 80 percent or better), compared with mail or telephone interviews, which are usually around 60 percent or lower (Goyder, 1986). Another advantage is that the interviewer can write down items that may be too sensitive to ask—like a person's race or income—and make notes on what he or she observes, such as house type, possessions, and so forth. Finally, the in-person interview allows for immediate feedback so the interviewer is able to probe when a respondent is having trouble with a response.

There are important ethical, environmental, and economic considerations that should be followed when conducting an in-person interview. The respondents are not anonymous in the strictest sense of anonymity and thus, as a researcher, you should provide some guarantee that the identity of the respondent, his or her name and address, will be kept in strictest confidence or not even be noted. Second, you must consider where you will send

TABLE 11.2   A Comparison of Telephone, Mail and Face-to-Face Surveys on Selected Criteria

	MAIL	TELEPHONE	FACE-TO-FACE
Cost per response	low[a]	medium	high
Speed of initiation	medium	high	low
Speed of return	low	high	medium
Number of interviews completed	low	high	high
Design constraints	medium	high	low
Convenience for respondent	high	medium	low
Risk of interviewer bias	low	medium	medium
Interview intrusiveness	low	high	high
Administrative bother	low	low	high
Survey control	medium	high	high
Anonymity of response	high	medium[b]	low

[a]Recently, mail costs have risen to such an extent that the cost difference between mail and telephone today is small.

[b]In the case of random-digit dialing, responses may actually be anonymous.

Source: M. Singletary (1994). *Mass communication research: Contemporary methods and applications.* New York: Longman, p. 153. Reprinted with permission.

an interviewer to gather data. Random sampling requires that all possible respondents be included in your sample—including those living in undesirable and even dangerous neighborhoods—and they must be interviewed if selected. You must also take into consideration possible unpleasant weather and vicious animals when conducting the in-person interview. One final consideration is cost. Of all interviewing methods, the in-person interview is the most expensive: interviews are generally longer than other methods, requiring more paper and time; interviewers or interviewees must be transported to and from the interview site, adding to hourly costs; and considerable effort is required to set up the interviews and, when an interview is not completed, the interview needs to be rescheduled.

Mail Surveys.   Mail surveys are virtually free of interviewer effects because the respondent answers a paper questionnaire he or she receives in the mail. However, some of the advantages of the in-person interview are not available with this method: there is no possibility for feedback or for probing; observations of the respondent and his or her environment are not possible; and the response rate is lower. In a simple, domestic survey, a 60 percent response rate will be fine, but lower rates should be expected in "snowball" or international studies (as low as 15 percent).

Mail surveys are usually cheaper to conduct and have the advantage of respondent anonymity, which takes care of some of the ethical concerns expressed earlier. This is especially helpful when the questions you ask are sensitive. When a person is asked to respond to a sensitive question, he or she may be reluctant to do so in person and may even distort the answer to make it socially desirable. For example, suppose you wanted to study the potential conflict married couples have over money matters. If you went up to someone's door and started asking questions regarding this, what would happen? Outside of the respondent's actual refusal to participate in the research, you would be likely to get answers stating that they (the couple) have no conflict. They would say so because it is not socially desirable to admit to money problems, let alone conflict, especially to strangers.

Mail survey costs generally fall into three areas. First, there is the cost of duplicating the questionnaire for each participant (something that need not be done for in-person or telephone interviews, which might use a response sheet for each respondent). Mail surveys should include a cover letter explaining the purpose of the survey and indicating its importance, the questionnaire, and a return envelope. Second, there is the cost of mailing. Generally, using 2003 postage rates, a two-page survey with cover letter and return envelope will cost about $1.25 to mail. Third, there is the cost of a second mailing to participants who have not returned the questionnaire, usually done in the form of a postcard reminder. Total costs for a single respondent may run between $1.25 (simply mailing the materials without return postage or a reminder mailing) to over $4.00 (initial mailing with return postage, a postcard reminder, and a follow-up mailing with return postage). A sample of 100 respondents could cost about $400.00.

Telephone Interviews.   Telephone interviews strike a happy medium between in-person and mail surveys. They are very inexpensive (at least with local samples), easy to conduct, and not very time-consuming—no need to wait for questionnaires to be returned nor spend time driving around town to go door-to-door. They allow for feedback, yet minimize some in-person interviewer effects. They also have the advantage of guaranteeing some anonymity, if the respondents are assured of such and believe it. However, they typically do not generate the high response rate achieved by in-person interviews.

Telephone surveys have become the most used data-collection technique. Most researchers have access to several telephones, they can train their interviewers and be at the interview location while the data are collected, and *most* respondents have telephones. You can also contact people in problem or dangerous areas via telephone. The problems of anonymity can be overcome via random digit dialing techniques so that the interviewer can tell the respondent that his or her telephone number was selected at random. You can also stratify your sample by requesting that a "man in the house," the "person of voting age," or "the person watching television at your household" respond to the questionnaire.

Telephone surveys only select as participants individuals with access to telephones. Not everyone has a telephone or access to one, thus a telephone survey only surveys people who can afford or want a telephone. Second, the advent of answering machines has made contacting respondents difficult—and when long-distance calling is required, more expensive. Third, the advent of computerized telephone marketing "surveys" has turned off many potential participants. Only a few years ago being contacted to participate in a survey was a rare occurrence; now people are contacted almost daily. Thus, it is important to identify the survey's purpose early in the introduction, and to reinforce the idea that you are not selling anything. Finally, technology has made it possible for computers rather than people to conduct telephone interviews. Most of us have been polled by computer, asking to press "1" if we agree or "2" if we disagree with a statement. This impersonal form of data gathering has made it more difficult to get respondents to participate in telephone surveys.

Group Interviews.   At times it is appropriate to conduct survey research in a group setting. The focus group (see Chapter 9) serves as an example of when group interviews may be conducted. Group interviews allow you to conduct in-person and mail surveys simultaneously. Advertising, public relations, marketing, and organizational communication research is often conducted via group interview where participants are interviewed and complete questionnaires in the field or some neutral setting. Group interviews are appropriate when you are attempting to gauge attitudes toward some product or an attitude stimulus on video or audiotape. The technique is also appropriate when surveying children or people who may have problems with language.

"New" Techniques.   Technology has provided new techniques for information gathering via surveys. At least two deal with the personal computer. One method, **disk-by-mail survey**, sends respondents the survey questionnaire on disk and requires that respondents complete the questionnaire on their computers and send the disk back for analysis (Wimmer & Dominick, 2003). A major problem lies in system formatting and the ability of respondents to read the disk and file(s) and write back to that same disk. A second method uses e-mail as the mail medium (Saris, 1991). Sophisticated questionnaires have been developed that use attractive, graphically based questions that require the respondent to simply complete an electronic form and send it back with the click of a mouse or key. Along this same line, fax-back surveys have been employed (e.g., Garrison, 1995). Fax-back surveys may be either mailed out and the completed questionnaire faxed back to the researcher or faxed to respondent and returned by either mail or fax. E-mail and fax-back surveys have a major problem with anonymity, as do any form of computerized mail (e.g., Hickson, Stacks, & Greeley-Padgett, 1998). These techniques are probably more suited for organizational settings where people have daily access to computers.

Maximizing Response Rates

In all forms of surveys you want to get as many people to respond as you possibly can to ensure that your sample matches the population in the best possible way. We have already mentioned some techniques, but two more things need to be added.

First, you should always make the survey convenient and pleasant for the respondent. Ask yourself if you would be interested in this topic, if you would have the time to complete the survey, would the day and hour that the survey is being administered be convenient for you if you were contacted? Is the context (home, office, school, church) a suitable one for conducting this survey? Would another place be better? These are all considerations you must make before contacting your first interviewee.

Second, while there will be people who are reluctant to complete the survey, you can use the well-known **norm of reciprocity** (Roloff, 1987) to your advantage in getting people to respond. This norm means that when you give someone something, they feel *obligated* to return the favor. Thus, if you give or promise to give an incentive or a reward to a participant, you will increase the likelihood that they will reciprocate. Being friendly and pleasant is a form of reward. Always indicate how respondents' individual help is a valuable part of your important research. It may cost a bit, but you can offer to send respondents a copy or summary of the research. Another technique that is used in mail survey research is to include

---

MINI-PROJECT:

How would you conduct a survey that seeks to answer the following research questions: (1) Is there a parking problem on campus? (2) If so, what has contributed to the parking problem? and (3) What should be done to alleviate the problem?

---

a small monetary reward, usually a dollar bill attached to the survey. Putting a small pencil in the envelope not only adds an incentive for reciprocity, but can make it convenient for respondents to fill out the questionnaire when they get it (avoiding the problem of them misplacing or forgetting to fill it out).

A third way to increase return rates is to contact respondents before they are actually questioned. Riffe (1988, 1990) used this technique in a mail survey of state legislatures and obtained a very respectful return rate with a population very hard to get responses from. The same can be done for telephone interviews, contacting respondents and setting up a time when responding to the survey would be convenient. The downside of this, however, is the time and cost of the initial contact.

STRUCTURING THE SURVEY

The foregoing discussion about data collection has pointed out the need to provide some structure to the survey. You have to have either an interview schedule or a questionnaire to ensure that each respondent gets the same interview so that you can compare responses across people.

Survey Types

An **interview schedule** is a guideline for asking questions in-person or over the telephone. A **questionnaire** contains the exact questions and measures an interviewer uses to survey through the mail, in person, or by telephone. The interview schedule differs from a questionnaire only in that precise measures are not given to the respondent; instead, guidelines are provided the interviewer for eliciting the requested information. Both can be used in any data-collection method, but each has its own advantages.

Suppose you are interested in getting an idea about the communication patterns physicians have with terminally ill patients. You have examined the literature in the area and found that there is no adequate description of the types of experiences patients have. You have no knowledge of such matters yourself and few ideas for the kinds of experiences or precise messages that might be exchanged between a physician and patient. Since you are engaging in rather preliminary work, and you do not have concrete ideas of what constitutes key messages, you want to explore the patient's experiences to find out what they are. Therefore, you develop a series of topics you want to cover. You want to find out what the patient's relationship with the doctor has been. So, you might begin by asking how often they have seen the physician. Then you might ask them what happened during the visits.

As they begin to relate their experiences they may tell you that they had trouble with one of the visits. You are now cued by the respondent and may ask, "What kind of trouble?" You have asked a question that was dependent on the earlier response. You may not have identified this issue if it were not for the loose nature of the interview. Thus, this example points out the main advantage of using a schedule: You are able to gain insight and some depth into the area chosen. You also get the respondent's experiences in his or her own words. (Here you must consider how to record the data—writing notes, using a tape recorder, or even videotaping.)

The disadvantage with the interview schedule is found in interpretation. Although interpretation across respondents may be difficult, you have the advantage of finding new topics brought to your attention by the respondent or probe for further information. The interview schedule is most amenable to humanistic or exploratory research in which you want to concentrate on individuals and are not overly concerned about generalizing to a larger population. Note, however, that the selection of respondents can be as scientific as ever.

The most commonly used method in communication research is the second type, the *questionnaire*. With a questionnaire, the interviewer has a list of precise questions to ask the respondent (see Box 11.2 and Box 11.3). These questions can be either closed or open-ended. **Closed** questions are similar to multiple-choice test questions in that responses are provided from which the interviewee may select the most appropriate. **Open-ended** questions are similar to essay or short-answer questions, allowing the respondent to answer in any way he or she wishes. An example might be the type of questions mentioned earlier in reaction to the nuclear war film study. One way to tap viewer reaction would be to ask the closed question, How much did watching the film affect you emotionally? Responses might be provided as: A Lot, Somewhat, or Not at All. If you wanted more general responses, however, you would use an open-ended question, such as, "How has viewing the film, *Schindler's List*, affected you emotionally?" and let the respondent say whatever he or she wants. Answers to the open-ended question require some type of categorization and content analysis. But the interviewer should record the responses exactly, or as nearly so as possible: "Saddened, shocked." "Just feel that the treatment of Jewish citizens was awful, is senseless." "Hadn't affected me." "No." "Trouble sleeping and thought provoking—very thought provoking—very frightening—worth watching." Obviously, you may have trouble quantifying these responses as they differ in type and magnitude of feeling.

Typically you will use both open-ended and closed-ended questions in a questionnaire. For instance, you may ask a person's age (open-ended) and their marital status (Married, Never Married, Divorced, Separated, Widow/Widower—closed-ended). In general, it takes longer and your responses are less easily analyzed with open-ended questions. Thus, a typical survey contains only a couple of open-ended questions, usually addressing the most important issues that the survey is examining.

You must train your interviewers more with open-ended questions, making certain that they write down *all* that was said. In some instances you may wish to begin with a closed-ended question, use it as a **filter**, and then, depending on response, go to the open-ended question. (For example, the closed-ended question might be, "Do you smoke?" with

BOX 11.2
TELEPHONE CONSTRUCT SURVEY

DEPARTMENT OF COMMUNICATION ARTS CONSTRUCT SURVEY
(ALL OF YOUR INSTRUCTIONS ARE IN CAPITAL LETTERS. DO NOT READ THEM ALOUD. WRITE CODE NUMBERS ON ANSWER SHEET. WRITE RESPONSES TO OPEN QUESTIONS VERBATIM ON ANSWER SHEET. WRITE ALL COMMENTS MADE BY RESPONDENTS AS CLEARLY AS YOU CAN). PLEASE NOTE: FOR THE NUMBER CODED QUESTIONS, A REFUSAL TO ANSWER THE QUESTION IS ALWAYS MARKED AS '8'.

Hello. Is this the _____ residence? May I speak to _____? I'm with the Institute for Communication Research at the University. We are doing a survey on American politics. Your name was drawn in a random sample and we would like to talk with you for a few minutes. Okay?

1. Are you registered to vote?

   YES...............1
   NO 2
   DK...............7

2. Do you consider yourself a Democrat, Republican, an Independent, or what?

   DEMOCRAT...1
   REPUBLICAN 2
   INDEPENDENT 3
   OTHER..4
   DK...7

We are going to ask you a series of questions about political leaders. Please respond with the first answers that come to mind.

3. Is there anything you particularly like or dislike about the president? (PROBE FOR UP TO SEVEN RESPONSES).
4. Is there anything that you particularly like or dislike about the governor? (PROBE!)
5. Is there anything that you particularly like or dislike about your senator? (PROBE!)
6. Is there anything that you particularly like or dislike about the mayor? (PROBE!)

Thank you very much. We would like to conclude by asking you a few questions about yourself for statistical purposes.

7. How many days a week do you read a newspaper?

   CODE NUMBER OF TIMES_____

(continued)

BOX 11.2   CONTINUED

8. How many days a week do you watch the news on television?

   CODE NUMBER OF TIMES_____

9. What do you consider to be your chief source of information about political leaders?
10. What is the highest level of education that you have completed?

   NO FORMAL EDUCATION 1
   COMPLETED GRADE SCHOOL 2
   SOME HIGH SCHOOL.....................3
   COMPLETED HIGH SCHOOL 4
   SOME COLLEGE.....................5
   COMPLETED COLLEGE 6
   GRADUATE WORK OR DEGREE 7
   DK..9

11. What is the occupation of the principal wage earner in your household?
12. Do you generally see yourself as Liberal, Conservative, or Moderate?

   LIBERAL...................................1
   CONSERVATIVE 2
   MODERATE 3
   DK...7

13. In what year were you born?
14. Did you vote in the recent property tax referendum?

   YES 1
   NO 2
   DK..7

15. Did you vote in the recent City Commissioners election?

   YES 1
   NO 2
   DK..7

16. Did you vote in the last Presidential election?

   YES 1
   NO 2
   DK..7

17. How would you describe your religious affiliation?

   RECORD_____

18. Which of the following best describes your racial or ethnic identification. (READ ENTIRE LIST EXCEPT "OTHER").

    AFRICAN AMERICAN.............................1
    LATINO/MEXICAN AMERICAN..........2
    NATIVE AMERICAN 3
    WHITE/EUROPEAN AMERICAN........4
    ASIAN AMERICAN..................................5
    OTHER...6
    (SPECIFY) _____
    DK _____ 7

19. In an average week, how many conversations about politics do you engage in?

    RECORD _____

    (TERMINATE WITH: That concludes our interview. We certainly appreciate your taking the time to talk to us. Your opinion will be very helpful. Thank you.)

20. Record sex of respondent.

    FEMALE 1
    MALE 2
    DK...7

Yes, or No as response options. If the respondent replied "no," you would go to another question. If the respondent replied "yes," then you might ask, "What benefits do you get from smoking?")

Designing the Survey Questionnaire and Schedule

The following discussion closes out our coverage of the descriptive methodology. Based on what we discussed earlier, careful consideration must be given to both the content and structure of the survey and to the design of the individual items within each survey. Only through careful consideration and construction of questions can we be assured that the questions we ask reflect the general questions guiding our research. Further, the quality of the question will to a great extent dictate the quality of the response. Use the following as guidelines in constructing your own questionnaires.

Content and Structure.   Any interview or survey must include an introduction before the main questioning begins. Several things should be included in the introduction:

1. An introduction of the interviewer and the affiliation of the sponsor of the study is necessary. This serves as a credibility inducement and provides indication that the project is important. For instance, you might begin with, "Hello, I'm _____ calling from

■ ■ ■ ■ ■

BOX 11.3

MAIL SURVEY—GUARANTEE OF FAIR TREATMENT (GFT) SURVEY

Dear Associate,

A Ph.D. candidate from the University of California, Santa Barbara is writing her dissertation on fairness in the workplace and would appreciate it if you would help her and your hotel by completing this survey. She is interested in your feelings about the company's *Guarantee of Fair Treatment (GFT) Policy*, which is your suggestion and complaint procedure. If you have a problem or complaint, GFT allows you to tell your immediate supervisor. If you do not get your problem straightened out with your supervisor, then you are free to see your manager or Executive Committee Member. If you are still not satisfied, then he or she will arrange for you to see your General Manager or Director of Human Resources. If the problem is still not resolved to your satisfaction, then the matter will be referred to your Regional Director of Human Resources.

Even if you have never used the *Guarantee of Fair Treatment (GFT) Policy* process, please take a few minutes to complete this survey. Your participation will help the company improve its ability to share information with its associates about *GFT*, and your responses will provide important information on how *fairly* you feel the company is treating its associates.

The Ph.D. candidate is collecting all of the surveys and analyzing the results; therefore, no one from the company will be looking at individual surveys. All of your responses will be kept *confidential* and will not be associated with you personally at any time. The survey will take about 15 minutes to complete. If you wish to make any additional comments, there is a separate sheet included in the middle of the survey. When you are finished, please put the entire survey in the attached envelope and place it in the box provided.

Thank you for your assistance.

Note: GFT refers to Guarantee of Fair Treatment.

Where do you get your information about the company's Guarantee of Fair Treatment (GFT) policy? (Circle all that apply)

Personnel manual	Memos	Executive Committee Member
Bulletin boards	Associates	Human Resources Director
Newsletter	Manager	Other _____
General Manager	Immediate Supervisor	

Who has used the company's Guarantee of Fair Treatment (GFT) to make a complaint, solve a problem, or settle a disagreement? (Circle all that apply)

Myself   Someone I know personally   Someone I heard about

How many times have *you* used the company's GFT to resolve a problem or settle a disagreement?

0   1   2   3   4   5   Other _____

Please indicate how strongly you agree or disagree with the following statements about the company's Guarantee of Fair Treatment (GFT). We are interested in your feelings even if you have never used the GFT process. (Circle *one* answer for each question).

	STRONGLY AGREE	AGREE	NEUTRAL	DISAGREE	STRONGLY DISAGREE
1. The information I receive about GFT is *clear*	1	2	3	4	5
2. The information I receive about GFT is *useful*	1	2	3	4	5
3. I receive enough information about GFT	1	2	3	4	5
4. I often discuss GFT with other company associates	1	2	3	4	5
5. I understand the GFT policy	1	2	3	4	5
6. I would feel comfortable using the GFT process	1	2	3	4	5
7. The company's GFT process is an effective way to discuss complaints, solve problems or settle disagreements	1	2	3	4	5
8. If I had a problem or complaint, I would be willing to use GFT	1	2	3	4	5
9. Using GFT will harm my relationship with my *immediate supervisor*	1	2	3	4	5
10. Using GFT will harm my relationship with my *co-workers*	1	2	3	4	5
11. I am satisfied with GFT at the company	1	2	3	4	5
12. The GFT policy at the company is fair	1	2	3	4	5

Have *you, someone you know,* or *someone you heard about* ever used the company's Guarantee of Fair Treatment (GFT) process (discussed a problem or complaint with a supervisor or another member of management)?

(continued)

BOX 11.3   CONTINUED

YES   NO → → → → | Skip to question #31 on the next page & continue with survey | → → → → → → → → → → → → → → → → →

(If you answered yes) Indicate how strongly you agree or disagree with the following statements about your or another associate's experiences with the GFT process. (Circle *one* answer for each question).

	STRONGLY AGREE	AGREE	NEUTRAL	DISAGREE	STRONGLY DISAGREE
13. Associate had an opportunity to present his/her views	1	2	3	4	5
14. Associate felt he/she was able to influence the decision	1	2	3	4	5
15. Supervisor/manager listened to associate's concerns	1	2	3	4	5
16. Supervisor/manager treated associate in a polite manner	1	2	3	4	5
17. Supervisor/manager was neutral and unbiased	1	2	3	4	5
18. Supervisor/manager had accurate information about the problem	1	2	3	4	5
19. Supervisor/manager treated associate with respect	1	2	3	4	5
20. Supervisor/manager applied the same procedures to this associate as he/she did with others who used this process	1	2	3	4	5

Source: B. Christine Shea, (1995). "Non-union grievance systems: The effects of procedural fairness, distribution fairness, outcome, and supervisor relationships on employee perception of organizational fairness and support." Dissertation, University of California, Santa Barbara, 1995.

the University of _____." This introduction should be written and followed carefully by each interviewer. It provides both a name for the respondent to refer to and the sponsoring agency. Interviewees should only use their first names; avoid giving respondents your full name and if asked, refer them to the researcher or individual supervising the study.

2. An explanation of the nature of the questions to be asked. This need not be lengthy or specific, but should provide some indication of the subject matter to be requested of the respondent. For example, if you were doing a study of the effects of a televised debate on political attitudes, you might say, "We're doing a study of people's feelings about the current political campaign." It is important, however, not to give away any hypotheses or specific research questions that might cue the respondent as to how to answer.

3. An estimate of the amount of time it will take the respondent to finish the survey. Keep in mind that each interview or respondent will differ in the amount of time it takes him or her to complete the information, estimate a reasonable amount of time (5 to 10 minutes is normal, unless the questions are very detailed or open-ended).

4. A request for the respondent's participation. Do not assume that a person will help you; ask for his or her help. If he or she refuses, offer thanks anyway (see Chapter 3).

5. A statement about how they were selected for the study. If they were selected at random, be sure to state that.

6. A guarantee of confidentiality and/or anonymity.[1]

7. Uses to be made of the data. Will it be prepared for a class project? A convention paper? For publication? A business report?

8. An expression of gratitude for their participation.

In the introduction, as well as throughout the survey, the interviewer should act the same way with each respondent. Every effort should be made to make the experience as pleasant as possible, even if the respondent becomes rude and abusive. After the respondent has agreed to participate, the interviewer immediately begins questioning.

Constructing a good questionnaire is challenging (see Box 11.4). It is an art *and* a science. Unless you have a reason for beginning with background information, avoid asking demographic questions or sensitive questions early in the questionnaire. Respondents may refuse to answer when you ask their race, educational level, age, income, and so forth; or if you ask about a controversial issue. It is best to begin with a simple and interesting question and work to get the respondent rolling through the questionnaire. For the rest of the questionnaire (and interview schedule), you should keep the following in mind when developing the questions: pace (the questions need to flow smoothly—how long it takes to go through each question or block of questions), ordering (keep question sequences logical, have one set lead to the next and do not have one question suggest a particular answer to a subsequent question), interesting (in terms of the questions themselves, their wording, and with regard to the interviewer's friendly, upbeat and professional manner). Finally, make sure that you obtain all the information you need.

To complete the questionnaire and to control the amount of relevant communication from the respondent, questions must be put together so that the interviews are paced to finish within the planned time limit. Interviewers must be instructed to move along

■ ■ ■ ■ ■

BOX 11.4

TELEPHONE SURVEY—IMAGE SURVEY

Hello, my name is _____, and I'm conducting a local marketing survey of attitudes toward American automobile dealers. Would you mind helping us out? The survey only takes a few minutes. (IF YES, CONTINUE; IF NO, THANK THE INDIVIDUAL AND HANG UP)

1. When you think of automobile dealers located in the greater Mobile, Alabama area, which *dealers* come to mind? (LIST IN ORDER PRESENTED)
2. If you were thinking about buying a new car, would you consider buying that car from:

    a. Grady Buick   Yes = 1   No = 0
    b. Trendwell Ford   Yes = 1   No = 0
    c. Bullard Oldsmobile   Yes = 1   No = 0
    d. Trail Pontiac   Yes = 1   No = 0

3. Have you ever bought—or know someone who has bought—a new automobile from Grady Buick? Yes = 1   No = 0

    IF YES: Were you—or they—pleased with the

    a. Product   Yes = 1   No = 0
    b. Salespeople   Yes = 1   No = 0

4. I'm going to read you a list of things people look for in a new car. Please tell me which of the following car makes you consider to be the *best* for each category (NOTE: NO PARTICULAR MODEL):

    BUICK = 1; FORD = 2; OLDSMOBILE = 3; PONTIAC = 4

    (READ THE CATEGORY AND THEN THE LIST, ABOVE, AND RECORD THE NUMBER)

    a. Looks   g. Quality
    b. Styling   h. Durability
    c. Size   i. Speed
    d. Fits Your needs j. Power
    e. Economy   k. Comfort
    f. Serviceability   l. Cost

5. What type of service do you think you would receive from a new car dealer in the greater Mobile area?

    EXCELLENT = 7; VERY GOOD = 6; GOOD = 5; UNCERTAIN = 4; BAD = 3; VERY BAD = 2; TERRIBLE = 1

6. Have you had any new automobile problems that have not been satisfactorily taken care of by your dealer? Yes = 1   No = 0

IF YES:

a. Which dealer (WRITE IN NAME)
b. What was the problem (WRITE IN PROBLEM)

DEMOGRAPHICS
Finally, I would like to ask you a few questions for statistical purposes.

7. What is your age? (FILL IN AGE IN YEARS)
8. How many years of formal education have you completed?

0–8 years	1	1–2 years of college	4
1–2 years of HS	2	3–4 years of college	5
3–4 years of HS	3	more than 4 years of college	6

9. Could you please tell me your *household* income before taxes? Which category do you fit?

Under $10,000	1	$31,000–$40,000	4
$11,000–$20,000	2	$41,000–$50,000	5
$21,000–$30,000	3	$51,000–$60,000	6
		over $60,000	7

10. What is your present marital status?

Single, never married	1	Separated	4
Married	2	Widowed	5
Divorced	3		

11. How many cars do you own? (WRITE IN NUMBER)
12. What is the age of your newest car (YEARS IN NUMBER)

What is your racial or ethnic identification?

African American	1	White (Euro American)	4
Mexican American/Latino	2	Native American	5
Asian American	3	Other	6

13. (RECORD RESPONDENT'S SEX HERE)

Male   0
Female   1

Thank you, that concludes our interview.

from question to question, and not get sidetracked on irrelevant issues brought up by the respondent. When a respondent spends too much time talking, you or the interviewer may have to interject that you have to go on to the next question. Overly long replies are often a problem with telephone surveys because the respondent cannot be guided with nonverbal behavior.

Ordering is important for pace, as well as ensuring that the respondents are not biased to give answers to questions toward the end of the interview as a result of questions asked near the beginning. For instance, suppose you want to measure a variety of campaign issues discussed in an election. But you also are interested in determining who is a viable candidate. You do not want to ask issue questions before you ask about the person's preference for candidates. The issues identified in your questionnaire, even if they were not normally associated with a candidate, may become salient in determining who a viable candidate is.

Suppose you wanted to find out what people thought of Diane Feinstein, California Senator, for president of the United States, but you also wanted to know if there was any connection between certain environmentally related issues and people's attitudes toward presidential candidates. You know that Senator Feinstein marched in a protest march in California for a "green" proposition. If you started your questionnaire with a question asking what the respondent thought about Feinstein's participation in the protest march, you have made that issue an important one for evaluating her. After all, the respondent probably would not have been aware of that fact, and given that they are now made aware of it, this knowledge may influence their evaluation of her later in the questionnaire.

Keeping interest is sometimes difficult, especially with either relatively complicated or relatively uninteresting topics. Questions about television viewing are relatively interesting and usually keep people's interest; questions on political ideology may not. You should avoid redundancy in question content and form to keep the respondent interested enough to complete the questionnaire (something that is essential so you have the full range of data you need to answer your research question[s] or hypotheses). You may have to occasionally include some throw-away questions that will not be analyzed but are designed to keep interest. This is particularly true when working with children. In many instances the researcher needs to ask questions that appear quite similar but are different. To a child, and less so to an adult, they may appear the same. Thus, they may tire of answering and therefore would either answer them all in the same way, skip some, or quit altogether. Therefore, you might include questions about their favorite television shows (which would not be analyzed) and perhaps schedule a break during which they could stand and stretch for a few minutes.

Making certain you get all the information you need is sometimes one of the most difficult tasks. You want to make sure that each respondent finishes the questionnaire, but you also need to make sure there is an answer for *every single question* within the questionnaire. To do this, a little encouragement on the part of the interviewer is sometimes required. With a reluctant respondent, an interviewer might have to say, "If you had to give some opinion, what would it be?" You should strategically place such prompts within the questionnaire, especially when you are almost finished with the major questions and transitioning to demographic information. It sometimes helps to use transitions between major bodies of questions, such as "Now we are going to ask you a few questions about . . ."

Designing the Questions. Designing questions requires careful consideration of a variety of factors that may lead to erroneous findings. Questions need to be direct, clear, and unambiguous. One or more questions should be used for each area you wish to study. Questions that contain two parts (referred to as *double-barreled* because the respondent may respond to either or both of the parts rather than the one idea you are attempting to analyze; see Chapters 6 and 7) may be ambiguous and should be avoided. Examples of *bad* questions include:

1. Do you think the United States should support Spain and the European Community?
2. What is your attitude about the President and his morals?
3. Do you believe in America and vote?

Instead, each question could be split in two. For example, you might ask, "What is your attitude toward the President?" and follow up with a second question asking "What is your attitude toward his morals?"

Leading questions also produce poor results. They are the questions that most often bias the respondent in a certain direction. Examples of leading questions include:

1. Don't you think that rich university professors should be denied a pay raise?
2. Isn't it true that most Southerners are bigots?
3. Do you think the Brotherhood March was successful?

Question 1 claims that university professors are rich. Question 2 implies by the phrase, "Isn't it true," that Southerners *are* bigots. And, question 3 has included "brotherhood," a term that some respondents may find emotionally loaded. Instead, the questions should be phrased:

1. Do you think university professors should be denied a pay raise?
2. Are Southerners more bigoted than Midwesterners?
3. Do you think the march of June 15th in San José was successful?

As discussed earlier, you also must guard against social desirability, even within a question. You must be careful to word questions so that the respondent does not give answers just to please you or others.

Chapter 6 and 7 examined measurement theory and scale construction. Because survey research often seeks to ascertain and describe the effects of intervening variables such

MINI-PROJECT:

Create a two-page survey of students that seeks to assess attitudes toward MTV, VH1, and CMT. Include the introduction and credibility induction, questions, and demographics.

as attitudes, beliefs, and values, measurement becomes very important. In designing your questionnaire, the type of survey becomes very important. In an in-person interview you might include closed-ended questions in any form (Likert-type, semantic differential, multidimensional, Thurstone, Guttman) because you or the interviewee are present and can ensure that the scales are being filled out correctly. In a mail survey, all forms of closed questions can be used if carefully explained in instructions. In telephone surveys, however, closed questions must be kept simple. Imagine, for example, how you would explain to a respondent that you wanted responses for 15 semantic differential scales measuring the persuasiveness of a particular medium. It certainly would be difficult. Telephone surveys typically contain Likert-type scales, scales that can be responded to easily. Aside from Likert-type scales, simple nominal or ordinal scales, and open-ended questions work best in telephone interviews.

Some Likert-type questions can be very complex, requiring several responses. Consider a survey on job satisfaction that asked a number of Likert-type (Strongly Agree to Strongly Disagree) questions about job satisfaction. Your project, however, is concerned with perceptions of job satisfaction when the respondent first began the job and at the present time. The questions should be asked and the respondent asked to respond first whether she Strongly Agreed, Agreed, Neither Agreed nor Disagreed, Disagreed, Strongly Disagreed when she first began the job and then again at the present time (see Figure 11.1).

Demographic questions are important. In analyzing your data you will want to break down your data by different demographic categories. Because many people are hesitant to provide information about themselves, demographic questions should be placed at the end of the questionnaire. At times, however, demographics such as age or voter registration are required openers. A researcher with an election survey does not want to discover after a 20-minute interview that the respondent is 16 years old. Transitioning to demographic questions is best done with a simple statement, such as: "For statistical purposes, I'd like to ask you a few questions about yourself." And then continue. For very personal questions, such as income, it is best to ask respondents to indicate an income or salary range: Is your annual pretax income under $10,000, between $11,000 and $20,000, between $21,000 and $30,000 and so forth (see Figure 11.2). Age is always hard to get; most people do not like to give out

Instructions:
Please help us in understanding how satisfied you are with your job now and when you first began it. Using the scales provided, please indicate how satisfied your were when you first began your current job and how satisfied you are with that job now. Please respond by indicating that you Strongly Agree (**SA**), Agree (**A**), Neither Agree Nor Disagree (**N**), Disagree (**D**), or Strongly Disagree (**SD**), with each statement.

	WHEN I BEGAN MY JOB	MY JOB NOW
My job is fun.	SA A N D SD	SA A N D SD
My job is challenging.	SA A N D SD	SA A N D SD
I hate my job.	SA A N D SD	SA A N D SD

FIGURE 11.1   Likert-type scale measuring job satisfaction at two times.

MINI-PROJECT:

An Associated Press story in summer 2001 was titled: "Study: Spankings Sting but Hurt Doesn't Last." The article reported that from 1968 to 1980 100 middle-class white families were interviewed, tested, and observed by teams of psychologists when their children were aged 4, 9, and 14. They reported that the "majority of families disciplined their preschool children by using mild to moderate spanking." The researchers stated that mild to moderate spanking had no negative effect on the cognitive, social, or behavioral skills of the youngsters and found no difference between them and the 4 percent of parents who disciplined their children frequently and impulsively. Those children were found not to be socially well adjusted and were more likely to have behavioral problems. What factors can you identify that are problems with this report and study and the conclusions that were drawn?

their age, but will readily answer the question, "In what year were you born?" or "Are you between 18 and 35?" (an age category used by radio rating services such as Arbitron), and so forth.

"NEW" SURVEY TECHNIQUES

A number of "new" survey techniques have been employed recently. Three of particular note—for their methodological and ethical concerns—include the "journalistic" survey, the "push poll," and the "persuasive survey."

"Journalistic" Surveys

A new technique, the "journalistic" telephone surveys or opinion polls, which are sponsored by many local television stations (as well as CNN and newspapers), also has problems, especially in the area of social desirability. These television stations typically ask one question and require the viewer to call one of two telephone numbers to indicate if they agree or disagree. Many times the anchor will read the question to the audience; in so doing, he or she may bias the results through vocal or facial expression, or by the fact that it follows a news story on the issue in question.

In addition to social desirability, these surveys and polls have other equally serious problems. First, many of the questions asked are neither well written nor pretested. Second, the results are invalid because they do not keep track of how many times a particular person responds. Another problem should be apparent by now: The sample is self-selected, therefore the principles of randomization discussed earlier cannot apply and the sample is no longer reflective of an identifiable population. Unless carefully constructed, such surveys are largely worthless.

When others report the results of such surveys and polls, remember to look for the following things: (1) the question as it was asked, (2) the number of respondents, (3) how the respondents were selected, (4) how the respondents were contacted (by telephone, in person, by mail), (5) the error rate (3 percent, 5 percent, 10 percent), (6) who sponsored or

FIGURE 11.2   Sample demographic questions.

Now, for statistical purposes, I'd like to ask you some questions about yourself.

In what year were you born?

Please mark the category that best describes your total family income during the last year:

___ Less than $10,000
___ $10,001-$20,000
___ $20,001-$35,000
___ $35,001-$50,000
___ $50,001-$65,000
___ $65,001-$80,000
___ $80,001-$95,000
___ $95,001-$110,000
___ More than $110,000

What is your racial or ethnic identification?

___ White
___ Black
___ Asian

What is your marital status?

___ single, never married   ___ divorced
___ married   ___ separated
___ widow/widower

How many years of formal education have you completed?

___ 0–8 years   ___ 1–2 years of college
___ 1–2 years of high school   ___ 3–4 years of college
___ 3–4 years of high school   ___ more than 4 years of college

---

cosponsored the survey or poll, and (7) what social desirability factors might have been present. You should include the same information when reporting your own surveys.

Persuasive and Push Poll Surveys.   Two pseudoscientific and highly questionable techniques have arisen in recent years with the advent of telephone survey methodology, persuasive and "push poll" surveying. The most controversial one became part of national concern during the 1996 presidential and congressional campaigns. With this technique, instead of trying to elicit unbiased information from a respondent, the telephone surveyor designs questions that insinuate or implicate that the political opponent is unfit for office. For instance, the so-called pollster might ask "Isn't it a shame that candidate Seagate accepts money from tobacco companies?" Or, worse yet, "Isn't it morally wrong when candidate Jones had sex with her secretary?" when the candidate has been accused, but not found guilty.

MINI-PROJECT:

BUSH, GORE, TV, AND CHADS

The 2000 Presidential election was full of examples in which the knowledge of social science research aids in understanding what occurred. Remember that the networks seemed to pin the election on the outcome of the Florida vote, first declaring Gore the winner, then retracting and declaring Bush the winner. Then, there was controversy about the so-called "butterfly ballots" that looked like figure X. These punch-out ballots were analyzed by machines that read the little holes that people punched out. A controversy arose over whether the machines could read ballots that were partially punched out. The media developed a lexicon for telling the varying ways that the ballots were punched. There were "chads," the area to be punched out. There were "dimpled" chads, where there was a small hole in the middle of the paper that was to be punched out. There were "pregnant" chads, where there was a bulge in the paper within the hole. There were even "two and three corner" chads, meaning that the paper was clinging to the hole area by a small piece of paper.

Then the different counties decided on different procedures for hand-counting the ballots. Perhaps you remember the TV images of a man holding the ballot up to the light to see the chad. Sometimes there were three people who examined each chad and then made a decision on how the voter had voted. Then there were decisions made about "intent," or whether people had intended to vote for Gore but had misread the ballot and voted for Buchannon. Secretary of State Harris even imposed a deadline on counting the ballots.

The news media incorrectly reported the outcome of the Florida election too early on election night. The nationwide polls leading up to the final vote had George W. Bush far ahead of Albert Gore in the national popular vote, when Al Gore, in the end, received the highest vote.

What measurement issues can you identify with what happened in the election of 2000?

A more subtle technique is using a presumed survey format to market or sell a specific product. The phone interviewer might start with seemingly innocent questions such as, "How many TVs do you have in your house?" or, "When you last purchased a television, what features were you looking for?" These questions might be asked by a true social science researcher. However, this survey, sponsored by ACME TV company, then states "ACME TV has the highest Consumer Reports rating of any TV on the market, did you know that?" Thus, the interviewer has attempted an act of persuasion on the respondent, and did not engage in truly ethical social science research. The goal was not the betterment of society, as noted in earlier chapters, but the betterment of a particular person or company.

OTHER CONSIDERATIONS

This chapter has introduced descriptive social science research, primarily through the use of survey methodology. It should be remembered that the selection methods introduced can be used by both the humanistic researcher and the social science researcher. In closing out this chapter, a few comments need to be made. First, you are probably different than your sample. Your education and interests may differ from those you seek to describe. Imposing your own feelings and ideas on their responses will not provide the impartial analysis you need. Always remember that although you are like some of your respondents in some ways, you are not much like some of your respondents in others. If you are conducting a survey, remember that you have *a lot* of information about the subject of your survey while many of your respondents may not. In addition, your vocabulary may not be suitable for your respondents. This is, of course, obvious in research dealing with children, but even adults may have trouble with the vocabulary of college students. Take special care to avoid jargon. Replace terms that may be stated more directly and more clearly with simpler, less obtuse terms. A respondent who does not understand a term in a question will most likely try to fake it to save face; thus, you may have an invalid response.

Before surveying your sample, pretest the questionnaire on your classmates, or, preferably, on a subset of the population under study. Ask for feedback during a session following the pretest administration of the questionnaire. Get reactions, ask how they interpreted each question, and find out if they have comments about the questions. You will find this extremely helpful in designing the final draft of your questionnaire.

APPLYING KNOWLEDGE IN COMMUNICATION

The survey is a fairly inexpensive way of assessing attitudes, values, and beliefs and in evaluating a message's effectiveness. Given today's technological advances, surveys are becoming not only an important research and evaluation tool, but they are also being used to provide almost instantaneous evaluation of ongoing opinions about current events.

A variety of examples of published survey research can demonstrate how surveys are useful in answering research questions and hypotheses. The following are examples from mass media, interpersonal, intercultural, organizational, and public relations to illustrate the application of survey research to communication studies.

Hoffner and Haefner (1993) were interested in children's strategies for coping with distressful news coverage of the Persian Gulf War. They found it beneficial to interview a *convenience sample* of 80 children, aged 8 to 12 enrolled in third to sixth grades. Seventy-six percent of the sample was classified as White, 10 percent Black, 9 percent Asian, and 5 percent Hispanic. The sample was taken at a large midwestern university elementary school. Among several hypotheses, they expected that children would use cognitive coping strategies—defined as reinterpretation and distraction—rather than seeking social support for their distress. These results were supported, most strongly for older children.

A second study by Dumlao and Botta (2000) examined the conflict style that fathers used with their young adult children. They gave a questionnaire to 211 university students at both a midwestern and a southeastern university. The respondents were given a survey that had 16 Likert items that measured family communication patterns and 28 items that measured conflict styles. They found that individuals with laissez-faire fathers had lower accommodation and collaborating styles of conflict than those whose fathers were not laissez-faire.

Organizational studies have also benefited by survey research. A study on the influence of information giving and information receiving during job transitions illustrates this. Kramer, Roberts, and Turban (1995) hypothesized that people who receive higher levels of information when they first acquire a new job will have higher levels of positive adjustment than people who do not. In addition, they were interested in whether people who received the information without soliciting it were more satisfied than those who had to seek information. They sampled a retail food store in a medium-sized midwestern city that was moving to a new location. All 175 employees (a *census* for the store, but not for the general population of new employees) were given a survey with their paychecks several weeks after the new store opened. The response rate was 43 percent due to vacations, employee status not fitting the description, or failure to pick up their paycheck on the designated day. The questionnaire included a variety of Likert-type items and items about which part of the company the employee worked in. Results generally indicated that receiving unsolicited information was associated with positive employee self-report or outcomes.

Brown and Rancer (1993) were interested in public relations methods of British and American practitioners. They presented four models that demonstrated a "mind set" of public relations practice and wanted to discover whether or not (a *research question*) the two countries had different or similar conceptions of public relations. To answer their question, they *randomly* mailed questionnaires to a sample of 570 public relations practitioners chosen from *Business Week's* top 1,000 companies and from *O'Dwyer's Directory of Public Relations Firms* in the United States. They also selected 505 British public relations practitioners at random from a respected directory of British firms. A total of 31 percent of the surveys were returned completed. They found that a two-way symmetrical model that uses bargaining, negotiation, and resolution was preferred by practitioners in both countries instead of other models that stressed media attention, public information, or persuasion as public relations techniques.

McDermott (1992) investigated the relationship between communication patterns and alienation among foreign college students. He did a census survey of 398 foreign students at a large U.S. university. Host culture behaviors of hostile communication, avoidance of communication, and norm attacking were related to alienation. The avoidance of communication by foreign students and communicating that they did not like living in the United States correlated with social isolation.

Survey methodology, however, is simply that—it surveys how people perceive or think about someone or something at a particular point in time. We can make certain inferences about the larger populations within allowed sampling or response error based on the survey sample size. However, this methodology cannot establish a cause-effect relationship; there are too many unknowns to be able to say via a survey that message "A" **causes** people to behave in some manner. For that we must turn to the last methodology covered in this book, the experiment. Before doing so, however, it is important to note that much of what we have discussed in sampling and survey methodology is applied to the experiment.

SUMMARY

This chapter has introduced a form of research that is very popular. Almost every time a major political figure makes an important speech, surveys are conducted to gauge reaction to both the speaker and the message. By understanding what survey research does, and the questions it answers, you should be prepared to evaluate those findings. Further, you have the necessary information to begin to conduct your own research. This chapter has attempted to provide information about how to collect survey data, whether it be by questionnaire or interview.

This methodology can be used by the historian and rhetorician as well as the social scientist. Understand also that survey research is rigorous; it provides a way of identifying how people think and feel about a subject and *begins* to address the question of causation. In sum, this quantitative research method allows you to begin to understand how variables may relate to each other and—in particular—describe their isomorphism with real-life settings.

PROBES

1. Survey methodology seeks to canvas a number of people to gain insight into their perceptions regarding selected variables or concerns. If you were asked to critique this method as a way of gaining understanding about human behavior, what would you say? What does survey research tell us that other methods do not? What limitations are placed on the survey researcher? Are these limitations important?

2. One of the more complex areas of survey research deals with the sampling design. Assume for a moment that you want to know who will be the next president of the student body. What type of design would best provide the data with which to answer that question? What if you wanted to establish how the students at your college or university had voted over time—which design(s) would you choose? What if you wanted to know how a particular group of people, say business students, voted over time?

3. What does it take to conduct *good* survey research? Does the researcher have to concern him- or herself with more than just questionnaire development? What are the needs of interviewer training? What about the type of interviewing method proposed? If you were going to interview people about a marketing concern in the local area, what method would be *best*? What method would be *worst*? Why?

4. What is a double-barreled question? What problems do we have with such questions? Thinking back to Chapter 7 (Measuring Instruments), what are the *best* types of questions for a mail survey? A telephone survey? An in-person survey?

5. There are several minimal things that should be dealt with when reporting the results of a survey. What are they? Which is *most* important? Why? Which have you observed to be violated the most? Why might it be violated? How would you report the results of a survey, for instance, on the five o'clock news?

RESEARCH PROJECTS

1. The mass media have been using surveys for a number of years in establishing "Q-ratings" of on-air talent. How would you conduct a study that sought to answer the question: "Who is the best known local weatherperson?"

2. Conduct a survey of alumni regarding their perceptions of the communication program at your school.

3. For the school newspaper, conduct a survey on student perceptions of the local student government association.

4. Test the effectiveness of an advertising or public relations campaign with survey methodology.

5. Assess the motivation of workers in an organization with survey methodology. Assess management's approach to motivation and see if workers' perception is similar to that of management.

SUGGESTED READING

Babbie, E. R. (1995). *Survey research*, 7th ed. Belmont, CA: Wadsworth.

Backstrom, C. H., & Hursh, G. D. (1981). *Survey research.* 2nd ed. New York: Macmillan.

Bradburn, N. M., & Sudman, S. (1979). *Improving interview method and questionnaire design.* San Francisco: Jossey-Bass.

Frey, J. H. (1983). *Survey research by telephone.* Beverly Hills, CA: Sage Publications.

Garrison, B. (1995). *Computer-assisted reporting.* Mahwah, NJ: Lawrence Erlbaum Associates.

Payne, S. L. (1951). *The art of asking questions.* Princeton, NJ: Princeton University Press.

Roll, C. W., Jr., & Cantril, A. H. (1972). *Polls: Their use and misuse in politics.* New York: Basic Books.

NOTE

1. This is a requirement of any federally funded research project and many private funding agencies.

REFERENCES

Brown, R. E., & Rancer, A. S. (1993). Congruence of orientations toward public relations: A cross-cultural comparison of British and American practitioners. *World Communication, 22,* 1–6.

Dumlao, R., & Botta, R. A. (2000). Family communication patterns and the conflict styles young adults use with their fathers. *Communication Quarterly, 48,* 2, 174–189.

Garrison, B. (1995). *Computer-assisted reporting.* Mahwah, NJ: Lawrence Erlbaum Associates.

Goyder, J. (1986). Survey on surveys: Limitations and potentialities. *Public Opinion Quarterly, 50,* 27–41.

Hickson, M. L., & Stacks, D. W. (1992). *NVC: Nonverbal communication studies and applications*, 3rd ed. Dubuque, IA: Brown & Benchmark.

Hickson, M. L., Stacks, D. W., & Greeley-Padgett, M. (1998). *Organizational communication in the personal context: From interview to retirement.* Needham Heights, MA: Allyn & Bacon.

Hoffner, C., & Haefner, M. J. (1993). Children's strategies for coping with news coverage of the Gulf War. *Communication Research Reports, 10,* 171–180.

Kramer, M. W., Roberts, R. C., & Turban, D. B. (1995). Information-receiving and information-giving during job transitions. *Western Journal of Communication, 59,* 151–170.

McDermott, S. T. (1992). Communication factors in alienation among foreign students. *World Communication, 21,* 2, 41–49.

McPeek, R. W., & Edwards, J. D. (1975). Expectancy

disconformation and attitude change. *Journal of Social Psychology, 96,* 193–208.

Riffe, D. (1988). A comparison of news media and other sources of information for Alabama legislators. *Journalism Quarterly, 65,* 46–53.

Riffe, D. (1990). Media roles and legislators' news media use. *Journalism Quarterly, 67,* 323–329.

Roloff, M. E. (1987). Communication and reciprocity within intimate relationships. In M. E. Roloff & G. R. Miller (Eds.), *Interpersonal processes: New dimensions in communication research* (pp. 11–38). New-bury Park, CA: Sage.

Saris, W. E. (1991). *Computer-assisted interviewing.* Newbury Park, CA: Sage.

Wimmer, R. D., & Dominick, J. R. (2003). *Mass media research: An introduction,* 6th ed. Belmont, CA: Wadsworth.

THE "TRUE" COMMUNICATION EXPERIMENT

OBJECTIVES

By the end of this chapter you should be able to:

1. Describe when experimental methodology is appropriate for communication research.

2. Describe a causal relationship between two communication variables.

3. Explain why an experiment advances our knowledge of communication variables and relationships.

4. Describe the "classic" laboratory experiment.

5. Conduct an experiment—structure the experiment, establish "conditions," and collect your data.

6. Explain the limitations associated with the experiment.

7. Discuss alternative approaches to deception.

8. Describe why an experiment, properly conducted, has the potential to provide the strongest evidence possible that two or more concepts, or variables, are related in a particular way.

The experiment is surely one of the most ingenious creations in human history. The logic is elegant. To observe what effect a particular concept or **independent variable** has on a **dependent variable**, you create two situations in which all factors are made constant except the independent variable, which is carefully *manipulated* to take on different values. Then the effect of this manipulation on the dependent variable is carefully observed (*measured*). If the researcher has been successful in holding other relevant factors constant, observed differences in the dependent variable may be attributed to the changes (*manipulations*) of the independent variable. Few ideas are simpler or more straightforward than the logic that underlies the experiment. Many of the advances in the sciences, ranging from physics and chemistry to educational and social psychology to communication, have come from the skillful application of the experiment.

The value of the experimental method lies in the *rigor* of the comparisons that are made possible. **Comparisons** are fundamental to establishing empirical relationships between variables, and, therefore, are fundamental to scientific inquiry. For example, if we want to know if the amount of self-disclosure in a relationship is related to the amount of relational satisfaction experienced by partners, we need to *compare* relationships with varying amounts of disclosure to see if they differ in amount of satisfaction. If we want to know if one type of organizational culture results in higher productivity than others, we need to *compare* various organizational cultures to see if they differ in productivity. If we want to know if exposure to political campaign advertising has an effect on voting, we need to *compare* the voting behavior of voters with high exposure to political ads with those of voters who have lower amounts of exposure. If we want to know if wearing seat belts saves lives, we need to, *compare* states with high and low seat belt use to see if they have differing levels of deaths in traffic accidents. Whenever we want to know the relationship between variables we need to make comparisons; this is true whether the method used is field observation, survey, or an experiment.

What the experiment allows us to do is make more carefully *controlled*, more *systematic*, more *rigorous* comparisons. By comparing two sets of circumstances that are identical, or more realistically, highly similar in *every* respect, except with regard to the independent variable, the effects of that variable can be *isolated*. Because experiments can allow careful, rigorous comparisons, they provide you, the researcher, with a uniquely powerful tool for establishing the relationships between concepts (*variables*) under study.

We treat experimental methodology in two chapters. We do so for several reasons. In this chapter we emphasize the fundamental logic of the experiment. We begin by describing the advantages of the experiment and then examine the critical link found in all research methods—asking the appropriate research question. After this we examine how the experiment *controls* potential sources of error (called, more technically, error *variance*) to make the analysis of proposed or predicted relationships as pure as possible. Then we describe, step-by-step, the procedures involved in conducting the laboratory experiment.

Chapter 13 extends the study of experiments to **quasi-experiments**, and attempts to show that the elegant logic and power of the experiment has widespread applicability outside the laboratory.

ADVANTAGES

Experiments have two related strengths or advantages over *all* other research methods. Of all methods, experiments can provide the best evidence that two variables are, in fact, related. And, importantly, in those situations where we want to make **causal statements** about the relationship between variables, the experiment provides the strongest possible evidence that a particular independent variable *causes* an effect on a dependent variable. Secondly, if two independent variables both appear to be related to a dependent variable, the experiment provides a means of sorting out whether one or both of our independent concepts or variables are related to the dependent variable; and, if both are related, an experiment can tell us if one of the variables is more powerfully related to the dependent variable.

ESTABLISHING RELATIONSHIPS

Establishing relationships among variables is the core of scientific inquiry. This idea is so vital to understanding science and empirical research that special emphasis is justified. Theories are composed of systematic statements about the nature of relationships between variables and, as discussed in Chapter 2, the purpose of scientific inquiry is the creation of theory. The statements contained in a theory provide explanations for, and allow predictions about, the phenomenon the theory is about. All communication theories contain statements of the relationships among variables.[1] Useful theories define variables and state their interrelationships in ways that are consistent with actual observation. Theories that do not do this are not useful. Thus, the very purpose of empirical research can be viewed as establishing whether variables in theories are, in fact, related or not.

Of course, there are a variety of sources of evidence that can be marshaled to determine if variables are related in the way stated by a theory. *The most powerful form this evidence can take comes from the results of a well-conducted experiment.* Whenever we make observations that indicate two variables are related, there exists the possibility that the observed relationship is **spurious**—that the apparent relationship lacks validity; it is false. In other words, a spurious relationship is one that has a third variable that influences the dependent variable. If an experiment, properly conducted, indicates that a particular independent and dependent variable are related, we can be confident that, at least within the context of the procedures and the rigor with which the experiment was conducted, the relationship is not spurious. Rather, the variables are indeed related. Let's examine why.

Assume for a minute that we have a theory about the relationship between touching behavior and interpersonal attraction. Specifically, we believe that some individuals engage in more casual touching of other people than do other individuals. Furthermore, our theory states that those who engage in high amounts of casual touching will be better liked than will individuals who engage in low amounts of touching. One way to test this theory would be to conduct a **field study**. This approach would involve making observations in a naturally occurring environment, such as in a college dorm, sorority or fraternity house, or a public place where many people congregate. We would observe the communicative behaviors in the particular environment(s) chosen, taking particular care to note the amount of touching engaged in by the persons being observed.

After a period of time we might be able to categorize those in the environment(s) according to the quantity of their casual touching of others. Some individuals would be "high touchers," others would be "moderate touchers," and yet others would be "low touchers." Next, we would need to assess our dependent variable—how well liked by others in the environment (those who are being touched or at least seeing the touching) are each of the individuals who are doing the touching. The amount of interpersonal attraction could be measured (*operationalized*) in a variety of ways (see Chapters 6 and 7). We could count the number of people with whom our touchers communicated. We could measure the total amount of time they spent talking to others. We could conduct interviews with the participants and ask how well liked was each of our touchers. Better, we could do all three, and have the opportunity to obtain a more valid measure of the participants' amount of attraction for our high, medium, and low touchers. This is one use of the term *triangulation*.

Assume that our observations confirm that the variables *touching* and *interpersonal attraction* are related. The high touchers are the most liked, the low touchers are the least liked, and the moderate touchers fall in the middle. Our theory, then, is supported by our observations. However, we still must be quite cautious in concluding that touching is actually the variable that accounts for the differences in the amount of interpersonal attraction felt for our high, medium, and low touchers. This is so because there are *many* other variables that might be related *both* to the amount of touching and to interpersonal attraction; each of these unknown, unmeasured, and almost limitless numbers of variables could be accounting for what we have observed.

For example, some people are more friendly and outgoing than others. These individuals probably communicate with more people, perhaps smile more, have more eye contact, more open body postures, better senses of humor, and so on, all in *addition* to engaging in more touching of others.[2] Each of these other behaviors or variables, or all of them, could be accounting for the observed relationship between touching and interpersonal attraction. It is possible that the amount of touching is just incidental, that it has no effect *whatsoever* on how well liked someone is. It is even possible that, other factors being equal, touching is negatively related to interpersonal attraction, that high touching makes someone less attractive, but that other behaviors associated with high touching overcome the negative impact of touching (i.e., smiling, eye contact, increased posture). Although seemingly unlikely, it is possible that the high touchers are liked better *in spite of* engaging in large amounts of touching.

Extraneous Variables

In a natural setting where these observations were made the researcher has little, if any, control over **extraneous variables**—variables that although present, are not the focus of the study. Extraneous variables muddy up the waters and make it difficult to observe clearly the relationships between the independent and dependent variables. Controlling for extraneous variables is the major advantage that experiments have over field studies and surveys. In the experiment, extraneous variables are held *constant* across the various conditions (manipulations of the independent variable[s]), and thus the effects of the independent variable are the same in *each* experimental condition. In our example, imagine if our field researcher could somehow magically hold all variables *except* touching and interpersonal attraction constant. Everyone would be *equally* friendly and outgoing, would communicate with the same people, would smile the same amount, have equal amounts of eye contact and open body postures, and have equally well-developed senses of humor, and on and on, regardless of their amount of touching. If all possible extraneous variables could be made equal and the high touchers were still found to be better liked than their low or moderate touching counterparts, then you would be in an excellent position to conclude that touching and interpersonal attraction are related as predicted by our theory. That is what an experiment attempts to do.

The Classic Experimental Design

How might an experiment to address this question be conducted? Sixty people could, one by one, be brought into your environment—your *laboratory*—and be randomly assigned to either the **experimental group** (touch) or to a **control group** (no touch). This ensures that the two groups consist of people who had an equally likely chance of being in either group. There is no systematic bias in selecting people for either group. Each participant could be introduced to a **confederate**, an individual who, although appearing to the participant to be simply another participant, is actually someone who is working for you, the researcher. Next, the partners, one a naïve participant and the other the confederate working for the researcher, could be given tasks in which they must sit together at a table for an hour or more and solve a series of problems cooperatively.

All confederates in the study would be carefully trained to behave identically in both the touch and no-touch conditions, except that in the experimental group (the touch group), the confederate would casually touch the participant in subtle, natural ways. In the control group the confederate would not touch the participant. Additionally, based on observation or the research literature, the number of touches would be carefully planned, practiced, and introduced during the experimental sessions.[3]

■ ■ ■ ■ ■

MINI-PROJECT:

What are some relationships that are important to communication researchers? Identify at least three variables that are important to the area of communication you are most interested in. Examples might include physical attraction, type of message, medium employed in sending a message, and so forth. Based on a quick review of the literature, (a) what casual relationships have been found and (b) what other (extraneous) variables have been controlled in establishing these relationships? Which extraneous variable would concern *you* the most?

After completing the tasks, each participant's degree of liking for their new friend, the confederate, would be assessed. For example, they could be given a questionnaire that asked such questions as: "If you were required to work on a similar problem-solving task in the future, how much would you like to work with your partner from this session?" "How much would you like to spend time with your partner in another setting?" Scaled response options ranging from Not at All to Very Much could be provided. Or, Likert-type scales, such as those devised by McCroskey and McCain (1974) that measure peer attraction on three levels, could be used to check the created scales' validity and to assess the dependent variable:

1. I think he(she) could be a friend of mine.
   Strongly Agree ____ : ____ : ____ : ____ Strongly Disagree

2. I think he(she) is quite handsome/pretty.
   Strongly Agree ____ : ____ : ____ : ____ Strongly Disagree

3. I couldn't get anything accomplished with him(her).
   Strongly Agree ____ : ____ : ____ : ____ Strongly Disagree

Thus, the degree of liking for the partner could be assessed and the responses of those in the experimental (touch) group could be compared to those of the control (no touch) group.

If the participants were assigned to the two groups at random, if the other conditions (such as amount of confederate smiling) were indeed successfully held constant in both conditions, and if the difference between the two groups' average amounts of liking for the confederate was large enough that statistical analysis indicated that the interpersonal attraction difference was not a result of random chance, you could conclude that the variables touch and interpersonal attractiveness were related, *at least for these participants and under these conditions.* This careful manipulation of touch increases the **rigor** of the study and provides the strongest possible evidence that touch does increase attraction, as predicted by our propositional statement, our theory.

The **design** of this simple two-group experiment is generally referred to as a **classic experiment**. It is shown symbolically as Design 12.1. The **R** represents the fact that the participants have been randomly assigned to the two conditions of the experiment. The **X** is used to refer to exposure to a stimulus of some kind. While in this case it represents exposure to a confederate who engages in a substantial amount of touching, this simple and elegant logic could be applied to many other independent and dependent variables.

For example, the effects of independent variables such as the content of communication messages, the communication channel through which information was received, the

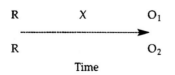

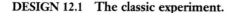

DESIGN 12.1 The classic experiment.

characteristics of the person delivering the message—in short, anything to which research participants are exposed, or not—could be assessed by observing the effect of the manipulation on any theoretically relevant dependent variable. Note, however, that the X is not by itself an independent variable because it does not vary; it is a constant, representing only one level of a variable. If there were other levels of the variable (for example, high, medium, low touch) as examined in the next chapter, there would be other lines composed of R's and X's. An **O** refers to an observation, that is, measurement. Symbols that appear on the left represent events that precede in time events represented by symbols on the right. The X's and O's on the same horizontal rows are applied to the same group of individuals or objects. This notation system was first presented in 1963 by two educational psychologists, Donald T. Campbell and Julian C. Stanley. This notation system is general, flexible, and useful, and we shall rely on it, as do most social scientific research books, to illustrate and clarify various experimental and quasi-experimental designs.[4]

The classic experimental design provides a graphic illustration of what has been said verbally. Note the rigor of the comparisons allowed by the design and the resulting *potential* confidence that may be placed in the results. (We say potential because the experiment still must be carefully conducted. It is not the design *per se* that allows confidence; rather, it is the design, plus the care with which all aspects of the experiment are conducted.) In Design 12.1 we see two groups of participants, illustrated by the two horizontal lines, the members of which have been randomly assigned, indicated by the R. One group then receives the experimental stimulus, exposure to the confederate who engages in high amounts of touching, represented by the X. The second group does not receive the experimental stimulus, represented by the absence of an X. Each group's degree of interpersonal attraction for the confederate is observed (measured)—as represented by O_1 and O_2—and determines if the variables are indeed related; and the strength of the observed relationship can also be assessed. The researcher compares the score of interpersonal attraction for group O_1 with O_2.

ESTABLISHING CAUSATION

The final goal of theory building is to establish *causal relationships* between variables. Researchers want to assert that variable X causes a change in the value taken by variable Y. Just as experiments have the potential to provide evidence that two variables are related, experiments also have the potential to establish that two variables are causally related. *Experiments are the only way that causation can be determined.* Survey research can only establish covariation.

Criteria for Establishing Causation

Three criteria need to be met to provide convincing evidence of causality. First, *the variables need to be shown to be empirically related to one another*. A change in the value of one variable (of course, the independent variable which is manipulated in an experiment) must result in a change in the value of the other variable, the dependent variable. This is referred to as *covariation*. If touch and liking are related, a change in the amount of touching results in a change in the amount of liking. If smoking causes cancer, increases in smoking leads to increases in the incidence of cancer. If violence on television causes violence in society, then increases in violence on television should lead to increases in violence in society. Unless the two variables covary they cannot be causally related.

Second, *the effect must follow the cause in time.* When we run our electric can opener, our cats come running into the kitchen. Since the can opener was started first, the running cats cannot be the cause of the can opener being used. While this second criterion is conceptually simple, sometimes establishing time order is difficult. The problem is not unlike the thorny issue posed by the question, "Which came first, the chicken or the egg?" Concerning touching and liking, it could be that people who are already well-liked respond by emitting more touching behaviors than those who are less well-liked. Similarly, perhaps it is the violent tendencies of individuals that results in their choosing to view television programs with violent content, rather than the opposite. In both examples, the variable that was thought to be the cause might be the effect. In other words, which of the variables was independent and which was dependent might be confused.

Establishing time order is especially difficult when both variables are attributes of individuals that may have taken a lifetime to develop. Self-esteem and communication apprehension are two variables that are **inversely related**. Individuals who have high self-esteem tend to have low communication apprehension, and vice-versa. But which came first? Maybe people who have communication apprehension receive negative feedback and that leads to low self-esteem. Or, people with low self-esteem may be afraid to speak, and thus have communication apprehension. The time order between these variables is not apparent. This is a limitation of the experimental method. Attributes of individuals cannot normally be manipulated. And, when they are measured, care must be taken to establish theoretically the expected causal ordering *prior* to the research.

Finally, to establish causality, possible alternative explanations that could account for the observed relationship between two variables must be discounted. Specifically, *the relationship cannot be accounted for by a third variable.* In other words, is there something else, some other variable, that could be causing covariation of both the independent and dependent variables? Recall that this would make the relationship spurious. This is the most difficult criterion to meet. For example, the number of bars located in towns and cities shows high correlation with the number of churches. Towns that have only a few bars also have only a few churches. Towns with many bars also have many churches. It might be tempting to conclude that churchgoers are heavy drinkers, or vice versa. Or that churches spring up to combat the evil caused by bars. Or that bars spring up to combat the good caused by churches. In reality, a third variable—town size—accounts for both the number of bars and the number of churches. The apparent church/bar relationship is spurious.

Meeting the Causation Criteria

A well-conducted experiment can meet all three criteria necessary to establish causation. The experiment does so by ensuring that covariation occurs, shows definitively that the manipulation of the independent variable occurred before the changes in the dependent variable, and that extraneous variables have been controlled through such techniques as random assignment of participants to conditions and ensuring that everything is the same, is held constant, except the manipulation of the independent variable.

Covariation.   First, if the dependent variable takes on different values in the experimental and control groups, covariation has been shown. The variables are related empirically.

Randomization.   Second, prior to the manipulation of the independent variable, the value taken by the dependent variable is made equal in both the experimental and the control group by randomly assigning participants to both the experimental and the control groups. An important distinction needs to be made between a random *sample* and *random assignment*. The purpose of sampling is to draw a subgroup from a population that is *representative* of the population. Drawing a sample from a population at random provides a means of increasing the likelihood that the sample is indeed representative of the population from which it is drawn (see Chapter 10).

Participants in experiments are rarely drawn at random from any population. Rather, they are almost always availability or convenience samples (see Chapter 10). However, once the sample is in hand, regardless of the method by which its members were obtained, random *assignment* refers to the method by which participants are assigned to the various conditions in the experiment. If *every* participant has an equal opportunity of ending up in *each and every* experimental condition, then random assignment has been achieved. (We will have more to say about how random assignment is accomplished in practice when we discuss the steps in conducting an experiment.)

To illustrate how random assignment equalizes the initial value of the dependent variable, suppose, for example, that we were interested in assessing the impact of a particular type of persuasive argument on attitudes toward smoking in public places. Initially, before any of our participants are assigned to a condition and before they hear any persuasive message about smoking, they will have a variety of views on this topic. How do we know that it is our message and not their initial views that result in the observed changes? By randomly assigning the participants we can be confident, within the limits of statistical probability, that the two groups are about equal in terms of their preparticipation attitudes. Some participants will be in favor of smoking in public places, others will be more neutral, and still others will be against it. By randomly assigning the participants to treatment and control groups we can be sure that each of these different attitudes will be represented *about equally in each group* and without any preselection bias. Therefore, any substantial differences that are observed after the receipt of the persuasive message can be attributed to the messages themselves. Remember, time order has been established because the manipulation of the independent variable preceded the change in the dependent variable.

Control.   Finally, an experiment can allow the elimination of extraneous variables as the cause of observed differences on the dependent variable. A critical determinant of whether an experiment can rule out *all possible* alternative explanations for the relationship between the variables under study is the extent to which the effects of other variables are controlled by being made equal in both the experimental and control groups.

How are the effects of all possible extraneous variables made equal? This is accomplished in two ways. First, all the conditions under which the experiment is run are made as similar as possible. Let us take the example of a researcher studying the impact of the use of humor in a persuasive speech on the effectiveness of the speech. If she were conducting an experiment on the effects of the use of humor in a persuasive speech, the only thing that would be varied across conditions would be the humor in the speech. Thus, in both "humor" and "no humor" conditions, the speaker would be the same, the room and audience sizes would be the same, the introduction would be the same. The researcher would attempt to make even seemingly irrelevant factors the same in both conditions. Time of day, for example, might not seem important, but it is possible that the participants might find the speech funnier and therefore more (or less) persuasive in the morning than right after lunch. *Any* differences between the experimental and control conditions, besides the purposefully manipulated independent variable, are potential rival explanations for any observed differences on the dependent variable. Conditions must be made as nearly identical as is possible.

Second, conditions in the experimental and control groups are made equal by randomly assigning participants to conditions. This point was made earlier when illustrating how an experiment establishes that the manipulation of the independent variable occurs earlier in time than any changes in the dependent variable. However, an understanding of the importance of randomization is so essential to understanding how an experiment can provide the best possible evidence that two variables are related that it deserves special emphasis. In fact, randomization is so important that Campbell and Stanley only apply the word *experiment* to studies in which participants have been randomly assigned to experimental conditions. The term *quasi*-experiment is used to describe those studies that, although identical in other respects, have been unable to randomize subjects (Campbell & Stanley, 1963).

Assume that in our study of the effects of humor on persuasion the theme of our persuasive speech is that basketball players are better athletes than participants in other sports. All sorts of extraneous variables that may affect how they feel about this topic and how susceptible they may be to being influenced by a humorous or nonhumorous speech on the topic are floating around in our participant pool. An obvious extraneous variable is their initial feelings about the theme of the speech. Before hearing the speech the participants are likely to have all sorts of differing views on this theme. Some probably think that it is true, that basketball players are the best athletes; others may think that football or soccer or baseball players are better athletes than basketball players. Others may have no opinion whatsoever and, in fact, may not even care. Of course, we want to be sure that we get an equal number of participants holding all these views in both the humorous and nonhumorous speech conditions. If the humor condition was full of participants who already agreed with the theme of the speech and the nonhumor condition was full of participants who thought football players were most athletic, these differing views would likely account for any differences on the dependent variable. Random assignment takes care of this problem. It assures that those in both the humor and nonhumor conditions will have about equal initial feelings on the speech topic.

It may not be so obvious how other extraneous variables could affect the outcome of the experiment. Some participants might be taller than others and therefore more receptive to a particular kind of speech about basketball, a sport in which height is an advantage. The list of ways in which our pool of participants differ is almost endless—some have high self-esteem, others low; some are affluent, others poor; some are high media users, others low; some are Republicans, others Democrats; and on and on. Any of these seemingly irrelevant variables *could* influence how someone feels about the theme of our speech and/or his or her susceptibility to a humorous or nonhumorous speech on this particular theme. How can we rule out this endless list of extraneous variables, each of which represents an alternative explanation of any observed relationship between the independent variable (use of humor) and dependent variable (attitude towards the speech topic)? The answer, once again, is random assignment of participants to conditions. If the number of participants is large enough, usually about 60 in a classic two-group experiment, random assignment ensures that the participants in both the experimental and control groups will be highly similar, within the limits of statistical probability, in *every* way, which may affect the outcome of the experiment. We will say it again. Random assignment ensures that the groups will be highly similar in *all possible ways*. Thus, random assignment allows *all* possible alternative variables to be ruled out as alternative explanations for the observed relationship between the independent and dependent variables. A study in which we have high confidence in the results, as they apply at that point in time, to our participants, using our operationalizations of the independent and dependent variables can be said to have high *internal validity*. In other words, internal validity means that we can be assured that variable *A* is related to variable *B*. A well-conducted true experiment has the potential to have the highest possible internal validity of any research technique.

Summary

An experiment provides the strongest possible evidence that two variables are related—stronger than field studies or surveys. However, to conduct such an experiment you must be able to accomplish five things: (1) Assign participants randomly to both experimental and control conditions; (2) structure the environments in the various conditions so that they are similar in every respect; (3) expose one group of participants to one level of the independent variable (usually called a **treatment**) and expose the other groups to the other levels of the independent variable, that is, to a different treatment or treatments; (4) employ a control group(s), which receive(s) no treatment; and (5) measure the dependent variable so that the effect of the independent variable on the dependent variable can be assessed. In short, to conduct a rigorous experiment—what we will call, as do Campbell and Stanley (1963), a *true* experiment—you must have a great deal of control over the experimental participants and

MINI-PROJECT:

Design a classic laboratory experiment that will test for the effect of photographs in mail advertisements. Provide (a) your design, (b) your independent and dependent variable(s), (c) how you would manipulate the independent variable, (d) what comparisons would be made, and (e) what extraneous variables may be potential problems.

their environment. This means that, in general, the most rigorous experiments take place in your carefully structured environment, the laboratory.

QUESTIONS APPROPRIATE FOR EXPERIMENTS

As noted in Chapter 1, the first step in conducting any research project is selecting a research question. Reviewing this process is important because selecting a good research question can be one of the most difficult parts of the entire research process.

Questions about human communication are plentiful. One of the things we like about our discipline and that differentiates it from, say, chemistry, is that we can study the social world around us. Ideas for interesting, important, and researchable questions about human communication can come from many sources. They can come from examining previous research literature, from classroom discussions, from reading a popular magazine, from asking someone for a date, from a conflict with a roommate or coworker from watching politics; in short, research questions may come from almost any life experience.

Selection Criteria Appropriate for Experimental Questions

Once a question has been selected (and the related literature reviewed), an appropriate method to answer it needs to be devised. The method should always follow the question, not the reverse. While it is extremely difficult to state hard-and-fast rules that assert which questions are appropriate for experimental method and which ones are not, we will suggest a few guidelines.

Experiments are particularly appropriate for research when the aim is to provide explanations for phenomena by establishing causal relationships between variables; for sorting out real relationships from spurious ones. Relatively narrow, focused questions lend themselves to experimentally derived answers. If we were interested in the causes of relationship satisfaction, a broad question, we probably would be better off, at least initially, observing or interviewing individuals involved in relationships than we would in conducting an experiment. On the other hand, if we wanted to know how accurate married couples were in detecting lying by their partner, a more focused question, we might be able to address this question with an experiment.

Many questions can be addressed using different methods, each with its own set of advantages and disadvantages. A theoretical proposition that is supported empirically over and over with different methods is one in which you can have a good deal of confidence. Examples include the propositions that smoking causes cancer and media violence causes violence by children. These questions have been addressed using many methods, including experiments. As noted in Chapter 9, the examination of the same basic research question using several different methods is called *triangulation*.

A good many questions simply are not amenable to experimentation. Exploratory investigations into new areas are probably best tackled with other methods: field studies, focus group interviews, surveys, and so on. Obviously, questions about past events, such as the impact or content of President Roosevelt's fireside chats, are not likely to be appropriate for experimentation. Similarly, questions involving large populations of people are not appropriate for experiments. How Americans feel about an international space mission to Mars is better answered via survey methodology.

Finally, if it is not possible to manipulate a variable, that variable cannot be the independent variable in an experiment. For instance, suppose we are interested in the accumulated effects of exposure to TV violence on aggressive behavior. We cannot take infants and expose half of them to violent programming until they are in their teens and not expose the other half to TV. This is why questions such as "What is the impact of violence in the media on violent behavior in society?" are so difficult to answer. They are easily subject to experimentation, but must be addressed with other methods, methods that have lower internal validity than laboratory experiments. Many variables of interest to communication researchers are characteristics or attributes of people. These variables may have taken a lifetime of experience to create. **Attribute variables** must be measured (see e.g., Kerlinger, 2000). Examples of attribute variables include: physical characteristics such as sex, height, body shape, physical attractiveness, and psychological characteristics such as attitudes, values, self-esteem, Machiavellianism, self-monitoring, and androgyny. All of these variables may be treated as independent variables, but since they must be measured and not manipulated, doing so involves conducting a survey, not an experiment.

We should note, however, that the impact of an attribute variable *on others*, as opposed to on those who possess the attribute, can sometimes be manipulated. For example, the impact of a person's physical attractiveness on others could be studied by exposing people to individuals of varying levels of attractiveness. Or the effect of differing levels of self-esteem in a relationship could be studied by training a confederate to *behave* as if he or she had a high or low self-concept—and then observing the effects of this manipulation on the participant.

THE LABORATORY EXPERIMENT

Theoretically, communication experiments, like other kinds of communication research, can be conducted in any environment in which human beings or their artifacts are present. In practice, however, most experiments take place in the experimenter's laboratory. A laboratory study is often contrasted with a *field study*. If a study is conducted with people in a location where they are routinely and normally present, it is generally called a field study. Thus, research conducted in shopping malls, in businesses or organizations, in public school classrooms, in short, any environment in which the research participants are present naturally is taking place *in the field*. On the other hand, if the research participants are brought into *your* environment, it is called a *laboratory* study. Thus, if participants are moved from where they would otherwise be and brought to a place under your *control*, the research is taking place in the laboratory.

The distinction between laboratory and field studies is not an either/or dichotomy, but rather should be conceived as existing on a continuum ranging from pure field research to pure laboratory research. If a researcher causes people to report individually at a specified time to a special facility called the Communication Research Lab, attaches them to a galvanic skin response (GSR) machine, and then measures their degree of physiological arousal as they are exposed to various erotic and/or violent television programming, the research would be an example of relatively pure laboratory research. On the other hand, if you phoned the participants in their homes and asked them questions about their reactions to a particular television show, it would be an example of relatively pure field research. Many studies fall somewhere in the middle of the continuum. For example, if members of an organization were brought into a room that was at their place of work, but which they did not normally visit, to fill out a questionnaire, the setting would have some of the elements of a field study and some of a laboratory study.

With rare exceptions, true experiments, that is those that meet the four criteria discussed earlier—random assignment, conditions held constant, manipulation of the independent variable(s), and systematic measurement of the dependent variable(s)—occur only in the laboratory. With this in mind, we present the basic steps in conducting an experiment.

To conduct a laboratory experiment you must: (1) present to the participants a plausible cover story; (2) assign participants randomly to conditions; (3) manipulate the independent variable(s) while holding other conditions constant; (4) measure the dependent variable and the success of the manipulation of the independent variable; and (5) debrief the participants. We will address, briefly, each of these, in turn.

The Cover Story

The phrase *cover story* implies, quite accurately, that experiments can involve deception. Frequently the deceptions are matters of omission, such as when participants are not provided with complete information about the research. For example, participants are not routinely told that they are, in fact, participating in an experiment in which other participants are receiving a different experimental stimulus. Other times the deception involves outright misrepresentation of fact. In either case, research participants are typically quite curious to know all about the research. The requirements of obtaining informed consent (see Chapter 3) prior to allowing individuals to volunteer to participate necessitates telling the participants in *general* terms what participation involves. However, if the participants knew *exactly* what was being studied, this knowledge would be likely to affect their behavior and invalidate the results. The cover story is designed to make all features of the experiment plausible to the participant, yet maintain any deception that may be necessary to obtain responses similar to those that would be obtained if the participants actually were confronted with this same situation in their normal lives.

A relatively simple cover story might be used in an *intra-audience* effects study. Intra-audience effects refer to the impact that audience response to an advertisement, for example, or some other kind of stimulus, has on *other* audience members. Participants in this study could be students enrolled in basic communication classes. They would be brought into the laboratory during a regular class meeting. In this case the laboratory consists of a large classroom-like room, which already has about 12 participants seated randomly about, waiting for the research to start. In reality, these individuals are confederates, individuals working with and trained by you, the researcher. Specifically, they will provide either positive or negative feedback to the advertisement to which they are exposed. The cover story might state that the purpose of the research is to examine people's reactions to various advertisements (slightly untrue) and explains that the individuals already in the room also are participants who happened to be enrolled in another communication course meeting at the same time (patently untrue).

Depending on the needs of the experiment, cover stories may be simple or elaborate. The counterattitudinal advocacy experiments described in Chapter 3 had extremely elaborate cover stories and typically included several levels of deception embedded within one another. Other cover stories may be very straightforward and simply state in general, but truthful terms, what is being studied. Because it provides a potential difference in how the participants may react to the experimental stimulus, the cover story is always reported in the method section of an experimental study so that others can replicate it exactly as it was conducted.

Assign Participants Randomly to Conditions

The experimental and control groups need to be made as nearly equal as possible in every possible way. This is done through random assignment of participants to conditions. Each person must have an equal probability of being assigned to both the experimental and control groups. This can be accomplished by flipping a coin, pulling names from a thoroughly shaken hat, assigning those with even Social Security numbers to one condition and those with odd numbers to the other, or, probably best, through the use of a table of random numbers. With the random numbers table, the first person may be assigned the first number in the table, the second is assigned the second, and so on. If there are two groups in the experiment, those with even numbers would be assigned to one group and those with odd numbers to the other. If there were three groups, those with numbers ending in 1, 2, or 3 could be assigned to one group, those with numbers ending in 4, 5, or 6 could be assigned to the second group, and those with numbers ending in 7, 8, 9 could be assigned to the third group. Those with numbers ending in 0 would be reassigned another number. If one group received one-third of the participants before a second group, those subsequently assigned to the full group would be randomly assigned to one of the two remaining groups, and so on, until all groups had equal numbers of randomly assigned participants. With a little thought and creativity, a table of random numbers can be used to assign people randomly to conditions, regardless of the number of conditions. Most computer statistical packages now have a random number generator that can be used in place of the random numbers tables found in most statistics books.

MINI-PROJECT:

You and a classmate are interested in determining how clothing influences compliance-gaining (getting people to do something for you). You decide to try to solicit money while wearing different types of clothing. Design this experiment and create an effective cover story. How will you debrief your participants?

Assigning **intact classes**, or those participants who arrive first to an experimental session, to one group and other intact classes, or those who arrived later, to a second group does *not* constitute random assignment. Similarly, participants should not be allowed to select for themselves to which of several groups he or she will be assigned. On the surface it may seem perfectly random to allow participants to choose for themselves whether to participate on, for example, a Wednesday or Thursday night, and to then administer the experimental treatment on one of these nights and the control condition on the other. However, it could well be that something is systematically different about people who select one night over another. And, this possibility creates a potential extraneous variable, a rival explanation for any differences observed on the dependent variable between the experimental and control groups. Therefore, if a research project must be run over several days, each condition should run each day to ensure that random assignment is achieved.

Manipulation of the Independent Variable

Once people are randomly assigned to conditions, the members of each group must be exposed to the various levels of the independent variable. Aronson and Carlsmith (1954) in a thorough, detailed paper on experimentation emphasize three concerns faced by the experimenter as he or she tries to operationalize the independent variable. The first asks what specific event corresponds to your theoretical independent variable. That is, the operationalization of the independent variable needs to capture some of the meaning of the conceptual definition of the variable. For example, if the independent variable is audience feedback, what specific behaviors in a given situation constitute positive and negative feedback? If the variable is a fear appeal message, what specific message content constitutes high and low fear appeals? If the variable is relationship disengagement strategies, what specific strategies are consistent with the variable's conceptual definition? Or, if the variable is physical distance between interactants, how are participants made to assume various distances?

Second, how can the levels of the variable be presented to the participants to produce the maximum effect? The impact of a variable that exists in the real world can seldom be recreated in the communication researcher's laboratory. You can show films that either do or do not depict violent content, but however violent the laboratory stimulus, it pales before the hundreds and hundreds of hours of exposure to violent media content available to people outside the laboratory. Similarly, the audience feedback that could plausibly be emitted by students listening to a speech in a classroom setting is probably negligible in intensity and effect compared to the audience response possible at a political rally, sporting event, or rock concert. Thus, your task is to expose the participants to the levels of the independent variable in as powerful a form as possible.

Finally, Aronson and Carlsmith note that on occasion the manipulation of the independent variable may tip off "cooperative" participants to provide the responses that they think you want. This is also a problem during the measurement phase of an experiment.

Unfortunately there are few, if any, widely accepted techniques for manipulating a particular independent variable. Although studying previous research in an area as part of the literature review may provide clues about how to proceed, you must frequently create unique manipulations to fit your situation. Aronson and Carlsmith note that there are basically two ways to present the manipulation of an independent variable: Participants can be presented with a set of *instructions or an event* of some kind. Assume that we are interested in assessing the effect the height of a person has on perceptions of his or her credibility in a job interview setting. A **verbal instructions** manipulation might involve telling participants that the male job candidate whose credentials they were examining was either 5′3″ or 6′3″ tall. An **event manipulation** would involve actually presenting the participants with a job candidate who was actually either 5′3″ or 6′3″ tall. Clearly, an event manipulation will, in general, be more realistic and have more impact than an instruction manipulation. Not surprisingly, Aronson and Carlsmith argue for event manipulations whenever possible.

An especially realistic and effective event manipulation was carried out by Stiff and Miller (1986) in their study of lying and truthful communication behavior. They needed to create a situation in which participants either lied or told the truth as they were being interrogated.[5] Participants were told in the cover story that the purpose of the research was to study "dyadic problem solving." Thus, it seemed quite natural to the participants when they were placed with another participant (really a confederate) and given a problem to solve. Further, they were told that the pair of participants that scored the highest on the problem-solving task would receive a substantial financial reward. Soon after each dyad had begun work on the task, the researcher was called out of the room. For half the dyads the confederate proceeded, as instructed by the researcher, to attempt to convince the participant to cheat on the task by looking at the answer, which had been conveniently left in a folder on the researcher's desk. (Almost all participants in this condition did collaborate in the cheating episode.) For the other half of the participants, cheating was not induced; that is, the confederate and the participant simply completed the task together. The researcher then returned, scored the completed task, and feigned great surprise at how well they had done. The participants were subsequently interrogated about how they had done so well. Of course, half of the participants, those who had been induced to cheat, were forced to lie in response to the interrogator's questions. This technique resulted in a realistic and relatively powerful manipulation. Note also the role of the cover story in setting up a situation that allowed a smooth and plausible manipulation of the independent variable.

As important as presenting a valid and powerful manipulation of the independent variable to participants is, it is equally important to take great care to assure that this is the *only* difference between what happens to those in the groups that make up the conditions of the experiment. Participants must be treated identically, or as nearly identically as possible, in every other way. Thus, for example, in Stiff and Miller's experiment, the researcher was called out of the room in *both* the lying and truthful conditions; and the confederate was carefully trained to behave in the same ways in both conditions, except for the cheating incident. Further, the person who interrogated the participants was *unaware* as to whether a particular participant had cheated or not. Sometimes, care is taken to assure that even the experimenters—anyone a part of the research team who comes into contact with the participants—are unaware of the experimental condition of which specific participants are a part. This is called a **double-blind experiment** and is done to reduce *demand* biases that the experimenter may introduce by unconsciously treating participants in different conditions differently. Equal care in holding conditions constant is taken in every well-controlled experiment.

Measuring the Dependent Variable and Assessing the Success of Manipulation of the Independent Variable

All of the measures discussed in Chapters 6 and 7 have potential applicability for assessing the impact of the experimental manipulation on the dependent variable. Basically, there are two kinds of dependent measures: **paper and pencil measures**, in which participants respond to scales and/or open-ended questions; and **behavioral measures**, which can be unobtrusive, that is, the participant is unaware that he or she is being measured. Unfortunately, the measurement process has the potential to tip off the true purpose of the experiment to the participants, which, in turn, could influence their responses. Thus, if the experiment involves deception, the measurement procedure frequently needs either to appear to the participant to be consistent with the cover story, to be unobtrusive, or to appear to be unrelated to the research project entirely.

Thus, for example, in studies of the effectiveness of various persuasive messages, the relevant dependent measure could be embedded in a large attitude survey distributed in class a week or so after the exposure to the experimental stimulus. In the Stiff and Miller (1986) deception experiment, participants were surreptitiously videotaped as they lied or told the truth, and their behaviors were later coded by observers. In a study on the impact of personal space violations and persuasion, Stacks and Burgoon (1981) administered the attitude-change questionnaire as part of a larger study being conducted on campus at the same time. The actual attitude scales were buried amid ten other attitude statements. They informed their participants that because so many students were participating in their study (the cover story concerned an examination of human-human and human-machine interaction) the researchers conducting the attitude survey wanted to canvas them also. They even went so far as to ask if any of their participants had completed the survey before. Debriefings indicated that the cover story worked for both the procedures and the posttest attitude measure.

Whenever possible, it is important to assess the success of the manipulation of the independent variable by directly measuring participants' perceptions of this variable. Such measures are called **manipulation checks**. For example, if source credibility has been manipulated, the measuring instrument would include a direct measure of participant perceptions of source credibility. If the amount of conflict in a small group discussion was manipulated, member perceptions of the amount of conflict present would be assessed. Manipulation checks are especially important whenever the results of an experiment indicate that an independent and a dependent variable are *not* related. Whenever such an outcome is observed there are two possible explanations: Either the variables really *are* related, but something about the procedures of this particular experiment failed to allow this relationship to be revealed empirically, *or*, the theory is wrong and the variables are not related. The purpose of the manipulation check is to provide evidence bearing on these explanations. If the independent variable and dependent variable are *not* found to be related and the manipulation check indicates that the manipulation was perceived as intended, this evidence suggests that the theory *may* be wrong.[6] On the other hand, if the manipulation check demonstrates that the manipulation was *not* perceived as intended, then this is evidence that the experiment has not provided a good test of the theory, that the procedures were inadequate.

Debriefing

In Chapter 3 we emphasized the importance of the debriefing for ethical reasons—specifically, to undo any deception, restore or maintain a positive relationship between the experimenter and the participant, and to make research participation a positive educational experience for the participant. Here, we will briefly mention a fourth purpose: to provide you with information about the efficacy of the experimental procedures. Was the participant suspicious about the research? What did he or she think was the reason for the research? Why did he or she display that particular behavior? Answers to questions such as these can help you make adjustments to the procedures (particularly if they are asked in sessions following participation in a pilot test of the experimental procedures), make corrections in the procedures used in future research, and even provide clues relevant to the accuracy and thoroughness of the theory being tested. As noted earlier, Stacks and Burgoon used the debriefing to check if participants were suspicious of the procedures, especially the additional "survey" completed at the end of the study. Debriefing, then, is more than an ethical consideration; it has practical applications also.

ROLE-PLAYING AS AN ALTERNATIVE TO DECEPTION IN EXPERIMENTS

Role-playing involves telling participants about a situation and asking them to pretend that they are really in that situation. Role-playing can be used as an experimental method because different groups of people can be asked to imagine that they find themselves in different circumstances. There are two reasons why you might use role-playing as an alternative to deception in an experiment: ethical reasons and practical reasons. We will discuss ethics first.

Ethical Concerns

Although we discussed the ethical treatment of human participants in research projects in some detail in Chapter 3, the impression should not be created that once considered, ethics can be put on the back burner. Rather, ethical concerns are an integral part of all phases of research projects. This point can be made well now, in the context of discussing experiments, because experiments frequently involve deception. Whenever we lie to a research participant it is a serious matter. The deception must be justified on the grounds that (1) there is no reasonable alternative that will allow you to answer the research question(s), (2) neither the deception nor its revelation during the debriefing will bring serious harm to the participant, and (3) the research question is an important one and the knowledge gained by answering it is substantial.

Social psychologist Herbert Kelman (1967) has been an outspoken critic of the use of deception. He argues that:

> Serious ethical issues are raised by deception *per se* and the kind of use of human beings it implies. . . . Yet we seem to forget that the experimenter-subject relationship, whatever else it is—is a *real* interhuman relationship, in which we have a responsibility toward the subject as another human being whose dignity we must preserve. (p. 5)

Kelman goes on to advocate role-playing as an alternative to deception. But the problem with role-playing, as a research methodology, is that it provides information about what people *think* they would do, not necessarily what they would do if actually confronted with a particular situation. As Freedman (1969) notes, "experimental results are not always easy to predict; people do not always behave the way that they or we expect them to" (p. 110).

Nonetheless, some research questions may involve deceptions that are so severe that role-playing is the only alternative to abandoning the research question entirely. If, for example, we were interested in assessing the impact of a serious news event, we could not falsely tell participants that certain serious events, such as, for example, a major earthquake in California, had occurred. In such a situation role-playing would be our only alternative. We should add that the more realistic the role-playing situation we are able to create, the more valid will be the data our pretending participants provide.

Practical Concerns

Some important independent variables simply cannot be operationalized adequately in the laboratory. For example, suppose we were interested in which of several relationship dissolution strategies resulted in the least damage to the self-concept of the disengagee. We simply could not realistically bring in 100 intimate couples, assign half to one condition and the other half to another condition and then enlist one partner as a confederate and have him or her use one or the other strategy to end the relationship, then measure the other partner's self-concept. Even if this procedure were not patently unethical, it would be impossible to conduct this, and many other communication studies, for purely practical reasons. In such situations, role-playing may be an alternative. If we ask people to imagine a situation, such as a date with their intimate partner, make the situation as realistic as possible, and ask them to imagine that their partner then ended the relationship with one of the strategies, we may obtain results approximating those of actual relationship disengagement.

LIMITATIONS OF THE LABORATORY EXPERIMENT

Type of Questions

Many questions simply are not amenable to experimentation. As noted earlier, exploratory investigations into new areas are probably best answered with other methods, such as field studies and focus groups. Questions involving large populations of people—such as, How do Americans feel about the creation of a Palestinian state in the Middle East?—similarly are not appropriate for experiments.

MINI-PROJECT:

Using what is called a "realistic role-play scenario," Hocking, Turk, and Ellinger (1999) reported that both male and female participants whose partner insisted on using a condom during their first-time sexual intercourse felt more positively about the sexual experience, about their partners, about the relationship, and about themselves. Apparently, at least for a first-time sexual encounter, sexually active college students prefer that a condom be used. And when a condom is used they feel better about the sexual experience; that their partner has behaved more responsibly; that there is more respect for this person, that their partner cares more about them, that the relationship is more intimate; and is likely to be long-term, rather than when no condom was used. Apparently, sexually active college students like partners who behave responsibly and they are well aware that using a condom is the correct thing to do.

The Hocking et al. study was widely reported in the media, including a full page description in the May, 2000, issue of *Shape* magazine (p. 61). The *Shape* paragraph was noteworthy in that, of approximately 50 mentions in the print and broadcast media, this was the only article that attempted to both describe the method *and* name of the researcher, allowing anyone to find the research itself, as well as report the results of the research.

Obtain both the *Shape* magazine report and the original research report. Evaluate both. Was this use of role playing as an experimental methodology valid? Do you believe that the results are valid? Would couples engaged in first-time sex feel toward their partners the same way that participants in this research did? The full reference is: Hocking, J. E., Turk, D. T., & Ellinger, A. (1999). The effects of partner insistence on condom usage on perceptions of the partner, the relationship, and the experience. *Journal of Adolescence, 22*, 355–367.

Generalizability of Findings

Laboratory experiments frequently are conducted in a highly contrived environment, one that may bear little resemblance to the circumstances typically faced by individuals as they communicate in their normal lives. This **artificiality**, especially when extreme, requires that great caution be used in generalizing the findings to more realistic circumstances. However, as sociologist George C. Homans (1961) notes, "The laws of human behavior are not repealed when a man leaves the field and enters the laboratory" (p. 81). With this weakness in mind, we should strive to make the laboratory environment as realistic as possible.

A related concern involves the population from which participants in laboratory experiments are typically drawn. Earlier, the importance of sampling was emphasized. It was noted that the ability to generalize from samples to populations was limited by the sampling procedures and estimates of sampling error. You learned that probability samples are most likely to be representative of, and thus generalizable to, the population from which they are drawn. Are participants in most communication research randomly drawn, and from what population do they come? They are almost always an *availability sample*—and most commonly an availability sample of undergraduate college students. Is this problem so serious that it eliminates our ability to generalize the findings to other populations? Not nearly to the extent that some critics of experimentation would suggest. The key question is: Are college students, and even more specifically, volunteers enrolled in introductory communication courses, different, *with regard to the variables being studied*, than human beings in general?

Assume for a moment that we are interested in determining the effect of taking a pin and pricking a person's finger on the production of blood on the fingertip. Does it matter whether we use a college student or not? Of course not. Blood is going to appear, no matter who we study. Now take an example of something we might actually study. Are individuals involved in intimate relationships that are characterized by high amounts of self-disclosure more satisfied in these relationships than those who are in relationships that have lower amounts of self-disclosure? Although this is an empirical question, we are going to venture an answer based on the use of reason. Our best guess is that in many ways, and specifically in this case with regard to self-disclosure and relational satisfaction, college students are a lot like other human beings. Most relationships observed between communication variables in samples drawn from college students probably exist in other human beings, even in populations from which our sample was not randomly drawn. Unless there is a good reason to think that college students are different with regard to the variables under study than the population to which we want to generalize the findings, it is reasonable, in our opinion, to proceed to generalize.

This is not to say that caution in generalizing our findings should not be exercised. Caution is fundamental to science. Limitations on findings should be emphasized, weaknesses and artificiality should be pointed out explicitly; caveats should abound; results should be interpreted conservatively and generalized cautiously. Whenever possible, findings should be replicated using different (and more realistic) methods (triangulation of the results based on the use of different methods) and populations. Until the results of such replications are available, claims of relationships between variables should be met with skepticism. *However*, experimental results should not be dismissed casually, simply because the research context was the laboratory and the sample studied consisted of college students.

Weakness of the Independent Variable

Kerlinger (2000) asserts that "the greatest weakness of the laboratory experiment is probably the lack of strength of the independent variables" (p. 367). In spite of Stiff and Miller's (1986) success at creating a realistic situation in which participants lied or told the truth, the consequences for the participant of being caught in the lie were minor compared to that which would exist in many normal life situations. If caught, they would have lost the financial reward they thought they were about to receive and would perhaps have suffered considerable embarrassment. Compare this to being caught lying to one's spouse about being involved in an extramarital affair, or to the IRS about an income tax return.

Communication can have powerful effects in our daily lives. Communication can create elation or depression; it can cause or prevent love or hate; it can change significant attitudes and behaviors. Yet these powerful outcomes are rarely, if ever, obtainable with the relatively weak manipulations of independent variables that are possible in the laboratory. Thus, if a variable *can* be shown to have an effect in a laboratory, this might well be taken as evidence that this variable will have even more powerful effects in our daily lives.

APPLYING KNOWLEDGE IN COMMUNICATION

The classic or laboratory experiment has been used in communication research for over 50 years. Its major goal is to establish causal relations between communication variables that will then be tested in the field under less stringent conditions. The laboratory experiment is the only methodology that truly allows you to state a causal relationship between variables. Although survey researchers are tempted to state that one variable affected another over time, they really do *not* know if a measured outcome was due to the variable of interest or some other variable that was left unmeasured.

SUMMARY

This chapter introduced what may be the ultimate form of research: the laboratory experiment. In particular, we have introduced the classic experiment, the true laboratory experiment. The experiment, a controlled manipulation of an independent variable whose effects are measured on a dependent variable, allows us to go one step further in the research process: We not only gain understanding, but we now can predict the relationships between the effects of the independent and dependent variable. The experiment is a systematic, controlled, and rigorous test of the relationships between variables. It permits us to make statements of causation.

The chapter also introduced the procedures and concerns of experimental researchers. A general overview of the laboratory experiment was provided, with emphasis on establishing the cover story, random assignment, manipulation of the independent variable(s), dependent variable measurement, and deception and debriefing. Finally, an alternative method to deception was discussed and the limitations and disadvantages of the method presented.

PROBES

1. What advantages does the experimental method present the communication researcher compared to field studies? Compared to surveys? What are the disadvantages?

2. The experiment addresses empirical questions. Based on your area of interest, what are some *significant* research questions amenable to the experimental method? Why are they more appropriate to this method than others?

3. The concepts of control and causation are important to experiments. Why? Can you establish causation without control? Why or why not? What do you give up to achieve control?

4. What are the ethical implications of the well-designed experiment? Are there certain research questions that might be unethical to test using experimental method? From your area of interest, what questions might *not* be ethically appropriate for experimental testing? Why?

5. Suppose that you are interested in the possibility that violence on television contributes to spousal abuse. Design an experiment to test this relationship; what is your independent variable? What are the levels or conditions you will use? Set up your experimental procedures by first using a pencil and paper dependent

measure and then by a behavioral dependent measure. What cover story will you use? What

type of debriefing will you employ? Critique your study.

RESEARCH PROJECTS

1. Conduct a review of the literature in an area of communication that interests you. What types of causal statements can be made about the variables in that area? What hypotheses might you deduce for further experimental testing? What limitations are found in the area based on the research reviewed?

2. Conduct a communication experiment. Based on what you have learned in other communication classes, create a simple study that manipulates one variable with two levels (manipulated and control conditions) and assesses the vari-

able (or lack of the variable) on an appropriate dependent variable. Randomly choose some friends to "participate" in a class project and run the study. If possible, enter the dependent variable's data into a computer and run the appropriate statistical tests (see Part III). Write up your study as an 8-to-10 page paper.

3. Design a manipulation to assess how gender affects credibility. Use a written manipulation to check this. Give an example of a debriefing to your experiment.

SUGGESTED READING

Broom, G., & Dozier, D. (1990). *Using research in public relations: Applications to program management.* Englewood Cliffs, NJ: Prentice-Hall.

Campbell, D. T., & Stanley, J. C. (1963). *Experimental and quasi-experimental designs for research.* Chicago: Rand McNally.

Jones, R. A. (1985). *Research methods in the social and behavioral sciences.* Sunderland, MA: Sinauer Associates. See especially Chapters 7, 8, & 9.

Keppel, G. (1991). *Design and analysis: A researcher's handbook,* 3rd ed. Englewood Cliffs, NJ: Prentice-Hall.

Kerlinger, F. N. (2000). *Foundations of behavioral research,* 3rd ed. New York: Holt, Rinehart and Winston.

Miller, G. R. (1970). Research settings: Laboratory experiments. In P. Emmert and W. D. Brooks (Eds.), *Methods of research in communication* (pp. 77–104). Boston: Houghton Mifflin.

Pavlik, J. (1987). *What public relations research tells us.* Beverly Hills, CA: Sage.

Rosenthal, R. *Experimenter effects in behavioral research,* 2nd ed. New York: Halsted Press, 1976.

Wesley, B. H. (1989). The controlled experiment. In G. H. Stempel, III, & B. H. Wesley (Eds.), *Research methods in mass communication* (pp. 196–217), 2nd ed. Englewood Cliffs, NJ: Prentice-Hall.

NOTES

1. We are defining theory here as we did in Chapter 2 (see also: Kerlinger, 1986, p. 9).

2. For a discussion of such variables and their impact see Hickson and Stacks (1992).

3. For a good study that used touches as the independent variable, see Pressner (1978).

4. This paper has become one of the most influential and widely cited contributions to research methodology

in the social sciences. The treatment of research design presented in this book, like those in many of the methodology books published in the last twenty years, is based on Campbell and Stanley's (1963) treatment. For those students particularly interested in experimental design, this reading is essential.

5. This procedure was originally used by Exline, Thibaut, Hickey, and Gumpert (1970).

6. It is not *definitive* evidence; no one study, by itself, can determine conclusively whether a theory is correct or incorrect. Rather, each study adds evidence to patterns that ultimately increase the confidence with which conclusions are drawn. See Chapter 2 for a review of the process of science.

REFERENCES

Aronson, E., & Carlsmith, J. M. (1954). Experimentation in social psychology. In G. Lindzey & E. Aronson (Eds.), *Handbook of social psychology* (vol. 2, pp. 1–79). Reading, MA: Addison Wesley.

Campbell, D. T., & Stanley, J. C. (1963). Quasi-experimental design for research on teaching. In N. L. Gage (Ed.), *Handbook of research on teaching.* Chicago: Rand McNally.

Exline, R. V., Thibaut, J., Hickey, C. B., & Gumpert, P. (1970). Visual interaction in relation to Machiavellianism and an unethical act. In R. Christie & F. Geis (Eds.), *Studies in Machiavellianism* (pp. 53–75). New York: Academic Press.

Freedman, J. L. (1969). Role-playing: Psychology by consensus. *Journal of Personality and Social Psychology, 13,* 110.

Hickson, M., III, & Stacks, D. W. (1992). *NVC: Nonverbal communication studies and applications,* 3rd ed. Dubuque: William C. Brown.

Hocking, J. E., Turk, D. T., & Ellinger, A. The effects of partner insistence on condom usage on perceptions of the partner, the relationship, and the experience. *Journal of Adolescence, 22,* 355–367.

Homans, G. C. (1961). *Social behavior: Its elementary forms.* New York: Harcourt, Brace, & World. As cited in Miller, G. R. (1970). Research settings: Laboratory studies. In P. Emmert & W. D. Brooks (Eds.), *Methods of research in communication* (pp. 77–104). Boston: Houghton Mifflin.

Kelman, H. C. (1967). Use of human subjects: The problem of deception in social psychological experiments. *Psychological Bulletin, 67,* 1–10.

Kerlinger, F. N. (2000). *Foundations of behavioral research,* 3rd ed. New York: Holt, Rinehart, & Winston.

McCroskey, J. C., & McCain, T. A. (1974). The measurement of interpersonal attraction. *Speech Monographs, 41,* 261–266.

Pressner, B. (1978). *The therapeutic implications of touching during articulation therapy.* Unpublished M. A. Thesis, University of Florida.

Stacks, D. W., & Burgoon, J. K. (1981). The role of nonverbal behaviors as distracters in resistance to persuasion in interpersonal contexts. *Central States Speech Journal, 32,* 61–73.

Stiff, J. B., & Miller, G. R. (1986). Come to think of it . . . : Interrogative probes, deceptive communication, and deception detection. *Human Communication Research, 12,* 339–357.

CHAPTER THIRTEEN

EXPERIMENTAL STRATEGIES AND DESIGNS

OBJECTIVES

By the end of this chapter you should be able to:

1. Explain when you would use a more complex experimental design than the classic experiment.
2. Describe and discuss the differences in the various "true" and "quasi-" experimental designs.
3. Describe the sources that may invalidate an experiment.
4. Explain how various sources of experimental invalidity are accounted for.
5. Explain the rationale for using factorial experimental design in communication research.
6. Design a multifactorial study.
7. Explain and draw an interaction effect.

Communication is complex. Most of the field's theories involve multiple variables and multiple theoretical propositions. Thus, studies are rarely done as true experiments with just one treatment group compared with a control group. Research titles often reflect this complexity by listing all the variables under study. For instance, Bernstein (2000) wrote an article titled: "The Effects of Message Theme, Policy Expectations, and Candidate's Gender." Another by Rocca and Vogl-Bauer (1999) also reflects this multivariate approach: "Trait Verbal Aggression, Sports Fan Identification, and Perception of Appropriate Sports Fan Communication." These examples point out that it is often necessary to move beyond the simple univariate, true experimental design.

To do this, research often requires trade-offs between what you really want to accomplish with a study—to learn—and what you can realistically impose on the variables and participants in the study. This chapter examines the impact of such trade-offs on the rigor and control of the experiment. We begin with a review of some previous material, then we move to an examination of what Donald T. Campbell and Julian C. Stanley (1963) have termed quasi-experimental design. We will then examine more complex "true" experimental designs and, finally conclude with a discussion of the advantages and limitations of these more complex experiments.

As we noted in Chapter 12, comparisons are central to establishing the relationships between variables, and therefore central to scientific inquiry. The most rigorous comparisons are possible in well-controlled experiments in which participants are randomly assigned to experimental and control groups; conditions are held constant, except for the manipulated independent variable, and the effect of the manipulation on the dependent variable is observed. This is the classic laboratory experiment. This ideal experiment is usually possible only in the laboratory.

However, for a variety of reasons, there are many times when we want to study the relationships between variables but cannot meet this ideal. We cannot design and conduct a true experiment that adequately addresses our research question. Sometimes we are unable to assign participants to conditions at random. Sometimes we are unable to hold conditions constant in two groups. Sometimes we are unable to manipulate a particular independent variable. Under these circumstances we may have no alternative (other than to choose a different research question) but to conduct a study that has some of the elements of a rigorous laboratory experiment, that resembles the design of such an experiment and allows us to make comparisons that help us answer our research question, but falls short of meeting all the criteria of the true experiment. Such studies are called **quasi-experiments**.

QUASI-EXPERIMENTAL DESIGN

Quasi-experiment is a broad term that refers to any research project in which, although one or more features of a true experiment are *not* present, the effect of an independent variable is studied by making comparisons between groups exposed to different levels of the independent variable. Subsumed under quasi-experiments are field experiments, in which a researcher is able to manipulate a variable in a natural setting, and natural experiments, in which the researcher is able to observe the effects of some naturally occurring event. True experiments and quasi-experiments have the same basic goal: to study the relationships between variables. The quasi-experiment, however, attempts to approximate the rigorous comparisons allowed by a true experiment as closely as possible. As the number of features present in a true experiment that are absent in a quasi-experiment increase (i.e., as the resemblance between the two is diminished), the confidence that can be placed in the results must be reduced accordingly. We begin our discussion of quasi-experiments with an attempt to apply the logic of experimentation to a naturally occurring event.

The Dow Jones Industrial Average of the New York Stock Exchange, the most widely followed index of stock price movements, has fluctuated with great variance in recent years. Stock prices in general, and "the Dow" in particular, are widely assumed to be indicative of the economic health of the country. The 2002 drop was taken as almost irrefutable evidence that the long run of the bull (rising) market and of a healthy, growing economy was over. Journalists, politicians, and many ordinary people spent considerable time discussing possible causes of this event. Democrats in Congress said the cause was the President's economic policies, tax cuts for the rich, and so on. The President blamed the crash on the Democrats' unwillingness to enact his economic policies fully, such as agreeing to even deeper cuts in domestic spending.

What caused the stock market fluctuation? It could be many factors, some combination of them, or none of them. We do not know, and worse, we do not have a good way to find out. The problem is that we do not have anything with which to compare the stock market fluctuation, and the circumstances that preceded it. We do not know what would have happened to the stock market if the President had different economic policies, or if the Democrats had agreed to more domestic cuts, or if the trade deficit had been smaller. There is no convenient set of different circumstances against which to compare what we know actually happened. And, as noted in Chapter 12, comparisons are essential to establishing with confidence that variables are related. In turn, the kinds of comparisons that a particular experimental design allow us to make are what differentiates true experiments from quasi-experiments, inferior from superior designs. A research design is a structure or model of the relationships among variables being studied in a research project. As noted in Chapter 12, it is the design's structure that allows us to make comparisons that warrant confidence in the conclusions about the relationships being studied.

In Chapter 12 we demonstrated the design of the classical experiment. In the following sections we will continue to illustrate various designs using Campbell and Stanley's (1963) notation system. Recall that an R represents random assignment, and the lack of an R means there has not been random assignment. An X is used to refer to a stimulus of some kind, often referred to as a treatment. It could represent an economic policy, an editorial, rock music, a speech, an advertisement—in short, anything to which research participants are exposed. An O refers to an observation, that is, a measurement. The X's and O's on the same horizontal rows are applied to the same individuals or objects. The main criterion by which designs are examined is the rigor of the comparisons that can be made. We now examine how a variety of designs, which when used in research, stack up in terms of this criterion.

One-Shot Case Study

Many decisions and conclusions are made on the basis of this first design, the one-shot case study. School districts will institute a program, say The Dare Program, and claim that it has caused a decrease in drug use. Similarly, the sheriff's department will set up alcohol checkpoints, saying they reduce drunk driving. However, despite these claims, the one-shot case study is the weakest design we will discuss. The weakest and simplest design presented by Campbell and Stanley is the one-shot case study (see Design 13.1). This design can be used in two forms: The X can happen first and then the O is observed, or the O is observed and then the researcher goes looking for an X. In the first form, something is made to happen or is observed happening naturally and something else is observed. For example, to study the impact of an advertisement, you might expose a group of participants to it and then measure their attitudes toward the product. The researcher wants to attribute the post-advertisement attitudes to the impact of the advertisement. Unfortunately, this design does not allow such an attribution to be made. It really does not even qualify as a quasi-experimental design. The reason: No comparisons are possible and therefore this design provides no evidence about the impact of the advertisement. The participants' post-ad attitudes might be a result of anything.

The other form of this design is that something happens and then, after the fact, you go looking for causes, a *post hoc* (after the fact) explanation of the relationship between stimulus and observation. Examples of use of this design are not hard to find. In each case you observe an outcome and then look for events that preceded the event to which to attribute causality. In the earlier stock market example, you observe a 500-point drop in the Dow Jones Average and look for the X's that explain the drop. Frequently, there is a strong temptation to conclude that because something preceded something else in time, it must be the cause of what it preceded—that if X preceded Y, X must have caused Y. This is especially true when the causal relationship is one that is consistent with our preconceived prejudices or is in our political self-interest. Thus, when something bad happens, as with the stock market crash, we find politicians conveniently and confidently attributing the cause to the X's created by the other party.

Other examples might include a study in which a psychotic killer is interviewed in prison and indicates that he viewed pornography as an adolescent. The interviewer then concludes that exposure to pornography causes violent behavior. But, even assuming the killer is being truthful, we do not know what the individual's behavior would have been if his life had been identical in every way, except with regard to exposure to pornography. Even though we can infer that there are some similarities, we have not controlled the study on that variable. Or, a researcher finds that 984 out of 1,000 pregnant, unwed teenaged girls conceived their babies (O) while listening to rock music (X) and concludes that rock music

Time

DESIGN 13.1   One-shot case study.

causes premarital sexual activity. Even assuming that the statistic is factual, there is no way to know if these mothers would have ended up pregnant if the rock music had been removed from their lives, or whether they would have conceived listening to country or hip hop music.

The problem with this design is fundamental: There is nothing against which to compare our observations, that is, the O. Thus, we are unable to conclude that the X and the O are related. We may speculate that they are, we may use other "methods of knowing" such as tenacity, intuition, or authority to conclude that they are, but scientifically we have no evidence that the X and the O are indeed related.[1] Therefore, this design is of little use to the communication researcher.

One Group Pretest-Posttest Design

To improve the design and raise it to the level of minimal scientific respectability we must be able to make at least one comparison. The "one group pretest-posttest" design allows for such a comparison (see Design 13.2).

With this design, observations are made both before and after exposure to a stimulus. For example, to study the effects of taking a course in public speaking on communication apprehension, we could measure student communication apprehension, then expose the students to the stimulus (the X—that is, they would take the course), and then measure apprehension a second time. This is an obvious improvement over the one-shot case study because we now can compare the audience's postcourse apprehension with their precourse apprehension. Any changes might be a result of taking the course and, therefore, *might* be attributed to the course. To the extent that we can confidently attribute any changes between O_1 and O_2 to X, our study has internal validity. *Internal validity* refers to whether a stimulus—the public speaking course in this case—had a known effect in this particular study. To the extent that observed results are attributable to the course, the study is internally valid. However, we emphasized the word "might" because there are other possible explanations that could account for the differences between O_1 and O_2. Each of these other explanations represents a threat to the study's internal validity.

Threats to Internal Validity. There may be other things, many other things, hundreds of other things, that happen to participants between a pretest (O_1) and a posttest (O_2) in an experiment besides exposure to the independent variable (the public speaking course in the previous example). In the public speaking study, the students could have observed a skilled speaker, or had a successful speaking experience in a nonclassroom setting, or undergone psychological counseling, or terminated a relationship, or begun a relationship, and so on—the list is endless. The point is not that any of these events necessarily had an impact on the

$O_1 \qquad X \qquad O_2$

Time

DESIGN 13.2 One group pretest-posttest design.

subsequent amount of communication apprehension experienced by the participants, but rather, *we do not know if they did or not.* Thus, all of these events are part of the participants' *history* between O_1 and O_2 and are threats to the study's internal validity (Campbell & Stanley, 1963). That is, they threaten the degree to which changes between O_1 and O_2 are known to be a result of X—the stimulus.

Second, the participants may simply change with the passage of time. They certainly will grow older, but also may become bored, sleepy, energetic, smarter, hungrier, and so on, completely independent of the fact that they are involved in a research study. Our public speaking students are likely to mature somewhat during the course of a 10- or 15-week term and this *maturation* process would occur whether they were enrolled in a public speaking course or not. Since this maturation process could result in reduced— or increased—communication apprehension, it is a threat to the study's internal validity.

Third, the *measurement* (or *testing*) of the participants at O_1 may affect the scores they receive on the second measure at O_2. Assume that we measured communication apprehension at O_1 by having each student make a speech, which was videotaped and shown to trained observers who coded a variety of verbal and nonverbal indicators of anxiety. At O_2, after completing the public speaking course, they deliver the speech again. Any difference between O_1 and O_2 could be a result of the speech made as part of O_1. Participants might display less (or more) anxiety at O_2 regardless of whether they took a public speaking course or not. Again, the point is not that the O_1 measurement necessarily affected the O_2 measurement, but rather that we do not know if it did, and thus it also is a threat to the study's internal validity. Alternatively, we might have measured communication apprehension with a paper and pencil measure. Responding to the Likert-type items on this measure might affect how someone would respond to these same items 10 to 15 weeks later. Perhaps they would cause some participants to dwell on their communication apprehension and this introspective process might affect the subsequent responses, even if they were not enrolled in the public speaking class. The effects of a measure on subsequent applications of the same measure is commonly called a *testing effect*, a term derived from educational research, where the effects of taking a test may have an effect on the scores of subsequent testing. Testing is a threat to the internal validity of Design 13.2.

Fourth, depending on the measurement technique selected, the rules for assigning numbers to observations may not be applied in exactly the same way at O_1 and O_2. For example, if the participants' speeches were being observed and coded for the amount of apprehension displayed, the observer might become bored or fatigued. This, and any other such changes, might affect the way the coders evaluate the O_2 speeches. Campbell and Stanley (1963) term this threat to internal validity *instrumentation*, "in which changes in the calibration of a measuring instrument or changes in the observers or scorers used may produce changes in the obtained measurements" (p. 5).

Fifth, if the participants have been *selected* to participate in the research because of their extreme scores on O_1, there is a tendency for them to receive less extreme scores at O_2. This is because extreme scores are extreme, in part, because of measurement unreliability; that is, random chance. If someone scores extremely well on an exam, they frequently do not do quite as well on the next one. Similarly, someone scoring extremely low on an exam will frequently do better the next time. In other words, extreme scores tend to regress toward the mean of all scores on a second testing. If all 4,000 freshmen entering a particular university were given a particular test for some variable, and those 50 students who scored the highest were selected for the study, it is almost certain that they would score lower on the second application of the measure, whether they took public speaking or not. (Thus, if you score high on the SAT or GRE, don't take it again in hopes of improving your score.) Campbell and Stanley (1963) call this phenomenon *statistical regression* because scores on the extreme of a normal curve by chance (error) are rare.

Sixth, some participants may drop out of the research project. If they did so randomly, that is, if those who were lost were representative of all the participants, this would not be a problem. The problem is that those who drop out may be systematically different in ways relevant to what is being studied from those who complete the project. In the public speaking study, it seems probable that those students who have severe communication apprehension are much more likely to drop the class than those who do not. These same students may be the ones who would have been the most affected by the experience of taking the class. However, since they are not around to provide scores at O_2, we would never know. One of your textbook authors collected data immediately following a speech, at 3 weeks, and then at 5 weeks, but he lost participants because people were absent from class. Their absence is a threat to the internal validity of the design. Campbell and Stanley (1963) label this threat *mortality*. We prefer the label *attrition*, since death is rarely the cause of a subject failing to complete a research project in the social sciences.[2]

Thus, while the pretest-posttest design is a marked improvement over the one-shot case study, it still possesses major threats to its internal validity. History, maturation, testing, instrumentation, selection, statistical regression, and attrition all provide potentially rival explanations for differences between O_1 and O_2, other than X.

Nonequivalent Group Comparison

The nonequivalent group—or static-group comparison design (see Design 13.3)—provides some good and some bad news for the internal validity of the experiment. The good news is that it allows us to rule out some of the alternative explanations; the bad news is that it opens the door to others.

In this design, a group of participants that have been exposed to a stimulus is compared to a group that has not. Consider the earlier example, in which we examined the impact of a public speaking course on communication apprehension. To answer the research question posed in that study (Does a course in public speaking change student's communication apprehension?) with a static-group comparison design, a group of students that had

■ ■ ■ ■ ■

MINI-PROJECT:

Many nonscientific interpretations of one-shot and pretest-posttest only designs make claims for causation. Examine your local papers and see how many times a survey has been interpreted as if it were either a one-shot case study or pretest-posttest only design. What sources of invalidity can you identify in the study?

$$X \qquad O_1$$
$$\cdots\cdots\cdots\cdots\cdots\cdots\cdots\longrightarrow$$
$$O_2$$

DESIGN 13.3 Nonequivalent group comparison.

a course in public speaking is compared to a control group that did not. To the extent that the groups are equivalent, except with regard to exposure to the stimulus, $O_1 - O_2$ differences can be attributed to the X. If the public speaking veterans have less communication apprehension, the researcher can conclude with some confidence that the class reduced communication apprehension.

How can we come to this conclusion? Assuming group equivalency, history is not a problem because extraneous events generally happened to both groups equally. Maturation is not a problem because both groups are measured at the same point in time, thus any maturation should be the same for both groups. Any instrumentation effect should affect both groups equally. Testing is not a problem because there is no pretest given. Statistical regression is eliminated as a possible rival explanation because, since both groups are measured only once, neither could be selected for participation based on their extreme scores.

However, some problems still exist. If, for instance, the stimulus caused some participants to drop out, as would likely be the case in the communication apprehension study, attrition would still be a problem; that is, the students high in communication apprehension might be inclined to drop the class, therefore dropping out of the research. Their counterparts in the control group would not be enrolled in the class so they would not drop out. Thus, the initially equivalent groups might become nonequivalent through attrition. But on the whole, assuming initial equivalency, this design looks pretty good. Unfortunately, the bad news is that we cannot assume equivalency. *Intact groups are almost always unique.* Every group has the potential to be different from other groups. And, it could be the fact that the groups are different that accounts for differences between O_1 and O_2, and not the fact that one group received the treatment—the X.

For example, students enrolled in a public speaking class are different from students not enrolled in such a course. In fact, we know that students who have extremely high communication apprehension will go to great lengths to avoid enrolling in such a class. It would not be surprising to find that students enrolled in an interpersonal communication class would report more communication apprehension as measured on the Personal Report of Communication Anxiety (PRCA) than students in the public speaking class. But this difference would not be because of the experience of taking the class—the X—it would be because of the method of selection of the participants. In this case they themselves have selected whether they are in the control group or the experimental group.

It may be that the two groups are quite similar; and, the more similar they are, the better this design. However, while we might marshal evidence that they are similar, without random assignment we will never know definitely that they are and, thus, the rigor of our comparisons is reduced.[3] Our O_1—O_2 comparison may really be comparing apples to oranges, cheese to Tuesday, seashells to Germans. The point is that the nonequivalency of the groups, the *selection* problem, provides a major threat to the internal validity of the design.

Any group that we find existing intact is likely to be different from any other group. Let us look at two examples. First, suppose you are interested in assessing the effects of the physical attractiveness of a model on attitude change toward the product being advertised. Two videotapes are made of a model making the same advertisement. In one condition the model's physical attractiveness has been lowered through the use of makeup. In the second condition the model has been made to be as physically attractive as possible. One version of the tape is shown to one intact advertising class, while the other is shown to another intact advertising class. After viewing the advertisement the students in both classes fill out a questionnaire on which they indicate their attitudes toward the product. On first glance it may appear that two advertising classes are likely to be highly similar. However, most certainly, they are not. Every event that happens in one class but not in the other contributes to the groups being nonequivalent, being different. For example, one class may have an instructor who emphasizes the importance of a type of advertising appeal, while the other does not. This could alter the effectiveness of the advertisement in that class. Or, perhaps the product was discussed in one class but not the other. The discussion could have systematically affected the participants' attitudes towards the product. What if the experiment took place the first day of class, before the groups had a chance to experience unique histories? What if one instructor was attractive and the other not so? One a female and the other a male? The groups might be equivalent, but without random assignment you would not know if they were or not. One section might have filled during preregistration, while the other section filled during a drop-add period. Any such factors could affect attitudes towards the advertisement. We simply do not know.

A second example: In 1996, the United States government allowed each state to increase the speed limit on rural interstate highways from 55 to 65 or more miles per hour. (The limit had been reduced to 55 miles per hour in 1974 as an energy conservation measure.) Opponents of the increase argued that the higher speed limit decreased highway safety and that states should keep the limit at 55 miles per hour. Nevertheless, many, but not all, states increased their speed limits. One way to examine the effect of increasing the speed limit (X) is to compare states that increased the speed limit (O_1) to those that did not (O_2). Doing so involves a quasi-experiment and, more specifically, since the independent variable is manipulated naturally and not by the researcher, this would be a *natural* experiment. To the extent that the states are equivalent in other ways that might contribute to interstate traffic deaths (weather, population, speeding enforcement, driver propensity for drunken driving, and so forth), a large difference observed in traffic deaths between the states might plausibly be attributed to the speed limit. However, while such an observed outcome can be taken as one piece of evidence for this conclusion, it is not definitive evidence because the states are not equivalent. To improve the design, we need to be able to provide evidence about how similar the two groups are. The nonequivalent group pretest-posttest design shown in Design 13.4 provides this evidence.

Nonequivalent Group Pretest-Posttest Design

We conclude our examination of quasi-experimental design with the nonequivalent group pretest-posttest design (Design 13.4). This design has been commonly used in all of the social sciences, including communication. Two groups exist intact: One group is assigned

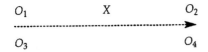

$$O_1 \qquad\qquad X \qquad\qquad O_2$$

$$O_3 \qquad\qquad\qquad\qquad O_4$$

DESIGN 13.4   Nonequivalent group pretest-posttest design.

to an experimental treatment and the other is assigned as a control. The more similar the two groups, the better this design. To provide evidence bearing on the degree of similarity between the two groups, the dependent variable is measured in both groups before and after the experimental group is exposed to the experimental stimulus. If the pretest measures O_1 and O_3 are highly similar, the comparison between the posttest measures (O_2 versus O_4) determines the results. To the extent that $O_1 - O_3$ differences are not the same as $O_2 - O_4$ differences, this outcome may be attributed with considerable confidence to the treatment, X.

In the example involving traffic deaths, if the states had similar levels of deaths prior to one state raising the speed limit and then this state had increased deaths, this would be better evidence that the speed limit and traffic deaths were related. As with the other examples, the addition of the pretest provides us with some control over history, maturation, testing, instrumentation, selection, and attrition. History is controlled, at least somewhat, because the treatment group can be compared to a nontreatment group that will be similar in many respects, except for exposure to the stimulus. The states may have different weather, different enforcement, and so on. Maturity is also controlled since similar amounts of driver maturation are likely. Testing and instrumentation are controlled for by comparing the control and treatment groups to see if any observable differences occurred because of either the materials used or the way in which they were administered. Attrition is known because we know how many participants we had when we began and how many we had when we ended. Selection is poorly controlled. The groups may be different with regard to their susceptibility to being influenced by the experimental stimulus. There is no problem due to statistical regression, unless the participants in one group have more extreme scores than those in the other groups.

Random assignment, in contrast, can assure equivalence not only in terms of the variables measured but in terms of all extraneous variables that were not measured as well. There are many other quasi-experimental designs we can study. An examination of the works of Campbell and Stanley (1963) is highly recommended to those interested in pursuing other, more complex designs (see Box 13.1). Nonetheless, while pretesting can help establish initial equivalence, it can do this only with regard to the variable measured in the pretest.

EXTERNAL VALIDITY

Before we turn to the more complex true experimental design, we need to discuss the other aspect of experimental validity: **external validity**. External validity concerns the questions of generalizability. As noted in Chapter 12, the results of most experiments must be generalized cautiously. In many cases we seek to begin a program of organized research in the laboratory,

■ ■ ■ ■ ■
BOX 13.1
SOURCES OF INTERNAL AND EXTERNAL INVALIDITY

Pre-Experimental Designs and True Experimental Designs

	Sources of Invalidity											
	Internal								External			
	History	Maturation	Testing	Instrumentation	Regression	Selection	Mortality	Interaction of Selection and Maturation, etc.	Interaction of Testing and X	Interaction of Selection and X	Reactive Arrangements	Multiple-X Interference
Pre-Experimental Designs:												
1. One-Shot Case Study $\quad X\ O$	−	−				−	−			−		
2. One-Group Pretest-Posttest Design $\quad O\ X\ O$	−	−	+	+	?	+	+	−	−			
3. Static Group Comparison $\quad \begin{array}{l}X\ O\\ \overline{}\ O\end{array}$	+	?	+	+	+	−	−	−				
True Experimental Designs:												
4. Pretest-Posttest Control Group Design $\quad \begin{array}{l}R\ O\ X\ O\\ R\ O\ \ \ O\end{array}$	+	+	+	+	+	+	+	+	−	?	?	
5. Solomon Four-Group Design $\quad \begin{array}{l}R\ O\ X\ O\\ R\ O\ \ \ O\\ R\ \ \ \ X\ O\\ R\ \ \ \ \ \ O\end{array}$	+	+	+	+	+	+	+	+	+	?	?	
6. Posttest-Only Control Group Design $\quad \begin{array}{l}R\ X\ O\\ R\ \ \ O\end{array}$	+	+	+	+	+	+	+	+	+	?	?	

Quasi-Experimental Designs

	Sources of Invalidity											
	Internal								External			
	History	Maturation	Testing	Instrumentation	Regression	Selection	Mortality	Interaction of Selection and Maturation, etc.	Interaction of Testing and X	Interaction of Selection and X	Reactive Arrangements	Multiple-X Interference
Quasi-Experimental Designs:												
7. Time Series $\quad O\ O\ O\ X\ O\ O\ O\ O$	−	+	+	?	+	+	+	+	−	?	?	
8. Equivalent Time Samples Design $\quad X_1O\ X_0O\ X_1O\ X_0O$ etc.	+	+	+	+	+	+	+	+	−	?	−	−
9. Equivalent Materials Samples Design $\quad M_aX_1O\ M_bX_0O\ M_cX_1O\ M_dX_0O$ etc.	+	+	+	+	+	+	+	+	−	?	−	−
10. Nonequivalent Control Group Design $\quad \begin{array}{l}O\ X\ O\\ \overline{O}\ \ \ \overline{O}\end{array}$	+	+	+	+	?	+	+	−	−	?	?	
11. Counterbalanced Designs $\quad \begin{array}{l}X_1O\ X_2O\ X_3O\ X_4O\\ X_2O\ X_4O\ X_1O\ X_3O\\ X_3O\ X_1O\ X_4O\ X_2O\\ X_4O\ X_3O\ X_2O\ X_1O\end{array}$	+	+	+	+	?	+	+	?	?	?	?	
12. Separate-Sample Pretest-Posttest Design $\quad \begin{array}{l}R\ O\ (X)\\ R\ \ \ X\ O\end{array}$	−	+	+	+	+	+	−	−	+	+	?	
12a. $\quad \begin{array}{l}R\ O\ (X)\\ R\ \text{---}\ X\ O\end{array}$	−	−	+	−	+	+	−	−	+	+	?	
12b. $\quad \begin{array}{l}R\ O_1\ (X)\\ R\ \ \ X\ O_2\ (X)\end{array}$	+	+	+	+	+	+	+	?	+	+	+	
12c. $\quad \begin{array}{l}R\ O_1\ X\ O_3\\ R\ O_1\ \ \ O_3\end{array}$	−	+	?	+	?	+	−	−	+	+	+	

Note: In the tables, a minus indicates a definite weakness, a plus indicates that the factor is controlled, a question mark indicates a possible source of concern, and a blank indicates that the factor is not relevant.

It is with extreme reluctance that these summary tables are presented because they are apt to be "too helpful," and to be depended upon in place of the more complex and qualified presentation in the text. No + or − indicator should be respected unless the reader comprehends why it is placed there. In particular, it is against the spirit of this presentation to create uncomprehended fears of, or confidence in, specific designs.

Source: D. T. Campbell & J. C. Stanley, *Experimental and Quasi-Experimental Designs for Research.* © 1963 by Houghton Mifflin Company. Used with permission.

where we can try to isolate our variables in as pure an environment as possible. However, how can we be sure that what we observe in our laboratory, which might involve some rather contrived and even unrealistic procedures, can be generalized to another setting and another participant population? External validity frequently creates a trade-off with concerns for internal validity. Designs that have high external validity may have lowered internal validity; designs that have high internal validity may have reduced external validity. As Campbell and Stanley (1963) note, "While internal validity is the *sine qua non* of the ultimate value of an experiment, and while the question of external validity, like the question of inductive inference, is never completely answerable, the selection of designs strong in both types of validity is obviously our ideal" (p. 5) and our goal.

MORE COMPLEX DESIGNS

So far, we have been talking about the simplest form of a true experiment—the classic two-group experiment in which one group receives an experimental stimulus and another group does not. The experimental and control groups are made equal through randomization and both groups are treated identically, except for their exposure to the independent variable, after which the dependent variable is measured. This same logic applies to more elaborate experiments. What we gain from the use of more complex true experimental design is both the potential to control all potential sources of invalidity and the possibility of testing more than one treatment within the study. For this reason, and because many times we use designs that are more complicated than the classic experiment, we now turn to more complex designs.

True Experimental Designs

Suppose that instead of an experimental and a control group, in which case the experimental stimulus would be present or absent, we have three levels of an independent variable: high, medium, and low. In our example of the experiment examining the effects of touching presented in Chapter 12 (the impact of touch and interpersonal attraction), we might have a high-touch condition, a moderate-touch condition, and a no-touch condition. This design is depicted in Design 13.5. If you kept the circumstances as nearly identical as possible in all three conditions—and randomly assigned participants to the three conditions—the effect of all three levels of the independent variable (high touch, moderate touch, control [no-touch]) could be assessed. Although there are practical limitations on the number of levels that feasibly might be manipulated in one experiment, the underlying logic generalizes to any number of levels of an independent variable.

$$
\begin{array}{lll}
R & X_1 & O_1 \\
R & X_2 & O_2 \\
R & & O_3
\end{array}
$$

---➤

DESIGN 13.5   **The three-group true experiment.**

Consider the following example. You are interested in assessing the effectiveness of six different approaches to teaching press release writing at one-day seminars. Your independent variable is the type of teaching approach; it consists of six different teaching approaches, or levels. You have a large pool of participants and randomly assign them to six groups. One group (X_1) receives lectures—that is, they hear lectures about how to write press releases. A second group (X_2) receives lectures and writes one press release. A third group (X_3) receives lectures, writes one press release, and receives feedback about the release from the instructor and the class. A fourth group (X_4) receives a lecture, writes the release, sees the release in print, and receives no other feedback. A fifth group (X_5) receives a lecture, writes the release, sees the release in print, and receives feedback about the release. A sixth group (X_6) receives no lecture, writes a press release, and receives no feedback. A week later, all participants write a press release under identical circumstances. The dependent variable is assessed by having experts evaluate the quality of the press releases. This design is shown in Design 13.6.

Again, the basic logic is identical to that of simpler designs. In a large enough group of participants, generally at least 30 per level for a total of 180 or more participants who are assigned at random, all six groups can be expected to be highly similar initially in all ways. Note that there is no control group in this design. This is perfectly acceptable if the research question or hypothesis concerns how the various treatments (types of writing training sessions in our example) differ from each other in terms of the dependent variable, and not how they differ from a situation in which participants receive no training whatsoever. If this latter question were important, the research should include a true control condition in which a group of randomly selected participants received none of the six one-day seminars that constituted the experimental conditions.

Factorial Experiments

So far our discussion of experimentation has assumed there is only one independent variable. However, the logic of the experiment is easily extended to more complex research problems in which the researcher wants to examine the independent and conjoint effects of two or more independent variables on one or more dependent variable(s). (Note: Any experiment—regardless of the design—can have multiple dependent variables.) An experiment that has at least two independent variables is called a **factorial experiment**. If two (or more) independent variables both appear to be related to a dependent variable, the experiment provides a means of sorting out whether only one or whether both of these independent variables are

R	X_1	O_1
R	X_2	O_2
R	X_3	O_3
R	X_4	O_4
R	X_5	O_5
R	X_6	O_6

--------------------------------➤

DESIGN 13.6   A six-group experiment.

MINI-PROJECT:

Assume that your instructor wants to know the best way to assess student knowledge of communication research methods. Of interest is which type of evaluation is best: quizzes, tests, or projects. Design an experiment that would test the research question: Which type of evaluation is best in research methods? In this case, you must carefully choose your dependent variable(s).

related to the dependent variable; and if both are related, an experiment can tell us which of the two independent variables is the more powerfully related. Let us examine how this is possible by exploring a classic use of the factorial experiment.

In the mid-1960s, James C. McCroskey (1969, 1986) conducted a series of experiments with the purpose of empirically examining the relationships between variables that were commonly suggested as advice in public speaking texts. One of his studies was designed to determine if the quality of evidence in a speech increased persuasive effectiveness. To test this research question, he constructed two speeches: one that used extremely good evidence to back up claims that were made—relevant statistics, and so on. The second speech was identical to the first, except that the evidence used was poor—irrelevant statistics, and so on. Groups of participants were randomly assigned to the two speech conditions, exposed to the speeches, and asked to indicate their attitudes toward the speech topic. Surprisingly, contrary to 2,000 years of prescriptive advice about public speaking, the quality of evidence did not affect attitudes toward the speech topic.

McCroskey tried again. It is hard to let the results of one experiment tell you that something seemingly this obvious is not true; that a theory consistent with common sense is deficient. He noted that, in his experiment, the speech had been attributed to a speaker who was perceived as highly credible by the participants. He speculated that perhaps source credibility (generally called *ethos* at that time) was so powerful that it made the quality of evidence irrelevant. To test this possibility he needed to examine simultaneously the effect of high- and low-quality evidence across different levels of source credibility (high and low). To do so he conducted a **2 × 2 factorial experiment**; that is, within the same study he manipulated both evidence quality (high and low) and source credibility (high and low). The design of his study is shown in Design 13.7, and also in Figure 13.1 using a graphic representation that shows the factorial nature of the design

$$R \qquad X_{1a} \qquad O_1$$
$$R \qquad X_{1b} \qquad O_2$$
$$R \qquad X_{2a} \qquad O_3$$
$$R \qquad X_{2b} \qquad O_4$$
$$\text{-------------------------->}$$

DESIGN 13.7   2 × 2 factorial design.

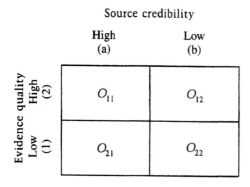

FIGURE 13.1   A 2 × 2 factorial design laid out.

more clearly. The first number following the X represents the first independent variable (evidence quality [see Figure 13.1]). The second letter represents the second independent variable (source credibility). Thus X_{1a} represents a treatment group in which randomly assigned participants are exposed to a speech with high-quality evidence delivered by a highly credible speaker. The X_{1b} represents a high-quality speech and a low-credible source; X_{2a} represents a speech with low-quality evidence delivered by a highly credible source; and, finally, X_{2b} represents low-quality evidence and a low-credible speaker.

Looking at Design 13.7 and Figure 13.1, the first factor represents the first independent variable—evidence quality. The fact that it is observed at two levels, as opposed to a three or some other number, means that there are two levels of evidence: high and low. (If the number were a three, it would mean that there were three levels of this variable, perhaps high, medium, and low.) The second factor represents the second independent variable (source credibility) and again, because it is composed of two levels, we know that there are two levels of this variable. Thus, by saying that the design is a 2 × 2 factorial experiment, we are saying that there are two independent variables, each of which has two levels. In this particular design, there are four experimental conditions, or cells. Each of the four groups of randomly assigned participants receives one of the four treatment combinations for that cell.

If McCroskey's speculation was correct, he would find that under conditions of high credibility, evidence quality would not make a difference. About equal amounts of attitude change toward the message topic would result. However, under conditions of low credibility, evidence quality would affect the amount of attitude change. Thus the $O_{1a} - O_{2a}$ comparison was expected to be negligible, while O_{1b} was expected to show relatively more attitude change than O_{2b}. In fact, these were the results. As a result of this experiment, and various replications conducted by McCroskey and his colleagues, we now know that evidence is an important factor in speech effectiveness, especially under conditions of low or moderate source credibility. Note that only by simultaneously manipulating both independent variables within the same experiment, was he able to answer his research question adequately; he had to conduct a factorial experiment to answer his question adequately.

McCroskey's research used the simplest factorial experiment possible—a two-by-two factorial design. Figures 13.2(a), 13.2(b), and 13.2(c) show, respectively, 2 × 3, 3 × 3, and 2 × 2 × 2 factorial designs. The 2 × 3 design has two independent variables, one with two

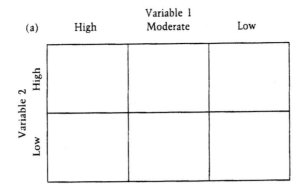

3 × 3 Factorial Design

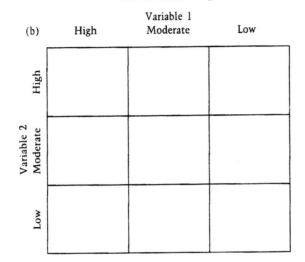

2 × 4 Factorial Design

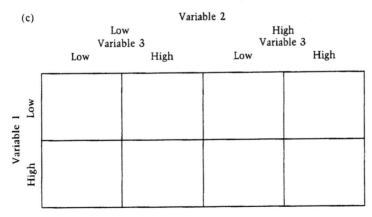

FIGURE 13.2   More complex factorial designs.

levels and the other with three levels, and a total of six separate conditions, or cells. The 3×3 factorial design has two independent variables, each with three levels, and a total of nine cells. The $2 \times 2 \times 2$ has three independent variables, each with two levels, and a total of eight conditions. Manipulation of three independent variables is the practical maximum number of variables that should be manipulated in one experiment. It is extremely difficult to interpret the results of more complex experiments.

Figure 13.3 shows a 2×2 factorial design with an offset control group. The control group is referred to as offset because it is not given a stimulus treatment. Design considerations allow for all the treatment conditions to be collapsed, that is, averaged, and compared against the control group or, when appropriate, each separate condition can be tested against the control, thus ensuring that the treatments—manipulations—not only differentiated between themselves but also against a group that received no treatment. Special statistical tests are required when employing an offset control group design, in particular the Dunnett's multiple t-test (Kirk, 1968, p. 94–95).

Determining the results of an experiment with one independent variable is simply a matter of comparing the scores in each of the groups. Typically, these scores are compared against what could have occurred by random chance. If the differences between the scores are so large that it is improbable that chance could account for them, the

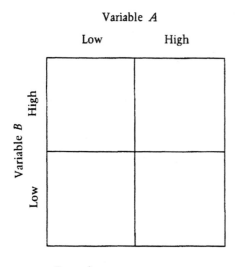

FIGURE 13.3   Factorial design with offset control group.

MINI-PROJECT:

Your instructor liked the study you designed earlier that tested the different evaluation techniques, now he or she wants to know if the differences occurred because of instruction or because of the particular type of class. Design an experiment that addresses this concern. (Can you do it by simply adding a control group or do you need to add additional experimental groups?)

difference is attributed to the manipulation of the particular independent variable under study. Determining the results of a factorial design experiment is similar, but involves more comparisons among groups.

Main and Interaction Effects.   Let us take the 2×2 design used by McCroskey as an example of the added complexity of factorial experiments. First, there is a result for evidence usage without accounting for credibility, just like doing a single-factor experiment, ignoring credibility. Second, there is a result for credibility, ignoring evidence quality. These results are determined by examining the means (the average of the responses for each level of the variable), respectively, at the bottom of the columns—O_{1c} versus O_{2c}—and at the end of the rows. For instance, low evidence had a mean of 30 and high evidence had a mean of 50. These comparisons, called **main effects**, allow the effects of the two independent variables to be examined without regard to the levels of the other independent variables (high versus low credibility main effect; high versus low evidence main effect). Figure 13.4(a) shows hypothetical means that would be interpreted as main effects for both variables. Figure 13.4(b) illustrates the results graphically. But notice that there are more complexities to this study. If we just visually examine Figure 13.4, it looks as though high evidence quality *combined* with high credibility is most effective with a mean of 60. It also appears that low evidence and low credibility are the least effective.

To determine if the effect of one independent variable is different, depending on the level of the other independent variable with which it is combined, requires an examination of the individual cell scores. Such an examination is called an **interaction effect** comparison. There are two kinds of interaction effects. One occurs if the *magnitude* or the size of the effect of one independent variable varies, that is, depends on the level of the other independent variable with which it is combined. Figures 13.5(a) and 13.5(b) shows hypothetical data for such an interaction effect. Note, also, a main effect is also shown for both independent variables. Interpretation of this would be that with a low-credible source, evidence quality made no difference on participants' attitudes toward the speech; for a highly credible source, however, high evidence quality produced more attitude change than low evidence quality.

The second type of interaction effect occurs if the direction of the effect of one independent variable is different, depending on the level of the other independent variable with which it is combined. A hypothetical example of such an outcome is shown in Figures 13.6(a) and 13.6(b). Note that in this example there is no main effect for either of the independent variables; that is, each cell produces significantly different attitude scores depending on the

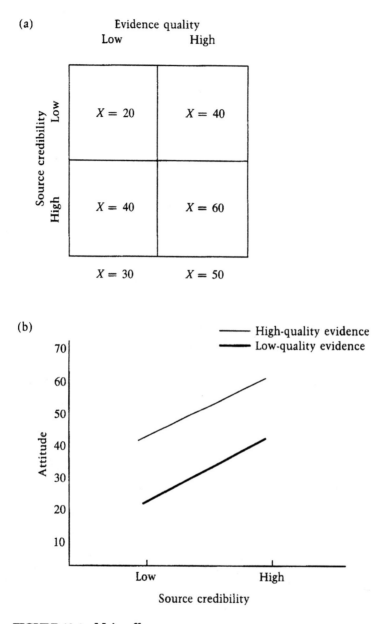

(a)

Evidence quality

		Low	High
Source credibility	Low	X = 20	X = 40
	High	X = 40	X = 60
		X = 30	X = 50

(b)

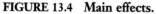

FIGURE 13.4   Main effects.

interactive effect of both independent variables. This interaction effect is sometimes called a **classic crossover or directive interaction effect**.

Thus factorial experiments provide the researcher with a powerful tool for examining simultaneously the relationship between several independent and dependent variables. Tests of more complex theories are made possible without the loss of the rigor provided by the true experiment.

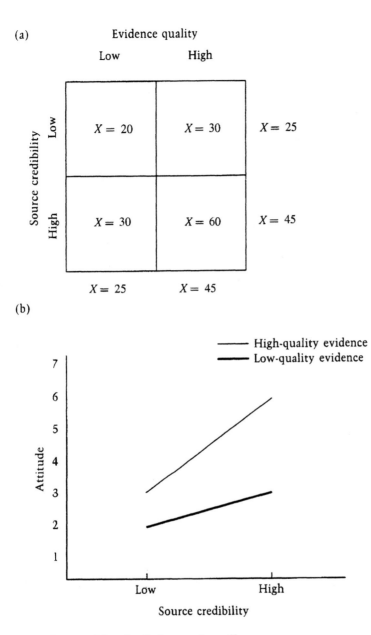

FIGURE 13.5   **Magnitude interaction effect.**

APPLYING KNOWLEDGE IN COMMUNICATION

There are many research questions in which quasi-experimental designs must be used, often due to a lack of resources or availability of participants. These studies are found in the communication literature and must be interpreted carefully; this is especially true in mass

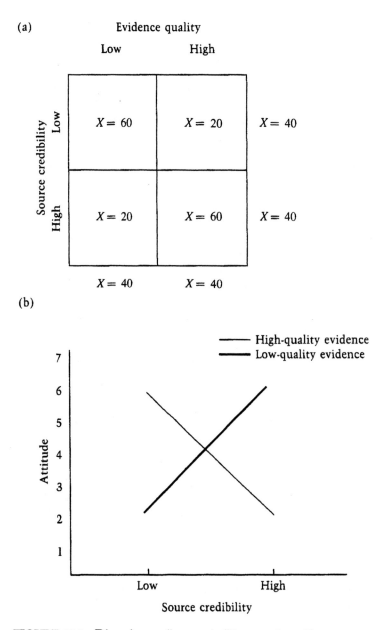

FIGURE 13.6   Direction or "crossover" interaction effect.

communication research where surveys are conducted over time to see if the media have influenced attitudes. It is important to understand that all research has limits and trade-offs. In the case of quasi-experimental studies we cannot be certain that a relationship exists (that one variable caused a change in another), because we have failed to exercise control over potential sources of invalidity and lack control. This book began with an emphasis on how knowledge is generated and science's—social science's—contribution to a knowledge base. We noted that we did not want to add false knowledge to our database and that we wanted as rigorous a test of theory as possible. Quasi-experimental research, although not usually as rigorous or as high in internal validity as the true experiment, can still be a powerful tool for testing the relationship between variables, that is, for testing communication theory. Sometimes the alternative is to simply guess about the nature of reality. Some empirical, albeit, imperfect evidence, provided about whether an independent and dependent variable are related gives us empirical evidence that transcends conventional wisdom.

While the true experiment may reduce external validity in an effort to increase internal invalidity it provides us with internal validity and it approximates attempts at achieving causation. This control often creates a problem in generalizing results beyond the immediate study—its participants, the laboratory setting, and the way the variables were operationalized and measured.

SUMMARY

The type of experimental design you choose will depend upon the research question you are attempting to answer. The rigor with which it is possible to answer the research question is directly affected by the extent to which you can make pure comparison of the effects of your independent variable on the dependent variable(s). True experimental designs can be as simple as a one-level treatment/control group experiment or as complicated as the factorial designs presented earlier. As we move from the carefully controlled environment of the laboratory to the field, we generally lose our ability to control for various sources of internal invalidity. Still, through careful consideration of the experimental design, some control is possible. Researchers attempt to be pragmatic yet construct the most rigorous design they can.

Due to the nature of the questions asked, some research must examine the impact of manipulating two or more independent variables simultaneously. These factorial designs are more complicated but follow directly from the true experimental designs discussed earlier.

This chapter has introduced several designs, quasi-experimental and more complex true experimental. There are many more. As researchers, we pick the design most appropriate to the research question or hypothesis. Experimental research, as noted previously, allows us not only to establish relationships, but also to establish causation among our relationships.

PROBES

1. Is internal validity more or less important than external validity? What is the tension between the two types of validity?

2. What research questions are best answered

from a quasi-experimental design? What can you do with this type of design that you cannot do with the true experiment? From your area of interest and reading, who has conducted quasi-experimental research? What have they found that they could not find with the true experiment?

3. When would you consider a factorial design experiment? Why would you even consider this type of design? Would an offset control group add anything to your study? Why or why not? Given this design, how many independent variables are you studying? How many

dependent variables are you assessing? How many levels of the independent variable do you have? Will there be any main effects? Any interactions? Why?

4. Think of a 2 × 3 factorial design that could be used in a study on teacher communication characteristics and student evaluations. What are the variables and what kinds of main effects and interaction effects would you expect?

RESEARCH PROJECTS

1. Find an experimental study in your area of communication that was conducted at least fifteen years ago and redesign it to meet what we know of the area today. If possible, conduct a small pilot of the redesigned study and write it up.

2. It is possible to evaluate a discipline's state or level by the type of research it conducts. What

is the state of communication based on the type of experimental research being reported in communication journals? Look at the complexity of experimental design as one indicator and the employment of quasi-experimental design as a second indicator. What conclusions can you draw based on the sophistication of study as compared to other social science disciplines?

SUGGESTED READING

Campbell, D. T., & Stanley, J. C. (1963). Quasi-experimental design for research on teaching. In N. L. Gage (Ed.), *Handbook of research on teaching.* Chicago: Rand McNally.

Kerlinger, F. N. (2000). *Foundations of behavioral research*, 4th ed. New York: Holt, Rinehart and Winston.

Kidder, L. H. (1981). Qualitative research and quasi-experimental frameworks. In M. B. Brewer and B. E. Collins (Eds.), *Scientific inquiry and the social sciences.* San Francisco: Jossey Bass.

Kirk, R. E. (1968). *Experimental design: Procedures for the behavioral sciences.* Belmont, CA: Brooks/Cole.

Ricken, H. W., & Boruch, R. F. (Eds.). (1974). *Social experimentation: A method for planning and evaluating social intervention.* New York: Academic Press.

Salwen, M. B., & Stacks, D. W. (Eds.) (1996). *An integrated approach to communication theory and research.* Mahwah, NJ: Lawrence Erlbaum Associates, Publishers.

NOTES

1. See sections on tenacity, authority, and intuition in Chapter 1.

2. Suggested by Jones (1985, p. 225).

3. Of course, even with random assignment we will never know absolutely definitively that the groups are highly similar. Random assignment is always subject to

the limits of probability. It is possible that all the individuals who are, for example, tall, will end up in one condition. However, it is extremely unlikely that, given adequate sample size, this will happen. With random assignment we will know as definitely as it is possible to know anything in science that the groups will be equal.

REFERENCES

Bernstein, A. G. (2000). The effects of message theme, policy explicitness, and candidate gender. *Communication Quarterly, 48,* 2, 159–173.

Campbell, D. T., & Stanley, J. C. (1963). Quasi-experimental design for research on teaching. In N. L. Gage (Ed.), *Handbook of research on teaching.* Chicago: Rand McNally.

Jones, R. A. (1985). *Research methods in the social and behavioral sciences.* Sunderland, MA: Sinauer Associates.

Kirk, R. E. (1968). *Experimental design: Procedures for the behavioral sciences.* Belmont, CA: Brooks/Cole.

McCroskey, J. C. (1969). A summary of experimental research on the effects of evidence in persuasive communication. *Quarterly Journal of Speech, 55,* 169–176.

McCroskey, J. C. (1986, April). *Individual scholar presentation.* Presented at the Southern Speech Communication Association Convention, Houston, Texas.

Rocca, K. A., & Vogl-Bauer, S. (1999). Trait verbal aggression, sports fan identification, and perceptions of appropriate sports fan communication. *Communication Research Reports, 16,* 3, 293–298.

PART III

MODES AND USES
OF ANALYSIS

Once we have acquired data from surveys, experiments, focus groups, interviews, or content analyses, what next? This section explores how we analyze the data gathered from quantitative methods. In so doing we address a topic about which many students seem most apprehensive: the manipulation of numbers. As we move through this section keep in mind that our aim is *understanding*. Understanding modes of analysis does not require the memorization of complex formulas, or difficult computations. Understanding requires that you make *intelligent* decisions about how to analyze the data you have collected and what conclusions, if any, you can draw from those analyses.

In preparing these chapters we have limited our discussions to those analytical tools you will most likely need in both reading others' research, and in proposing and conducting your own. This section provides you the *basic* information from which to work and provides hints of where to go for future help. Perhaps some students will find this introductory treatment interesting enough to enroll in a statistics class. Our approach, however, is to attempt to meet three important objectives: (1) We want you to understand what types of analysis you have available to you, (2) we want you to understand which types of analysis are most appropriate for your particular research question-hypothesis-theory, and (3) we want you to be able to interpret the results.

To meet these objectives we introduce you to data analysis. Where it is appropriate we provide you with formulas. We believe that being able to choose the most appropriate mode of analysis is more important than applying the specific formula or equation. Understanding how the results were obtained, however, helps to not only choose the correct analysis but also in interpretation. In general, our approach is conceptual, not computational.

Understanding also requires the ability to *read* the results of the analysis. Much like driving in a new area, you need a road map to guide you. Inability to read that map, however, precludes its usefulness. Thus, we will provide you with maps to interpreting printouts. Most researchers today use computers—at one time primarily mainframe computers, which have been replaced by equally powerful personal computers—to do their analyses. We present examples of printouts based on a popular personal computer program available in a student version; the *Statistical Package for the Social Sciences*—SPSS. The ability to read one package gives you the knowledge to read others; the advancement of the personal computer and the graphics based interface (GUI) has resulted in a standardization of sorts for output.

Chapter 14 introduces the concept of data and simple *description* of the data set. We discuss the way data points are arranged and how they spread. Modes of analysis discussed in this chapter include, for ordinal and nominal data, frequency and percentage, and for interval and ratio data, range, mean, mode, median, variance, standard deviation, standard error, and curvilinearity. Types of simple descriptive analysis covered include tabulation, crosstabulation and rank-order analysis. Presentation of descriptive analyses is also covered: Bar, frequency, fever, and pie charts are often used to communicate simple descriptive analyses in both academic and business applications.

Chapter 15 moves from simple description to inferential analysis and introduces *inferential* statistics. Specific statistical tools discussed include parametric tests such as *t*-tests, analysis of variance, correlation, and nonparametric tests such as the chi-square test and nonparametric correlation are also covered.

Chapter 16 is new to this edition. In it we try to give you a glimpse at some of the many practical applications and implications that are possible from a mastery of communication research. We suggest ways the methods you have learned in this book are useful tools in every arena of life. We believe that scientific thinking can help all aspects of the human experience, and this chapter challenges you to use your new knowledge of communication research. Chapter 16 is not a typical research methods book chapter. It is a collage of the ways science can help us to think critically.

Finally, Chapter 17 brings together the research process by focusing on the final product: the research report. This chapter brings us full circle. We began by asking questions and we end by examining the processes involved in reporting your answers and the formats appropriate for your report. In addition, we explore the differences between writing for an academic versus a business audience. Finally, we review the research process.

Part III, then, brings us to the climax of learning about research that generates quantified data. We began the journey by learning how research relies on theory, how theory leads to research questions, how questions lead to method, and, now, in turn, this section demonstrates how method leads to analysis. But remember, the research process does not end there. All research, especially social scientific research, is cumulative and ongoing. It serves to build toward more and better theory, further questions and research, still better theory, and on and on.

DESCRIPTIVE STATISTICS

OBJECTIVES

By the end of this chapter you should be able to:

1. Distinguish between categorical (nonparametric) and continuous (parametric) data.
2. Code data for statistical analysis.
3. Choose the appropriate descriptive statistical tool.
4. Run and interpret the following univariate statistics: frequencies, percentages, proportions, means, medians, modes, ranges, variances, standard deviations, and standardized (Z-scores) scores.
5. Present univariate statistics in both tabular and graphic form.
6. Explain and interpret the following bivariate statistics: crossbreaks, means by groups, correlational analyses.
7. Present bivariate statistics in both tabular and graphic form.

After data from a survey or an experiment have been collected, the results must be summarized, organized, and analyzed. **Statistics** is the branch of applied mathematics that provides the tools to accomplish these goals. Our experience has been that many communication students are intimidated by statistics and, perhaps because they believe that quantitative research methods and statistics are one and the same, even fearful of quantitative research methods in general. If you feel this way, several points may help allay your fears. First, statistics are merely *tools*, a set of techniques whose overall purpose is to help answer research questions. They are not an end in themselves, they are a means to understanding the results of a research study. They, in themselves, do not answer questions, but give you information to do so. Second, understanding most statistical analyses does not require high levels of mathematical sophistication. Rather, the ability to think conceptually—to understand the underlying logic of the tool—is more important than knowing specialized mathematical techniques. Third, data analysis—statistics—is a relatively small part, albeit an important part, of the overall research process. Identifying an important question, designing the study, and creating adequate operationalizations of the variables are all *more* important than data analysis. Why? If these stages of research are poorly carried out, if an unimportant research question is addressed, if the research design is seriously flawed or the variables are inadequately operationalized, all the sophisticated analysis in the world will not create a good study.

There are three major distinctions that are helpful in understanding statistical analyses used by social researchers. First, statistics are used to *describe* and to *infer*. The goal of **descriptive statistics** is the reduction and simplification of the numbers representing research to ease interpreting the results. There are ways to summarize your findings and make them clear to the readers of your report. They are usually the first step in data analysis as they give a preliminary picture of what your data looks like. However, for some types of data and research, they are the only analytical procedures that are done. For example, when we read that "participants in the experimental group had a mean (average) score of 4.2 on the dependent measure and participants in the control group had a mean score of 2.5," or that two variables "had a correlation of 0.45," we are being presented with *descriptions* of the results. **Inferential statistics**, on the other hand, have as their goal the presentation of information that allows us to make judgments. These judgments concern whether the research results observed in a sample *generalize* to the population from which the sample was drawn. Thus, when we hear that the difference between two groups' means was "significant at the .05 level" we are able to make *inferences* to the population from which the sample was drawn. Specifically, we know that there is less than a 5 percent chance that the result observed in the sample would *not* generalize to the population.

A second important statistical distinction concerns the *type of data* we are making inferences about or describing. We noted in Chapters 6 and 7 that measurement occurs at four levels: nominal, ordinal, interval, and ratio. Numbers resulting from nominal and ordinal measures are described, and inferences from samples to the population made, with one class of statistics: **nonparametric**. Numbers resulting from interval and ratio measures are treated with **parametric** statistics. Characteristics of populations are called parameters. Therefore, parametric statistics allow you to draw conclusions about population characteristics.

Third, we may describe, or make inferences about, nonparametric or parametric variables by themselves (**univariate**), as two variables relate to one another (**bivariate**), or as three or more variables interrelate (**multivariate**). Table 14.1 summarizes and gives examples of the kinds of statistics available to the researcher within each of the categories mentioned. In this chapter we present both nonparametric and parametric *descriptive* statistics.

We begin first by reviewing the types of data used in research, how that data is coded, and the use of computers in statistical analysis and reporting of results. After this we examine the nonparametric and parametric analyses available to make sense out of the numbers generated in the research.

TYPES OF DATA

As noted, measurement creates data consisting of one of four types—nominal, ordinal, interval, and ratio. For analytical purposes, data can be broken into two broad categories. Data that come from nominal categories (nominal measurement) or ordered categories (ordinal

TABLE 14.1 Examples of Types of Statistics

	DESCRIPTIVE (CHAPTER 14)		INFERENTIAL (CHAPTER 15)	
	NONPARAMETRIC	PARAMETRIC	NONPARAMETRIC	PARAMETRIC
Univariate (one variable)	Percentages Mode Range Rank Median	Mean Standard deviation	Confidence intervals (percent) e.g., 95% sure	Confidence intervals (range) Significance test
Bivariate (two variables)	Comparison of percentages Cross-tabulations Spearman rho correlation	Comparison of two means e.g., 4.5 > 3.1 Pearson correlation	Chi-square	*t*-test
Multivariate (three or more variables)	Comparison of percentages Crosstabs	Comparison of means Partial correlation Multiple regression	Chi-square	Analysis of variance Multivariate analysis of variance Factor analysis F-test

measurement) are classified as categorical, or *nonparametric*. These analytical tools rely on establishing proportions or percentages based on simple categorization principles. Data from interval or ratio measures are classified as continuous, or *parametric*. They are assigned some arbitrary (interval) or absolute (ratio) zero point. Parametric analysis examines the dispersion of the data as it varies from the mean or its central tendency, where most of the respondents lay. In parametric statistics we use the mathematics of the normal curve, the normal random distribution of scores around a mean that approximates a bell-shaped curve.

If, for instance, our purpose in conducting a research project is to ascertain if a woman might be elected president, we might consider a survey of registered voters. Our survey would include some basic information about the sample. Here, nominal and ordinal measures come into play. They help us to classify people into groups, and provide frequency and percentage data about the sample.

Box 14.1 presents some of the variables we might consider in surveying people about voting. Note that some of the variables are measured at the nominal level (sex, race, marital

---

BOX 14.1
CATEGORIZING DATA

Sex: ____Male (1)   ____Female (2)
Age: ____Years
Race: ____Euro American (1)   ____African American (2)
           ____Asian American (3)   ____Hispanic/Mexican American (4)
           ____Other (5)
Income After Tax: $_____
Years of Education: ____Years
Highest Degree Earned: ____High School   ____Community College
                             ____University   ____Graduate Degree
                                                  ____No Degree
Occupation:_____
Years on the job: ____Years
Married?   ____Yes   ____No
(or
Marital Status: ____Married   ____Single   ____Divorced)

Instructions: Please circle the response which best reflects how you feel about the following statements. Circling SA means that you strongly agree with the statement, A means that you agree with the statement, N means that you neither agree nor disagree with the statement, D means that you disagree with the statement, and SD means that you strongly disagree with the statement.

SA   A   N   D   SD   Voting is important.
SA   A   N   D   SD   The next president of the United States should be a woman.

status), others at the ordinal (education) or interval ("voting is important") level, and still others at the ratio level (income after taxes). The nominal and ordinal data are analyzed with nonparametric statistics; the interval and ratio data with parametric statistics.

Several variables could be treated as nonparametric *or* parametric. For example, although age is a ratio variable, ranging from 18 years (remember, our question concerns voting behaviors and people must be at least 18 years of age to vote) to the age of the oldest voter, we could also place age in one of several ordinal categories:

___under 20   ___20–30   ___31–40
___41–50   ___51–60   ___over 60

But remember that reducing the level of measurement means that you cannot use statistics that are as powerful or precise.

This category system suggests that people under 20 should be grouped together, as should be people over 60, and that there are naturally occurring breaks that are meaningful in answering the particular research question. It also suggests that there is some reason for placing those between 20 and 60 in categories of ten-year increments. How "age" is defined will determine the category system. Although age is normally a ratio measure, we defined it here as ordinal; we ordered the age groups from youngest to oldest. As noted in earlier chapters, income levels are often similarly grouped because it is sensitive information.

Consider the ways we can approach the survey's attitudinal statements. Responses to the statement, "Voting Is Important," for instance, consist of Strongly Agree, Agree, Neither Agree nor Disagree, Disagree, and Strongly Disagree. We could treat each as a category and count the number of respondents who Strongly Agree, Agree, Disagree, Strongly Disagree, or Neither Agree nor Disagree with the statement. Our analysis would take the percentage or proportion of respondents falling in each category. Or, we could treat the responses as continuous data, assigning numbers to the intervals as Strongly Disagree = 1, Disagree = 2, Neither Agree nor Disagree = 3, Agree = 4, and Strongly Agree = 5. This scale, as noted in Chapter 7, is a Likert-type measure, one that is treated as interval data.

Table 14.2 presents examples of data types found within categorical and continuous data. Note that as we move from nominal to ratio measures, precision increases. But, it is sometimes more difficult to get participants to respond to more complex measurement scales. Sometimes we must consider trading precision (interval and ratio measures) for accuracy and reliability (nominal and ordinal measures).

■ ■ ■ ■ ■

MINI-PROJECT:

Take two of the sample measurement instruments presented in Chapters 7 and 11. First, indicate whether each measure is parametric or nonparametric. Second, indicate what level of data is represented: nominal, ordinal, interval, or ratio. How can you convert an ordinal measure to an interval or ratio?

TABLE 14.2 Categorical and Continuous Data Levels of Measurement

DATA TYPE	MEASUREMENT LEVEL	EXAMPLE
Categorical (Nonparametric statistics)	Nominal	Sex (Male = 1/Female = 2) Race (White = 1/Black = 2)
	Ordinal	Larger > Smaller Agree > Disagree
Continuous (Parametric statistics)	Interval	Agree (5) to Disagree (1) Believe (5) to Disbelieve (1)
	Ratio	Age Hours of television viewing

DISTRIBUTIONS

Regardless of what type of data you collect, it will be distributed in some way. When describing research findings, we frequently find both continuous and categorical or discreet, types of data, although as Kerlinger & Lee (2000) notes, quantitative social science research seems more predisposed to continuous data than frequency data. A quick perusal of communication research articles might find, however, that categorical data analysis is more common in mass communication and marketing than in interpersonal and organizational research. Political communication research, for instance, reports many categorical descriptions of how people perceive different candidates. Communication education research also employs categorical data analysis (reporting types of activities, books in use, types of basic courses) and how educators use different educational strategies in the classroom. Public relations and journalist research often reports content analysis. Usually such studies employ descriptive, nonparametric analysis.

We now turn to the question of how to use data to answer research questions. We discuss computer packages, how to prepare for the analysis, identify the various descriptive statistics available, and interpret what they mean. We begin with nonparametric data descriptors.

Table 14.3 presents a fictitious subset of data for the questionnaire found in Box 14.1. In this data set we have two variables, sex and score1 (the first column contains the *participant number*). For the rest of this chapter we present calculations based on a statistical program available for the personal computer: *Statistical Package for the Social Sciences (SPSS)*.

SPSS is representative of most modern statistical packages available on the personal computer, and was one of the first mainframe statistical packages to be made widely available to researchers. Other popular personal computer statistical packages with long research histories include SAS and BMD. As mainframe programs, each was difficult to learn, each had different ways of entering and "reading" the data once it was entered, and offered slightly different statistical treatments. Generally, researchers used the program on which they were trained. Today, however, the personal computer and its graphics based interface

TABLE 14.3   Sample Data Set[a]

	DATA LINES	
1	1	5
2	2	5
3	1	4
4	2	4
5	1	4
6	2	3
7	1	3
8	2	3
9	1	3
10	2	3
11	1	2
12	2	2
13	1	2
14	2	1
15	1	1
16	2	9
17	1	9
18	2	9

[a]*Note:* Response number (1–18), sex (1 = Male, 2 = Female), and data (interval scale: 1 = Strongly Disagree, 2 = Disagree, 3 = Neither Agree nor Disagree, 4 = Agree, 5 = Strongly Agree).

(GUI) have changed all of that. Modern statistical packages offer similar ways of entering data, offer similar statistical analyses, and now provide advanced graphics packages that allow you to not only analyze your data, but also present camera-ready tables and graphics. We will employ those capabilities in this and the next chapter.

The personal computer has opened statistical packages to everyone. There are over 100 statistical packages available on Windows and/or Apple-based computers. Some are very simple, much like the standard calculator available at any drug store for under $10; others are very complex and much more expensive. SPSS, SAS, and BMD represent the high-end statistical program—their basic modules (statistical programs) run about $500, and a complete version as high as $1500. SPSS has a student version that costs about $90: it runs basic statistical analyses and limits you to no more than 50 variables, but allows you 1,500 participants. Box 14.2 lists a variety of computer packages available to you.

Our choice is SPSS, mainly because it is available in a student version and because most popular personal computer-developed programs have imitated SPSS's data entry and output formats. It also provides excellent table and graphic support. While the full version (basic, advanced, and professional modules) takes up over 20 MB of disk space and requires a minimum 12 MB RAM, the student version only requires about 5 MB and requires 4 MB RAM. SPSS also provides all the basic statistical analyses needed and offers very good support (Stacks, 1996).

■ ■ ■ ■ ■

BOX 14.2
STATISTICAL SOFTWARE AVAILABLE FOR THE PERSONAL COMPUTER

STATISTICAL SOFTWARE	OTHER SOFTWARE[a]
CRCSSIZ	*Database*
GAUSS	Access
GLIM	FoxPro
Hyperstat	dBase
JMP	
KwikStat	*Spreadsheet*
MacAnova	Excel
MiniTab	LOTUS 123
NCSS	
SAS	
Sigmastat	
SIMSTAT	
SPSS	
Statistica	
STPLAN	
SYSTAT	

[a]Software with the potential to do basic and advanced statistical tests.

Regardless of the computer program you use, your first step in conducting statistical analyses is to prepare the data for entry in the computer. The screen shots listed in this and the next chapter come from the Statistical Package for the Social Sciences (SPSS). Like all major computer programs, new versions of SPSS are released regularly and it is possible that the version you use will have slightly different setup procedures (commands that tell the program what analyses to perform) and output (visual displays of the results). These changes will be minor and almost always make an already easy-to-use program even simpler. We provide these SPSS screen shots merely as examples to give the reader a "feel" for the way the program works. Excellent "Help" comes with SPSS to aid the user in performing exactly those analyses that he or she wants to perform.

Modern data entry is similar to entering data into a spreadsheet. Figure 14.1 is a "screen shot" of the data from Table 14.3. Note how simple the data look. Each variable has been named and decisions made regarding labels and missing data entered. To enter the data, you simply put your cursor on an empty cell and enter the data and either tab over to the next cell or enter to the next "case" (participant's data) or line. SPSS will name the variable "var001" unless you tell it to do otherwise. To name it yourself double click on the "var001." Doing so opens to a different window in which you can change the type of data (column width and whether the variable represents numeric—1, 2, 3 . . .

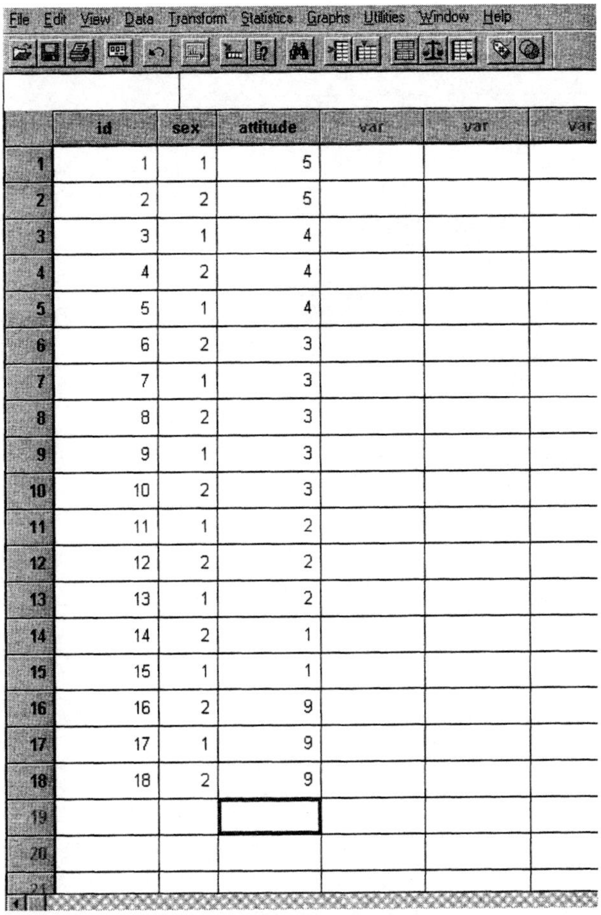

	id	sex	attitude	var	var	var
1	1	1	5			
2	2	2	5			
3	3	1	4			
4	4	2	4			
5	5	1	4			
6	6	2	3			
7	7	1	3			
8	8	2	3			
9	9	1	3			
10	10	2	3			
11	11	1	2			
12	12	2	2			
13	13	1	2			
14	14	2	1			
15	15	1	1			
16	16	2	9			
17	17	1	9			
18	18	2	9			
19						
20						

FIGURE 14.1   SPSS data grid—SPSS Base.

,—alphanumeric—SA, female, high—or other types of variables), the variable name and enter value labels ("id;" "sex," 1 = male, 2 = female; and "attitude," 1 = SA, 2 = A, 3 = U, 4 = D, 5 = SD), your missing-data code ("9," a blank cell is also identified as missing data), and the column format (column width and alignment). For the most part, we will only use the labels and missing-data commands. You will always enter numeric data to be statistically analyzed, not alpanumeric.

CODING DATA FOR ANALYSIS

Before the data can be analyzed it must be coded. Coding requires that you systematically take the responses from the questionnaires, scales, or observers' check sheets and assign numbers to them. For example, our scale might consist of responses to a yes/no question.

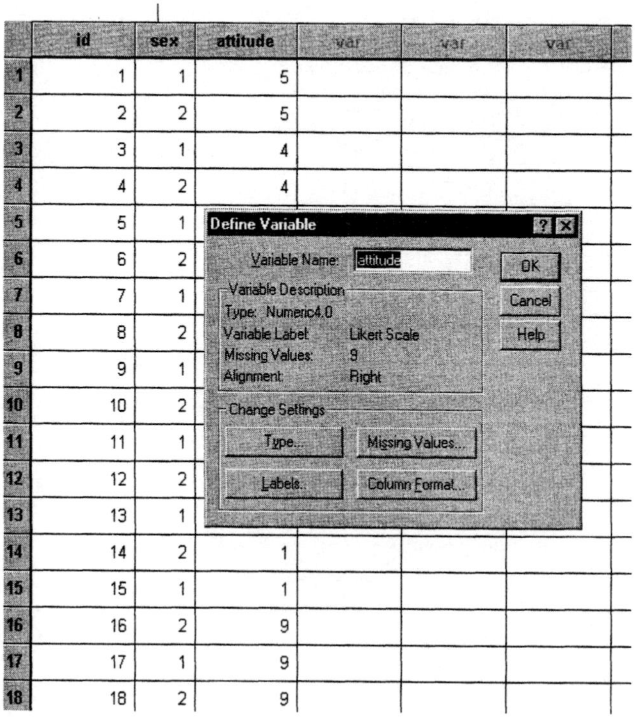

	id	sex	attitude	var	var	var
1	1	1	5			
2	2	2	5			
3	3	1	4			
4	4	2	4			
5	5	1				
6	6	2				
7	7	1				
8	8	2				
9	9	1				
10	10	2				
11	11	1				
12	12	2				
13	13	1				
14	14	2	1			
15	15	1	1			
16	16	2	9			
17	17	1	9			
18	18	2	9			

Define Variable dialog box:

Variable Name: attitude

Variable Description
Type: Numeric4.0
Variable Label: Likert Scale
Missing Values: 9
Alignment: Right

Change Settings
Type...   Missing Values...
Labels...   Column Format...

OK   Cancel   Help

FIGURE 14.2   Defining a variable—SPSS Base.

We might enter this on the coding form as Y and N but we usually enter it as 1 (Yes) and 2 (No) because we can use the numerical indications in statistical programs. Usually, *the simpler the coding, the fewer the errors.* The researcher prepares a coding sheet that has a grid where data may be entered. Then the data is transferred from the handwritten grid to the computer program. Errors are the major problem with coding data and the data must be carefully proofread after transfer to the coding sheet and again after being entered into a computer file. SPSS will allow you to see the actual value labels in lieu of their numeric entries, but this should not be done until all the data have been entered and checked for errors.

Sometimes a respondent or participant fails to answer a question or complete a scale. Most computer programs today allow us to enter a special notation for missing data. Typically, we use a 9 or 99 or some other number that is not part of the scale we use to represent missing data. These programs then compute the analysis without including an entry for the missing case. As a general rule, it is best to code the data using numbers (1 for male, 2 for female; 1 for Euro American, 2 for African American, 3 for Asian American; and so forth) and then add values or labels later. Although most computer packages allow for both alphabetical and numeric data, many analyses require the data to be entered as numbers only.

The key to coding data is to establish a coding system (much like that discussed in Chapter 8) that includes all possible ranges when the data are categorical. When the data are continuous, the actual numbers can be entered. Be sure the numbers you assign to items correspond to their meaning. For instance, suppose you are measuring attitudes toward Madonna. One item reads "Madonna is a talented singer" with a Strongly Agree to Strongly

Disagree response scale. You assign a 5 to the Strongly Agree and a 1 to the Strongly Disagree. You have another question that is reversed to avoid response bias (i.e., someone is just going to mark down one side of all the items). Let us say that you the next item reads "Madonna's lyrics are oversimplified." In order to keep your data consistent, you must code the Strongly Agree as a 1 instead of a 5.

Once the data have been coded and entered into the computer, we are ready for analysis.

DESCRIBING NONPARAMETRIC DATA

Nonparametric data, as was noted earlier, are data that have been placed in mutually exclusive categories. These analyses range from *univariate* analysis, in which only one variable is examined, to *multivariate* analysis, or **contingency analysis**, where two or more variables are analyzed simultaneously (c.f., Babbie, 1995; Kerlinger & Lee, 2000). Our focus will be limited to univariate and bivariate (two variable) analysis, but the principles can be extended to multivariate analysis. We will present each of these in turn.

For the purposes of our discussion, suppose that we are interested in studying how voters feel about a woman being elected president. Our research question might be: Do males and females differ in their feelings about a woman president? The best method to answer this question is to survey randomly selected voters.

Univariate Descriptive Analysis

When conducting a univariate descriptive analysis we analyze the ways our respondents scored on one variable. Table 14.4 presents a simple univariate analysis conducted by run-

TABLE 14.4 Frequency Output—SPSS Base

STATISTICS

	N	
	VALID	**MISSING**
Sex of Respondent	18	0

SEX OF RESPONDENT

		FREQUENCY	**PERCENT**	**VALID PERCENT**	**CUMULATIVE PERCENT**
Valid	1 male	9	50.0	50.0	50.0
	2 female	9	50.0	50.0	100.0
	Total	18	100.0	100.0	
Total		18	100.0		

ning a frequency analysis off the "Descriptive Statistics" command of SPSS. It analyzes the sample according to the category, *sex*. As you can see, there were nine males and nine females. These statistics are simply the **frequency distribution**; that is, the number of responses that fall in each category. We could analyze the same data as **percentages**, assuming that the total number is finite, and then describe the data in terms of **proportions**. We find that one half (50 percent) of our sample is male and the other half is female. Both descriptions tell us something about the sample.

Table 14.5 presents the categorical analysis of the Likert-type scale described earlier. Listed in one column are all possible responses, including those who failed to respond. Notice that while the frequencies are the same, the percentages differ. In the case of Table 14.5, our analysis would conclude that 27.8 percent of the respondents were undecided about electing a woman president. Notice that the figures in columns Percent and Valid Percent are identical; that is, the results are calculated as if *any* response, in any category, should be tabulated. All 18 respondents were included in the analysis. Actually, only those who responded (15 of the 18 respondents) should be included in the analysis. The Valid Percent column in Table 14.6 differs from the Percent column in that the former takes into account respondents classified as Missing, Incomplete, or Other.

We can visualize the univariate analysis by examining the frequencies in ways other than reported percentages. Figure 14.3 presents one such analysis of the data, a *bar chart*.

TABLE 14.5   Frequency Output with No Missing Values—SPSS Base

STATISTICS

	N	
	VALID	**MISSING**
ATTITUDE Likert Scale	18	0

ATTITUDE LIKERT SCALE

		FREQUENCY	**PERCENT**	**VALID PERCENT**	**CUMULATIVE PERCENT**
Valid	1 SD	2	11.1	11.1	11.1
	2 D	3	16.7	16.7	27.8
	3 U	5	27.8	27.8	55.6
	4 A	3	16.7	16.7	72.2
	5 SA	2	11.1	11.1	83.3
	9	3	16.7	16.7	100.0
	Total	18	100.0	100.0	
Total		18	100.0		

TABLE 14.6   Frequency Output With Missing Values—SPSS Base

STATISTICS

	N	
	VALID	**MISSING**
ATTITUDE Likert Scale	15	3

ATTITUDE LIKERT SCALE

		FREQUENCY	**PERCENT**	**VALID PERCENT**	**CUMULATIVE PERCENT**
Valid	1 SD	2	11.1	13.3	13.3
	2 D	3	16.7	20.0	33.3
	3 U	5	27.8	33.3	66.7
	4 A	3	16.7	20.0	86.7
	5 SA	2	11.1	13.3	100.0
	Total	15	83.3	100.0	
Missing	9	3	16.7		
	Total	3	16.7		
Total		18	100.0		

We see that more people respondend as "Undecided." Furthermore, an equal number of respondents agreed and disagreed with the statement, as was the case of those "Strongly Disagreeing" and "Strongly Agreeing." In a second eyeball analysis, the bar chart provides not only the frequency of responses, but also the percentages and proportions (percent × 100) associated with each category. These descriptive tools show the responses visually. Interpretation, assigning meaning to the responses, is still up to you.

We can also visualize the Likert-like data in terms of a pie chart (see Figure 14.4). A pie chart divides each response as part of a circle and can be represented as a simple pie or wedges can be "exploded" for emphasis. To create a pie chart you must first select "graphs" on the command bar, then select "pie," and then define it. Once it has been produced, you double click on the chart, select the slice to be exploded, and select the "explode" tool. These graphical displays usually do not appear in academic reports, but they are useful for presentations.

Bivariate Analysis

Usually, the data must be divided into subgroups to describe the results of the research adequately. It may be informative to report the number or percentage of males and females who responded differently to the Likert-type statement concerning electing a woman president.

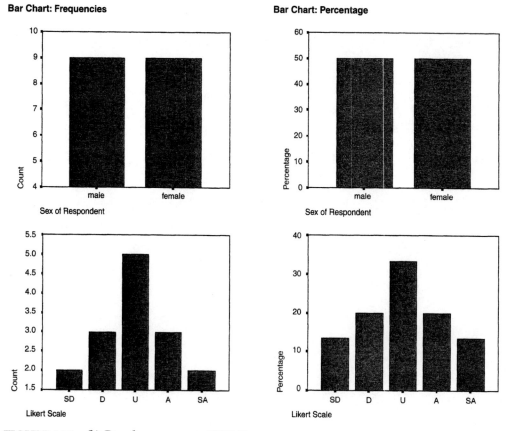

FIGURE 14.3   (b) Bar chart output—SPSS Base.

By breaking sex into two categories and reanalyzing the data, it is possible to address this question. Table 14.7 presents a 2 (M-F) × 5 (Strongly Agree to Strongly Disagree) **contingency table**. This table shows how males and females responded to the attitude statement.

To get this analysis, select Descriptive Statistics from the command bar and then "crosstabs." Select "sex" as your column and "attitude" as your row. This produces the table shown in Table 14.8. There are several ways to interpret this table. First, we can examine the frequency of males and females who responded to the statement and the resulting percentages or proportions. As a general rule, it is best to establish your independent variable as the columns (usually there are fewer categories with this variable and this makes for easier reading) and the dependent variable's categories as the rows. Initial eyeball examination of the data indicates that eight males (53.3 percent of the sample) and seven females (46.7 percent of the sample) responded to the statement. Analysis also indicates that two people (13.3 percent) strongly agreed, three people (20.0 percent) agreed, three people (20.0 percent) disagreed, two people (13.3 percent) strongly disagreed, and five people (33.3 percent) were undecided about a woman being elected president. This analysis is the same as conducting two univariate analyses, one for sex and one for attitude.

Analysis of the **crossbreaks**, or a comparison of the frequency of responses in individual cells, provides three types of analysis (Kerlinger & Lee, 2000). In each case the individual cell frequencies (number of males choosing each response category and number of females doing the same) will remain the same, what changes are the percentages or proportions. If you are concerned with describing how *each* cell related to the *total*, you would interpret the last statistic in the cell, which shows that 6.7 percent of the males (1 out of 15) strongly disagreed with the statement, as did the same percentage of females. Twenty percent of the females, however, were undecided; as were 13.3 percent of the males.

The second way to interpret this table is by analyzing each cell as a percent of each column. Here descriptions of the data focus on how each sex responded (percent of SEX). For males, 12.5 percent strongly disagreed, 25.0 percent disagreed, 25.0 percent agreed, 12.5 percent strongly agreed with the statement, and 25.0 percent neither agreed nor disagreed. For females, the percentages differ: 14.3 percent strongly disagreed, disagreed, strongly agreed, or agreed with the statement; 42.9 percent neither agreed nor disagreed. You could also further collapse the rows and analyze which sex was uncertain about the statement, agreed with it, or disagreed with it. Your focus, however, is on how each sex responded to the statement.

The third analysis shows each cell as a percentage of each *row*. Here we are interested in how each response category differs between males and females (percent of ATTITUDE). Thus, 50 percent of the males and 50 percent of the females strongly disagreed with the statement, the same percentages as with males and females who strongly agreed with it. Of the males, 66.7 percent disagreed, compared to 33.3 percent of the females. The same per-

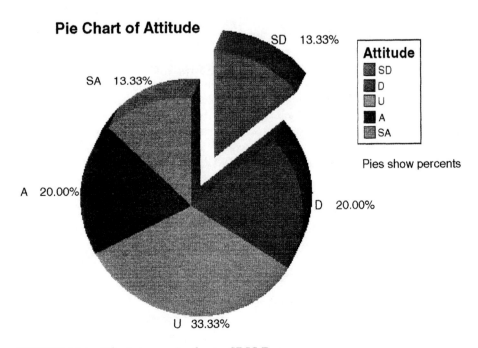

FIGURE 14.4   Obtaining a pie chart—SPSS Base.

TABLE 14.7 Contingency Table

	SEX	
SCORE	MALE	FEMALE
Strongly agree		
Agree		
Undecided		
Disagree		
Strongly disagree		

centages of males and females (66.7 percent and 33.3 percent) agreed with it. And, 40 percent of the males were undecided about electing a woman president, as compared with 60 percent of the females.

Before completing this section we need to note two things. First, it is important that you report how many responses were not included in the tables, or were classified as missing. If there were 100 respondents to a survey and only 97 responded to a particular question, then that should be indicated in the table. In the text of your report, you should explain why the figures differ. Missing responses, errors in coding, inability to properly code response are some of the reasons you may offer to account for any differences. Second, contingency tables can be confusing to construct and interpret. We have presented two *simple* cases consisting of only two variables with limited categories. We could just as easily have added a third variable, perhaps whether or not the respondents were married (just two levels or categories, Married and Not Married) and created a *multivariate* analysis. We would now have *six* potential tables to analyze: three for those married and three for those not married. Or, as shown in Table 14.9, the interrelationships between the three variables could be displayed in a considerably more complex table.

DESCRIBING PARAMETRIC DATA

What do we know about the data presented in Table 14.3, other than how many people—the number, percent, or proportion—responded to the categories Strongly Agree, Agree,

TABLE 14.8   SPSS Contingency Analysis Output—SPSS Base

ATTITUDE LIKERT SCALE * SEX SEX OF RESPONDENT CROSSTABULATION

			SEX SEX OF RESPONDENT		
			1 MALE	2 FEMALE	TOTAL
ATTITUDE Likert Scale	1 SD	Count	1	1	2
		% of ATTITUDE Likert Scale	50.0%	50.0%	100.0%
		% of SEX Sex of Respondent	12.5%	14.3%	13.3%
		% of Total	6.7%	6.7%	13.3%
	2 D	Count	2	1	3
		% of ATTITUDE Likert Scale	66.7%	33.3%	100.0%
		% of SEX Sex of Respondent	25.0%	14.3%	20.0%
		% of Total	13.3%	6.7%	20.0%
	3 U	Count	2	3	5
		% of ATTITUDE Likert Scale	40.0%	60.0%	100.0%
		% of SEX Sex of Respondent	25.0%	42.9%	33.3%
		% of Total	13.3%	20.0%	33.3%
	4 A	Count	2	1	3
		% of ATTITUDE Likert Scale	66.7%	33.3%	100.0%
		% of SEX Sex of Respondent	25.0%	14.3%	20.0%
		% of Total	13.3%	6.7%	20.0%
	5 SA	Count	1	1	2
		% of ATTITUDE Likert Scale	50.0%	50.0%	100.0%
		% of SEX Sex of Respondent	12.5%	14.3%	13.3%
		% of Total	6.7%	6.7%	13.3%
Total		Count	8	7	15
		% of ATTITUDE Likert Scale	53.3%	46.7%	100.0%
		% of SEX Sex of Respondent	100.0%	100.0%	100.0%
		% of Total	53.3%	46.7%	100.0%

TABLE 14.9   More Complex Contingency Table

SCORE	MARRIED		NOT MARRIED	
	MALE	FEMALE	MALE	FEMALE
Strongly agree				
Agree				
Undecided				
Disagree				
Strongly Disagree				

Disagree, Strongly Disagree, or Uncertain regarding our question? If we want to examine the characteristics of the data for the entire sample we can begin by asking what the central tendencies of the respondents' answers are and how much dispersion there is in the scores.

Figure 14.5 presents the same data as Table 14.3, but graphically as a *histogram*. Note that it approximates the *normal curve* discussed in Chapter 10. In this case there are five scores at the midpoint of the Likert-type scale (3), three scores on either side (2 or 4), and two scores at the extremes (1 or 5). This is a *frequency distribution* of the data. Two people answered 1.0 on the scale; five answered 3.0, or neutral, on the scale. It tells us at a glance that there is a score that is the *average* response. Obviously, not all data will be normally distributed. Note that three people failed to respond to the statement. The ramifications of missing data will be more apparent later, for now we omit them from the analysis.

How would you describe the data in Figure 14.6? One way is to describe the data distributed over the entire scale. Our first descriptive analysis is visual: We can label it in at least two ways—by degree of *flatness* (bell-shaped, peaked, or flat) or by the degree of *skewness* of the data (the peakedness of the data to one side of the midpoint of the scale or the other).[1] In this case we see two peaks, meaning it is bimodal. Figure 14.7 indicates five possible descriptions of the data. Note that our data distribution is *normal*; that is, it is bell-shaped and equally distributed on both sides of the peak.

If two of the scores were shifted from 4 to 2 we would skew the curve toward the higher end of the scale. This curve is described as having a positive skew. Why? We label the curve by the direction of the *tail* away from the peak. If the data cluster at the negative end of the scale, the skewness is positive; if the data cluster at the positive end, the skewness is negative.

MINI-PROJECT:

You are interested in how an upcoming campus event will be perceived. You believe that under-class students will be more positive about the event than upper-class students. Conduct a survey among your friends (at least 10 under-class and 10 upper-class students) about an upcoming event on campus. Ask them to respond to three five-point Likert-type statements (SA, A, U, D, SD) that gauge their attitude toward this event and three seven-point semantic differential statements about the event (excited-unexcited, sad-happy, valuable-worthless), code the data, enter it into a computer program, and conduct all possible analyses. Prepare a report with appropriate tables and graphics for presentation.

Univariate Indicators: Mean, Median, Mode

Now that we have graphically described the data, we want to describe the average score for our sample (see Table 14.10). There are three indices of *central tendency* that provide information about the average response.

Histogram with Normal Curve Imposed

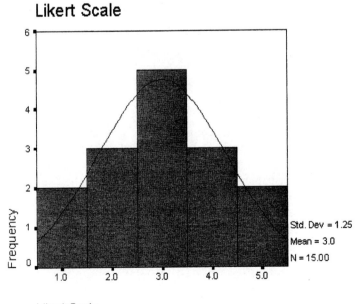

FIGURE 14.5   Histogram with normal curve imposed—SPSS Base.

FIGURE 14.6 **Graphic representation of hypothetical data.**

```
                X
                X
        X       X               X
        X       X               X
X       X               X       X
X       X               X       X
X       X               X       X

1       2       3       4       5
```

The **arithmetic mean** is one type of average response. It is calculated by summing all scores and then by dividing by the number of scores:

$$M = \frac{\Sigma X}{N}$$

where M is the mean (sometimes represented as X, or "x-bar"), Σ (sigma) is the notation for summation, X are the individual scores, and N is the number of scores being summed.

By adding all data for ATTITUDE from our survey data and dividing by 15 (the number of people *answering* the question), we get a mean response of 3.00. *Extremes in the data influence the mean response.* Two scores of 8 will make the mean a poor indicator of what was found.

Sometimes it is best to examine the data for another kind of central tendency: the **mode**. If we were interested in which TV show is watched most often, we would use the mode. The mode is the most frequently occurring score. In this example it happens to be the same as the mean, 3.00. Some data sets will have more than one mode, in this case we might describe the data as being bimodal or even trimodal (see Figure 14.8). If the sample yielded six people responding to the statement as undecided and another six as strongly disagreeing, then the data would be described as bimodal (two modes of six responses each). The mean is always influenced by the mode and by all other scores; in contrast, the mode is uninfluenced by small numbers of extreme scores.

The third measure of central tendency is the **median**. The median is the score representing the midpoint of all scores. It is the score above which lie one-half of the scores and below which lie the other half of the scores. Our median also is 3.00 (remember, the scores are "normally" distributed, which means the curve is bell-shaped). In this case the median is a whole number; that is, there are an odd number of participants and the midpoint fell on one score. Where there are an even number of scores, you take the average (or mean) of the two scores that fall around the midpoint (a median of 3.5, for instance).

Understanding Dispersion: Range, Standard Deviation, and Standard Score

A second way to describe data is to examine how the data points or scores spread out around the mean. Put another way, we can describe how the data are dispersed between the highest and lowest points. These are three commonly used indices of the distribution. The **range** is simply the difference between high and low scores. Since we have scores between 1 and 5, our range is 4 (5 − 1 = 4).

While the range tells us the distance between data points, it does not tell us much about how the scores are dispersed. A more precise analytical tool is the **standard deviation** (usually signified as *s* or *σ*). It provides us with a more workable description of the data. It also has another advantage—the standard deviation can be used to estimate the number of responses that lie within the various points of the data:

$$(s) \text{ or } (\sigma) = \frac{\sqrt{\Sigma(X - M)^2}}{N}$$

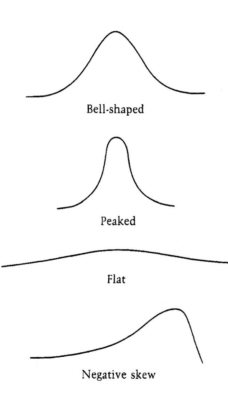

Bell-shaped

Peaked

Flat

Negative skew

Positive skew

FIGURE 14.7   Possible graphic distribution of continuous data.

TABLE 14.10   Parametric Statistics—SPSS Base

WITH "MISSING DATA" INCLUDED

STATISTICS

| | N | | | | | Std. | | | | |
	Valid	Missing	Mean	Median	Mode	Deviation	Variance	Range	Minimum	Maximum
ATTITUDE Likert Scale	18	0	4.00	3.00	3	2.57	6.59	8	1	9

WITHOUT "MISSING DATA"

STATISTICS

| | N | | | | | Std. | | | | |
	Valid	Missing	Mean	Median	Mode	Deviation	Variance	Range	Minimum	Maximum
ATTITUDE Likert Scale	15	3	3.00	3.00	3	1.25	1.57	4	1	5

The standard deviation tells us how dispersed the data points are from the mean. The more closely the scores cluster around the mean, the more reliable is your analysis and the smaller the standard deviation will be. Calculation of the standard deviation is not difficult, you simply subtract the average score from each score, square the result, and sum the *deviations*. You then divide this score by the number of scores. The standard deviation tells us how normally dispersed the data are in a bell-shaped, normal distribution. A more general measure of dispersion is the **variance**, which is calculated from the standard deviation. The variance (s^2 or σ^2), then, is the square of the standard deviation (see Table 14.11).

The variance is based on the mathematics of a normal, bell-shaped distribution. If we have data that end up in that distribution, we can use the mathematics of the area of that distribution to determine how likely it is that scores will be described by the mean. In other words, mathematical theory allows us to statistically determine how much error or chance plays in drawing conclusions about how descriptive the mean is. The smaller the variance, the more compact the curve is around the mean. A mean with a small variance is a better indicator of the data than a mean that has a less compact distribution, and thus a higher variance.

The normal curve was introduced in Chapter 10 as predictable areas under the curve where scores might be expected to fall (see Figure 14.9). In our example the curve obtained was normal, it was bell-shaped and tapered out symmetrically at both ends. This curve yielded a standard deviation of 1.21 ($\sigma^2 = 1.47$), where the number of scores that fall between ±1.21 points from the mean response (3.00) accounted for 68 percent of the total number of scores, or between 1.79 and 4.21. As Figure 14.9 demonstrates, over two-thirds (68 percent) of the scores should fall within one standard deviation on either side of the mean. Ninety-five percent of the scores should fall within two standard deviations of that mean.

The standard deviation provides an index of how the majority of the scores spread out around (deviate from) the mean. Additionally, it provides one more tool for data description. Suppose for a moment that we have not *one* but *two* measures of respondent attitudes toward something. The first is the Likert-type, five-point measure we have been describing. The second is a semantic differential scale consisting of seven equal-appearing intervals. How can scores derived from two different scales be compared? We might want to know how the two scores describe the same attitude object. Obviously, the 5-point and 7-point measures will yield different distributions. Are we comparing apples to oranges? A **standardized score** provides us with a way of describing the attitudes by translating each individual score into a score that reflects standard deviation units.

To *standardize* the scores so that they may be described together, a simple calculation is necessary. The **Z-score**, or standardized score, takes each participant's score, subtracts the mean from it, and then divides that number by the variable's standard deviation:

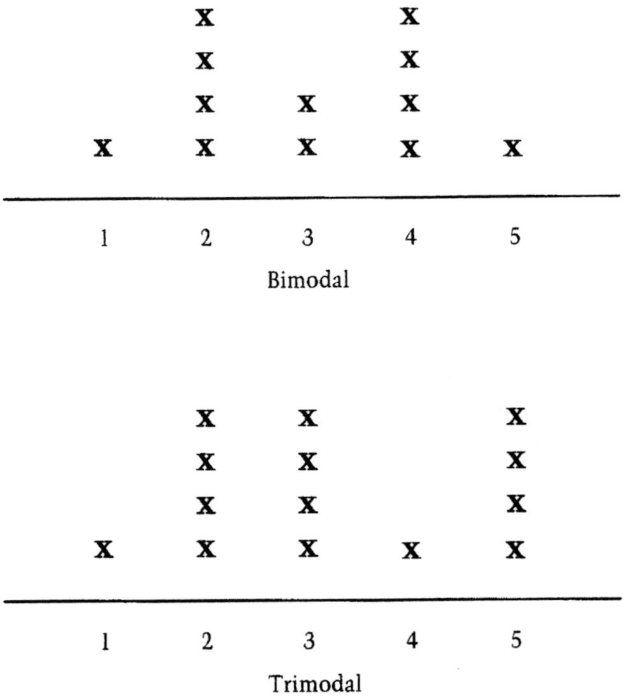

FIGURE 14.8   **Bimodal and trimodal distributions.**

TABLE 14.11   VARIANCE CALCULATIONS[a]

PARTICIPANT	SCORE	MEAN	$X - M$	$(X - M)^2$
1	5	3	2	4
2	5	3	2	4
3	4	3	1	1
4	4	3	1	1
5	4	3	1	1
6	3	3	0	0
7	3	3	0	0
8	3	3	0	0
9	3	3	0	0
10	3	3	0	0
11	2	3	−1	1
12	2	3	−1	1
13	2	3	−1	1
14	1	3	−2	4
15	1	3	−2	4
Σ(sum)	45		0	22

[a]Note: $\sigma^2 = \dfrac{22}{15} = 1.47$.

$$Z = \frac{X - M}{\sigma}$$

In our example, the mean response for the 15 people answering was 3.00 and the standard deviation, 1.21. We can calculate Z-scores for each participant and then take the mean of those scores, providing a standardized mean score for comparative or descriptive purposes. Suppose, for instance, that a score on the Likert-type measure was a 2.00, subtracting the mean from this (2.00 − 3.00) produces a numerator of −1.00, dividing this score by 1.21 yields a Z-score of −.826. Assume that a score on the semantic differential measure was a 3.00 and the standard deviation for the measure was a 2.42. The standardized score for the semantic differential would be ([3 − 4] ÷ 2.42) or −.413. Both standardized scores describe the score as falling within one standard deviation *below* the mean response. You can do the same for all the scores on each measure.

For example, what if we have scores for ten people on two different measures reflecting beliefs and attitudes toward a persuasive message? The data may have been gathered from an experiment in which the participants were exposed to a persuasive message employing high fear appeals. Table 14.12 presents both the attitude measure scores (a belief scale ranging from 1 to 11 and a 7-point semantic differential scale tapping attitude toward the speech). By standardizing the scores we can better describe how the sample perceived the high fear appeal. Note the similarities between the Z-scores among the participants. Note also the discrepancy when the participants evaluated the speech differently on the two scales (participants 3 and 10).

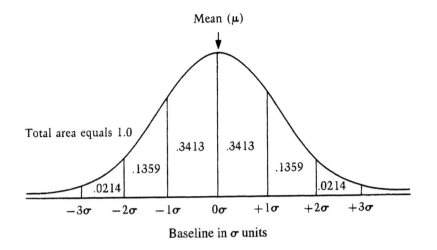

FIGURE 14.9   The normal curve.

We can conduct a bivariate type parametric analysis by examining how different groups of people respond to our questions. Assuming, for instance that we wanted to show how males and females differed on our attitude scale, we would describe the mean response of males and the mean response of females. To do so, we would select "Analyze" from the SPSS command bar, then select "compare means," and "means." We would then identify our independent variable—sex—and our dependent variable—attitude (see Figure 14.12). The results are found in Table 14.13.

Summary

Describing single parametric variables provides us with a starting point in our research. A research report will frequently include means, standard deviations, and ranges. This allows the reader to examine other research that describes similar circumstances and make comparisons. Although social scientists make regular use of descriptive analyses, purely descriptive studies are still rather rare because reporting single variable average responses, responses that cluster around some central tendency of the sample or population, do not ad-

MINI-PROJECT:

Take the data gathered from the parametric mini-project (page 345) and run the appropriate descriptive statistics. Compute Z-scores for each of the six attitude scales (three Likert-type and three semantic differential). Report the findings in tables and discuss what you found about underclass and upper-class student attitudes toward the event.

TABLE 14.12   Z-score for Two Attitudinal Measures

PARTICIPANT	BELIEF SCORE[a]	Z SCORE	ATTITUDE SCORE[b]	Z SCORE
1	2	−1.022	2	−0.909
2	4	−0.292	3	−0.303
3	3	−0.657	1	−1.515
4	6	0.438	4	0.303
5	2	−1.022	3	−0.303
6	11	2.262	7	2.121
7	5	0.073	3	−0.303
8	7	0.803	5	0.909
9	3	−0.657	3	−0.303
10	5	0.073	4	0.303
	Mean	4.80	Mean	3.50
	Std Dev	2.74	Std Dev	1.65

[a]Scale = 1 (low belief) to 11 (high belief).
[b]Scale = 1 (low attitude) to 7 (high attitude).

equately answer the research question. Sometimes it is more important to know the distribution of responses than the average response. When researchers are more interested in the frequency with which the participants are able to name candidates, categorical analyses may be more appropriate. Consider, for instance, what it means to report that the average family consists of 2.33 people; unless you are trying to describe the variance in family size, a categorical response is more appropriate here. On the other hand, reporting that 22.3 percent of the respondents reported earning between $15,000 and $19,999 a year may be less revealing than knowing that the average respondent earned $24,242.54, with the sample's median income reported as $26,500. And almost always, descriptions of the results for single variables do not adequately answer complex research questions. Usually it is necessary to analyze the relationship between two or more variables, a topic to which we now turn.

Scatter Diagrams (Scattergrams)

A useful graphic depiction of the relationship between two variables is the scatter diagram, or *scattergram*. One of the two variables is represented by the X axis, while the other is represented by the Y axis. Each respondent's score on both variables is plotted and the resulting pattern of points on the graph provides the opportunity to inspect its relationship visually. Figure 14.10 shows a series of hypothetical scattergrams. Scattergram (a) shows a positive correlation of 1.00; the plotted points fall perfectly along a straight line. Note that the individual with the highest score on variable 1 also had the highest score on variable 2; the individual with the next highest score on variable 1 also had the next highest on variable

TABLE 14.13   Output for Mean Score Analysis—SPSS Base

CASE PROCESSING SUMMARY

	CASES					
	INCLUDED		EXCLUDED		TOTAL	
	N	PERCENT	N	PERCENT	N	PERCENT
ATTITUDE Likert Scale * SEX Sex of Respondent	15	83.3%	3	16.7%	18	100.0%

REPORT

ATTITUDE	LIKERT SCALE	
1 male	Mean	3.00
	N	8
	Std. Deviation	1.31
	Median	3.00
	Minimum	1 SD
	Maximum	5 SA
	Range	4
	Variance	1.714
2 female	Mean	3.00
	N	7
	Std. Deviation	1.29
	Median	3.00
	Minimum	1 SD
	Maximum	5 SA
	Range	4
	Variance	1.667
Total	Mean	3.00
	N	15
	Std. Deviation	1.25
	Median	3.00
	Minimum	1 SD
	Maximum	5 SA
	Range	4
	Variance	1.571

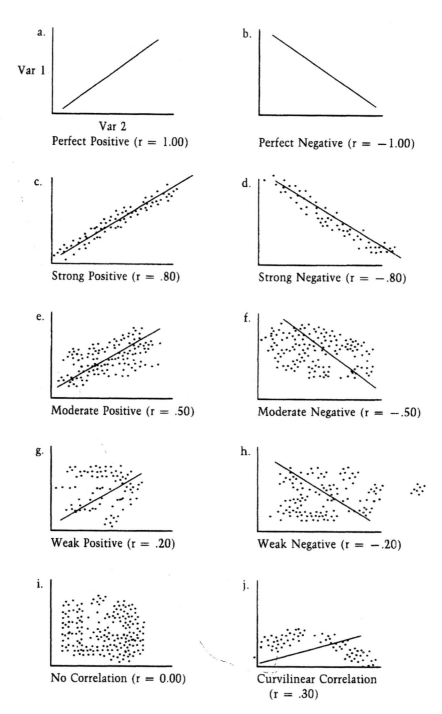

FIGURE 14.10   Scattergrams and correlations.

2, and so on, for all the individuals measured. Scattergram (b) shows a negative correlation of –1.00. Again, the points fall along a straight line; however this time the individual with the highest score on variable 1 had the *lowest* score on variable 2, and so on, for all the individuals. Both of these scattergrams show a *perfect* relationship between variables 1 and 2.

Scattergrams (c) and (d) show, respectively, strong correlations of ±.80. Note that some of the plotted points deviate from the straight line. Scattergrams (e) and (f) show moderate correlations of ±.50. Deviations from the straight line, aberrations, have increased. The plots in scattergrams (g) and (h), which show weak correlations of ±.20, indicate many wide deviations from the straight line.

Scattergram (i) shows the case when two variables are *not* related. There is no systematic pattern whatsoever—only randomness. An individual's score on one variable is unrelated to his or her score on the other. The correlation is *zero*.

Finally, scattergram (j) shows a curvilinear correlation; that is, two variables are related in a positive fashion for low to moderate scores, but as scores represented by plots on the X axis continue to increase from moderate to high, scores on the Y axis begin to go down again. A curve results. Note that although the pattern is very regular and very closely follows a curving line, the correlation is quite low: .30. This is because the Pearson correlation coefficient assumes that variables will be *linearly* related; it assumes that as one variable increases, the other either increases *or* decreases, not increases *and* decreases. *The Pearson correlation provides no information about curvilinear relationships.* There are coefficients designed to assess curvilinear relationships. Thus, the scattergram becomes an important analytic technique, providing information that the correlation cannot: Specifically, information about the *shape* of the relationship (Pedhazur, 1997).[3]

BIVARIATE CORRELATIONAL ANALYSIS

As we have noted repeatedly, the purpose of science is to build theories that state the way in which variables are *related*. Probably no statistic in all of empirical communication research has been more widely employed than the **Pearson r,** (the Pearson correlation coefficient). This statistic provides an index of the extent to which ordered pairs of observations (measurements) covary or share variance; that is, the correlation tells us if and to what degree individual scores on two variables are related.

Parametric correlations range from +1.00 through 0 to –1.00, from a perfect positive correlation, to no correlation, to a perfect negative correlation. Seldom, however, do we find perfect positive or negative correlations in the social sciences, but to the extent that respondents who score high on one variable also score high on the second, correlations will be positive. Thus height and weight are usually positively correlated because tall people tend to weigh more than shorter people. Self-disclosure and the degree of trust in the person to whom the disclosure is addressed are usually positively correlated; that is, people self-disclose more to people they trust highly than they do to those whom they trust less. Thus, self-disclosure and trust are positively correlated. On the other hand, if people who score high on one variable score low on the second variable, or vice versa, the variables are negatively correlated. High blood pressure and longevity are negatively correlated; people with high blood pressure do not live as long as those with lower blood pressure. Communication apprehension and success in many professions such as law, teaching, and sales are negatively correlated. People with high communication apprehension do not do as well in these professions as those with lower levels of apprehension. Correlations are computed on continuous data. They are only done on interval and ratio data.

The correlation coefficient is determined by fitting a line to the actual scattergram scores. If the line does not fit the scores well, there is error around the line, which is represented by the scatter points. A correlation of 0.0 indicates that the line does not describe the data in a meaningful way—there is no recognizable pattern or association between the two variables. On the other hand, if the scores are very close to the line, there is a sizable correlation because there is almost no error.

Of course, sometimes tall people are quite skinny and light, whereas a short person may be plump and heavy. Occasionally individuals will self-disclose to those they do not trust and will withhold disclosures from those they do. A few people with high blood pressure will live to ripe old ages, whereas some with lower blood pressure will die at younger ages. And, some individuals with high communication apprehension will do well in law or teaching or sales, whereas others with low apprehension will do poorly in these professions. These aberrations reduce the strength of the correlation. As the number of aberrations increase, the resulting correlations will move toward zero. And, in fact, if the two variables were unrelated, the correlation would be close to zero (Pedhazur, 1997).[3]

What constitutes a strong versus a moderate versus a weak correlation? Interpretation guidelines are somewhat arbitrary and vary with both the type of study undertaken and the purpose of the analysis. For example, if we used a correlation to estimate the reliability of two related measures, we would look for a good correlation of .70, while a .85 correlation or higher would be considered excellent. On the other hand, if the relationship between theoretical variables was being examined in an exploratory study, we might be pleased to find *any* correlation. According to Guilford (1954), a correlation of ±.20 is labeled "slight," representing an almost negligible relationship. With this in mind, when examining relationships between two variables, correlations below ±.30 are *sometimes* considered weak or slight, with a small but definite relationship; ±.40 to ±.70 are moderate, with a substantial relationship; ±.70 to ±.90 are considered high, and correlations above ±.90 are very high and very dependable. Correlations that are "high" are rare in communication research, except among similar measures.

However, the judgment about what the size of the correlation means depends on what is being studied. One of the "strongest" correlations in television effects is the correlation for the relationship of televised violence and aggressive behavior in children. Most researchers have identified a correlation of about .25. That is considered a fairly strong correlation. This is because other factors also contribute to violence in children, such as parental behaviors, friends' behaviors, music lyrics, and so forth.

The Correlation Matrix

A correlation matrix is a table that presents the correlations among three or more variables. Each variable's correlation with every other variable is shown. If there were five variables being measured in a survey, variable 1 could be correlated with variables 2, 3, 4, and 5.

Variable 2 could be correlated with variables 1, 3, 4, and 5, and so on. With five variables there are ten different correlations. With ten variables there are 45 separate correlations.[4] Table 14.14 shows a simple correlation matrix. In addition to the correlation itself, correlation matrices frequently contain the sample size (e.g., $n = 85$; 85 would be the number of *pairs* of scores used to calculate a particular correlation).

Nonparametric Correlations

The Pearson correlation is a parametric statistic and thus requires interval or ratio data. Correlation techniques are also available for both nominal and ordinal data. Probably the most commonly used correlation for ordinal data is the **Spearman rho rank** correlation. This technique is employed when the scores to be correlated are rank ordered (e.g., Rosenthal & Rosnow, 1984, pp. 212–222). Other nonparametric correlations found include **Kendall's *Tau-b***. There are specific correlations available for special cases, such as when the data for one variable are continuous and the data from the second are dichotomous (point-biserial) (e.g., Rosenthal & Rosnow, 1984, pp. 212–222).

Running a Correlational Analysis

To obtain a correlation between two or more variables you select "Analyze" from the SPSS command bar and "correlate." The window that comes up next provides you with your various options. For the most part, you will run bivariate correlations. Suppose you have conducted an analysis of attitudes toward possible candidates for mayor. You asked respondents a series of Likert-type statements and now wonder how they correlate. As the data can be treated as either categorical or continuous, you could run the Pearson *r*, Kendall's *Tau-b*, or Spearman, depending on the assumptions you made about the data—or you could run all three to see if they differ (see Table 14.15).

A final note on correlation: Correlation is *not* causation. It is important to remember that there are three criteria for the establishment of causality (see Chapters 12 and 13): co-variation, time order, and ruling out alternative explanations. Correlation provides evidence bearing only on the first of these criteria, *covariation*. It could be that the relationship is spurious, that a third variable is causing the observed relationship. Or, it could be that the variable thought to be the cause and the variable thought to be the effect are reversed. Correlation, by itself, does help determine time order.

TABLE 14.14   Sample Correlation Matrix

	(1)	(2)	(3)	(4)	(5)
(1) Monetary donations	1.00	.10	−.08	.09	.25
(2) Age		1.00	.08	.29	.19
(3) Sex			1.00	.26	.10
(4) Times voted				1.00	.94
(5) Political activity					1.00

TABLE 14.15 Correlation Matrices—SPSS Base

CORRELATION

		Q1	Q2	Q3	Q4	Q5	Q6	Q7	Q8	Q9	Q10
Pearson	Q1	1.000	.871	.757	.669	.654	.422	.488	.050	.746	.693
Correlation	Q2	.871	1.000	.767	.683	.656	.450	.502	−.008	.711	.688
	Q3	.757	.767	1.000	.795	.771	.653	.696	.128	.784	.758
	Q4	.669	.683	.795	1.000	.792	.586	.686	.110	.762	.709
	Q5	.654	.656	.771	.792	1.000	.693	.738	.233	.799	.761
	Q6	.422	.450	.653	.586	.693	1.000	.705	.210	.601	.653
	Q7	.488	.502	.696	.686	.738	.705	1.000	.203	.676	.693
	Q8	.050	−.008	.128	.110	.233	.210	.203	1.000	.259	.269
	Q9	.746	.711	.784	.762	.799	.601	.676	.259	1.000	.855
	Q10	.693	.688	.758	.709	.761	.653	.693	.269	.855	1.000

NONPARAMETRIC CORRELATION

		Q1	Q2	Q3	Q4	Q5	Q6	Q7	Q8	Q9	Q10
Kendall's	Correlation Q1	1.000	.827	.698	.600	.599	.392	.456	.095	.676	.619
tau-b	coefficient Q2	.827	1.000	.696	.596	.590	.411	.460	.041	.627	.610
	Q3	.698	.696	1.000	.740	.727	.603	.656	.151	.723	.696
	Q4	.600	.596	.740	1.000	.743	.540	.647	.122	.695	.639
	Q5	.599	.590	.727	.743	1.000	.643	.701	.219	.742	.689
	Q6	.392	.411	.603	.540	.643	1.000	.648	.208	.547	.583
	Q7	.456	.460	.656	.647	.701	.648	1.000	.183	.620	.636
	Q8	.095	.041	.151	.122	.219	.208	.183	1.000	.217	.229
	Q9	.676	.627	.723	.695	.742	.547	.620	.217	1.000	.802
	Q10	.619	.610	.696	.639	.689	.583	.636	.229	.802	1.000
Spearman's	Correlation Q1	1.000	.862	.756	.661	.662	.443	.512	.110	.740	.688
rho	coefficient Q2	.862	1.000	.755	.656	.655	.464	.516	.049	.691	.680
	Q3	.756	.755	1.000	.791	.783	.654	.710	.174	.789	.771
	Q4	.661	.656	.791	1.000	.788	.588	.704	.139	.756	.711
	Q5	.662	.655	.783	.788	1.000	.688	.752	.247	.801	.761
	Q6	.443	.464	.654	.588	.688	1.000	.685	.230	.606	.647
	Q7	.512	.516	.710	.704	.752	.685	1.000	.204	.682	.705
	Q8	.110	.049	.174	.139	.247	.230	.204	1.000	.247	.261
	Q9	.740	.691	.789	.756	.801	.606	.682	.247	1.000	.860
	Q10	.688	.680	.771	.711	.761	.647	.705	.261	.860	1.000

■ ■ ■ ■ ■

MINI-PROJECT:

Using the data collected earlier in the chapter, what relationships do you find between the Likert-type and semantic differential measures? If they are measuring the same thing, then their variance accounted for should be high, is it?

APPLYING KNOWLEDGE IN COMMUNICATION

All quantitative communication research involves some form of descriptive analysis. We almost always try to describe the sample we have drawn by its demographic characteristics, and we report them as descriptive statistics. When you read a report of a survey or experiment or even a focus group, it is informative to know how many males and females participated, what their average age was, how many were married or divorced or unmarried, and so forth.

Any good research study will provide the descriptive backbone against which you can gauge it. Often, when we will find that a particular portion of population is underrepresented, we do this via descriptive statistics. At times we must be careful about interpreting the percentages, proportions, means, or other descriptive statistics based on the number (n) of respondents. Remember that 90 percent of 10 doctors is not the same as 90 percent of 100 doctors; both represent a statistical finding of 9 out of 10, but with larger numbers, we can be more certain that the findings are representative.

Finally, descriptive statistics in tabular and graphic form are used in making formal presentations of results. In business you may only present a summary of findings, complete with a series of tables and charts. In academia, however, you not only present the descriptive findings, but also those that allow you to infer to the larger population, as we discuss in Chapter 15.

SUMMARY

This chapter introduced the concepts of data analysis and data interpretation. It also has introduced the most elementary form of data analysis: descriptive analysis. Descriptive analysis has as its goal the simplification of research results so that patterns can be detected and conclusions made regarding those patterns. We noted that descriptive analysis is an important first step in most research; we also noted that some type of descriptive analysis is found in all research, even if it is just describing the sample.

We observed that data can take on two basic forms or types: categorical or continuous. Categorical data are representative of nominal or ordinal category systems. Continuous data are representative of interval or ratio scale data. They describe the sample or population differently. When describing a sample containing continuous data, we rely on measures of central tendency, usually the mean and median. We can also describe the data as to their dispersion through the range, the variance, and the standard deviations. We can display our data graphically and describe their skewness and peakedness.

Sometimes our research questions are more appropriately answered with a categorical analysis. Categorical analysis establishes categories from which we can describe our sample. Simple frequency counts and calculation of percentages and proportions can be used to describe how the population falls into each category. We noted that there were several types of analysis available: Univariate analysis allows you to examine how scores fall across the categories of one particular variable, whereas bivariate or multivariate analysis breaks the analysis into finer distinctions. Finally, we noted that the correlation coefficient allows us to establish a simple relationship between two variables.

PROBES

1. In what ways can statistics be used in communication research? Are there methods where statistics, in general, are *never* employed? If you think so, which? Why?

2. What descriptive statistics would be appropriate for assessing your classmates?

3. What is meant by nonparametric analysis? When might you employ a nonparametric analysis? What might this analysis tell you about the data you collected? What inferences can you make?

4. When we measure via continuous data we rely on parametric statistics. What do these statistics tell us that nonparametric statistics do not? When and where might we want to use such statistics?

5. Differentiate between the use of univariate and bivariate statistics. How do the parametric and nonparametric tools discussed differ with each type of analysis? When would you use one and not the other?

RESEARCH PROJECTS

1. Ask your instructor for some of the data he or she has collected and analyzed. Conduct the same analyses and see if you come up with the same results.

2. Conduct a survey or focus group for a campus group that needs to find out about attitudes toward them or is trying to market something (often clubs, sororities and fraternities, and even departments will find something for you to study). Analyze the data and prepare the appropriate tables and graphs for presentation.

3. Conduct a study of undergraduates about their perceptions of research methods as a class. What do they think about having to take it? What do they expect to get out of it? Do these perceptions seem to differ by year in school? By experience outside the classroom (internships or actual jobs in communication)? Present your findings.

SUGGESTED READING

Huck, S. W., Cormier, W. H., & Bounds, W. G., Jr. (1974). *Reading statistics and research*. New York: Harper & Row.

Kerlinger, F. N. & Lee, H. B. (2000). *Foundations of be-*havioral research, 4th ed. New York: Harcourt.

Pedhazur, E. J. (1997). *Multiple regression in behavioral research: Explanation and prediction*, 3rd ed. New York: Holt, Rinehart & Winston.

Phillips, J. L., Jr. (1973). *Statistical thinking: A structural approach*. San Francisco: W. H. Freeman.

Rosenthal, R., & Rosnow, R. L. (1984). *Essentials of behavioral research: Methods and data analysis*. New York:

McGraw-Hill.

Williams, F. & Monge, E. (2001). *Reasoning with statistics: How to read quantitative research*, 5th ed. New York: Holt, Rinehart & Winston.

NOTES

1. For an excellent, yet readable treatment of distribution shapes and skewness, see Williams & Monge (2001), pages 35–38.

2. There are statistical techniques for examining nonlinear relationships that are beyond the scope of this book. See Pedhazur (1982), pp. 404–435.

3. For a detailed presentation of the formula for the Pearson correlation see Pedhazur (1982), pages 12–44. The formula is:

$$r_{xy} = \frac{N \sum XY - (\sum X)(\sum Y)}{\sqrt{N \sum X^2 - (\sum X)^2} \, N \sum Y^2 - (\sum Y^2)}$$

where N is the number of pairs of observations, X and Y are the individual scores on the two variables, and $\sum$ means "sum to what follows."

4. The formula for determining the number of correlations is $N(n - 1) \div 2$, where n is the number of variables and N the number of respondents.

REFERENCES

Babbie, E. (1994). *The practice of social research*, 7th ed. Belmont, CA: Wadsworth.

Guilford, J. P. (1954). *Fundamental statistics in psychology and education*. New York: McGraw-Hill.

Kerlinger, F. N. & Lee, H. B. (2000). *Foundations of behavioral research*, 4th ed. New York: Harcourt.

Pedhazur, E. J. (1982). *Multiple regression in behavioral research: Explanation and prediction*, 2nd ed. New York: Holt, Rinehart & Winston.

Rosenthal, R., & Rosnow, R. L. (1984). *Essentials of behavioral research: Methods and data analysis*. New York: McGraw-Hill.

Stacks, D. W. (1996). Spss 7.0 for Windows 95. *World Communication*, 25, 108–109.

Williams, F. & Monge, P. (2001). *Reasoning with statistics: How to read quantitative research*, 5th ed. New York: Holt, Rinehart & Winston.

INFERENTIAL STATISTICS

OBJECTIVES

By the end of this chapter you should be able to:

1. Differentiate between descriptive and inferential statistics and their use in communication research.

2. Discuss the difference between a research question and a hypothesis and the difference each makes in terms of interpreting an inferential statistical test.

3. Describe and explain the Chi-Square test for nonparametric data and when and how it should be employed for a given research question or hypothesis.

4. Explain the concepts of variance and how it relates to parametric inferential statistical tests.

5. Describe and explain the t-test, one-way, and multifactor Analysis of Variance tests for parametric data and when and how they should be employed for a given research question or hypothesis.

6. Run the appropriate statistical tests for a given research question or hypothesis; interpret appropriate statistical tables and graphics.

In Chapter 14 we examined statistics as percentages and proportions, measures of central tendency, variability, and correlations. These statistics provide descriptions of the samples studied. Most often, however, the researcher is interested in knowing if the results observed for a sample are indicative of the population. (See Chapter 10 for a review of sampling.) **Inferential statistics** allow the researcher to make this determination.

Before examining specific statistical methods, we need to look at the reason for employing inferential statistics. What is the purpose of inferential statistics? When we observe that two variables are related in a sample, the question arises: Are the variables related in the larger population from which the sample was drawn?

Suppose a researcher is interested in determining the average number of hours of television children watch in her home town. She draws a sample from her home town that represents all of the children. From past research, she knows that the average U.S. child watches 3.5 hours per day. In order for her to have confidence that her sample represents her home town, she has to draw an inference (hence, inferential statistics) about whether her sample approximates the national mean of 3.5 hours. Thus she presents the hypothesis that the mean for her town is 3.5 hours. To test this hypothesis, she determines what a distribution of a large sample of means would look like. Recall that we know the characteristics of a bell-shaped, normal curve. We know that 68 percent of the time our sample score would fall within one standard deviation and 95 percent would fall within two. Thus she has an estimate of the probability that the mean she finds in her home town will be similar enough to the population mean to accept her hypothesis. If her findings, her mean, are too divergent, then she will have to reject her hypothesis.

We can also do the same procedure with two or more variables.

How do we decide if our sample represents the population? It is on inferential statistics that we base this decision. Let us return for a moment to the classic true experimental design discussed in Chapter 12. Suppose that we conduct an experiment in which one group of 30 participants receives an experimental treatment—say exposure to an advertisement advocating a particular product—while a second group of 30 serves as a control and receives an unrelated message. Then both groups are given a questionnaire that contains semantic differential scales measuring attitudes toward the product. The results indicate that the *mean* scores of the people in the experimental group is 5.5 (on a 7-point scale), while the mean for those in the control group is 4.5, a difference of 1.0. Thus, it looks at first glance as if the independent (exposure to the advertisement) and dependent variables (attitude toward the product) are systematically related. Exposure to the advertisement apparently changed attitudes. Inferential statistics allows us to state the **probability** that our observed difference of 1.0 was the result of exposure to the persuasive message, or alternatively, that it was the result of sampling error, or random chance.

An observed result in a study is said to be **statistically significant** if sampling error accounts for the result in fewer than a specified number of cases (usually 5 percent) if the study were run over and over again. In other words, 95 percent of the time we would come up with the same result. This chapter deals with several basic tests of statistical significance. There are inferential statistics to test the statistical significance for both nonparametric and parametric analyses. Thus, we can estimate the probability that research results such as percentages, frequencies, correlations, and differences between means are the results of the fact that the variables under study represent *with some probability* the population from which the sample studied was drawn.

USING STATISTICS TO TEST HYPOTHESES

Inferential statistics tell us whether the results that we have observed in our study are indicative of what would have been obtained if we had studied the population from which the sample (the group we have studied) was drawn. When conducting a research study we attempt to predict the relationships between variables. Thus, our statistical *analyses* are tests of the hypothesized relationships among variables of interest. Hypothesis testing involves four steps: (1) specifying the hypothesis to be tested, (2) picking a desired significance level for the tests, (3) calculating the appropriate statistics and probability levels, and (4) concluding whether the null hypothesis is rejected or not. We will examine each.

Specifying the Research Hypothesis

As we have noted in earlier chapters, a hypothesis is a statement of a relationship among two or more variables. It is a *prediction* of how the variables are related. As the values for an independent variable change, the hypothesis predicts what will happen to the values for the dependent variable. Examples include:

1. Individuals who have had a course in public speaking will experience less communication apprehension than individuals who have not.
2. Increases in amount of touching will result in increases in liking of the toucher.
3. As readability difficulty increases, newspaper readership decreases.
4. Participants exposed to an advertisement that contains a single vivid example of a homeless person's situation will be more favorably disposed toward helping the homeless in general than will participants exposed to a message that contains abstract statistics about the homeless.

Specifying the Null Hypothesis

Although it may seem somewhat odd, classical statistical inference hypotheses such as these are tested by predicting that the variables are *not* related, and then examining the probability that this prediction is false. These predictions of no relationship are called **null hypotheses**. The researcher hopes that the null hypothesis will be rejected and the alternative, or theoretical hypothesis, will be supported. The null hypothesis is tested because an assumption of science is that, logically, a hypothesis can never be proved; it can only be disproved. Remember, the researcher is judging the sample and making an inference about its correspondence with a larger population. That is a process of induction. You probably know the rule about inductive reasoning—it can only support an argument, not prove it. Thus, the null hypothesis is tested in an effort to reject it, providing evidence for its alternative. For the previous examples the null hypotheses would be:

1. Individuals who have had a course in public speaking will experience the same amount of communication apprehension as individuals who have not.
2. Increases in amount of touching will result in no change in liking of the toucher.
3. As readability difficulty increases, newspaper readership is unaffected.
4. Participants exposed to a message that contains a single vivid example of a homeless person's situation will feel equally favorable toward helping the homeless in general as participants exposed to a message that contains abstract statistics about the homeless.

Once the hypothesis has been stated, a decision must be made regarding the level of error we will tolerate in testing the null hypothesis; that is, we must specify a level of confidence for our statistical tools or specify an accepted level of significance.

Specifying a Significance Level

The level of significance specified in a research study represents the confidence we have in our predictions. Convention among communication researchers calls for using a .05 level of significance. If the results are said to occur by chance *no more than* 5 times out of 100 then those results are statistically significant. Put another way, we would say that selection of the *.05* level of significance expresses confidence that our findings occur due to expected differences *95 percent* of the time and that chance accounts at most only *5 percent* of the time. Some researchers report their level of significance as an *alpha* (α) or *"p" level*; thus, we might report a particular test being significant at the $\alpha = .05$ or $\alpha = .01$ level (*99 percent* probability, or *1 percent* chance).

We have now expressed the degree to which we believe our results provide a basis for rejecting the null hypothesis. What is so magical about the .05 level of significance? Actually, nothing; the figure is commonly accepted as being appropriate. You might want to be more stringent about the amount of error you will accept in your results. In this case you might specify the .01 level of significance; chance could now account for the observed results at most only 1 time in 100. Perhaps your research is still at the exploratory stage and the accepted .05 level of significance is too stringent. You might choose to increase your probability of error to .10, or allowing chance to account for the results as often as 10 times out of 100 occurrences.

There is no magic significance level. Accepted levels include .05, .01, and .10 in some instances. The .05 and .01 levels of significance approximate two and three standard deviations from a mean; thus, they represent the "tail" ends of the probability curve (Kerlinger & Lee, 2000). (For a review of the probability curve, see Chapters 10 and 14.)

It is important to remember that the level of significance *does not* give us any indication of how strongly our independent and dependent variables are related. It just provides us with the likelihood or probability that our sample represents the population. You will see some researchers assume that a *p* level of .001 is somehow more important than one of .05. That is an *incorrect interpretation*, so beware.

Research Questions versus Hypotheses

How you interpret your level of significance is confounded by whether your research hypothesis predicts simple differences or establishes direction. For instance, suppose that you predicted that males and females differed in their evaluations of physically attractive females. This statement suggests that males and females will differ, but not which sex will perceive the attractive female as "more" attractive (as indicated on some measure). Like the research question, this is a **two-tailed test of significance** (see Figure 15.1). In actual practice you have said that some differences will be found, but you have not specified how the differences will occur, so the sample results could end up at either tail of the curve.

If you had hypothesized that males would score higher on your measure than females, the test for significance would be **one-tailed** (see Figure 15.1). In other words, specification of direction or magnitude in a hypothesis gives you a better chance for significance (the area under the curve indicating significance is larger) than when you simply make a claim of difference. In some ways you are rewarded for making the specific prediction, but in actual practice, the two-tailed test simply must account for differences at *both* ends of the probability curve, while the one-tailed test is looking for results at one and only one end of the probability curve.

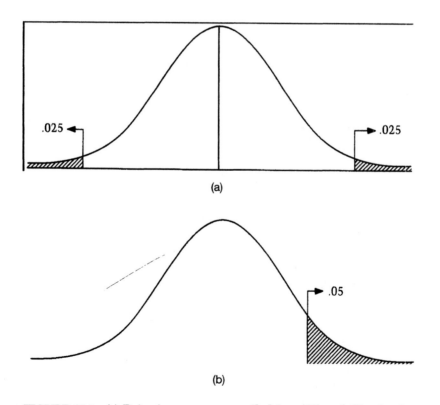

(a)

(b)

FIGURE 15.1 (a) Rejection curve: two-tailed ($\alpha = .05$) and (b) rejection curve: one-tailed ($\alpha = .05$).

Research questions, like nondirectional hypotheses, are usually examined as if they are two-tailed. Practically, this means that the level of significance is .025 (.05 ÷ 2) for *either* end of the probability curve. If your theory is developed enough to specify direction or magnitude then a one-sided test is appropriate; otherwise it is not. Williams (1992) says:

> A one-tailed test is never used (or should never be used) unless there is very good reason to make a directional prediction. This reason is not especially a function of wanting to make directional predictions, but is mainly based on the confidence that an outcome in the opposite direction will not be obtained. If a one-tailed test is made in the absence of such confidence, the researcher is assuming the hazard of never really testing statistically an outcome that would be opposite to the predicted direction. (p. 72)

This leads us to the two types of error possible when we test hypotheses.

Type I and Type II Errors

There are two basic mistakes researchers can make when interpreting statistical tests of their hypotheses or research questions (see Figure 15.2). A **Type I error** occurs when a researcher claims that relationships exist when in fact they do not. This is an inappropriate rejection of the null hypothesis. A **Type II error** is just the opposite. The researcher fails to reject the null hypothesis and claims that relationships do not exist when in fact they do. Both types of error are important and are to be avoided. In general, error is associated with sample size. As illustrated in Figure 15.3, the larger the sample, the smaller the probability of Type I error. Thus, we might note that the **power** of the test, *the ability to detect differences that are truly different, is a function of sample size.*

All good computer programs provide both the obtained statistical test values and their levels of significance. Reading of statistical printouts requires an understanding of two things: *calculated values* and *degrees of freedom*. An understanding of these two things is necessary whether you do your statistical tests manually or use a computer. Both parametric and nonparametric statistical tests use similar concepts, although the labels may differ.

Fundamental to inferential analysis is the understanding of **degrees of freedom**, correction factors that allow for a type of probability to be computed and analyzed. Degrees of

The relationships are really:

	True	False
You find the relationships: True	No problem	Type II error
You find the relationships: False	Type I error	No problem

FIGURE 15.2   Relationship of Type I and Type II error to research.

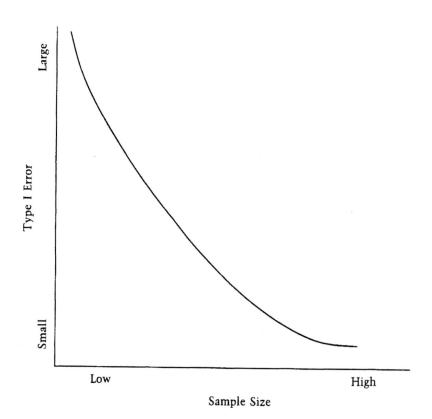

FIGURE 15.3   Relationship of Type I error to sample size.

Source: After Fred N. Kerlinger (1986). *Foundations of Behavioral Research.* 3rd ed. (New York: Holt, Rinehart & Winston), p. 117. Reprinted by permission.

freedom provide information about the "latitude of variation a statistical problem has" (Kerlinger, 1986, p. 155). The assumption is that, by holding one condition, group, or category constant, we can predict what the other conditions will be.

The concept is actually quite simple; for instance, suppose you have predicted that males will be more apprehensive about writing than females. Knowing one group's score and the total score, we can predict the female group's score. In other words, by noting the degrees of freedom we can then calculate scores from the nonfree condition. You will need to know how many degrees of freedom are associated with your test in order to interpret the results.

Statistical tests yield calculated values. These may be in the form of *F*-values, *t*-values, *r*-values, Chi-square values, or whatever. Calculated values are tested by taking into account the particular degree(s) of freedom (df) associated with the specific analysis. This is the **critical value** that the calculated statistic must equal or surpass to be significant at the designated level of significance. In general, if we are testing only one independent and one dependent variable, we will have only 1 degree of freedom to calculate because we know the value of the second group.

Assume that your study examined the impact of the sex of speaker (male, female) and message intensity (high, moderate, low) on persuasiveness. The degrees of freedom for this test would be sex of speaker = 1 (2 groups – 1), message intensity = 2 (3 groups – 1), and the interaction of message intensity and sex of speaker = 2 ($2_{[3 \text{ groups} - 1]} \times 1_{[2 \text{ groups} - 1]}$). In reporting our statistical test for each *effect* we first find the appropriate column for degrees of freedom (often labeled, "df") for the groups or categories. Then the degrees of freedom for the sample (N – 1) is calculated. If we tested 31 people, our df_{sample} would be 30.

Assumptions

Before we look at specific statistical tests, we need to look at several assumptions statistical tests make about data. Although different statistical analyses interpret them differently, we should note that inferential statistics assume that for both the sample and the population the variables of interest are independent, each variable is normally distributed, and that the variances for all groups are equal. **Independence** simply means that any participant selected in the sample does not preclude another participant's selection (see Chapter 10). **Normality** refers to the shape of the data distribution (Are the data found under a normal dispersion or a curve?), as would be the data in the population. Our sample's data for each variable are normally distributed, as are the population's data. Finally, if the sample is representative of the population, each group's variance will be equal, thus meeting the **equality of variance** assumption. To the degree that our data do *not* meet these assumptions, we introduce error to our analyses.

Summary

Statistical analysis that goes beyond description and tests for differences between groups is frequently a necessary step in answering research questions. In testing for differences among participants, you must make decisions regarding how you will approach your problem. We noted that you will derive hypotheses or state research questions and then test these relationship statements by the null hypothesis, or hypothesis of no difference. Depending on the level of theory or confidence in relationship development, you establish a probability level with which you feel comfortable. Finally, you test the data by the appropriate test and compare the test statistic to a stored (tabled) value.

We can now turn to inferential analyses. The first set of tests examined will be nonparametric. These are analyses appropriate for *both* dependent and independent variables

■ ■ ■ ■ ■

MINI-PROJECT:

Examine the literature in your particular communication area and describe the *kinds* of hypotheses or research questions being asked. Do they indicate differences, magnitude, or direction for particular variables? Which? From a statistical analysis perspective, how complicated has this research become?

that are composed of *only* categorical data. After this we will examine parametric analyses, which consist of continuous data dependent variables and categorical independent variables.

NONPARAMETRIC STATISTICS

As you recall from Chapter 6, the way we operationalize our variables requires us to make certain decisions. One of those decisions is whether the data collected will be categorical or continuous. Categorical data are derived from nominal or ordinal measurement. This choice also affects later analysis decisions. As we saw in Chapter 14, categorical data analysis provides gross distribution analysis; continuous data analysis allows measures of central tendency and dispersion. If your variables are categorical, the *appropriate* data analysis tests are nonparametric. To understand better what nonparametric tests are and what they can do we will discuss their advantages and limitations and examine specific nonparametric tests.

Advantages and Limitations

Roger Kirk (1968) suggests the advantages of nonparametric analyses are three-fold. First, nonparametric tests are fairly simple to conduct. However, with the advent of computerized statistical packages, the value of this advantage has diminished. Second, nonparametric tests are less restricted by their assumptions about the data. Nonparametric tests can be conducted on "non-normal" populations—populations with large variances, for instance, or skewed data.[1] Third, in experimental designs, nonparametric analyses are appropriate where parametric (continuous) analyses are not. This last advantage comes from the ability of the nonparametric analysis to use a "crossbreak type analysis" in an experiment or survey. A crossbreak analysis allows us to see the percentage of responses of various kinds in each experimental condition or cell.

There are also serious limitations to nonparametric analysis. One limitation stems from the advantages: Nonparametric tests cannot tell us as much about differences between groups or categories as can parametric tests. Because the level of measurement is nominal or ordinal, the analysis will be less refined. We only know that scores or observations are found in particular categories—in terms of the count or frequency of occurrence—but we have no real way of assessing the *relationships* between the scores and observations and the categories. This causes difficulty in attributing differences when they are found. Finally, power (the probability of Type II error) is low. The probability of accepting your null hypothesis when in fact it is false is increased with nonparametric tests.

Although there are many nonparametric tests, we will cover only a few. These include **Chi-square tests** and measures of association.

Testing for Differences: The Chi-Square Test

Probably the most used of all nonparametric tests, the Chi-square (we use the notation χ^2 in equations) tests for differences between the frequency of occurrence between different categories. In general, there are two types of Chi-square tests: simple or *one-sample* (univariate) tests and *two-sample* (bivariate) tests. We will begin with the one-sample test.

One-Sample Chi-Square Test.   The one-sample Chi-square examines the differences in the category selection when the sample has been selected for purposes of homogeneity; that is, people are expected to fall into categories based on some common characteristic. Assume, for instance, that we are interested in the occurrence of communication apprehension in writing students. We could survey students enrolled in writing courses on a measure designed to tap perceptions of communication apprehension. Although there are several parametric indices that might interest us, we are mainly concerned with placing students into one of three categories: highly communication apprehensive, moderately communication apprehensive, and lowly communication apprehensive. Furthermore, we are interested in whether highly apprehensive students enroll in public speaking courses.

The nonparametric test will examine the proportions of students falling into each category. These students, as in our case, are the **observed frequency** per category of apprehension. The students will fall into either high, moderate, or low apprehension categories. But, there is an **expected frequency**, which is how many students we expect to fall into each category. Usually, we would expect an equal number in each category, but we need to specify the expected frequency to do a chi-square.

After considerable research we derive the following hypothesis:

There will be fewer high communication apprehensive students enrolled in writing courses than moderate communication apprehensive students and more low communication apprehensive students than moderate apprehensives.

Note that our hypothesis is directional, it specifies that there will be more people in two groups than in one group. For this one-tailed test we will set our level of significance at $\alpha = .05$.

The distributions of 66 students who participated in the study by enrolling in the courses are found in Table 15.1 (obtained via SPSS by running the "frequencies" statistic). Reading the table is straightforward: 4.5 percent of the sample report high communication apprehension, 36.4 percent report moderate communication apprehension, and 59.1 percent report low communication apprehension.

A simple inspection of the data indicates that there are different frequencies in the three categories. But are they significantly different *statistically*? That is, could our results be the result of sampling error? To test for differences between the categories we must calculate the chi-square statistic. Calculation of the Chi-square is fairly simple. Table 15.1 reports the computer-generated chi-square statistic. Of importance are the "cases observed" and the "expected" columns.

The table was produced by clicking on "Analyze" on the command line, then "Nonparametric Tests," and "Chi-Square." Once the Chi-Square window is opened, select the appropriate variable (APP) and expected range and values and run the program.

The *Observed N* column reflects the number of participants placed in each category. The *Expected N* column reflects the theoretically expected frequency. What we test for in the Chi-square is the *difference* between expected and observed frequencies.

TABLE 15.1   Frequency Output of Hypothetical Data—SPSS Base

STATISTICS

	N	
	VALID	MISSING
APP Degree of Apprehension	66	0

APP DEGREE OF APPREHENSION

		FREQUENCY	PERCENT	VALID PERCENT	CUMMULATIVE PERCENT
Valid	1 High	3	4.5	4.5	4.5
	2 Moderate	24	36.4	36.4	40.9
	3 Low	39	59.1	59.1	100.0
	Total	66	100.0	100.0	
Total		66	100.0		

ONE-SAMPLE CHI-SQUARE OUTPUT—SPSS BASE

NPAR TESTS CHI-SQUARE TEST FREQUENCIES

APP DEGREE OF APPREHENSION

	OBSERVED N	EXPECTED N	RESIDUAL
1 High	3	22.0	−19.0
2 Moderate	24	22.0	2.0
3 Low	39	22.0	17.0
Total	66		

TEST STATISTICS

	APP DEGREE OF APPREHENSION
Chi-Square[a]	29.727
df	2
Asymp. Sig.	.000

[a] 0 cells (.0%) have expected frequencies less than 5. The minimum expected cell frequency is 22.0.

Although the computer calculates the expected frequencies, it is important you understand how they are computed. (Remember, the expected frequency is what is expected if the independent variable has had no effect—the null hypothesis.) In this case the expected frequency is simply the number of observations divided by number of categories. In our case we have 66 cases observed and 3 categories: expected = (66 ÷ 3) = 22. If we had 60 cases our expected frequency per category would be (60 ÷ 3) = 20.

Calculation of the chi-square (χ^2) takes each category and subtracts the expected from the observed, squares that difference, and divides it by the expected frequency:

$$\chi^2 = \frac{(O - E)^2}{E}$$

Or, in our case,

$$\chi^2 = [(3 - 22)^2 \div 22] + [(24 - 22)^2 \div 22] + [(39 - 22)^2 \div 22] = 29.72.$$

Our Chi-square calculated value is 29.72, but is that a value higher than the tabled value? We first calculate the degrees of freedom associated with the statistic. The formula for one-sample Chi-square is the *number of categories minus 1*, or (3 – 1) = 2 in our case. The critical value Chi-square for the α = .05 for 2 degrees of freedom is 3.84. Since 29.72 is greater than 3.84, we can interpret the categories as being statistically significantly different. This information was provided by the computer-generated values listed in Table 15.1. The χ^2 value calculated is 29.727, the degrees of freedom (df) is 2 and the significance level is .000—this is smaller than .05 (.000 is *less* than .05)—which is reported as "Asymp. Sig."

But which groups are different? Here the chi-square analysis reveals a limitation. Inspection of the frequencies clearly indicates that there were fewer high apprehensive students than those who indicated moderate or low degrees of apprehensiveness. Examining the residual column in Table 15.1 provides further information. The **residual** is simply the difference between the observed and expected frequencies. Notice that the residuals are calculated as –19, +2, and +17 for the high, moderate, and low apprehensive categories. We might interpret these as follows: Both high and low apprehensive groups differed from expected frequencies, with far fewer high apprehensives than expected and far more low apprehensives than expected. The frequency of moderates was not greatly different than expected.

Two-Sample Chi-Square Tests.   The two-sample Chi-square test adds a second set of categories from a second sample and is equivalent to the descriptive statistic, cross-break. Suppose that we have access to a course in which no writing is done; instead, the students enrolled in this course simply to learn about communication and have no written assignments except their examinations. If we were to give them the same communication apprehension measure, would they differ from the speaking course students?

The results of this analysis are found in Table 15.2, which presents a 2 (course) × 3 (apprehension) crosstabulation design similar to those presented in Chapter 13. To obtain the table you would select "Analyze" from the SPSS command bar, then "Descriptive Statistics" as though you were going to run a crosstabulation, then select "Crosstabs."

TABLE 15.2   Two-Group Chi-Square Output—SPSS Base

CROSSTABS: APPREHENSION LEVEL BY COURSE TYPE

CASE PROCESSING SUMMARY

	CASES					
	VALID		MISSING		TOTAL	
	N	PERCENT	N	PERCENT	N	PERCENT
APP Degree of Apprehension * COURSE Course Type	160	100.0%	0	.0%	160	100.0%

APP DEGREE OF APPREHENSION * COURSE COURSE TYPE CROSSTABULATION

			COURSE COURSE TYPE		
			1 NON-WRITING	2 WRITING	TOTAL
APP Degree of Apprehension	1 High	Count	8	3	11
		Expected Count	6.5	4.5	11.0
		% of APP Degree of Apprehension	72.7%	27.3%	100.0%
		% of COURSE Course Type	8.5%	4.5%	6.9%
		% of Total	5.0%	1.9%	6.9%
	2 Moderate	Count	51	24	75
		Expected Count	44.1	30.9	75.0
		% of APP Degree of Apprehension	68.0%	32.0%	100.0%
		% of COURSE Course Type	54.3%	36.4%	46.9%
		% of Total	31.9%	15.0%	46.9%
	3 Low	Count	35	39	74
		Expected Count	43.5	30.5	74.0
		% of APP Degree of Apprehension	47.3%	52.7%	100.0%
		% of COURSE Course Type	37.2%	59.1%	46.3%
		% of Total	21.9%	24.4%	46.3%
Total		Count	94	66	160
		Expected Count	94.0	66.0	160.0
		% of APP Degree of Apprehension	58.8%	41.3%	100.0%

TABLE 15.2   Continued

CHI-SQUARE TESTS

	VALUE	DF	ASYMP. SIG. (TWO-TAILED)
Pearson Chi-Square	7.540[a]	2	.023
Likelihood Ratio	7.591	2	.022
Linear-by-Linear Association	6.829	1	.009
N of Valid Cases	160		

[a] 1 cells (16.7%) have expected count less than 5. The minimum expected count is 4.54.

SYMMETRIC MEASURES

		VALUE	APPROX. SIG.
Nominal Measures	Contingency Coefficient	.212	.023
N of Valid Cases		160	

To obtain the needed statistics you must make two more selections. First, select "Statistics" and another window opens; we selected "Chi-Square" and the "Coefficient of Contingency" statistics. Next, select "Cells" and from that window select all the "Counts" and "Percentages" options. Finally, select "OK" to run the test. (Note: We could have selected only "Counts" and not have the percentages computed, but when interpreting the table we would need those statistics; thus, we asked for as much analysis as possible to avoid unnecessary computer runs later.)

The table provides the observed frequencies ("Count") in each of the six possible categories; the category, column, and row percentages; the marginals; and the expected frequencies. Also given are the computer-calculated Chi-square value, the degrees of freedom, and the level of significance for the test.

Calculation of the two-sample Chi-square is similar to that of the one-sample test. In this case the expected frequencies are a little more complicated to calculate. Expected frequencies are the result of multiplying the row and column **marginals** (or totals for each row and column) for that particular category and then dividing the result by the total frequencies for the table. Thus, the expected frequencies for the category, high/non-speaking is (11 [row frequency] × 94 [column frequency] ÷ 160 [total frequency]), or 6.5. Each particular category's expected frequency must be calculated and then the chi-square calculated. In this case

$$\chi^2 = ([8 - 6.5]^2 \div 6.5) + ([3 - 4.5]^2 \div 4.5)$$
$$+ ([51 - 44.1]^2 \div 44.1) + ([24 - 30.9]^2 \div 30.9)$$
$$+ ([35 - 43.5]^2 \div 43.5) + ([39 - 30.5]^2 \div 30.5) = 7.54$$

MINI-PROJECT:

You have been asked by a friend in student government to conduct an attitude survey on parking problems on campus. Of concern are commuters, dorm dwellers, and fraternity and sorority members' attitudes toward a new parking policy. You have done so and have reported the following table to your friend. She asks, "There appear to be some differences in opinion between the groups, are they really different?" To answer this you need to conduct inferential statistics. Enter the data into the computer and answer her. **HINT:** You will have to take the tabled data and create a "coding sheet" to correctly input it.

Opinion on Parking

LIVING ACCOMMODATIONS	APPROVE	DISAPPROVE	NO OPINION
Commuters	5	20	15
Dorm dwellers	20	5	5
Greeks	10	10	10

The degrees of freedom associated with this particular chi-square take into account variation due to both rows *and* columns. The formula for degrees of freedom is (columns − 1) × (rows − 1). In our case the degrees of freedom associated with the 2 × 3 table are (2 − 1) × (3 − 1) or 2. Comparing this against the critical value stored in the computer indicates that 7.540 (the "Pearson Chi-Square") is greater than that value. Note, too, that the computer provides you with the more conservative, two-tailed test. It also provides you with advanced statistical tests. For our purposes, all we need is the Pearson χ^2 statistic. The conclusion is that some cells are significantly different than would be theoretically expected. Interpretation of the Chi-square could end here. However, we can go one step further and examine the relationships between categories.

We have already examined the frequency of occurrence for the writing course (see Table 15.1). We can now do the same for the nonwriting course. Table 15.2 also presents the observed frequency, expected frequency, and residuals for the three categories of apprehension found in the nonwriting course (high = 8 vs. 6.5; Moderate = 51 vs. 44.1; and Low = 39 vs. 30.5). The Chi-square calculated is significant (30.149 with 2 degrees of freedom). Here we may infer that the moderate and high apprehensive students differed from the expected frequencies but the lows did not. We could, of course, run Chi-squares between courses to see if the frequency of high apprehensives differs from course to course, and then do the same with moderate apprehensives and the same with low apprehensives. Your decision to do so, however, is dependent on your research question and hypotheses (see Table 15.2.) (Notice that the observed frequencies differed significantly from theoretical expectations only for the *moderately* apprehensive student.)

Problems Associated with Chi-Square.   The chi-square test is very sensitive to sample size (effect size, E.F.). When the number of expected frequencies is less than 5 in a category, the chi-square value and level of significance may be incorrect. Some computer programs will warn you if this problem exists. Table 15.2 warns us that one cell was found with an expected frequency less than 5. The table tells us that this accounted for 16.7 percent of the categories or cells, and gives us the *minimum* effect size for all cells.

Kerlinger & Lee (2000) suggests that for 2 × 2 chi-squares a correction of .5 from the absolute difference between expected and observed frequencies *before squaring* corrects for this (this is the Yates Correction as calculated automatically by SPSS). For designs greater than two columns or two rows, this correction is not necessary; nor, for that matter are all statisticians convinced that the correction is necessary at all. The correction, however, almost always yields a smaller chi-square value. Use of the correction is considered a conservative approach to the analysis.

Coefficient of Contingency.   What we have found so far is that differences have occurred, but we do not know about the *magnitude* of the differences. Here the coefficient of contingency can be of help.[2] This statistic provides a *relative* measure of magnitude of the relationship between variables on a 0.00 to +1.00 scale. Its calculation is simply the square root of the chi-square value divided by that value plus the total observed frequencies:

$$C = \frac{x^2}{x^2 + N}$$

For the one-sample test of the writing course, C is the square root of (29.727 ÷ 95.727) = .55. A C of .49 was obtained for the nonwriting course. For the two-sample test C was only .21 (see Table 15.2). Note, however, that the *direction* of relationship is not assessed. That is, we do not know if the relationship is positive or negative; we only know the relative degree of relationship. This is a severe limitation.

Interpreting Chi-Square Results.   Interpretation of the Chi-square test, like that of most nonparametric tests, is not easy. Care must be taken in making conclusions, especially if the test for magnitude indicates less than moderate (<.30) association. The best way to interpret the data is first to calculate the Chi-square statistics, then the percentages, and then the measure of association. Use all the information you have to make such decisions as to which category or categories are making the difference.[3]

Summary

Nonparametric analyses are appropriate when the data collected are categorical. The Chi-square test was examined, both in one-sample and two-sample formats, where the test statistic examines whether the frequency of scores or observations into categories is statistically greater than the expected frequency, assuming no effect for the variable(s) under study. Finally, the coefficient of contingency statistic, a rough measure of association related to nonparametric statistics was examined. The advantages and limitations of the nonparemetric analysis were also discussed for each nonparametric statistic examined.

The next section examines a more powerful set of analytical tools: parametric analyses. Based on measures of central tendency and following the assumptions of normality and equal (homogeneous) variances, parametric statistics provide powerful tools for data analysis.

PARAMETRIC ANALYSIS

Some extremely important inferential statistics are based on examining variance. Historically, the results of experiments were almost always analyzed through these methods. These techniques are used for studying the various sources of variance associated with a *dependent* variable consisting of interval or ratio data. Our goal here is to present a conceptual treatment of these methods, keeping formulas to a minimum. After the basic ideas of variance have been explained, we will turn to the very practical matter of reading and interpreting these methods; focusing on the dependent variable's mean responses, which may differ according to the levels or conditions associated with the independent variable. We begin by re-examining variance, move to the *t*-test, a simple **ANOVA** (analysis of variance), then, finally, to the more complex multiple factor ANOVA.

Variance

Whenever we measure a variable, different numbers will result. Whether we measure height or cognitive complexity or amount of positive self-disclosure, or any variable, different people receive different scores—they vary. This variability is called *variance* (s^2 or σ^2). We have already introduced the statistical concept of variance, but its importance to parametric analysis of data requires a short review. The variance of any measure is defined as follows:

$$\text{variance} = \frac{\Sigma(X - M)^2}{N - 1}$$

where X is each individual's score, M is the mean of all scores, and N is the number of scores. In other words, this formula says that the mean of all scores is subtracted from each score, then these deviation scores are squared, added together, and finally divided by the number of scores minus one. (You will recall from Chapter 14 that if we took the square root of this result we would have the standard deviation, another measure of dispersion.)

In an experiment, if we took *all* the scores on the dependent measure and calculated the variance we would come up with the total variance. Of course, we do not actually cluster these scores together as one group of data; rather, they are grouped together within the various experimental conditions. ANOVA sorts out the sources of variation into its component parts. Some of the variability is due to *error*. Participants who are in the same experimental condition, yet who receive different scores, are the sources of this error. From the experimenter's point of view, participants in each experimental condition were all treated identically; thus, he or she does not know why they vary on the dependent variable measurement, yet they do. Thus, some of the total variance, specifically this **within-group variance**, is due to error. However, some of the total variability may be due to the fact that the independent variable had an effect on the dependent variable. If participants in one group had a mean of 4.5 (on a 7-point scale) and those in the other had a mean of 5.5, this is **among-group variance**—this difference of 1.0 is systematic variance. Thus, the **total variance** consists of two parts, systematic (among group) and random, or error (within group), variance:

$$V_{total} = V_{b(etween)} + V_{e(rror)}$$

If the systematic source of variance (among group) is larger than the error variability (within groups), the ANOVA will indicate that the independent variable accounted for the difference between the means. Because ANOVA is an inferential statistic, the differences reflect not *only* this particular *sample*, but *also* the *population* from which the sample was drawn. On the other hand, if the error variance is larger than the systematic variance, then the group mean differences are probably due to sampling error.

How do we calculate which source of variance is larger? The within-group variance (error) is divided into the among-group variance (systematic):

$$F = \frac{V_b}{V_e}$$

The result is an *F*-ratio, a value that can be looked up in a table of critical values to determine the statistical significance of the differences among means. If the results of the experiment were due to sampling error, or put another way, if the null hypothesis that there was no difference among the means of the groups in the population is accurate, we would expect the error variance and the systematic variance to be about equal, and the *F*-ratio would be about 1.0. However, as the systematic variance increases in relation to the error variance, our *F*-value increases, as does the probability of achieving significance. The following examples illustrate this point:

V_b is small and V_e is large: no significance   (15.1)
V_b is large and V_e is equally large: no significance   (15.2)
V_b is small and V_e is equally small: no significance   (15.3)
V_b is large and V_e is smaller: *significance*   (15.4)

As indicated, no significance will be obtained if the variance between groups and within groups is equal, regardless of whether the variance is large or small. Any differences in the means observed in the sample do not reflect population differences. It also follows, as shown in (15.1), that if the variance within groups is larger than the variance between groups, no significance will be found. Significance is *only* obtained when the variance is larger among groups than within groups.

The *t*-Test

Probably the most often used *simple* parametric test is the *t*-test. The *t*-test is limited by several assumptions. First, the dependent variable must be continuous, it must consist of interval or ratio data, such as Likert-type or semantic differential measurement. Second, the dependent variable can have two and only two levels—that is, it is usually nominal (sex: male or female) or ordinal (score: high or low). And, third, it is used only when there are 100 or fewer observations (N is less than or equal to 100).

The t-test tests for differences between means. Within-cell variation is used to calculate an estimate of the sampling error. This estimate, called the **standard error of the mean**, is used in the denominator in an equation while the difference between the two means is in the numerator:

$$t = \frac{M_1 - M_2}{\text{standard error}}$$

The result is a t-value that expresses in standard error units how far apart the two means are. If they are about 1.68 or more standard error units apart, the difference is significant at the .05 level (one-tailed with more than 40 observations, [df > 40]).

Suppose, for instance, that you had hypothesized that advertising focusing on sports would be rated higher by males than by females. You create an advertisement that relies heavily on a sports motif—large males actively engaged in sport watched by stereotypically made-up females as cheerleaders and observers—and show it to 20 randomly selected male and female students. You measure the sample's attitude toward the advertisement via a Likert-type scale, giving you a dependent variable ranging from 1 (dislike the advertisement very much) to 5 (like the advertisement very much). The appropriate test statistic is the t-test. The dependent variable is interval, the independent variable consists of two and only two levels, and the number of observations (sample) is small ($N = 20$). The results are in Table 15.3.

To produce Table 15.3, we would select "Analyze" from SPSS's command bar and then "Compare Means." In the "Compare Means" window, we have several choices. This study's independent variable consisted of independent samples (the participants were either males or females), so an "independent samples t-test" is the appropriate test. After we have identified our dependent and independent variables, we must define the independent variable's values, in this instance we had coded males as "1" and females as "2." We could have used "M" and "F," but it is easier to enter numeric data. Under Options, set our significance level at 95 percent. As with the nonparametric tests, the degrees of freedom can be computed quickly. In SPSS's case the degrees of freedom is the number of observations minus 2 ($N - 2$), or $20 - 2 = 18$.

The output in Table 15.3 includes a number of group statistics. It provides us with the mean and number of observations for each group: males scored the advertisement a 4.20 out of a possible 5.00, while females scored it a 2.00 out of 5.00. Each group's standard deviation and stand error of the mean is also provided. The output also provides Levene's Test for Equality of Variances (Norusis, 1992). The Levene's Test in this case tells us that the assumption of equality of variance holds—there are no significant differences ($p > .05$) between the male and female group variances. Had there been a significant difference in variances, we would have had to recompute the dependent variables to account for this (which is conceptually beyond the scope of this treatment, but pragmatically requires you to interpret a different line in the output—the one where the degrees of freedom are not whole numbers).

TABLE 15.3 *t*-Test for Independent Groups Output—SPSS Base

GROUP STATISTICS

	SEX	N	MEAN	STD. DEVIATION	STD. ERROR MEAN
ATTITUDE	1 Male	10	4.20	.79	.25
	2 Female	10	2.00	.82	.26

INDEPENDENT SAMPLES TEST

	LEVENE'S TEST FOR EQUALITY OF VARIANCES		*t*-TEST FOR EQUALITY OF MEANS						
								95% CONFIDENCE INTERVAL OF THE MEAN	
	F	SIG.	*t*	df	SIG. (TWO-TAILED)	MEAN DIFFERENCE	STD. ERROR DIFFERENCE	LOWER	UPPER
ATTITUDE Equal variances assumed	.037	.850	6.128	18	.000	2.20	.36	1.45	2.95
Equal variances not assumed			6.128	17.979	.000	2.20	.36	1.45	2.95

Most important is the "*t*-test for Equality of Means." In this case we find that males liked the advertisement significantly more than did females. The results would be reported as means, "A significant difference was found for sex ($t = 6.128$, df = 18, $p < .05$), with males rating the advertisement higher than females."

There are times when we sample the same group twice, such as in a pretest and posttest design. The *t*-test for this case is called a "paired samples *t*-test." Suppose that you were interested in how students' attitudes toward an unknown group's music video were, both before and after seeing the video. You were interested in seeing how much difference the video made on liking the group. To test the video, you recruited at random 20 students and measured their pre-exposure attitude towards the group, exposed them to the music video, then measured them again with the same measure. To run the paired *t*-test, you would select "Analyze," "Compare Means," and then "Paired Samples *t*-test." You would then select the variables representing the pretest and posttest (each must be a separate variable). As seen in Table 15.4, the results indicate that exposure to the video increased the students' liking of the group ($t = 2.44$, df = 19, $p < .05$). The degrees of freedom, unlike the independent samples test, is computed as $N - 1$, or $20 - 1 = 19$.

Finally, there are times when you may have obtained scores on a standardized test and would like to know if your group was different than the "norm." Use the example about TV viewing by children that was discussed at the beginning of this chapter. The "One-Sample *t*-Test" will compute your sample's score and test it against the normative score you provide (Table 15.5). In this case you compared your group's pre-exposure to the video attitude toward the group to one published in a music industry publication ($M = 3.00$) and found a significant difference between your sample's pre-exposure evaluation of the group ($M = 2.00$) and a national survey of students' attitudes toward the group after the video was produced ($t = -4.359$, df = 19, $p < .05$). Your sample liked the group less after watching the video than the national average did. Note that the t computed

TABLE 15.4   *t*-Test for Paired Groups Output—SPSS Base

PAIRED SAMPLES STATISTICS

		MEAN	N	STD. DEVIATION	STD. ERROR MEAN
Pair 1	PRE	2.90	20	1.17	.26
	POST	2.00	20	1.03	.23

PAIRED SAMPLES CORRELATIONS

		N	CORRELATION	SIG.
Pair 1	PRE & POST	20	−.132	.579

PAIRED SAMPLES TEST

		PAIRED DIFFERENCES						
		MEAN	STD. DEVIATION	STD. ERROR MEAN	95% CONFIDENCE INTERVAL OF THE DIFFERENCE		t	df	SIG. (TWO-TAILED)
					LOWER	UPPER			
Pair 1	PRE-POST	.90	1.65	.37	.13	1.67	2.438	19	.025

TABLE 15.5   One Sample *t*-Test Output—SPSS Base

ONE-SAMPLE STATISTICS

	N	MEAN	STD. DEVIATION	STD. ERROR MEAN
POST	20	2.00	1.03	.23

ONE-SAMPLE TEST

TEST VALUE = 3.00

	t	df	SIG. (TWO-TAILED)	MEAN DIFFERENCE	95% CONFIDENCE INTERVAL OF THE DIFFERENCE	
					LOWER	UPPER
POST	–4.359	19	.000	–1.00	–1.48	–.52

was *negative* in this case. Actually, the sign makes no difference, it simply indicates that the larger of the two means was first in the equation.

One-way ANOVA

One-way ANOVAs are used when there is one independent variable that has more than two levels or conditions. They are also unaffected by the sample size assumption. This statistic takes the average within-group variability in each experimental condition and compares it with the average among-group variability. In experiments involving three or more groups, if the overall *F*-test yields significance, subsequent tests that examine the pairs of mean differences need to be performed to determine which mean differences account for the significant *F*-value. Most computer programs offer several group comparison tests as a follow-up to the analysis; how these are conducted will be discussed later. Table 15.6 shows the output of a one-way ANOVA with three groups and hypothetical data that failed to reveal significant results; Table 15.7 shows the same experiment with data that achieved significance. In each instance the descriptive statistics are outputted first (see Chapter 14).

The one-way ANOVA table is read as follows. The first column shows the Source of Variation. There are always two sources of variation for a one-way ANOVA: among groups and within groups. The among-groups variation is that attributable to the experimental treatments; the within-groups variation is error. The second column shows the *sums of squares* (SS) associated with each source of variation. The sums of squares are the results of the numerator in the formula for the variance ($\Sigma[X - M]^2$). The third column indicates the *degrees of freedom* associated with the analysis (abbreviated "df"), which is the number of groups minus 1, or 2 in this case. The total number of degrees of freedom is always the

TABLE 15.6   One-Way Analysis of Variance Output—SPSS Base

DESCRIPTIVES

		N	MEAN	STD. DEVIATION	STD. ERROR	95% CONFIDENCE INTERVAL FOR MEAN LOWER BOUND	UPPER BOUND	MINIMUM	MAXIMUM
SCORE 2 GROUP	1	10	1.90	.32	1.00E–01	1.67	2.13	1	2
	2	10	1.90	.57	.18	1.49	2.31	1	3
	3	10	2.00	.00	.00	2.00	2.00	2	2
	Total	30	1.93	.37	6.67E–02	1.80	2.07	1	3

ANOVA

		SUM OF SQUARES	df	MEAN SQUARE	F	SIG.
SCORES 2	Among Groups	6.66E–02	2	3.333E–02	.237	.791
	Within Groups	3.800	27	.141		
	Total	3.867	29			

number of participants minus 1. In this hypothetical example there were 10 participants per experimental condition, for a total of 30. Thus, there are 29 total degrees of freedom. These are then partitioned into two subsets, with two being assigned to the among-groups source of variation (3 groups minus 1 = 2) and the remaining 27 being left to the within-groups variation (error). The *mean square* (MS), which is also the variance, is the sum of squares divided by the degrees of freedom. Note that the variance is so small here that exponential notation must be used. (Since the sums of squares can be calculated by multiplying the mean square by the degrees of freedom, some computer programs omit the sums of squares column.) The next column is the obtained *F*-value. As shown earlier, this is calculated by dividing the mean square associated with the among-groups source of variation by the mean square associated with the within-groups source of variation. Finally, the level of probability is printed. This is the significance level with which to associate the *F*-value.

Obtaining a one-way ANOVA from SPSS begins with selecting "Analyze" on the command bar and then selecting "Compare Means." The "One-way ANOVA" is then selected and the next window asks the dependent variables (you can analyze more than one dependent variable at a time) and the factor—the independent variable you are testing. One option you need to check is "descriptives," which gives you the top portion of the printout and allows you to visually examine the pattern of means for each level of the independent variable (we will examine *post hoc* options later).

Table 15.7 illustrates an example of a hypothetical significant one-way ANOVA. Note that the mean square among groups is 7.90 and the mean square within groups is much smaller, 1.074. Thus, the calculated *F*-value of 7.355, with 2 and 27 degrees of freedom is significant at beyond the .05 level (.003 is much smaller than .05). This is interpreted as meaning that differences among the means shown in the cells of the experiment are so large that they could have been obtained by random chance in fewer than 3 cases in 1,000. An examination of these means intuitively supports this interpretation. Assuming the hypothetical data represent responses to a 5-point scale, mean differences of between 1 and 4 scale points seem quite large. Thus, it is highly *probable* that the results of the experiment are *not* a result of sampling error. They do generalize to the population.

The differences shown in Table 15.6 are not statistically significant. Note that the mean squares among and within are identical; that is, the variances within and among conditions are equal. Thus the *F*-value is 1.0. Again, this is consistent with an examination of the cell means that are shown below the ANOVA table. They differ only by fractions of a scale point. Note that the ANOVA table, by itself, does not reveal which cells have higher scores, or which cells are significantly different from each other. ANOVA source tables and tables that show cell means are necessary to interpret the results of the experiment.

TABLE 15.7   Significant One-Way Analysis of Variance Output—SPSS Base

DESCRIPTIVES

			N	MEAN	STD. DEVIATION	STD. ERROR	95% CONFIDENCE INTERVAL FOR MEAN — LOWER BOUND	95% CONFIDENCE INTERVAL FOR MEAN — UPPER BOUND	MINIMUM	MAXIMUM
SCORE	GROUP	1	10	2.20	.92	.29	1.54	2.86	1	4
		2	10	3.50	1.27	.40	2.59	4.41	2	5
		3	10	3.90	.88	.28	3.27	4.53	2	5
		Total	30	3.20	1.24	.23	2.74	3.66	1	5

ANOVA

		SUM OF SQUARES	df	MEAN SQUARE	F	SIG.
SCORE	Among Groups	15.800	2	7.900	7.355	.003
	Within Groups	29.000	27	1.074		
Total		44.800	29			

Multiple Factor ANOVA

In Chapter 13 we introduced the notion of the factorial experiment—an experiment with two or more independent variables—and gave examples of the various factorial designs, such as the 2×2, 3×2, and $2 \times 2 \times 2$. We showed how the results of such experiments are interpreted, in part, by examining the patterns of the means obtained, and further, how graphs help display these patterns visually. We say "in part" because the patterns of means provide descriptive statistics only. As with the one-way ANOVA, we still do not know if these patterns are a result of our manipulations of the independent variables or, alternatively, of sampling error. Factorial ANOVA is the statistical tool that helps us decide whether we can make inferences from the patterns of means observed in the sample *to the* population from which the sample was drawn. Like the one-way ANOVA, the factorial ANOVA is based on the idea that the total variance of a data set can be divided into component parts. However, the factorial ANOVA has more parts. An ANOVA with two independent variables has the following components contributing to the total variance:

$$V_{total} = V_A + V_B + V_{A \times B} + V_{error}$$

As can be seen from this conceptual formula, the error variance still comes last, but the between-group variance has now been divided into (1) the variance associated with variable A, (2) the variance associated with variable B, and (3) the variance associated with the interaction of variables A and B. A factorial ANOVA table reflects these increased sources of systematic variance, but otherwise is conceptually similar to a one-way ANOVA table. The only difference is that there are two or more (depending on the number of independent variables) additional sources of systematic variation.

Suppose, for instance, that you hypothesized that a press release written in moderately intense and active style (public relations style) would be more accepted than one written from a journalistic style (low intensity and passive style). Further, you hypothesized that including a photo of the writer would increase message acceptance. Your study has two main effects (*message*, PR or journalistic style, and *photo*, included or absent). You create a message and alter its language intensity and tense to create the PR or journalistic style and then duplicate it as if it were a newspaper clipping with either a photo of the writer or no photo. You then randomly distribute the "clipping" to 40 people who complete an instrument designed to evaluate its acceptance on a scale of 1 (low) to 100 (high).

Obtaining the ANOVA in SPSS requires that you select "Analyze" from the command bar, then "General Linear Model" (on some older packages you would select "ANOVA") and "Univariate". This opens a new window, where you indicate your independent variables and their levels (1 or 2, for PR or journalist and photo or no photo) and the dependent variable. You also select "Means and counts" from "Options" to produce the cell means table for interpretation of the ANOVA statistics.

Table 15.8 shows a source table for a 2 (message) $\times$ 2 (photo) factorial design experiment, which contains the results of a 2×2 ANOVA. The within-groups source of variation remains unchanged from the one-way ANOVA error—the numbers in this row still reflect the variance of scores within each individual cell. However, the between-groups variance that characterized the one-way ANOVA has now been divided into three parts. The independent variable *message* can be a source of dependent variable variation.

TABLE 15.8   ANOVA Output with Post Hoc Comparisons—SPSS Base

ANOVA

CASE PROCESSING SUMMARY[a]

CASES

INCLUDED		EXCLUDED		TOTAL	
N	PERCENT	N	PERCENT	N	PERCENT
40	100.0%	0	.0%	40	100.0%

[a] EVAL by MESSAGE, PHOTO

CELL MEANS[a]

		EVAL	
MESSAGE	PHOTO	MEAN	N
1	1	90.50	10
	2	83.20	10
	Total	86.85	20
2	1	77.70	10
	2	51.20	10
	Total	64.45	20
Total	1	84.10	20
	2	67.20	20
	Total	75.65[b]	40

[a] EVAL by MESSAGE, PHOTO

[b] Grand Mean

ANOVA[a]

			HIERARCHICAL METHOD				
			SUM OF SQUARES	df	MEAN SQUARE	F	SIG.
EVAL	Main Effects	(Combined)	7873.700	2	3936.850	90.283	.000
		MESSAGE	5017.600	1	5017.600	115.068	.000
		PHOTO	2856.100	1	2856.100	65.499	.000
	2-Way Interactions	MESSAGE* PHOTO	921.600	1	921.600	21.135	.000
	Model		8795.300	3	2931.767	67.234	.000
	Residual		1569.800	36	43.606		
	Total		10365.100	39	265.772		

[a] EVAL by MESSAGE, PHOTO

(continued)

TABLE 15.8 Continued

ONEWAY

ANOVA

		SUM OF SQUARES	df	MEAN SQUARE	F	SIG.
EVAL	Among Groups	8795.300	3	2931.767	67.234	.000
	Within Groups	1569.800	36	43.606		
	Total	10365.100	39			

POST HOC TESTS

MULTIPLE COMPARISONS

DEPENDENT VARIABLE: EVAL
LSD

(I) GROUP	(J) GROUP	MEAN DIFFERENCE (I – J)	STD. ERROR	SIG.	95% CONFIDENCE INTERVAL	
					LOWER BOUND	UPPER BOUND
1	2	7.30*	2.953	.018	1.31	13.29
	3	12.80*	2.953	.000	6.81	18.79
	4	39.30*	2.953	.000	33.31	45.29
2	1	–7.30*	2.953	.018	–13.29	–1.31
	3	5.50	2.953	.071	–.49	11.49
	4	32.00*	2.953	.000	26.01	37.99
3	1	–12.80*	2.953	.000	–18.79	–6.81
	2	–5.50	2.953	.071	–11.49	.49
	4	26.50*	2.953	.000	20.51	32.49
4	1	–39.30*	2.953	.000	–45.29	–33.31
	2	–32.00*	2.953	.000	–37.99	–26.01
	3	–26.50*	2.953	.000	–32.49	–20.51

* The mean difference is significant at the .05 level.

ONEWAY

ANOVA

		SUM OF SQUARES	df	MEAN SQUARE	F	SIG.
EVAL	Between Groups	8795.300	3	2931.767	67.234	.000
	Within Groups	1569.800	36	43.606		
	Total	10365.100	39			

POST HOC TESTS

MULTIPLE COMPARISONS

DEPENDENT VARIABLE: EVAL
SCHEFFE

(I) GROUP	(J) GROUP	MEAN DIFFERENCE (I – J)	STD. ERROR	SIG.	95% CONFIDENCE INTERVAL LOWER BOUND	95% CONFIDENCE INTERVAL UPPER BOUND
1	2	7.30	2.953	.126	–1.36	15.96
	3	12.80*	2.953	.002	4.14	21.46
	4	39.30*	2.953	.000	30.64	47.96
2	1	–7.30	2.953	.126	–15.96	1.36
	3	5.50	2.953	.340	–3.16	14.16
	4	32.00*	2.953	.000	23.34	40.66
3	1	–12.80*	2.953	.002	–21.46	–4.14
	2	–5.50	2.953	.340	–14.16	3.16
	4	26.50*	2.953	.000	17.84	35.16
4	1	–39.30*	2.953	.000	–47.96	–30.64
	2	–32.00*	2.953	.000	–40.66	–23.34
	3	–26.50*	2.953	.000	–35.16	–17.84

* The mean difference is significant at the .05 level.

HOMOGENEOUS SUBSETS

EVAL

SCHEFFE[a]

GROUP	N	SUBSET FOR $\alpha = .05$ 1	SUBSET FOR $\alpha = .05$ 2
4	10		
3	10	77.70	
2	10	83.20	83.20
1	10		90.50
Sig.		.340	.126

Means for groups in homogeneous subsets are displayed.

* Uses Harmonic Mean Sample Size = 10.000.

The independent variable *photo* can also be a source. (As noted in Chapter 13, these are called *main effects*.) Finally, the *interaction* of variables A and B can be a source of variation. Thus, there are three different tests of statistical significance in this table. In this example all obtained significant F-values ($F_{[message]}$ = 90.283, df = $1_{[between]}$; and $36_{[within]}$; $F_{[photo]}$ = 115.068, df = $1_{[between]}$; and $36_{[within]}$; $F_{[interaction]}$ = 65.499, df = $1_{[between]}$, and $36_{[within]}$. Note that these results are consistent with the cell means. Message has main effect means of 90.50 and 83.20, a difference of 7.30 points. Photo main effect means are 77.70 and 51.20, a difference of 26.50. Examination of the individual cell means reveals that the magnitude or the direction of the effect of one variable varies with the level of the other variable with which it is combined. Thus, it makes sense that interaction effects were revealed in the ANOVA. Note that to interpret the results of an ANOVA fully requires both an examination of the ANOVA source table *and* an examination of a table of means. The question remains, however, as to which cell means are truly different, this test requires a second step.

A Priori and Post Hoc Tests of Pairs of Cell Means

In a complex experiment in which there are three or more experimental conditions, it is frequently necessary to conduct tests of statistical significance between pairs of cell means. Suppose, for example that we conduct an ANOVA and the results indicate overall significance. How do we know which of the group means, if any, are significantly different from the other. If, before the data were collected, we had specifically predicted that one cell will differ from another, we can conduct an *a priori* test, a planned comparison to see if the two means differ in the population. Planned comparisons are liberal tests in the sense that they minimize the likelihood of Type II error (falsely accepting the null hypothesis) and maximize the likelihood of Type I error (false rejection of the null hypothesis). Because we had a theory, a hypothesis, that predicted which cell means would differ from which other cells, we can use procedures that maximize our chances of obtaining significant results for a given comparison.

Multiple Comparison Tests

A priori *t*-test: The *t*-test is the most liberal *a priori* test. As noted earlier, however, the *t*-test is limited to two levels of an independent variable. One further limitation is the assumption that it is an independent test—that is, when you employ the *t*-test, it has as an assumption that the test is only being run *once*. So, if you have a comparison between Cell A and Cell B, then between B and C, you have already tested B's value. In our example the main effects approximate the *t*-test, but the interaction has *four*, not two cells, thus the *t*-test is not appropriate.

Post hoc, or *multiple comparison*, tests are appropriate when specific differences between cell means are not predicted ahead of time; rather, the researcher wants to examine several, or even all possible cell mean comparisons. The number of comparisons possible is calculated by the now familiar formula: $n(n-1) \div 2$, where n is the number of experimental conditions or cells. Thus, in the three-group experiment there are three possible comparisons: group 1 versus group 2; group 1 versus group 3; group 2 versus group 3, or [3 (3 − 1)]

÷ 2 = 3 comparisons. For a 3×2 factorial experiment, there would be 6 cells and 12 possible cell mean comparisons—$[6(5-1)] \div 2 = 12$; for a $3 \times 2 \times 2$ factorial experiment there are 12 cells and 55 possible comparisons—$[12(12-1)] \div 2 = 55$.

Since achieving the .05 level of significance means that an observed outcome could be a result of sampling error in 1 case in 20, if we conducted 100 t-tests of significance, we would expect about five significant results by chance alone. Clearly, we are in grave danger of committing Type I error in such a case—of thinking we have found a significant relationship when actually we have found sampling error. This problem is addressed by using more *conservative* tests whenever we are conducting post hoc or multiple comparisons. These tests, if properly applied, can provide us with what is called **experiment-wise error protection**. Experiment-wise protection means that we can be sure that no matter how many multiple, post hoc comparisons we conduct, the chance that any *one* of them will be statistically significant is still .05. We are protected against Type I error. However, the price of conducting many post hoc tests, and thus having to use these conservative tests, is the increased probability of Type II error—of failing to identify mean differences that actually *are* indicative of mean differences in the population. Therefore, theory should be used to make a priori predictions whenever possible.

Although discussions of the various post hoc tests are beyond the scope of this book, many computer packages offer the researcher several alternative ways to test for differences between cells; therefore, a short discussion of what is offered may help to understand and interpret the output of the ANOVA.

Only after obtaining a significant interaction effect, you would run a one-way ANOVA. Obtaining the one-way ANOVA is no different than before, except you must make another decision—which multiple comparison test to use. The most liberal is the Student-Newman-Keuls (S-N-K) test (it will find differences between cell means if any are there, but is open to Type I error). The most conservative (it protects from Type I error and is very rigorous—the cell means must really be different) is the Scheffe. The LSD offers some Type I and Type II protection; it is more conservative than S-N-K, but more liberal than Scheffe.[4]

Since you had hypothesized an interaction effect, you also planned for the appropriate multiple comparison analysis. With most computer packages you have to do one of two things—either code the interaction term into one variable with four levels or use the compute statement and create a new variable. Of the two options, the former is easier. The four cells and their means in our "clipping" study are represented on the next page, with cells identified as "groups" 1 (photograph, PR active message) through 4 (no photograph, journalistic passive message).

After the one-way ANOVA table has been produced, most computer packages will list the cell means and indicate which are significantly different from the others. Table 15.9 demonstrates the output from three such tests. The cells are identified in a matrix format and those cells that differ significantly from each other are indicated by an asterisk (*). As indicated, all four cell means in our "clipping" example are significantly different in the S-N-K analysis; in the LSD analysis cells 2 and 3 do not differ significantly; and in the Scheffe analysis, not only are cells 2 and 3 nonsignificant, but also cells 1 and 2 (the Scheffe output also provides a visual indication of which cells are "homogeneous," or not different). Thus, in interpreting our "clipping" study we could say that both message style and inclusion of

TABLE 15.9   Output for a Dunnett's Control Group Comparison—SPSS Base

ANOVA

		SUM OF SQUARES	df	MEAN SQUARE	F	SIG.
EVAL	Between Groups	8804.120	4	2201.003	58.949	.000
	Within Groups	1680.200	45	37.338		
	Total	10484.320	49			

POST HOC TESTS

MULTIPLE COMPARISONS

DEPENDENT VARIABLE: EVAL
DUNNETT (TWO-SIDED)[a]

					95% CONFIDENCE INTERVAL	
(I) GROUP	(J) GROUP	MEAN DIFFERENCE (I – J)	STD. ERROR	SIG.	LOWER BOUND	UPPER BOUND
1	5	15.90*	2.733	.000	8.98	22.82
2	5	8.60*	2.733	.010	1.68	15.52
3	5	3.10*	2.733	.619	–3.82	10.02
4	5	–23.40*	2.733	.000	–30.32	–16.48

* The mean difference is significant at the .05 level.

[a] Dunnett *t*-tests treat one group as a control, and compare all other groups against it.

Message

		PR/Active	JN/Passive
Photo	Photo	1 90.50	2 83.50
	No Photo	3 77.70	4 51.20

MINI-PROJECT:

Conduct a survey of freshman and senior communication majors regarding their attitudes toward research methods classes in the major. Ask each their student classification and their intended areas of study (divide it arbitrarily between mass and non-mass communication either by academic major or intended occupation, include non-majors as "other"). Code the data into the computer and conduct the appropriate parametric analyses to test the hypothesis that senior communication majors will be more favorable to the class than will be freshmen majors, who will be more favorable than non-major freshmen.

a photo makes a difference in message acceptance (S-N-K), or we could say that for *some* combinations there are significant differences in message acceptance.

In Chapter 13 we noted that there is a special post hoc test for control group comparisons. The Dunnett's *t*-test tests each cell mean against the control group's mean in a way that protects the analysis from Type I error. SPSS's one-way ANOVA lets you conduct this analysis. Suppose that you had a control group in the "clipping" study. Participants in this condition would receive no message at all, just the evaluation of message topic. The output is found in Table 15.9. All four groups were significantly different than the control, with the passive/no photo group evaluating the message lower than the control.

APPLYING KNOWLEDGE IN COMMUNICATION

The use of inferential statistics in communication research has increased in recent years. This increase is a function of two things: an increasing sophistication in communication *theory* and the advent of the personal computer. When the discipline was just asking questions about communication use, descriptive analyses were appropriate; however, as communication researchers developed theories of communication variables and communication effects, their testing of hypotheses of magnitude and direction differences required them to move to inferential tests. As theories became more sophisticated, so, too, did the statistical analyses. Researchers now test the interactive effect of communication variables on a multitude of dependent variables, requiring the use of multifactor analysis of variance and other advanced statistical tools.

Finally, it should be noted that inferential statistics are sometimes used outside of "academic" research. Much of what we see in the "real world" application of communication research, however, does not include reporting the inferential statistics. If the results were not significant, some companies and organizations will be reluctant to release accurate findings. What inferential statistics gives the communication researcher is a degree of confidence that the results were due to the theoretical presence of the independent variable(s) in his or sample. When reporting simple descriptive statistics for a client—whether they be from a survey, content analysis, focus group, or experiment—the ability to say with confidence that the differences found are real comes from the inferential analyses. As one of your authors tells his students—when your boss asks you how sure you are that your results reflect the population, you can be 95, 99, or 99.9 percent certain, depending on the level of significance you established in your analyses. If your job was on the line, wouldn't you want to be at least 95 percent sure that what you reported was not due to some type of error?

SUMMARY

This chapter introduced the concepts of inferential statistical analysis. We noted that inferential statistics go one step further in analyzing the data collected in research, allowing the researcher to test whether the sample's results are indicative of the larger population from which it was drawn.

We began with a general discussion of what inferential statistics do. We then examined the related concepts of hypotheses, probability, and error. Hypotheses, null and otherwise, and research questions were examined in light of inferential analysis; probability was reexamined, and Type I and Type II error were discussed. With these interrelated concepts in mind, the logic behind the statistical table was discussed with the concepts of critical values, tabled values, and degrees of freedom explored.

Nonparametric and parametric inferential statistics were then covered. We began with an examination of the Chi-square statistic as a way of examining univariate (one-sample) and bivariate (two-sample) nonparametric research. We then examined Analysis of Variance and a priori and post hoc multiple comparisons as analytical procedures for parametric tests of differences, both in terms of the one-way ANOVA (univariate) and the multiple factor ANOVA (bivariate and multivariate). This chapter introduced more advanced analysis techniques. Remember that this is an introductory treatment of a complex area. An in-depth understanding of the assumptions discussed earlier, the various nonparametric and parametric statistical analyses, and more advanced statistics (such as multiple regression and multivariate analysis of variance) require other courses.

PROBES

1. What is the purpose of the null hypothesis? Why do we test it?

2. How do hypotheses and research questions differ in the way probability operates in the use and interpretation of inferential statistics? Is it important to let the readers of research know whether the test statistic was tested one-tailed or two-tailed? Why?

3. What is the relationship between Type I and Type II error? Why are researchers concerned with both types of error? How does each affect the way in which we can interpret research

findings? How can we control for Type I error in our design considerations?

4. What types of research are *best* analyzed via nonparametric analyses in your area of interest? Why? Can you think of any univariate and bivariate examples from the research you have read? Are they used appropriately? Why or why not? What limitations exist in analyzing nonparametric data? Why are they limitations?

5. What types of research are *best* analyzed via parametric analyses in your area of study? Why? When might you want to use a *t*-test?

Why a *t*-test instead of an Analysis of Variance? When should we use a multiple comparison test? When might a researcher use a liberal multiple comparison test? Why? What is the major difference between a post hoc and an a priori test? Why might a conservative researcher, even when an a priori test might be appropriate, choose to test for significance between means with a post hoc test like Scheffe?

RESEARCH PROJECTS

1. A shortcoming of some communication research is a failure to account for differences in gender or ethnicity as an independent variable. Find a fairly simple published research study and conduct it again; this time, however, include the participant's gender as an independent variable and see if the interaction between gender and the tested independent variable becomes significant and what that does to any conclusions drawn from the study.

2. This project examines the use/misuse of control group comparisons. First, conduct a literature review to see how many experimental studies actually use the appropriate control group comparison (Dunnett's *t*-test) and how many use the most liberal (S-N-K) method. Second, conduct a simple 2 × 2 factorial experiment and include a control group in your design. (You could use gender as one variable and dichotomize scores on another measure for your independent variables.) Code the data, enter it into the computer, and then analyze your results appropriately (ANOVA, one-way with Dunnett's *t*-test) and inappropriately (ANOVA, one-way with S-N-K).

3. Use your research and statistical abilities to help a student group or club with collecting and analyzing data for a class or competitive proj-ect. If you have an advertising or public relations major, then there should be an AD GROUP or PRSSA chapter, both of which may participate in national competitions requiring research. If not, check with the campus radio or television station and see if they have a project that could use your expertise. Design, run, and conduct the appropriate analyses for them and write up a report (see Chapter 17) that they will understand.

SUGGESTED READING

Kerlinger, F. N. (1986). *Foundations of behavioral research*, 3rd ed. New York: Holt, Rinehart & Winston.

Kirk, R. E. (1968). *Experimental design procedures for the behavioral sciences*. Belmont, CA: Brooks/Cole.

Williams, F. & Monge, P. (2001). *Reasoning with statistics: How to read quantitative research*, 5th ed. New York: Holt, Rinehart & Winston.

NOTES

1. Kerlinger & Lee (2000), notes, however, that this "advantage" really is not a reason for using nonparametric analysis. He suggests that any time variances from groups drawn randomly from a population are greatly different, nonparametric analysis is just as prone to error as is parametric analysis.

2. For a more in-depth discussion, see Kerlinger (1986), pages 158–159, or Williams & Monge (2001), pages 138–139.

3. For an excellent example of the use of the chi-square statistic, see Michael J. Beatty (1987).

4. For an excellent review of these tests, see Hays (1963), Winer (1971), Kirk (1968), and Kerlinger & Lee (2000).

REFERENCES

Beatty, M. J. (1987). Communication apprehension as a determinant of avoidance, withdrawal, and performance anxiety. *Communication Quarterly, 35,* 202–217.

Hays, W. (1963). *Statistics.* New York: Holt, Rinehart & Winston.

Kerlinger, F. N. & Lee H. B. (2000). *Foundations of behavioral research,* 4th ed. New York: Holt, Rinehart & Winston.

Kirk, R. E. (1968). *Experimental design procedures for the behavioral sciences.* Belmont, CA: Brooks/Cole.

Norusis, M. J. (2000). *SPSS for Windows Base System User's Guide.* Englewood Cliffs, NJ: Prentice-Hall.

Williams, F. (1992). *Reasoning with statistics: How to read quantitative research,* 4th ed. New York: Holt, Rinehart & Winston.

Williams, F. & Monge, P. (2001). *Reasoning with statistics: How to read quantitative research,* 5th ed. New York: Holt, Rinehart & Winston.

Winer, B. J. (1971). *Statistical principles in experimental design,* 2nd ed. Chicago: McGraw-Hill.

CHAPTER SIXTEEN

APPLICATIONS OF COMMUNICATION RESEARCH

OBJECTIVES

By the end of this chapter you should be able to:

1. Understand how to conduct a small applied communication or marketing study.
2. Understand how the principles of communication science apply in everyday life.
3. Understand focus groups well enough to the point that you could conduct a study using this method.
4. Explain the strengths and weaknesses of case studies as a research and teaching tool.
5. Identify biased survey questions.
6. Explain why there is no machine that will reveal if someone is lying or telling the truth.
7. Explain why comparisons are fundamental to science and to human reasoning.
8. Know when to be skeptical of claims.

We hope that you have gained some measure of mastery of communication research.[1] What good is this mastery? In this chapter we hope to answer that question. Ideas as an end in themselves can be beautiful, but for the college graduate in the twenty-first century, value is placed on a person's ability to process and analyze information. This chapter presents two contexts in which you can use what you have learned: (1) at work as you make your living; and (2) away from work, applying critical thinking skills as you process information from the media and elsewhere. Ultimately, the goal of this chapter is to illustrate the ways in which communication research can improve our lives in the many roles we play, as consumers, voters, workers, parents, friends—as concerned, constructive, and happy people. As you read about the application of communication research on the job, you may become a better consumer of information and vice versa. This chapter is a collage of the interrelationships between science, the methods and techniques presented, and critical thinking in life's many arenas, because we believe scientific thinking affects all aspects of the human experience.

CONDUCTING COMMUNICATION RESEARCH ON THE JOB

Realistically, if a person with a degree in the communication field becomes involved in empirical social research on the job, it is probably going to be in what is generally called "marketing research." It is highly likely that you will need to understand the results of marketing research conducted by others, or quite possibly, you might conduct marketing research—applied communication research—yourself. Marketing research is simply empirical research of any sort, including the use of topics and methodologies presented in this book, for a commercial purpose. Its goal is specific, whereas scientific research has as its goal the development of theories that will create the potential to explain, predict, and control human behavior to improve the human condition. The goal of marketing research is to find out what goods and services consumers want and how to design messages to persuade them to spend money and/or time. Simply put, *marketing* is bringing sellers (be they commercial or public service) and buyers together. Marketing *research* is figuring out how to do this. As Zimond and d'Amnico (2000) put it,

> The basic function of bringing marketers (suppliers) together with consumers (buyers) cannot be accomplished without communication. . . . Effective marketers carefully select both message and media when they communicate the value of what they offer to potential customers. (pp. 7–8)

How does the marketer "carefully select" messages and media? Research.

Marketing research involves the same tools as standard scientific communication research. The terminology may be different, but the principles remain the same. Instead of generating propositional statements about the relationship between abstract variables to generate knowledge that has widespread applications, the goal of the marketing researcher is to generate statements that apply to a specific product or service and specific audience or consumer.

There is very little in this book that applies to scientific research but does not apply to marketing research. Measurement reliability, for example, is fundamental and necessary to assess a participant's attitude towards a theoretical concept or to a brand of cereal or to a car. Intercept sampling, a nonprobability technique, has the same advantages and disadvantages in all kinds of research. For example, intercept sampling (a type of convenience sampling), such as stopping people as they exit a movie theater, would be a poor way to predict how the entire community felt about an upcoming election, but it would be an ideal way to find out how they felt about the movie they had just seen. As in communication science, the marketing researcher's methodology will be determined by the research question.

A marketing researcher would use the library and the Internet to find out what is already known about his or her product and its market and the ways it has been sold to consumers. The researcher might use qualitative research techniques such as in-depth interviews, unobtrusive field observations, or focus groups. He or she might conduct quantitative phone, face-to-face, or self-administered surveys, or the researcher might conduct a field or even a laboratory experiment. Let's begin with an example of a simple marketing experiment.

APPLIED EXPERIMENTS

One of the most famous marketing studies ever conducted was a laboratory experiment.[2] In the early 1930s, Cheskin asked participants, drawn from a pool of potential consumers, to evaluate identical products in different packages. One package featured triangles on the outside whereas the other had circles. Four-fifths (80 percent) of the participants preferred the product that came from a package with circles.

Other early experiments had participants try identical underarm deodorants presented in different color combinations. Although the deodorants were identical, results indicated that one color scheme was evaluated as having better fragrance, more effectiveness at controlling odor, and less skin irritation. A communication scientist might have conducted these same experiments, but circles, triangles, and color schemes would have been operationalizations of abstract concepts, and assessments of effectiveness would provide the means of measuring a theoretically important dependent variable. The interest would not be in the effects of circles, triangles, and colors *per se*, but in the relationships between the underlying theoretical constructs. The marketing researcher would want to know how to package the product in a way that maximizes its attractiveness to consumers.

Issues of control and random assignment are as critical to the internal validity of marketing experiments as to theoretical research. If the deodorant research was conducted on a college campus and residents of a men's dorm were given a deodorant with a brown color scheme while residents of a women's dorm were presented the product in a blue color scheme, it could be that women, in general, simply liked the product better; the color had no effect. The correct approach, as we learned in Chapter 12, would be to randomly assign all of the participants to the two conditions. If the sample size was large enough, random assignment would make the two groups reasonably similar in every way, including sex. About an equal number of men and women would end up with the deodorant in each color scheme. If differences in their preferences were observed, then this result could be confidently attrib-

■ ■ ■ ■ ■ ■

MINI-PROJECT:

Improve on Cheskin's simple two-group experiment by using a 2 × 2 factorial design, which is displayed in Figure 13.3. Your study could reveal the answers to many more questions than which color scheme was most appealing. You could simultaneously find out if males and females prefer different color schemes by randomly assigning all of the participants to one of four conditions. Design this experiment and imagine that you are a marketing researcher presenting your study to a potential client who may hire you to find out how to best package a new deodorant.

uted to the color scheme and not to an extraneous variable. You should recognize the flawed approach of using men's and women's dorms instead of random assignment, as explained in Chapter 12.

MARKETING RESEARCH AS A VIABLE CAREER

Marketing research is a *multi-billion dollar* a year industry in our multi-trillion dollar economy. We are not referring to *marketing*, which involves much more than research (advertising budgets, timely transportation of products, and so on); we are referring only to marketing *research*. Larger companies may have a marketing research department and rarely outsource a study. Small- to medium-sized firms may hire marketing research firms to do research, as needed, but they may occasionally conduct their own market research. Let us imagine for a moment that you work for such a firm.

CONDUCTING AN ON-THE-JOB MARKETING SURVEY

Let's suppose that in a few years you have a job in the marketing department of a small company. Perhaps your department consists of your boss and seven coworkers. Your boss has been instructed to provide information to the manufacturing division about how many widgets will be needed in the next year. Heretofore, your boss has hired marketing research firms to do this type of research. However, it would help the company and minimize costs if this question could be answered "in-house." Your boss's job, and yours, may depend on the accuracy of the answer. What are your options? How can you answer this question?

You would perhaps begin with archival research to see how many widgets were sold last year. Let's assume that your company sold 3,528 widgets last year, and thus far this year, they have been selling at a somewhat slower rate. It might be adequate to simply track sales and estimate the number you will need based on the archival and ongoing data. However, unsold widgets are expensive, so you certainly do not want to manufacture more than you will need. On the other hand, if a salesperson comes in with an order for 100 widgets late next year, you want to have them available. Yours is not the only company who makes this state-of-the art widget. How can you predict accurately the number you will need? A survey of your widget customers would probably be the best way to more accurately make this prediction.

Your boss comes in one morning and asks who in your work group would be willing to head up this small marketing study. If you raised your hand and asked, "What kind of sampling frame is available to us?" your boss would almost certainly be impressed that you had asked such a sophisticated question. You probably would soon be the person heading up this study and the rising star within your work group. Of course, what you have asked for is the actual list of potential customers, companies, and ultimately the people within them who could project their need for your product in next year.

It might be adequate to ask your sales people for their projections of widget sales. But they might have a social desirability response bias just like any respondent in any survey. They might overestimate sales to be sure that there were enough widgets available to fill their orders or for other reasons. If only 28 companies had bought all of the 3,528 widgets, a census would be feasible. (Of course, you would also try to ascertain if the customer base may be expanded.) You would contact key personnel at each of these companies and assess buying intentions for the next year. Common sense advice about clear unambiguous questions apply here, just as in scientific research.[3]

However, if 1,000 or more companies had bought your product, you may not have the resources to contact them all. You would probably want to draw a sample (a subset of the names on the sampling frame) and phone as many customers as your resources allowed. A table of random numbers could come in handy. If you had the resources to complete 100 interviews in the time allotted, a systematic random sample would work well. You could randomly choose one of the first ten names on the list and then call every tenth customer thereafter. Probability theory, and the attendant statistics, could be applied to estimate widget demand for next year. You would be wise to keep all of your data and next year compare the respondents' stated intentions with their actual purchases. In this way, over a number of years you may be able to develop a formula or model to adjust future survey results to increase prediction accuracy. The process could and does become quite sophisticated. You might, for example, discover that the number of widgets purchased each year when averaged with the findings of your survey resulted in increasingly precise predictions.

If you became a researcher with the necessary skills and tools to accurately predict product sales, in a few years you might soon be making twice as much money as a marketing researcher rather than an entry-level trainee. This research does not differ from scientific research other than the fact that different questions are being asked and answered. The material in this book and this course are useful in many jobs.

Knowledge of research methods can also be enormously valuable in evaluating applied research presented to you by others. If your firm had outsourced a marketing study, your ability to understand the results of that study and to identify its strengths and weaknesses could be highly useful employment skills.

FOCUS GROUPS: A MAJOR MARKETING RESEARCH TOOL

In Chapter 8, in the context of presenting various qualitative methods, we explained the use of *focus groups*. Whereas running formal focus groups is relatively rare as the sole methodology in theoretical research, it is frequently and increasingly the method of choice in marketing research. Because of its flexibility, simplicity, and sometimes low cost, the method is being applied to a wide range of research questions and goals. Focus groups may be used at the beginning stage of research to stimulate ideas about the possible solution to a problem or as a last stage to, for example, discuss the appeal of several different marketing strategies.

Because the method does not provide participants with preconceived categories in which to provide answers, the results of focus groups may be unexpected. This can be of great heuristic value in discovering things the researcher had not thought about.

The essential idea of the focus group is to bring groups of about five to fifteen participants from the relevant population together in a nonthreatening, relaxed atmosphere in which they will feel free to state their honest opinions. Their answers are usually recorded, and frequently transcribed, and analyzed for patterns and themes. Participants are often paid to participate ($20 to $100 for a two-hour session is not unusual). It obviously is going to require more incentive for some participants than others. College students may be perfectly happy to participate for $20 and a nice meal; a group of physicians might have to be flown to a vacation spot with their families by a drug company to obtain participation (a practice that has come under increased scrutiny in recent years due to the possibility that the trip may be an inducement for the doctor to view the drug favorably and therefore it may become the prescription recommended by the doctor for a particular medical problem).

Because the focus groups may be the only research method described in this book that you may use in a future job, we will illustrate the method by describing a focus group study in which one of us participated. This study will allow us to make a number of points about the applications and practical value of communication research.

THE UNEXPECTED: THE ARMY'S "BE ALL YOU CAN BE" CAMPAIGN

Between 1940 and 1973 the United States relied on a draft to obtain military service personnel. However, beginning in 1973, national policy has been to rely on an all-volunteer force to meet military staffing requirements. Thus military service advertising has become a part of American daily advertising fare. The U.S. Army spent more than $40 million in 1984 to attract volunteers. Most of the money was devoted to the most comprehensive and extensive advertising campaign ever used by the U.S. military, the army's "Be All You Can Be" campaign. The campaign, which emphasized rewards to the enlistee such as salaries, job training, adventure, self-actualization, and camaraderie, was perceived to be so successful that it lasted the entire decade of the 1980s, and after a break of several years, continued in the 1990s.

In the mid-1980s the army wanted to find out how they might be more successful at persuading active duty soldiers to reenlist, rather than having to continually attract and retain so many new recruits. The product being "marketed" was military service. They hired Professor Leonard Shyles to conduct research to find out how to sell their product to accomplish this objective. As Shyles and Hocking (1990) state:

> Focus groups were selected as the basic research method because of the flexibility offered in question design and follow-up, the in-depth qualitative nature of the data generated, and the potential for more one-on-one interviews. In addition, focus groups allowed respondents to describe their reactions and feelings in their own words, rather than in merely responding in prestructure categories created by the investigator. (p. 372)

Shyles used both probability and purposeful sampling to obtain a representative and feasible sample. First, in consultation with army researchers, twelve army bases were selected from four regions of the country (*purposeful*). A sampling frame of soldiers who were within 8 to 12 months of expiration of their term of service was created at each base (*purposeful*), and 45 names were selected at random off each list (*probability*). Thirty names were selected based on their availability to participate on the days that Shyles would be visiting a particular base (*purposeful*).[4]

"Finally, twelve focus groups, each with ten members, were formed. All twelve groups were asked about their reasons for joining the army, their uses of the media, and several other questions about their reenlistment plans" (Shyles and Hocking, 1990, p. 371). During a small part of the two-hour sessions the soldiers were shown six television advertisements, including the "Be All You Can Be" ads and an ad with another theme. After viewing the ads the soldiers were asked questions such as: "What are your feelings about these advertisements?" "How do Army TV advertisements compare to other advertisements?" "Do you think the advertisements present a realistic picture of the Army?"

Both Shyles and Hocking read all twelve transcripts which had been created directly off the taped discussions. There were no positive comments about the "Be All You Can Be" advertisements: The "Results" section of the paper consists of six pages of direct quotes from the respondents. The following are representative.[5]

- I yell at it. Because there are about three of [the Be All You Can Be Ads] that are in my MOS [military occupational specialty] and it's the biggest bunch of bull I've ever seen. (p. 374)
- I was highly upset [by the ads]. I'm still upset. (p. 374)
- When I see ads that offer opportunities in my MOS, they just depress me. (p. 375)
- They show stuff we don't ever have and we'll never get. We see stuff that's never gonna happen. (p. 375)
- The advertisements are true for some, but very very few. Percentage wise it'd be small. One percent. (p. 375)
- All the [Be All You Can Be] commercials are very deceptive, almost to the point of lying. (p. 376)
- Those commercials are a lot different from the way it is. People are getting buffaloed. (p. 376)
- The ones about education are false. (p. 377)
- Most of the commercials are lies. (p. 377)
- I came in to do telecommunication and I'm not doing that. As far as school, I was told that while in the Army you can go to school, you can take classes, but that's not true ... (p. 378)

The authors concluded that the "Be All You Can Be" advertising campaign was at best making claims that were *perceived* by active duty soldiers to be false.[6] The authors suggested that these ads may damage soldiers' morale and decrease the chance of reenlistment. Their "Implications" section provided advice to the Army and made an overt value judgment about the ads. Shyles and Hocking clearly differentiated between the data—the verbal responses of the soldiers—and their interpretations and opinions. So, there is a need to be careful here, because the line between results and interpretation can be fuzzy. A good consumer of a research report will look for this line as they critically process this information. Shyles and Hocking (1990) wrote:

> For both ethical and practical reasons, we feel that these results suggest a number of steps that the Army should consider. First, altering the [Be All You Can Be] campaign to make promises that are more consistent with what can reasonably be expected for most soldiers; and/or second, making more of a good-faith effort to deliver on the promises. Ethically, it is simply wrong to induce young Americans to join in the service of their country with misleading claims that are likely to be true for only a small portion of those who enlist . . . (p. 381)
> . . . if the Army persists in using offers of training in a specific field of interest, it is incumbent upon the Army to do more to make good on the advertised promises. (p. 382)
> Future recruitment advertisements should be designed with a concern for both effectiveness and honesty. (p. 383)

Soon after the research was published, Shyles received a phone call from a high-level executive in the advertising agency which designed the "Be All You Can Be" campaign. The firm, one of the world's largest, was not pleased. According to Shyles, a conversation in which the advertising executive wanted to know about every detail of the research ensued. The executive became increasingly angry.[7] The campaign involved tens of millions of dollars and near the end of the one-hour conversation the advertising executive demanded a retraction and threatened a lawsuit. Shyles offered to retract the article under one condition: that he be presented with two replications of the research conducted by independent scientists who had no financial interest in the outcome and which would be published in reputable peer-reviewed scientific journals. He went so far as to offer to conduct one of these replications at the ad agency's expense. The conversation ended abruptly, and not only were Shyles and Hocking not sued, neither researcher ever again received a communication from the advertising agency.

Soon thereafter the "Be All You Can Be" ads stopped running, and when the slogan appeared in ads some years later they were altered to include more qualifications and caveats. Words such as "may," "some," and "possible" had been added. This episode illustrates a number of important points about focus groups in particular and science and its applications more generally.

First, focus groups have more potential to find the unexpected than other kinds of research. In an experiment, only three results are possible: (1) A hypothesis that a particular independent variable will be positive or negatively related to a dependent variable may be correct; (2) there may be no relationship between these variables; or, (3) the variables may be related in the opposite way than that predicted by the hypothesis. The purpose of focus groups is not usually to test hypotheses, and that is the case with regard to the study described. The researcher had no idea that the "Be All You an Be" ads apparently angered soldiers, and the fact that they asked about reactions to the ads at all was only a small part of a much broader study. The Army had paid Shyles to "find out how we can get soldiers to reenlist," a wide-ranging question. Nearly 30 hours of discussion was transcribed, and the topics and opinions ranged far and wide. The negative attitudes toward the "Be All You Can Be" ads were completely unanticipated. This finding was interesting, useful, and a valuable surprise to the researchers, to the journal reviewers and editors, and potentially to the advertising agency, although the agency may not have agreed about the "value" of the results.

Second, focus groups are not usually complicated. Knowledge of special statistical tools or the ability to use computers played no role in the study. Feasibility is a concern for any researcher asking any research question. The most difficult task Shyles faced was obtaining access to soldiers, and the Army cooperated fully with him to find a sample from the relevant population. We do not mean to suggest that anyone, without training, can do high quality focus group research. However, this example should help show the feasibility of conducting useful applied empirical research. Anyone who has this book could conduct a study similar to that conducted by Shyles and Hocking (1990).

Third, many people view social research as lacking relevance. A commonly held belief is that research appears in obscure academic journals and few studies impact the real world in a meaningful way. The "Be All You Can Be" example shows the possibility of a significant effect of just one study. Even though the journal in which the research appeared, *Armed Forces and Society*, sits on few coffee tables, research that is published, that becomes part of public knowledge, is widely available and readily found. Shyles and Hocking published their study in 1990, before the Internet and before databases such as Lexis/Nexis and Psy Info were as nearby as your computers. Research published in the new millennium is much more easily found, a trend that is sure to continue.

Although it is tempting to conclude that this one article *caused* the suspension and subsequent changes in the "Be All You Can Be" campaign, you know that simply because one event preceded another in time it is not adequate evidence to conclude that the first caused the second. There is no control group against which to compare subsequent events. From the perspective of answering the question "Did this article temporarily stop and change the "Be All You Can Be" advertising campaign?" the research design is weak, an X followed by an O—a stimulus (*the published article*) followed by an observation, a measurement (*the suspension of the campaign*). The report of the research may or may not have influenced these outcomes—there is no way of knowing for sure—but the possibility is certainly there.[8]

Finally, this episode illustrates again the argument that empiricism provides a mechanism for providing the strongest possible evidence for answering questions of fact. Remember how quickly the phone conversation between Shyles and the advertising agency executive ended when Shyles suggested that the research be replicated? Shyles and Hocking quoted soldiers stating that the advertising agency and the Army appeared to be lying. Why were they willing to essentially state that the United States Army was lying? Hocking and Shyles (1990) had the data to back it up. The results of their research was clear-cut; the research itself and the underlying philosophy that places a high value on empiricism provides a very firm ground for making a claim. The article jeopardized a $40 million advertising campaign and, although the agency that designed that campaign was apparently angry about the article, they had difficulty arguing with the results of good research. It is our speculation that the advertising executive realized that the research results were correct and the last

---

MINI-PROJECT:

Find an interesting question that will help a local non-profit group such as a homeless shelter, animal shelter, or a college organization and set up a focus group to answer the question. Be as rigorous as possible at every stage: sample selection, appropriate inducements for participation, room set-up, facilitator training, question design, follow-up probes, and data analysis and conclusions. Present a report to the group.

---

thing he wanted was any more attention brought to the issue (or, perhaps, he did not have the skills of a communication researcher to evaluate information properly, unlike you).

APPLICATIONS OF COMMUNICATION RESEARCH AS AN AID TO CRITICAL THINKING: SCIENCE AND REASON

Science is much more than "a good way to find stuff out." Science, and how it applies to human behavior, is a way of thinking, a perspective, a way to view the world, a lens through which we can see, organize, and evaluate the ideas and information with which we are inundated.

Science is not the only way, nor necessarily always the best way of discerning knowledge, to be sure. Often authorities tell us what and how to think. Sometimes the Bible or Koran or our doctor or lawyer provide the bases for the choices we make, for the way we lead our lives. They are convenient and necessary means of knowing. However, empiricism and science differentiate us from our ancestors who burned witches and from some contemporaries who live in ignorance without the benefit of scientific methods. Ultimately, we believe that human reason, augmented by appropriate authority and reason, is how we should proceed to live our lives. Our purpose is to paint a picture of some of the ways that communication science can be applied as a useful thinking tool, an aid to critically processing information.

MINI-PROJECT:

Find archival data about the Army's actual use of the "Be All You Can Be" advertising campaign before and after the publication of the Shyles and Hocking (1990) study. Is there systematic evidence for our hypothesis that the article impacted the advertising campaign?

The single most important notion of human reasoning and of science is identical: the notion of a **comparison**. How will you know whether you have received a high grade in this class? A "92," an "A," a "70," or an "F" are meaningless by themselves. Only comparisons of your grade to the grades that others receive or with grades you receive in other classes provides meaning to your grade in this class. How do you know if this paragraph is dull or interesting? By comparing it to other paragraphs in this book, to paragraphs in your rhetoric or chemistry book, or perhaps by comparing it to the opening paragraph of *The Catcher in the Rye*.

How do we know if a manipulated (independent) variable in an experiment caused a change in the measured (dependent) variable? By comparing the scores of the dependent variable. The reasoning is identical, and this notion of comparison forms the core of critical human thinking. Integrating scientific thinking into our everyday lives might be viewed as simply "tightening up," so to speak, of the comparisons we make. By overtly acknowledging and thinking about the relevant bases for a comparison that fits a particular situation, we can become better critical thinkers.

We have emphasized the complementary nature of the humanities and science. The famous poem, "The Road Not Taken," by Robert Frost may help illustrate the importance of comparisons and control groups.

Two roads diverged in a yellow wood
And sorry I could not travel both
And be one traveler, long I stood
And looked down as far as I could
To where it bent the undergrowth;

Then took the other, as just as fair,
And having perhaps the better claim.
Because it was grassy and wanted wear;
Though as for that the passing there
Had worn them really about the same,

And both that morning equally lay
In leaves no step had trodden black.
Oh, I kept the first for another day!
Yet knowing how way leads on to way,
I doubted if I should ever come back.

I shall be telling this with a sigh
Somewhere ages and ages hence:
Two roads diverged in a wood, and I—
I took the one less traveled by,
And that made all the difference

Frost is a great poet, but a challenged social scientist. There is absolutely no way of ever knowing if traveling the less-traveled path had any effect on *anything*. No comparison is possible, so one can never know which path was better.[9]

You decided to go to a particular college or university. We hope you are happy with your choice. But if you are not, perhaps a good way to look at it is that things could be a lot worse. Each of our lives is a case study. Our sample size is one ($N = 1$), because we only have experience with one college; not many others. We do not know how things would have turned out if we had made different choices. Our lot could be better or worse than it is whenever we think, "I should have gone to the University of [other school you considered]." We should remember that we have no data with which to compare our outcomes. Russell Jones (1985) has called this the "unfounded implicit baseline comparison" fallacy. We choose simply to "love the one we're with," that is, to be happy with the choices we have made.

$N = 1$: CASE STUDIES AS A TEACHING TOOL

The notion of comparison is fundamental to all aspects of education, business, and life. A widely used teaching tool in communication, business, and other disciplines is the *case study*. Usually, a specific instance of a company or an organization is presented that has a serious problem. The technique involves exploring in detail how the company dealt with the problem. Examples of both bad and good outcomes are usually presented, the point being that actions taken by company A did not solve the problem, whereas those taken by company B did. The point is that when one is confronted with a similar situation, you should do what company B did. This is a fine pedagogical tool, and we do not mean to criticize it, except to emphasize that a case study is only as valuable as a real or imagined control problem with which to compare the single case being studied. Single case studies, like our lives, have no control group. A case study includes so many unique details that it is impossible to know which of them caused the outcome of interest. Case studies involve viewing situations holistically. We can only guess about what specifics contributed to the outcomes.

In Small Group Communication classes two case studies are frequently presented as a kind of quasi-experiment to illustrate the idea of Group Think. *Group Think* is the notion that pressures towards conformity, isolation, illusions of invulnerability, and other factors can cause groups to make bad decisions. The Bay of Pigs is presented as a bad decision by the group of men advising President John F. Kennedy in 1961. The United States supported covertly an invasion of Cuba by exiled Cuban dissidents that had disastrous consequences. The intent of the invasion, the overthrow of Fidel Castro, was not accomplished, many of the invaders were captured and killed, and President Kennedy appeared to many to be incompetent. At best, the incident was an embarrassment to him and to the United States. Many Small Group Communication books tell us that Group Think by Kennedy's group of advisors caused this bad decision.

In 1962, the Soviet Union began placing missiles with nuclear capabilities in Cuba that were within range of Washington, D.C. This incident is known as the *Cuban missile crisis* and was depicted in the movie *Thirteen Days*. The fact that we are alive and here reading and writing books is evidence that Group Think did not occur during the *Cuban missile crisis*—that avoiding group think resulted in a wise decision by essentially this same group of men. In the Cuban missile crisis, among other stops, outside advisors were brought in and members of the group were assigned the role of "Devil's Advocates" to emphasize potential flaws in any decision. Did the avoidance of Group Think save humankind during the Cuban missile crisis? No one really knows, but the example is considered useful only because a comparison is possible. We have a kind of quasi-experiment. The Bay of Pigs and the Cuban missile crisis were similar in some important ways—essentially the same men were involved, as were Cuba and John F. Kennedy—and therefore a comparison is possible. The same group of men worked together through similar situations (a national crisis) and seemed to use different decision-making techniques and obtained different outcomes. The fact that a comparison is possible adds enormously to the credibility of these events as support for the *Group Think* hypothesis.

Whenever a single case study is presented there is no control group. Perhaps the behaviors that are attributed to causing a positive outcome did so, but perhaps not. In addition, we do not know which of the many behaviors taken by the involved individuals had positive and negative effects. As noted, a case study involves a holistic presentation of a situation and how it was dealt with. A case study can be a wonderful pedagogical tool. It may help us to think about things in new ways. The case study may have great heuristic value. Case studies can help scientifically in that they may be a source of good hypotheses that can be tested using controls in a laboratory. However, science requires rigorous comparisons, and simple case studies that describe only one situation are not scientific research, except perhaps as a way to generate ideas for study.

In 1984, one of the most successful business self-help books ever written, *In Search of Excellence*, was published. The author, Tom Peters, presents a series of case studies of companies that had achieved *excellence*. He interviewed key executives at each firm and carefully "documented" why the company had achieved excellence. One of the companies was IBM. IBM, for years referred to as "Big Blue," was presented as the pinnacle of excellence. The message was clear: Do it the IBM way and excellence would result. Peters had no control group. His design was X (IBM Culture)–O (IBM's performance); no comparison was possible. He had evidence that IBM was a highly successful company; it had never laid off a worker, its stock value had never taken a significant sustained drop, and its profits had predictably and steadily increased. He also had a lot of qualitative data in the form of interviews with IBM managers—the book is one of the primary sources of the concept of "corporate culture."

Peters tell us that IBM had a "Culture of Excellence." The implication was that there was a causal relationship between IBM culture and IBM success. However, Peters had no control group. There were less successful companies that perhaps had different "cultures." But because these companies also differed in so many *other* ways from IBM, for example, they did not sell typewriters and computers, there was no way to confidently attribute their different levels of success to any one factor, including the "corporate culture" concept.

Peters notes in his book the stability of IBM's culture. Therefore, it is a pretty safe assumption that that same culture was around later when IBM nearly went bankrupt. Its stock went from about $175 to near $40. (Unexpected at the time, to be sure, but trivial when compared to Enron's breathtaking drop from $80 a share to 28 cents in less than a year.) IBM's 400,000 employees in the mid 1980s numbered less than 200,000 by the early 1990s. Whatever IBM was doing right and wrong, Peters seems to have missed it. Books like *In Search of Excellence* should be read critically. Scientific thinking or re-thinking can be applied very effectively as we consume this kind of information. "As compared to what?" is among the most profound questions ever asked. It is an especially good question to bear in mind when examining case studies, but we suggest you ask it often in other contexts as well.

SCIENCE AND THE MEDIA

A big part of how scientific thinking may be applied in our day-to-day lives is as consumers of research presented in the media. This has historically been more true of print media, but now with the proliferation of the Internet and 24-hour news channels, it is difficult, if not impossible, to go through a day, whether we read or not, without hearing information that requires mental energies to process.

Most of us believe in a general way that more of a good thing is better than less, and this certainly applies to sample size in survey research. A survey of 4,000 respondents would seem to be better than one with 400 respondents. Well, not always. As discussed in Chapter 10, an equally important concern is *how* the sample is selected. A probability sample, in which every respondent has the same opportunity of being selected, provides more valuable information than a sample in which participants *self-select*, that is, decide for themselves whether or not to participate. Consider the following example. The numbers are embellished and rounded but the study is real and the results were widely reported in the media in the late 1970s.

A researcher wanted to know how satisfied women were in their marriages and how faithful their husbands had been. She mailed about 100,000 survey questionnaires to married women and asked them questions about these issues. Now let's pretend that *you know* the answer to this question. You know the *parameter*, the percentage of women in the population whose husbands have cheated, and this number is 4 percent. Four percent of all adult married or formerly married women have caught their husbands having extramarital affairs and are consequently dissatisfied in these marriages.

Therefore, we know that most women, 96,000 of those who received the survey in the mail, or 96 percent, are satisfied with their marriages and have not caught their husbands in extramarital affairs. These potential respondents found the survey to be silly, treated it as junk mail, and discarded it as most people do with most junk mail. However, the other 4,000 respondents who *have* caught their husbands cheating are extremely interested that someone is finally studying something they know something about: marital infidelity. These respondents are pleased to take the trouble to answer the researchers' questions, voice their dissatisfaction, and tell the researcher about the jerks to whom they are or were married. They enthusiastically fill out the surveys and mail them back.

What did the results show? One hundred percent of women are dissatisfied in their marriages and the cause appears to be marital infidelity. (Note: We have exaggerated the percentages to make the point, but the actual research suggested that three-quarters of all husbands had cheated.) The sample size is 4,000! That seems impressive to noncritical consumers of this information. Many of these consumers may know that the outcome of elections in which over 100 million people vote are predicted with sample sizes about half that size: $N = 2,000$. The results of this sociologist's study were published in a book and widely publicized. She visited many talk shows discussing her findings, stating that most American wives were unhappy in their marriages and most husbands engaged in extramarital affairs. Her sample of 4,000 women said so!

Her findings were worse than worthless. They were harmful and may have caused a good bit of unjustified suspicion and marital strife. Some happy marriages may have been put at risk because of this egregiously bad research that was widely reported in the media.

If 4 percent was the real population parameter, we would be about 95 percent sure that a true probability sample of 4,000 would have found that about 4 percent (+/− 1 percent) of American women had cheating husbands and were dissatisfied in their marriages. Hopefully, even the most naive talk show host and viewer would question the extraordinarily high percentage of cheating husbands in the actual incident. But one never knows; as John Fogerty wrote in a sarcastic song about television, "I know its true, cause I saw it on TV."

A PARTICULARLY DANGEROUS AREA OF SURVEY BIAS: QUESTION WORDING

In Chapter 11 we emphasized the importance of question construction. Because of its importance we revisit the issue here. If a question is clear and unambiguous and asked the same way consistently, the answer is likely to be reliable. However, as noted in Chapter 6, a question may be highly reliable (i.e., repeated application yields the same results) but not valid (i.e., not measure what it purports to measure). A biased question, asked repeatedly, will yield similar answers. But biased questions may not reflect the true view of the respondent. Please consider the following examples.

- Do you believe that Yellowstone National Park should be expanded so that animals that roam off the park grounds during winter in search of food won't be slaughtered by waiting hunters?
- Do you believe that the rights guaranteed in the Constitution of the United States to sportsmen should apply in the areas around Yellowstone National Park?
- Do you think that a woman such as yourself, your sister, or your daughter should be allowed to choose whether or not to have children?
- Do you think that the Constitution should be amended to prevent the murder of unborn babies?

MINI-PROJECT:

Locate the book that describes this infidelity study ((Sherry Hecht) use your library skills) and obtain various media reports of the author's research and examine how her results were filtered and presented in magazines such as *Newsweek*, *Time*, *Cosmopolitan*, *Redbook*, and others. Prepare a short oral report for your class based on your findings.

MINI-PROJECT:

The bias in the example questions is fairly obvious. Can you write neutral questions about each of these issues? It can be quite difficult to write neutral questions, and biased questions are sometimes easier to write than neutral questions. In general, the less a respondent knows about an issue, the easier it is to write a question that will elicit the desired answer because the question can fill in the void of missing information, pointing the respondent towards the desired answer. Pick another issue and write biased and neutral questions about an important issue on your campus.

- Should the government do more or less to help children in our country from going to bed hungry?
- Should the government provide more or less money for people on welfare who refuse to work?
- Should the Constitution of our country be changed so that those who would burn that flag and desecrate the men and women who have died defending it may no longer do so?
- Should the First Amendment of the Constitution of the United States be changed to limit free speech?

As we discussed in Chapter 11, double-barreled questions that ask about two items in one question can easily be used to obtain biased answers. The bias results from combining an unpopular, or little-known feature, with a more popular one is even more problematic. For example:

- Should we increase defense spending on training our military service personnel so that they will be ready to fight and return alive, and on missile defense?
- Do you support cutting unnecessary pork barrel defense spending so the money can be used to support our men and women whose lives are at stake in the Middle East and our president?
- Do you support better training and support for police officers so that they may keep our city and streets safe from criminals, and longer sentences for dope users?

In addition to question wording, there are five more issues to be concerned with. When interpreting the results of a survey or poll there are at least five related questions that should immediately come to mind as we assess its validity:

1. Who paid for the research and by whom are the results being released?
2. Are the questions worded clearly and unambiguously?
3. Were the questions worded neutrally?
4. What was the sample size?
5. How was the sample selected?

SCIENCE, MYTHS, AND NONSENSE

The word "science" has been associated with all sorts of chicanery and outright hogwash. Science is obviously a loaded and powerful word. Some "science" is nonsense. The media present messages, for example, from infomercials, that tell us that this or that is true because science tells us it is so. We know of no better example of chicanery than the beliefs and claims made regarding the polygraph or "lie detector."

The media is full of stories that make reference to the polygraph, commonly thought of as a lie detector (e.g., "O.J. passed a lie detector test." "Jon Benet Ramsey's parents passed the test." ["An accused local pedophile] refused to take the test.") The notion that there is a specific response, either physiologically or behaviorally, that is a reliable and valid indication of whether someone is telling the truth or lying is perhaps one of the single most harmful myths remaining in our culture. This myth is akin to believing that a god throwing a spear is the cause of thunder.

A polygraph is widely known as a "lie detector." How accurate are polygraph exams at detecting lies? The answer very much depends on whom you ask. Although widespread use of the polygraph for such purposes as pre-employment screening have been outlawed for most jobs since 1988, use of the lie detector remains entrenched in police agencies, in the military, in the legal profession, and in the government. Even today, it is used on suspected terrorists, kidnappers, and financial consultants and it is suggested for use on senators (2002). Individuals who benefit from their existence state that the polygraph, when administered by a well-qualified *polygrapher* (the name of someone trained to administer the exam), is at least 98 percent accurate. Highly regarded polygraphers routinely claim 99 percent. The polygrapher for the Athens, Georgia, police department stated that he had conducted over 1,000 exams and had never made an error.[10] Testimony before a state legislature indicated that a polygrapher had administered 20,000 exams and never made a mistake. These claims are folly. One of the publications that has published many pro-polygraph articles over the years is titled, *Journal of Police Science and Administration?* (emphasis ours). The word "science" is most surely a misnomer in this context, but, as noted earlier, the word can have a powerful rhetorical effect. It adds credibility to the publication.

The space available here cannot begin to do justice to the harm and abuse that have resulted from the various uses of the polygraph examinations. A distinguished psychologist, David T. Lykken,[11] has worked for over forty years trying to understand all aspects of lie detection. His efforts are thoroughly described in his book, *A Tremor in the Blood: Uses and Abuses of the Lie Detector* (Lykken, 1998). This book should receive a Pulitzer Prize. It is must reading for anyone who has an association with lie detectors or polygraphs or has any interest in the topic, or for someone who would like to go on an intellectual joy ride while swooping to an understanding of how an entire society can be duped by pseudo "science." Lykken reviews virtually all known research about lie detection with brilliant scientific rigor. He concludes that there exists no credible evidence for the reliability or validity of the test and that the available good empirical evidence indicates that the test identifies liars from individuals who are telling the truth at about what would be expected by random chance. He states that "it is madness for courts or federal police or security agencies to rely on polygraph results" and that belief in the polygraph is "a deeply entrenched mythology that children come to accept along with Santa Claus and the Easter Bunny" (p. 279).

Lykken's book should be required reading by every lawyer in the country, starting with the Supreme Court of the United States.

Why does the polygraph myth—what the late Senator Sam Erwin called, "twentieth century witchcraft"—survive? It could have a lot to do with *money*, a topic to which we shall return. In exchange for a fee of $40,000, a former psychologist turned polygrapher tested John DeLorean (a famous case in the 1970s) and found him to be innocent of selling a large quantity of cocaine. The man who tested DeLorean was one of the most famous polygraphers in the world and is on record as stating that the polygraph is 100 percent accurate. Later, a "highly qualified FBI polygrapher" ("qualified polygrapher" is a wonderfully ironic oxymoron) who had witnessed videotapes of DeLorean accepting money for drugs found DeLorean to be "lying" when he administered the test.

Are the people who constitute the polygraph industry charlatans and bad people preying on the rest of us? No, they probably believe what they say. As Lykken explains in meticulous detail, polygraphers almost never receive objective evidence about the accuracy of their tests. They certainly do see many individuals who failed their exam found guilty of a crime and many who passed walk free. However, they almost never have access to "ground truth"—the way it really is. They have no way to know whether they are right or wrong. Writes Lykken of the polygrapher, "he (sic) is in the position of the astrologer who believes in what he is doing but almost never has a chance to actually test whether his predictions are correct or not" (p. 73). To anyone who has spent years of their lives believing in and administering polygraph exams, Lykken's book would be a tough read.

It should also be noted that although most members of the relevant scientific community agree with Lykken, there are some trained psychologists—social scientists—who believe the test has some value. The value may well be this: The polygraph can be a rhetorical tool, a device which may help elicit confessions from guilty suspects (and, sadly, even in some cases, from innocent ones as well). If a subject, or suspect, can be convinced that the test is infallible, that it is impossible to beat, and if the person is guilty (and especially if exhausted and frightened), the polygraph test can be an effective stage prop to elicit a confession.

The sad truth about the polygraph is that innocent people go to jail and lose jobs, marriages, or court cases because they have failed a polygraph exam. On the other side of the coin, rapists, murderers and spies go free because the exam shows them to be innocent. In fact, there was a recent case in which a member of the American Central Intelligence Agency (CIA) was able to sell vital national secrets to their Soviet, now Russian, counterparts, the KGB, for over twenty years because he had repeatedly passed polygraph exams (the Aldrich Ames debacle; if interested, simply type Aldrich Ames into any Internet search engine).

In the mid-1980s the United States Congress took a hard look at the polygraph industry and despite much testimony of the type described above—"20,000 exams, zero errors"—concluded the test so unreliable (and therefore, invalid) that they outlawed the then most widespread use of the polygraph: the *preemployment polygraph screening interview*. Oddly, the Employee Polygraph Protection Act, which was signed into law by President Ronald Reagan in 1988, exempts the government and certain businesses such as those involving security service firms from the prohibition of using the polygraph. If you understand the logic behind the fact that a pseudo-scientific practice ("twentieth century witchcraft") is so fraught with errors as to be outlawed, but the FBI *can and does* require its own agents to take the test, please contact us immediately so that we may include this information in the fourth edition of *Communication Research*. Lacking a law banning polygraphs, Professor Lykken recommends civil litigation by people who are wronged by polygraph exams. We recommend that you obtain his book, read it, and provide it and the evidence within as the reason for your refusal to *ever* submit to any polygraph exam.

MONEY, SCIENCE, AND THE MEDIA

Whenever large amounts of money are mixed with empiricism, you should be especially skeptical of the reported results. We would apply this suggestion to infomercials, to political polls paid for by politicians, to studies about nicotine addiction paid for by tobacco companies, to medical wonder drugs funded by drug companies, and even to the results of large publicly funded grants. Grants that fund research that get results, that make progress, are renewed. Dead ends are not. It costs money to do research, but when the researcher stands to make more money if the research turns out one way over another, pull that hat of skepticism down a little more tightly.

We have been preaching skepticism pretty hard. Please do not lose sight of the fact that the media can bring us both accurate and inaccurate information about scientific findings. On December 21, 2001, the Associated Press put out a story that stated that a group of three brothers, Drs. Cameron, Farr, and Ceana Nezhat, had been fired by Stanford University for falsifying research data. The doctors, gynecologists, had practices in Atlanta and California and were well known for developing high-tech, minimally invasive techniques to treat endometriosis and infertility in women. Endometriosis is a condition that causes infertility. The doctors used endoscopies, which employ instruments for visualizing the interior of hollow organs. One of the reasons the doctors were unusually well known is that for over a decade they had retained public relations firms to publicize their claim of near miracle results, primarily in magazines aimed at women in their thirties and forties. Woman from all over the country flew to Atlanta, and later, to Palo Alto, California, home of Stanford University, and paid fees in the $5,000 to $10,000 range for the one hour procedure. Detractors, other gynecologists, the doctor's peers, had attacked this procedure as dangerous and unethical for over a decade.

This incident illustrates two points that are relevant. First, the incident illustrates the potential that money has to taint scientific research. According to an article in *The American Lawyer* (Frankel, 2001), the doctors had a stake in a company that made a device called a "laparoscope." The purpose of the article with the fabricated data was to garner acceptance of the device by the medical community. The company subsequently sold for $40 million soon after the article appeared in 1992. Whenever large sums of money are at stake, depending on the results of empirical research, we believe special vigilance is appropriate.

Second, the incident illustrates the value of the public nature of scientific research. The three doctors fought for seven years to prevent the release of hospital records, claiming patient confidentiality, even though no patients were named in the records. Until the original data could be examined, allegations of scientific fraud remained merely allegations. The data were the records of 16 surgical procedures. Dr. Nicolos Spirtos, former head of Stanford University's gynecology department, examined these records expecting to find minor discrepancies between the article and the records. Spirtos states, "Oh my God, there isn't one match with what they published, They don't even have the ages right." The doctor's review of the article concludes: "When information was missing or did not fit [the Nezhats'] desired picture, it was invented or altered to provide readers with the impression that this experimental [medical] procedure could be safely performed and with minimal risk." In fact, the experimental procedure requires one patient to empty a sack attached to her body every time she relieves herself for the rest of her life, but the article states, "no complications" resulted. It is easy to see why the Nezhat brothers did not want the hospital records examined, and the case appears to be a perfect example of why we should be skeptical of research that provides the researcher with a financial incentive for certain results to be obtained or when the researcher refuses to provide the original research data on which the results are based. The results of research conducted by a researcher who refuses to produce the original data are also suspect.

One might wonder how such a case of abuse could escape investigative journalism for so long. Frankel (2001) states that all of the allegations and evidence had been sent to the producers of the top-rated investigative journalism TV show. However, the producer's wife had apparently been successfully treated by one of the brothers and they had subsequently become friends. As evidence was sent to the producer he sent it directly to his friend who turned it over to his lawyers, who, in turn, wrote threatening letters to each of 16 physicians who were prepared to testify against the Nezhats in a malpractice suit. The incident would seem to make an excellent case study for a class in media ethics.

The media had served the Nezhats' purpose, but ultimately also contributed to their downfall. They had employed public relations firms to publicize their practice. Small articles had appeared in women's magazines and the news weeklies touting their success.[12] However, it was the media who published allegations against the Nezhats, perhaps helping Stanford University to decide to appoint a blue ribbon panel to investigate the doctors. Ultimately, it was the media—the Associated Press—who reported the removal of the Nezhats from the Stanford faculty.

A FINAL WORD ABOUT MONEY

We will take small license and talk for a moment about the role that money plays in the larger purpose of this book: to help the reader become a more skilled and critical information

■ ■ ■ ■ ■

MINI-PROJECT:

Using your skills at using the Internet, archival research, and open records laws, read the article in *American Lawyer* (Frankel, 2001) about the Nezhat case and then trace how the media impacted the case. Should the Nezhats be practicing medicine? Would you allow these world-renowned surgeons to operate on you, your mother, sister, or daughter? What could have prevented these misdeeds by the researchers?

processor. The polygraph myth and the Nezhat story are clear examples of money influencing scientific information. However, money enters into other areas as well.

In Chapter 2 we mentioned that for several days after the space shuttle *Challenger* exploded in 1986, the government was collecting all available data in an inductive effort to find clues for the cause of the disaster and that there was open speculation that we would never know. We now know that the likely cause of this tragedy was well known by a small number of engineers and NASA officials from the moment of the explosion. Memos had been written by scientists and engineers begging that the launch be delayed until the clearly identified problem with the O-rings could be solved. However, those in charge of the "go" decision were under pressure to produce a successful launch as millions of school children watched. Concern for funding for NASA appears to be at the core of the decision to launch.

As we write this it is hard to ignore the disgrace of the bankruptcy of the Enron Corporation and other scandals involving corporations. Although it is unclear how the Enron and WorldCom scandals will unfold, we know a lot, and it is all in one way or another linked to money. We do know that one of the (formerly) most-respected accounting firms in the world, Arthur Anderson, certified Enron as being the seventh most valuable company in the country months before the company went bankrupt, and that Arthur Anderson was also receiving tens of millions of dollars in consulting fees from Enron.

Our point is to emphasize the role that money should play as we process information. The political scandal that will define twentieth century political chicanery will almost surely be Watergate. In the early 1970s, two reporters for the *Washington Post*, Bob Woodward and Carl Bernstein, were central in unraveling the Watergate case, which eventually led to the resignation of President Richard Nixon. Woodward and Bernstein had a mysterious source, named Deep Throat, guiding their inquiry. Over and over Deep Throat advised them to: "Follow the money."

We will conclude our applications chapter by adding one more rule of thumb to our question, "As compared to what?" This question is: "Who makes money?" When the answers to that question affects your life, we suggest you ask it often.

SUMMARY

In this chapter we have attempted to provide a mere glimpse at some of the ways that the methods presented in this book may actually be used. Our examples skim the surface of the potential that scientific thinking can contribute to our lives. Two questions emerged as having reoccurring pragmatic importance: "As compared to what?" and "Who makes money?"

There are few do's or don'ts or "can't miss" principles when it comes to processing incoming information and deciding what is true or false. The best advice we can offer is to arm yourself with as many tools of critical thinking as possible. A doctor who only had one diagnostic tool or knew how to do only one thing would not be allowed to practice medicine. Similarly, in this chapter we have attempted to show some of the ways that experiments, surveys, and focus groups can be applied to help us in our jobs and as concerned, constructive, happy citizens.

PROBES

1. What kinds of jobs could you obtain when you graduate in which doing research will help you succeed? For example, what percentage of the potential jobs will be easier to obtain if you can do focus group research? A survey? An experiment?

2. What have you been taught in other courses that have relied on case studies that perhaps should now be critically revisited?

3. Why do so many people still put a lot of faith in polygraph exams? Do you know anyone who has taken a polygraph examination? If so, how did it turn out? If polygraph exams are so inaccurate that they are illegal for most purposes, such as pre-employment interviews, how come the FBI still uses them to test their own agents?

4. What role did money play in the Enron scandals and WorldCom? Does money seem to be involved whenever there is a crime or a scandal? Do any recent scandals rival Enron, which went bankrupt in late 2001, and WorldCom, whose fraudulent bookkeeping was uncovered in mid-2002? Did any of the Enron executives who made, collectively, over a billion dollars selling their stock, have to give any of it back to the thousands of people and investment funds that lost billions of dollars? Did anyone go to jail or otherwise accept responsibility?

RESEARCH PROJECTS

1. How would you find out how to recruit young men and women to join the military if you were brought in as a communication consultant? What would you do and what would you subsequently advise? Role-play a meeting in which you try to sell the Army or Navy your services as an applied communication or marketing researcher.

2. Conduct an applied communication study to find out how a club on your campus can attract more members and student activity dollars.

3. Approach the Graduate or Undergraduate Coordinator of your department and interview him or her about how your department recruits students. Based on the information obtained in the interview, design a research project to find out how to help your department attract more students.

4. Approach the director of general studies courses such as "Public Speaking," "Interpersonal Communication," or "Introduction to Public Relations." Obtain permission to survey students in this class about their degree of satisfaction with the course and what changes should be made, if any. You could also use focus groups. Of course, you would want to be sure that if you had only one or two focus groups that each group had students from many different sections of the general studies course.

5. Go to the newsstand and browse current periodicals that have small reports of scientific research. Track down the original study on which the report was based, study it carefully, and critique the magazine's use of this research, as well as the original research itself. Bonus: e-mail the author of the article to obtain their opinion regarding whether they feel their research was accurately described.

6. Cheskin did a true two-group experiment in which he found that one color scheme was preferred by consumers of a deodorant over another. Design a 2×2 factorial experiment that manipulates both color scheme and some other aspect of the packaging (see Figure 13.3). Design a study that uses a 2×2 factorial design to improve on the one conducted by Cheskin.

7. Obtain a copy of Professor David Lykken's book on lie detection. Interview a police detective about the use of the polygraph and base some of your questions on what you learn from Lykken's book.

SUGGESTED READING

Bearden, W. O., & Netemeyer, R. G. (1998). *Handbook of marketing scales*, 2nd ed. Thousand Oaks, CA: Sage Publications.

Costa, J. A. & Bamossy, G. J. (Eds.). (1995). *Marketing in a multi cultural world*. Thousand Oaks, CA: Sage.

Crask, M., Fox, R. J., & Stout, R.G. (2002). *Marketing research: Principles and applications*, 2nd ed. New York: Wiley.

Edmonds, H. (1996). *AMA complete guide to marketing research for small businesses*. Lincoln, IL: NTL Business Books.

Gilovich, T. (1991). *How we know what isn't so: The fallibility of human reason in everyday life*. New York: The Free Press.

Peters, T. (1984). *In search of excellence*. New York: Warner Books.

Lykken, D. T. (1998). *A tremor in the blood: Uses and abuses of the lie detector*. Reading, MA: Perseus Books.

Radner, B., & Radner, M. (1982). *Science and unreason*. Belmont, CA: Wadsworth.

Shermer, M. (1997). *Why people believe weird things: Pseudoscience, superstition, and other confusions of our time*. New York: W.H. Freeman and Company.

Skinner, B. F. (1983). *A matter of consequences*. New York: Knopf.

Storr, A. (1996). *Feet of clay: A study of gurus*. New York: Free Press Paperbacks.

Zikmund, W. G., & d'Amico, M. (2000). *Marketing: Creating and keeping customers in an e-commerce world*. Dallas, TX: Southwest College Publishing.

NOTES

1. Or soon will be, if you are reading this chapter first.

2. These examples come from Crask et al. (2002).

3. As discussed in Chapter 2, science is research that is published and available for everyone to see, with theory building as the goal. Most marketing research is proprietary, that is, owned by the company that pays for it. However, you are conducting rigorous empirical research, and it might be useful to your career to occasionally use the word "science" as you described your work (e.g., "You drew a scientifically valid sample").

4. In particular, this last step violates pure probability theory, but most research, especially field studies, require compromises between perfection and feasibility—researchers always do the best they can do to conduct perfect research, but rarely or never succeed. However, as discussed in Chapter 2, the *Method* section of a scientific research report allows the reader to openly see the flaws of the research; in marketing research, the researcher may or may not call these flaws to the attention of the client. If, in a future job, you are in the role of client, an excellent application of this book and this course would be knowing appropriate and relevant questions to ask of the researcher you have hired or are considering hiring. If you are in the role of researcher, the ethical thing to do would be to include flaws in your report to the client. However, as money is involved, some people may find this hard to do. If you were hiring a marketing researcher to do a study for your firm, your evaluations of his or her credibility of the research should, necessarily *increase* if the researcher makes known to you specific weaknesses of the research and attendant caveats.

5. These comments were made in 1987 and are probably not representative of what would be obtained today, post September 11.

6. Were the soldiers unhappy or were they just venting against the Army in general? The research showed another type of ad, specifically one that emphasized patriotism as a reason for serving. Comments about this ad included: "[the ad] is true." "I like it better." (p. 378) "[the ad] gives you a sense of pride" (p. 379).

7. Personal communication with John Hocking, February 2002.

8. In fact, Iraq invaded Kuwait in late 1990, soon after this article appeared, and the Gulf War began in January 1991. This provides a pretty substantial rival "X" to explain discontinuation of the ads. In Campbell and Stanley's terms, "history" would be the threat to the internal validity of the study, that is, another event during the time frame of the research threatens the confidence in the conclusion that it was the article which caused the change in the ads run by the Army during this time.

9. The idea for using the Robert Frost poem comes from Russell A. Jones (1985).

10. Personal communication with John Hocking, March 1990.

11. Most of the material about the polygraph comes from Lykken (1998).

12. As of this writing, mid 2002, the Nezhats have medical practices in Atlanta and in the San Francisco Bay area.

REFERENCES

Crask, M., Fox, R. J., & Stout, R. G. (2002). *Marketing research: Principles and applications*, 2nd ed. New York: John Wiley & Sons.

Frankel, A. (2001). *The American Lawyer*, June 4, 2001 (cited in law.com).

Jones, Russell A. (1985). *Research methods in the social and behavioral science*. Sunderland, MA: Sinaver Associates.

Lykken, D. T. (1998). *A tremor in the blood: Uses and abuses of the lie detector*. Reading, MA: Perseus Books.

Shyles, L. & Hocking, J. E. (1990). The Army's "Be all you can be campaign." *Armed Forces and Society*, *16*(3), 369–383.

Zikmund, W. G., & d'Amico, M. (2000). *Marketing: Creating and keeping customers in an e-commerce world*, 7th ed. Dallas, TX: Southwest College Publishing.

CHAPTER SEVENTEEN

DISSEMINATING INFORMATION: WRITING AND PRESENTING RESEARCH

OBJECTIVES

By the end of this chapter you should be able to:

1. Explain the process by which research is written.
2. Explain and demonstrate the differences in style: APA and MLA (in-line and footnote/endnote).
3. Create tables and graphs for presentation.
4. Write an academic research proposal.
5. Write a nonacademic research proposal.
6. Create an oral research presentation.
7. Discuss the research process in general.

We have come full circle. The analysis of data gathered by whatever methodology, including qualitative methods, should yield new *questions*, questions arising from the answers to earlier questions. In sum, the quest is a continuous one; one we might even call the *never-ending process for knowledge, understanding, and prediction*. But, in reality, the research process is only nine-tenths complete. We began with a question derived from theory, selected the methodology most appropriate to collect the data to answer the question, and then analyzed the data. We now face the final step in making the results—including the theoretical rationale, method, analysis, and interpretation—available to others for further scrutiny. In completing this last step, we hope to move the research to the next plateau and add to the body of knowledge we know as science.

This chapter examines that final step. It also serves as a review of the process of research, and as such, is the culmination of a long journey from conceptualizing a problem, reviewing the relevant literature, posing the research question, selecting the most appropriate methodology, designing the research and collecting the data, and analyzing and interpreting the data collected. But data collection and analysis is not the last step in a research project, preparing the research report for dissemination and presentation is.

There are at least two different types of research reports, the **academic report** and the **business report**. The academic report is like a term paper, it takes a 360-degree approach, beginning with a question posed from some theoretical understanding of the problem and ending with a set of new questions to answer based on that theoretical perspective (see Figure 17.1). This report is complete with title, abstract, introduction, literature review, formal statement of hypotheses or research questions, method, results, and discussion sections (see Table 17.1). The business report is an abbreviated form of the academic report, consisting of a title, summary of important literature as an introduction—to include questions or hypotheses where appropriate—and method, followed by

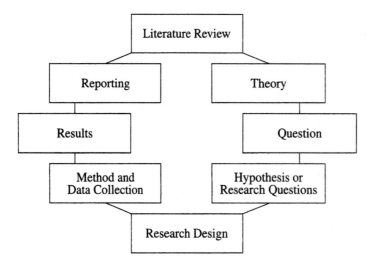

FIGURE 17.1 The academic research cycle.

TABLE 17.1   The Academic Research Report

Title
Abstract
Introduction
Literature Review
Hypotheses or Research Question
Method
Results
Discussion

tables and figures presenting the results in as visually pleasing a mode as possible, and recommendations based on the results (see Table 17.2). The business report rarely includes inferential statistical reporting or tables, instead it seeks to describe what was found; inferential statistics are used to establish your degree of certainty in the answers (sampling and statistical error).

Both academic and business research are often presented to interested parties. Academic research is for other researchers who both know the research process and engage in their own research programs. Business research presentations are to managers and board members who will use the information in making decisions regarding a product or idea. In either case, an effective visual presentation of the research, usually through slides or overheads that (a) provide main point illustration and (b) present the study's *descriptive* statistics, enhances the audience's understanding of the study and adds to its impact.

PREPARING THE FINAL PRODUCT

For many researchers—academic and nonacademic—the final step of writing and presenting the results is the hardest. The research must be carefully reviewed and scrutinized before it can be published or presented. Even in informal in-house presentations of research there are certain guidelines that help make the presentation as accurate as possible, and, at

TABLE 17.2   The Business Report

Title
Abstract
Introduction
Method
Results
Recommendations

the same time, allow for comparison with other research. Let us begin by examining the importance of written research to the research process.

Importance of Writing to the Research Process

There are many reasons for writing and disseminating the results of research. The first is obvious: Data and interpretation of that data sitting in a computer file or on a desk do not help others addressing the same problems. One of the reasons for conducting research in any methodology is to let others know what has been found. The desire to share knowledge should be basic to the research process, and this sharing comes from disseminating the findings of research to others, either in the form of published articles, monographs, and books, through presentations at professional societies and organizations, or through formal and informal presentations to interested parties. In any case, the research must be written in a clear and accurate manner to ensure that the results and interpretations are clearly understood by interested others.

Second, *academic* research is written to advance the state of the knowledge about communication. In writing to advance theory, we seek to understand the relationships between variables. Which variables are related? In what ways? To what degree? Each research project disseminated to the field—and to other fields interested in the type of research or research questions we may be addressing—adds one more piece of evidence to our database of knowledge concerning human communication. Research that does not get disseminated does not contribute to this knowledge base. Business research adds to the knowledge base about a particular product or idea; it is not widely disseminated, but instead is used to make decisions regarding promotions, products, or services.

Third, and we believe this to be of major importance to academic researchers, dissemination of research allows for more informed and better teaching. As new research becomes available we change—modify or intensify—our views of how the world should be structured. This process is essential in relating communication to students. Teachers are constantly revising their views of the essential *process* of communication through the knowledge of the research base(s) of their field and for research contributed by other fields. A similar business purpose is found here. Dissemination of research within the organization or agency helps to structure, modify, or solidify how others perceive a product, promotion, idea, or service. The research process is essential to making *good* business decisions.

Fourth, writing serves *personal* purposes. (1) It is gratifying to see the end product of much labor and love (and sometimes grief) disseminated to interested others. Publication and presentation become an important part of life, and not only for the academic researcher—the business researcher also reports his or her findings within the organization. (2) Disseminating the final reports enhances professional reputation. Although this may seem far from the original reasons for conducting research discussed in the first section of this book, professional reputations and livelihoods are an end product of the research process. This is especially true in academia; however, more and more, as we become an increasingly information-based society, the ability to produce and disseminate research will create careers. Examples of research-based careers include political polling, economic forecasting, marketing research, and advertising/media effect research, to name but a few.

Finally, as Raymond K. Tucker, Richard L. Weaver, II, and Cynthia Berryman-Fink (1981) point out, researchers "write for writing's sake" (pp. 231–232). That is, the process of writing helps us clarify the presentation of our research—academic or otherwise—by ensuring that the focus is clear and the ideas are fully supported. Furthermore, the process of writing itself may serve a heuristic function; it may bring to mind new ideas or explanations that may have been lost among all the facts and ideas behind the research. Many times new or better tests of the theory come from the writing stage; entirely new theories often originate at this stage. Writing, then, may serve as a way to balance the research from beginning to end, to bring the process of research full circle and motivate further theory and study.

Why write? There are many reasons, but from our perspective the most important reason is the dissemination of research in a timely and professional manner, one that allows for close scrutiny and replication. Writing the findings of a research project is the next step in a continuing *program* of research. Research, then, begets research.

WRITING THE ACADEMIC RESEARCH REPORT

The process of writing academic research reports differs slightly from other forms of writing. The process of research reporting is much more formal than other forms of writing. There are certain elements that must be included in a research report, elements that may differ from method to method, such as identification of participants and definitions of variables. There are also approved **styles** for the way in which research is reported. Each particular discipline typically approves of one or more **style sheets** or manuals that researchers follow in reporting their research. The academic communication discipline, for instance, allows much more flexibility in the style sheets followed, typically differing between journal and association, than does the American Psychological Association (APA) or the Modern Language Association (MLA), each of which has its own particular style.

Style Sheets

There are a variety of style sheets and manuals available to the researcher. The communication discipline typically follows those of the Modern Language Association (*MLA Style Sheet*), the American Psychological Association (*Publication Manual of the American Psychological Association*), or a derivation of one or the other.[1] In many journals the major format of one of these two style sheets is followed, but with minor modifications; these modifications are typically specified in the journal's editorial statement. By reading the different journals you should get a feel for the different style sheets appropriate for your area of study or methodology.

A major difference between these particular styles is the way they approach citation. As discussed in Chapter 3, all contributions by others must be carefully and fully credited. The American Psychological Association's *Publication Manual* (2001) requires that references be in an in-line form of citing sources in parentheses. The APA style sheet (5th edition) requires that you cite sources by name and date within the particular line of text (e.g., "Sargent, 2002"). Even notes that add to or explain things are cited in-line (e.g., "Note 1"). Box 17.1 presents a sample of APA style.

BOX 17.1
SAMPLE APA STYLE

Both rhetorical and communication scholars have recently considered the relationships between the way in which the human brain functions and how human beings communicate (Note 1). In *Symbolic Inducement and Knowing: A Study of the Foundations of Rhetoric*, Gregg (1984) suggests that a far more comprehensive view of the epistemic function of rhetoric is possible when "the principle of symbolic discrimination from the neurological level is recognized" (p. 44). Similarly, Chesebro (1984) has argued that a neurophysiological view is especially useful when explaining the "epistemological functions of media in cultural systems." Likewise, Shedletsky (1981, 1983) has isolated more specific relationships among language usage, information processing, and cerebral activity within the human brain. Such explorations suggest that far more detailed examinations of the influence of brain hemispheres might now be appropriately considered in terms of specific variables such as source perception, message perception, and message intensity.

NOTES

1. This is taken from Stacks & Sellers (1986).

REFERENCES

Chesebro, J. W. (1984). The media reality: Epistemological functions of media in cultural systems. *Critical Studies in Mass Communication, 2*, 111–130.

Gregg, R. (1984). *Symbolic inducement and knowing: A study of the foundations of rhetoric*. Columbia, SC: University of South Carolina Press.

Shedletsky, L. J. (1981). Cerebral asymmetry for aspects of sentence processing. *Communication Quarterly, 29*, 3–11.

Shedletsky, L. J. (1983). Cerebral asymmetry for aspects of sentence processing: A replication and extension. *Communication Quarterly, 31*, 78–84.

Stacks, D. W., & Sellers, D. E. (1986). Toward a holistic approach to communication: The effect of "pure" hemispheric reception on message acceptance. *Communication Quarterly, 34*, 266–285.

The *MLA Handbook for Writers of Research Papers* (Gibaldi, 2000) also calls for references to be cited in-line. Unlike APA, MLA referencing does not include the date of publication (e.g., "Stacks and Hocking"). MLA also provides for cites to be *footnoted*, with reference citations placed in the text of the report as superscript numbers. (Usually footnotes are treated as *endnotes* in the draft report and are listed on a separate page at the end of the manuscript.) MLA style allows for substantive additions and comments, as well as the actual source of the material. Boxes 17.2a and 17.2b provide samples of MLA style.

BOX 17.2A
SAMPLE MLA STYLE (IN-LINE REFERENCING)

Both rhetorical and communication scholars have recently considered the relationships between the way in which the human brain functions and how human beings communicate.[1] In *Symbolic Inducement and Knowing: A Study of the Foundations of Rhetoric*, Gregg (44) suggests that a far more comprehensive view of the epistemic function of rhetoric is possible when "the principle of symbolic discrimination from the neurological level is recognized." Similarly, Chesebro has argued that a neurophysiological view is especially useful when explaining the epistemological functions of media in cultural systems." Likewise, Shedletsky (*Cerebral*; *Replication*) has isolated more specific relationships among language usage, information processing, and cerebral activity within the human brain. Such explorations suggest that far more detailed examinations of the influence of brain hemispheres might now be appropriately considered in terms of specific variables such as source perception, message perception, and message intensity.

NOTES

1. This is taken from Stacks and Sellers.

WORKS CITED

Gregg, Richard. *Symbolic Inducement and Knowing: A Study of the Foundations of Rhetoric* (Columbia, SC: University of South Carolina Press, 1984).
Chesebro, James W. "The Media Reality: Epistemological Functions of Media in Cultural Systems," *Critical Studies in Mass Communication*, 2 (1984): 111–130.
Shedletsky, Leonard J. "Cerebral Asymmetry for Aspects of Sentence Processing," *Communication Quarterly*, 29 (1981): 3–11.
———. "Cerebral Asymmetry for Aspects of Sentence Processing: A Replication and Extension," *Communication Quarterly*, 31 (1983): 78–84.
Stacks, Don W., and Daniel E. Sellers, "Toward a Holistic Approach to Communication: The Effect of 'Pure' Hemispheric Reception on Message Acceptance," *Communication Quarterly*, 34 (1986): 266–285.

There are other differences between APA and MLA styles. In MLA style the references are called "Works Cited," whereas the APA style refers to "References," both of which are bibliographic in content. Each has its own way of presenting source information. For notes, for example, MLA uses superscripted numbers in both text and the Note section; APA uses in-line referencing. However, APA (5th edition, 2001) has reverted back to superscripted notation for footnotes. Each style sheet has its own peculiarities and should be consulted frequently. This book, like most communication journals, has used a little of each.

■ ■ ■ ■ ■

BOX 17.2B

SAMPLE MLA STYLE—4TH EDITION (ENDNOTE OR FOOTNOTE)

Both rhetorical and communication scholars have recently considered the relationships between the way in which the human brain functions and how human beings communicate.[1] In *Symbolic Inducement and Knowing: A Study of the Foundations of Rhetoric*, Gregg suggests that a far more comprehensive view of the epistemic function of rhetoric is possible when "the principle of symbolic discrimination from the neurological level is recognized."[2] Similarly, Chesebro has argued that a neurophysiological view is especially useful when explaining the "epistemological functions of media in cultural systems."[3] Likewise, Shedletsky has isolated more specific relationships among language usage, information processing, and cerebral activity within the human brain.[4] Such explorations suggest that far more detailed examinations of the influence of brain hemispheres might now be appropriately considered in terms of specific variables such as source perception, message perception, and message intensity.

NOTES

1. This is taken from Don W. Stacks and Daniel E. Sellers, "Toward a Holistic Approach to Communication: The Effect of 'Pure' Hemispheric Reception on Message Acceptance," *Communication Quarterly, 34* (1986): 266–285.
2. Richard Gregg, *Symbolic Inducement and Knowing: A Study of the Foundations of Rhetoric* (Columbia, SC: University of South Carolina Press, 1984): 44.
3. James W. Chesebro, "The Media Reality: Epistemological Functions of Media in Cultural Systems," *Critical Studies in Mass Communication, 2* (1984): 111–130.
4. Leonard J. Shedletsky, "Cerebral Asymmetry for Aspects of Sentence Processing," *Communication Quarterly, 29* (1981): 3–11; and Leonard J. Shedletsky, "Cerebral Asymmetry for Aspects of Sentence Processing: A Replication and Extension," *Communication Quarterly, 31* (1983): 78–84.

Style sheets serve an important purpose in research reports. They allow a form of standardization and control over what could be a very individualized process. Imagine, for instance, an experiment being reported in free verse or iambic pentameter. The style sheet sets forth the required minimums of presentation and, as noted earlier, may be modified to meet the particular needs of specific groups.

Organization of the Report

Regardless of the style sheet followed, all research reports are organized in specific ways. The researcher, whether qualitative or quantitative, follows the general outline of introduction, body, and concluding statement. The specifics may differ by method, but in general the following outline provides a good starting point:

   I. Rationale
      A. Introduction
         1. Goal or purpose
         2. Significance of research
      B. Review of literature
         1. Review of related literature
         2. Statement of research question/hypothesis
  II. Method
      A. Research participants
      B. Procedures followed
      C. Measures used
 III. Results
 IV. Discussion
      A. Significance
      B. Flaws—limitations and qualifications
      C. Conclusion and extension of theory
      D. Future research

In addition, the report should have a title page, a short abstract that presents the essential information such as basic theory, method employed, and results; references; and explanatory tables and figures.

In organizing and writing the report, use of **subheads**—subtitles of sorts—help to maintain a flow and direction of the writing. This book has employed the use of three levels of subheads within each chapter. Headers serve two functions: the *outline* function keeps the material in order and the *orienting* function tells the reader whether the material is a major idea, secondary idea, or even a tertiary idea. Experienced writers use subheads to maintain flow and coherence in their writing.

All academic research reports are *formal* presentations. Most style sheets suggest that the use of the first person be avoided; hence, the "I" becomes "the researcher" or "we." The report should be grammatically and syntactically correct, conforming to the rules and prescriptions of the language in which it is written (not all research is written in English—or American English). The report should flow with internal summaries and transitional sentences bridging the various sections of the report. Supporting evidence (tables and figures) should be discussed within the body of the report and, in unpublished reports, should include a statement as to where the table or figure should be inserted (see Figure 17.2):

> The means, as presented in Table 1, indicate that, although significant differences were not obtained for all analyses, the *pattern* of the means was as predicted: traditional males were most persuaded, traditional females followed next, nontraditional males next, nontraditional females being least persuaded by the message.

Introduction.   The specific format followed in writing the results of a research project will differ according to the method you follow. For our purposes, we will look in more detail at the required elements of an experimental study. The introduction, obviously, introduces the reader to the general area of study and the importance of the study. Many times the problem

FIGURE 17.2 Example of a statistical table.

SEX (BIOLOGICAL/PSYCHOLOGICAL)	MEAN*	STD DEV.
Female		
Traditional	5.1	1.32
Nontraditional	2.2	0.98
Male		
Traditional	6.8	1.11
Nontraditional	4.6	1.62

* Responses to a scale of persuasibility with ranging from strongly agree (7) to strongly disagree (1) with the attitude statement.

that the research addresses is stated formally in the introduction. Most of the time, however, the introduction serves to acquaint the reader with the variables under study and prepares the reader for the rest of the report.

Literature Review.   In Chapter 4 we discussed the literature review as a method in and of itself. All research reports, including the experimental report, contain a review of the literature—documents published or presented—that was used to formulate the general research question. The literature review formally presents the logic behind the theory or previous research or descriptions of the phenomenon under study. Supporting materials, often reduced to explanatory figures and tables, are frequently acceptable additions to the literature review, which also serves as a potential base for future research. Again, in some instances, the literature review may be the final written project. The literature review should culminate in a *formal* statement of the research question(s) explored and/or hypotheses to be tested. Although it may differ according to style sheet, the research questions and hypotheses should be clearly set off in the report and stated as formal relationships between the variables under study.

For example, the literature review may seek to identify reasons for a possible relationship between two variables, say receiver sex and persuasibility. The literature review would describe the previous research for each variable and show why the relationship was expected. The literature review should serve as a transition between the actual literature review and the statement of the question, for example:

Based on this discussion the following research question was addressed.

Or, for the hypothesis:

Based on theory and the preceding discussion, the following hypotheses were derived.

Frequently, the research questions and hypotheses are then stated as formal questions of relationships or predictions of relationships:

RQ₁: What is the relationship between sex of interviewer and expected distancing in interview situations?

RQ₂: What is the relationship between interviewer rate of speech and perceptions of interviewer credibility?

H₁: Male interviewees will be more disturbed by male interviewers adopting socially inappropriate seating distance than will female interviewees.

H₂: Speakers with faster-than-normal rates of delivery will receive higher evaluations of benevolence and trustworthiness than will speakers with slower-than-normal delivery rates.

The statement of research questions and hypotheses serves as a transition between theory and method in the report. The way in which the research question or hypothesis is stated may also help determine the methodology chosen to answer the questions or test the relationships between variables. *Remember*, however, both the literature review and statement of research questions and/or hypotheses are stated prior to conducting the research. Often, as is the case of a research proposal or prospectus that seeks to conduct research, these have already been formally stated. (We cover the proposal/prospectus later in this chapter.)

Method.   Critical to an understanding of the research and the results is a clear and concise description of the methodological design employed, the operationalization of the variables under study, the participants, and the procedures followed. In writing the method section keep in mind that someone should be able to *replicate* the research based on the way it is described in this section. The method section should begin with a statement of the particular methodology employed, whether it be experimental, survey, content analytic, or whatever. For example, suppose that our study explores the relationship of two independent variables (biological sex and message—language—intensity) and one dependent variable (persuasibility). We might begin the method section by stating that the "experimental design employed in this study was a 2 (sex of receiver—male or female) × 2 (level of message intensity—high or low) factorial design with off-set control." This tells the reader that there were two independent variables in the experimental manipulation, the levels they took, and that a control group, which received no manipulation, was included in the design.

After the design has been explained, the participants should be described. It may be necessary to report demographic variables, although this practice is not as prevalent today as it once was. Typically, the number of male and female participants and where they were drawn from is important: "100 students, 50 male and 50 female, enrolled in beginning public speaking courses volunteered to serve as participants in this study." Or, "50 male volunteers from a large Midwestern university participated in the study." Of importance is that the reader know *who* participated in the study, how many there were, and any important distinguishing characteristics (e.g., university versus high school students, males versus females).

A careful description of the variables employed in the study must be included in the method section. Here you would describe how you operationalized the independent variables (sex could be *biological sex*, psychological sex orientation—*androgyny*—if used might be operationalized as scores on the *Bem Sex Role Inventory*; distance as "the thigh-to-thigh seated distance adopted by the participant from the confederate"). Dependent variables should be described in terms of the type of data employed (e.g., number of violent themes in prime-time television, responses to a semantic differential or Likert-type scale). When describing the dependent variables you should include the bipolar terms employed in a semantic differential scale: "Persuasion was measured via responses to 7-step semantic differential scales which tapped the evaluation dimension of attitude. Scales were bounded by *Good-Bad*, *Valuable-Worthless*, *Foolish-Wise*, and *Pleasant-Unpleasant*." Likewise, we would need to know the number of intervals in any scale and how they were operationalized (Strongly Agree, Agree, Undecided, Disagree, Strongly Disagree). Here, a reader could take your description and replicate the materials and manipulations employed.[2] Any messages employed should also be described in this section.

Finally, the procedures employed in the study should be briefly described. Again, the procedures should be stated in such a way that others can evaluate, and be able to replicate the research. As was discussed in Chapter 12, if the research required participants to report to a room, engage in a conversation, and then complete the dependent measure(s), this procedure should be outlined:

> Participants reported to the communications lab ostensibly to participate in an interview study concerning the basic speech course in which he or she was enrolled. Each was provided with a copy of the Subjects Signed Consent Form, which detailed the supposed reasons for the study and a basic overview of the procedures. After indicating that he or she understood the project and agreed to participate, each participant was taken to a second room where the "interviewer" was waiting. In reality, the interviewer was a confederate who "interviewed" all participants. The confederate was a female carefully trained in interview method, who asked the same questions of all participants and maintained the same vocal, facial, and gesticular communication throughout the study.
>
> The interview room was set up to approximate a standard interview room. The confederate sat behind a table with several résumés on it. The interviewee was shown one of two chairs, both situated across from the confederate, and told to sit down, and that the interview would begin shortly.
>
> After a few seconds the confederate arose and closed the door "accidentally" left open by the researcher. This manipulation allowed the confederate to adopt one of the two distance manipulations: norm—back behind the desk—or close—the other chair adjacent to the participant. The interview was then conducted with the confederate asking a series of pretested questions regarding participation in the basic speech course in which the student was enrolled.
>
> Immediately after the interview each participant was told that the real purpose of the research was to study *interviewer* behavior and asked if he or she would mind taking a few minutes to evaluate his or her interviewer via a series of scales. Upon completion of the dependent measures each participant was debriefed as to the real purpose of the research, afforded the opportunity to ask questions, and signed a statement indicating that he or she had read the debriefing statement, had a chance to discuss the study, and would remain silent as to its true purpose until later in the semester.

Based on this description a reader could replicate or improve upon the study. Where deemed necessary, figures that displayed the procedures or layout of the "lab" can be included.

Results.   The results section presents the data analyses in both tabular and discussion format. Tables such as graphs, lists of means or data points, and charts should be included to make the reporting easier to follow. Tables and graphs, however, are less important than the written description of the analyses. Tables for instance, make little sense without a written explanation as to what the data—numbers, points, and so on—mean. The important thing to remember is that by themselves, *numbers in tables and graphs have no meaning*—they must be interpreted by the researcher.

Each hypothesis or research question should be addressed, beginning with the statistical method employed, the established alpha-level (α), and all relevant statistical information included. Suppose that we had completed the study created for the method section. We may have hypothesized that interviewees would rate the confederate as more professional when she stayed behind the desk. We would report the findings of the *t*-test between distance (norm-close) on professionalism (7-step semantic differential scaled bounded by Professional-Unprofessional) as follows (see Figure 17.3):

> Hypothesis 1, that interviewees would perceive the interviewer as more professional when she remained at the norm, was tested with a *t*-test on the professionalism scale as the dependent variable and distance (norm or close) as the independent variable. Interviewers were rated as significantly more professional ($t = -4.51$, df = 87, $p < .05$, one-tailed) when they maintained the expected norm than when they deviated to the close distance (the means are found in Table 1).

Notice that the results are simply presented, no discussion is offered. The results section should address the findings and provide the relevant information so that the reader can understand which analyses were employed and what the findings were.

Discussion.   The final section typically begins with a short summary of the research: what was done and its importance to further understanding communication. Theoretical issues of import may be reviewed here, bringing them back into focus and reestablishing the purpose of the research. The discussion section serves to integrate the results with the theoretical rationale presented earlier. The discussion interprets the findings, extends them to other situations (if appropriate), and offers possible alternative explanations if the hypotheses were not supported. The discussion section should also include a frank discussion of any flaws or limitations to the research, especially in light of the findings.

FIGURE 17.3   Reporting of inferential statistics.

TABLE 1
MEANS FOR DISTANCE AND PROFESSIONALISM

VARIABLE	MEAN*	STD ERR
Norm	6.32	1.22
Close	3.61	0.88

* (p < .05)

Finally, the discussion should suggest future research and the implications of such research for the field. In cases where the research is very complicated, a short summary of the research might end the discussion.

Tidying Up.   There are three final elements to the research report remaining. First, the report should have a *title*. The title should reflect the purpose of the research and may reflect also the methodology employed. In instances where the study is part of a program of research, it might be indicated in the title, such as, "Power in the Classroom, II" or "Further Tests of the Mass Communication Writing Apprehension Measure (MCWAM)." Although it differs by style sheet, the title (and the names of the researchers and any other pertinent information) should appear on a title page, and on the first page of text. Second, the research should include an *abstract* of the study, usually 100 to 250 words, which serves as a preview of the study and includes the important findings (see Chapter 4). The abstract also may include key words, which index the research (such as Sex Differences, Proxemics, Violations of Expectations, Communication Apprehension). Placement of the abstract differs by style sheet, some require it on a separate sheet placed between the title page and text, others on the title page, and still others as the first page of text.

Finally, all research reports must be fully *referenced*. It is the writer's responsibility to give clear and fair credit to others' works (see Chapter 3). The reference section usually is found at the end of the report and may include substantive statements that further explain points or arguments made in the report's body. Again, style sheets and journals differ on how references are presented.

WRITING THE NONACADEMIC RESEARCH REPORT

The nonacademic research report offers its readers an abbreviated version of the academic research report. The typical nonacademic research report does not include inferential statistics, instead it describes the study's results. Most nonacademic research reports have a title page, a body (the "executive summary"), and a series of tables or graphs. The term, "executive summary" should be kept in mind as you approach the nonacademic research report. The body often contains a short abstract of the most significant results, followed closely by a brief rationale for the study's purpose and method of data collection. For example, if you were conducting a survey for a particular product you might begin the body as follows:

> The present study was conducted to identify attitudes toward the use of ATM machines and potential problems for the imposition of a "user's fee" when an ATM card is used in a nonmember bank's ATM machine. A telephone survey of 385 randomly selected residents of the greater Miami area was conducted the first week of January 1999. Participants were randomly selected from the Miami/Dade County telephone directory. Beginning on Monday, calls were made on five consecutive nights from 5:00 P.M. until 10:00 P.M. Participants were screened for inclusion with the following question: Do you have a bank ATM card? If they answered in the affirmative, the interview was conducted (see Appendix A). Each interview took approximately 8 minutes.

The rest of the report usually consists of the results. In most cases you begin with demographics, then univariate results, then bi- or multivariate results. Results are typically presented in frequency tables, crosstabulations, and tables of means.

The nonacademic research report may end with the results, but may also include a recommendations section. The recommendation section is written in nonstatistical terms and its content is often derived from the researcher's use of inferential statistics. Rarely, for example, will ANOVA, statistically significant, variance, or other statistical terms be presented.

The nonacademic research report differs from its academic counterpart by its simplicity and its general descriptive nature. The academic report is published and made available to researchers around the world—people who can make critical assessment of the study's theoretical base, methodology, analyses, and conclusions. The nonacademic report is often a confidential document, one that is interpreted by the researcher via one-on-one contact or a small group presentation.

VISUAL AND ORAL PRESENTATIONS

Technological advances have made reporting research more than simply writing a report. Today's researcher often includes slides and overhead transparencies of research findings in his or her reporting. (Some of these even make their way into the written reports, too.) Slides, Powerpoint displays (see Box 17.3), and overheads are audiovisual elements of the research presentation. The presentation is typically an abbreviated (usually 10 to 15 minute) presentation of the study. Audiovisuals should be simple, direct, and easy to read. A table of figures that has 10 columns and 50 rows will be neither readable nor intelligible. Audiovisuals summarize the data and present results in either numerical or word form. The data presented in Figure 17.3 could be used as an audiovisual.

What might constitute an audiovisual presentation's visuals? Typical presentations include:

- Title slide
- Outline of major concepts and definitions
- Hypotheses or research questions
- Sample and sample selection
- Method employed and any important features
- Results
- Important conclusions

Each slide or overhead should contain a succinct summary of the section it covers in the written report; the data thrown up on the screen is only the most important—things that you want to emphasize or dramatize. At one time, content was only numbers and words, and sometimes a graphic artist would be called in to create charts, sometimes in color. Today, however, photographs and illustrations are included. A rule of thumb, however, is to make your audiovisuals as simple as possible. Let them enhance your presentation, not become the presentation itself.

434

BOX 17.3
VISUAL PRESENTATION—SLIDES (MICROSOFT POWERPOINT)

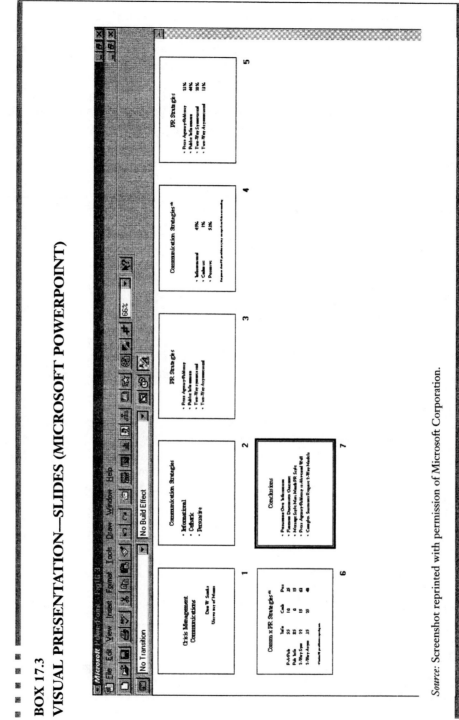

Source: Screenshot reprinted with permission of Microsoft Corporation.

As noted, at one time graphic artists would be brought in to create the slides or over-heads. Today, however, laser and ink jet printers and software allow you to create your own audiovisuals. Programs such as *Freelance Graphics*, *PowerPoint*, and *Persuasion* not only allow you to create slides and overheads, but with the aid of a computer and projection device you can also automate them. Add a voice system and you have a packaged "slide show."

THE RESEARCH PROSPECTUS/PROPOSAL

The way in which the research report is written is reflected in the purpose of the report. To this point we have assumed that the report reflects a completed research project. However, there is another type of research writing that is important, the research *proposal* or *prospectus*. The research proposal/prospectus follows the same general outline as provided earlier; however, it differs in that the method, results, and discussion are presented for discussion *prior* to the conduct of the research. In addition, in many areas it tends to be more detailed than the final report (see Box 17.4). The introduction and literature review, which culminate in the statement of research questions and/or hypotheses, are similar to the research report, typically taking about the same amount of space, but the method, procedures, and results are stated in the future tense ("Differences will be measured by . . . ." "Data will be analyzed via regression analysis." "Appropriate tables and figures will present the data obtained in the study."). The discussion section presents how the results will be discussed if hypotheses are supported or not supported. The proposal/prospectus is used to help identify any weaknesses in the proposed research prior to the actual acquisition of data. It also serves to prepare the researcher for the final report. In academic situations, a proposal or prospectus is normally required before conducting the research needed for advanced degrees or when applying for funding to conduct the research. Specific funding organizations have specific guidelines that must be followed, as do universities and colleges for masters' theses and doctoral dissertations.

APPLYING KNOWLEDGE IN COMMUNICATION

Perhaps more important than anything else, writing the research report may have as much to do with your credibility as a researcher as your theory, methods, and analyses. A well-written or well-presented research study adds much to the study of communication—any other field for that matter. Different academic outlets have different requirements—they follow different style sheets or adopt parts of major style sheets that fit their research—and you must be aware of them. For instance, most social scientific-based communication journals follow some form of APA style, while those steeped in the humanities tend toward MLA (and, even then, toward the older, footnoted-endnoted style).

As good as your research is, it must be disseminated to others. This means that you must be able to communicate what you wrote in a concise, understandable, and appropriate manner. Believe it or not, this may be the hardest part of the research process. As Hickson, Stacks, and Amsbary (1993) reported, the average number of publications for *communication* researchers who have published at least once in a recognized *communication* journal in a researcher's lifetime is **1.86**; the mode is 1 (and how many did not publish at all is unknown).

BOX 17.4

PROPOSAL/PROSPECTUS OUTLINE

In writing up a proposal to conduct research, answer the following questions as they pertain to your project.

I. Introduction (Statement of the Problem)
  A. What is the goal of the research project?
  B. What is the problem, issue, or critical focus to be researched?
  C. What are the important terms, what do they mean?
  D. What is the significance of the problem or issue?[1]
    1. Do you want to test a theory?
    2. Do you want to extend a theory?
    3. Do you want to test competing theories?
    4. Do you want to test a method or methodology?
    5. Do you want to replicate a method or methodology?
    6. Do you want to replicate a previous study?[2]
    7. Do you want to correct previous research that was conducted in an inadequate manner?
    8. Do you want to resolve inconsistent results from earlier studies?
    9. Do you want to solve a practical problem?
II. Review of Literature
  A. What does previous research reveal about the problem or issue?
  B. What is the theoretical framework for the investigation?
  C. Are there any complementary frameworks?[3]
  D. Are there any competing theoretical frameworks?
  E. What is (are) the research question(s) or hypothesis(es)?
    1. Clearly separate the research questions/hypotheses.
    2. Clearly state the research questions/hypotheses.
III. Participants/Materials
  A. Who (what) will provide (constitute) the data for the research?
  B. For quantitative research:
    1. What is the population being studied?
    2. Who will comprise the participants or respondents of the research?
    3. What is the sample size?
    4. What are the characteristics of the sample?
    5. Which sampling techniques will be used?
    6. If experimental research:
      a. How will participants be assigned to cells?
      b. What safeguards have you provided?
      c. Present a sample consent form and debriefing form in an appendix.
  C. For qualitative research:
    1. What materials and/or information are necessary to conduct the research?
    2. How will they be obtained?
    3. What special problems can be anticipated in acquiring needed materials and information?

    4. What are the limitations in the availability and reporting of materials and information?

IV. Methodology
  A. What methods or techniques will be used to collect the data?
  B. What procedures will be used to apply the methods or techniques?
    1. Be specific.
    2. Be practical.
    3. Be conservative.
  C. What are the limitations of this methodology?
  D. For quantitative research:
    1. What are the variables?
    2. The dependent variables?
    3. The independent variables?
    4. How will the variables be manipulated, controlled, measured, and/or observed?
    5. What instrument(s) (scales) will be used?
      a. If developed by others:
        (1) How reliable and valid are they?[4]
        (2) Why use this instrument or scale rather than others?
      b. If developing an instrument for this research project:
        (1) How will the scales be developed?
        (2) What format will be used?
        (3) How will reliability and validity be assessed?
        (4) Why develop a new scale or instrument?
  E. If an experiment:
    1. What factors will affect the study's internal validity?
    2. What factors will affect the study's external validity?
    3. How will plausible rival hypotheses be minimized?
  F. If historical/critical:
    1. What sources of bias will exist?
    2. How will bias be controlled?
  G. Will any ethical principles be jeopardized?
    1. If so, with what ramifications?
    2. If so, how will participants be informed of the true nature of the study?
    3. Will participants be debriefed? Given a copy of the results?
    4. Provided the name of someone to talk with if problems ensue?

V. Data Analysis
  A. How will the data be analyzed?
  B. If quantitative research, what statistics will be employed?
  C. What criteria will be used to determine if the hypotheses are supported? (alpha-level?)
  D. If a pilot study was conducted, what was learned:
    1. About the question?
    2. About the data to be gathered?
    3. About the methodology:
      a. Did the pilot study consist of another method?
      b. Which?

(continued)

BOX 17.4   CONTINUED

          c. What did it find?
- VI. Conclusions
  - A. How will the final research report be organized?
  - B. In what form?
    1. Text?
    2. Tables?
    3. Figures?
    4. Bibliographies?
  - C. What are the time deadlines imposed?
    1. For completing the literature review?
    2. For collection of the data?
    3. For analysis of the data?
    4. For writing the report?
- VII. Summary (1 paragraph)

NOTES

1. Obviously, you may only answer one or two of these questions, but look at all to see what is appropriate.
2. In this case, why? What was wrong or flawed with the previous study? Or is it a case of time being the variable—things have changed over the ___-year period?
3. Here, be certain to point out any theoretical models developed if conducting a participant observation study or, in the case of content analysis, you may use already extant category systems.
4. Present other research reporting reliability and validity information. Be sure to indicate weaknesses in the scales and what you will do to improve them.

Source: Adapted from Rebecca B. Rubin, Alan M. Rubin, and Linda J. Piele, *Communication Research: Strategies and Sources* (Belmont, Calif.: Wadsworth, 1986), 46–48. © Copyright 1986 by Wadsworth, Inc. Reprinted by permission of the publisher.

To be a part of the research process and the research community, it is your responsibility—duty—to publish your findings. Becoming a good writer has to do with knowing the style and understanding what editors are looking for as much as anything else.

But we do more than simply publish our research in journals that other researchers read. You will make presentations to clients and bosses that must be clear and concise. They will have as much trouble understanding methodology and statistical analysis as you did coming into your first methods course. You must be as simple and concise as your methods teacher was. You will not only be presenting research, but also teaching them what is appropriate and how to interpret what you have given them. Doing so today is easier than before; you have statistical packages and presentational software built into your computer that allow you great flexibility. You can transfer data between statistical packages and spreadsheets for simplified presentation if necessary; you can insert tables and graphs into reports and presentational audiovisual slides or overheads. You can even create multimedia presentations. However, all this is mere flash if you cannot explain what the numbers you came up with mean.

SUMMARY

The culmination of the research project is found in its write-up. The writing stage is often perceived as the most difficult and time-consuming part of the research. Writing, however, is important because it allows the researcher to review his or her findings and ensure that the logic and focus of the study are appropriate. In addition, the writing stage often yields unexpected dividends in the form of new insights and alternative explanations. In writing the research report or proposal, a general form should be followed that includes an introduction, a literature review, a method section, a results section, and finally, a discussion and interpretation of the findings. Style manuals or style sheets have different requirements, but all follow the same basic outline. The actual style of the report may be dictated by the audience for whom the report is written.

GENERAL REVIEW OF THE RESEARCH PROCESS

The purpose of this final section is to review the process of research. In Part I of this book we examined the relationships between theory and research. Part II introduced the various methods researchers use to answer the research questions generated in the quest to further understand human communication and its effects. And, in Part III, we examined how researchers make sense out of the quantitative data they gather as the research study is conducted. The purpose of research, in the end, is to add knowledge to what we already know about human behavior. In this case, of course, we are examining *human communicative behavior*.

Research begins with the identification of some area of communication that is both important and of interest to the researcher. As should be gathered by now, there are many areas of interest from which we can pose significant research questions. Throughout the book we have tried to indicate as many areas of interest as possible; the chapter Mini-Projects and Probes were written in such a way as to get you—the reader—involved in areas of your particular interest; the Research Projects suggested possible research avenues. Once an area of potential interest has been identified we move to the next step in the research process.

All research requires an understanding of previous study and thought. This stage of the research process consists of reading all material—books, journal articles, papers, data bases, and so forth—relevant to the area of interest. Here, of course, we are talking about library research and a review of the previous literature. At this stage we sometimes formalize our study by writing a prospectus, proposal, or area paper. All this work culminates in the *literature review*, which sets both the theory and tone of the research project being considered. From this literature review the research questions and hypotheses are generated, perhaps the most critical step in the research process.

The research question determines which method is selected to conduct the research. Selection of the most appropriate method is an important step. Here the researcher must decide his or her approach to the study, based, of course, on the type of question being asked. If the researcher is interested in assessing the communication from a particular event, person, or time, then historical and/or critical method is most appropriate. On the other hand, if the researcher is interested in the examination of an ongoing event, describing how people perceive an event or communication, or attempting to understand the relationships between communication variables, he or she will choose one of the following methodologies: participant-observation, focus group, in-depth interview, content analysis, survey, or experimental. Whatever the method a researcher chooses, however, it is important to remember that the research question should suggest the method, not the other way around.

Once the method has been chosen, procedures for conducting the study must be established. Regardless of methodology employed, creation of research procedures are critical to the study's success. Here we are talking about the plan of attack, the identification of materials necessary to conduct the research (documents in some instances, creation of scales in others). At this stage of the research process the social scientist must make some important decisions. How will the study be conducted? Where? What amount of control is necessary? How many people will be questioned or participate in the study? At this stage the researcher must create the instruments for the collection of data; whether that data comes from qualitative methods or experiments, it must be assessed for validity and reliability. For the survey or experimental study, questions and scales must be created and tested. Confederates and/or interviewers must be trained and procedures tested. Finally, the sample must be selected and its representativeness noted. Once all this planning, pretesting, and testing has been completed, the researcher can move to data collection, the next step.

Depending on the research method selected, collecting the materials from which to draw conclusions may take a day, a week, or a year. Regardless of the method employed, data collection is an exciting, if not the most exciting stage of research. The data from which the research questions or hypotheses are tested or answered are assembled during this stage of the process, so before long the researcher has answers to his/her questions and hypotheses. An exciting prospect indeed!

In the experiment, at least two additional features of the data collection stage must be addressed. First, as noted above, research participants must be chosen. These participants must be apprised of the study through the *consent form*. They must be provided a way out of the study if they so desire. Second, participants who complete the study must be debriefed. Both steps are crucial to a well-conducted and ethical experiment. In conducting survey research the researcher may offer copies of the findings to the participants at a later time. This information must be sent after the study has been completed.

Once all the data has been collected the research has entered the analysis process. At this stage the researcher uses whatever analytical procedures and tools are available to make sense out of the data acquired. In some methods this typically requires that the data be coded into the computer and statistical analyses computed. In others, the acquired data may be compared against some theoretical model, assessed against what others have found, and their logic employed in drawing their conclusions or compared against certain aesthetic principles. Regardless of method, however, all data—for example, observations, scales, documents—must be analyzed before any meaningful conclusions can be drawn from the research.

Once the study has been conducted, the data analyzed, and conclusions drawn about the research questions, the results must be made public. Here the researcher, according to the conventions of his or her discipline, writes the research report. This report establishes a rationale for the research, reviews previous literature, states the research questions and hypotheses, describes the method employed in the collection of the data and the results, and then discusses the research. This stage of the process is extremely important. Here the researcher contributes to knowledge generation, to theory construction. The final report, in whatever way made public, may ultimately end up impacting on others and may provide the data necessary for their examination of communication behavior. The final report also identifies future areas of research, based on the findings of this study and its limitations and qualifications.

Is the research process now over? No. This project should set the stage for the next. The next project will set the stage for another. Research is a true process, it never ends. Conducting research is an exciting adventure in understanding how and why people communicate. It may be difficult, but it is extremely rewarding work.

By now you should have the necessary information and skills to conduct a research project in your particular interest area. It is hoped, too, that you can now make critical analyses of others' research, assessing where the method and procedures were good and where they were bad. We hope that your study of research methods will, in the end, make you a more informed and educated consumer of the ever-increasing amounts of research being disseminated daily. We also hope that some of you will be bitten by the research bug and go on to examine significant problems and areas of interest in your area of communication.

PROBES

1. Why is writing and presenting research so difficult?

2. How well written is the research in your area of communication? Could an "average" person read and understand it? What minimal knowledge do you need to understand the research in that area?

3. How difficult is it to take a research study that has been written for an academic audience and revamp it for a more general audience?

4. In actuality, for the researcher, how different is the nonacademic research presentation? Is the research process actually any different than for the academic presentation?

5. How different is the research proposal format from that of any research report? What is the one major difference?

RESEARCH PROJECTS

1. Conduct a content analysis of research in your area of interest with the idea of answering the research question: "How well written is the academic research report?"

2. For an outside-of-class client, write up a nonacademic research report and then give that report verbally in class.

3. Have research articles or presentations changed in the last 30 years? Design a study to answer this question, conduct it, write up your findings, and then submit them for presentation to the appropriate professional group.

SUGGESTED READING

Gibaldi, J. (2000). *MLA handbook for writers of research papers*, 5th ed. New York: Modern Language Association of America.

Publication manual of the American Psychological Association, 5th ed. (2001). Washington, DC: American Psychological Association.

Rubin, R. B., Rubin, A. M., & Piele, L. J. (2000). *Communication research: Strategies and sources*, 5th ed. Belmont, CA: Wadsworth.

Ward, J., & Hansen, K. A. (1993). *Search strategies in mass communication*, 2nd ed. New York: London.

NOTES

1. An excellent Web site that shows how the various style sheets are used in communication (and includes updated cites for online referencing) can be found at: http://www.uiowa.edu/~commstud/resources/citation.html. The Web site is also known as "Karla's Guide to Citation Guides" (Tonella, 1998). A second source for different citations is found in *Easy Writer: A Pocket Guide* (Lundsford, Connors & Horowitz, 1997).

2. In many instances the researcher reports, via a footnote, that the materials are available from him or her or offers more information about the construction of the measure or the operationalization of the manipulations.

REFERENCES

Gibaldi, J. (2000). *MLA handbook for writers of research papers*, 5th ed. New York: Modern Language Association of America.

Hickson, M., III, Stacks, D. W., & Amsbary, J. H. (1993). Active prolific scholars in communication studies: Analysis of research productivity, II. *Communication Education, 42*, 223–233.

Lundsford, A., Connors, R., & Horowitz, F. E. (1997). *Easy writer: A pocket guide*. New York: St. Martin's Press.

Publication manual of the American Psychological Association, 5th ed. (2001). Washington, DC: American Psychological Association.

Sargent, J. (2002). Topic avoidance: Is this the way to a more satisfying relationship? *Communication Research Reports, 19*(2), 175–182.

Tonella, K. (1998). Guide to citation guides. <http://www.uiowa.edu/~commstud/resources/citation.html>.

Tucker, R. K., Weaver, R. L., II, & Berryman-Fink, C. (1981). *Research in speech communication*. Englewood Cliffs, NJ: Prentice-Hall.

σ see standard deviation, s.

σ^2 see variance, s^2.

χ^2 the statistic associated with the Chi-Square nonparametric test ($\chi^2 = (O - E)^2 \div E$)

2 × 2 factorial experiment an experiment with two variables, each of which contains two levels (a 3 × 3 factorial experiment would have two variables with three levels each).

a priori method use of reasoning to answer a question before a factual observation.

abstraction a general concept that defines what something "is" through language.

academic report the final step in the research process whereby a theoretical question has been tested and formally written up for an academic audience, complete with theory, statistics, and limitations.

adductive an approach to historical research in which the process of inquiry is neither deductive nor inductive; it takes the form of answering specific questions, so that a satisfactory explanatory "fit" is obtained.

alpha (α) the significance level of an inferential statistical test.

annotated bibliography a listing of sources with a short (usually one or two sentences) description of each document.

anonymity ensuring that no one, including the researcher, knows who gave which responses in a research project.

ANOVA Analysis of Variance, a parametric statistic that tests for differences among means for groups.

APA style sheet a format used for the writing of research findings published by the American Psychological Association.

application error in measurement, error attributable to lack of control over how the measure was distributed or completed.

archives documents, as in historical/rhetorical-critical research; a technique found in unobtrusive measurement.

argument the use of reason and evidence to persuade someone that a policy is correct.

arithmetic mean (M) a parametric statistic, a measure of central tendency, one type of average response; mean; ($M = \sum X \div N$).

artificiality an outcome of laboratory experiments, which are frequently conducted in a highly contrived environment, one that may bear little resemblance to the circumstances typically faced by individuals as they communicate in their normal lives.

attitude an intervening variable; a predisposition to respond to something.

attitude (attitudinal) object the stimulus that caused a person to form an attitude.

attitude scales measurement of an intervening variable that theoretically predisposes people to respond to the attitude object.

attribute variables variables, such as sex, that must be measured, not manipulated.

attrition a potential threat to experimental validity, when participants *may* drop out of the research project for some unknown reason; mortality.

authority (1) a source of some kind that has established knowledge and shares it with us; (2) from documentary research; the credibility of a document and its author.

behavioral measures measures that directly measure behaviors, not attitudes and predispositions.

bibliographic study a humanistic method that focuses on documentary research and the creation of information bases.

bibliography a listing of all the sources found in a documentary search listed in alphabetical order.

bivariate statistics descriptions or inferences about two nonparametric or parametric variables as they relate to one another.

Boolean operators a programming language used in documentary searches that limit or expand the searches based on the combination of key words.

business report the final step in the research process whereby a summary of the study is presented to a lay audience.

case study direct observations of an event, interviews with participants before, during, or after it, and a host of other data-gathering techniques.

category in content analysis, the part of the system where the content (unit of analysis) is placed; to be valid, category systems must be exhaustive and exclusive.

category sources of invalidity in content analysis, the degree to which categories overlap; problems where categories are not mutually exclusive and exhaustive.

causal statements statements made about the relationship between two variables, that one variable makes the other change in predictable ways.

census (1) an examination of all possible units, people, or items in a population; (2) questioning or testing *every* member of a population.

central tendency in parametric statistics, the tendency of individual scores (numbers) to disperse around a group mean (average); it provides information about the *average* response.

character from content analysis, a unit of analysis that is usually defined as an individual or defined as being composed of specific communicative behaviors identified with a specific type of person.

characteristic see **parameter**.

chi-square tests inferential statistical tests for nonparametric data.

chronology of events a historical time pattern that looks at events through some system of setting dates or timetable.

classic crossover interaction effect a direct interaction effect whereby both variables are affected by levels of the other.

classic experiment from Campbell and Stanley (1963), a design with a control group known for its elegance and control over extraneous variables.

closed questions questions asked in a survey that are similar to multiple-choice test questions in that responses are provided from which the interviewee may select the most appropriate.

cluster sampling a form of random sampling that breaks the sample into representative subsamples, or clusters.

coding the process of assigning meaning to some communication behavior, message, or observation.

coefficient alpha a reliability statistic for interval and ratio measures that tells the researcher how consistent the respondents are in their responses. Also known as Chronbach's alpha.

cohort a shared characteristic, such as age.

cohort trend design a type of longitudinal survey that examines people from the same subgroup of the population over time.

communication research the patient, systematic study to learn new "things" about communication.

communication roles from participant-observation, roles are expected behaviors that people take in an interaction.

communication routines from participant-observation, routines are the expected behaviors people take when periodically interacting in a *particular* environment.

communication rules from participant-observation, rules are unwritten behaviors dictated by the norms present as established by the group.

comparisons from experimental methodology, when we observe (measure) something that has been affected by manipulation of an independent variable; comparisons are fundamental to establishing relationships and, ultimately, causation.

confederate (1) a person who appears to be a participant but is actually working with the researcher and has been trained by the researcher; (2) a person who helps the researcher conduct an experiment with deception.

confidentiality ensuring that only the researcher knows who gave the responses in a research project.

construct a variable that is built by a researcher; a defined term in a theory.

construct validity whether a measure's items actually reflect *what* is being measured as determined by experts.

content analysis a research method or measurement technique that involves the systematic study of the content of communication messages; a systematic, objective, and quantitative method for measuring variables.

content validity whether a measure captures the content or the meaning of the variable being measured; an objective source of validity.

contingency analysis a statistical analysis where two or more variables are analyzed simultaneously; bivariate statistics; multivariate statistics.

contingency table a nonparametric analysis where two variables are displayed.

control (1) a critical criteria for causation in which a researcher has eliminated extraneous variables as the cause of observed differences on the dependent variable; (2) the researcher's ability to exclude all possible sources of change in a study except those manipulated to test the relationship between independent and dependent variables.

control group from experimental methodology, a group that received *no* manipulation or treatment.

convenience sampling a nonprobability sampling technique where you sample from a population or universe that is convenient to you.

covariation a criteria for causation whereby changes in an independent variable correspond to changes in the dependent variable.

cover story the description of research in an experiment that intentionally deceives the participant and makes him or her ignorant of the true purpose of the research.

criterion variable the variable the research wants to predict from changes in an antecedent variable.

criterion-related validity a measure is valid to the extent that it enables the researcher to predict a score on some other measure or to predict a particular behavior of interest.

critic a researcher who attempts to apply some established ethical or aesthetic principles to a situation in an effort to answer a question of value.

critical analysis a rhetorical study requiring description that uses rhetorical theory to evaluate and interpret the meaning of an event.

critical method part of the humanistic approach to historical research and an extension of the tests of internal evidence or criticism the researcher uses when examining the question of how well the act was accomplished.

critical value an established value that a calculated statistic must equal or surpass to be significant at a designated level of significance.

crossbreak analysis a nonparametric analysis that compares the frequency of responses in individual cells.

cross-sectional design a survey design that takes a cross section of a population to study *at a given time*; it takes a "snapshot" of the population.

cumulative scale a measurement scale that assumes that when you agree with a scale item you will also agree with items that are less extreme (see also Guttman scale).

data anything that is observed and recorded.

databases a computer program that stores and retrieves data.

debriefing informing a research participant after the study what the actual purpose of the study was and then answering any questions that person may have about the study.

deception the practice of establishing a cover for a study that, while close to the study's actual purpose, is not true.

deductive theory theory which presumes a relationship between particular variables ahead of time and then deduces a testable hypothesis; the theory precedes the research.

definitional sources of invalidity a source of invalidity in content analysis determined by misdefined units of analysis.

degrees of freedom (df) a correction factor in inferential statistics that allows you to predict one outcome by holding another constant; $(n - 1)$.

demand cues the sometimes subtle, unconscious cues that the researcher may emit to let the participant figure out what the researcher wants to find.

demographic data data that differentiates between groups of people or things.

dependent variable depends on the independent variable for its value.

description a stipulation of what a variable, concept, or construct refers to.

descriptive research a method of gathering information in such a way as to paint a picture of what people think or do.

descriptive statistics the reduction and simplification of data to describe results.

design in an experiment, the laying out of conditions and manipulations in such a way as to test for relationships among variables.

didactic criticism rhetorical criticism model where the critic is interested in the particular communicator and how he or she uses communication as a tool.

direction interaction effect when the effect of one independent variable is different, depending on the level of the other independent variable with which it is combined.

double-barreled question a question that attempts to measure two things at the same time; part of instrumental error.

double-blind experiment an experiment where the study administrator and confederates are not told which conditions are actually being manipulated at the time of the manipulation.

empirical model from participant-observation, a

model based on the observations made of a particular group of people, organization, or event.

empirical questions   questions capable of being verified or refuted by measurement.

epistemology   the study of how we come to know things. It deals with how individuals and groups come to believe what they believe. Includes tenacity, authority, intuition, and science.

equal appearing interval scale   a scale with predefined values associated with each statement; for example, a Likert scale.

equality of variance   a statistical assumption that sample and population's data are equally distributed.

ethical absolutism   the belief that ethical judgments are absolutely right or wrong, true or false, regardless of the situation or the beliefs of the individual.

ethical relativism   the belief that all ethical judgments are equally valid because they depend on the situation in which the judgment is being made and the personal ethical beliefs of the individual making the judgment.

ethics   questions the value about whether something is right or wrong.

ethnomethodology   a study of how people make sense out of the situations in which they find themselves.

event manipulation   an experimental manipulation that actually presents the participants with a stimulus rather than telling them what the stimulus will be (observing an attractive or unattractive female anchor reading news). See also **verbal instructions**.

expected frequency (*E*)   in the chi-square nonparametric test, the theoretically expected number of objects or people who are expected to be placed in a given category.

experiment-wise error protection   a multiple comparison inferential statistic that allows us to be sure that no matter how many multiple, post hoc comparisons we conduct, the chance that any *one* of them will be statistically significant remains the same. We are protected against Type I error.

explanation   the specification of the *relationships* between variables. If we know the conditions under which events will occur, we can say that we have explained the event. The answer to the question "Why?"

external evidence   concerns the following questions: Is the information the real thing? Is it genuine? Is it authentic?

external validity   concerns the questions of generalizability of a study's findings.

extraneous variables   variables that although present, are not the focus of the study.

extrinsic factors   used in rhetorical criticism to describe and analyze the period in which the communication occurred; describe the audience, both in terms of the intended and the real audience; describe the occasion for the speech is then described and analyzed; describe and analyze the speaker (or organization), giving attention to the speaker's background and training; and describe and analyze the communication itself.

F   the test statistic for a one-way or multiple factor Analysis of Variance.

face validity   whether a measure appears, on the face of itself, to be valid. A source of validity.

facilitator   an individual who guides a focus group.

factor analysis   a statistical technique that identifies groupings of scale items. Used in establishing construct validity for new indices and for marketing research.

factorial experiment   an experiment that has at least two independent variables.

facts   things that are observable and can be verified.

field experiments   a type of quasi-experiment in which a researcher is able to manipulate a variable in a natural setting.

field study   a research methodology that involves making observations in a naturally occurring environment, such as participant-observation or in-depth interviewing.

filter question   a question which is used by a researcher to move the respondent from one question to another.

focus group   a qualitative/descriptive methodology where a group of people are collected through some method that discuss some topic of concern to a researcher.

frequency distribution   the number of responses that fall in a category in a nonparametric analysis; can be analyzed as numbers, percentages, or proportions.

generalizability   the ability of research to be extended beyond the actual study.

Gopher   an online program that allows you to visit remote computer sites to obtain documents.

grand theories   generalize to a global society and presumed to hold over a long period of time.

Guttman scale   a unidimensional scale that assumes (1) unidimensionality and (2) that people, when faced with a choice, will also choose items less intense than the one chosen. See also **cumulative scale** and

scalogram.

Hawthorne effect   a finding that resulted when research participants changed their behaviors because they felt they were being part of a study—were being observed.

heuristic   providing new ideas or questions to examine.

historical document   any evidence the researcher uses to establish or help explain the event, person, or institution under study.

historical facts   what is known about a thing, event, or person at a particular time that may change with later knowledge.

history   a potential threat to experimental validity, what *may* occur between observations (O) in an experiment.

human communication   communication between two or more people.

humanism   an attitude or philosophy in which human beings are of paramount importance, that human interests and values are worthy of study as ends in themselves.

humanistic   one of two dominant approaches to communication research, uses rhetorical-historical-critical approaches to research.

humanistic research   research that takes a qualitative approach; research aimed at understanding someone or something in depth rather than according to some grouping construct or norm.

hypothesis   a statement of the concrete relationship between variables.

hypothesis testing theories   limited in scope of content, as well as in the group of people under investigation.

ideographic model of explanation   an approach that is interested in identifying as many factors that contribute to a particular event as possible, even if these factors are unique to the event.

independence   a statistical assumption that any participant selected in the sample does not preclude another participant's selection.

independent variable   the variable that is the cause of, the antecedent to, or the predictor of, the dependent variable.

in-depth interview   a qualitative/descriptive method where the interviewer spends considerable time talking to a respondent.

inductive theory   theory that presumes the selection of a particular communication phenomenon and observes every identifiable variable that might conceivably be related to the phenomenon; in short, the research precedes the theory.

inferential statistics   statistical analyses that test if the results observed for a sample are indicative of the population; the presentation of information that allows us to make judgments whether the research results observed in a sample *generalize* to the population from which the sample was drawn.

information processing   selectively choosing or discarding, combining or synthesizing, finding or creating, and most importantly, evaluating information to reach conclusions.

informed consent   informing participants *basically* of what they will be doing in a study (especially an experiment) in such a way that they may decide on participation.

in-person survey   a survey conducted face-to-face.

instrumental error   in measurement, error that occurs because the measuring instrument was poorly written.

instrumentation   a potential threat to experimental validity, when changes in the measuring instrument or changes in observers or scorers used *may* produce changes in the obtained measurements.

intact classes random assignment   not a condition of actual random assignment; when used appropriately, participants in a given class will be randomly assigned to conditions *within* the class, not the entire class assigned to a condition.

intact group   a group chosen for an experiment because it is convenient and composed of people who were *not* assigned to a particular condition at random.

intensive interview   see **in-depth interview**.

interaction effect comparison   an examination of the effects of an independent variable as effected by the levels of the other independent variables.

internal consistency   the amount of agreement a measure's items have with each other.

internal evidence   an evaluation of the actual message, concerning what the source *meant* to communicate.

internal validity   whether a variable has a demonstrated effect in *the particular study being conducted*.

interval measures   data that have equal appearing intervals; scores of 1 and 5 are known to be 4 units apart in interval data.

intervening variables   variables that come between independent and dependent variables.

interview schedule   a guideline for asking questions in person or over the telephone.

interviewer effects those outcomes that are produced in the responses as a result of behaviors of the interviewer, which may bias the answers a respondent provides.

intrinsic factors used in rhetorical criticism for the analysis of the communication itself and the evidence with which it was constructed.

intuition a source of knowledge where the truth tends to be self-evident.

inversely related a relationship between two variables where a change in one variable causes the other variable to change in the opposite way: as we increase the effect of one variable, the other variable's measured outcome is *reduced*.

isomorphic results have a one to one correspondence with theory or observations.

item from content analysis, a unit of analysis that consists of an entire communication message.

journal a document produced by a professional organization that reflects the ideas and interests of that organization; it typically presents abstract technical and theoretical information.

journalistic surveys a survey technique in which a poll or survey is sponsored by a media source.

key words terms or words that set the scope of a documentary search.

key words/terms descriptors that help in searching for documents.

known group a focus group technique where participants are selected because of their position in the organization.

Kuder-Richardson Formula 20 a reliability statistic for nominal and ordinal measures that tells the researcher how consistent the respondents are in their responses. Also known as KR-20.

laboratory experiment an experimental methodology that carefully controls for all possible intervening or extraneous variables.

latent content from content analysis methodology, an analysis of the underlying idea, thesis, or theme of content; the deeper meanings that are intended or perceived in the message or observation; see also **theme** and **character**.

lateral think an approach to historical research that takes a wider view of the problem, as in adductive reasoning.

Likert-type scale an equal appearing scale that asks participants to react to the statement on a range of responses from favorable to unfavorable. See also **summated rating scale**.

listserv an automated discussion list found online.

literature review a type of documentary research that presents the *relevant* literature pertaining to your topic.

longitudinal design a survey design that allows for observations over time; it permits statements about which variables occur first, but does *not* allow statements of causation (what caused a particular effect)—the design is descriptive, not causative.

magnitude interaction effect when the size of the effect of one independent variable varies, depending on the level of the other independent variable with which it is combined.

mail survey a survey mailed to respondents, who complete the survey and mail it back.

main effects an examination of the effects of an independent variable without regard to the levels of the other independent variables.

manifest content from content analysis methodology, an analysis of the actual content of a message; the content exactly as it appears; see also **word, character, time and space**, and **item**.

manipulated operational definition an operational definition stated in much detail so that other researchers can evaluate the research procedures and repeat the study.

manipulation checks assessing the success of an experimental manipulation of the independent variable by directly measuring participants' perceptions of the variable.

marginals in the chi-square nonparametric test, totals for each row and column for that particular category.

maturation a potential threat to experimental validity; what occurs over the passage of time independent of the study.

measured operational definition an operational definition stating the procedures used to measure the concept under study.

measurement unreliability measurement that is nonsystematic and characterized by randomness.

median (Md) a parametric statistic, a measure of central tendency, the 50th percentile or midpoint of all responses.

meta-analysis an analysis of literature in an area that

has been studied *quantitatively*; it provides information on the comparative effectiveness of a number of studies that may influence a given area.

middle-range theories concern only a particular group in society, or may be particular in content and universal in the groups to which they generalize.

MLA style sheet a format used for the writing of research findings published by the Modern Languages Association.

mode (Mo) a parametric statistic, a measure of central tendency, the most frequently occurring response; a variable may be multi-modal—have more than response that is responded to equally.

moderator see **facilitator**.

mortality a potential threat to experimental validity, when participants *may* drop out of the research project for some unknown reason; attrition.

multidimensional scaling a measurement scale that draws an analogy between a physical space and distances and a similar space and distances in our minds.

multivariate statistics descriptions or inferences about three or more nonparametric or parametric variables as they interrelate.

mutually exclusive category from content analysis, a coding system where a particular entry will fall into one and only one category.

natural experiments a type of quasi-experiment in which the researcher is able to observe the effects of some naturally occurring event.

neutral point in measurement scales, a point midway between extremes; in Likert-type scales, usually defined as "neither agree nor disagree" (preferred), "uncertain," or "undecided."

nominal measurement assigning numbers to categories that have *qualitative* rather than quantitative differences.

nomothetic model of explanation an approach that is interested in relatively few factors that provide explanations for a broad range of human behavior.

nonequivalent group comparison design a quasi-experimental design where two intact groups are compared; also known as a static-group comparison design.

nonequivalent group pretest-posttest design a quasi-experimental design where two intact groups are pretested and posttested and comparisons made between pretests, posttests, and for any differences between pre- and posttest measures.

nonparametric statistics statistical analysis where numbers resulting from nominal and ordinal measures are described; measures that represent categories of people, events, or things.

nonprobability sampling sampling from certain known subpopulations; also known as **purposive sampling**.

norm of reciprocity a strategy that offers research participants some reward or favor for their participation in a research project.

normality a statistical assumption that the peakedness of the data distribution is normally distributed (as in the normal curve) and is the same for data in the population.

null hypotheses the actual testing relationship that no difference exists between conditions; statistical tests seek to *reject* the null hypothesis in favor of the research hypothesis of difference.

O in experimental design is used to refer to an observation, that is, a measurement.

observed frequency (O) in the chi-square nonparametric test, the number of objects or people who *are placed* in a given category.

offset control group an experimental group that is *not* given *any* stimulus treatment; it is offset from the design.

one group pretest-posttest only design a quasi-experimental design where one group is pretested and then posttested and a comparison of scores made.

one-shot case study a quasi-experimental design where one group is simply observed either before or after some event.

one-tailed test of significance a statistical test for a hypothesis that predicts that differences will be of a certain magnitude and in a particular direction.

open-ended questions a measurement technique where no predetermined response options are provided; questions asked in a survey are similar to essay or short-answer questions, allowing the respondent to answer in any way he or she chooses.

operational definition (1) defines variables with such specificity and concreteness that they make scientific research possible; (2) specifies the procedures the researcher uses to observe the variable; both the independent and dependent variables require operational definition.

ordinal measures   data that differentiate between groups based on someone or thing having more or less of whatever is being measured than some other person or thing.

original event   the actual communication event that has occurred; the "IT."

outsourcing   contracting work outside of a firm.

panel design   a type of longitudinal survey which measures the *same* individuals over *time*.

paper and pencil measures   experimental measures to which participants respond via scales and/or open-ended questions.

paradigm   a dominant way of conceptualizing a phenomenon, of approaching it methodologically, and of looking for solutions to research problems (Kuhn).

parameter   in sampling, a characteristic of a population that is of interest.

parametric statistics   statistical analysis where numbers resulting from interval and ratio measures are described and inferences from samples to the population made; statistical techniques employed on interval and ratio data; measures that represent a continuum of data that at minimum appear to be equally distant apart.

participant-observation   a qualitative research method that directly involves the researcher in the research process as both participant in the communication event and observer of that event.

Pearson r   (1) (Pearson correlation coefficient) a parametric statistic that provides an index of the extent to which ordered pairs of observations (measurements) covary or share variance; (2) a statistical measure of relationship (correlation) between two interval or ratio measures.

percentages   a nonparametric statistic of the number of each group divided by the total in all groups.

periodicity   a bias found in systematic sampling based on the way in which the items are chosen because of their location in the population.

personal interview survey   a survey method where questions are asked orally.

persuasive survey   a survey technique that seeks to sell or market a product rather than seek information about that product or market.

physical traces   an unobtrusive measure that examines the weathering of sites for behavior and use.

pilot test   a preliminary data-gathering effort for

the purpose of examining the research procedures, including the measures used, in order to correct any problems before the full study is conducted.

polygraph exam   an unreliable, nonvalid technique to assess whether people tell the truth or lie.

population   a group of people, objects, events, or things that a researcher is interested in studying that share some *characteristic*; a universe in content analytic or rhetorical-critical studies.

post hoc   "after the fact"; usually refers to statistics used after the primary analysis is completed.

power   the ability to detect differences that are truly different, is a function of sample size.

prediction   the ability of a theory to specify relationships between independent and dependent variables.

primary evidence   evidence from the source itself; testimony, documents, and evidence that comes from those engaged in the activities of the period.

primary source   documentary material that comes from original sources; the research as presented by the author in whatever form it was originally distributed to the public.

probability   a statistical outcome that tells the researcher the likelihood that a sample's finding can be inferred to the larger population.

probability sample   a sampling technique where the chance for selecting a member of a population is known.

probability sampling   respondents are selected as randomly as possible; that is, every person in the population should have an equal chance of being chosen.

probability theory   a statistical theory that provides the researcher with an estimate of the sampling error and confidence in responses in a survey.

proportions   a nonparametric statistic of the number of each group divided by the total for a finite number.

purposive sampling   see **nonprobability sampling**.

push poll   a survey technique that begins innocently, then asks the respondent a question implying questionable behavior or outcome of a person or product.

qualitative approach   when research questions focus on single events, as ends in themselves.

quantitative approach   when research questions focus

on many related events as ways of describing the event.

quasi-experiment an adaptation of the laboratory experiment that does not control all possible intervening or extraneous variables.

quasi-experimental design any research project in which, although one or more features of a true (classic) experiment are not present, the effect of an independent variable is studied by making comparisons among groups exposed to different levels of the independent variable.

questionnaire a measurement instrument that contains the exact questions and measures an interviewer uses to survey through the mail, in person, or by telephone.

questionnaire survey a survey method where questions are asked—and answered—via a written format.

questions of definition a question that seeks to clarify what the particular communication variable, event, or process is.

questions of fact describe the world as it is according to what we know at that time.

questions of policy describe the world in terms of what should be done.

questions of value describe the world in terms of a continuum of "goodness" to "badness."

quota sampling a nonprobability sampling technique where you sample from a population by using the known *characteristics* of the population as a guide to the selection of participants.

R in experimental design, a representation of the fact that the participants have been randomly assigned to the two conditions of the experiment.

random sampling a sampling technique that allows all possible units, people, or items in a population to have an equal chance of being chosen for study.

random selection a sampling technique whereby each person or object in a population or universe has an equal chance of being chosen.

randomization in experimental method, the random assigning of participants to conditions so that all participants have an equal chance of being in any one condition.

randomness in measurement, measurement that is inconsistent, not systematic.

range a parametric statistic, a measure of central tendency, the difference between high and low scores.

rank ordered ordinal data that have been ranked according to some criteria, such as larger to smaller,

younger to older.

ratio measures data that meet interval criteria, but also have *a meaningful absolute zero point.*

reference in research, the citing or giving others credit for their work.

referents specific meanings to which the word can refer.

reliability the extent to which measurement yields numbers (data) that are consistent, stable, and dependable.

reportive definition reports how a particular term has been customarily used, that is, what the conventional meaning for a term is.

research hypothesis a statement that predicts changes in the dependent variable(s) will occur in specified ways due to the independent variable(s).

research methodology a way of inquiry; may be qualitative or quantitative.

research question (1) **good**: a question the researcher hopes to address through research that will advance his or her knowledge of the world. (2) **right**: a question whose answer is important.

residual in the chi-square nonparametric test, the difference between the observed and expected frequencies $(O - E)$.

response rate from survey methodology, the number of participants *actually* reached who *completed* an interview.

response set a pattern the respondent might get into based on simply marking down one side or the middle.

rhetoric the humanistic study of persuasive discourse.

rhetorical criticism a critical analysis of communication discourse through message context and content as it relates to evaluating, describing, analyzing, and interpreting persuasive messages.

rigor the amount of control in a research study; the ability to generalize with credibility.

rigor the amount of control in an experimental study; it serves as an indication that a manipulation is effective.

risk the potential psychological or physical damage a research participant may face while participating in a research project.

role-playing an experimental manipulation that involves telling participants about a situation and asking them to pretend that they are really in that situation; an alternative to deception.

rules of scholarship   giving appropriate credit for ideas, reporting the results of research in an impartial and complete way, and describing openly and honestly any flaws or weaknesses in research procedures.

s   see **standard deviation**.

s^2 see **variance**.

sample   a selected subgroup of a population or universe.

sample size   the number of people or objects selected from a population or universe for study.

sampling   the process by which content or participants are drawn from a population or universe; see also **random sampling, convenience sampling**, and **stratified sampling**.

sampling error   in measurement, error that is attributable to the people who complete the measurement instrument; in drawing a sample, failure to include entire population in drawing participants for a study.

sampling frame   set criteria for deciding on the characteristics of a sample.

sampling sources of invalidity   in content analysis, problems with the drawing of a sample from some population or universe.

scale   a form of measurement composed of items that reflect some underlying concept and may range from a single item to hundreds of items.

scalogram   a Guttman scale.

scholarship   the reporting of research results in a prescribed manner.

scientific   one of two dominant approaches to communication research, uses a social scientific research approach.

scientific explanation   the specification of the relationships between independent and dependent variables.

scientific research   carefully controlled and defined observations that can be repeated again and again.

secondary evidence   evidence from those of the time period who may have observed but did not actually engage in the activities in question; also represents sources whose credibility or testimony you cannot personally verify through access to primary sources.

search engine   computer program developed to conduct very rapid key word searches on the Internet.

secondary sources   another source referencing the primary source; documents that are compilations of others' original work.

self-correctiveness   a part of the process of science, where rules of procedure increase the chances that if mistakes are made they will be identified and corrected.

semantic differential scale   a general scaling technique for measuring the meaning that an "object" has for an individual.

semantic space   the idea that people evaluate objects along spatial continua.

skepticism   in humanistic research, the acceptance or rejection of a document or the testimony of a source.

skip interval   found in systematic sampling; the number of occurrences that are skipped between selected units or people in selecting a sample.

snowball sampling   a nonprobability sampling technique employed when you do not know much about the population you are attempting to study and use identified participants to identify new participants.

snowball technique   a technique for drawing a sample or finding interviewees that asks participants to identify other participants.

social norms   from participant-observation, a question to be answered about the community or group being observed.

Spearman rho rank   a nonparametric statistic that measures the correlation between two categorical variables.

spreadsheets   a computer program that stores and computes data like a financial registrar.

spurious relationship   a finding that the apparent relationship lacks validity; it is false.

standard deviation   (s or σ) a parametric statistic, a measure of central tendency that tells us how dispersed the data points are from the mean.

standard error of the mean   the standard error, the within-cell variance associated with the t-test.

standardized score   (Z-score) a parametric statistic, a way of describing a variable by translating each individual score into a score reflecting standard deviation units.

static group comparison design   a quasi-experimental design where two intact groups are compared; also known as a nonequivalent group comparison design.

statistical analysis program   a computer program that stores, retrieves, and performs complex statistical procedures on data.

statistical regression   a potential threat to experimental validity, when participants score highly (or lowly) on an initial measure and then *may* score somewhat less (or more) on later measures.

statistically significant a decision made based on the probability that a research finding is caused by the independent variable and not through random chance; typically set by convention at a 95 percent (or $p < .05$) probability level; see also **alpha (α)**.

statistics the branch of applied mathematics that provides the tools to summarize, organize, and analyze the results of a quantitative study.

stipulative definition involves specifying how a term will be used—to what it will refer.

stratified sampling a form of random sampling that is concerned with selecting a sample that have an identifiable characteristic or segment of interest.

study of sources a humanistic method of study that examines those with whom someone has studied (teacher, mentor) or someone acknowledged as influential in the subject's life.

style sheets a format used for the writing of research findings; see also **APA style sheet, MLA style sheet**.

subheads subtitles of sorts—help to maintain a flow and direction of the writing.

subjects those upon whom a study has been conducted; a pejorative term indicating that a researcher has "subjected" someone to something without their being able to do anything about it.

summated rating scale a scale with statements that yield responses that range from favorable to unfavorable toward an object.

surviving objects the printed, written, and oral materials that may be of relevance and can be authenticated.

symbol a name, utterance, part of speech, or other unit that represents something else.

symptom criticism a rhetorical criticism model that approaches the communication event or person as a symptom of some larger social concern.

systematic measurement measurement where repeated applications yield identical responses.

systematic sampling a form of random sampling that selects units, people, or items based on some systematic criteria, every sixth occurrence for example.

t the test statistic; a *t*-test.

TELNET an online program that allows you to access remote computers.

tenacity things people believe simply because people have always believed them.

tertiary evidence evidence based on the accounts of the primary source; not to be trusted.

tertiary source a reporting of secondary source's report of the primary source.

testing a potential threat to experimental validity, what occurs when the measurement of participants at O_1 *may* affect the scores they receive on the second measure at O_2.

test-retest a method designed to assess reliability over time with the same test.

thematic criticism rhetorical criticism model where the critic is interested in how the communication is constructed.

theme a unit of analysis found in content analysis that deals with latent message content—an idea, concept, or thesis.

theoretical model from participant-observation, a model based on the literature, which provides an understanding of what we expect to be observed given this particular group of people, organization, or event.

theory Statements about the relationships among abstract variables.

threats to internal validity potential sources that may invalidate an experiment's findings because the researcher *does not know* if they impacted on the results.

Thurstone scale a scale with predefined values associated with each statement. An **equal appearing interval scale**.

time and space from *historical method*, a historical time pattern that looks at events that occurred at a particular time and in a particular place or space. From *content analysis*, a unit of analysis that reflects some physical or temporal measure.

time pattern a way of looking at history; see also **chronology of events** and **time and space**.

total variance consists of two parts, systematic (between group) and random or error (within group) variance in inferential statistics.

tradition from documentary research; that which our culture presents to us.

treatment in an experiment, a group that receives a manipulation. A condition may have several treatments, such as a touch condition with high, moderate, and low touch.

trend design a type of longitudinal survey that allows you to collect *different* samples at *different* points in time.

triangulation   employing two or more research methods for the purpose of verifying data.

t-**test**   an inferential parametric statistic that tests for differences between two means.

two-tailed test of significance   a statistical test for a hypothesis that predicts that some differences will be found, but without specifying how the differences will occur; if $\alpha = .05$ ("one tailed,") then $2\alpha = 0.25$ ("two tailed").

Type I error   error that occurs when a researcher claims that relationships exist when in fact they do not; an inappropriate rejection of the null hypothesis.

Type II error   error that occurs when a researcher claims that a relationship does not exist when in fact one does, an inappropriate acceptance of the null hypothesis.

units of analysis   an element of content analysis; the thing that is actually counted; such as a **word, theme, character, time and space,** and **item.**

univariate statistics   descriptions or inferences about nonparametric or parametric variables by themselves.

universe   a population of messages studied in content analysis.

unobtrusive measures   a measurement technique whereby the research passively observes behavior without the studied person's knowledge.

validity   the extent that scales or questions measure what they are thought to measure. See also **criterion-related validity, content validity, face validity,** and **construct validity.**

variance   (s^2 or σ^2) a parametric statistic, a measure of central tendency that is a more general measure of dispersion from which the standard deviation is calculated, the square of the standard deviation.

verbal instructions   experimental manipulation that involves telling participants what they will be observing or doing.

volunteer sampling   A nonprobability sampling technique that uses volunteers as participants.

WAIS (Wide Area Information Search)   a powerful on-line documentary search tool that you use when you seek access to databases.

within-group variance   that part of the variance that is associated with error in inferential statistics.

word   from content analysis, a unit of analysis that can include units consisting of names, utterances, parts of speech, and so forth.

χ in experimental design, this is used to refer to exposure to a stimulus or treatment of some kind.

Z-score   see **standardized score.**